25 CBSE Class 10 Mathematics (Standard)

Chapter-wise, Topic-wise & Skill-wise

Previous Year Solved Papers (2013 - 2023) with Value Added Notes

DISHA™
Publication Inc

DISHA Publication Inc.
A - 23, FIEE Complex,
Okhla Industrial Area Phase-II, New Delhi-110020
Tel: 49842349/ 49842350

By:

Raghvendra Kumar Sinha
Dileep Singh

Typeset By
DISHA DTP Team

CONTENTS

3rd Level of Division : Skillwise Division

Each Question in the topic has been further divided skillwise using following codes:

- **K** Knowledge
- **U** Understanding
- **Ap** Application
- **A** Analysis

Trend Analysis (Year 2023-2019)

CBSE All India & Delhi

S. No.	Chapter Name	Year of Examination								
		2023		2022		2021	2020		2019	
		All India	Delhi	(All India) Term-I	(All India) Term-II		All India	Delhi	All India	Delhi
1.	Real Numbers	3	3	7		Not Held in 2021 due to Covid-19 Pandemic	3	3	3	3
2.	Polynomials	2	3	5			2	4	1	1
3.	Pair of Linear Equations in Two Variables	2	2	7			3	2	2	3
4.	Quadratic Equations	2	3		2		3	1	3	2
5.	Arithmetic Progressions	3	3		2		3	4	2	3
6.	Triangles	4	3	9			4	6	3	3
7.	Coordinate Geometry	4	3	7			4	4	3	3
8.	Introduction to Trigonometry	3	3	6			4	4	3	3
9.	Some Applications of Trigonometry	1	2		2		2	2	1	1
10.	Circles	5	4		2		2	1	1	1
11.	Areas Related to Circles	1	2	5			3	1	1	1
12.	Surface Areas and Volumes	2	2		2		2	3	2	2
13.	Statistics	3	1		3		3	3	3	2
14.	Probability	3	4	4			3	3	1	2
	Total no. of Questions	**38**	**38**	**40**	**13**		**41**	**41**	**26**	**26**

Note: In this book all 25 papers (Years 2023-2013) including CBSE sample papers 2021-22, 2022-23 & 2023-24 are divided as per latest CBSE chapter-wise, topicwise & skill-wise – K (= Knowledge based), U (= Understanding), Ap (= Application based) & A (= Analysis) marked below the question.

Chapter 1 Real Numbers

Topic-1: The Fundamental Theorem of Arithmetic

1 Multiple Choice Questions

1. If two positive integers a and b are written as $a = x^3y^2$ and $b = xy^3$, where x, y are prime numbers, then the result obtained by dividing the product of the positive integers by the LCM (a, b) is **[CBSE Sample Paper 2023-24, K]**

(a) xy (b) xy^2

(c) x^3y^3 (d) x^2y^2

2. The ratio of HCF to LCM of the least composite number and the least prime number is: **[Delhi 2023, Set-I, K]**

(a) 1 : 2

(b) 2 : 1

(c) 1 : 1

(d) 1 : 3

3. Let a and b be two positive integers such that $a = p^3q^4$ and $b = p^2q^3$, where p and q are prime numbers. If HCF(a,b) $= p^mq^n$ and LCM(a,b) $= p^rq^s$, then $(m + n)(r + s) =$

[CBSE Sample Paper 2022-23, U]

(a) 15

(b) 30

(c) 35

(d) 72

4. The exponent of 5 in the prime factorisation of 3750 is

[All India 2022, Term-I, U]

(a) 3 (b) 4

(c) 5 (d) 6

5. What is the greatest possible speed at which a girl can walk 95 m and 171 m in an exact number of minutes ?

[All India 2022, Term-I, Ap]

(a) 17 m/min (b) 19 m/min

(c) 23 m/min (d) 13 m/min

6. Three alarm clocks ring their alarms at regular intervals of 20 min, 25 min and 30 min respectively. If they first beep together at 12 noon, at what time will they beep again for the first time ? **[All India 2022, Term-I, Ap]**

(a) 4 : 00 pm (b) 4 : 30 pm

(c) 5 : 00 pm (d) 5 : 30 pm

7. The greatest number which when divides 1251, 9377 and 15628 leaves remainder 1, 2 and 3 respectively is

[All India 2022, Term-I, A]

(a) 575 (b) 450

(c) 750 (d) 625

8. If a and b are two coprime numbers, then a^3 and b^3 are

[All India 2022, Term-I, K]

(a) Coprime

(b) Not coprime

(c) Even

(d) Odd

9. If n is a natural number, then $2(5^n + 6^n)$ always ends with

[All India 2022, Term-I, K]

(a) 1 (b) 4

(c) 3 (d) 2

10. The LCM of two numbers is 2400. Which of the following cannot be their HCF ?

[All India 2022, Term-I, U]

(a) 300 (b) 400

(c) 500 (d) 600

11. $\sqrt{n}$ is a natural number such that n > 1.

Which of these can DEFINITELY be expressed as a product of primes? **[CBSE CFPQ 2022, A]**

(i) $\sqrt{n}$ (ii) n (iii) $\frac{\sqrt{n}}{2}$

(a) only (ii)

(b) only (i) and (ii)

(c) all (i), (ii) and (iii)

(d) (cannot be datermined without knowing *n*)

12. The HCF of k and 93 is 31, where k is a natural number. Which of these CAN be true for SOME VALUES of k?

(i) *k* is a multiple of 31. **[CBSE CFPQ 2022, A]**

(ii) *k* is a multiple of 93.

(iii) *k* is an even number.

(iv) *k* is an odd number.

(a) only (ii) and(iii)

(b) only (i), (ii) and (iii)

(c) only (i), (iii) and (iv)

(d) all (i), (ii), (iii) and (iv)

13. The ratio of LCM and HCF of the least composite and the least prime numbers is

[CBSE Sample Paper 2021-22, Term-I, U]

(a) 1 : 2 (b) 2 : 1 (c) 1 : 1 (d) 1 : 3

14. If LCM(x, 18) = 36 and HCF(x, 18) = 2 then x is

[CBSE Sample Paper 2021-22, Term-I, K]

(a) 2 (b) 3 (c) 4 (d) 5

15. If sum of two numbers is 1215 and their HCF is 81, then the possible number of pairs of such numbers are

[CBSE Sample Paper 2021-22, Term-I, K]

(a) 2 (b) 3 (c) 4 (d) 5

16. The LCM of two prime numbers *p* and $q (p > q)$ is 221. Find the value of $3p - q$.

[CBSE Sample Paper 2021-22, Term-I, K]

(a) 4 (b) 28 (c) 38 (d) 48

17. The sum of exponents of prime factors in the prime-factorisation of 196 is **[All India 2020, K]**

(a) 3 (b) 4 (c) 5 (d) 2

18. The total number of factors of a prime number is

[Delhi 2020, K]

(a) 1 (b) 0 (c) 2 (d) 3

19. The HCF and the LCM of 12, 21, 15 respectively are

[All India 2023, Set-II(s), Delhi 2020, K]

(a) 3, 140 (b) 12, 420 (c) 3, 420 (d) 420, 3

2 *Assertion Reason/Two Statement Type Questions*

20. **Assertion (A) :** The number, 5^n cannot end with the digit 0, where n is a natural number.

Reason (R) : Prime factorisation of 5 has only two factors, 1 and 5. **[All India 2023, A]**

(a) Both Assertion (A) and Reason (R) are true and Reason (R) is the correct explanation of Assertion (A).

(b) Both Assertion (A) and Reason (R) are true and Reason (R) is not the correct explanation of Assertion (A).

(c) Assertion (A) is true but Reason (R) is false.

(d) Assertion (A) is false but Reason (R) is true.

21. **Assertion (A):** If product of two numbers is 5780 and their HCF is 17, then their LCM is 340

Reason (R): HCF is always a factor of LCM

[CBSE Sample Paper 2022-23, A]

(a) Both Assertion (A) and Reason (R) are true and Reason (R) is the correct explanation of Assertion (A).

(b) Both Assertion (A) and Reason (R) are true and Reason (R) is not the correct explanation of Assertion (A).

(c) Assertion (A) is true but Reason (R) is false.

(d) Assertion (A) is false but Reason (R) is true.

4 Very Short Answer Questions (1 Mark)

22. Using prime factorisation, find HCF and LCM of 96 and 120. **[All India 2023, K]**

23. Two numbers are in the ratio 2 : 3 and their LCM is 180. What is the HCF of these numbers? **[Delhi 2023, K]**

24. If HCF (336, 54) = 6, find LCM (336, 54). **[All India 2019, K]**

25. What is the HCF of smallest prime number and the smallest composite number? **[All India 2018, K]**

5 Short Answer Questions (2 or 3 Marks)

26. National art convention got registrations from students from all parts of the country, of which 60 are interested in music, 84 are interested in dance and 108 students are interested in handicrafts. For optimum cultural exchange, organisers wish to keep them in minimum number of groups such that each group consists of students interested in the same artform and the number of students in each group is the same. Find the number of students in each group. Find the number of groups in each art form. How many rooms are required if each group will be allotted a room? **[CBSE Sample Paper 2023-24, Ap]**

27. Show that 6^n can not end with digit 0 for any natural number 'n'. **[All India 2023 Set-II, U]**

28. Find the HCF and LCM of 72 and 120. **[All India 2023 Set-II, U]**

29. The traffic lights at three different road crossings change after every 48 seconds, 72 seconds and 108 seconds respectively. If they change simultaneously at 7 a.m., at what time will they change together next? **[All India 2023, Ap]**

30. M and N are positive integers such that $M = p^2q^3\ r$ and $N = p^3q^2$ where, p, q, r are prime numbers.
Find LCM (M, N) and HCF (M, N). **[CBSE CFPQ]**

31. Write the smallest number which is divisible by both 306 and 657. **[All India 2019, V]**

32. Find HCF and LCM of 404 and 96 and verify that HCF × LCM = Product of the two given numbers. **[All India 2018, K]**

33. Find the greatest number of six digits exactly divisible by 18, 24 and 36. **[All India 2017, Term-I, K]**

34. Is it possible that HCF and LCM of two numbers be 24 and 540 respectively. Justify your answer. **[Delhi 2016, Term-I, K]**

35. Show that numbers 8^n can never end with digit 0 for any natural number *n*. **[Delhi 2016, Term-I, K]**

36. Can be number 6^n, *n* being a natural number, end with the digit 5? Give reasons. **[All India 2015, Term-I, K]**

Topic-2: Revisiting Irrational Numbers

Multiple Choice Questions

1. If $p^2 = \frac{32}{50}$, then p is a/an [All India 2023 Set-II, K]
   (a) whole number (b) integer
   (c) rational number (d) irrational number
2. If $a^2 = 23/25$, then a is
   [CBSE Sample Paper 2021-22, Term-I, K]
   (a) rational (b) irrational
   (c) whole number (d) integer

Assertion Reason/Two Statement Type Questions

3. **Statement A (Assertion):** If $5+\sqrt{7}$ is a root of a quadratic equation with rational coefficient, then its other root is $5-\sqrt{7}$.
   Statement R (Reason) : Surd roots of a quadratic equation with rational coefficients occur in conjugate pairs.
   [All India 2023 Set-II, U]
   (a) Both Assertion (A) and Reason (R) are true; and Reason (R) is the correct explanation of Assertion (A).
   (b) Both Assertion (A) and Reason (R) are true; but Reason (R) is not the correct explanation of Assertion (A).
   (c) Assertion (A is true but Reason (R) is false.
   (d) Assertion (A) is false but Reason (R) is true.

Very Short Answer Questions (1 Mark)

4. Find a rational number between $\sqrt{2}$ and $\sqrt{3}$.
   [Delhi 2019, K]

Short Answer Questions (2 or 3 Marks)

5. Prove that $\sqrt{2}$ is an irrational number.
   [Delhi 2019, CBSE Sample Paper 2023-24, K]
6. Prove that $\sqrt{3}$ is an irrational number.
   [All India 215, Term-I, Delhi 2023, All India 2023, K]
7. Show that $5 + 2\sqrt{7}$ is a irrational number, $\sqrt{7}$ is given to be an irrational number. [All India 2020]
8. Prove that $2 + 5\sqrt{3}$ is an irrational number, given that $\sqrt{3}$ is an irrational number.
   [CBSE Sampe Paper 2022-23(s), All India 2019, K]
9. Given that $\sqrt{2}$ is irrational, prove that $(5+3\sqrt{2})$ is an irrational number. [All India 2018, K]

Long Answer Questions (4 or 5 Marks)

10. Prove that $\sqrt{5}$ is an irrational number.
    [All India 2020, K]

Hints & Solutions

Topic-1: The Fundamental Theorem of Arithmetic

1. **(b)** xy^2 **(1 Mark)**

2. **(a)** $\frac{\text{HCF(least composite no, Least prime no.)}}{\text{LCM(least composite no, Least prime no.)}}$

$\Rightarrow \frac{\text{HCF}(4, 2)}{\text{LCM}(4, 2)} = \frac{2}{4} = \frac{1}{2}$ **(1 Mark)**

3. **(c)** 35 **(1 Mark)**

4. **(b)** Given number is 3750.

Prime factorisation of 3750 = $5 \times 5 \times 5 \times 5 \times 2 \times 3$

$= 5^4 \times 2^1 \times 3^1$

5	3750
5	750
5	150
5	30
2	6
3	3
	1

Exponent of 5 = 4. **(1 Mark)**

a^m, a = *base*

m = *exponent*

5. **(b)** Given, distances covered by girl are 95m and 171m.

$95 = 5 \times 19$

$171 = 3 \times 3 \times 19$

H.C.F of (95, 171) = 19

Girl can cover maximum distance 19m in 1 min. Therefore, the speed is 19m/min. **(1 Mark)**

6. **(c)** Given, regular intervals are 20 min, 25 min and 30 min.

L.C.M of (20, 25, 30) = $2 \times 5 \times 2 \times 3 \times 5$

= 300 min.

2	20, 25, 30
5	10, 25, 15
2	2, 5, 3
3	1, 5, 3
5	1, 5, 2
	1, 1, 1

They beep together at 12 noon, then they beep after 300 minutes again.

$300 \text{ min} = \frac{300}{60} = 5 \text{ h}$

All clocks will beep again together at 5 : 00 pm.

(1 Mark)

7. **(d)** Three numbers are 1251, 9377, 15628 and the respective remainders are 1, 2 & 3.

$(1251 - 1) = 1250$

$(9377 - 2) = 9375$

$(15628 - 3) = 15625$

H.C.F of (1250, 9375, 15625) is shown below.

$1250 = 2 \times 5 \times 5 \times 5 \times 5$

$9375 = 3 \times 5 \times 5 \times 5 \times 5 \times 5$

$15625 = 5 \times 5 \times 5 \times 5 \times 5 \times 5$

H.C.F of (1250, 9375, 15625) = $5 \times 5 \times 5 \times 5 = 625$

Therefore, the greatest no. is 625. **(1 Mark)**

8. **(a)** Given a and b are coprime, whose H.C.F is 1.

Then, a^3 & b^3 also the coprime numbers.

Whose H.C.F is 1. **(1 Mark)**

9. **(d)** Number $2(5^n + 6^n)$ contains power n to the base 5 and 6.

For every $n \in N$ 5^n ends with 5 and 6^n ends with 6.

Sum of 5 & 6 is 11, then $2 \times 11 = 22$.

Therefore, the number always ends with 2. **(1 Mark)**

10. **(c)** LCM = 2400

HCF of two numbers will always divide the LCM of two numbers.

Factors of 2400 = 2 × 2 × 2 × 2 × 2 × 3 × 5 × 5

2 × 2 × 5 × 5 × 3 = 300

2 × 2 × 5 × 5 × 3 × 2 = 600

2 × 2 × 5 × 5 × 2 × 2 = 400

As per options, it will give all numbers except 500.

(1 Mark)

11. 2 (b) **(1 Mark)**

12. 3 (c) **(1 Mark)**

13. **(b)** Least composite number is 4 and the least prime number is 2. LCM (4, 2) : HCF(4, 2) = 4 : 2 = 2 : 1

(1 Mark)

14. **(c)** LCM × HCF = Product of two numbers

36 × 2 = 18 × x

72 = 18x

4 = x

x = 4 **(1 Mark)**

15. **(c)** Since HCF = 81, two numbers can be taken as 81x and 81y,

ATQ

81x + 81y = 1215

or x + y = 15

which gives four co prime pairs-

1, 14

2, 13

4, 11

7, 8

Such pair of numbers are, (81, 1134) (162, 1053) (324, 891) and (567, 648) **(1 Mark)**

16. **(c)** LCM of two prime numbers = product of the numbers

221 = 13 × 17.

So p = 17 & q = 13

∴ 3p – q = 51 – 13 = 38 **(1 Mark)**

17. **(b)** $196 = 2^2 \cdot 7^2$, sum of exponents = 2 + 2 = 4

(1 Mark)

18. **(c)** Prime number have two factor 1 and itself.

(1 Mark)

19. **(c)** $12 = 2^2 \times 3$; $21 = 3 \times 7$; $15 = 3 \times 5$

HCF = 3

$LCM = 2^2 \times 3 \times 5 \times 7 = 420$ **(1 Mark)**

20. **(d)** The number 5^n end with multiple of 5 for all $n \in N$

⇒ R : Prime factorisation of 5 are 1, 5 **(1 Mark)**

21. **(b)** Both Assertion (A) and Reason (R) are true and Reason (R) is not the correct explanation of Assertion (A)

(1 Mark)

22. $96 = 2^2 \times 3 \times 2^3 = 2^5 \times 3$

$120 = 2^2 \times 3 \times 5 \times 2 = 2^3 \times 3 \times 5$ **(½ Mark)**

$HCF = 2^3 \times 3 = 24$; $LCM = 2^5 \times 3 \times 5 = 480$ **(½ Mark)**

23. Let No. are 2x, 3x

Product of No. = LCM × HCF ⇒ 2x × 3x = 180 × x

$6x^2 = 180x \Rightarrow \boxed{x = 30} \Rightarrow HCF = 30$ **(1 Mark)**

24. Given, HCF (336, 54) = 6

We know,

HCF × LCM = Product of numbers

⇒ 6 × LCM = 336 × 54

$\Rightarrow LCM = \frac{336 \times 54}{6} = 336 \times 9 = 3024$ **(1 Mark)**

25. As smallest prime number = 2

and smallest composite number = 4 **(½ Mark)**

∴ HCF of 2 and 4 = 2

Hence HCF of smallest prime number and smallest composite number is 2. **(½ Mark)**

26. Number of students in each group subject to the given condition = HCF (60, 84, 108) **(½ Mark)**

HCF (60, 84, 108) = 12 **(½ Mark)**

Number of groups in music $= \frac{60}{12} = 5$ **(½ Mark)**

Number of groups in dance $= \frac{84}{12} = 7$ **(½ Mark)**

Number of groups in handicrafts $= \frac{108}{12} = 9$ **(½ Mark)**

Total number of rooms required = 5 + 7 + 9 = 21

(½ Mark)

27. If the number 6^n, for any n, were to end with digit zero, then it would be divisible by 5. That is, the prime factorisation of 6^n would contain the prime number 5. **(1 Mark)**

This is not possible because $6^n = (2\times3)^n$, so the only prime numbers in the factorisation of 6^n are 2 and 3.

So, the uniqueness of the fundamental theoram of Arithmetic guarantees that there are no other prime number other than 2 and 3 in the factorisation of 6^n so there is no natural "n" for which 6^n ends with digit zero. **(1 Mark)**

28. We have

$72 = 2^3 \times 3^2$ **(1 Mark)**

$120 = 2^3 \times 3 \times 5$ **(1 Mark)**

29. Take the LCM of given time

$48 = 2^4 \times 3;\ 72 = 2^3 \times 3^2;\ 108 = 2^2 \times 3^3$ **(1 Mark)**

Then, LCM = 2 × 2 × 2 × 2 × 3 × 3 × 3 = 432

After 432 seconds, they will change simultaneously.

⇒ 432 seconds = 7 min 12 sec

Time = 7 : 07 : 12 am **(1 Mark)**

30. LCM $= p^3q^3r$ **(1 Mark)**

HCF $= p^2q^2$ **(1 Mark)**

31. Smallest number which is divisible by 306 and 657 is,

LCM (657, 306)

657 = 3 × 3 × 73

306 = 3 × 3 × 2 × 17 **(1 Mark)**

LCM = 3 × 3 × 73 × 2 × 17 = 22338 **(1 Mark)**

For LCM take each prime factor with highest power in all then multiply it.

32.

2	404
2	202
101	101
	1

2	96
2	48
2	24
2	12
2	6
3	3
	1

∴ 404 = 2 × 2 × 101

96 = 2 × 2 × 2 × 2 × 2 × 3 **(1 Mark)**

HCF of 404 and 96 = 2 × 2 = 4

LCM of 404 and 96 = 4 × 101 × 2 × 2 × 2 × 3

= 9696

HCF × LCM = 4 × 9696 = 38784

Product of numbers = 404 × 96 = 38784

Hence verified that

HCF × LCM = Product of the two numbers. **(1 Mark)**

33. LCM of 18, 24 and 36 is 72

```
72)999999(13888
   999936
       63
```

(1 Mark)

∴ Required number = 9,99,936. **(1 Mark)**

HCF will be find when we have to find greatest (maximum) number wich exactly divide the given number.

34. HCF = 24

LCM = 540

Now, $\frac{\text{LCM}}{\text{HCF}} = \frac{540}{24} = 22.5$ not an integer **(1 Mark)**

Since LCM is always a multiple of HCF, hence two numbers cannot have HCF and LCM as 24 and 540 respectively. **(1 Mark)**

35. If 8^n ends with 0, then it must have 5 as a factor.

But prime factor of 8^n is 2.

$\therefore \quad 8^n = 2^n \times 2^n \times 2^n$ **(1 Mark)**

From the fundamental theorem of arithmetic, the prime factorisation of every composite number is unique.

$\therefore$ 8^n can never ends with 0. **(1 Mark)**

36. No, because $6^n = (2 \times 3)^n = 2^n \times 3^n$, so the only primes in the factorisation of 6^n are 2 and 3, and not 5. **(2 Marks)**

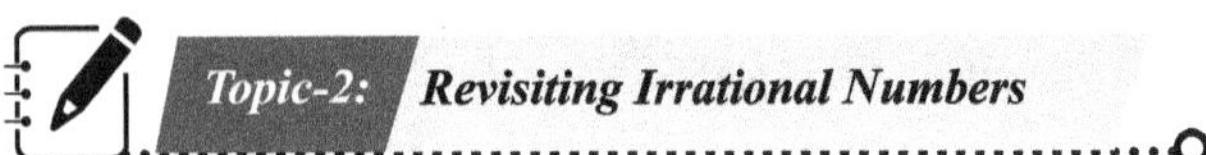

Topic-2: Revisiting Irrational Numbers

1. **(c)** $p^2 = \frac{32}{50}$

$\Rightarrow p^2 = \frac{16}{25}$

$\Rightarrow p = \pm\frac{4}{5}$

P is in the form of $\frac{a}{b}$, where "a" and "b" are integers having no common factor other than 1, also $q \neq 0$.

(1 Mark)

2. **(b)** $a^2 = \frac{23}{25}$, then $a = \frac{\sqrt{23}}{5}$, which is irrational.

(1 Mark)

3. **(b)** **(1 Mark)**

4. Since, $\sqrt{2}$ = 1.414.... and $\sqrt{3}$ = 1.732 ... **(½ Mark)**

Hence, the rational number between $\sqrt{2}$ and $\sqrt{3}$ is 1.5 or $\frac{3}{2}$.

(½ Mark)

There are infinite rational numbers between any two irrational numbers.

5. Let us assume, to the contrary, that $\sqrt{2}$ is rational.

So, we can find integers a and b such that $\sqrt{2} = \frac{a}{b}$ where a and b are coprime. **(½ Mark)**

So, $b\sqrt{2} = a$.

Squaring both sides, we get $2b^2 = a^2$.

Therefore, 2 divides a^2 and so 2 divides a. **(½ Mark)**

So, we can write a = 2c for some integer c.

Substituting for a, we get $2b^2 = 4c^2$, that is, $b^2 = 2c^2$.

This means that 2 divides b^2, and so 2 divides b.

(½ Mark)

Therefore, a and b have at least 2 as a common factor.

But this contradicts the fact that a and b have no common factors other than 1. **(½ Mark)**

This contradiction has arisen because of our incorrect assumption that $\sqrt{2}$ is rational.

So, we conclude that $\sqrt{2}$ is irrational.

6. **(a)** Let $\sqrt{3}$ is rational no. So $\sqrt{3}$ can be written as

$\sqrt{3} = \frac{p}{q}$, $q \neq 0$, HCF (P, q) = 1 **(½ Mark)**

i.e. p ≠ q are co-prime to each other

Squaring both sides

$3 = \frac{p^2}{q^2} \Rightarrow p^2 = 3q^2$ **(1 Mark)**

$\Rightarrow$ 3 is a factor of p^2...(i)

$\Rightarrow$ 3 is a factor of p...(ii) **(½ Mark)**

So p = 3 m from (i), where m is any integer. $p^2 = 9m^2$

$3q^2 = 9m^2$

$q^2 = 3m^2$

$\Rightarrow$ 3 is factor of $q^2 \Rightarrow$ 3 is a factor of q

HCF (p,q) ≠ 1 contradicts our & supposition. So is irrational. **(1 Mark)**

7. ***Topper's Answer***

Let us assume to the contrary that $5+2\sqrt{7}$ is rational.
Then $5+2\sqrt{7}$ is of the form $\frac{p}{q}$ where p and q are co-primes and $q \neq 0$.

$$\frac{p}{q} = 5+2\sqrt{7}$$

$$\frac{p}{q} - 5 = 2\sqrt{7}$$

$$\frac{p-5q}{2q} = \sqrt{7}$$

$\frac{p-5q}{2q}$ is rational as p and q are integers

This contradicts the given fact that $\sqrt{7}$ is irrational.
∴ Our assumption is wrong.
$5+2\sqrt{7}$ is irrational //
Proved.

8. Let $2 + 5\sqrt{3} = r$, where, r is rational number.

$\Rightarrow (2 + 5\sqrt{3})^2 = r^2$ **(½ Mark)**

$\Rightarrow 4 + 75 + 20\sqrt{3} = r^2$

$\Rightarrow 79 + 20\sqrt{\ } = r^2$ **(½ Mark)**

$\Rightarrow 20\sqrt{3} = r^2 - 79$

$\Rightarrow \sqrt{3} = \frac{r^2-79}{20}$ **(½ Mark)**

Since r is rational number therefore $r^2 - 79$ is also rational number $\Rightarrow \frac{r^2-79}{20}$ is a rational number. So, $\sqrt{3}$ must also be a rational number.

But $\sqrt{3}$ is an irrational number (Given).

So, our assumption is wrong.

$2+5\sqrt{3}$ is an irrational number.

Hence proved. **(½ Mark)**

9. Let $5+3\sqrt{2}$ be a rational number

$\Rightarrow 5+3\sqrt{2} = \frac{p}{q}$, **(½ Mark)**

where p and q are coprime integers and $q \neq 0$

$\Rightarrow 3\sqrt{2} = \frac{p}{q} - 5 = \frac{p-5q}{q}$

$\Rightarrow \sqrt{2} = \frac{p-5q}{3q}$ **(1 Mark)**

Since p & q are integers

$\Rightarrow \frac{p-5q}{3q}$ is a rational number **(½ Mark)**

But $\sqrt{2}$ is irrational.

We know that an irrational number cannot be equal to a rational number.

$\Rightarrow$ Our supposition is wrong that $5+3\sqrt{2}$ is a rational number.

Hence $5+3\sqrt{2}$ is irrational. **(1 Mark)**

Note

Addition of a rational and an irrational number is an irrational number.

10. Let $\sqrt{5}$ is rational number

$\therefore \sqrt{5} = \frac{p}{q}$, **(1 Mark)**

where p and q are coprime integers and $q \neq 0$.

$$\sqrt{5} = \frac{p}{q} \Rightarrow p = \sqrt{5}q$$

Squaring both sides

$p^2 = 5q^2$ ...(i) **(1 Mark)**

So, p^2 is divisible by 5

Then p is also divisible by 5

Let $p = 5$ m **(½ Mark)**

Putting in (i)

$(5m)^2 = 5q^2 \Rightarrow 25m^2 = 5q^2 \Rightarrow q^2 = 5m^2$ **(½ Mark)**

So, q^2 is divisible by 5

Then q is also divisible by 5 **(½ Mark)**

Thus, p and q both divisible by 5 but p and q are coprime integers.

By contradiction.

$\sqrt{5}$ is irrational number.

Hence, proved. **(½ Mark)**

Chapter 2 Polynomials

Topic-1: *Geometrical Meaning of the Zeroes of a Polynomial*

1 *Multiple Choice Questions*

1. The given linear polynomial y = f(x) has

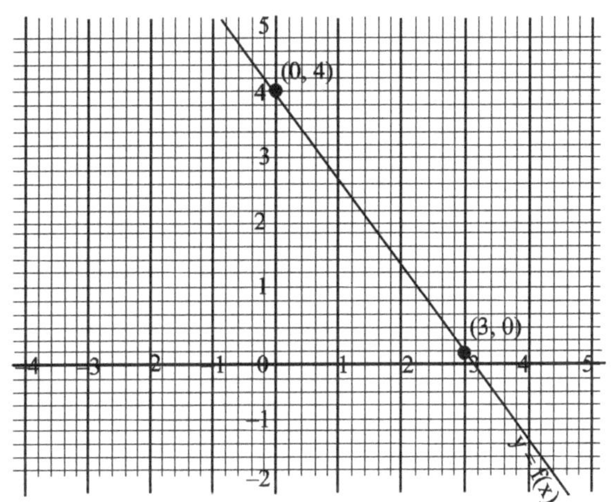

[CBSE Sample Paper 2023-24, Ap]

(a) 2 zeros

(b) 1 zero and the zero is '3'

(c) 1 zero and the zero is '4'

(d) No zero

2. The number of polynomials having zeroes –1 and 2 is:

[All India 2023, Set-I, K]

(a) exactly 2

(b) only 1

(c) at most 2

(d) infinite

3. In figure, the graph of a polynomial P(x) is shown. The number of zeroes of P(x) is

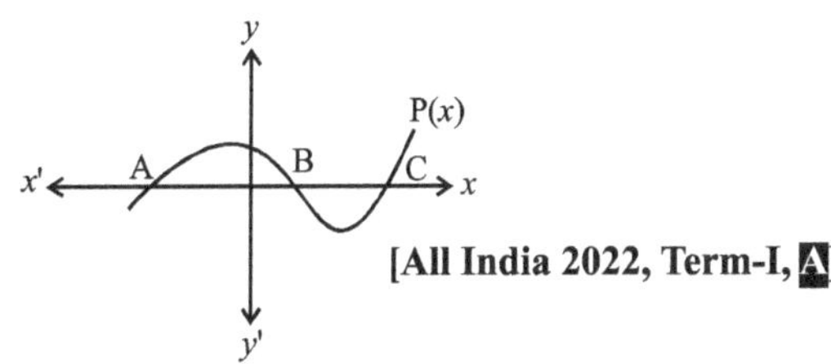

[All India 2022, Term-I, A]

(a) 1

(b) 2

(c) 3

(d) 4

4. If x –1 is a factor of the polynomial $p(x) = x^3 + ax^2 + 2b$ and a + b = 4, then **[All India 2022, Term-I, Ap]**

(a) a = 5, b = –1 (b) a = 9, b = –5

(c) a = 7, b = –3 (d) a = 3, b = 1

5. If one of the zeroes of the quadratic polynomial $x^2 + 3x + k$ is 2, then the value of k is **[Delhi 2020, Ap]**

(a) 10 (b) –10 (c) –7 (d) –2

5 *Short Answer Questions (2 or 3 Marks)*

6. A teacher asked 10 of his students to write a polynomial in one variable on a paper and then to handover the paper. The following were the answers given by the students :

[All India 2020, A]

$2x + 3, 3x^2 + 7x + 2, 4x^3 + 3x^2 + 2,$

$x^3 + \sqrt{3x} + 7, 7x + \sqrt{7}, 5x^3 - 7x + 2,$

$2x^2 + 3 - \frac{5}{x}, 5x - \frac{1}{2}, ax^3 + bx^2 + cx + d, x + \frac{1}{x}$

Answer the following questions:

(i) How many of the above ten, are not polynomials ?

(ii) How many of the above ten, are quadratic polynomials ?

7. Show that x = 2 is a root of $2x^3 + x^2 - 7x - 6$ **[Delhi 2014 Term-I, Ap]**

Topic-2: Relationship between Zeroes and Coefficients of a Polynomial

Multiple Choice Questions

1. The number of quadratic polynomials having zeroes –5 and –3 is **[All India 2023, Set-II, K]**

(a) 1

(b) 2

(c) 3

(d) More than 3

2. If α and β are the zeroes of the polynomial $x^2 - 1$, then the value of (α + β) is **[All India 2023, Set-II, K]**

(a) 2

(b) 1

(c) –1

(d) 0

3. If the zeroes of the quadratic polynomial

$x^2 + (a + 1)x + b$ are 2 and –3, then

[All India 2023, Set-II, Ap]

(a) a = – 7, b = –1

(b) a = 5, b = –1

(c) a = 2, b = –6

(d) a = 0, b = –6

4. If α, β are zeroes of the polynomic $x^2–1$, then value of (α + β) is : **[Delhi 2023, U]**

(a) 2

(b) 1

(c) –1

(d) 0

5. If α, β are the zeroes of the polynomial $p(x) = 4x^2 - 3x - 7$, then $\left(\frac{1}{\alpha}+\frac{1}{\beta}\right)$ is equal to : **[Delhi 2023, Ap]**

(a) $\frac{7}{3}$

(b) $\frac{-7}{3}$

(c) $\frac{3}{7}$

(d) $\frac{-3}{7}$

6. If α and β are the zeros of a polynomial $f(x) = px^2 - 2x + 3p$ and α + β = αβ, then p is

[CBSE Sample Paper 2022-23, A]

(a) –2/3

(b) 2/3

(c) 1/3

(d) –1/3

7. The graph of a polynomial P(x) cuts the x-axis at 3 points and touches it at 2 other points. The number of zeroes of P(x) is **[All India 2022, Term-I, U]**

(a) 1

(b) 2

(c) 3

(d) 5

8. A quadratic polynomial, the product and sum of whose zeroes are 5 and 8 respectively is

[All India 2022, Term-I, A]

(a) $k[x^2 - 8x + 5]$

(b) $k[x^2 + 8x + 5]$

(c) $k[x^2 - 5x + 8]$

(d) $k[x^2 + 5x + 8]$

9. If α, β are the zeroes of the quadratic polynomial $p(x) = x^2 - (k + 6)x + 2(2k - 1)$, then the value of k, if $\alpha + \beta = \frac{1}{2}\alpha\beta$, is **[All India 2022, Term-I, U]**

(a) –7

(b) 7

(c) –3

(d) 3

10. If 2 and $\frac{1}{2}$ are the zeros of $px^2 + 5x + r$, then

[CBSE Sample Paper 2021-22, Term-I, A]

(a) $p = r = 2$ (b) $p = r = -2$

(c) $p = 2, r = -2$ (d) $p = -2, r = 2$

Q11 - 15 are based on Case Study

The figure given alongside shows the path of a diver, when she takes a jump from the diving board. Clearly it is a parabola.

Annie was standing on a diving board, 48 feet above the water level. She took a dive into the pool. Her height (in feet) above the water level at any time 't' in seconds is given by the polynomial h(t) such that $h(t) = -16t^2 + 8t + k$.

11. What is the value of k?

[CBSE Sample Paper 2021-22, Term-I, A]

(a) 0

(b) –48

(c) 48

(d) $\frac{48}{-16}$

12. At what time will she touch the water in the pool?

[CBSE Sample Paper 2021-22, Term-I, A]

(a) 30 seconds

(b) 2 seconds

(c) 1.5 seconds

(d) 0.5 seconds

13. Rita's height (in feet) above the water level is given by another polynomial p(t) with zeroes –1 and 2. Then p(t) is given by-

[CBSE Sample Paper 2021-22, Term-I, A]

(a) $t^2 + t - 2$

(b) $t^2 + 2t - 1$

(c) $24t^2 - 24t + 48$

(d) $-24t^2 + 24t + 48$

14. A polynomial q(t) with sum of zeroes as 1 and the product as –6 is modelling Anu's height in feet above the water at any time t(in seconds). Then q(t) is given by

[CBSE Sample Paper 2021-22, Term-I, K]

(a) $t^2 + t + 6$ (b) $t^2 + t - 6$

(c) $-8t^2 + 8t + 48$ (d) $8t^2 - 8t + 48$

15. The zeroes of the polynomial $r(t) = -12t^2 + (k-3)t + 48$ are negative of each other. Then k is

[CBSE Sample Paper 2021-22, Term-I, K]

(a) 3 (b) 0 (c) –1.5 (d) –3

16. The zeroes of the polynomial $x^2 - 3x - m(m+3)$ are

[All India 2020, K]

(a) m, m + 3 (b) –m, m +3

(c) m, –(m + 3) (d) –m, –(m + 3)

17. The quadratic polynomial, the sum of whose zeroes is –5 and their product is 6, is **[Delhi 2020, Ap]**

(a) $x^2 + 5x + 6$ (b) $x^2 - 5x + 6$

(c) $x^2 - 5x - 6$ (d) $-x^2 + 5x + 6$

18. If α, β are the zeroes of $f(x) = x^2 - 5x + b$ and $\alpha - \beta = 1$, then b is **[Delhi 2014, Term-I, U]**

(a) 1 (b) 6 (c) 4 (d) 0

Very Short Answer Questions (1 Mark)

19. If one zero of the polynominal $p(x) = 6x^2 + 37x - (k-2)$ is reciprocal of the other, then find the value of k.

[Delhi 2023, U]

20. p and q are zeroes of the polynomial $2x^2 + 5x - 4$

Without finding the actual values of p and q, evaluate $(1-p)(1-q)$. Show your steps. **[CBSE CFPQ 2022, K]**

21. $p(x) = 2x^2 - 6x - 3$. The two zeroes are of the forms:

$\frac{3 \pm \sqrt{k}}{2}$; Where k is a real number

use the relationship between the zeroes and coefficients of a polynomial to find the value of k, Show your steps.

[CBSE CFPQ 2022, K]

22. Find the distance between tha zeroes of the polynomial $f(x) = 2x^2 - x - 6$. Show your steps.

[CBSE CFPQ 2022, U]

23. Find the value of k for which the roots of the equation $3x^2 - 10x + k = 0$ are reciprocal of each other.

[Delhi 2019, U]

5 *Short Answer Questions (2 or 3 Marks)*

24. If α, β are zeroes of quadratic polynomial $5x^2 + 5x + 1$, find the value of **[CBSE Sample Paper 2023-24, Ap]**

1. $\alpha^2 + \beta^2$
2. $\alpha^{-1} + \beta^{-1}$

25. If the zeroes of the polynomial $x^2 + px + q$ are double in value to the zeroes of the polynomial $2x^2 - 5x - 3$, then find the values of p and q.

[CBSE Sample Paper 2022-23, U]

26. Find the sum and product of the roots of the equation $2x^2 - 9x + 4 = 0$ **[Delhi 2023, K]**

27. Find the discriminant of the quadratic equation $4x^2 - 5 = 0$ and hence comment on the nature of roots of the equation **[Delhi 2023, K]**

28. Find a quadratic polynomial whose zeroes are reciprocals of the zeroes of the polynomial

$f(x) = ax^2 + bx + c,\ a \neq 0,\ c \neq 0.$ **[Delhi 2020, Ap]**

29. Find the zeroes of the quadratic polynomial

$7y^2 - \frac{11}{3}y - \frac{2}{3}$ and verify the relationship between the zeroes and the coefficients. **[All India 2019, A]**

30. Find the value of k such that the polynomial $x^2 - (k+6)x + 2(2k-1)$ has sum of its zeros equal to half of their product. **[Delhi 2019, A]**

31. Quadratic polynomial $2x^2 - 3x + 1$ has zeroes as α and β. Now form a quadratic polynomial whose zeroes are 3α and 3β. **[Delhi 2016, Term-I, A]**

32. If α and $\frac{1}{\alpha}$ are the zeroes of the polynomial $P(x) = 4x^2 - 2x + k - 4$, then find the value of k.

[All India 2015, Term-I, Ap]

33. Find the zero(es) of the polynomial $x^2 - 3$ and verify the relationship between the zero(es) and the coefficients.

[All India 2015, Term-I, U]

Long Answer Questions (4 or 5 Marks)

34. If α and β are the zeroes of the quadratic polynomial $f(x) = 2x^2 - 5x + 7$, find a polynomial whose zeroes are $2\alpha + 3\beta$ and $3\alpha + 2\beta$. **[Delhi 2014, Term-I, Ap]**

Case Based Questions (4 Marks)

35. In a pool at an aquarium, a dolphin jumps out of the water travelling at 20 cm per second. Its height above water level after t seconds is given by $h = 20t - 16t^2$. **[All India 2023, Ap]**

Based on the above, answer the following questions.

(i) Find zeroes of polynomial $p(t) = 20t - 16t^2$.

(ii) Which of the following types of graph represents p(t)?

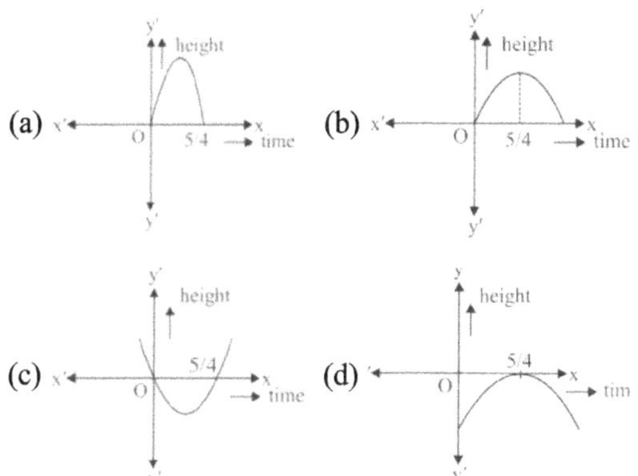

(iii) (a) What would be the value of h at $t = \frac{3}{2}$? Interpret the result. **[All India 2023, A]**

OR

(iii) (b) How much distance has the dolphin covered before hitting the water level again?

Hints & Solutions

Topic-1: Geometrical Meaning of the Zeroes of a Polynomial

1. **(b)** 1 zero and the zero is '3' **(1 Mark)**

2. **(d)** Polynomial define in factor form

$K(x + 1)(x - 2) = 0$

$\Rightarrow K(x^2 - 2x + x - 2) = 0 \Rightarrow K(x^2 - x - 2) = 0$

So infinite many Polynomial having zeroes –1, and 2 **(1 Mark)**

Note

If α, β are the roots/zeros of the Polynomial then the Polynomial is $k(x - a)(x - b)$ where $k \in R$

3. **(c)**

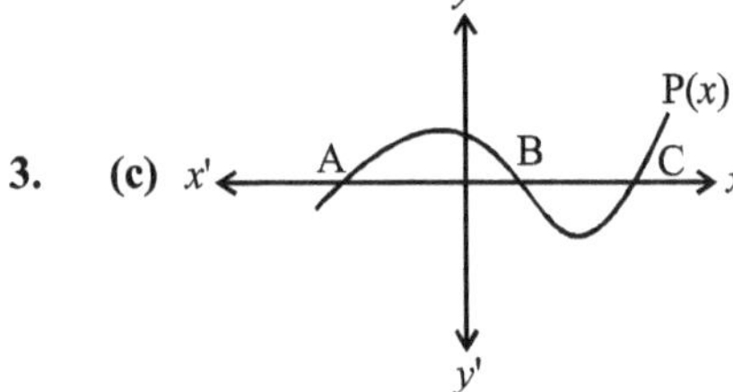

Graphs intersects at three points A, B and C. Then, the number of zeroes are 3. **(1 Mark)**

4. **(b)** $p(x) = x^3 + ax^2 + 2b$

If $(x - 1)$ is the factor of the polynomial p(x)

then x = 1 is the zero of the polynomial & p(1) = 0

put x = 1 in the polynomial p(x).

$p(1) = 1 + a + 2b = 0$

$a + 2b = -1$ ....(i)

$a + b = 4$ ....(ii)

Subtract (ii) from (i)

$$\begin{array}{r} a + 2b = -1 \\ \underline{-a + \; b = 4} \\ b = -5 \end{array}$$

From (ii)

$a + b = 4 \Rightarrow a - 5 = 4 = \boxed{a = 9}$ **(1 Mark)**

5. (b) $(2)^2 + (3)2 + k = 0 \Rightarrow k = -10$ **(1 Mark)**

6.

Polynomials	Not polynomials	Quadratic polynomials
$2x + 3$ $3x^2 + 7x + 2$ $4x^3 + 3x^2 + 2$ $7x + \sqrt{7}$ $5x^3 - 7x + 2$ $5x - \frac{1}{2}$ $ax^3 + bx^2 + cx + d$	$x^3 + \sqrt{3x} + 7$ $2x^2 + 3 - \frac{5}{x}$ $x + \frac{1}{x}$	$3x^2 + 7x + 2$

(i) Number of not polynomials = 3 **(1½ Marks)**

(ii) Number of quadratic polynomials = 1 **(1½ Marks)**

7. $p(x) = 2x^3 + x^2 - 7x - 6$

$p(2) = 2(2)^3 + (2)^2 - 7(2) - 6$

$= 16 + 4 - 14 - 6 = 0$

Hence x = 2 is a root of p (x). **(2 Marks)**

Note

The value of polynomial is zero at x = a then x = a is called zero or root of polynomial

Topic-2: Relationship between Zeroes and Coefficients of a Polynomial

1. **(d)** Let the factors of the polynomial be (x + 5) and (x + 3). Then the polynomial can be written as: $(x + 5)(x + 3) = x^2 + 8x + 15$

Hence, any quadratic polynomial having which fits in the condition will be in form of $k(x^2 + 8x + 15)$, where k is real number. **(1 Mark)**

2. **(d)** The given polynomial is a quadratic polynomial, in the form of $ax^2 + bx + c = 0$.

For a quadratic polynomial with zero α and β.

$$\alpha + \beta = \frac{-b}{a} \text{ and } \alpha\beta = \frac{c}{a}$$

In the equation $x^2 - 1 = 0$, a = 1, b = 0 and c = –1

$$\alpha + \beta = \frac{-(0)}{1} = 0$$ **(1 Mark)**

3. **(d)** For a quadratic polynomial $ax^2 + bx + c$, the roots α, ß are related to the coefficient a, b, c as

$$\alpha + \beta = \frac{-b}{a}$$

$$\alpha\alpha\beta = \frac{c}{a}$$

$$2 + (-3) = \frac{-(a+1)}{1}$$

$$-1 = -(a + 1)$$

$$a = 0 \quad \text{and} \quad 2(-3) = \frac{b}{1}$$

$$-6 = b$$

Hence, a = 0, b = –6 **(1 Mark)**

4. **(d)** $f(x) = x^2 - 1 = x^2 - (1)^2 = (x - 1)(x + 1)$

$x = 1, 1 \Rightarrow \alpha = 1, \beta = -1$

$\alpha + \beta = 1 + (-1) = 0$ **(1 Mark)**

5. **(d)** $p(x) = 4x^2 - 3x - 7 \Rightarrow 4x^2 - 7x + 4x - 7$

$\Rightarrow x(4x - 7) + 1(4x - 7) \Rightarrow x = -1, 7/4$

$$\Rightarrow \frac{1}{\alpha} + \frac{1}{\beta} = \frac{1}{-1} + \frac{4}{7} = \frac{-7+4}{7} = \frac{-3}{7}$$ **(1 Mark)**

6. **(b)** 2/3 **(1 Mark)**

7. **(d)** When polynomial P(x) cuts the x-axis at 3 points and touches the x-axis at 2 points, then there are two pairs of equal roots of the polynomial P(x).

Intersecting graph with x-axis, then the total number of roots = 3.

Total number of distinct roots when touches the x-axis = 2.

Total number of zeroes = 3 + 2 = 5. **(1 Mark)**

Note

When graph cuts the x-axis then it is considered as one zero & when touches it considered as two equal zeroes.

8. **(c)** Given product and sum of zeroes are 5 and 8 respectively.

$P(x) = x^2 - Sx + P$

Here, S = 5, P = 8

$P(x) = x^2 - 5x + 8$

Therefore, $k[x^2 - 5x + 8]$ is the required polynomial. **(1 Mark)**

Note

When we multiply the quadratic polynomial with 'k' then it will also considered as quadratic polynomial.

9. **(b)** $p(x) = x^2 - (k + 6)x + 2(2k - 1)$

$$\alpha + \beta = \frac{-b}{a}$$

$$\alpha + \beta = \frac{(k+6)}{1} = k + 6$$

$$\alpha\beta = \frac{c}{a} = 2(2k-1)$$

$$\alpha + \beta = \frac{1}{2}\alpha\beta \Rightarrow (k+6) = \frac{1}{2} \times 2(2k-1)$$

$k + 6 = 2k - 1$

$\boxed{7 = k}$

Therefore, the value of k is 7. **(1 Mark)**

10. **(b)** Sum of zeroes $= 2 + \frac{1}{2} = \frac{-5}{p}$

i.e. $\frac{5}{2} = \frac{-5}{p}$. So p = –2

Product of zeroes $\left(\frac{c}{a}\right) = 2 \times \frac{1}{2} = \frac{r}{p}$

i.e. $\frac{r}{p} = 1$ or r = p = – 2 **(1 Mark)**

11. **(c)** Initially, at t = 0, Annie's height is 48ft

So, at t =0, h should be equal to 48

$h(0) = -16(0)^2 + 8(0) + k = 48$

So k = 48 **(1 Mark)**

12. **(b)** When Annie touches the pool, her height = 0 feet

i.e. $-16t^2 + 8t + 48 = 0$ above water level, it can be written as $2t^2 - t - 6 = 0$

$2t^2 - 4t + 3t - 6 = 0$

$2t(t - 2) + 3(t - 2) = 0$

$(2t + 3)(t - 2) = 0$

i.e. $t = 2$ or $t = \frac{-3}{2}$ **(1 Mark)**

Since time cannot be negative, so t = 2 seconds

13. **(d)** $t = -1$ & $t = 2$ are the two zeroes of the polynomial p(t)

then k (t^2 – (Sum of the roots) t + Product of the roots)

$k(t^2 - t - 2)$

ot $t = 0$, height is 48 so,

$k(0 - 0 - 2) = 48$

or $-2k = 48$ or $k = -24$

Hence polynomial p(t) is $-24(t^2 - t - 2) = -24t^2 + 24t + 48$ **(1 Mark)**

14. **(c)** A polynomial q(t) with sum of zeroes as 1 and the product as –6 is given by

$q(t) = k(t^2 - (\text{sum of zeroes})t + \text{product of zeroes})$

$= k(t^2 - 1t + -6)$ ...(i)

When t = 0 (initially) q(0)= 48ft.

$q(0) = k(0^2 - 1(0) - 6) = 48$

i.e. $-6k = 48$ or $k = -8$

Putting $k = -8$ is equation (i), reqd. polynomial is

$-8(t^2 - 1t + (-6))$

$= -8t^2 + 8t + 48$ **(1 Mark)**

15. **(a)** When the zeroes are negative of each other,

sum of the zeroes = 0

So, $\frac{-b}{a} = 0$

$-\frac{(k-3)}{-12} = 0$

$+\frac{k-3}{12} = 0$

$k - 3 = 0,$

i.e. $k = 3$. **(1 Mark)**

16. **(b)** $x^2 - (m+3)x + mx - m(m+3) = 0$

$\Rightarrow x[x - (m+3)] + m[x - (m+3)] = 0$

$\Rightarrow (x + m)[x - (m+3)] = 0$

$\therefore x + m = 0$ | $x - (m+3) = 0$

$x = -m$ | $x = m + 3$ **(1 Mark)**

17. **(a)** $p(x) = x^2 - (\alpha + \beta)x + \alpha.\beta = x^2 + 5x + 6$ **(1 Mark)**

18. **(b)** $\alpha + \beta = 5, \alpha\beta = b.$

$(\alpha - \beta)^2 = (\alpha + \beta)^2 - 4\alpha\beta = (5)^2 - 4b$

$\Rightarrow (1)^2 = 25 - 4b$

$\Rightarrow 4b = 24$

$b = 6$ **(1 Mark)**

19. Let one zero = α, other = $\frac{1}{\alpha}$

Now Product of zeros $\Rightarrow \frac{c}{a}$

$\alpha \times \frac{1}{\alpha} = \frac{-(k-2)}{6} \Rightarrow 6 = -k + 2 \Rightarrow 4 = -k \; \boxed{k = -4}$

(1 Mark)

20. Expands $(1 - p)(1 - q)$ to get $1 - (p + q) + pq$.

Find the sum of the zeroes as $\frac{5}{2}$ **(½ Mark)**

Find the product of the zeroes as $\frac{-4}{2} = -2$

Use the above steps to find the value of $(1 - p)(a - q)$ as

$1 - \left(-\frac{5}{2}\right) - 2 = \frac{3}{2}$ **(½ Mark)**

21. Write the equation for the product of zeroes as:

$\left(\frac{3+\sqrt{k}}{2}\right)\left(\frac{3-\sqrt{k}}{2}\right) = \frac{-3}{2}$ **(½ Mark)**

Simplifies the above equation and writes:

$$\frac{9-k}{4}=\frac{-3}{2}$$

Solves the above equation and finds the value of k as 15.

(½ Mark)

22. Factorises f(x) as (x – 2) (2x + 3).

Writes f(x) = 0 and finds the coordinates of the zeroes as (2, 0) and $\left(\frac{-3}{2},0\right)$ **(½ Mark)**

Finds the distance between the zeroes as $\frac{7}{2}$ units.

(½ Mark)

23. Let the roots of the equation $3x^2 - 10x + k = 0$ are α & $1/\alpha$.

Now, product of the roots is,

$\alpha.\frac{1}{\alpha}=\frac{k}{3} \Rightarrow k=3.$ **(1 Mark)**

24. Let $P(x) = 5x^2 + 5x + 1$ **(½ Mark)**

Then, $\alpha+\beta=\frac{-b}{a}=\frac{-5}{5}=-1$

$\alpha\beta=\frac{c}{a}=\frac{1}{5}$ **(½ Mark)**

$\alpha^2+\beta^2=(\alpha+\beta)^2-2\alpha\beta$ **(½ Mark)**

$=(-1)^2-2\left(\frac{1}{5}\right)$ **(½ Mark)**

$=1-\frac{2}{5}=\frac{3}{5}$ **(½ Mark)**

$\alpha^{-1}+\beta^{-1}=\frac{1}{\alpha}+\frac{1}{\beta}$

$=\frac{(\alpha+\beta)}{\alpha\beta}=\frac{(-1)}{\frac{1}{5}}=-5$ **(½ Mark)**

25. Let α and β be the zeros of the polynomial $2x^2 - 5x - 3$

Then $\alpha + \beta = 5/2$ **(½ Mark)**

And $\alpha\beta = -3/2$. **(½ Mark)**

Let 2α and 2β be the zeros $x^2 + px + q$ **(½ Mark)**

Then $2\alpha + 2\beta = -p$

$2(\alpha + \beta) = -p$

$2 \times 5/2 = -p$ **(½ Mark)**

So $p = -5$ **(½ Mark)**

And $2\alpha \times 2\beta = q$

$4\alpha\beta = q$

So $q = 4 \times -3/2 = -6$ **(½ Mark)**

26. sum of roots $=\frac{-b}{a}=\frac{-(-9)}{2}=\frac{9}{2}$

Product of roots $=\frac{c}{a}=\frac{4}{2}=2$ **(2 Marks)**

27. $4x^2 - 5 = 0$

Comparing with $ax^2 + bx + c = 0$

$a = 4, b = 0, c = -5$

Discriminant $= b^2 - 4ac$

$\Rightarrow (0)^2 - 4 \times 4 \times (-5)$

$= 0 + 80 = 80 = +ve > 70$

Nature of roots are real & distinct **(2 Marks)**

28. $\because \quad f(x) = ax^2 + bx + c, a \neq 0, c \neq 0$

$\therefore \quad \alpha+\beta=\frac{-b}{a}, \alpha\cdot\beta=\frac{c}{a}$ **(1 Mark)**

Zeroes of required quadratic polynomial are $\frac{1}{\alpha}$ and $\frac{1}{\beta}$

$\therefore \alpha^{-1}+\beta^{-1}=\frac{1}{\alpha}+\frac{1}{\beta}=\frac{\alpha+\beta}{\alpha\beta}=\frac{-b/a}{c/a}=\frac{-b}{c}$

$\alpha^{-1}\beta^{-1}=\frac{1}{\alpha}\cdot\frac{1}{\beta}=\frac{1}{\alpha\beta}=\frac{1}{c/a}=\frac{a}{c}$ **(1 Mark)**

$\therefore$ Quadratic polynomial

$P(x) = k[x^2 - (\alpha^{-1} + \beta^{-1})x + \alpha^{-1}\cdot\beta^{-1}]$

$= k[x^2 - \left(\frac{-b}{c}\right) x + \frac{a}{c}]$

$= k\left[\frac{cx^2 + bx + a}{c}\right]$

$= cx^2 + bx + a$ [Let k = c] **(1 Mark)**

Note

If zeroes of quadratic polynomial is same but opposite in sign then sum of zeroes is zero. If zeroes of quadratic polynomial is reciprocal to each other then product of zeroes is one.

29. $7y^2 - \frac{11}{3}y - \frac{2}{3} = 0$

$21y^2 - 11y - 2 = 0$

$21y^2 - 14y + 3y - 2 = 0$

$7y(3y - 2) + 1(3y - 2) = 0$

$(3y - 2)(7y + 1) = 0$

$y = \frac{2}{3}, -\frac{1}{7}$ **(1½ Marks)**

So, zeroes are $\frac{2}{3}, -\frac{1}{7}$

Verification: On comparing $7y^2 - \frac{11}{3}y - \frac{2}{3}$ with $ax^2 + bx + c$, we get

$a = 7, b = -\frac{11}{3}, c = -\frac{2}{3}$

Sum of zeroes $= \frac{2}{3} - \frac{1}{7} = \frac{14-3}{21} = \frac{11}{21}$

$\frac{-b}{a} = \frac{-\left(-\frac{11}{3}\right)}{7} = \frac{11}{21}$

$\therefore$ Sum of zeroes $= \frac{-b}{a}$.

Product of zeroes $= \frac{2}{3} \times \frac{-1}{7} = \frac{-2}{21}$

$\frac{c}{a} = \frac{\frac{-2}{3}}{7} = \frac{-2}{21}$

$\therefore$ Product of zeroes $= \frac{c}{a}$ **(1½ Marks)**

Hence verified.

30. Let α and β are the zeros of the polynomial

$x^2 - (k + 6)x + 2(2k - 1)$.

given, $\alpha + \beta = \frac{\alpha\beta}{2}$ **(1 Mark)**

$\Rightarrow k + 6 = \frac{2(2k-1)}{2}$ $[\because \alpha + \beta = k + 6 \text{ and } \alpha.\beta = 2(2k-1)]$

$\Rightarrow k + 6 = 2k - 1 \Rightarrow 6 + 1 = 2k - k \Rightarrow k = 7$.

Therefore, the value of k is 7. **(1 Mark)**

Note

If α and β are zeroes of any quadratic polynomial in indeterminate x, then the polynomial is $x^2 - (\alpha + \beta)x + \alpha\beta$.

31. If α and β are the zeroes of $2x^2 - 3x + 1$, then

$\alpha + \beta = \frac{-b}{a}$

$\Rightarrow \alpha + \beta = \frac{3}{2}$ **(1 Mark)**

and $\alpha\beta = \frac{c}{a}$

$\Rightarrow \alpha\beta = \frac{1}{2}$ **(1 Mark)**

New quadratic polynomial whose zeroes are 3α and 3β is:

P(x) = K(x^2 – (Sum of the roots)x + Product of the roots)

$= K(x^2 - (3\alpha + 3\beta)x + 3\alpha \times 3\beta)$

$= K(x^2 - 3(\alpha + \beta)x + 9\alpha\beta)$

$= K\left(x^2 - 3\left(\frac{3}{2}\right)x + 9\left(\frac{1}{2}\right)\right)$

$= K\left(x^2 - \frac{9}{2}x + \frac{9}{2}\right)$

$= \frac{K}{2}(2x^2 - 9x + 9)$

Hence, required quadratic polynomial is

$$P(x) = (2x^2 - 9x + 9) \text{ (take K = 2)} \quad \textbf{(1 Mark)}$$

32. Since, α and $\frac{1}{\alpha}$ are the zeroes of the polynomial

$P(x) = 4x^2 - 2x + k - 4$

So, $\alpha \times \frac{1}{\alpha} = \frac{k-4}{4}$

$\Rightarrow \quad 1 = \frac{k-4}{4} \Rightarrow k = 8$ **(2 Marks)**

If one zero of quadratic polynomial $p(x) = ax^2 + bx + c$ is reciprocal to other then product of zeroes will be 1 i.e $a = c$.

33. Recall the identity $a^2 - b^2 = (a - b)(a + b)$. Using it, we can write:

$x^2 - 3 = (x - \sqrt{3})(x + \sqrt{3})$

So, the value of $x^2 - 3$ is zero when $x = \sqrt{3}$

or $x = -\sqrt{3}$

Therefore, the zeroes of $x^2 - 3$ are $\sqrt{3}$ and $-\sqrt{3}$

Now, sum of zeroes

$= \sqrt{3} - \sqrt{3} = 0 = \frac{-(\text{Coefficient of } x)}{\text{Coefficient of } x^2}$ **(1 Mark)**

Product of zeroes

$= (\sqrt{3})(-\sqrt{3}) = -3 = \frac{-3}{1} = \frac{\text{Constant term}}{\text{Coefficient of } x^2}$ **(1 Mark)**

If quadratic polynomials $p(x) = ax^2 + bx + c$ have $b = 0$ then zeroes are equal and opposite in sign.

34. Since, α and β are zeroes of polynomial
$f(x) = 2x^2 - 5x + 7$.

So, $\alpha + \beta = -\left(-\frac{5}{2}\right) = \frac{5}{2}$ and $\alpha\beta = \frac{7}{2}$ **(1 Mark)**

Let S and P denote respectively the sum and product of zeroes of the required polynomial. Then, polynomial is $p(x) = k(x^2 - Sx + P)$

$S = (2\alpha + 3\beta) + (3\alpha + 2\beta) = 5(\alpha + \beta)$

$= 5 \times \frac{5}{2} = \frac{25}{2}$ and, $P = (2\alpha + 3\beta)(3\alpha + 2\beta)$

$\Rightarrow P = 6(\alpha^2 + \beta^2) + 13\alpha\beta$

$= 6\alpha^2 + 6\beta^2 + 12\alpha\beta + \alpha\beta$

$= 6(\alpha + \beta)^2 + \alpha\beta$

$\Rightarrow P = 6 \times \left(\frac{5}{2}\right)^2 + \frac{7}{2} = \frac{75}{2} + \frac{7}{2} = 41$ **(2 Marks)**

Hence, the required polynomial is given by
$p(x) = k(x^2 - Sx + P)$

or, $p(x) = k\left(x^2 - \frac{25}{2}x + 41\right)$, where k is any non-zero real number.

$P(x) = 2x^2 - 25x + 82$ **(1 Mark)**

If both zero of quadratic polynomial are same but opposite sign then sum of zeroes are zero.

35. (i) $P(t) = 0$

$\Rightarrow 20t - 16t^2 = 0 \Rightarrow t(20 - 16t) = 0 \Rightarrow t = \frac{20}{16} = \frac{5}{4}, t = 0$

$\Rightarrow t = 0, \frac{5}{4}$ **(1 Mark)**

(ii) Let $P(t) = y, t = x$

$\Rightarrow y = 20x - 16x^2 \Rightarrow y = -(16x^2 - 20x)$

That is similar to parabola $y = -(x - a)^2$

At, $t = 0, \frac{5}{4} \Rightarrow P(t) = 0$

Both condition are similar to option (a) **(1 Mark)**

Equation of parbola can be in the form of

$y^2 = \pm 4ax, x^2 = 4ay$

(iii) (A) At t = 3/2,

$$h = 20\times\frac{3}{2} - 16\times\frac{9}{4}$$

$h = -6$

This means that the dolphin will be 6 cm inside the water at $t = \frac{3}{2}$. **(2 Marks)**

OR

(iii) (B) At the water level when dolphin hits water, $t = \frac{5}{4}$.

and velocity v = 20 cm/sec.

Since, $v = \frac{\text{distance}}{\text{time}} = \frac{d}{t}$

$\Rightarrow 20\times\frac{5}{4} = d$

$\Rightarrow d = 25$ cm **(2 Marks)**

Chapter 3 Pair of Linear Equations in Two Variables

Topic-1: *Consistency / Inconsistency of pair of Linear Equations*

1 *Multiple Choice Questions*

1. The lines representing the given pair of linear equations is non–intersecting. Which of the following statements is true? **[CBSE Sample Paper 2023-24, U]**

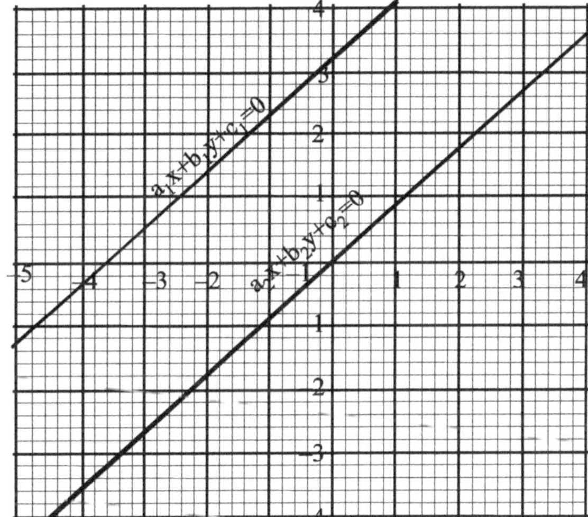

(a) $\frac{a_1}{a_2}=\frac{b_1}{b_2}=\frac{c_1}{c_2}$

(b) $\frac{a_1}{a_2}=\frac{b_1}{b_2}\neq\frac{c_1}{c_2}$

(c) $\frac{a_1}{a_2}\neq\frac{b_1}{b_2}=\frac{c_1}{c_2}$

(d) $\frac{a_1}{a_2}\neq\frac{b_1}{b_2}\neq\frac{c_1}{c_2}$

2. The pair of equations $ax + 2y = 9$ and $3x + by = 18$ represent parallel lines, where a, b are integers, if: **[All India 2023, K]**

(a) $a = b$
(b) $3a = 2b$
(c) $2a = 3b$
(d) $ab = 6$

3. The pair of linear equations $2x = 5y + 6$ and $15y = 6x - 18$ represents two lines which are : **[Delhi 2023, K]**

(a) Intersecting
(b) parallel
(c) coincident
(d) either intersecting or parallel

4. If the system of equations $3x + y = 1$ and $(2k - 1)x + (k - 1)y = 2k + 1$ is inconsistent, then $k =$ **[CBSE Sample Paper 2022-23, K]**

(a) –1 (b) 0
(c) 1 (d) 2

5. Two lines are given to be parallel. The equation of one of the lines is $3x - 2y = 5$. The equation of the second line can be **[All India 2022, Term-I, U]**

(a) $9x + 8y = 7$
(b) $-12x - 8y = 7$
(c) $-12x + 8y = 7$
(d) $12x + 8y = 7$

6. If a pair of linear equations given by $a_1x + b_1y + c_1 = 0$ and $a_2x + b_2y + c_2 = 0$ has a unique solution, then which of the following is true? **[CBSE CFPQ, 2022, K]**

(a) $a_1a_2 = b_1b_2$
(b) $a_1b_2 \neq a_2b_1$
(c) $\frac{a_1}{a_2}=\frac{b_1}{b_2}$
(d) $\frac{a_1}{a_2}\neq\frac{b_1}{b_2}$

7. The value of k for which the lines $5x + 7y = 3$ and $15x + 21y = k$ coincide is **[CBSE Sample Paper 2021-22, Term-I, K]**

(a) 9 (b) 5
(c) 7 (d) 18

8. One equation of a pair of dependent linear equations is $-5x + 7y = 2$. The second equation can be **[CBSE Sample Paper 2021-22, Term-I, K]**

(a) $10x + 14y + 4 = 0$
(b) $-10x - 14y + 4 = 0$
(c) $-10x + 14y + 4 = 0$
(d) $10x - 14y = -4$

9. The number of solutions of $3^{x+y} = 243$ and $243^{x-y} = 3$ is **[CBSE Sample Paper 2021-22, Term-I, A]**
(a) 0 (b) 1
(c) 2 (d) infinite

10. The value of k for which the system of linear equations $x + 2y = 3$, $5x + ky + 7 = 0$ is inconsistent is **[All India 2020, K]**
(a) $-\frac{14}{3}$ (b) $\frac{2}{5}$
(c) 5 (d) 10

11. The value of k for which the system of equations $x + y - 4 = 0$ and $2x + ky = 3$, has no solution, is **[Delhi 2020, K]**
(a) –2 (b) ≠2
(c) 3 (d) 2

Short Answer Questions (2 or 3 Marks)

12. Find the value(s) of k so that the pair of equations $x + 2y = 5$ and $3x + ky + 15 = 0$ has a unique solution. **[All India 2019, K]**

13. Find c if the system of equations $cx + 3y + (3-c) = 0$; $12x + cy - c = 0$ has infinitely many solutions? **[Delhi 2019, U]**

14. Given the linear equation $3x + 4y = 9$. Write another linear equation in these two variables such that the geometrical representation of the pair so formed is : **[All India 2017, Term-I, U]**
(i) intersecting lines
(ii) coincident lines

15. For which values of p and q. will be following pair of linear equations have infinitely many solutions?
$4x + 5y = 2$
$(2p + 7q)x + (p + 8q)y = 2q - p + 1.$
[Delhi 2014, Term-I, K]

Topic-2: Graphical Method of Solution of a Pair of Linear Equations

Multiple Choice Questions

1. The lines $x = a$ and $y = b$, are **[CBSE Sample Paper 2021-22, Term-I, K]**
(a) intersecting
(b) parallel
(c) overlapping
(d) None of these

2. Given below is the graph representing two linear equations by lines AB and CD respectively. What is the area of the trignale formed by these two lines and the line x = 0? **[CBSE Sample Paper 2021-22, Term-I, U]**

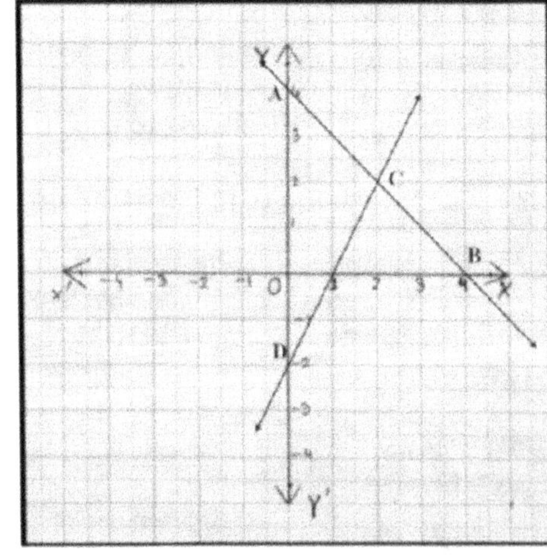

(a) 3sq. units
(b) 4sq. units
(c) 6sq. units
(d) 8sq. units

Short Answer Questions (2 or 3 Marks)

3. Determine graphically the coordinates of the vertices of a triangle, the equations of whose sides are given by $2y - x = 8$, $5y - x = 14$ and $y - 2x = 1$. **[Delhi 2020, A]**

Long Answer Questions (4 or 5 Marks)

4. For uttarakhand flood victims two sections A and B of class X contributed 1,500. If the contribution X-A was 100 less than that of IX-B, find graphically the amounts contributed by both the sections. **[All India 2017, Term-I, A]**

5. Solve graphically the pair of linear equations $3x - 4y + 3 = 0$ and $3x + 4y - 21 = 0$
Find the coordinate of the vertices of triangular region formed by these lines and x–axis. Also calculate the area of this triangle. **[All India 2017, Term-I, A]**

6. Draw the graphs of the pair of linear equations :
$x + 2y = 5$ and $2x - 3y = -4$
Also find the points where the lines meet the x-axis.
[Delhi 2016, Term-I, A]

7. Draw the graphs of the equations $x - y + 1 = 0$ and $3x + 2y - 12 = 0$. Determine the co-ordinates of the vertices of the triangle formed by these lines and the x-axis and shade the triangular region. Also calculate the area of the triangle so formed. **[All India 2015, Term-I, A]**

8. Solve the following system of linear equations graphically:
$3x + y - 12 = 0$ and $x - 3y + 6 = 0$
Shade the region bounded by these lines and the x-axis. Also find the ratio of areas of triangles formed by the given lines with x-axis and y-axis. **[Delhi 2014, Term-I, A]**

Topic-3: Substitution Method of Solving a Pair of Linear Equations

1 Multiple Choice Questions

1. The point of intersection of the line represented by $3x - y = 3$ and y-axis is given by **[All India 2023, Set-II, K]**
   (a) (0, –3)
   (b) (0, 3)
   (c) (2, 0)
   (d) (–2, 0)

2. The values of x and y satisfying the two equations $32x + 33y = 34$, $33x + 32y = 31$ respectively are: **[All India 2022, Term-I, K]**
   (a) –1, 2 (b) –1, 4
   (c) 1, –2 (d) –1, –4

5 Short Answer Questions (2 or 3 Marks)

3. In Fig. ABCD is rectangle. Find the values of x and y. **[All India 2018, U]**

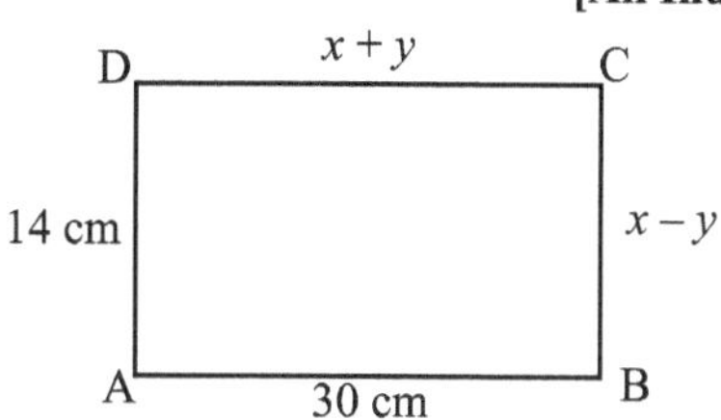

Topic-4: Elimination Method of Solving a Pair of Linear Equations

1 Multiple Choice Questions

1. In a ΔABC, ∠A = $x°$, ∠B = $(3x - 2°)$, ∠C = $y°$. Also ∠C – ∠B = 9°, The sum of the greatest and the smallest angles of this triangle is **[All India 2022, Term-I, U]**
   (a) 107° (b) 135°
   (c) 155° (d) 145°

2. If $217x + 131y = 913$, $131x + 217y = 827$, then $x + y$ is **[CBSE Sample Paper 2021-22, Term-I, U]**
   (a) 5 (b) 6
   (c) 7 (d) 8

5 Short Answer Questions (2 or 3 Marks)

3. Solve : $\frac{2}{\sqrt{x}} + \frac{3}{\sqrt{y}} = 2$; $\frac{4}{\sqrt{x}} - \frac{9}{\sqrt{y}} = -1$, x, y > 0 **[CBSE Sample Paper 2023-24, U]**

4. If $49x + 51y = 499$, $51x + 49y = 501$, then find the value of x and y. **[CBSE Sample Paper 2022-23, K]**

5. Shown below is a pair of linear equations.
$x + 0.999y = 2.999$
$0.999x + y = 2.998$ **[CBSE CFPQ, 2022, U]**
   (i) Without finding the values of x and y, prove that $x = y = 1$.
   (ii) Find the values of x and y. Show your work.

6. If $2x + y = 23$ and $4x - y = 19$, find the value of $(5y - 2x)$ and $\left(\frac{y}{x} - 2\right)$. **[All India 2020, Ap]**

7. Solve the following pair of linear equations :
$3x - 5y = 4$
$2y + 7 = 9x$ **[All India 2019, K]**

Topic-5: Simple Situation Problems

Multiple Choice Questions

1. 3 chairs and 1 table cost ₹900; whereas 5 chairs and 3 tables cost ₹2,100. If the cost of 1 chair is ₹x and the cost of 1 table ₹y, then the situation can be represented algebraically as **[All India 2023, Set-II, Ap]**
   (a) $3x + y = 900, 3x + 5y = 2100$
   (b) $x + 3y = 900, 3x + 5y = 2100$
   (c) $3x + y = 900, 5x + 3y = 2100$
   (d) $x + 3y = 900, 5x + 3y = 2100$

2. The ratio of a two-digit number and the sum of its digits is 7:1. How many such two-digit numbers are possible? **[CBSE CFPQ, 2022, Ap]**
   (a) 1
   (b) 4
   (c) 9
   (d) (infinitely many)

Case Study

A book store shopkeeper gives books on rent for reading. He has variety of books in his store related to fiction, stories and quizzes etc. He takes a fixed charge for the first two days and an additional charge for subsequent day. Amruta paid ₹ 22 for a book and kept for 6 days, while Radhika paid ₹ 16 for keeping the book for 4 days.

Assume that the fixed charge be ₹ x and additional charge (per day) be ₹ y.

Based on the above information, answer any four of the following questions.

3. The situation of amount paid by Radhika, is algebraically represented by **[All India 2022, Term-I, Ap]**
   (a) $x - 4y = 16$ (b) $x + 4y = 16$
   (c) $x - 2y = 16$ (d) $x + 2y = 16$

4. The situation of amount paid by Amruta, is algebraically represented by **[All India 2022, Term-I, Ap]**
   (a) $x - 2y = 11$ (b) $x - 2y = 22$
   (c) $x + 4y = 22$ (d) $x - 4y = 11$

5. What are the fixed charges for a book? **[All India 2022, Term-I, Ap]**
   (a) ₹ 9 (b) ₹ 10
   (c) ₹ 13 (d) ₹ 15

6. What ar=e the additional charges for each subsequent day for a book ? **[All India 2022, Term-I, Ap]**
   (a) ₹ 6 (b) ₹ 5
   (c) ₹ 4 (d) ₹ 3

7. What is the total amount paid by both, if both of them have kept the book for 2 more days ? **[All India 2022, Term-I, Ap]**
   (a) ₹ 35 (b) ₹ 52
   (c) ₹ 50 (d) ₹ 58

Short Answer Questions (2 or 3 Marks)

8. The sum of a two–digit number and the number obtained by reversing the digits is 66. If the digits of the number differ by 2, find the number. How many such numbers are there? **[Delhi, 2014, Term-I, CBSE Sample Paper 2023-24, Ap]**

9. A train covered a certain distance at a uniform speed. If the train would have been 6 km/h faster, it would have taken 4 hours less than the scheduled time. And, if the train were slower by 6 km/hr ; it would have taken 6 hours more than the scheduled time. Find the length of the journey. **[CBSE Sample Paper 2022-23, Ap]**

10. Anuj had some chocolates, and he divided them into two lots A and B. He sold the first lot at the rate of ₹2 for 3 chocolates and the second lot at the rate of ₹1 per chocolate, and got a total of ₹400. If he had sold the first lot at the rate of ₹1 per chocolate, and the second lot at the rate of ₹4 for 5 chocolates, his total collection would have been ₹460. Find the total number of chocolates he had. **[CBSE Sample Paper 2022-23, Ap]**

11. A father's age is three times the sum of the ages of his two children. After 5 years his age will be two times the sum of their ages. Find the present age of the father. **[Delhi 2019, Ap]**

12. A fraction becomes 1/3 when 2 is subtracted from the numerator and it becomes 1/2 when 1 is subtracted from the denominator. Find the fraction. **[Delhi 2019, Ap]**

13. A 2-digit number is seven times the sum of its digits. The number formed by reversing the digits is 18 less than the given number. Find the given number. **[Delhi 2018, Ap]**

14. The present age of a father is three years more than three times the age of his son. Three years hence the father's age will be 10 years more than twice the age of the son. Determine their present ages. **[All India 2020, Ap]**

15. A part of monthly hostel charge is fixed and the remaining depends on the number of days one has taken food in the mess. When Swati takes food for 20 days, she has to pay ₹ 3,000 as hostel charges whereas Mansi who takes food for 25 days ₹ 3,500 as hostel charges. Find the fixed charges and the cost of food per day.

[All India 2017, Term-I, Ap]

16. 4 chairs and 3 tables cost ₹ 2100 and 5 chairs and 2 tables cost ₹1750. Find the cost of one chair and one table separately. **[Delhi 2016, Term-I, Ap]**

17. Aftab tells his daughter, 'Seven years ago, I was seven times as old as you were then. Also, three years from now, I shall be three times as old as you will be." Represent this situation as a pair of linear equations in two variables. **[All India 2015, Term-I, Ap]**

18. Form the pair of linear equations representing the following situation:

10 students of class ten took part in science quiz and the number of girls is 4 more than the number of boys.

[Delhi 2014, Term-I, Ap]]

19. The sum of the digits of a two digit number is 12. The number obtained by interchanging the digits exceeds the given number by 18. Find the number. **[Delhi 2014, Ap]**

Long Answer Questions (4 or 5 Marks)

20. In a class test, the sum of Arun's marks in Hindi and English is 30. Had he got 2 marks more in Hindi and 3 marks less in English, the product of the marks would have been 210. Find his marks in the two subjects.

[All India 2019, Ap]

21. Form the pair of linear equations in the following problem and find their solutions (if they exist) by any algebraic method :

Places A and B are 100 km apart on a highway. One car starts from A and another from B at the same time. If the cars travel in the same direction at different speeds, they meet in 5 hours. If they travel towards each other, they meet in 1 hour. What are the speeds of the two cars?

[Delhi 2014, Ap]

Case Based Questions (4 Marks)

22. A coaching institute of Mathematics conducts classes in two batches I and II and fees for rich and poor children are different. In batch I, there are 20 poor and 5 rich children whereas in batch II, there are 5 poor and 25 rich children. The total monthly colletion of fees from batch I is ₹9000 and from batch II is ₹26000. Assume that each poor child pays ₹x per month and each rich child pays ₹y per month.

[All India 2023, Set-II, Ap]

Based on the above information, answer the following questions:

(i) Represent the information given above in terms of x and y.

(ii) Find the monthly fee paid by a poor child.

OR

Find the difference in the monthly fee paid by a poor child and a rich child.

(iii) If there are 10 poor and 20 rich children in batch II, what is the total monthly collection of fees from batch II?

23. Two schools 'P' and 'Q' decided to award prizes to their students for two games of Hockey ₹ x per student and cricket ₹ y per student. School 'P' decided to award a total of a`9,500 for the two games to 5 and 4 students respectively; while school 'Q' decided to award ₹ 7,370 for the two games to 4 and 3 students respectively.

Based on the above information, answer the following questions: **[Delhi 2023, Ap]**

(i) Represent the following information algebraically (in terms of x and y).

(ii) (a) What is the prize amount for hockey?

OR

(b) Prize amount on which game is more and by how much?

(iii) What will be the total prize amount if there are 2 students each from two games?

Hints & Solutions

Topic-1: Consistency / Inconsistency of pair of Linear Equations

1. (b) $\frac{a_1}{a_2} = \frac{b_1}{b_2} \neq \frac{c_1}{c_2}$ **(1 Mark)**

2. (d) Given here, ax + 2y = 9 ...(i)

3x + by = 18 ...(ii)

For parallel, $\frac{a_1}{a_2} = \frac{b_1}{b_2} = \frac{c_1}{c_2}$. So, to make cofficient equal, multiply(i) eq. by (ii).

or 2ax + 4y = 18, 3x + by = 18

Given pair are parallel if

2a = 3, b = 4 ⇒ 2ab = 12 ⇒ ab = 6 **(1 Mark)**

3. (c) 2x – 5y = 6; 6x – 15y = 18

Here $\frac{a_1}{a_2} = \frac{b_1}{b_2} = \frac{c_1}{c_2}$ (coincident lines) **(1 Mark)**

4. (d) 2 **(1 Mark)**

5. (c) Given, line is $3x - 2y = 5$

Take line $-12x + 8y = 7$

$-4(3x - 2y) = 7$

$3x - 2y = -\frac{7}{4}$

General form: ax + by = c; ax + by = c'

Therefore, the other parallel line is $-12x + 8y = 7$. **(1 Mark)**

6. (b) **(1 Mark)**

7. (a) For lines to coincide: $\frac{a_1}{a_2} = \frac{b_1}{b_2} = \frac{c_1}{c_2}$

so, $\frac{5}{15} = \frac{7}{21} = \frac{-3}{-k} \Rightarrow \frac{3}{k} = \frac{1}{3} \Rightarrow k = 9$ **(1 Mark)**

8. (d) Second equation be λ times of the first equation

–2(–5x + 7y = 2) gives 10x – 14y = –4.

Now $\frac{a_1}{a_2} = \frac{b_1}{b_2} = \frac{c_1}{c_2} = -2$ **(1 Mark)**

9. (b) $3^{x+y} = 243 = 3^5$

So x + y = 5 ...(1)

$243^{x-y} = 3$

$(3^5)^{x-y} = 3^1$

So 5x – 5y = 1 ...(2)

Since : $\frac{a_1}{a_2} \neq \frac{b_1}{b_2}$, so unique solution **(1 Mark)**

10. (d) $\frac{1}{5} = \frac{2}{k} \neq \frac{-3}{7}$ $\left[\because \text{For inconsistent } \frac{a_1}{a_2} = \frac{b_1}{b_2} \neq \frac{c_1}{c_2}\right]$

$\Rightarrow k = 10$ **(1 Mark)**

11. (d) $\frac{a_1}{a_1} = \frac{b_1}{b_2} \neq \frac{c_1}{c_2}$ [For no solution]

$\frac{1}{2} = \frac{1}{k} \neq \frac{-4}{3} \Rightarrow k = 2$ **(1 Mark)**

12. ∵ Given pair of equations have a unique solution.

$\therefore \frac{a_1}{a_2} \neq \frac{b_1}{b_2}$ **(1 Mark)**

$\frac{1}{3} \neq \frac{2}{k}$

$k \neq 6$

k can have any value except 6. **(1 Mark)**

13. Since, system of equations,

$cx + 3y + (3 - c) = 0$; $12x + cy - c = 0$ has infinite many solutions.

Hence, $\frac{c}{12} = \frac{3}{c} = \frac{3-c}{-c}$ ...(1)

Take first two equations, ⇒ $c^2 = 36$ **(1 Mark)**

⇒ c = ± 6.

Therefore, the values of c are ± 6. **(1 Mark)**

But c = – 6 does not satisfy the equation (1).

Hence, the required value of c is only 6. **(1 Mark)**

14. Given linear equation is $3x + 4y = 9$

(i) For intersecting line $\frac{a_1}{a_2} \neq \frac{b_1}{b_2}$

∴ Intersecting line is $3x - 6y = 10$ **(1 Mark)**

(ii) For coincident line $\frac{a_1}{a_2} = \frac{b_1}{b_2} = \frac{c_1}{c_2}$

∴ Coincident line is $6x + 8y = 18$ **(1 Mark)**

15. Here, $\frac{a_1}{a_2} = \frac{4}{2p+7q}$

$\frac{b_1}{b_2} = \frac{5}{p+8q}$

$\frac{c_1}{c_2} = \frac{2}{2q-p+1}$ **(1 Mark)**

For pair linear equations to have infinitely many solutions

$\frac{a_1}{a_2} = \frac{b_1}{b_2} = \frac{c_1}{c_2}$

So, $\frac{4}{2p+7q} = \frac{5}{p+8q} = \frac{2}{2q-p+1}$

So, $\frac{4}{2p+7q} = \frac{5}{p+8q}$ and $\frac{4}{2p+7q} = \frac{2}{2q-p+1}$

i.e., $4p + 32q = 10p + 35q$ and **(1 Mark)**

$8q - 4p + 4 = 4p + 14q$

i.e., $6p + 3q = 0$ and $8p + 6q = 4$

i.e., $q = -2p$ (1) and $4p + 3q = 2$ (2)

Substituting the value of q obtained from equation (1) in equation (2), we get $q = 2$

Putting $q = 2$ in (1) we get $p = -1$

So, for $p = -1$, $q = 2$, the given pair of linear equations will have infinitely many solution. **(1 Mark)**

Topic-2: *Graphical Method of Solution of a Pair of Linear Equations*

1. **(a)** Lines x = a is a line parallel to y axis and y = b is a line parallel to x axis. So they will interest. **(1 Mark)**

2. **(c)** Required area is area of triangle ACD

$- \times$ base $\times$ height $= \frac{1}{2} \times AD \times H$

$= \frac{1}{2} \times 6 \times 2 = 6$ sq. units **(1 Mark)**

3. $2y - x = 8$

x	0	–8	–4
y	4	0	2

$5y - x = 14$

x	–4	1	6
y	2	3	4

$y - 2x = 1$

x	0	1	2
y	1	3	5

(1 Mark)

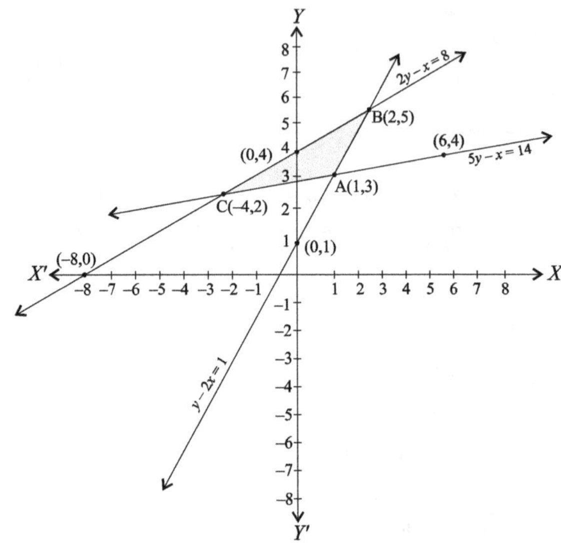

Coordinates of vertices of triangle be A(1,3), B(2,5) and C(–4,2) **(2 Marks)**

4. Let amounts contributed by two sections X-A and X-B be ₹ x and ₹ y.

Now, A.T.Q. $x + y = 1{,}500$ ...(i)

x	0	1500
y	1500	0

$y - x = 100$ ...(ii)

x	0	–100
y	100	0

(1 Mark)

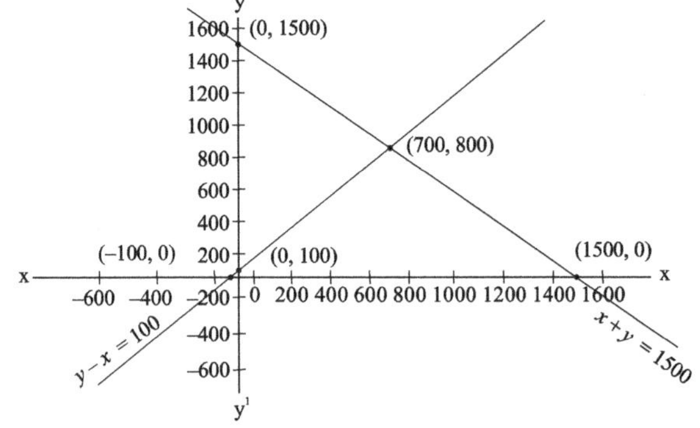

(2 Marks)

Point of intersection = (700, 800)

Hence $x = 700$ and $y = 800$ **(1 Mark)**

5. $3x - 4y + 3 = 0$

x	–1	3	7
y	0	3	6

$3x + 4y - 21 = 0$

x	7	3	–1
y	0	3	6

(1 Mark)

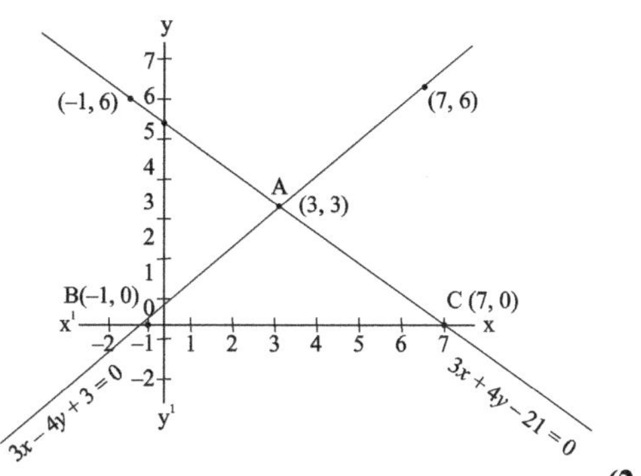

(2 Marks)

Since both lines intersect at (3, 3)

∴ Solution is

$x = 3, y = 3$

Vertices of triangle ABC are

A (3, 3), B (–1, 0) and C(7, 0)

Area of triangle ABC

$= \frac{1}{2} \times 8 \times 3 = 4 \times 3 = 12$ sq. units. **(1 Mark)**

6. $x + 2y = 5$

$\Rightarrow y = \frac{5-x}{2}$

x	1	3	5
y	2	1	0

$2x - 3y = -4$

$\Rightarrow \quad y = \frac{2x+4}{3}$

x	1	4	–2
y	2	4	0

(1 Mark)

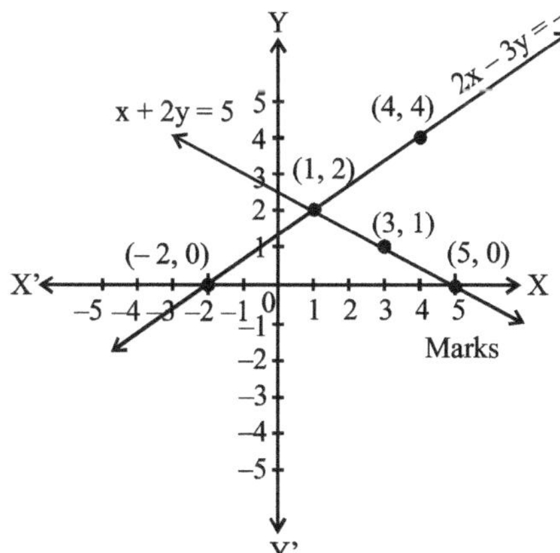

(2 Marks)

Lines meet x-axis at (5, 0) and (–2, 0) respectively.

(1 Mark)

7. Table for values

For $x - y + 1 = 0$

x	0	–1
y	1	0

For $3x + 2y - 12 = 0$

x	0	4
y	6	0

(1 Mark)

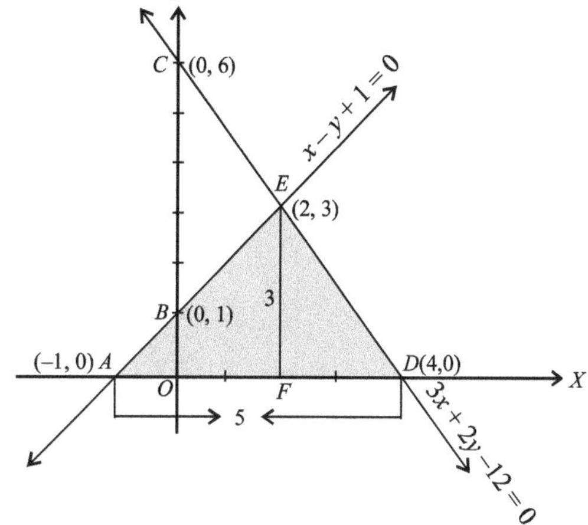

(2 Marks)

Plot the point $A(-1, 0)$, B (0, 1) and join them to get the graph of line $x - y + 1 = 0$.

Now plot the point $C(0, 6)$, $D(4, 0)$. Join them to get the graph of line $3x + 2y - 12 = 0$.

The two lines meet in $E(2, 3)$ and this is the graphic solution of given equations. Also, the two lines meet x-axis in $A(-1, 0)$ and $D(4, 0)$ as shown in figure.

∴ Required vertices of triangle are $A(-1, 0)$, $D(4, 0)$ and $E(2, 3)$. The triangular region is shaded in figure.

Further note that

$AD = AO + OD = 1 + 4 = 5$ units

and $EF = 3$ units

∴ Area of triangles $ADE = \frac{1}{2}(AD)(EF)$

$= \frac{1}{2}(5)(3) = \frac{15}{2}$ square units. **(1 Mark)**

8. Consider both the equations, separately

$3x + y = 12$
$y = 12 - 3x$

$x - 3y = -6$
$3y = x + 6$
$y = \frac{x+6}{3}$

We make tables for both equations by giving the values to x.

$x = \frac{12-y}{3}$ $\qquad$ $y = \frac{x+6}{3}$

x	0	3	4
y	12	3	0

x	0	3	−6
y	2	3	0

(1 Mark)

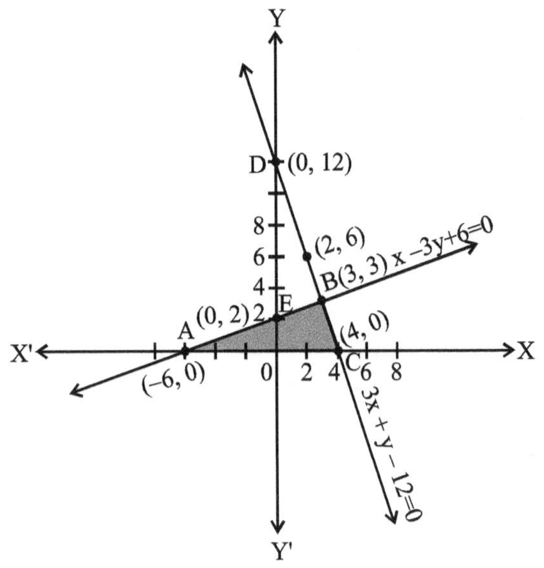

(2 Marks)

By plotting the points on the graph and joining them, we get that the lines intersect at B (3, 3)

$\therefore \quad x = 3, y = 3$

Area of triangle ABC formed by the lines with x-axis $= \frac{1}{2} \times \text{base} \times \text{corresponding height}$

$= \frac{1}{2} \times 10 \times 3 = 15$ sq. units

Area of triangle BDE

$= \frac{1}{2} \times 10 \times 3 = 15$ sq. units

Hence, required ratio = 1 : 1 **(1 Mark)**

When two non parallel lines does not intersect in graph then increase scale of graph.

Topic-3: Substitution Method of Solving a Pair of Linear Equations

1. (a) At Y-axis, the abscissa is 0.

Putting $x = 0$ in the equation $3x - y = 3$

$0 - y = 3$

$y = -3$

Hence, the coordinates of the point are (0, –3)

(1 Mark)

2. (a) $32x + 33y = 34$ ...(i)

$33x + 32y = 31$ ...(ii)

Apply substitution method.

$32x + 33y = 34$ {from (i)}

$33y = 34 - 32x$

$y = \frac{34}{33} - \frac{32}{33}x$ ...(iii)

Substitute the value of y in eq. (ii)

$33x + 32y = 31$

$33x + 32\left(\frac{34}{33} - \frac{32}{33}x\right) = 31$

$33x + \frac{1088 - 1024x}{33} = 31$

$1089x + 1088 - 1024x = 1023$

$65x = -65$

$x = -1$

From (iii)

$y = \frac{34}{33} - \frac{32}{33} \times (-1)$

$y = \frac{34 + 32}{33} = \frac{66}{33} = 2$

Therefore, the value of x and y are –1 and 2 respectively.

(1 Mark)

3.

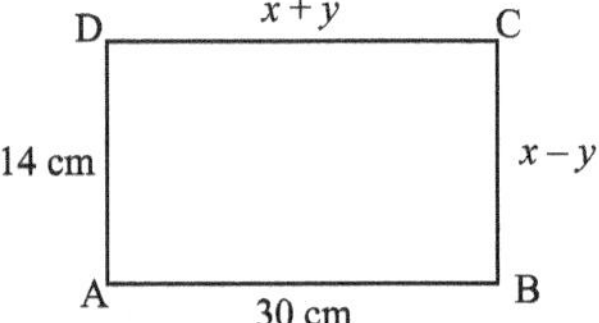

Since ABCD is a rectangle

$\Rightarrow \quad x + y = 30$ ...(i)

and $x - y = 14$ ...(ii) **(1 Mark)**

[$\because$ opposite sides of a rectangle are equal]

Adding equations (i) and (ii) we get

$2x = 44$

$x = \frac{44}{2} = 22$ **(1 Mark)**

Put $x = 22$ in equation (i).

$\Rightarrow \quad 22 + y = 30 \Rightarrow y = 30 - 22 = 8$

Hence $x = 22$ and $y = 8$. **(1 Mark)**

Topic-4: Elimination Method of Solving a Pair of Linear Equations

1. **(a)** Sum of all angles of triangle is 180°

$\angle A + \angle B + \angle C = 180°$

$x + 3x - 2 + y = 180°$

$4x + y = 182$ .... (i)

$\angle C - \angle B = 9°$ (Given)

$y - 3x + 2 = 9$

$-3x + y = 7$

$3x - y = -7$ .... (ii)

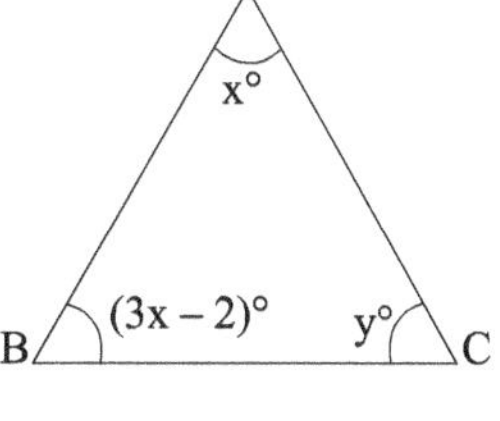

Add (i) and (ii)	From (ii)
$4x + y = 182$	$3x - y = -7$
$3x - y = -7$	$3 \times 25 - y = -7$
$7x = 175$	$75 + 7 = y$
$x = 25$	$y = 82°$

$\angle A = x° = 25° \rightarrow$ Smallest angle

$\angle B = (3x - 2)° = 3 \times 25 - 2 = 75 - 2 = 73°$

$\angle C = y° = 82° \rightarrow$ Greatest angle

Sum of $\angle A + \angle C = x + y$

$= 25 + 82$

$= 107°$ **(1 Mark)**

2. **(a)** Adding the two given equations we get:

$348x + 348y = 1740.$

So $x + y = 5$ **(1 Mark)**

3. Let $\frac{1}{\sqrt{x}} = m$ and $\frac{1}{\sqrt{y}} = n,$ **(½ Mark)**

Then the given equations become

$2m + 3n = 2$

$4m - 9n = -1$ **(½ Mark)**

$(2m + 3n = 2) \times -2 \Rightarrow -4m - 6n = -4$ ...(1)

$4m - 9n = -1 \Rightarrow 4m - 9n = -1$ ...(2)

Adding (1) and (2), we get $-15n = -5 \Rightarrow n = \frac{1}{3}$

(½ Mark)

Substituting $n = \frac{1}{3}$ in the equation $2m + 3n = 2$, we get:

$2m + 1 = 2 \Rightarrow 2m = 1 \Rightarrow m = \frac{1}{2}$ **(½ Mark)**

$m = \frac{1}{2} = \frac{\sqrt{1}}{x} = \frac{1}{2} \Rightarrow \sqrt{x} = 2 \Rightarrow x = 4$ **(½ Mark)**

and $n = \frac{1}{3} = \frac{1}{\sqrt{y}} = \frac{1}{3} \Rightarrow \sqrt{y} = 3 \Rightarrow y = 9$ **(½ Mark)**

4. Adding the two equations and dividing by 10, we get :

$x + y = 10$ **(½ Mark)**

Subtracting the two equations and dividing by –2, we get:

$x - y = 1$ **(½ Mark)**

Solving these two new equations, we get, $x = 11/2$

(½ Mark)

$y = 9/2$

(½ Mark)

5. (i) Subtracts the given equations and finds that $x - y = 1$

(1½ Marks)

(ii) Solves any two equations and finds the values of x and y as 2 and 1 respectively. **(1½ Marks)**

6. $2x + y = 23$ ...(i)

$4x - y = 19$ ...(ii)

Adding (i) and (ii) **(1 Mark)**

$2x + y = 23$

$4x - y = 19$

$6x \quad = 42$

$x = \frac{42}{6} = 7$ **(1 Mark)**

putting $x = 7$ in (i) we get

$2(7) + y = 23 \Rightarrow y = 23 - 14 = 9$

$\therefore \quad 5y - 2x = 5(9) - 2(7) = 45 - 14 = 31$

and $\frac{y}{x} - 2 = \frac{9}{7} - 2 = \frac{9-14}{7} = \frac{-5}{7}$ **(1 Mark)**

Mostly use ellimination method to solve two linear equations of two variables.

7. **Topper's Answer**

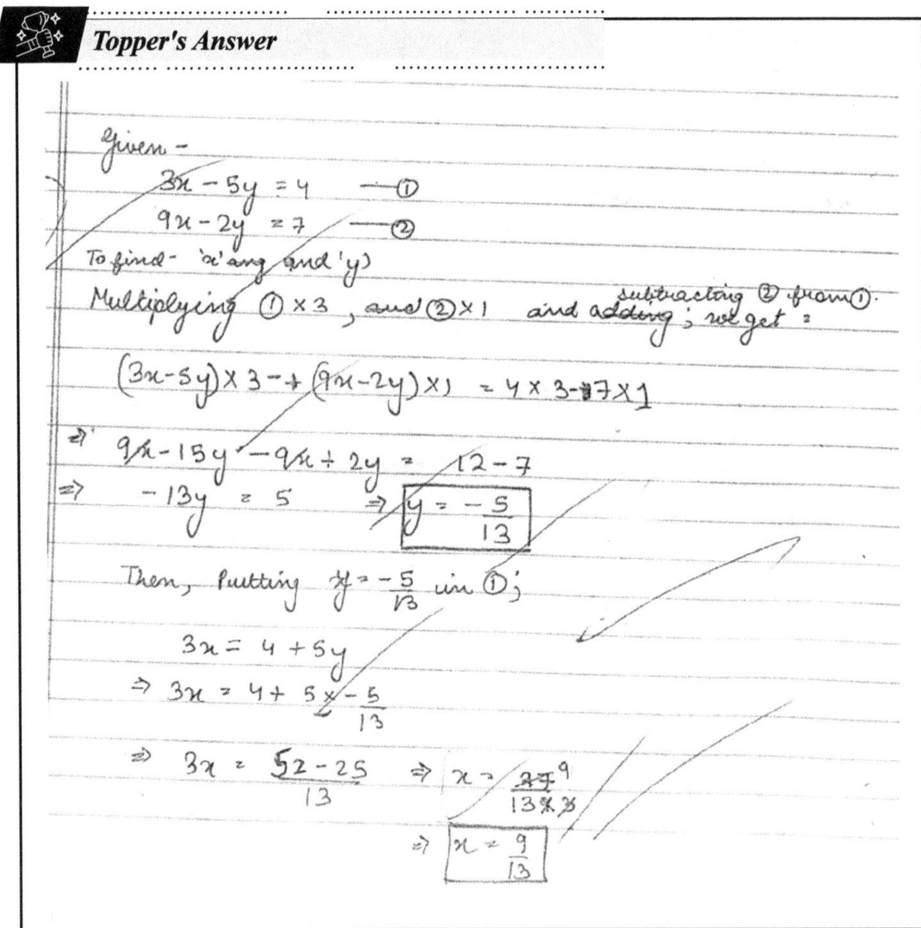

Topic-5: Simple Situation Problems

1. **(c)** 3 chairs + 1 table = ₹ 900

   5 chairs + 3 tables = ₹ 2100

   cost of 1 chair = ₹ x

   cost of 1 table = ₹ y

   Hence, $3x + y = 900$

   and $5x + 3y = 2100$ **(1 Mark)**

2. **(b)** **(1 Mark)**

3. **(d)** Let the fixed charge for first two days be ₹ x and additional charges be ₹ y per day.

   Radhika situation algebraically represented as

   $x + 2y = 16$. **(1 Mark)**

4. **(c)** According to question, Amruta situation represented as $x + 4y = 22$. **(1 Mark)**

5. **(b)** System of linear equations are represented as:

   $x + 4y = 22$ ...(i)

   $x + 2y = 16$ ...(ii)

   Subtract (ii) from (i) by using elimination method,

   $x + 4y = 22$

   $x + 2y = 16$

   $-\quad -$

   $2y = 6$

   $y = 3$

   From (ii)

   $x + 2y = 16 \Rightarrow x + 2 \times 3 = 16$

   $x + 6 = 16$

   $x = 10$

   Fixed charges is ₹ 10. **(1 Mark)**

6. **(d)** From solution Q. 43, the value of additional charges $y = 3$. **(1 Mark)**

7. **(c)** If both of them kept book for 2 more day at ₹ 3 per day then the total amount paid by both is represented as.

   Amount of 2 more days for Amruta = 2 × 3 = ₹ 6

   Amount of 2 more days for Radhika = 2 × 3 = ₹ 6

   Total amount paid by both = 22 + 16 + 6 + 6 = ₹ 50.

   (1 Mark)

8. Let the ten's and the unit's digits in the first number be x and y, respectively.

So, the original number = 10x + y

When the digits are reversed, x becomes the unit's digit and y becomes the ten's digit **(½ Mark)**

So the number obtain by reversing the digits = 10y + x

According to the given condition.

$(10x + y) + (10y + x) = 66$

i.e., $11 (x + y) = 66$ **(½ Mark)**

i.e., $x + y = 6$ ....(1)

We are also given that the digits differ by 2, **(½ Mark)**

therefore, either $x - y = 2$ ....(2) **(½ Mark)**

or $y - x = 2$ ....(3)

Case 1: If $x - y = 2$, then solving (1) and (2) by elimination, we get x = 4 and y = 2. **(½ Mark)**

In this case, we get the number 42.

Case 2: If $y - x = 2$, then solving (1) and (3) by elimination, we get x = 2 and y = 4. **(½ Mark)**

In this case, we get the number 24.

Thus, there are two such numbers 42 and 24.

9. Let the actual speed of the train be x km/hr and let the actual time taken be y hours. **(½ Mark)**

Distance covered is xy km If the speed is increased by 6 km/hr, then time of journey is reduced by 4 hours i.e., when speed is (x + 6)km/hr, time of journey is (y – 4) hours.

∴ Distance covered = $(x + 6)(y - 4)$

⇒ $xy = (x + 6)(y - 4)$

⇒ $4x + 6y - 24 - 0$

⇒ $2x + 3y - 12 = 0$ .....(i)

(½ Mark)

Similarly $xy = (x - 6)(y + 6)$

⇒ $6x - 6y - 36 = 0$

⇒ $x - y - 6 = 0$ ....(ii)

(½ Mark)

Solving (i) and (ii) we get x = 30 and y = 24 **(1 Mark)**

Putting the values of x and y in equation (i), we obtain

Distance = (30 × 24) km = 720 km.

Hence, the length of the journey is 720 km. **(½ Mark)**

10. Let the number of chocolates in lot A be x

And let the number of chocolates in lot B be y

(½ Mark)

∴ Total number of chocolates = x + y

Price of 1 chocolate = ₹2/3 , so for x chocolates = $\frac{2}{3}x$ and price of y chocolates at the rate of ₹1 per chocolate = y.

∴ by the given condition $\frac{2}{3}x + y = 400$ **(½ Mark)**

⇒ $2x + 3y = 1200$ ....(i)

Similarly $= x + \frac{4}{5}y = 460$ **(½ Mark)**

⇒ $5x + 4y = 2300$ ...(ii)

Solving (i) and (ii) we get

x = 300 and y = 200

∴ x + y = 300 + 200 = 500 **(1 Mark)**

So, Anuj had 500 chocolates. **(½ Mark)**

11. Let father's present age is *x* years and sum of the ages of his two children is *a* + *b* years. **(½ Mark)**

Given, $x = 3(a + b)$ ....(1)

After 5 years, **(½ Mark)**

$x + 5 = 2(a + 5 + b + 5) \Rightarrow x + 5 = 2(a + b + 10)$

Using equation (1), **(1 Mark)**

$x + 5 = 2\left(\frac{x}{3} + 10\right) \Rightarrow 3x + 15 = 2(x + 30)$

$\Rightarrow 3x + 15 = 2x + 60 \Rightarrow x = 45$ **(1 Mark)**

Therefore, the present age of the father is 45 years.

12. Let the fraction is $\frac{a}{b}$. **(½ Mark)**

According to the question,

$\frac{a-2}{b} = \frac{1}{3} \Rightarrow 3a \;\; 6 = b \Rightarrow 3a \;\; b = 6$ ....(1) **(½ Mark)**

and $\frac{a}{b-1} = \frac{1}{2} \Rightarrow 2a = b - 1 \Rightarrow 2a - b = -1$....(2) **(½ Mark)**

Subtracting eqn (2) by eqn (1),

$3a - b - 2a + b = 6 + 1 \Rightarrow a = 7$ and $b = 15$

Therefore, the fraction is $\frac{7}{15}$. **(½ Mark)**

13. $10x + y = 7(x + y) = 7x + 7y$

⇒ $3x = 6y$ ⇒ $x = 2y$ **(1 Mark)**

Number formed by reversing the digit yx

$10y + x = 10x + y - 18$ **(1 Mark)**

put x = 2y

⇒ $10y + 2y = 10 \times 2y + y - 18$

⇒ $21y = 18 + 12y$ ⇒ $y = 2$ ∴ $x = 2y = 2 \times 2 = 4$

The number is 42 **(1 Mark)**

14.

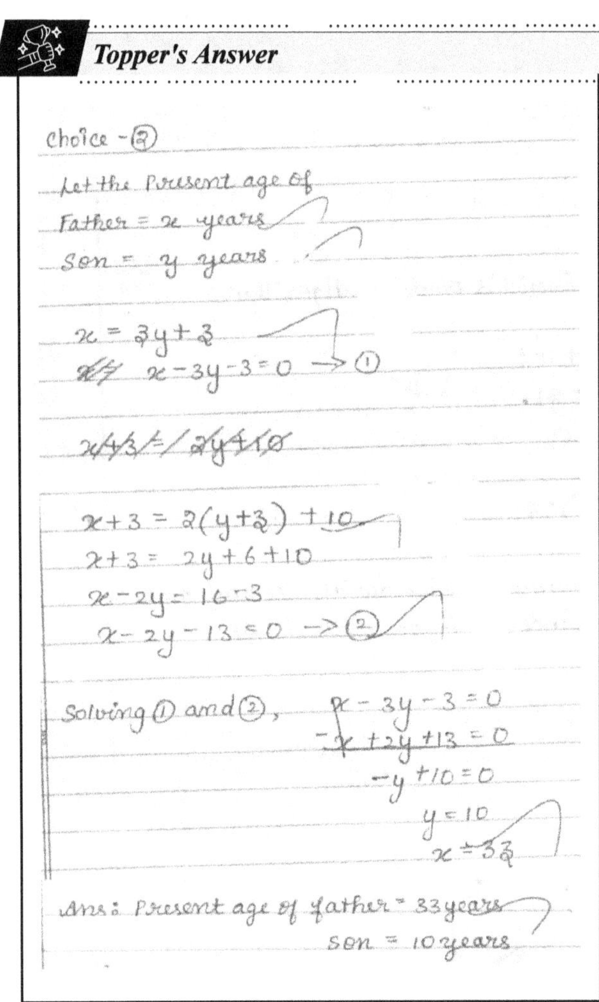
Topper's Answer

Choice - (2)

Let the Present age of
Father = x years
Son = y years

$x = 3y + 3$
$x - 3y - 3 = 0 \rightarrow (1)$

$x + 3 = 2(y+3) + 10$
$x + 3 = 2y + 6 + 10$
$x - 2y = 16 - 3$
$x - 2y - 13 = 0 \rightarrow (2)$

Solving (1) and (2),
$x - 3y - 3 = 0$
$-x + 2y + 13 = 0$
$-y + 10 = 0$
$y = 10$
$x = 33$

Ans: Present age of father = 33 years
son = 10 years

15. Let fixed charge be ₹ x and cost of food per day be ₹ y

$$x + 20y = 3000 \quad ...(i)$$
$$x + 25y = 3500 \quad ...(ii)$$

By using Elimination Method **(1 Mark)**

$$x + 25y = 3500$$
$$x + 20y = 3000$$
$$- \quad - \quad -$$
$$5y = 500$$

$\Rightarrow \quad y = 100$ **(1 Mark)**

$x + 20(100) = 3000$ From (i)

$\Rightarrow \quad x = 1000$

$\therefore \quad x = 1000$ and $y = 100$

Fixed charge and cost of food per day are ₹ 1000 and ₹ 100 **(1 Mark)**

16. Suppose cost of 1 chair = ₹ x and cost of 1 table = ₹ y

A.T.Q.

$$4x + 3y = 2100 \quad ...(i)$$
$$5x + 2y = 1750 \quad ...(ii)$$ **(1 Mark)**

Multiplying eqn. (i) by 2 and eqn. (ii) by 3,

$$8x + 6y = 4200 \quad ...(iii)$$
$$15x + 6y = 5250 \quad ...(iv)$$

Subtract eqn. (iv) from eqn. (iii) **(1 Mark)**

$$7x = 1050$$
$$x = 150$$

Substituting the value of x in (i), $y = 500$

Cost of chair and table = ₹150, ₹ 500 **(1 Mark)**

17. Let x and y be the ages of Aftab and daughter presently.

Seven years ago:

$x - 7 = 7(y - 7) \Rightarrow x - 7y + 42 = 0$ **(1 Mark)**

Three years from now:

$\therefore \quad x + 3 = 3(y + 3) \Rightarrow x - 3y - 6 = 0$ **(1 Mark)**

which is the required pair of linear equations.

18. Let number of boys = x and number of girls = y

$\therefore \quad x + y = 10$ and $y = x + 4$ **(1 Mark)**

$\Rightarrow$ Pair of linear equations for this problem is $x + y - 10 = 0$ and $x - y + 4 = 0$ **(1 Mark)**

19. Let x and y be the digits at unit's place and ten's place, then

Original number = $10y + x$

Number obtained by interchanging the digits

= $10x + y$ **(1 Mark)**

According to the condition, we have

$x + y = 12$ ...(1)

and $(10x + y) - (10y + x) = 18$ **(½ Mark)**

$9x - 9y = 18$

$x - y = 2$ ...(2)

Adding and subtracting (1) and (2), we get **(½ Mark)**

$2x = 14$ and $2y = 10$

$x = 7$ and $y = 5$

Hence, the original number

$= 10y + x$

$= 10(5) + 7$

$= 50 + 7$

= 57 **(1 Mark)**

20. Let Arun's marks in Hindi be x and in English be y. Then, according to question, we have **(1 Mark)**

$x + y = 30$ ...(1)

$(x + 2)(y - 3) = 210$ ...(2) **(1 Mark)**

From equation (1) put $x = 30 - y$ in equation (2)

$(30 - y + 2)(y - 3) = 210$ **(1 Mark)**

$\Rightarrow (32 - y)(y - 3) = 210$

$\Rightarrow 32y - 96 - y^2 + 3y = 210$

$\Rightarrow y^2 - 35y + 306 = 0$

$\Rightarrow y^2 - 18y - 17y + 306 = 0$

$\Rightarrow y(y - 18) - 17(y - 18) = 0$

$\Rightarrow (y - 18)(y - 17) = 0$

$\Rightarrow y = 18, 17$ **(1 Mark)**

Put y = 18 and 17 in equation (1), we get x = 12, 13. Hence, Arun's marks in Hindi can be 12 and 13 and in English his marks can be 18 and 17. **(1 Mark)**

21. Let the speed of two cars be x km/h an y km/h respectively. **(½ Mark)**

Case I: When two cars move in the same direction, they will meet each other at P after 5 hours.

The distance covered by car from A = $5x$ (Distance = Speed × Time) and distance covered by the car from B – 5y

$\therefore \quad 5x - 5y = AB = 100 \Rightarrow \quad x - y = \frac{100}{5}$

$\therefore \quad x - y = 20$ ...(i) **(1½ Marks)**

Case II: Whe two cars move in opposite direction, they will meet each other at Q after one hour.

The distance covered by the car from A = x

The distance covered by the car from B = y

$\therefore \quad x + y = AB = 100$

$\Rightarrow \quad x + y = 100$ ...(ii) **(1 Mark)**

Now, adding equations (i) and (ii), we have

$2x = 120 \Rightarrow x = \frac{120}{2} = 60$

Putting the value of x in equation (i), we get

$60 - y = 20 \Rightarrow -y = -40 \therefore y = 40$

Hence, the speeds of two cars are 60 km/h and 40 km/h respectively. **(1 Mark)**

When two cars move in same direction from different position then difference of their distance travel when they meet is equal to distance between them before start.

22. (i) Number of rich children in batch I = 5

Number of poor children in batch I = 20

Monthly fee collection from batch I = 9000

Amount that poor child pays = ₹ x

Amount that rich child pays = ₹ y

The equation corresponding to the situations is

$5y + 20x = 900 <$ (i) 0

Number of rich children in batch II = 25

Number of poor children in batch II = 5

Monthly fee collection from batch II = 26000

The equation corresponding to the situation is

$5x + 25y = 26000$ (ii) **(1 Mark)**

(ii) The equations are

$20x + 5y = 9000$

and

$5x + 25y = 26000$

Multiply equation $20x + 5y = 9000$ by 5

$100x + 25y = 45000$ (iii) **(1 Mark)**

Subtract equation (ii) from equation (iii)

$$\begin{array}{l} 100x + 25y = 45000 \\ 5x \quad + 25y = 26000 \\ - \quad - \quad\quad - \\ \hline 95x \quad\quad = 19000 \end{array}$$

$x = \frac{19000}{95}$

$\boxed{x = 200}$ **(1 Mark)**

Hence, the poor child pays ₹ 200 per month.

OR

As x = 200, substitute the obtained value of x in equation (i)

$5y + 20(200) = 9000$ **(1 Mark)**

$5y + 4000 = 9000$

$$5y = 5000$$
$$y = 1000$$

Difference in monthly fee paid by poor child and rich child = ₹1000 – ₹200 = ₹800 **(1 Mark)**

(iii) Monthly fee paid by poor children = ₹200

Monthly fee paid by rich children = ₹1000

Fee paid by 10 poor children = ₹200 × 10 = ₹2000

Fee paid by 20 rich children = ₹1000 × 20 = ₹20000

Total fee paid = ₹2000 + ₹20000

= ₹22000 **(1 Mark)**

23. (i) ATQ $5x + 4y = 9500 \rightarrow (1)$

$4x + 3y = 7370 \rightarrow (2)$ **(1 Mark)**

(ii) (a) Prize amount of Hockey = x

To solve this, use elimination method,

Multiply (1) by 3 & (2) by 4, we get **(1 Mark)**

$$15x + 12y = 28500$$
$$16x + 12y = 29480$$
$$-x = -980$$

$$\boxed{x = 980}$$

Prize amount of Hockey = ₹ 980. **(1 Mark)**

OR

(b) Prize amount for cricket = y

Put value of x in (1)[st] equation.

$5x + 4y = 9500$

$5(980) + 4y = 9500$ **(1 Mark)**

$\Rightarrow 4y = 9500 - 4900$

$\Rightarrow 4y = 4600$

$\boxed{y = 1150\text{RS}}$

Prize amount for cricket = 1150

Difference = 150 – 980

= ₹ 170. Total **(1 Mark)**

(iii) $2x + 2y = ?$

$2 \times 980 + 2 \times 1150 = 2\,(980 + 1150)$

$\Rightarrow 2130 \times 2$

$\Rightarrow$ ₹ 4260. **(1 Mark)**

Quadratic Equations

Topic-1: Quadratic Equations

Very Short Answer Questions (1 Mark)

1. Check whether the following equation is quadratic.
   (i) $(x-4)^3 + 20 = x^3 + 2x$ **[CBSE CFPQ 2022, U]**
   (ii) $\frac{2}{x^2} + 4x + 3 = 0$
   Justify your answer in each case.

2. If $x = 3$ is one root of the quadratic equation $x^2 - 2kx - 6 = 0$, then find the value of k. **[All India 2018, K]**

Topic-2: Solution of a Quadratic Equation by Factorisation

Multiple Choice Questions

1. The roots of the equation $x^2 + 3x - 10 = 0$ are: **[Delhi 2023, K]**
   (a) 2, –5 (b) –2, 5
   (c) 2, 5 (d) –2, –5

2. Let p be a prime number. The quadratic equation having its roots as factors of p is **[CBSE Sample Paper 2022-23, K]**
   (a) $x^2 - px + p = 0$
   (b) $x^2 - (p + 1) x + p = 0$
   (c) $x^2 + (p + 1) x + p = 0$
   (d) $x^2 - px + p + 1 = 0$

3. The roots of the quadratic equation $x^2 - 0.04 = 0$ are **[All India 2020, Ap]**
   (a) ± 0.2 (b) ± 0.02
   (c) 0.4 (d) 2

Short Answer Questions (2 or 3 Marks)

4. The sum of two numbers is 15. If the sum of their reciprocals is $\frac{3}{10}$, find the two numbers. **[All India 2023, Set-II, Ap]**

5. Find the solution(s) of the following equation.
   $$(y-1)(y-3)\left(\frac{1}{y-3}+\frac{2y}{y-1}\right) = 2; y \neq 1, 3$$
   Show your steps and give valid reasons. **[CBSE CFPQ, 2022 U]**

6. One of the solutions of the follwing equations is –7 where k is a constant. **[CBSE CFPQ, 2022, A]**
   $z^2 - kz - 28 = 0$
   (i) Find the value of k.
   (ii) Find the other solution.
   Show your steps.

7. Solve the quadratic equation for x:
   $x^2 - 2ax - (4b^2 - a^2) = 0$ **[All India 2022, K]**

8. Solve for x : $\frac{1}{x+4} - \frac{1}{x-7} = \frac{11}{30}, x \neq -4, 7.$ **[All India 2020, K]**

9. Solve for x :
   $$\frac{1}{x+1} + \frac{3}{5x+1} = \frac{5}{x+4}, x \neq -1, -\frac{1}{5}, -4$$
   [All India 2017 Term-II, U]

10. Solve for x : **[Delhi 2016, Term-II, K]**

$$\frac{2x}{x-3}+\frac{1}{2x+3}+\frac{3x \quad 9}{(x-3)(2x+3)}=0, \quad \neq 3,-\frac{3}{2}$$

11. Solve the following quadratic equation for x :

$4x^2+4bx-(a^2-b^2)=0$ **[All India 2015, Term-II, A]**

12. Solve for x :

$\sqrt{3}x^2-2\sqrt{2}x-2\sqrt{3}=0$ **[All India 2015, Term-II, A]**

13. Solve the equation $\frac{4}{x}-3=\frac{5}{2x+3}; x \neq 0,-\frac{3}{2}$, for x.

[Delhi 2014, Term-II], K

14. Solve the following quadratic equation for x :

$4\sqrt{3}x^2+5x-2\sqrt{3}=0$ **[All India 2013, U]**

6 *Long Answer Questions (4 or 5 Marks)*

15. Two water taps together can fill a tank in $9\frac{3}{8}$ hours. The tap of larger diameter takes 10 hours less than the smaller one to fill the tank separately. Find the time in which each tap can separately fill the tank.

[CBSE Sample Paper 2023-24, Ap]

16. To fill a swimming pool two pipes are used. If the pipe of larger diameter used for 4 hours and the pipe of smaller diameter for 9 hours, only half of the pool can be filled. Find, how long it would take for each pipe to fill the pool separately, if the pipe of smaller diameter takes 10 hours more than the pipe of larger diameter to fill the pool?

[CBSE Sample Paper 2022-23, Ap]

17. In a flight of 600km, an aircraft was slowed down due to bad weather. Its average speed for the trip was reduced by 200 km/hr from its usual speed and the time of the flight increased by 30 min. Find the scheduled duration of the flight. **[CBSE Sample Paper 2022-23, U]**

18. The sum of two numbers is 34. If 3 is subtracted from one number and 2 is added to another, the product of these two numbers becomes 260. Find the numbers.

[All India 2022, Term-II, U]

19. The hypotenuse (in cm) of a right angled triangle is 6 cm more than twice the length of the shortest side. If the length of third side is 6 cm less than thrice the length of shortest side, then find the dimensions of the triangle.

[All India 2022, Term-II, U]

20. Two taps running together can fill a tank in $3\frac{1}{13}$ hours. If one tap takes 3 hours more than the other to fill the tank, then how much time will each tap take to fill the tank ?

[All India 2017, Term-II , U]]

21. A passenger, while boarding the plane, slipped from the stairs and got hurt. The pilot took the passenger in the emergency clinic at the airport for treatment. Due to this, the plane got delayed by half an hour. To reach the destination 1500 km away in time, so that the passengers could catch the connecting flight, the speed of the plane was increased by 250 km/hour than the usual speed. Find the usual speed of the plane. What value is depicted in this question?

[Delhi 2016, Term-II , U]]

22. Find x in terms of a, b and c : **[Delhi 2016, Term-II , A]]**

$$\frac{a}{x-a}+\frac{b}{x-b}=\frac{2c}{x-c}, x \neq a,b,c$$

23. A train travels at a certain average speed for a distance of 54 km and then travels a distance of 63 km at an average speed of 6 km/h more than the first speed. If it takes 3 hours to complete the total journey, what is its first speed?

[All India 2015, Term-II, Ap]

24. The difference of two natural numbers is 5 and the difference of their reciprocals is $\frac{1}{10}$. Find the numbers.

[Delhi 2014, Term-II, Ap]

25. Solve the following for x : **[All India 2013, A]**

$$\frac{1}{2a+b+2x}=\frac{1}{2a}+\frac{1}{b}+\frac{1}{2x}$$

26. Sum of the areas of two squares is 400 cm^2. If the difference of their perimeters is 16 cm, find the sides of the two squares. **[All India 2013, U]**

Topic-3: Solution of a Quadratic Equation by Formula

Short Answer Questions (2 or 3 Marks)

1. Solve the quadratic equation: $x^2 - 2ax + (a^2 - b^2) = 0$ for x. **[All India 2022 ,Term-II, K]**

2. Write the discriminant of the quadratic equation $(x + 5)^2 = 2(5x - 3)$. **[All India 2019, K]**

3. Solve the quadratic equation $2x^2 + ax - a^2 = 0$ for x. **[Delhi 2014, Term-II, Ap]**

Topic-4: Relationship between Discriminant and Nature of Roots

Multiple Choice Questions

1. The nature of roots of the quadratic equation $9x^2 - 6x - 2 = 0$. **[CBSE Sample Paper 2023-24, Ap]**
   (a) No real roots
   (b) 2 equal real roots
   (c) 2 distinct real roots
   (d) More than 2 real roots

2. If the quadratic equation $ax^2 + bx + c = 0$ has two real and equal roots, then c is equal to : **[All India 2023, Set-II, Ap]**
   (a) $\frac{-b}{2a}$
   (b) $\frac{b}{2a}$
   (c) $\frac{-b^2}{4a}$
   (d) $\frac{b^2}{4a}$

Very Short Answer Questions (1 Mark)

3. Find the nature of roots of the quadratic equation $2x^2 - 4x + 3 = 0$. **[All India 2019, K]**

4. For what values of k, the roots of the equation $x^2 + 4x + k = 0$ are real? **[Delhi 2019, K]**

5. If the quadratic equation $px^2 - 2\sqrt{5}px + 15 = 0$ has two equal roots, then find the value of p. **[All India 2015, Term-II, A]**

Short Answer Questions (2 or 3 Marks)

6. If α and β are roots of the quadratic equation $x^2 - 7x + 10 = 0$, find the quadratic equation whose roots are α^2 and β^2. **[All India 2023, Set-II, Ap]**

7. Find the value of 'p' for which the quadratic equation $px(x - 2) + 6 = 0$ has two equal real roots. **[Delhi 2023, Ap]**

8. Write all the values of p for which the quadratic equation $x^2 + px + 16 = 0$ has equal roots. Find the roots of the equation so obtained. **[All India 2019, U]**

9. If $ad \neq bc$, then prove that the equation $(a^2 + b^2)x^2 + 2(ac + bd)x + (c^2 + d^2) = 0$ has no real roots. **[All India 2017, Term-II, U]**

10. For what value of k, are the roots of the quadratic equation $kx(x - 2) + 6 = 0$ equal ? **[All India 2013, Ap]**

Long Answer Questions (4 or 5 Marks)

11. Find the values of k for which the quadratic equation $(k + 4)x^2 + (k + 1)x + 1 = 0$ has equal roots. Also find these roots. **[Delhi 2014, Term-II, A]**

Topic-5: Day to Day Situation Problem

Short Answer Questions (2 or 3 Marks)

1. In a flight of 600 km, an aircraf was slowed down due to bad weather. The average speed of the trip was reduced by 200 km/hr and the time of flight increased by 30 minutes. Find the duration of flight. **[All India, 2020, Ap]**

2. In a flight of 600 km, an aircraft was slowed due to bad weather. Its average speed for the trip was reduced by 200 km/hr and time of flight increased by 30 minutes. Find the original duration of flight. **[Delhi 2020, Ap]**

3. A plane left 30 minutes late than its schedule time and in order to reach the destination 1500 km away in time, it had to increase its speed by 100 km//h from the usual speed. Find its usual speed. **[All India 2018, Ap]**

Long Answer Questions (4 or 5 Marks)

4. A motor boat whose speed is 18 km/h in still water takes 1 hour more to go 24 km upstream than to return downstream to the same spot. Find the speed of stream.

[CBSE Sample Paper 2023-24, A]

5. A train travels at a certain average speed for a distance of 54 km and then travels a distance of 63 km at an average speed of 63 km at an average speed of 6 km/h more than the first speed. If it takes 3 hours to complete the journey, what was its first average speed? **[All India 2023, A]**

6. Two pipes together can fill a tank in $\frac{15}{8}$ hours. The pipe with larger diameter takes 2 hours less than the pipe with smaller diameter to fill the tank separately. Find the time in which each pipe can fill the tank separately.

[All India 2023, A]

7. A train travels at a certain average speed for a distance of 63 km and then travels at a distance of 72 km at an average speed of 6 km/hr more than its original speed. If it takes 3 hours to complete journey, what is the original average speed? **[All India 2023, A]**

8. A motor boat whose speed is 18 km/h in still water takes 1 hr more to go 24 km upstream than to return downstream to the same spot. Find the speed of the stream.

[All India 2020, Ap]

Case Based Questions (4 Marks)

9. In the picture given below, one can see a rectangular in-ground swimming pool installed by a family in their backyard. There is a concrete sidewalk around the pool of width x m. The outside edges of the sidewalk measure 7 m and 12 m. The area of the pool is 36 sq. m.

[All India 2022, A]

(a) Based on the information given above, form a quadratic equation in terms of x.

(b) Find the width of the sidewalk around the pool.

Hints & Solutions

Topic-1: Quadratic Equations

1. (i) Writes that the equation is of degree 2 or writes that the simplified form is $-12x^2 + 46x - 44 = 0$, and hence it is quadratic.

(½ Mark)

(ii) Writes that the equation is not of degree 2 and hence it is not quadratic. **(½ Mark)**

2. As $x = 3$ is a root of the quadratic equation **(½ Mark)**

$x^2 - 2kx - 6 = 0$

$\therefore \quad (3)^2 - 2k(3) - 6 = 0$

$\Rightarrow \quad 9 - 6k - 6 = 0 \Rightarrow 3 - 6k = 0 \Rightarrow k = \frac{3}{6} = \frac{1}{2}$

Hence, the value of $k = \frac{1}{2}$ if $x = 3$ is a root of the quadratic equation $x^2 - 2kx - 6 = 0$. **(½ Mark)**

Every root must satisfy its equation.

Topic-2: Solution of a Quadratic Equation by Factorisation

1. **(a)** $x^2 + 3x - 10 = 0$, $a = 1$, $b = 3$, $c = -10$ **(1 Mark)**

Sum of roots is $= \frac{-b}{a}$, Product of roots $= \frac{c}{a}$

Check by options $\alpha + \beta = -3$, $\alpha\beta = -10$

Another Method:

$x^2 + 5x - 2x - 10 = 0 \Rightarrow x(x + 5) - 2(x + 5) = 0$

$\Rightarrow \quad (x + 5)(x - 2) = 0$

$\Rightarrow \quad x = -5, 2$

2. **(b)** $x^2 - (p + 1)x + p = 0$ **(1 Mark)**

3. **(a)** $x^2 - 0.04 = 0 \Rightarrow x^2 = 0.04 \Rightarrow x = \pm 0.2$ **(1 Mark)**

4. Let the numbers are x and y

ATQ

$x + y = 15$ (i) **(1 Mark)**

$\frac{1}{x} + \frac{1}{y} = \frac{3}{10}$ (ii) **(1 Mark)**

solving equation (ii)

$\frac{x+y}{xy} = \frac{3}{10}$

$\frac{15}{xy} = \frac{3}{10}$ [from equation (i)]

$xy = 50$ (iii)

$x = \frac{50}{y}$

substitute the obtained value of x in equation (i)

$\frac{50}{y} + y = 15$

$y^2 + 50 = +15y$

$\Rightarrow y^2 - 15y + 50 = 0$

$y^2 - 10y - 5y + 50 = 0$

$y(y - 10) - 5(y - 10) = 0$

$(y - 10)(y - 5) = 0$

$(y - 10) = 0$ or $(y - 5) = 0$

$y = 10$ or $y = 5$

When $y = 5, x = 10$

When $y = 10, x = 5$

The numbers are (10, 5) **(1 Mark)**

5. Simplifies the given equation as $2y^2 - 5y - 3 = 0$

(½ Mark)

Factorises the above equation as:

$(y - 3)(2y + 1) = 0$ **(1 Mark)**

Concludes that the solution of the original equation is $y = \frac{-1}{2}$ as $y \neq 3$. **(½ Mark)**

6. (i) Substitutes $z = (-7)$ in the given equation and finds the values of k as -3. **(1 Mark)**

(ii) Substitus $k = -3$ in the given equation and factorises the LHS as $(z + 7)(z - 4)$.

(½ Mark)

Concludes that the other solution is $z = 4$

(½ Mark)

7.

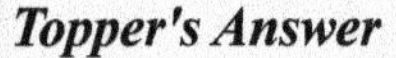

Topper's Answer

$x^2 - 2ax - (4b^2 - a^2) = 0$

$b^2 - 4ac = 4a^2 - 4[-(4b^2 - a^2)](1)$

$= 4a^2 - 4[-4b^2 + a^2]$

$= 4a^2 + 16b^2 - 4a^2$

$= 16b^2$

$x = \frac{-b \pm \sqrt{b^2 - 4ac}}{2a} = \frac{2a \pm \sqrt{16b^2}}{2(1)} = \frac{2a \pm 4b}{2}$

$\Rightarrow x = \frac{2a+4b}{2}$ $x = \frac{2a-4b}{2}$

$x = a+2b$ $x = a-2b$

8. $\frac{1}{x+4} - \frac{1}{x-7} = \frac{11}{30}$

$\Rightarrow \frac{(x-7)-(x+4)}{(x+4)(x-7)} = \frac{11}{30}$

$\Rightarrow \frac{x-7-x-4}{x^2-3x-28} = \frac{11}{30}$

$\Rightarrow \frac{-11}{x^2-3x-28} = \frac{11}{30}$

$\Rightarrow x^2 - 3x - 28 = -30 \Rightarrow x^2 - 3x + 2 = 0$ **(1 Mark)**

$\Rightarrow x^2 - 2x - x + 2 = 0$

$\Rightarrow x(x-2) - 1(x-2) = 0$

$\Rightarrow (x-1)(x-2) = 0$

$\Rightarrow x - 1 = 0$ | $x - 2 = 0$ **(1 Mark)**

$x = 1$ | $x = 2$

9. Given that, **(1 Mark)**

$\frac{1}{x+1} + \frac{3}{5x+1} = \frac{5}{x+4}, x \neq -1, \frac{-1}{5}, -4$

$\Rightarrow \frac{5x+1+3x+3}{(x+1)(5x+1)} = \frac{5}{x+4}$

$\Rightarrow (8x+4)(x+4) = 5(x+1)(5x+1)$

$\Rightarrow 8x^2 + 32x + 4x + 16 = 5(5x^2 + x + 5x + 1)$

$\Rightarrow 8x^2 + 36x + 16 = 25x^2 + 30x + 5$

$\Rightarrow 17x^2 - 6x - 11 = 0$ **(1 Mark)**

$\Rightarrow 17x^2 - 17x + 11x - 11 = 0$

$\Rightarrow 17x(x-1) + 11(x-1) = 0$

$\Rightarrow (17x + 11)(x - 1) = 0$

$\Rightarrow (17x + 11) = 0$ or $(x - 1) = 0$

$\Rightarrow x = \frac{-11}{17}$ or $x = 1$ **(1 Mark)**

10. $\frac{2x}{x-3} + \frac{1}{2x+3} + \frac{3x+9}{(x-3)(2x+3)} = 0$ **(1 Mark)**

$\frac{2x(2x+3)+(x-3)+(3x+9)}{(x-3)(2x+3)} = 0$

$\Rightarrow 4x^2 + 6x + x - 3 + 3x + 9 = 0$

$\Rightarrow 4x^2 + 10x + 6 = 0$

$\Rightarrow 2x^2 + 5x + 3 = 0$ **(1 Mark)**

$\Rightarrow 2x^2 + 2x + 3x + 3 = 0$

$\Rightarrow 2x(x + 1) + 3(x + 1) = 0$

$\Rightarrow (x + 1)(2x + 3) = 0$

$\Rightarrow x + 1 = 0$ or $2x + 3 = 0$

$\Rightarrow x = -1$ or $x = \frac{-3}{2}$

$\Rightarrow$ But $x \neq \frac{-3}{2}$

$\therefore x = -1$ is the solution **(1 Mark)**

Note

In order to find roots of equation, discriminant of the equation should be greater than 0 (D > 0)

11. $4x^2 + 4bx - (a^2 - b^2) = 0$ **(1 Mark)**

$4x^2 + 4bx = a^2 - b^2$

$x^2 + bx = \frac{a^2 - b^2}{4}$

Adding $\left(\frac{b}{2}\right)^2$ on both sides

$x^2 + 2\left(\frac{b}{2}\right)x + \left(\frac{b}{2}\right)^2 = \frac{a^2 - b^2}{4} + \left(\frac{b}{2}\right)^2$

$\left(x + \frac{b}{2}\right)^2 = \frac{a^2 - b^2}{4} + \frac{b^2}{4}$ $[\because (x + y)^2 = x^2 + y^2 + 2xy]$

$\left(\quad - \right) = \frac{a^2}{4} \Rightarrow x + \frac{b}{2} = \pm\frac{a}{2}$

$x = -\frac{b}{2} \pm \frac{a}{2} \Rightarrow x = -\frac{b-a}{2}$ or $x = -\frac{b+a}{2}$

Hence the roots are $-\frac{b-a}{2}$ or $-\frac{b+a}{2}$ **(1 Mark)**

Note

In a quadratic equation, $ax^2 + bx + c = 0$

Sum of roots $= \alpha + \beta = -\frac{b}{a}$

Product of roots $= \alpha\beta = \frac{c}{a}$

12. $\sqrt{3}x^2 - 2\sqrt{2}x - 2\sqrt{3} = 0$

$\Rightarrow \sqrt{3}x^2 - 3\sqrt{2}x + \sqrt{2}x - 2\sqrt{3} = 0$

$\Rightarrow \sqrt{3}x^2 - \sqrt{3}\sqrt{3}\sqrt{2}x + \sqrt{2}x - \sqrt{2}\sqrt{2}\sqrt{3} = 0$

$\Rightarrow \sqrt{3}x(x - \sqrt{6}) + \sqrt{2}\left(x - \sqrt{6}\right) = 0$

$\Rightarrow (x - \sqrt{6})(\sqrt{3}x + \sqrt{2}) = 0$

$\Rightarrow x - \sqrt{6} = 0$ or $\sqrt{3}x + \sqrt{2} = 0$

$\Rightarrow x = \sqrt{6}$ or $x = -\sqrt{\frac{2}{3}}$ **(2 Marks)**

13. $\frac{4}{x} - 3 = \frac{5}{2x+3}$

$\frac{4-3x}{x} = \frac{5}{2x+3}$

$(4 - 3x)(2x + 3) = 5x$ **(1 Mark)**

$-6x^2 + 8x - 9x + 12 = 5x$

$-6x^2 - x - 5x + 12 = 0$

$\Rightarrow 6x^2 + 6x - 12 = 0$

$x^2 + x - 2 = 0$ **(1 Mark)**

$x^2 + 2x - x - 2 = 0$

$\Rightarrow (x + 2)(x - 1) = 0$

$\Rightarrow x = -2$ or $x = 1$

Thus solution of given equation is –2, 1. **(1 Mark)**

Note

Sum of roots $= \alpha + \beta = -\frac{b}{a}$

Product of roots $= \alpha\beta = -$

14. $4\sqrt{3}x^2 + 5x - 2\sqrt{3} = 0$

$4\sqrt{3}x^2 + 8x - 3x - 2\sqrt{3} = 0$ **(1 Mark)**

$4x(\sqrt{3}x + 2) - \sqrt{3}(\sqrt{3}x + 2) = 0$

$(\sqrt{3}x + 2)(4x - \sqrt{3}) = 0$

$\sqrt{3}x + 2 = 0$ or $4x - \sqrt{3} = 0$

$x = -\frac{2}{\sqrt{3}}$ or $x = \frac{\sqrt{3}}{4}$

$x = -\frac{2\sqrt{3}}{3}$ or $x = \frac{\sqrt{3}}{4}$ **(1 Mark)**

15. Let the time taken by the smaller pipe to fill the tank = x hr.

Time taken by the larger pipe = (x – 10) hr **(½ Mark)**

Part of the tank filled by smaller pipe in 1 hour = $\frac{1}{x}$

Part of the tank filled by larger pipe in 1 hour = $\frac{1}{x-10}$

(½ Mark)

The tank can be filled in $9\frac{3}{8} = \frac{75}{8}$ hours by both the pipes together. **(½ Mark)**

Part of the tank filled by both the pipes in 1 hour = $\frac{8}{75}$

(½ Mark)

Therefore, $\frac{1}{x}+\frac{1}{x-10}=\frac{8}{75} \Rightarrow \frac{2x-10}{x(x-10)}=\frac{8}{75}$ **(1 Mark)**

$8x^2 - 230x + 750 = 0 \Rightarrow 4x^2 - 115x + 375 = 0$

$\Rightarrow (x-25) = 25, \left(x-\frac{15}{4}\right) = 0 \Rightarrow x = 25, \frac{15}{4}$ **(1 Mark)**

Time taken by the smaller pipe cannot be 15/4 = 3.75 hours, as the time taken by the larger pipe will become negative, which is logically not possible. **(½ Mark)**

Therefore, the time taken individually by the smaller pipe is 25 hours and the larger pipe will be 25 – 10 = 15 hours. **(½ Mark)**

16. Let the time taken by larger pipe alone to fill the tank = x hours

Therefore, the time taken by the smaller pipe = x + 10 hours **(½ Mark)**

Water filled by larger pipe running for 4 hours $=\frac{4}{x}$ litres

(1 Mark)

Water filled by smaller pipe running for 9 hours $=\frac{9}{x+10}$ litres

(½ Mark)

We know that

$\frac{4}{x}+\frac{9}{x+10}=\frac{1}{2}$ **(1 Mark)**

Which on simplification gives:

$x^2 - 16x - 80 = 0$

$x^2 - 20x + 4x - 80 = 0$

$x(x - 20) + 4(x - 20) = 0$

$(x + 4)(x - 20) = 0$

$x = -4, 20$ **(1 Mark)**

x cannot be negative.

Thus, x = 20

x + 10 = 30 **(½ Mark)**

Larger pipe would alone fill the tank in 20 hours and smaller pipe would fill the tank alone in 30 hours.

(½ Mark)

17. Let the usual speed of plane be x km/hr **(½ Mark)**

and the reduced speed of the plane be (x – 200) km/hr

Distance = 600 km [Given]

According to the question,

(time taken at reduced speed) - (Schedule time) = 30 minutes = 0.5 hours.

$\frac{600}{x-200}-\frac{600}{x}=\frac{1}{2}$ **(1 Mark)**

Which on simplification gives: **(1 Mark)**

$x^2 - 200x - 240000 = 0$

$x^2 - 600x + 400x - 240000 = 0$

$x(x - 600) + 400(x - 600) = 0$

$(x - 600)(x + 400) = 0$

$x = 600$ or $x = -400$ **(1 Mark)**

But speed cannot be negative. **(½ Mark)**

∴ The usual speed is 600 km/hr and **(½ Mark)**

the scheduled duration of the flight is $\frac{600}{600}$ = 1hour **(½ Mark)**

18. Let the two numbers are x and y.

$x + y = 34$ ... (i) **(1 Mark)**

$(x-3)(y+2) = 260$

$xy + 2x - 3y - 6 = 260$

$xy + 2x - 3y = 266$ ... (ii) **(1 Mark)**

Multiply eq. (i) with (iii).

$3x + 3y = 102$ ... (iii)

Add equations (ii) & (iii)

$$\begin{aligned} xy + 2x - 3y &= 266 \\ 3x + 3y &= 102 \\ \hline xy + 5x &= 368 \\ x(y+5) &= 368 \end{aligned}$$

$x(34 - x + 5) = 368$ $\begin{cases} \text{from (i)} \\ y = 34 - x \end{cases}$

$x(39 - x) = 368$

$-x^2 + 39x - 368 = 0$

$x^2 - 39x + 368 = 0$

$x^2 - 23x - 16x + 368 = 0$

$x(x - 23) - 16(x - 23) = 0$

$(x - 16)(x - 23) = 0$

$(x - 16) = 0, x - 23 = 0$

$x = 16, x = 23.$ **(1 Mark)**

From (i)

$x + y = 34$

put $x = 16, y = 34 - 16 = 18$

put $x = 23, y = 34 - 23 = 11$

Therefore, two numbers are (16, 18) and (23, 11).

(1 Mark)

19. Let the shortest side be x cm. (Let b)

hypotenuse = $(2x + 6)$ cm.

third side = $(3x - 6)$ cm = p (Let) **(2 Marks)**

Apply pythagoras theorem,

$H^2 = p^2 + b^2$

$(2x + 6)^2 = (3x - 6)^2 + x^2$

$4x^2 + 3b + 24x = 9x^2 + 3b - 3bx + x^2$

$10x^2 - 4x^2 - 36x - 24x = 0$

$6x^2 - 60x = 0$

$6x(x - 10) = 0$

$x = 0, x - 10 = 0$

$x = 10.$

Hence $b = 10$ cm

hypotenuse = $(2x + 6) = 2 \times 10 + 6 = 26$ cm.

and, $p = (3x - 6) = 3 \times 10 - 6 = 24$ cm. **(2 Marks)**

We need to assume the shortest side as base 'b'. So, third side will be perpendicular 'p'.

20. Let time taken by one tap to fill the tank = x hours

Then time taken by second tap to fill the tank = $(x + 3)$ hours

Part filled by first tap in 1 hour = $\frac{1}{x}$

Part filled by second tap in 1 hour = $\frac{1}{x+3}$ **(1 Mark)**

Part filled by both the taps in 1 hour

$= \frac{1}{x} + \frac{1}{x+3}$ ...(i) **(1 Mark)**

But, given that time taken by both the taps to fill the tank

$= 3\frac{1}{13} = \frac{40}{13}$ hr. **(1 Mark)**

$\Rightarrow \frac{1}{x} + \frac{1}{x+3} = \frac{13}{40}$

$\Rightarrow \frac{x+3+x}{x(x+3)} = \frac{13}{40}$

$\Rightarrow 40(2x + 3) = 13(x^2 + 3x)$

$\Rightarrow 80x + 120 = 13x^2 + 39x$

$\Rightarrow 13x^2 - 41x - 120 = 0$

$\Rightarrow 13x^2 - 65x + 24x - 120 = 0$

$\Rightarrow 13x(x - 5) + 24(x - 5) = 0$

$\Rightarrow (3x + 24)(x - 5) = 0$

$\Rightarrow x = -\frac{24}{13}$ or $x = 5$ **(1 Mark)**

But time cannot be negative therefore, taking $x = 5$, we get

Time taken by first tap to fill the tank = 5 hours and time taken by the second tap to fill the tank = 5 + 3 = 8 hours.

(1 Mark)

21. Let the usual speed of the plane be x km/h.

Let the time taken by the plane to reach the destination be t_1

$\therefore t_1 = \frac{1500}{x}$ $\left[\because \text{Time} = \frac{\text{Distance}}{\text{Speed}}\right]$ **(1 Mark)**

To reach the destination on time, the speed of the plane was increased to $(x + 250)$ km/hr.

$\therefore t_2 = \frac{1500}{x+250}$ **(1 Mark)**

$\Rightarrow t_1 - t_2 = 30$ min

$\Rightarrow \frac{1500}{x} - \frac{1500}{x+250} = 30$ **(1 Mark)**

$\Rightarrow \frac{1500(x+250) - 1500x}{x(x+250)} = \frac{1}{2}$

$\Rightarrow 750000 = x^2 + 250x$

$\Rightarrow x^2 + 250x - 750000 = 0$

$\Rightarrow x^2 + 1000x - 750x - 750000 = 0$

$\Rightarrow x(x + 1000) - 750(x + 1000) = 0$

$\Rightarrow (x + 1000)(x - 750) = 0$

$\Rightarrow x = -1000$ or $x = 750$ **(1 Mark)**

$\Rightarrow x$ cannot be negative.

So $x = 750$

$\therefore$ Usual speed of plane is 750 km/hr.

The value depicted in this question is that of humanity. The pilot has set an example of a good and responsible citizen of the society. **(1 Mark)**

22. $\frac{a}{x-a}+\frac{b}{x-b} = \frac{2c}{x-c}$

$\frac{a(x-b)+b(x-a)}{(x-a)(x-b)} = \frac{2c}{x-c}$

$\Rightarrow (x-c)[a(x-b)+b(x-a)] = 2c(x-a)(x-b)$

$\Rightarrow (x-c)[ax-ab+bx-ba] = 2c(x^2-bx-ax+ab)$

$\Rightarrow (x-c)[ax+bx-2ab] = 2c[x^2-bx-ax+ab]$

$\Rightarrow ax^2+bx^2-2abx-acx-bcx+2abc = 2cx^2-2bcx-2acx+2abc$

$\Rightarrow ax^2+bx^2-2cx^2 = 2abx-acx-bcx$ **(2 Marks)**

$\Rightarrow x^2(a+b-2c) = x(2ab-ac-bc)$

$\Rightarrow x^2(a+b-2c) - x(2ab-ac-bc) = 0$

$\Rightarrow x[(a+b-2c)x-(2ab-ac-bc)] = 0$

$\Rightarrow x = 0$ or $(a+b-2c)x = (2ab-ac-bc)$

$\Rightarrow x = 0$ or $x = \frac{2ab-ac-bc}{a+b-2c}$

$\therefore$ Roots of equation are $x = 0$ and $x = \frac{2ab-ac-bc}{a+b-2c}$

(2 Marks)

23. 54 km — 63 km

x km/hr — $(6+x)$ km/hr

Let average speed for 54 km distance be x km/hr

Then average speed to cover 63 km = $(x+6)$ km/hr

Total time = 3 hr

$\text{Time} = \frac{\text{Distance}}{\text{Speed}}$

$\frac{54}{x}+\frac{63}{x+6} = 3$ **(2 Marks)**

$\Rightarrow \frac{54(x+6)+63x}{x(x+6)} = 3$

$\Rightarrow 54x+324+63x = 3(x^2+6x)$

$\Rightarrow 117x+324 = 3x^2+18x$

$\Rightarrow 3x^2+18x-117x-324 = 0$

$\Rightarrow 3x^2-99x-324 = 0$

$\Rightarrow x^2-33x-108 = 0$

$\Rightarrow x^2-36x+3x-108 = 0$

$\Rightarrow x(x-36)+3(x-36) = 0$

$\Rightarrow (x-36)(x+3) = 0$

$\Rightarrow x-36 = 0$ or $x+3 = 0$

$\Rightarrow x = 36$ or $x = -3$ **(1 Mark)**

Speed cannot be negative

$\therefore x = 36$ km/hr

Therefore, the first speed of the train is 36 km/hr

(1 Mark)

24. Let x and y be two natural numbers

Such that x > y

$x - y = 5$ ...(1)

$\frac{1}{y}-\frac{1}{x}=\frac{1}{10}$

$\frac{x-y}{xy}=\frac{1}{10}$

$x - y = \frac{1}{10}(xy)$

$5 = \frac{1}{10}(xy)$

$xy = 50$ ...(2) **(1 Mark)**

From (1),

$x = 5 + y$ **(1 Mark)**

Putting the value of x in eq. (2)

$(y+5)y = 50$

$y^2+5y-50 = 0$

$y^2+10y-5y-50 = 0$

$y(y+10)-5(y+10) = 0$

$(y+10)(y-5) = 0$

$y+10 = 0$ or $y = 5$

$y = -10$ or $y = 5$ **(1 Mark)**

As y is natural number

$\therefore y = 5$

$x = y + 5$

$= 5 + 5 = 10$

Therefore, two natural numbers are 10 and 5. **(1 Mark)**

25. $\frac{1}{2a+b+2x} = \frac{1}{2a}+\frac{1}{b}+\frac{1}{2x}$

$\Rightarrow \frac{1}{2a+b+2x} = \frac{1}{2x}+\frac{1}{2a}+\frac{1}{b}$

$\Rightarrow \frac{1}{2a+b+2x}-\frac{1}{2x} = \frac{1}{2a}+\frac{1}{b}$ **(1 Mark)**

$\Rightarrow \frac{2x-2a-b-2x}{2x(2a+b+2x)} = \frac{b+2a}{2ab}$

$\Rightarrow \frac{-(2a+b)}{(2a+b+2x)2x} = \frac{2a+b}{2ab}$

$\Rightarrow \frac{-1}{(2a+b+2x)x} = \frac{1}{ab}$ **(1 Mark)**

$\Rightarrow (2a + b + 2x)x = -ab$

$\Rightarrow 2x^2 + xb + 2ax + ab = 0$

$\Rightarrow x(2x + b) + a(2x + b) = 0$

$\Rightarrow (x + a)(2x + b) = 0$

$\Rightarrow x + a = 0$ or $2x + b = 0$

$\Rightarrow x = -a$ or $x = \frac{-b}{2}$ **(2 Marks)**

26. Let side of first square be x and the side of another square be y

Perimeter of square = 4 x side

Difference in perimeter of two square:

$4x - 4y = 16$

$x - y = 4$

$x = 4 + y$ ...(1) **(1 Mark)**

Sum of areas of two squares

$x^2 + y^2 = 400$

$(4 + y)^2 + y^2 = 400$ (from (1)) **(1 Mark)**

$16 + y^2 + 8y + y^2 = 400$ $[(a + b)^2 = a^2 + b^2 + 2ab]$

$\Rightarrow 2y^2 + 8y + 16 - 400 = 0$

$\Rightarrow 2y^2 + 8y - 384 = 0$

$\Rightarrow y^2 + 4y - 192 = 0$

$\Rightarrow y^2 + 16y - 12y - 192 = 0$

$\Rightarrow y(y + 16) - 12(y + 16) = 0$

$\Rightarrow (y + 16)(y - 12) = 0$

$\Rightarrow y = -16$ or $y - 12 = 0$

$\Rightarrow y = 12$ **(1 Mark)**

Side cannot be negative. Therefore $y = 12$

$x = 4 + y$

$= 4 + 12 = 16$ cm

Side of first square = 16 cm

Side of second square = 12 cm **(1 Mark)**

Topic-3: Solution of a Quadratic Equation by Formula

1. Given, quadratic equation $x^2 - 2ax + (a^2 - b^2) = 0$.

Compare the above equation with general quadratic equation $ax^2 + bx + c = 0$

Here, $a = 1, b = -2a, c = (a^2 - b^2)$

$D = b^2 - 4ac$

$= (-2a)^2 - 4 \times 1 \times (a^2 - b^2)$

$= 4a^2 - 4a^2 + 4b^2 = 4b^2 > 0$ {real & distinct roots}

(1 Mark)

Apply quadratic formula,

$x = \frac{-b \pm \sqrt{D}}{2a} = \frac{-(-2a) \pm \sqrt{4b^2}}{2 \times 1}$

$x = \frac{2a \pm 2b}{2} = a \pm b$

Hence, $x = a + b$ and $x = a - b$ **(1 Mark)**

2. *Topper's Answer*

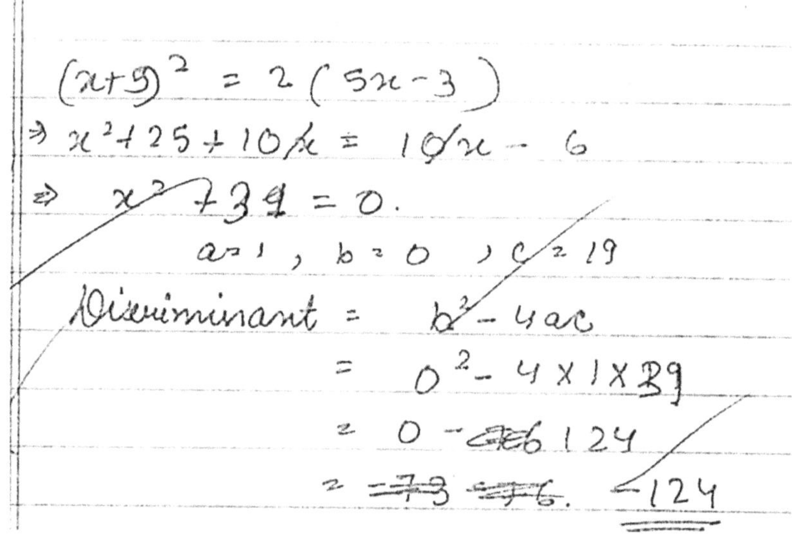

$(x+5)^2 = 2(5x-3)$

$\Rightarrow x^2 + 25 + 10x = 10x - 6$

$\Rightarrow x^2 + 31 = 0.$

$a = 1, \; b = 0, \; c = 19$

Discriminant $= b^2 - 4ac$

$= 0^2 - 4 \times 1 \times 31$

$= 0 - 124$

$= -124$

3. Standard form of quadratic equation:

$ax^2 + bx + c = 0$

Given quadratic equation:

$2x^2 + ax - a^2 = 0$

On comparing

$a = 2, b = a, c = -a^2$

$x = \dfrac{-b \pm \sqrt{b^2 - 4ac}}{2a}$ (Quadratic formula) **(1 Mark)**

$x = \dfrac{-a \pm \sqrt{a^2 - 4 \times 2(-a^2)}}{4}$

$= \dfrac{-a \pm \sqrt{9a^2}}{4} = \dfrac{-a \pm 3a}{4}$

$x = \dfrac{-a + 3a}{4} = \dfrac{a}{2}$ or $x = -\dfrac{a - 3a}{4} = -a$

$\therefore x = \dfrac{a}{2}$ or $x = -a$ **(1 Mark)**

If the discriminant $D = b^2 - 4ac$ is perfect square and a, b, c are rational then roots of the quadratic equation are rational.

Topic-4: Relationship between Discriminant and Nature of Roots

1. **(c)** 2 distinct real roots **(1 Mark)**

2. **(d)** For real and equal roots, D = 0

$D = b^2 - 4ac$

$\Rightarrow 0 = b^2 - 4ac$

$\Rightarrow b^2 = 4ac$

$\Rightarrow c = \dfrac{b^2}{4a}$ **(1 Mark)**

3. Given, $2x^2 - 4x + 3 = 0$

Here, $a = 2$, $b = -4$ and $c = 3$

$D = b^2 - 4ac = (-4)^2 - 4 \times (2)(3) = 16 - 24 = -8 < 0$

(1 Mark)

4. For real roots of the equation $x^2 + 4x + k = 0$,

$D \geq 0 \Rightarrow b^2 - 4ac \geq 0 \Rightarrow 16 - 4k \geq 0$

$\Rightarrow 4k \leq 16 \Rightarrow k \leq 4.$ **(1 Mark)**

If D is a perfect square, then the roots are rational.

5. $px^2 - 2\sqrt{5}\, px + 15 = 0$

Compare the given quadratic equation with equation $ax^2 + bx + c = 0$

$b = -2\sqrt{5}\,p, a = p, c = 15$

Since the given quadratic equation has two equal roots

$D = 0$ **(½ Mark)**

$\Rightarrow b^2 - 4ac = 0$

$\Rightarrow (-2\sqrt{5}p)^2 - 4p(15) = 0$

$\Rightarrow 20p^2 - 60p = 0$

$\Rightarrow p^2 - 3p = 0$

$\Rightarrow p(p - 3) = 0$

$\Rightarrow p = 0$ or $p - 3 = 0 \Rightarrow p = 3$ **(½ Mark)**

The graph of quadratic equation $ax^2 + bx + c = 0$ opens upwards if $a > 0$.

6. $x^2 - 7x + 10 = 0$

$x^2 - 5x - 2x + 10 = 0$

$x(x - 5) - 2(x - 5) = 0$

$(x - 2)(x - 5) = 0$

$(x - 2) = 0$ or $(x - 5) = 0$

$x = 2$ or $x = 5$ **(1 Mark)**

Hence the roots for $x^2 - 7x + 10 = 0$ are (2, 5).

Let $\alpha = 2$ and $\beta = 5$

Then, $\alpha^2 = 4$ and $\beta^2 = 25$ **(1 Mark)**

The equation with roots 25 and 4 is determined as follows:

$(x - 4)(x - 25) = 0$

$x^2 - 29x + 100 = 0$ **(1 Mark)**

7. Equal roots when $D = b^2 - 4ac = 0$

$p\,x\,(x - 2) + 6 = 0 \Rightarrow p\,x^2 - 2\,px + 6 = 0$

$a = P, b = -2p, c = 6$ **(1 Mark)**

$D = (-2P)^2 - 4 \times p \times 6 = 0$

$\Rightarrow 4\,p^2 - 24\,p = 0 \Rightarrow 4\,p\,(P - 6) = 0$

$\boxed{P = 0, P = 6}$ **(1 Mark)**

8. $x^2 + px + 16 = 0$

$\therefore a = 1, b = p, c = 16$

Given that quadratic equation has equal roots.

$\therefore D = 0$

$\Rightarrow b^2 - 4ac = 0$ **(1 Mark)**

$\Rightarrow p^2 - 4 \times 1 \times 16 = 0$

$\Rightarrow p^2 - 64 = 0$

$\Rightarrow p^2 = 64$

$p = \pm 8$ **(1 Mark)**

$\therefore$ Quadratic equation :

$x^2 + 8x + 16 = 0$

$(x+4)^2 = 0$

$x = -4, 4$

or $x^2 - 8x + 16 = 0$

$(x-4)^2 = 0$

$x = 4, 4.$ **(1 Mark)**

9. Given eqn is

$(a^2+b^2)x^2 + 2(ac+bd)x + (c^2+d^2) = 0$

We know, discriminant of the above quadratic equation

$D = B^2 - 4AC$

Thus, $D = [2(ac+bd)]^2 - 4(a^2+b^2)(c^2+d^2)]$ **(1 Mark)**

$= 4(a^2c^2 + b^2d^2 + 2abcd) - 4(a^2+b^2)(c^2+d^2)$

$= 4[a^2c^2 + b^2d^2 + 2abcd - a^2c^2 - a^2d^2 - b^2c^2 - b^2d^2]$

$= 4[a^2c^2 + b^2d^2 + 2abcd - a^2c^2 - a^2d^2 - b^2c^2 - b^2d^2]$

$= 4[2abcd - b^2c^2 - a^2d^2]$

$= -4[a^2d^2 + b^2c^2 - 2abcd]$

$= -4[ad - bc]^2$ **(1 Mark)**

But we know that,

$ad \neq bc$

$\Rightarrow (ad - bc) \neq 0$

$\Rightarrow (ad - bc)^2 > 0$

$\Rightarrow -4(ad-bc)^2 < 0$

$\Rightarrow D < 0$ **(1 Mark)**

Hence, given equation has no real roots.

If D < 0, then quadratic equation will have no real roots and if D = 0, the both the roots will be equal and real.

10. $kx(x-2) + 6 = 0$

$kx^2 - 2kx + 6 = 0$

$D = 0$ for equal roots

$D = b^2 - 4ac$

$\Rightarrow D = (-2k)^2 - 4(6)(k)$

$D = 4k^2 - 24k$ **(2 Marks)**

$4k^2 - 24k = 0$

$4k(k-6) = 0 \Rightarrow k = 0$ or $k = 6$

But $k \neq 0$ for quadratic equation.

$\therefore k = 6$ **(1 Mark)**

11. $(k+4)x^2 + (k+1)x + 1 = 0$

As quadratic equation has equal roots

$\therefore D = 0$ [D=Discriminant]

$b^2 - 4ac = 0$

Here $a = k + 4$

$b = k + 1$

$c = 1$

$(k+1)^2 - 4(k+4)(1) = 0$

$\Rightarrow k^2 + 2k + 1 - 4k - 16 = 0$

$\Rightarrow k^2 - 2k - 15 = 0$

$\Rightarrow k^2 - 5k + 3k - 15 = 0$

$\Rightarrow k(k-5) + 3(k-5) = 0$

$\Rightarrow (k-5)(5+3) = 0$

$\Rightarrow k - 5 = 0$ or $k + 3 = 0$

$\Rightarrow k = 5$ or $k = -3$ **(1 Mark)**

For k = 5

$(k+4)x^2 + (k+1)x + 1 = 0$

$9x^2 + 6x + 1 = 0$

$(3x+1)^2 = 0$

$x = \frac{-1}{3}, \frac{-1}{3}$ **(1 Mark)**

For k = –3

$(-3+4)x^2 + (-3+1)x + 1 = 0$

$x^2 - 2x + 1 = 0$

$(x-1)^2 = 0$

$x = 1, 1$ **(1 Mark)**

Hence, equal roots of the quadratic equation is either 1 or $\frac{-1}{3}$. **(1 Mark)**

Topic-5: *Day to Day Situation Problem*

1. Let duration of flight = t hr.

Distance = 600 km

$\therefore$ Average speed = $\frac{600}{t}$

New duration of flight = $t + \frac{30}{60} = \left(t + \frac{1}{2}\right)$ hr.

New speed = $\frac{600}{t+\frac{1}{2}} = \frac{1200}{2t+1}$ **(1 Mark)**

According to question,

$$\frac{600}{t}-\frac{1200}{2t+1}=200$$ **(1 Mark)**

$$\Rightarrow \frac{-1200t+600(2t+1)}{t(2t+1)}=200$$

$$\Rightarrow \frac{1200t-1200t+600}{2t^2+t}=200$$

$\Rightarrow$ $600 = 200(2t^2 + t)$

$\Rightarrow$ $2t^2 + t = \frac{600}{200} = 3$

$\Rightarrow$ $2t^2 + t - 3 = 0 \Rightarrow 2t^2 + 3t - 2t - 3 = 0$

$\Rightarrow$ $t(2t + 3) - 1(2t + 3) = 0 \Rightarrow (2t + 3)(t - 1) = 0$

$\therefore$ $t - 1 = 0$ | $2t + 3 = 0$

$t = 1$ | $t = \frac{-3}{2} = -1\frac{1}{2}$

$\because$ Time is not negative

$\therefore$ Duration of flight = 1 h **(1 Mark)**

2. Let the duration of the flight be t hours

Speed = $\frac{\text{Distance}}{\text{time}} = \frac{600}{t}$ km/h **(1 Mark)**

Duration of the flight due to slow down $t+\frac{30}{60}=t+\frac{1}{2}$

According to question

$$\frac{600}{t}-\frac{600}{t+\frac{1}{2}}=200$$ **(1 Mark)**

$$\Rightarrow \frac{3}{t}-\frac{3}{t+\frac{1}{2}}=1$$

$$\Rightarrow \frac{3(2t+1)-6t}{t(2t+1)}=1$$

$$\Rightarrow \frac{6t+3-6t}{t(2t+1)}=1$$

$$\Rightarrow \frac{3}{t(2t+1)}=1$$

$\Rightarrow$ $2t^2 + t - 3 = 0$

$\Rightarrow$ $2t^2 + 3t - 2t - 3 = 0$

$\Rightarrow$ $t(2t + 3) - 1(2t + 3) = 0$

$\Rightarrow$ $(2t + 3)(t - 1) = 0$

$t = 1$

Original duration of the flight is 1 hour. **(1 Mark)**

3. Let usual speed of aeroplane be x km/hr

$\therefore$ New speed of aeroplane = $(x + 100)$km/hr

Distance/covered = 1500 km

Original usual time $=\frac{1500}{x}$ hrs **(1 Mark)**

New time $=\frac{1500}{x+100}$ km / hr

New time $+\frac{30}{60}$ hr = Usual time

[As it got late by 30 minutes or $\frac{30}{60}$ hour]

$$\Rightarrow \frac{1500}{x+100}+\frac{1}{2}=\frac{1500}{x}$$ **(1 Mark)**

$$\frac{1}{2}=1500\left(\frac{1}{x}-\frac{1}{x+100}\right)=1500\left(\frac{x+100-x}{x(x+100)}\right)$$

$$\Rightarrow \frac{1}{2}=\frac{150000}{x^2+100x}\Rightarrow x^2+100x=300000$$

$\Rightarrow$ $x^2 + 100x - 300000 = 0$

$\Rightarrow$ $x^2 + 600x - 500x - 300000 = 0$

$\Rightarrow$ $x(x + 600) - 500(x + 600) = 0$

$\Rightarrow$ $(x + 600)(x - 500) = 0$

$\Rightarrow$ $x = -600$ or $x = 500$

Reject $x = -600$ as speed cannot be negative.

$\therefore$ Usual speed of aeroplane = 500 km /hr **(1 Mark)**

4. Let the speed of the stream be x km/h.

The speed of the boat upstream = (18 – x) km/h and the speed of the boat downstream = (18 + x) km/h. **(1 Mark)**

The time taken to go upstream $=\frac{\text{distance}}{\text{speed}}=\frac{24}{18-x}$ hours

The time taken to go downstream

$\frac{\text{distance}}{\text{speed}}=\frac{24}{18+x}$ hours **(1 Mark)**

According to the question, $=\frac{24}{18-x}-\frac{24}{18+x}=1$

(1 Mark)

$24(18 + x) - 24(18 - x) = (18 - x)(18 + x)$

$x^2 + 48x - 324 = 0 \Rightarrow (x - 6)(x + 54) = 0$

x = 6 or – 54 **(1 Mark)**

Since x is the speed of the stream, it cannot be negative.

Therefore, x = 6 gives the speed of the stream = 6 km/h.

(1 Mark)

5. D = 54 km

Let average speed be x.

Distance = 63 km

The average speed to cover distance = x + 6 **(2 Marks)**

Time taken = 3 hr

So, $\frac{54}{x}+\frac{63}{x+6}=3 \Rightarrow 54x + 324 + 63x = 3x^2 + 18x$

$\Rightarrow x^2 - 33x - 108 = 0 \Rightarrow (x-36)(x+3) = 0$

Then, x = 36 km/hr **(2 Marks)**

6. Time taken by larger dia pipe = x – 2

where x is time to fill smaller dia tap tank filled in one hour by both pipes = $\frac{8}{15}$ **(2 Marks)**

$\Rightarrow \frac{1}{x}+\frac{1}{x-2}=\frac{8}{15} \Rightarrow 3x - 30 = 8x^2 - 16x$

$\Rightarrow 8x^2 - 46x + 30 = 0 \Rightarrow (x-5)\left(x-\frac{3}{4}\right) = 0$

Then, x = 5 and, x – 2 = 5 – 2 = 3

Hence two pipe take 5 hours and 3 hours respectively.

(2 Marks)

Note

$\frac{\text{Distance}}{\text{Speed}} = \text{time}$

7. Speed of motor boat in still water = 18 km/hr

Let speed of stream be x km/hr

∴ Speed of motor boat going upstream

$= (18 - x)$ km/hr **(½ Mark)**

Speed of motor boat going downstream

$= (18 + x)$km/hr **(½ Mark)**

Distance travelled upstream and downstream is 24 km each.

Time for going upstream $= \frac{24}{18-x}$ hr **(1 Mark)**

Time for going downstream $= \frac{24}{18+x}$ hr

$\Rightarrow \frac{24}{18-x} = 1 + \frac{24}{18+x}$ (given) **(1 Mark)**

$\Rightarrow 24\left(\frac{1}{18-x} - \frac{1}{18+x}\right) = 1$

$\Rightarrow \frac{24(18+x-18+x)}{(18-x)(18+x)} = 0$

$\Rightarrow 24 \times 2x = 18^2 - x^2$

$\Rightarrow x^2 + 48x - 324 = 0$

$\Rightarrow x^2 - 6x + 54x - 324 = 0$

$\Rightarrow x(x-6) + 54(x-6) = 0$

$\Rightarrow (x-6)(x+54) = 0$

$\Rightarrow x = +6$ or $x = -54$

reject $x = -54$ as speed cannot be negative

∴ Speed of stream = 6 km/h **(1 Mark)**

Topper's Answer

For motorboat:
Speed in still water = 18 km/hr
Let speed of stream = x km/hr
Upstream speed = 18 − x km/hr
downstream speed = 18 + x km/hr.

$t = \frac{d}{s}$

$\frac{24}{18-x} - \frac{24}{18+x} = 1$

$24\left(\frac{1}{18-x} - \frac{1}{18+x}\right) = 1$

$\frac{18+x-18+x}{(18-x)(18+x)} = \frac{1}{24}$

$\frac{2x}{324-x^2} = \frac{1}{24}$

$48x = 324 - x^2$

$x^2 + 48x - 324 = 0$

$(x+54)(x-6) = 0$

$x = -54$ (invalid − speed cannot be negative)

$x = 6$

Ans: Speed of the stream = 6 km/hr.

8. Let Speed of train to travel 63 km be x km/hr

$\therefore$ Speed of train to travel next 72 km is $(x + 6)$ km/hr

(1 Mark)

As total time of journey is 3 hours

$$\Rightarrow \frac{63}{x}+\frac{72}{x+6}=3$$

$$\Rightarrow \frac{21}{x}+\frac{24}{x+6}=1$$ **(1 Mark)**

$$\Rightarrow \frac{21(x+6)+24x}{x(x+6)}=1$$

$$\Rightarrow 21x + 126 + 24x = x^2 + 6x$$

$$\Rightarrow x^2 - 39x - 126 = 0$$

$$\Rightarrow (x + 3)(x - 42) = 0$$

$$\Rightarrow x = -3 \text{ or } x = 42$$ **(1 Mark)**

Reject $x = -3$ as speed of train cannot be negative

$\therefore$ Original average speed = 42 km/hr **(1 Mark)**

9. ***Topper's Answer***

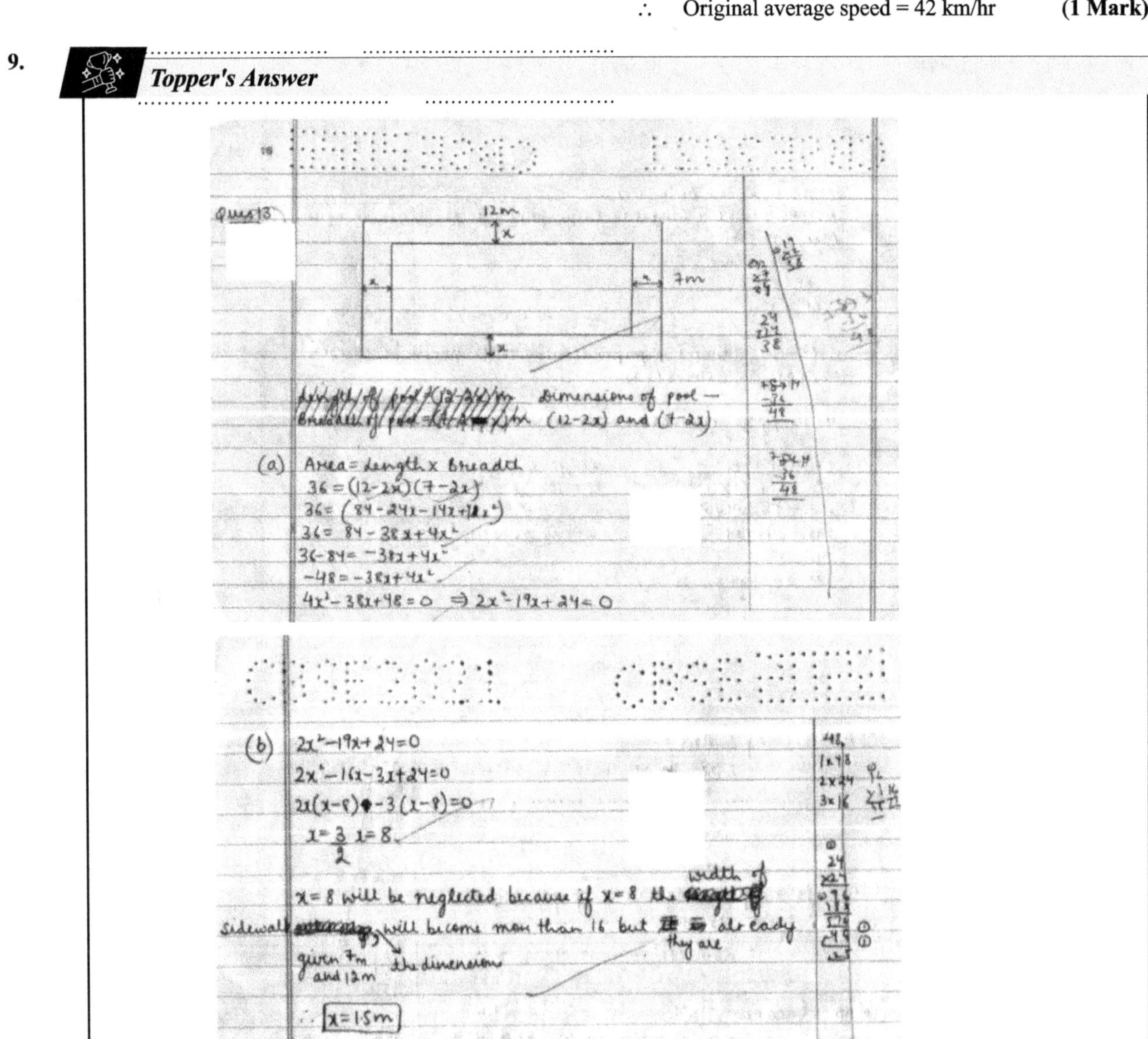

Chapter 5 Arithmetic Progressions

Topic-1: Arithmetic Progressions

1 Multiple Choice Questions

1. If k + 2, 4k – 6 and 3k – 2 are three consecutive terms of an A.P, then the value of k is: **[Delhi 2023, Ap]**

(a) 3 (b) – 3 (c) 4 (d) – 4

2. The common difference of the A.P. $\frac{1}{p}, \frac{1-p}{p}, \frac{1-2p}{p} A$, ... is **[All India 2013 (S), All India 2020, Ap]**

(a) 1 (b) $\frac{1}{p}$ (c) –1 (d) $-\frac{1}{p}$

3. The value of x for which 2x, (x + 10) and (3x + 2) are the three consecutive terms of an AP, is **[Delhi 2020, K]**

(a) 6 (b) –6 (c) 18 (d) –18

4. The first term of an AP is p and the common difference is q, then its 10th term is **[Delhi 2020, U]**

(a) q + 9p (b) p – 9q (c) p + 9q (d) 2p + 9q

2 Assertion Reason/Two Statement Type Questions

5. **Statement A (Assertion):** $-5, \frac{-5}{2}, 0, \frac{5}{2}$, ... is in Arithmetic Progression.

Statement R (Reason): The terms of an Arithmetic Progression cannot have both positive and negative rational numbers. **[CBSE Sample Paper 2023-24, U]**

(a) Both assertion (A) and reason (R) are true and reason (R) is the correct explanation of assertion (A)

(b) Both assertion (A) and reason (R) are true and reason (R) is not the correct explanation of assertion (A)

(c) Assertion (A) is true but reason (R) is false.

(d) Assertion (A) is false but reason (R) is true

4 Very Short Answer Questions (1 Mark)

6. $\sqrt{2}, \sqrt{18}, \sqrt{50}, \sqrt{98}...$ **[CBSE CFPQ 2022, K]**

In the above pattern in AP? Justify your answer.

7. Find the common difference of the Arithmetic Progression (A.P.) $\frac{1}{a}, \frac{3-a}{3a}, \frac{3-2a}{3a}, ...(a \neq 0)$ **[All India 2019, K]**

8. In an AP, if the common difference (d) = – 4, and the seventh term (a_7) is 4, then find the first term. **[All India 2018, Ap]**

9. What is the common difference of an A.P. in which $a_{21} - a_7 = 84$? **[All India 2017, Term-II, U]**

5 Short Answer Questions (2 or 3 Marks)

10. Find a and b so that the numbers a, 7, b, 23 are in A.P. **[All India 2022, Term-II, A]**

11. Show that $(a - b)^2$, $(a^2 + b^2)$ and $(a + b)^2$ are in A.P. **[Delhi 2020, K]**

6 Long Answer Questions (4 or 5 Marks)

12. The sum of four consecutive numbers in AP is 32 and the ratio of the product of the first and last terms to the product of two middle terms is 7:15. Find the numbers. **[Delhi 2020, U]**

Topic-2: nth Term of an AP

Multiple Choice Questions

1. Two APs have the same common difference. The first term of one of these is – 1 and that of the other is – 8. Then the difference between their 4th terms is

[CBSE Sample Paper 2023-24, K]

(a) 1 (b) –7

(c) 7 (d) 9

2. The 13th term from the end of the A.P. : 20, 13, 6, –1, ..., –148: **[All India 2023, Set-I, K]**

(a) 57 (b) –57 (c) 64 (d) –64

3. The common differences of the A.P. whose n^{th} term is given by $a_n = 5n - 7$ is : **[All India 2023, Set-I, A]**

(a) –7 (b) 7 (c) 5 (d) –2

4. The nth term of the A.P. a, 3a, 5a, ..., is

[All India 2020, U]

(a) na (b) (2n – 1)a

(c) (2n + 1)a (d) 2na

5. The first three terms of an AP respectively are 3y – 1, 3y + 5 and 5y + 1. Then y equals:

[Delhi 2014, Term-II, Ap]

(a) –3 (b) 4

(c) 5 (d) 2

Very Short Answer Questions (1 Mark)

6. How many two digits number are divisible by 3?

[Delhi 2019, U]

7. Find the 9th term from the end (towards the first term) of the A.P. 5, 9, 13, ..., 185. **[Delhi 2016, Term-II, Ap]**

5 Short Answer Questions (2 or 3 Marks)

8. Which term of the A.P. $-\frac{11}{2}, -3, -\frac{1}{2}, ...$ is $\frac{49}{2}$?

[All India 2022, Term-II, Ap]

9. 14, 21, 28, 35, ... and 26, 39, 52, 65, ... are two arithmetic progressions such that the pth term of the first arithmetic progression is the same as the qth term of the second arithmetic progression. **[CBSE CFPQ, 2022, U]**

Derive a relationship between p and q. Show your work.

10. In an A.P. given that the first term (a) = 54, the common difference (d) = –3, and the nth term $(a_n) = 0$. Find n and sum of first n terms (S_n) of the A.P.

[All India 2020, U]

11. Which term of the AP 3, 15, 27, 39, ... will be 120 more than its 21st term? **[Delhi 2019, A]**

12. Which term of the progression 20, $19\frac{1}{4}, 18\frac{1}{2}, 17\frac{3}{4}, ...$ is the first negative term ? **[All India 2017, Term-II, Ap]**

13. If the seventh term of an AP is $\frac{1}{9}$ and its ninth terms is $\frac{1}{7}$, find its 63rd term. **[Delhi 2014, Term-II, An]**

14. How many three-digit natural numbers are divisible by 7 ?

[All India 2013, U]

6 Long Answer Questions (4 or 5 Marks)

15. If m times the mth term of an Arithmetic Progression is equal to n times its nth term and $m \neq n$, show that the $(m + n)^{th}$ term of the A.P. is zero. **[All India 2019, U]**

16. Which term of the Arithmetic Progression –7, –12, –17, –22, ... will be –82 ? Is –100 any term of the A.P. ? Give reason for your answer. **[All India 2019, A]**

17. If the ratio of the sum of the first n terms of two A.Ps is (7n + 1) : (4n + 27), then find the ratio of their 9th terms.

[All India 2017, Term-II, U]

Topic-3: Sum of First n Terms of an AP

1. If the sum of the first n terms of an A.P be $3n^2 + n$ and its common difference is 6, then its first term is

[All India 2023, Set-II, Ap]

(a) 2 (b) 3

(c) 1 (d) 4

Assertion Reason/Two Statement Type Questions

2. **Assertion (A) :** a, b, c are in A.P. if and only if $2b = a + c$.

Reason (R) : The sum of first n odd natural numbers is n^2.

[Delhi 2023, K]

(a) Both Assertion (A) and Reason (R) are true and Reason (R) is the correct explanation of Assertion (A).

(b) Both Assertion (A) and Reason (R) are true and Reason (R) is not the correct explanation of Assertion (A).

(c) Assertion (A) is true but Reason (R) is false.

(d) Assertion (A) is false but Reason (R) is true.

Very Short Answer Questions (1 Mark)

3. If the mean of the first n natural number is 15, then find n. **[Delhi 2020, K]**

5 Short Answer Questions (2 or 3 Marks)

4. In an A.P., the sum of the first n terms is given by $S_n = 6n - n^2$. Find the 30th term.

[All India 2023, Set-II, Ap]

5. The sum of first 15 terms of an A.P. is 750 and its first term is 15. Find its 20th term. **[Delhi 2023, K]**

6. Rohan repays his total loan of ₹ 1,18,000 by paying every month starting with the first instalment of ₹ 1,000. If he increases the instalment by ₹ 100 every month, what amount will be paid by him in the 30th instalment? What amount of loan has he paid after 30th instalment? **[Delhi 2023, K]**

7. Find the sum of first 20 terms of an A.P. whose nth term is given as $a_n = 5 - 2n$. **[All India 2022 Term-II, K]**

8. The average of an Arithmetic Progression with 151 terms is zero. One of its terms is zero.

Which term of the Arithmetic Progression is zero? Show your steps. **[CBSE CFPQ 2022, U]**

9. Show that the sum of all terms of an A.P. whose first term is a, the second term is b and the last term is c is equal to $\frac{(a+c)(b+c-2a)}{2(b-a)}$. **[All India 2020, U]**

10. Solve the equation :

$1 + 4 + 7 + 10 + ... + x = 287$. **[All India 2020, K]**

11. If S_n the sum of first n terms of an AP is given by $S_n = 3n^2 - 4n$, find the nth term. **[Delhi 2019, Ap]**

12. Find the sum of first 8 multiples of 3. **[All India 2018, K]**

13. The first term of an A.P. is 5, the last term is 45 and the sum of all its terms is 400. Find the number of terms and the common difference of the A.P.

[All India 2017, Term-II, K]

14. How many terms of the A.P. 18, 16, 14, ... be taken so that their sum is zero? **[Delhi 2016, Term-II, K]**

15. If the sum of first 7 terms of an A.P. is 49 and that of its first 17 terms is 289, find the sum of first n terms of the A.P.

[Delhi 2016, Term-II, A]

16. The 14th term of an AP is twice its 8th term. If its 6th term is – 8, then find the sum of its first 20 terms.

[All India 2015, Term-II, U]

17. In an AP, if $S_5 + S_7 = 167$ and $S_{10} = 235$, then find the AP, where S_n denotes the sum of its first n terms.

[All India 2015, Term-II, U]

18. The first and the last terms of an AP are 5 and 45 respectively. If the sum of all its terms is 400, find its common difference. **[Delhi 2014, Term-II, Ap]**

19. Find the number of terms of the AP 18, 15½, 13, …., –49½ and find the sum of all its terms. **[All India 2013, Ap]**

6 *Long Answer Questions (4 or 5 Marks)*

20. The ratio of the 11th term to the 18th term of an A.P. is 2 : 3. Find the ratio of the 5th term to the 21st term. Also, find the ratio of the sum of first 5 terms to the sum of first 21 terms. **[All India 2023, Set-II, A]**

21. If the sum of first 6 terms of an A.P. is 36 and that of the first 16 terms is 256, find the sum of first 10 terms. **[All India 2023, Set-II, A]**

22. Find the common difference 'd' of an AP whose first term is 10 and the sum of the first 14 terms is 1505. **[All India 2022, A]**

23. Solve: $1 + 4 + 7 + 10 + ... + x = 287$ **[Delhi 2020, Ap]**

24. How many terms of the Arithmetic Progression 45, 39, 33, ... must be taken so that their sum is 180 ? Explain the double answer. **[All India 2019, K]**

25. If the sum of first four terms of an AP is 40 and that of first 14 terms is 280. Find the sum of its first n terms. **[Delhi 2019, U]**

26. The sum of four cosecutive numbers in an AP is 32 and the ratio of the product of the first and the last term to the product of two middle terms is 7 : 15. Find the numbers. **[All India 2018, Ap]**

27. A thief runs with a uniform speed of 100 m/minute. After one minute a policeman runs after the thief to catch him. He goes with a speed of 100 m/minute in the first minute and increases his speed by 10 m/minute every succeeding minute. After how many minutes the policeman will catch the thief. **[Delhi 2016, Term-II, Ap]**

28. Find the 60th term of the AP 8, 10, 12, ..., if it has a total of 60 terms and hence find the sum of its last 10 terms. **[All India 2015, Term-II, A]**

29. In an AP of 50 terms, the sum of first 10 terms is 210 and the sum of its last 15 terms is 2565. Find the A.P. **[Delhi 2014, Term-II, K]**

30. If the sum of first 7 terms of an AP is 49 and that of first 17 terms is 289, find the sum of its first n terms. **[All India 2013, A]**

7 *Case Based Questions (4 Marks)*

31. Manpreet Kaur is the national record holder for women in the shot–put discipline. Her throw of 18.86m at the Asian Grand Prix in 2017 is the maximum distance for an Indian female athlete. Keeping her as a role model, Sanjitha is determined to earn gold in Olympics one day. Initially her throw reached 7.56m only. Being an athlete in school, she regularly practiced both in the mornings and in the evenings and was able to improve the distance by 9cm every week.

During the special camp for 15 days, she started with 40 throws and every day kept increasing the number of throws by 12 to achieve this remarkable progress.

(i) How many throws Sanjitha practiced on 11th day of the camp? **[CBSE Sample Paper 2023-24, A]**

(ii) What would be Sanjitha's throw distance at the end of 6 weeks? **[CBSE Sample Paper 2023-24, K]**

OR

When will she be able to achieve a throw of 11.16 m?

(iii) How many throws did she do during the entire camp of 15 days? **[CBSE Sample Paper 2023-24, A]**

32. The school auditorium was to be constructed to accommodate at least 1500 people. The chairs are to be placed in concentric circular arrangement in such a way that each succeeding circular row has 10 seats more than the previous one. **[CBSE Sample Paper 2022-23, A]**

(i) If the first circular row has 30 seats, how many seats will be there in the 10th row?

[CBSE Sample Paper 2022-23, K]

(ii) For 1500 seats in the auditorium, how many rows need to be there? **[CBSE Sample Paper 2022-23, K]**

OR

If 1500 seats are to be arranged in the auditorium, how many seats are still left to be put after 10th row?

(iii) If there were 17 rows in the auditorium, how many seats will be there in the middle row?

[CBSE Sample Paper 2022-23, U]

Hints & Solutions

Topic-1: *2 Arithmetic Progressions*

1. **(a)** Consecutive terms of an A.P. means common difference is same. So,
$(4k - 6) - (k + 2) = (3k - 2) = (3k - 2) -- (4k - 6)$
$\Rightarrow$ $4k - 6 - 1 - 2 = 3k - 2 - 4k + 6$
$\Rightarrow$ $3k - 8 = -k + 4 \Rightarrow 3k + k = 8 + 4 \Rightarrow 4k = 12$
$\Rightarrow$ $k = 3$ **(1 Mark)**

2. **(c)** $d = \frac{1-p}{p} - \frac{1}{p} = \frac{1-p-1}{p} = \frac{-p}{p} = -1$ **(1 Mark)**

3. **(a)** $x + 10 - 2x = (3x + 2) - (x + 10)$
$\Rightarrow x = 6$ **(1 Mark)**

4. **(c)** $a_{10} = a + 9d = p + 9q$ **(1 Mark)**

Note

The nth term of a finite A.P. is $a_n = a + (n - 1)d$.

5. **(c)** Assertion (A) is true but reason (R) is false. **(1 Mark)**

6. Answers that the pattern is in AP. **(½ Mark)**
Mentions that the series is in AP because the common difference is the same which is $2\sqrt{2}$. **(½ Mark)**

7. $d = \frac{3-a}{3a} - \frac{1}{a} = \frac{3-a-3}{3a}$
$= \frac{-a}{3a} = \frac{-1}{3}$ **(1 Mark)**

Note

Common difference of A.P $= a_2 - a_1 = a_3 - a_2 = ...$

8. In an A.P., $d = -4$ and $a_7 = 4$
$\Rightarrow$ $a + 6d = 4 \Rightarrow a + 6(-4) = 4$
$\Rightarrow$ $a = 4 + 24 \Rightarrow a = 28$.
Hence first term of the AP is 28. **(1 Mark)**

Note

n^{th} term of an A.P. is $a_n = a + (n - 1)d$.

9. Let first term of AP be 'a' and its common difference be 'd'
$a_n = a + (n - 1)d$
$\Rightarrow$ $a_{21} = a + (21 - 1)d = a + 20d$
and $a_7 = a + (7 - 1)d = a + 6d$ **(½ Mark)**
given that, $a_{21} - a_7 = 84$
$\Rightarrow$ $(a + 20d) - (a + 6d) = 84$
$\Rightarrow$ $14d = 84$
$\Rightarrow$ $d = 6$
Thus, the required common difference of A.P. is '6'. **(½ Mark)**

10. Given a, 7, b, 23 are in A.P.
Then, there common difference will be equal.
$d = 7 - a = b - 7$
$7 - a = b - 7$
$a + b = 14$ .... (i) **(1 Mark)**
Similarly,
$b - 7 = 23 - b$
$2b = 30$
$b = 15$
From (i)
$a + 15 = 14$
$\boxed{a = -1}$
Required A.P = –1, 7, 15, 23 **(1 Mark)**

11. $a_2 - a_1 = (a^2 + b^2) - (a - b)^2$
$= a^2 + b^2 - a^2 - b^2 + 2ab$
$= 2ab$ **(1 Mark)**
$a_3 - a_2 = (a + b)^2 - (a^2 + b^2)$
$= a^2 + b^2 + 2ab - a^2 - b^2 = 2ab$ **(1 Mark)**
$\therefore$ $a_2 - a_1 = a_3 - a_2$
So, $(a - b)^2$, $(a^2 + b^2)$ and $(a + b)^2$ are in AP. **(1 Mark)**

12. Let the four consecutive numbers in A.P. are $(a - 3d)$, $(a - d)$, $(a + d)$ and $(a + 3d)$.
$\therefore$ According to question
$(a - 3d) + (a - d) + (a + d) + (a + 3d) = 32$
$\Rightarrow$ $4a = 32$
$\Rightarrow$ $a = 8$ ....(i) **(1 Mark)**
Now, $\frac{(a-3d)\times(a+3d)}{(a-d)\times(a+d)} = \frac{7}{15}$ **(1 Mark)**
$\Rightarrow$ $\frac{(8-3d)\times(8+3d)}{(8-d)\times(8+d)} = \frac{7}{15}$
$\Rightarrow$ $\frac{64-9d^2}{64-d^2} = \frac{7}{15}$
$\Rightarrow$ $15(64 - 9d^2) = 7(64 - d^2)$
$\Rightarrow$ $960 - 135d^2 = 448 - 7d^2$
$\Rightarrow$ $128d^2 = 512$

$\Rightarrow \quad d^2 = 4$

$\Rightarrow \quad d = \pm 2$ **(2 Marks)**

$\therefore$ Numbers are 2, 6, 10 and 14 or 14, 10, 6 and 2.

Three consecutive numbers in A.P. are a – d, a, a + d.

Topic-2: nth Term of an AP

1. **(c)** 7 **(1 Mark)**
2. **(d)** There is common difference d = –7
   Then series from end is, –148, –141, –134, ...20
   Where, a = –148, d = 7; 13th term = a + 12d
   = –148 + 12 × 7 = –148 + 84 = –64 **(1 Mark)**
3. **(c)** Given, $a_n = 5n - 7$; $a_1 = -2$, $a_2 = 3$
   Common difference (d) = $a_2 - a_1 = 3-(-2) = 5$ **(1 Mark)**
4. **(b)** $a_n = a + (n-1)d = a + (n-1)2a$
   $[\because d = 3a - a = 2a]$
   $= a + 2an - 2a = 2an - a = (2n-1)a$ **(1 Mark)**
5. **(a)** First 3 terms of AP:
   3y – 1, 3y + 5, 5y + 1
   Common difference will be same
   $d_1 = a_2 - a_1 = 3y + 5 - (3y - 1) = 6$
   $d_2 = a_3 - a_2 = 5y + 1 - (3y + 5) = 2y - 4$
   $d_1 = d_2 \Rightarrow 6 = 2y - 4 \Rightarrow 2y = 6 + 4$
   $2y = 10 \Rightarrow y = 5$ **(1 Mark)**

If a constant quantity is added or subtracted from an A.P., then resulting terms of the sequence are also in A.P. with same common difference.

6. The two digit numbers divisible by 3 are 12, 15, ..., 99, which forms an A.P with a = 12, d = 3 and a_n = 99 (where n is number of terms).
   We know that
   $a_n = a + (n-1)d \quad \Rightarrow 99 = 12 + (n-1)3$
   $\Rightarrow \dfrac{99-12}{3} = n - 1 \Rightarrow n = 29 + 1 \Rightarrow n = 30.$
   Therefore, there are 30 two digit numbers which are divisible by 3. **(1 Mark)**

Note

If l is last term of in a finite AP, then l = a + (n – 1)d

7. Given series is an AP
   Common difference, d = 9 – 5 = 4
   Last term, l = 185
   n^{th} term from end = l – (n – 1)d
   9th term from end = 185 – (9 – 1)4
   = 185 – (4 × 8)
   = 153 **(1 Mark)**

If A.P. has n terms then K^{th} term from end is equal to $(n-k+1)^{th}$ term from begining.

8. Given, AP = $-\dfrac{11}{2}, -3, -\dfrac{1}{2}$, ..., Let $a_n = \dfrac{49}{2}$
   where, $a = -\dfrac{11}{2}$, $d = -3 + \dfrac{11}{2} = \dfrac{5}{2}$ **(1 Mark)**
   Apply a_n term formula,
   $a_n = a + (n-1) \times d$
   $\dfrac{49}{2} = -\dfrac{11}{2} + (n-1) \times \dfrac{5}{2}$
   n = 12 + 1 = 13. **(1 Mark)**
9. $a_p = b_q$. **(1 Mark)**
   $a + (p-1) \times d_1 = b + (q-1) \times d_2$
   $14 + (p-1) \times 7 = 26 + (q-1) \times 13$
   $7p - 13q = 6$ **(1 Mark)**
10.

Topper's Answer

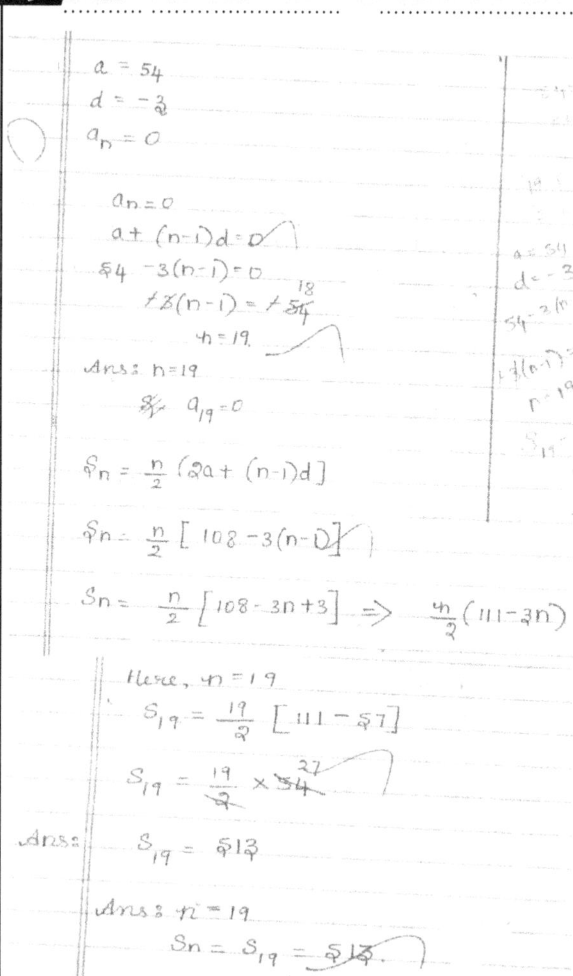

11. a = 3 and d = 15 – 3 = 12.

$a_{21} = 3 + (21 - 1) \times 12$

$= 3 + 240 = 243$ **(1 Mark)**

Let, $a_n = 243 + 120 = 363 = a + (n - 1)d$

$\Rightarrow 363 = 3 + (n-1)12 \Rightarrow \frac{360}{12} = n - 1 \Rightarrow n = 31$

(1 Mark)

Therefore, 31st term will be 120 more than its 21st term.

12. The given sequence is,

$20, 19\frac{1}{4}, 18\frac{1}{2}, 17\frac{3}{4}...$

This is an A.P. series

The first term, a = 20

And common difference

$d = 19\frac{1}{4} - 20 = \frac{77-80}{4} = \frac{-3}{4}$ **(1 Mark)**

Let the nth term of AP be the first negative term

$\Rightarrow \quad a_n < 0$

$\Rightarrow \quad a + (n-1)d < 0$

$\Rightarrow \quad 20 + (n-1)\left(-\frac{3}{4}\right) < 0$

$\Rightarrow \quad \frac{83}{4} - \frac{3n}{4} < 0$

$\Rightarrow \quad 83 - 3n < 0$

$\Rightarrow \quad 3n > 83$

$\Rightarrow \quad n > 27\frac{2}{3}$

$\Rightarrow \quad n \geq 28$

Thus the 28th term is the first negative term of given AP.

(1 Mark)

13. Let a and d be first term and common difference of AP respectively.

$a_7 = \frac{1}{9}, \quad a_9 = \frac{1}{7}$

$\because a_n = a + (n-1)d$

$a_7 = \frac{1}{9}$

$\Rightarrow a + (7-1)d = \frac{1}{9}$

$a + 6d = \frac{1}{9}$ ...(1)

$a_9 = \frac{1}{7}$

$a + 8d = \frac{1}{7}$ ...(2)

Subtracting equation (1) from (2)

$2d = \frac{1}{7} - \frac{1}{9}$

$2d = \frac{2}{63}$

$d = \frac{1}{63}$ **(1 Mark)**

Putting the value of d in equation (1)

$\Rightarrow \quad a + \left(6 \times \frac{1}{63}\right) = \frac{1}{9}$

$a = \frac{1}{9} - \frac{6}{63}$

$a = \frac{1}{63}$ **(1 Mark)**

$a_{63} = a + (63 - 1)d$

$= \frac{1}{63} + 62 \times \frac{1}{63} = \frac{63}{63} = 1$

$a_{63} = 1$

Thus, the 63rd term of the given AP is 1. **(1 Mark)**

14. Three digit natural numbers divisible by 7 are 105, 112 ... 994

Here $a = 105, d = 7$

$a_n = a + (n-1)d$ **(1½ Marks)**

$994 = 105 + (n-1)7$

$994 = 105 + 7n - 7$

$994 = 98 + 7n$

$7n = 994 - 98$

$7n = 896$

$n = 128$

∴ There are 128 three digit natural numbers divisible by 7. **(1½ Marks)**

If a, b, c are in AP, then $b = \frac{a+c}{2}$ and b is called the arithmetic mean of a and c.

15.

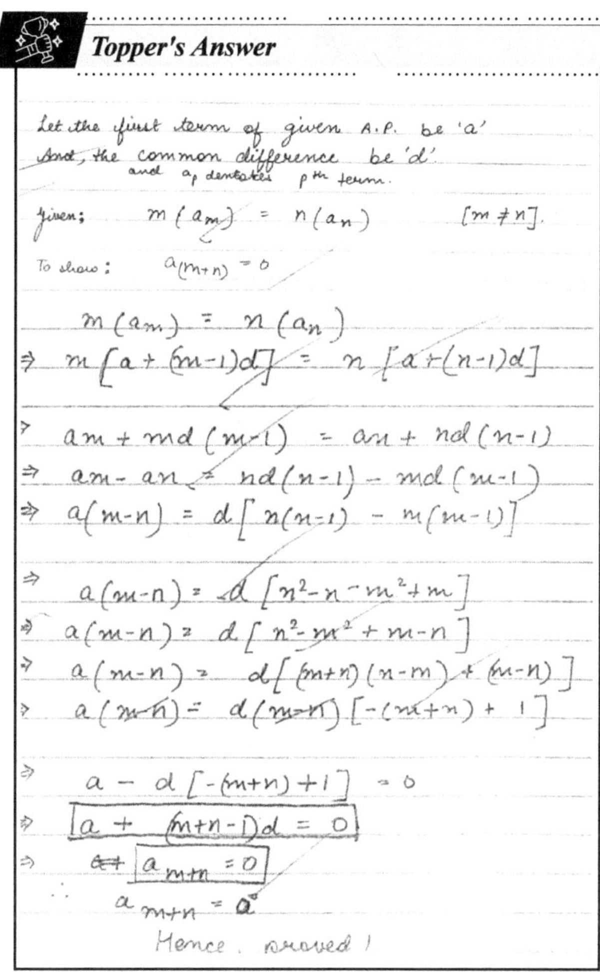

Topper's Answer

Let the first term of given A.P. be 'a'
And, the common difference be 'd'.
and a_p denotes p^{th} term.

Given; $m(a_m) = n(a_n)$ $[m \neq n]$.

To show: $a_{(m+n)} = 0$

$m(a_m) = n(a_n)$

$\Rightarrow m[a + (m-1)d] = n[a + (n-1)d]$

$\Rightarrow am + md(m-1) = an + nd(n-1)$

$\Rightarrow am - an = nd(n-1) - md(m-1)$

$\Rightarrow a(m-n) = d[n(n-1) - m(m-1)]$

$\Rightarrow a(m-n) = d[n^2 - n - m^2 + m]$

$\Rightarrow a(m-n) = d[n^2 - m^2 + m - n]$

$\Rightarrow a(m-n) = d[(m+n)(n-m) + (m-n)]$

$\Rightarrow a(m-n) = d(m-n)[-(m+n) + 1]$

$\Rightarrow a - d[-(m+n) + 1] = 0$

$\Rightarrow a + (m+n-1)d = 0$

$\Rightarrow a_{m+n} = 0$

$\therefore a_{m+n} = 0$

Hence proved!

16. The given A.P. is

$-7, -12, -17, -22, \ldots\ldots$

Here $a = -7$, $d = -12 - (-7) = -12 + 7 = -5$ **(1 Mark)**

Let $a_n = -82$

$a_n = a + (n-1)d$

$\Rightarrow -82 = -7 + (n-1)(-5)$

$\Rightarrow -82 = -7 - 5n + 5$

$\Rightarrow -82 = -2 - 5n$

$\Rightarrow -82 + 2 = -5n$

$\Rightarrow -80 = -5n$

$\Rightarrow n = 16$ **(1 Mark)**

Therefore, 16th term will be –82.

Let $a_n = -100$

Again, $a_n = a + (n-1)d$

$\Rightarrow -100 = -7 + (n-1)(-5)$

$\Rightarrow -100 = -7 - 5n + 5$

$\Rightarrow -100 = -2 - 5n$

$\Rightarrow -100 + 2 = -5n$

$\Rightarrow -98 = -5n$

$\Rightarrow n = \frac{98}{5}$

Since, the terms of given A.P. are integers

$\therefore$ The number of terms can not be in fraction.

Hence, –100 can not be the term of this A.P. **(2 Marks)**

17. Let a_1, a_2 be the first terms of given two A.P.'s and d_1 & d_2 be their common differences respectively.

Then, the sum of 'n' terms of first A.P. is,

$$S_n = \frac{n}{2}[2a_1 + (n-1)d_1] \quad \ldots(i)$$

For second A.P.

$$S'_n = \frac{n}{2}\{2a_2 + (n-1)d_2\} \quad \ldots(ii)$$

As per the question,

$$\frac{S_n}{S'_n} = \frac{7n+1}{4n+27} \quad \textbf{(1 Mark)}$$

Using eqn. (i) & (ii) we get,

$$\frac{\frac{n}{2}\{2a_1 + (n-1)d_1\}}{\frac{n}{2}\{2a_2 + (n-1)d_2\}} = \frac{7n+1}{4n+27}$$

$$\Rightarrow \frac{\{2a_1 + (n-1)d_1\}}{\{2a_2 + (n-1)d_2\}} = \frac{7n+1}{4n+27} \quad \ldots(iii) \quad \textbf{(1 Mark)}$$

Let, m^{th} terms of two A.P.s be a_m & a'_m

$\Rightarrow$ As the nth term of AP is given as,

$a_n = a' + (n-1)d$

Thus the ratio of mth terms of two A.P.s given as

$$\therefore \frac{a_m}{a'_m} = \frac{a_1 + (m-1)d_1}{a_2 + (m-1)d_2} \quad \textbf{(1 Mark)}$$

By multiplying with 2, we get,

$$\frac{a_m}{a'_m} = \frac{2a_1 + 2(m-1)d_1}{2a_2 + 2(m-1)d_2}$$

$$\Rightarrow \frac{a_m}{a'_m} = \frac{2a_1 + [(2m-1)-1]d_1}{2a_2 + [(2m-1)-1]d_2}$$

$$\Rightarrow \frac{a_m}{a'_m} = \frac{S_{2m-1}}{S'_{2m-1}} \quad \textbf{(1 Mark)}$$

$$\Rightarrow \frac{a_m}{a'_m} = \frac{7(2m-1)+1}{4(2m-1)+27} \quad \text{[Using eqn. (iii)]}$$

$$\Rightarrow \frac{a_m}{a'_m} = \frac{14m-7+1}{8m-4+27}$$

$$\Rightarrow \frac{a_m}{a'_m} = \frac{14m-6}{8m+23}$$

Substituting 'm' by 9 in above eqn. we get

$\Rightarrow \quad \frac{a_9}{a'_9} = \frac{14\times9-6}{8\times9+23} = \frac{120}{95}$

Hence, the ratio of 8th terms of two APs be 120 : 95 or 24 : 19 **(1 Mark)**

If a and b are two positive real numbers, Arithmetic mean $= \frac{a+b}{2}$.

Topic-3: Sum of First n Terms of an AP

1. **(d)** Since , the sum $3n^2 + n$ is true for any value of n hence let n = 5

$S_5 = 3(5)^2 + 5$
$= 80$

The sum of n terms in AP is calculate d by formula

$$S_n = \frac{n}{2}[2a+(n-1)d]$$

$$S_5 = \frac{5}{2}[2a+(5-1)6]$$

$$80 = \frac{5}{2}[2a+24]$$

32 = 2a + 24

2a = 8

$\boxed{a = 4}$ **(1 Mark)**

2. **(b)** a, b, c are in A.P. i.e. b – a = c – b

$\boxed{2b = a + c}$ & 1 + 3 + 5 + …… + n

$Sn = \frac{n}{2}[20 + (n-1)d] = \frac{n}{2}[2 \times 1 + (n-1)2]$

$= \frac{n}{2}[2 + 2n - 2] = \frac{n}{2} \times 2n = n^2$ **(1 Mark)**

3. Sum of first n natural number = 1 + 2 + 3 .... + n

$$= \frac{n}{2}(a+l) = \frac{n}{2}(1+n) = \frac{n(n+1)}{2}$$

$\text{Mean} = \frac{n(n+1)}{2\cdot n} = \frac{n+1}{2} = 15 \Rightarrow n = 29$ **(1 Mark)**

4. Given $S_n = 6n - n^2$

We know, $T_n = S_n - S_{n-1}$ **(1 Mark)**

$\Rightarrow T_{30} = S_{30} - S_{29} = 6(30) - (30)^2 - (6(29) - (29)^2)$

$= 180 - 900 - 174 + 841$

$= -53$ **(1 Mark)**

Note

If S_n be the sum of n terms of an AP then its nth term is $t_n = S_{n-1} - S_{n-1}$

5. Given $S_{15} = 750$, a = 15, n = 15

$S_n = \frac{n}{2}[2a + (n-1)d]$

$750 = \frac{15}{2}[30 + (14)d]$

$\Rightarrow 100 = 30 + 14d \Rightarrow 70 = 14d \boxed{d = 5}$ **(1 Mark)**

$a_{20} = a + 19d = 15 + 19 \times 5 = 15 + 95$

$a_{20} = 110$ **(1 Mark)**

6. $S_n = 1,18,00$, a = 1000, d = 100

$a_{30} = a + (30-1)d = 1000 + 29 \times 100$

$= 1000 + 2900 = 3900$ [30th installment] **(1 Mark)**

$S_{30} = \frac{n}{2}[2a + (n-1)d] = \frac{30}{2}[2 \times 1000 + (30-1)100]$

$= 15[2000 + 2900] = 4900 \times 15$

$= 73,500$

Amount of loan still paid by Rohan after 30th instalements

$\Rightarrow 118000 - 73500 = 44500$ **(1 Mark)**

$a_n = a + (n-1)d$

7. Given, $a_n = 5 - 2n$

Put n = 1

$a_1 = 5 - 2 \times 1 = 5 - 2 = 3$

Put n = 20

$a_{20} = 5 - 2 \times 20 = 5 - 40 = -35$ **(1 Mark)**

$S_n = \frac{n}{2}[a + a_n]$

Here, n = 20

$S_{20} = \frac{20}{2}[3 - 35]$

$= \frac{20}{2} \times (-32) = -320$ **(1 Mark)**

$S_{20} = -320$

8. $S_n = 0$.

$\frac{n}{2}[2a + (n-1)d] = 0$

a + 75d = 0. **(½ Mark)**

Assumes the xth term to be zero and writes the equation for the term as:

a + (x – 1) d = 0 **(½ Mark)**

Uses a = –75 d in the above equation to write:

–75 d + xd – d = 0 **(½ Mark)**

Solves the above equation and finds the value of x as 76. **(½ Mark)**

9. First term = a

Second term = b

Last term (a_n) = c **(1 Mark)**

d = b – a

$\because \quad a_n = a + (n-1)d$

$c = a + (n-1)(b-a)$ **(1 Mark)**

$$\frac{c-a}{b-a} = n-1$$

$$n = \frac{c-a}{b-a} + 1 = \frac{c-a+b-a}{b-a}$$

$$\Rightarrow \quad n = \frac{c+b-2a}{b-a}$$

$$S_n = \frac{n}{2}(a+l) = \frac{(b+c-2a)}{2(b-a)}(a+c)$$

[$\because$ l = last term]

Hence, proved. **(1 Mark)**

10. $\because \quad a_2 - a_1 = 4 - 1 = 3$

$a_3 - a_2 = 7 - 4 = 3$

Since, $a_2 - a_1 = a_3 - a_2$

$\therefore$ Given sequence are in A.P. whose a = 1, d = 3, l = x and $S_n = 287$

$a_n = a + (n-1)d \Rightarrow x = 1 + (n-1)3$

$$n - 1 = \frac{x-1}{3}$$

$$n = \frac{x-1}{3} + 1 = \frac{x-1+3}{3} = \frac{x+2}{3}$$ **(1 Mark)**

$$S_n = \frac{n}{2}(a+l)$$

$$287 = \frac{(x+2)}{2\times 3}(1+x)$$

$287 \times 6 = (x+2)(1+x)$

$1722 = x^2 + 3x + 2 \Rightarrow x^2 + 3x - 1720 = 0$

$x^2 + 43x - 40x - 1720 = 0$ **(1 Mark)**

$x(x+43) - 40(x+43) = 0$

$(x-40)(x+43) = 0$

$x - 40 = 0$ | $x + 43 = 0$

$x = 40$ | $x = -43$

(Negative value is not possible because each terms is positive)

Hence, x = 40 **(1 Mark)**

When each terms of A.P multiply by 2 then it is also are in A.P.

11. Given $S_n = 3n^2 - 4n$

n^{th} term of the AP is $S_n - S_{(n-1)}$

$= 3n^2 - 4n - [3(n-1)^2 - 4(n-1)]$ **(1 Mark)**

$= 3n^2 - 4n - 3(n-1)^2 + 4(n-1)$

$= 3n^2 - 4n - 3n^2 - 3 + 6n + 4n - 4 = 6n - 7.$

Therefore, n^{th} term of the AP is 6n – 7. **(1 Mark)**

12. First 8 multiples of 3 form an AP with a = 3 and d = 3

3, 6, 9, ...

We know $S_n = \frac{n}{2}\left[2a + (n-1)d\right]$ **(1 Mark)**

$$\therefore \quad S_8 = \frac{8}{2}\left[2\times 3 + (7)3\right]$$

$S_8 = 4(6 + 21) = 4 \times 27 = 108$

Hence sum of first 8 multiples of 3 is 108. **(1 Mark)**

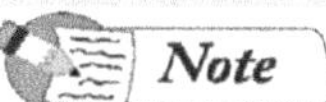

It can be also solved by simple method

$S = 3 + 6 + 9 + 12 + ... + 24$

$= 3(1 + 2 + 3 + ... + 8)$

$= 3 \times \frac{8\times 9}{2}$

$= 108$

13. Given that

$a_1 = 5$

$a_n = 45$

$S_n = 400$

We know that,

$a_n = a + (n-1)d$

$45 = 5 + (n-1)d$

$\Rightarrow \quad (n-1)d = 40 \quad ...(i)$ **(1 Mark)**

Now, sum of n terms

$$S_n = \frac{n}{2}\left[(2a + (n-1)d\right]$$

$$400 = \frac{n}{2}\left[2\times 5 + (n-1)d\right]$$

$$\Rightarrow \quad \frac{800}{n} = [10 + 40] \text{ ...using eqn. (i)}$$

$$n = \frac{800}{50} = 16$$ **(1 Mark)**

Putting n = 16 in eqn. (i) we get

$(16-1)d = 40$

$$\Rightarrow \quad d = \frac{40}{15} = \frac{8}{3}$$

Hence the common difference of AP is $\frac{8}{3}$ and number of terms are 16. **(1 Mark)**

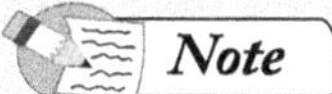

The above also can solved as,

$$S_n = \frac{n}{2}(a+l) \Rightarrow 400 = \frac{n}{2}(5+45) \Rightarrow n = 16$$

$$\because l = a + (n-1)d \Rightarrow 45 = 5 + (16-1)d \Rightarrow d = \frac{8}{3}$$

14. AP : 18, 16, 14 ...

Sum = 0 (given)

Common difference, d = 16 – 18 = –2

First term, a = 18 **(1 Mark)**

$S_n = \frac{n}{2}[2a + (n-1)d]$

$0 = \frac{n}{2}[(2 \times 18) + (n-1)(-2)]$

$\Rightarrow n[36 - 2n + 2] = 0$

$\Rightarrow n[38 - 2n] = 0$

$\Rightarrow n = 0$ or $38 - 2n = 0$

$\Rightarrow n = \frac{38}{2} = 19$

$\Rightarrow$ n cannot be 0

$\Rightarrow$ So, n = 19

Sum of 19 terms will be 0 **(1 Mark)**

15. Let first term and common difference of an A.P. be a and d.

$S_7 = 49$

$S_n = \frac{n}{2}[2a + (n-1)d]$

$S_7 = \frac{7}{2}[2a + (7-1)d]$

$49 = \frac{7}{2}[2a + 6d]$

$14 = 2a + 6d$

$a + 3d = 7$ ...(1) **(1 Mark)**

$S_{17} = 289, S_{17} = \frac{17}{2}[2a + (17-1)d]$

$\Rightarrow 289 = \frac{17}{2}[2a + 16d]$

$\Rightarrow 289 = \frac{17}{2} \times 2[a + 8d]$

$a + 8d = \frac{289}{17} = 17$

$a + 8d = 17$ ...(2)

Subtracting (2) from (1)

$\Rightarrow 5d = 10$

$\Rightarrow d = 2$ **(1 Mark)**

Substituting the value of d in (1)

a = 1

$S_n = \frac{n}{2}[2a + (n-1)d]$

$= \frac{n}{2}[2(1) + (n-1)2]$

$= \frac{n}{2}[2 + (n-1)2]$

$= n[n] = n^2$

Sum of n terms of AP is n^2 **(1 Mark)**

16. n^{th} term of an AP is given as

$a_n = a + (n-1)d$

$a_{14} = 2a_8$

$a + (14-1)d = 2[a + (8-1)d]$

$a + 13d = 2[a + 7d]$

$a + 13d = 2a + 14d$

$a + d = 0$ ...(1) **(1 Mark)**

$a_6 = -8 \Rightarrow a + (6-1)d = -8$

$\Rightarrow a + 5d = -8$ ...(2) **(1 Mark)**

Subtracting equation (1) from (2)

$a + 5d - (a + d) = -8 - 0$

$4d = -8$

$d = -2$

Putting the value of d in (1)

$a - 2 = 0 \Rightarrow a = 2$

$\therefore S_{20} = \frac{20}{2}[2a + (20-1)d]$

$= 10[2 \times 2 + 19 \times (-2)]$

$= -340$ **(1 Mark)**

Note

If common difference of an arithmetic progression is negative, then nature of progression is in decreasing order.

17. Sum of n terms in an A.P. is

$Sn = \frac{n}{2}[2a + (n-1)d]$

$S_5 + S_7 = 167$

$\frac{5}{2}[2a + (5-1)d] + \frac{7}{2}[2a + (7-1)d] = 167$

$5a + 10d + 7a + 21d = 167$

$12a + 31d = 167$ ...(1) **(1 Mark)**

Also $S_{10} = 235$

$\Rightarrow \frac{10}{2}[2a + (10-1)d] = 235$

$\Rightarrow 5[2a + 9d] = 235$

$\Rightarrow 2a + 9d = 47$ ...(2) **(1 Mark)**

Multiplying equation (2) by 6

$12a + 54d = 282$ ...(3)

Subtracting (1) from (3)

$$\begin{array}{r} 12a + 54d = 282 \\ \underline{\overset{-}{}12a \overset{}{+} 31d = \overset{}{}167} \\ 23d = 115 \end{array}$$

$d = 5$

Substituting value of d in (2)

$2a + 9(5) = 47 \Rightarrow 2a + 45 = 47 \Rightarrow 2a = 2 \Rightarrow a = 1$

$\therefore$ Given AP is 1, 6, 11, 16, ... **(1 Mark)**

Sum of n terms is also given as $S_n = \frac{n}{2}[a + l]$

18. Let a be the first term and d be the common difference.

Given that a = 5

Last term $a_n = 45$

Sum of all terms $S_n = 400$

$a_n = a + (n - 1) d$

$45 = 5 + (n - 1) d$

$40 = (n - 1) d$ ...(1)

$\Rightarrow S_n = \frac{n}{2}[a + a_n]$ **(1 Mark)**

$\Rightarrow 400 = \frac{n}{2}[5 + 45]$

$\Rightarrow n = \frac{400 \times 2}{50}$

$\Rightarrow n = 16$ **(1 Mark)**

Substituting the value of n in (1)

$40 = (16 - 1)d$

$\Rightarrow d = \frac{40}{15} = \frac{8}{3}$

$\therefore$ Common difference is $\frac{8}{3}$. **(1 Mark)**

The sum of two terms that are equidistant from either end of an AP is constant.

Tr + T(n – r) + 1 = constant

19. AP: 18, 15–, 13, ..., $-49\frac{1}{2}$

Here a = 18

$d = a_2 - a_1$

$= 15\frac{1}{2} - 18$

$= \frac{31}{2} - 18$

$= \frac{31 - 36}{2} = -\frac{5}{2} = -2.5$

$a_n = -49\frac{1}{2}$

$a + (n - 1)d = -49\frac{1}{2}$

$18 + (n - 1)(-2.5) = -\frac{99}{2}$

$18 - 2.5n + 2.5 = -49.5$

$-2.5n = -49.5 - 20.5$

$-2.5n = -70$

$n = 28$ **(1½ Marks)**

Sum of n terms is given as

$S_n = \frac{n}{2}[2a + (n - 1)d]$

$S_n = \frac{28}{2}[2(18) + (n - 1)(-2.5)]$

$= 14[36 - 2.5n + 2.5]$

$= 14[38.5 - 2.5(28)]$

$= 14(-31.5)$

$= -441$

$\therefore$ Sum of 28 terms = –441 **(1½ Marks)**

Another formula of sum of n terms of A.P, $Sn = \frac{n}{2}(a + l)$, where l is last term.

20. The nth term of an AP is calculated by the formula

$a_n = a + (n-1)d$

Where n = number of terms

d = common difference of AP

a = first term of AP

For 11th term, n = 11

$a_{11} = a + (11-1)d$

$= a + 10d$

For 18th term, n = 18 **(1 Mark)**

$a_{18} = a + (18-1)d$

$= a + 17d$

$\frac{a_{11}}{a_{18}} = \frac{a + 10d}{a + 17d} = \frac{2}{3}$ [given]

$\Rightarrow 3a + 30d = 2a + 34d$ [on cross multiplication]

$\Rightarrow \boxed{a = 4d}$ (i) **(1 Mark)**

5th term of AP is calculated as

$a_5 = a + 4d$

21st term of AP is calculated as

$a_{21} = a + 20d$

$$\frac{a_5}{a_{21}} = \frac{a+4d}{a+20d}$$

$$= \frac{4d+4d}{4d+20d}$$ [from equation (i)]

$$= \frac{8}{24} \quad \frac{1}{3}$$ **(½ Mark)**

Sum of n terms of an AP is $S_n = \frac{n}{2}\left[2a+(n-1)d\right]$

For 5 terms, the sum is

$$S_5 = \frac{5}{2}\left[2a+(5-1)d\right]$$

Substituting a = 4d from equation (i)

$$S_5 = \frac{5}{2}[2(4d)+4d]$$

$$= \frac{5}{2}\times 12d$$

$S_5 = 30d$ **(1 Mark)**

Similarly, the sum of 20 terms is

$$S_{21} = \frac{21}{2}[2a+20d]$$

$$= \frac{21}{2}[8d+20d]$$

$= 21 \times 14d$ **(1 Mark)**

$$\frac{S_5}{S_{21}} = \frac{30d}{21\times 14d} = \frac{5}{49}$$

Hence the $S_5 : S_{21} = 5 : 49$ **(½ Mark)**

21. Sum of n terms of an AP is

$$S_n = \frac{n}{2}\left[2a+(n-1)d\right]$$

For the first six terms, n = 6

$$S_6 = \frac{6}{2}\left[2a+(6-1)d\right]$$

$36 = 3[2a + 5d]$

[Given that sum of first six terms is 36]

$12 = 2a + 5d$ (i) **(1 Mark)**

For first 16 terms, n = 16

$$S_{16} = \frac{16}{2}\left[2a+(16-1)d\right]$$

$256 = 8[2a + 15d]$

[Given that sum of first 16 terms is 256]

$32 = 2a + 15d$ (ii) **(1 Mark)**

Subtracting equation (i) from equation (ii)

$2a + 15d = 32$

$2a + 5d = 12$

− − −

$10d = 20$

$d = 2$ **(1 Mark)**

Substituting the obtained value of d in equation (i)

$12 = 2a + 5(2)$

$2a = 12 - 10$

$2a = 2 \Rightarrow a = 1$ **(1 Mark)**

Sum of first 10 terms is calculated as

$$S_{10} = \frac{10}{2}\left[2a+(10-1)d\right]$$

$S_{10} = 5[2 + 9(2)]$

$S_{10} = 100$ **(1 Mark)**

Hence the sum of first 10 terms is 100.

22.

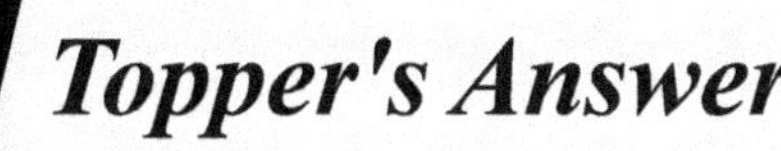

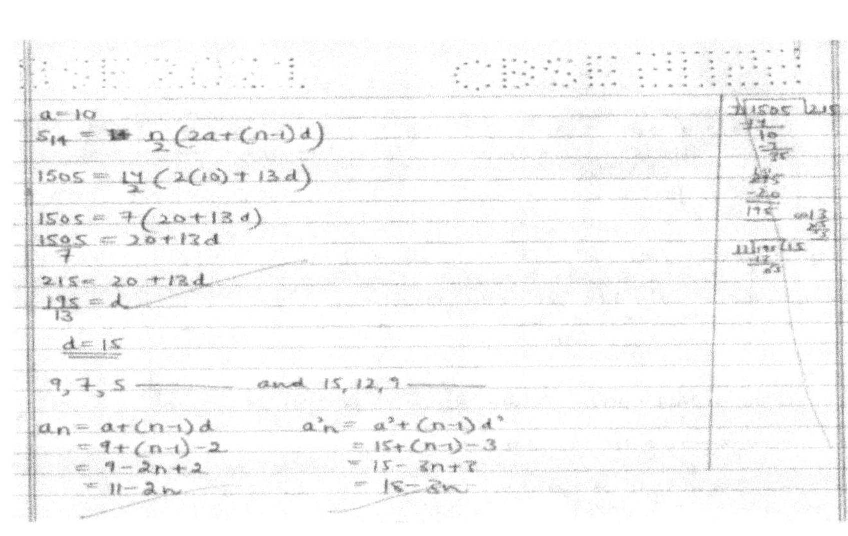

a = 10

$S_{14} = \frac{n}{2}(2a+(n-1)d)$

$1505 = \frac{14}{2}(2(10)+13d)$

$1505 = 7(20+13d)$

$\frac{1505}{7} = 20+13d$

$215 = 20+13d$

$\frac{195}{13} = d$

d = 15

9, 7, 5 —— and 15, 12, 9 ——

$a_n = a+(n-1)d$ $\quad a'_n = a'+(n-1)d'$

$= 9+(n-1)-2$ $\quad = 15+(n-1)-3$

$= 9-2n+2$ $\quad = 15-3n+3$

$= 11-2n$ $\quad = 18-3n$

23. $a_2 - a_1 = 4 - 1 = 3$

$a_3 - a_2 = 7 - 4 = 3$

$\therefore$ 1, 4, 7, 10 .... x are in A.P. **(1 Mark)**

$a = 1, d = 3, a_n = l = x$ and $S_n = 287$

$a_n = a + (n - 1)d$

$x = 1 + (n - 1)3 = 1 + 3n - 3$

$n = \frac{x+2}{3}$ **(1 Mark)**

$S_n = \frac{n}{2}(a + l)$

$287 = \frac{(x+2)}{6}(1 + x)$

$1722 = x^2 + 3x + 2$ **(1 Mark)**

$x^2 + 3x - 1720 = 0 \Rightarrow x^2 + 43x - 40x - 1720 = 0$

$x(x + 43) - 40(x + 43) = 0 \Rightarrow (x - 40)(x + 43) = 0$

$\therefore$ $x - 40 = 0$ or $x + 43 = 0$

$x = 40$ $\quad x = -43$ (Not possible) **(1 Mark)**

24. The given Arithmetic progression

45, 39, 33, ...

Here $a = 45, d = 39 - 45 = -6$

Let $S_n = 180$

$\Rightarrow \frac{n}{2}[2a + (n - 1)d] = 180$ **(1 Mark)**

$\Rightarrow \frac{n}{2}[2 \times 45 + (n - 1)(-6)] = 180$

$\Rightarrow \frac{n}{2}[90 - 6n + 6] = 180$

$\Rightarrow n(96 - 6n) = 360$

$\Rightarrow 96n - 6n^2 = 360$

$\Rightarrow 6n^2 - 96n + 360 = 0$

$\Rightarrow 6(n^2 - 16n + 60) = 0$

$\Rightarrow n^2 - 16n + 60 = 0$

$\Rightarrow n^2 - 10n - 6n + 60 = 0$

$\Rightarrow n(n - 10) - 6(n - 10) = 0$

$\Rightarrow (n - 10)(n - 6) = 0$

$\Rightarrow n = 10, 6$ **(2 Marks)**

$\therefore$ Sum of first 10 terms = Sum of first 6 terms = 180

Hence, it means that the sum of all terms from 7th to 10th is zero. **(1 Mark)**

When A.P in decreasing order and we have to find the first negative number then use condition $a_n < 0$.

25. Sum of first four terms of an AP is 40.

$\frac{4}{2}[2a+(4-1)d]=40$ where, a is the first term of the AP and d is the common difference.

$2[2a + 3d] = 40$ or $2a + 3d = 20$ ...(1) **(1 Mark)**

Sum of first 14 terms is 280.

$\therefore \frac{14}{2}[2a+(14-1)d]=280$

or $2a + 13d = 40$ ...(2) **(1 Mark)**

Subtracting eqn (1) from eqn (2),

$10d = 20 \Rightarrow d = 2$

Substitute d = 2 in eqn (1), we get, a = 7 **(1 Mark)**

$\therefore$ The sum of its first n terms,

$$S_n = \frac{n}{2}[2\times7+(n-1)2] = \frac{n}{2}\times2[7+n-1]$$
$$= n(n + 6).$$ **(1 Mark)**

Sum of kth terms from end = $S_n - S_{n-k}$
where n is number of terms.

26. Let four consecutive terms of an AP be a – 3d, a – d, a + d and a + 3d

Now $a - 3d + a - d + a + d + a + 3d = 32$ [Given]

$\Rightarrow 4a = 32$

$\Rightarrow a = \frac{32}{4} = 8$

So, a = 8 **(1 Mark)**

Now $\frac{(a-3d)(a+3d)}{(a-d)(a+d)} = \frac{7}{15}$ [Given]

$\Rightarrow \frac{a^2-9d^2}{a^2-d^2} = \frac{7}{15}$ **(1 Mark)**

$\Rightarrow \frac{8^2-9d^2}{8^2-d^2} = \frac{7}{15}$

$\Rightarrow 15(64 - 9d^2) = 7(64 - d^2)$

$\Rightarrow 15 \times 64 - 135d^2 = 7 \times 64 - 7d^2$

$\Rightarrow (15 - 7) \times 64 = 135d^2 - 7d^2$

$\Rightarrow 8 \times 64 = 128d^2$

$d^2 = \frac{8\times64}{128}$

$\Rightarrow d^2 = 4$

$\Rightarrow d = \pm 2$ **(1 Mark)**

Case I, a = 8, d = 2

$\therefore$ 4 numbers are $8 - 3 \times 2, 8 - 2, 8 + 2, 8 + 3 \times 2$

or 2, 6, 10, 14

Case II, a = 8, d = –2

4 numbers are 14, 10, 6, 2 **(2 Marks)**

Five consecutive terms of an AP are a-2d, a-d, a, a+d and a+2d.

27. Let the policeman catches the thief after t min.

Uniform speed of the thief = 100 m/min

$\therefore$ Distance covered by thief in (t + 1) min

= Speed × Time

= 100 × (t + 1)

= 100 (t + 1) metres. **(1 Mark)**

Distance covered by policeman in t minutes = Sum of t terms of an AP with first term 100 and common difference 10

$= \frac{t}{2}[2 \times 100 + (t-1)10]$ $\left[\because S_n = \frac{n}{2}(2a+(n-1)d\right]$

$= t[100 + 5(t - 1)]$

$= t[5t + 95] = 5t^2 + 95t$ **(2 Marks)**

When policeman catches thief

$5t^2 + 95t = 100(t + 1)$

$\Rightarrow 5t^2 + 95t = 100t + 100$

$\Rightarrow 5t^2 - 5t - 100 = 0$

$\Rightarrow t^2 - t - 20 = 0$

$\Rightarrow t^2 - 5t + 4t - 20 = 0$

$\Rightarrow (t - 5)(t + 4) = 0$

t = 5 or t = –4

Time cannot be negative

$\therefore$ t = 5

$\therefore$ Policeman catches the thief after 5 minutes.

(2 Marks)

28. The given AP is :

8, 10, 12, ...

Here, a = 8, d = 10 – 8 = 2

n^{th} term of an AP is,

$a_n = a + (n - 1)d$

$\therefore a_{60} = a + (n - 1)d$ **(1 Mark)**

$= 8 + (60 - 1)^2$

$= 8 + 59 \times 2 = 126$

$a_{51} = a + (51 - 1)d$

$= 8 + 50 \times 2 = 108$ **(1 Mark)**

Sum of last 10 terms: $a_{51} + a_{52} + ... + a_{60}$

Now, first term $A = a_{51} = 108$, d = 2

Sum of n terms:

$$S_n = \frac{n}{2}[2A + (n - 1)d]$$

$$S_{10} = \frac{10}{2}[2 \times 108 + (10 - 1)2]$$

$= 5[216 + 18] = 5 \times 234 = 1170$

$\therefore$ Sum of last 10 terms = 1170 **(2 Marks)**

29. Let a and d be the first term and common difference of an A.P respectively.

n^{th} term of an AP, $a_n = a + (n - 1)d$

$$S_n = \frac{n}{2}[2a + (n-1)d]$$

$S_{10} = 210$

$$\frac{10}{2}[2a + (10 - 1)d] = 210$$

$2a + 9d = 42$ ...(1) **(1 Mark)**

15th term from last term is $(50 - 15 + 1 = 36^{th})$

36th term from beginning

$a_{36} = a + 35d$ **(1 Mark)**

$\therefore$ Sum of last 15 terms $= \frac{n}{2}[2a_{36} + (15 - 1)d]$

$$2565 = \frac{15}{2}[2(a + 35d) + 14d]$$

$2565 = 15[a + 35d + 7d]$

$171 = a + 42d$ ...(2) **(1 Mark)**

Solving equation (1) and (2), we get

a = 3

d = 4

$\therefore$ AP is 3, 7, 11, 15 .... 199 **(1 Mark)**

30. $S_n = \frac{n}{2}[2a + (n - 1)d]$

$S_7 = 49$

$$S_7 = \frac{7}{2}[2a + (7 - 1)d]$$

$$\Rightarrow 49 = \frac{7}{2}[2a + 6d]$$

$\Rightarrow 14 = 2a + 6d$

$\Rightarrow a + 3d = 7$ ...(1) **(1 Mark)**

$S_{17} = 289$

$$S_{17} = \frac{17}{2}[2a + (17 - 1)d]$$

$$\Rightarrow 289 = \frac{17}{2}[2a + 16d]$$

$\Rightarrow 34 = 2a + 16d$

$\Rightarrow a + 8d = 17$ ...(2) **(1 Mark)**

Subtracting equation (1) from (2)

$$\begin{array}{r} a + 8d = 17 \\ a + 3d = 7 \\ - \quad - \quad \\ \hline 5d = 10 \\ d = 2 \end{array}$$

a + 3d = 7

$\Rightarrow a + 3(2) = 7$

$\Rightarrow a = 1$

$$S_n = \frac{n}{2}[2(1) + (n - 1)(2)]$$

$= \frac{n}{2}[2 + 2(n - 1)] = n[1 + n - 1] = n^2$ **(2 Marks)**

31. (i) $x = 11$

Number of throws during camp. $a = 40$; $d = 12$

$t_{11} = a + 10d$

$= 40 + 10 \times 12$

$= 160$ throws **(1 Mark)**

(ii) $a = 7.56$ m; $d = 9$cm $= 0.09$ m **(½ Mark)**

$n = 6$ weeks **(½ Mark)**

$t_n = a + (n - 1) d$ **(½ Mark)**

$= 7.56 + 6(0.09)$

$= 7.56 + 0.54$ **(½ Mark)**

Sanjitha's throw distance at the end of 6 weeks = 8.1 m

OR

$a = 7.56$ m; $d = 9$cm $= 0.09$ m

$t_n = 11.16$ m **(½ Mark)**

$t_n = a + (n - 1) d$ **(½ Mark)**

$11.16 = 7.56 + (n - 1) (0.09)$

$3.6 = (n - 1) (0.09)$ **(½ Mark)**

$n - 1 = \frac{3.6}{0.09} = 40$ **(½ Mark)**

$n = 41$

Sanjitha's will be able to throw 11.16 m in 41 weeks.

(iii) $a = 40$; $d = 12$; $n = 15$

$S_n = \frac{n}{2}[2a + (n-1)d]$ **(½ Mark)**

$S_n = \frac{15}{2}[2(40) + (15-1)(12)]$

$= \frac{15}{2}[80 + 168]$

$= \frac{15}{2}[248] = 1860$ throws **(½ Mark)**

32. (i) Since each row is increasing by 10 seats, so it is an AP with first term $a = 30$, and common difference $d = 10$. **(½ Mark)**

So number of seats in 10th row $= a_{10} = a + 9d$

$= 30 + 9 \times 10 = 120$ **(½ Mark)**

(ii) $Sn = \frac{n}{2}(2a + (n-1)d)$ **(½ Mark)**

$1500 = \frac{n}{2}(2 \times 30 + (n - 1)10)$

$3000 = 50n + 10n^2$

$n^2 + 5n - 300 = 0$ **(½ Mark)**

$n^2 + 20n - 15n - 300 = 0$

$(n + 20)(n - 15) = 0$ **(½ Mark)**

Rejecting the negative value, $n = 15$ **(½ Mark)**

OR

No. of seats already put up to the 10th row $= S_{10}$

$S_{10} = \frac{10}{2}\{2 \times 30 + (10-1)10)\}$

$= 5(60 + 90) = 750$ **(1 Mark)**

So, the number of seats still required to be put are $1500 - 750 = 750$ **(1 Mark)**

(iii) If no. of rows = 17

then the middle row is the 9th row **(½ Mark)**

$a_8 = a + 8d$

$= 30 + 80$

$= 110$ seats **(½ Mark)**

6 Chapter Triangles

Topic-1: Similar Figures

Multiple Choice Questions

1. $\Delta ABC \sim \Delta PQR$. If AM and PN are altitudes of ΔABC and ΔPQR respectively and $AB^2 : PQ^2 = 4 : 9$, then AM : PN = **[CBSE Sample Paper 2022-23, U]**
   (a) 3 : 2
   (b) 16 : 81
   (c) 4 : 9
   (d) 2 : 3

2. $\Delta ABC \sim \Delta PQR$. If AM and PN are altitudes of ΔABC and ΔPQR respectively and AB^2: $PQ^2 = 4 ; 9$, then AM : PN = **[CBSE Sample Paper 2021-22, Term-I, K]**
   (a) 16 : 81
   (b) 4 : 9
   (c) 3 : 2
   (d) 2 : 3

3. ΔABC is such that AB = 3 cm, BC = 2cm, CA = 2.5 cm. If $\Delta ABC \sim \Delta DEF$ and EF = 4cm, then perimeter of ΔDEF is **[CBSE Sample Paper 2021-22, Term-I, U]**
   (a) 7.5 cm (b) 15cm (c) 22.5 cm (d) 30cm

Short Answer Questions (2 or 3 Marks)

4. In Fig, $\angle ACB = 90^o$ and $CD \perp AB$, prove that $CD^2 = BD \times AD$. **[Delhi 2019, U]**

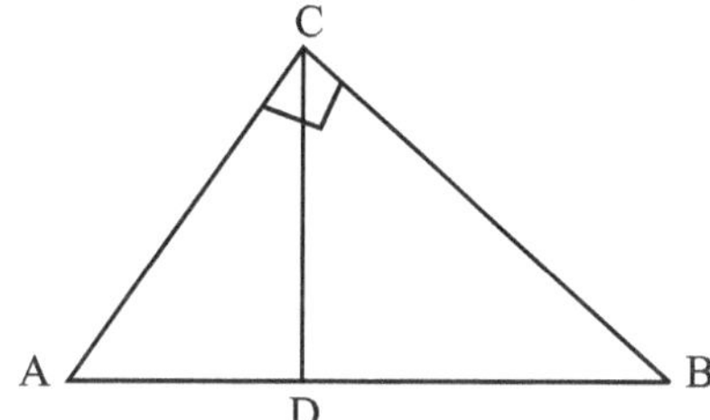

5. Prove that the ratio of the perimeters of two similar triangles is equal to the ratio of their corresponding sides. **[Delhi 2016, Term-I, U]**

Topic-2: Basic Proportionality Theorem (Thales Theorem)

Multiple Choice Questions

1. In Δ ABC, DE || AB. If AB = a, DE = x, BE = b and EC = c. **[CBSE Sample Paper 2023-24, U]**

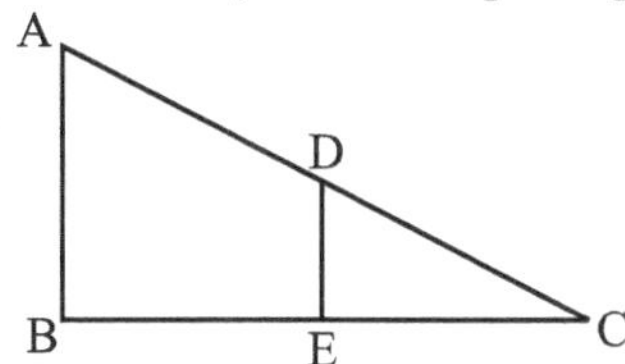

   (a) $\frac{ac}{b}$ (b) $\frac{ac}{b+c}$
   (c) $\frac{ab}{c}$ (d) $\frac{ab}{b+c}$

2. In the given figure, DE||BC. If AD = 3 cm, AB = 7 cm and EC = 3 cm, then the length of AE is **[All India 2023, Set-II, Ap]**

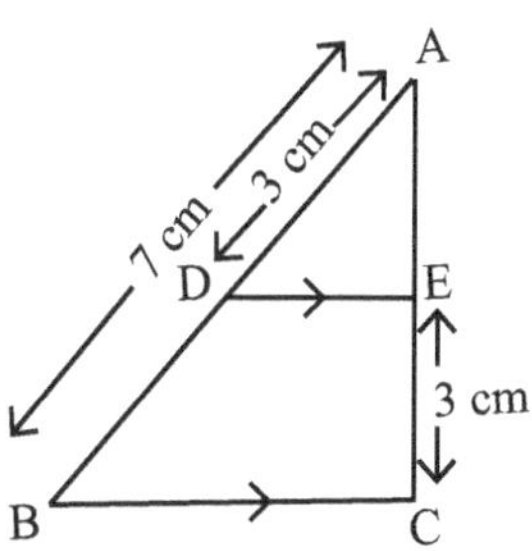

   (a) 2 cm (b) 2.25 cm
   (c) 3.5 cm (d) 4 cm

3. In ΔABC and ΔDEF, $\frac{AB}{DE} = \frac{BC}{FD}$. Which of the following makes the two triangles similar? **[All India 2023, A]**

(a) ∠A = ∠D (b) ∠B = ∠D

(c) ∠B = ∠E (d) ∠A = ∠F

4. In ΔABC, PQ || BC. If PB = 6 cm, AP = 4 cm, AQ = 8 cm, find the legnth of AC. **[Delhi 2023, A]**

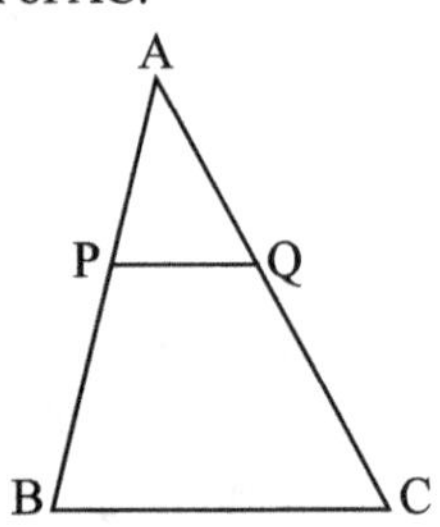

(a) 12 cm (b) 20 cm (c) 6 cm (d) 14 cm

5.

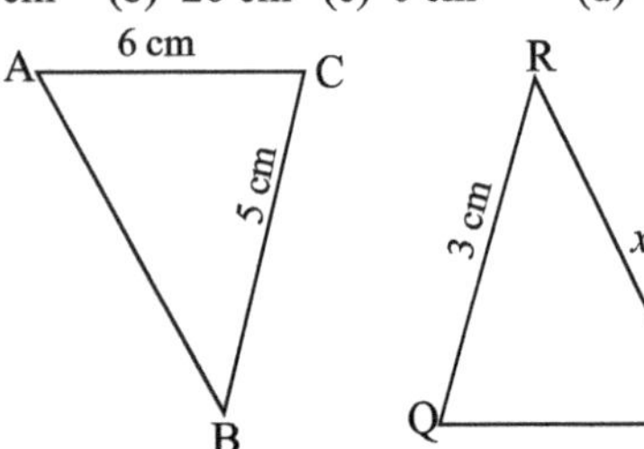

In the given figure, ΔABC ~ ΔQPR. If AC = 6 cm, BC = 5 cm, QR = 3 cm and PR = x; then the value of x is: **[Delhi 2023, U]**

(a) 3.6 cm (b) 2.5 cm (c) 10 cm (d) 3.2 cm

6. In the given figure, DE || BC, AE = a units, EC = b units, DE = x units and BC = y units. Which of the following is true? **[CBSE Sample Paper 2022-23, A]**

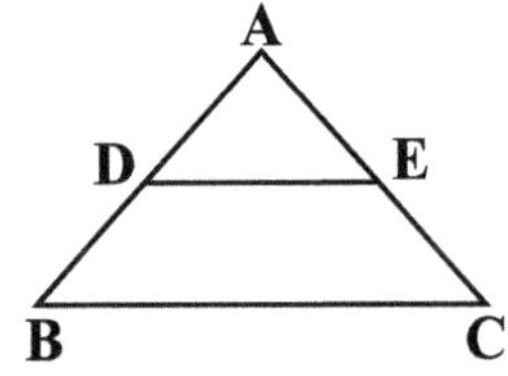

(a) $x = \frac{a+b}{ay}$ (b) $y = \frac{ax}{a+b}$

(c) $x = \frac{ay}{a+b}$ (d) $\frac{x}{y} = \frac{a}{b}$

7. Which of the following are DEFINITELY similar to each other? **[CBSE CFPQ 2022, U]**

(a) any two rhombuses

(b) any two right triangles

(c) any two regular pentagons

(d) any two isosceles triangles

8. In the figure, if DE || BC, AD = 3cm, BD = 4cm and BC = 14 cm, then DE equals

[CBSE Sample Paper 2021-22, Term-I, Ap]

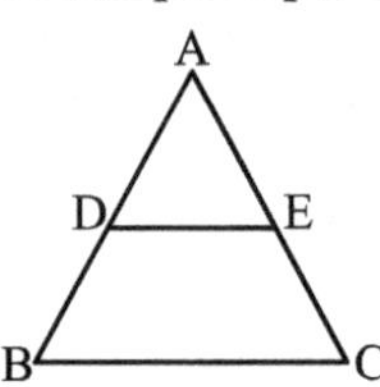

(a) 7cm (b) 6cm (c) 4cm (d) 3cm

Very Short Answer Questions (1 Mark)

9. In Figure, DE || BC. Find the length of side AD, given that AE = 1·8 cm, BD = 7·2 cm and CE = 5·4 cm. **[All India 2019, A]**

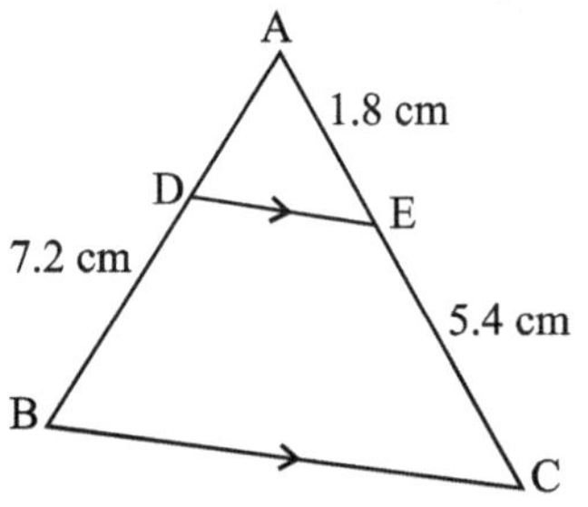

10. In Δ*ABC*, *DE* || *BC*, find the value of *x*.

[All India 2017, Term-I, Ap]

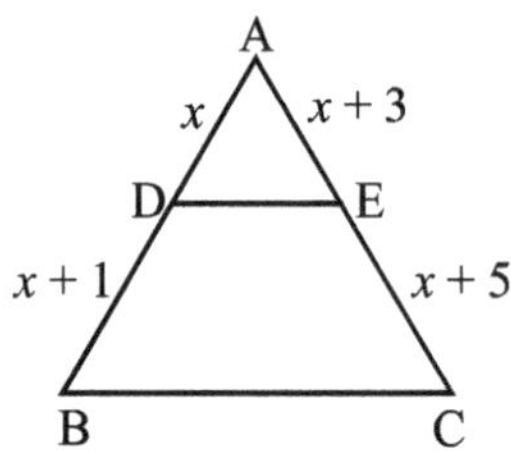

11. Any point *O*, inside Δ *ABC*, is joined to its vertices. From a point *D* on *AO*, *DE* and *DF* are drawn so that *DE* || *AB* and *EF* || *BC* as shown in figure. Prove that *DF* || *AC*.

[All India 2015, Term-I, Ap]

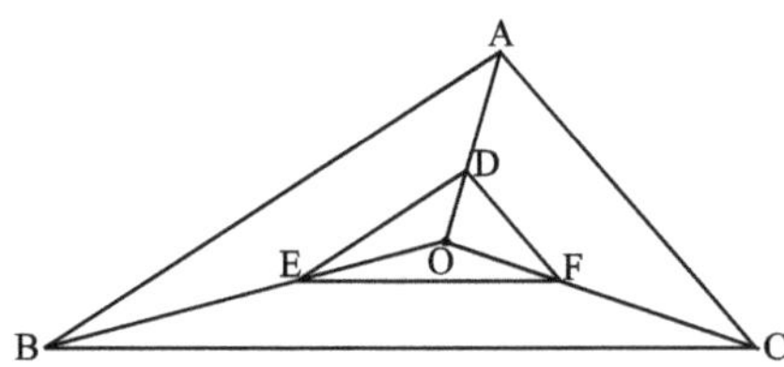

Short Answer Questions (2 or 3 Marks)

12. In the given figure, ABC is a triangle in which DE||BC. If AD = x, DB = $x - 2$, AE = $x + 2$ and EC = $\;\; - x$ then find the value of x. **[All India 2023, Set-II, Ap]**

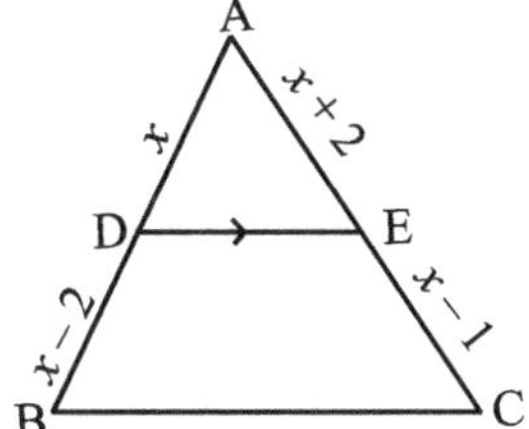

13. Diagonals AC and BD of trapezium ABCD with AB||DC intersect each other at point O. Show that $\frac{OA}{OC} = \frac{OB}{OD}$.

[All India 2023, Set-II, Ap]

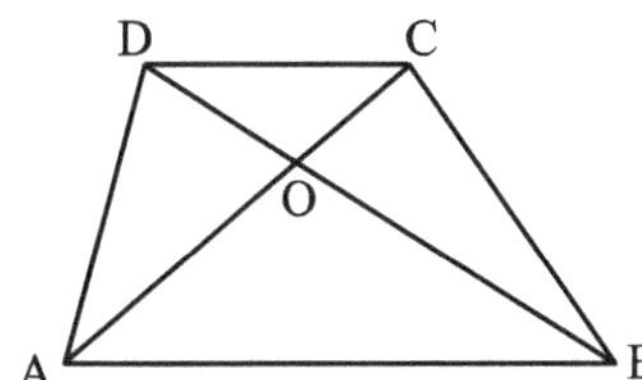

14. In the given figure, CD is the perpendicular bisector of AB. EF is perpendicular to CD. AE intersects CD at G. Prove that $\frac{CF}{CD} = \frac{FG}{DG}$. **[All India 2023, Set-I, U]**

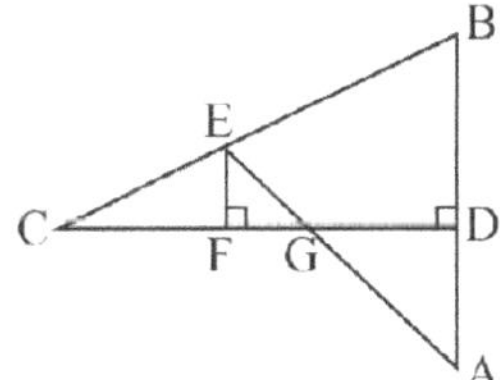

15. In fig., ABC and DBC are two triangles on the same base BC. If AD intersects BC at O, show that

$$\frac{ar(\Delta ABC)}{ar(\Delta DBC)} = \frac{AO}{DO}$$ **[All India 2020, K]**

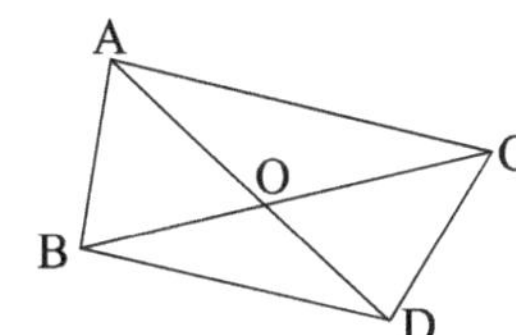

16. In fig. 6, if AD ⊥ BC, then prove that $AB^2 + CD^2 = BD^2 + AC^2$ **[All India 2020, K]**

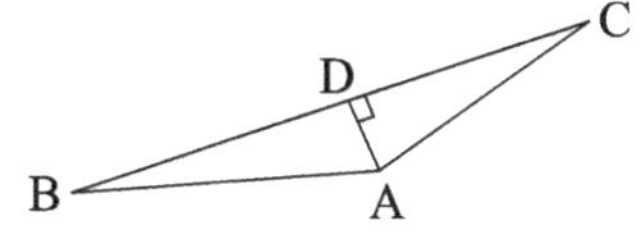

17. In Fig., if ΔABC ~ ΔDEF and their sides of lengths (in cm) are marked along them, then find the lengths of sides of each triangle. **[All India 2020, A]**

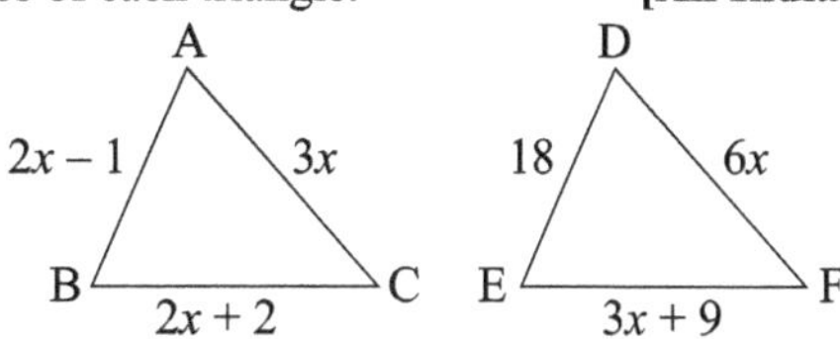

18. In the given Figure, DE || AC and DF || AE.

Prove that $\frac{BF}{FE} = \frac{BE}{EC}$

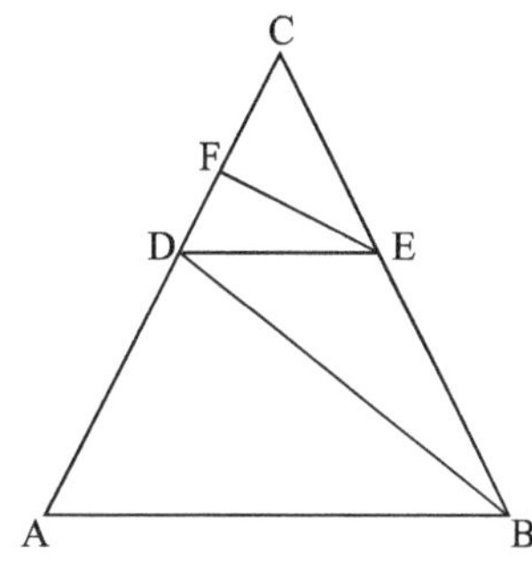

[All India 2020, U]

19. In Fig, DE || AC and DC || AP. Prove that $\frac{BE}{EC} = \frac{BC}{CP}$

[Delhi 2020, A]

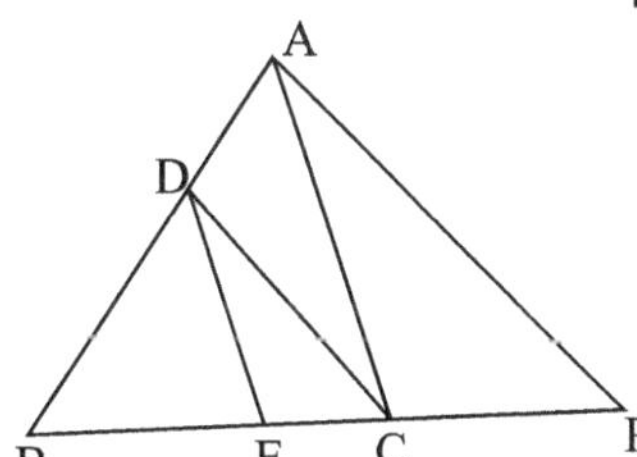

20. In Fig., two tangents TP and TQ are drawn to a circle with centre O from an external point T. Prove that ∠PTQ = 2 ∠OPQ. **[Delhi 2020, A]**

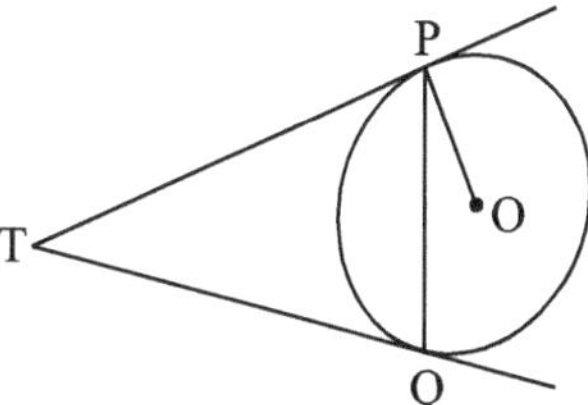

21. If Fig., $\angle D = \angle E$ and $\frac{AD}{DB} = \frac{AE}{EC}$, prove that ΔBAC is an isosceles triangle. **[Delhi 2020, K]**

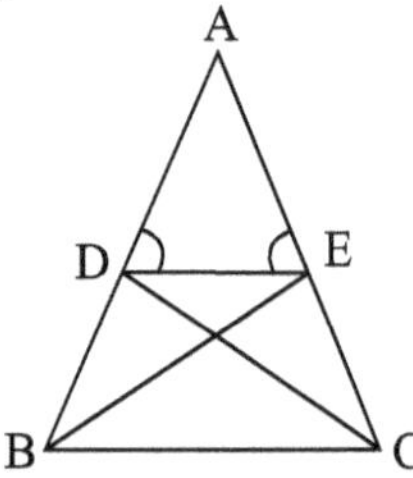

22. In ΔABC, if X and Y are points on AB and AC respectively such that $\frac{AX}{XB} = \frac{3}{4}$, $AY = 5$ cm and $YC = 9$ cm, then state whether XY and BC parallel or not. **[All India 2017, Term-I, U]**

23. In the given figure, $\Delta ABC \sim \Delta PQR$. Find the value of $y + z$. **[Delhi 2016, Term-I, K]**

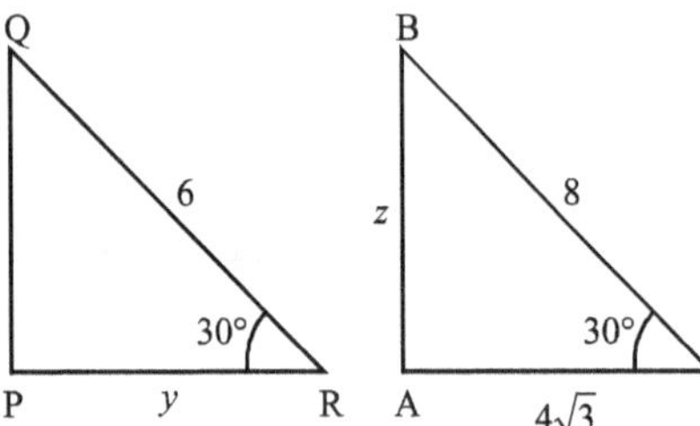

24. In figure, $AB \parallel DE$ and $BD \parallel EF$. Prove that $DC^2 = CF \times AC$.

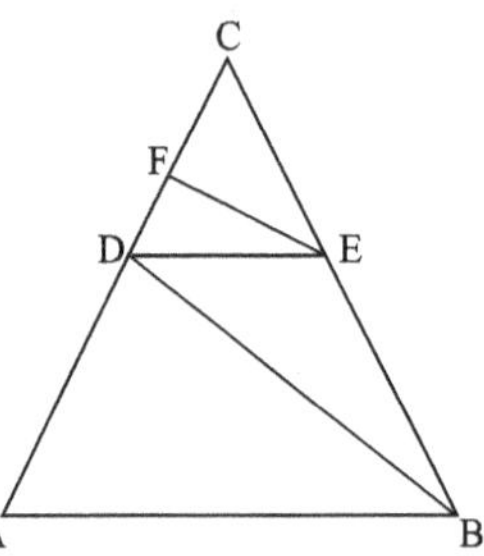

[Delhi 2014, Term-I, A]

6 Long Answer Questions (4 or 5 Marks)

25. (a) State and prove basic proportionality theorem.

(b) In the given figure $\angle CEF = \angle CFE$. F is the midpoint of DC. Prove that $\frac{AB}{BD} = \frac{AE}{FD}$

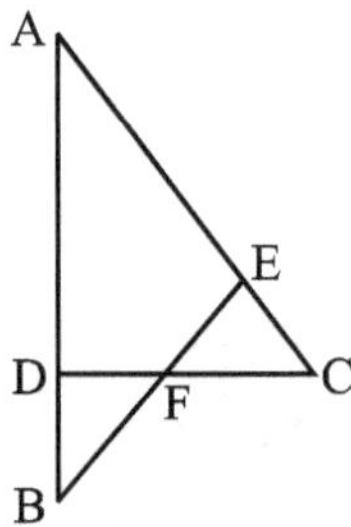

[CBSE Sample Paper 2023-24, U]

26. Prove that if a line is drawn parallel to one side of a triangle intersecting the other two sides in distinct points, then the other two sides are divided in the same ratio. Using the above theorem prove that a line through the point of intersection of the diagonals and parallel to the base of the trapezium divides the non parallel sides in the same ratio. **[All India 2019, A]**

27. If a line is drawn parallel to one side of a triangle to intersect the other two sides in distinct points, then prove that the other two sides are divided in the same ratio. **[All India 2019, A]**

28. In a ΔABC, the mid-points of sides BC, CA and AB are D,E and F respectively. D, E and F are joined to form four triangles. Prove that all four triangles are similar to ΔABC.

[All India 2017, Term-I, Ap]

Topic-3: Similarity and Criteria for Similarity of Triangles

Multiple Choice Questions

1. If $\Delta PQR \sim \Delta ABC$; PQ = 6 cm, AB = 8 cm and the perimeter of ΔABC is 36 cm, then the perimeter of ΔPQR is **[All India 2023, Set-II, K]**
   (a) 20.25 cm (b) 27 cm
   (c) 48 cm (d) 64 cm
2. ABCD is a trapezium with AD || BC and AD = 4cm. If the diagonals AC and BD intersect each other at O such that AO/OC = DO/OB =1/2, then BC = **[CBSE Sample Paper 2022-23, U]**
   (a) 6cm (b) 7cm
   (c) 8cm (d) 9cm
3. In ΔABC and ΔDEF, $\angle F = \angle C$, $\angle B = \angle E$ and AB = $\frac{1}{2}$ DE. Then the two triangles are **[All India 2022, Term-I, A]**
   (a) Congruent, but not similar
   (b) Similar but not congruent
   (c) Neither congruent nor similar
   (d) Congruent as well as similar
4. In fig., PA, QB and RC are each perpendicular to AC. If $x = 8$ cm and $z = 6$ cm, then y is equal to **[All India 2022, Term-I, K]**

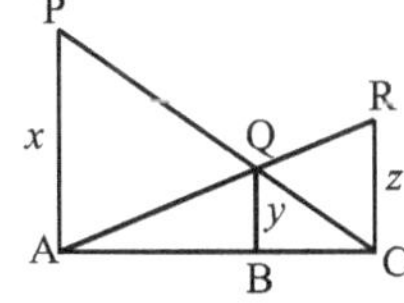

   (a) $\frac{56}{7}$ cm (b) $\frac{7}{56}$ cm
   (c) $\frac{25}{7}$ cm (d) $\frac{24}{7}$ cm
5. In the given figure, $\angle ACB = \angle CDA$, AC = 8cm, AD = 3cm, then BD is **[CBSE Sample Paper 2021-22, Term-I, Ap]**

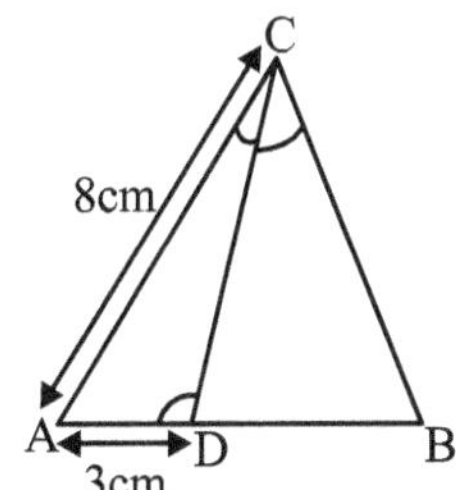

   (a) $\frac{22}{3}$ m (b) $\frac{26}{3}$ m
   (c) $\frac{55}{3}$ cm (d) $\frac{64}{3}$ m
6. Sides AB and BE of a right triangle, right angled at B are of lengths 16 cm and 8 cm respectively. The length of the side of largest square FDGB that can be inscribed in the triangle ABE is **[CBSE Sample Paper 2021-22, Term-I, K]**

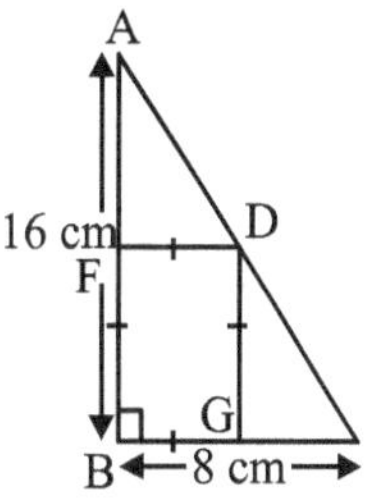

   (b) $\frac{32}{3}$ cm (b) $\frac{16}{3}$ cm
   (c) $\frac{8}{3}$ cm (d) $\frac{4}{3}$ cm

Question (7-11) Based on Case Study

A farmer has a field in the shape of trapezium. whose map with scale 1 cm = 20 m, is given below :

The field is divided into four parts by joining the opposite vertices.

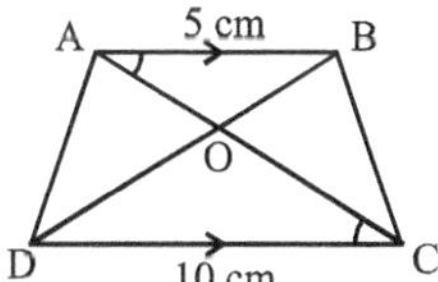

Based on the above information, answer any four of the following questions.

7. The two triangular regions AOB and COD are **[All India 2022, Term-I, A]**
   (a) Similar by AA criterion
   (b) Similar by SAS criterion
   (c) Similar by RHS criterion
   (d) Not similar
8. The ratio of the area of the ΔAOB to the area of ΔCOD, is **[All India 2022, Term-I, K]**
   (a) 4 : 1 (b) 1 : 4
   (c) 1 : 2 (d) 2 : 1

9. If the ratio of the perimeter of ΔAOB to the perimeter of ΔCOD would have been 1 : 4, then

[All India 2022, Term-I, Ap]

(a) AB = 2 CD
(b) AB = 4 CD
(c) CD = 2 AB
(d) CD = 4 AB

10. If in Δs AOD and BOC, $\frac{AO}{BC} = \frac{AD}{BO} = \frac{OD}{OC}$, then

[All India 2022, Term-I, Ap]

(a) ΔAOD ~ ΔBOC
(b) ΔAOD ~ ΔBCO
(c) ΔADO ~ ΔBCO
(d) ΔODA ~ ΔOBC

11. If the ratio of areas of two similar triangles AOB and COD is 1 : 4, then which of the following statements is true?

[All India 2022, Term-I, U]

(a) The ratio of their perimeters is 3 : 4.
(b) The corresponding altitudes have a ratio 1 : 2.
(c) The medians have a ratio 1 : 4.
(d) The angle bisectors have a ratio 1 : 16.

4 *Very Short Answer Questions (1 Mark)*

12. Two triangles are similar if their corresponding sides are ____________. **[All India 2020, Ap]**

13. In the figure, if *DE* || *BC*, then find the value of *x*.

[All India 2015, Term-I, K]

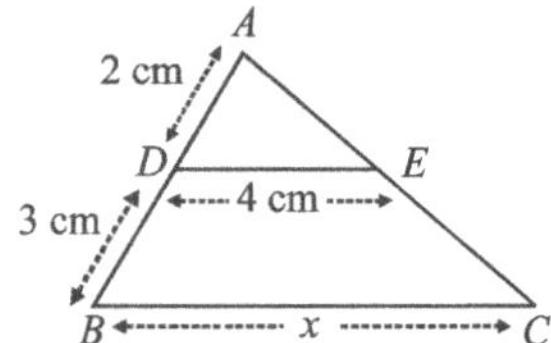

5 *Short Answer Questions (2 or 3 Marks)*

14. ABCD is a parallelogram. Point P divides AB in the ratio 2:3 and point Q divides DC in the ratio 4:1. Prove that OC is half of OA. **[CBSE Sample Paper 2023-24, U]**

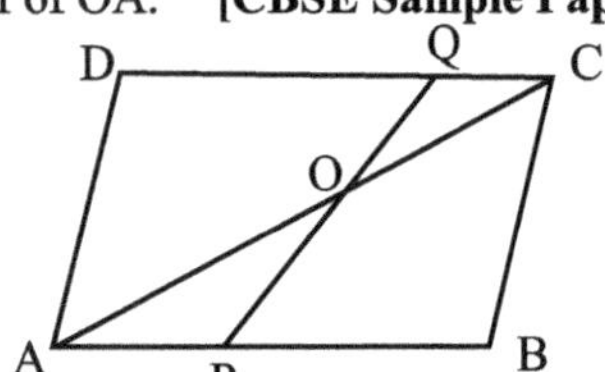

15. In the given figure, E is a point on the side CB produced of an isosceles triangle ABC with AB = AC. If AD ⊥ BC and EF ⊥ AC, then prove that ΔABD ~ ΔECF.

[All India 2023, Set-II, U]

16. In the given figure below, $\frac{AD}{AE} = \frac{AC}{BD}$ and ∠1 = ∠2. Show that ΔBAE~ ΔCAD .**[CBSE Sample Paper 2022-23, A]**

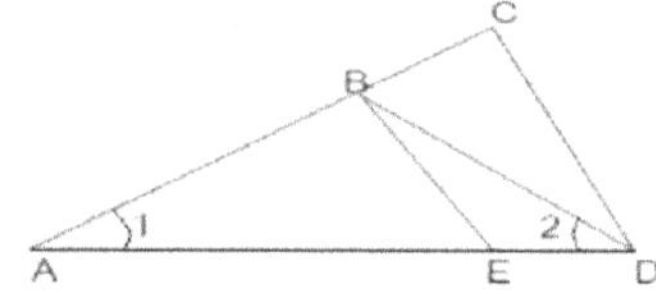

17. In the figure below, OPQ is a triangle with OP = OQ. RS is an arc of a circle with centre O.

[CBSE CFPQ 2022 U]

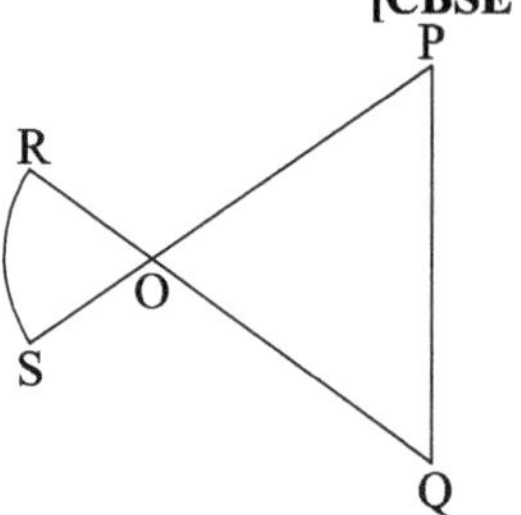

(Note: The figure is not to scale.)
Triangle OSR is similar to triangle OPQ.
Is the above statement true or false? Justify your reason.

18. Two right triangles ABC and DBC are drawn on the same hypotenuse BC and on the same side of BC. If AC and BD intersect at P, prove that AP × PC = BP × DP.

[All India 2019, Ap]

19. AD and PM are medians of triangles ABC and PQR respectively where ΔABC ~ ΔPQR. Prove that $\frac{AB}{PQ} = \frac{AD}{PM}$.

[All India 2019, Ap]

20. In the figure ABCD is a rectangle and E is the middle point of BC. DB and AE interesect at F. Prove that DF = 2 FB and AF = 2FE. **[All India 2017, Term-I, Ap]**

21. In Fig., if *PQ* || *RS*, prove that Δ *POQ* ~ Δ *SOR*

[All India 2015, Term-I, Ap]

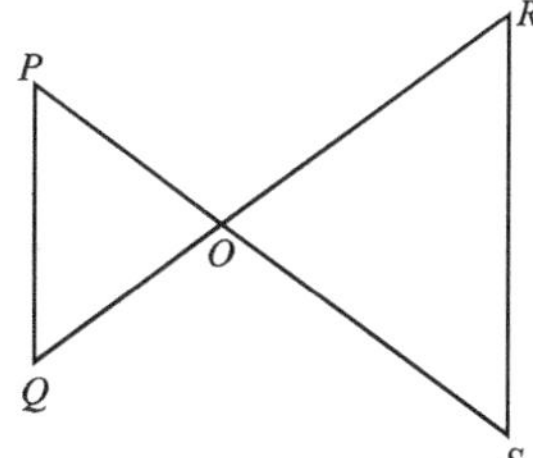

22. P and Q are point on sides AB and AC respectively of $\Delta\, ABC$. If $AP = 3$ cm. $PB = 6$ cm, $AQ = 5$ cm and $QC = 10$ cm, show that $BC = 3\, PQ$. **[Delhi 2014, Term-I, U]**

Long Answer Questions (4 or 5 Marks)

23. In the given figure, ∠ADC = ∠BCA; prove that ΔACB ~ ΔADC. Hence find BD if AC = 8 cm and AD = 3 cm.

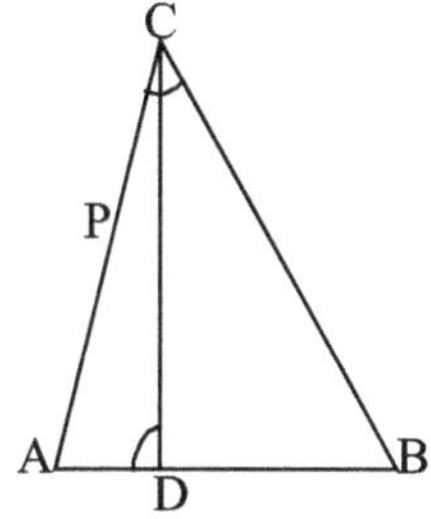

24. If a line is drawn parallel to one side of a triangle to intersect the other two sides in distinct points, then prove that the other two sides are divided in the same ratio. **[Delhi 2023, Ap]**

25. ΔABC is right angled at C. If p is the length of the perpendicular from C to AB and a, b, c are the lengths of the sides opposite $\angle A$, $\angle B$ and $\angle C$ respectively, then prove that $\frac{1}{p^2} = \frac{1}{a^2} + \frac{1}{b^2}$ **[All India 2017, Term-I, Ap]**

26. In the given figure, ΔABC and ΔDBC are on the same base BC. AD and BC intersect at O. Prove that $\frac{ar(\Delta ABC)}{ar(\Delta DBC)} = \frac{AO}{DO}$. **[All India 2017, Term-I, A]**

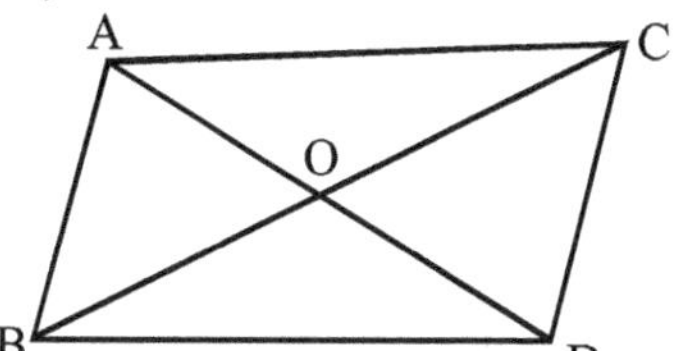

27.

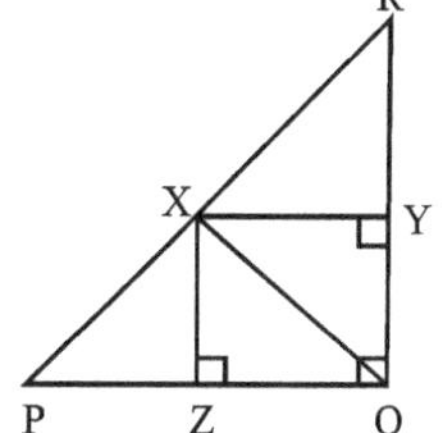

ΔPQR is right angled at Q. $QX \perp PR$, $XY \perp RQ$ and $XZ \perp PQ$ are drawn. Prove that $XZ^2 = PZ \times ZQ$.

[Delhi 2016, Term-I, U]

Hints & Solutions

Topic-1: Similar Figures

1. **(d)** 2 : 3 **(1 Mark)**
2. **(d)** Ratio of altitudes = Ratio of sides for similar triangles
   So AM : PN = AB : PQ = 2 : 3. **(1 Mark)**
3. **(b)** Ratio of perimeter's of two similar triangle
   = Ratio of their corresponding sides

$$\frac{\text{perimeter of } \Delta ABC}{\text{perimeter of } \Delta DEF} = \frac{BC}{EF}$$

$$\frac{7.5}{\text{perimeter of } \Delta DEF} = \frac{2}{4}.$$ So perimeter of ΔDEF = 15 cm

(1 Mark)

4.

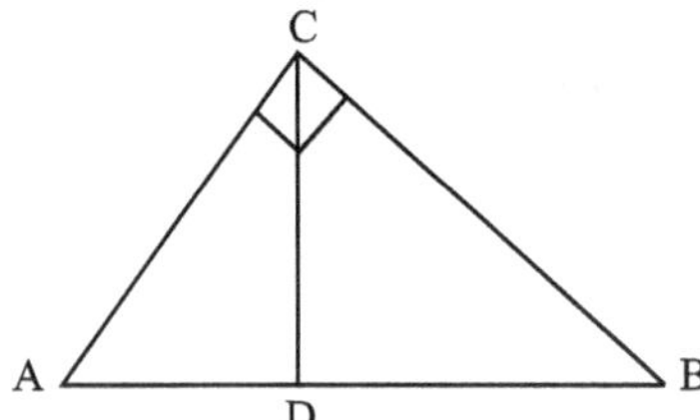

Since, a perpendicular is drawn from the vertex of the right angle of a right triangle to the hypotenuse then triangles on both sides of the perpendicular are similar to the whole triangle and to each other.

Hence, $\Delta ACD \sim \Delta ABC$ ...(i) **(1 Mark)**

and $\Delta ABC \sim \Delta CBD$ ...(ii)

from (i) and (ii)

$$\Delta ACD \sim \Delta CBD \Rightarrow \frac{CD}{BD} = \frac{AD}{CD}$$

$\Rightarrow CD^2 = AD \times BD$ **(1 Mark)**

Using eqn (1),

$AB.AD - (AD)^2 = (CD)^2$

$\Rightarrow AD\,(AB - AD) = (CD)^2$

$\Rightarrow AD \times DB = (CD)^2 \Rightarrow (CD)^2 = BD \times AD.$ **(1 Mark)**

5. Given : $\Delta ABC \sim \Delta PQR$

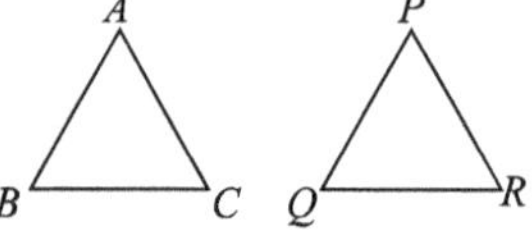

To prove :

$$\frac{\text{Perimeter of } \Delta ABC}{\text{Perimeter of } \Delta PQR} = \frac{AB}{PQ} = \frac{BC}{QR} = \frac{AC}{PR}$$

Proof : Given that $\Delta ABC \sim \Delta PQR$

then by similarity property,

$$\frac{AB}{PQ} = \frac{BC}{QR} = \frac{AC}{PR} = K \text{ (say)} \quad ...(i)$$

$\Rightarrow AB = KPQ, BC = KQR, AC = KPR$ ...(ii) **(1 Mark)**

Now, $$\frac{\text{Perimeter of } \Delta ABC}{\text{Perimeter of } \Delta PQR} = \frac{AB + BC + AC}{PQ + QR + PR}$$

$$= \frac{KPQ + KQR + KPR}{PQ + QR + PR} \quad \text{[From (ii)]}$$

$$= \frac{K(PQ + QR + PR)}{PQ + QR + PR}$$

$$= K = \frac{AB}{PQ} = \frac{BC}{QR} = \frac{AC}{PR} \quad \text{[From (i)]}$$ **(1 Mark)**

Note

If $\frac{AB}{PQ} = \frac{BC}{QR} = \frac{AC}{PR}$ *then by addendo method*

$$\frac{AB}{PQ} = \frac{BC}{QR} = \frac{AC}{PR} = \frac{AB + BC + AC}{PQ + QR + PR}$$

Topic-2: Basic Proportionality Theorem (Thales Theorem)

1. **(b)** $\frac{ac}{b+c}$ **(1 Mark)**
2. **(b)** From the figure, it is clear that BD = 4 cm
   According to basic proportionality theorem

$$\frac{AD}{BD} = \frac{AE}{EC}$$

$$\frac{3}{4} = \frac{AE}{3}$$

$$AE = \frac{9}{4} = 2.25 \text{ cm}$$ **(1 Mark)**

3. **(b)** Given, $\frac{AB}{DE} = \frac{BC}{FD}$

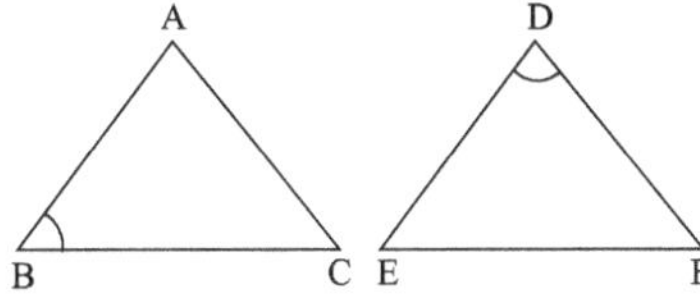

In AB and BC, $\angle B$ is common

And In DE and FD, $\angle D$ is common

For similar triangle $\angle B = \angle D$ **(1 Mark)**

4. **(b)** By basic proportionality theorem

when PQ || BC,

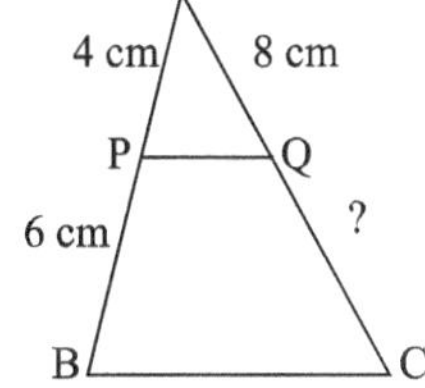

$$\frac{AP}{PB} = \frac{AQ}{QC} \Rightarrow \frac{4}{6} = \frac{8}{QC}$$

$$\Rightarrow QC = 8 \times \frac{6}{4} \Rightarrow QC = 12 \text{ cm}$$

Now, AC = AQ + QC

$\Rightarrow$ 8 + 12 = 20 cm **(1 Mark)**

5. **(b)** $\Delta ABC \sim \Delta QPR \Rightarrow \frac{AC}{QR} = \frac{BC}{PR} \Rightarrow \frac{6}{3} = \frac{5}{x}$

$$\Rightarrow x = 5 \times \frac{3}{6} = 2.5 \text{ cm}$$ **(1 Mark)**

6. **(c)** $\frac{ay}{a \quad b}$ **(1 Mark)**

7. **(c)** **(1 Mark)**

8. **(b)** Since DE || BC, $\Delta ABC \sim \Delta ADE$

(By AA rule of similarity)

Let $\frac{AD}{AD + BD} = \frac{DE}{BC}$

So $\frac{AD}{AB} = \frac{DE}{BC}$ i.e., $\frac{3}{7} = \frac{DE}{14}$. So DE = 6 cm **(1 Mark)**

9. $\because$ DE || BC

By Thales theorem,

$$\frac{AD}{BD} = \frac{AE}{EC}$$ **(½ Mark)**

$$\frac{AD}{7.2} = \frac{1.8}{5.4}$$

$$AD = \frac{1.8 \times 7.2}{5.4} = 2.4 \text{ cm}$$ **(½ Mark)**

10. As $DE \parallel BC$

$\therefore$ $\frac{AD}{DB} = \frac{AE}{EC}$ (By B.P.T.)

$\Rightarrow$ $\frac{x}{x+1} = \frac{x+3}{x+5}$

$\Rightarrow$ $x^2 + 5x = x^2 + 4x + 3$

$\Rightarrow$ $x = 3$ **(1 Mark)**

11.

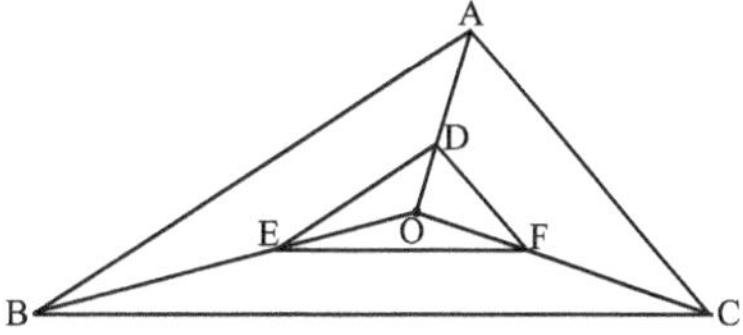

In ΔOAB, $DE \parallel AB$

$\Rightarrow$ $\frac{OD}{AD} = \frac{OE}{EB}$ [Basic proportionality theorem] ... (1)

Again in ΔOBC, $EF \parallel BC$

$\Rightarrow$ $\frac{OE}{EB} = \frac{OF}{FC}$ [Basic proportionality theorem] .... (2)

From (1) and (2), we get, $\frac{OD}{AD} = \frac{OF}{FC}$

As in ΔOAC, $\frac{OD}{AD} = \frac{OF}{FC} \Rightarrow DF \parallel AC$

[$\because$ In a triangle if a line divides the two sides in the same proportion then it is parallel to the third side.] **(1 Mark)**

12. According to BPT

$$\frac{x}{x-2} = \frac{x+2}{x-1}$$

$$x^2 - x = x^2 - 4$$

$$x = 4$$ **(2 Marks)**

13. Consider ΔAOB and ΔCOD

$\angle AOB = \angle COD$ [vertically opposite angle]

$\angle ABO = \angle CDO$ [Since AB||DC with BD as traversal, alternate angle are equal]

Similarly

$\angle BAO = \angle DCO$ [Alternate angle]

$\therefore \Delta AOB \sim \Delta COD$ **(1 Mark)**

As we know that if 2 triangles are similar, then corresponding sides are proportional.

Hence

$\frac{AO}{CO} = \frac{OB}{OD}$ **(1 Mark)**

14. In ΔEFC and ΔBDC

$\angle EFC = \angle BDC = 90°$ $\angle ECF = \angle BCD$

by similarity $\Delta EFC \sim \Delta BDC$

$\Rightarrow \frac{EF}{BD} = \frac{CF}{DC}$ **(1 Mark)**

In ΔEGF and ΔDGF

$\angle EGF = \angle DGA$, $\angle EFG = \angle GDA$

by similarity $\Delta EGF \sim \Delta DGA \Rightarrow \frac{EF}{AD} = \frac{FG}{DG}$

And AD = BD so, $\frac{FC}{DC} = \frac{FG}{DG}$ **(1 Mark)**

15. Construction: Draw $AM \perp BC$ and $DN \perp BC$.

Proof: In ΔAMO and ΔDNO

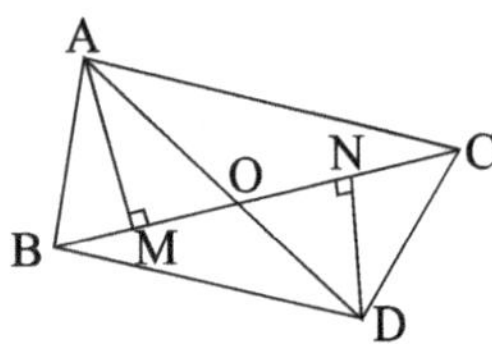

$\angle AMO = \angle DNO = 90°$ (By construction)

$\angle AOM = \angle DON$ (V.O.A)

$\therefore$ By AA-similarity

$\Delta AMO \sim \Delta DNO$ **(1 Mark)**

$\therefore \frac{OA}{OD} = \frac{AM}{DN}$ ...(i)

$$\frac{ar(\Delta ABC)}{ar(\Delta DBC)} = \frac{\frac{1}{2} \times BC \times AM}{\frac{1}{2} \times BC \times DN} = \frac{AM}{DN}$$

$\frac{ar(\Delta ABC)}{ar(\Delta DBC)} = \frac{OA}{OD}$ [From (i)]

Hence, proved. **(1 Mark)**

16. Given: In ΔABC, $AD \perp BC$

To prove: $AB^2 + CD^2 = BD^2 + AC^2$

Proof: In right ΔABD

$AB^2 = AD^2 + BD^2$

$\Rightarrow AD^2 = AB^2 - BD^2$ ...(i)

In right ΔADC

$AC^2 = AD^2 + CD^2$

$\Rightarrow AD^2 = AC^2 - CD^2$ ...(ii)

From (i) and (ii)

$AB^2 - BD^2 = AC^2 - CD^2$

$AB^2 + CD^2 = AC^2 + BD^2$ **(2 Marks)**

Hence, proved.

17. $\because \Delta ABC \sim \Delta DEF$

$\therefore \frac{AB}{DE} = \frac{BC}{EF} = \frac{AC}{DF}$

$\Rightarrow \frac{2x-1}{18} = \frac{2x+2}{3x+9} = \frac{3x}{6x}$ **(1 Mark)**

$\Rightarrow \frac{2x-1}{18} = \frac{3x}{6x}$	$\frac{2x+2}{3x+9} = \frac{3x}{6x}$
$\Rightarrow \frac{2x-1}{18} = \frac{1}{2}$	$\frac{2x+2}{3x+9} = \frac{1}{2}$
$\Rightarrow 2x - 1 = \frac{1}{2} \times 18$	$4x + 4 = 3x + 9$
$\Rightarrow 2x = 9 + 1$	$4x - 3x = 9 - 4$
$\Rightarrow 2x = 10$	$x = 5$
$\Rightarrow x = 5$	

(1 Mark)

In ΔABC

$AB = 2x - 1 = 10 - 1 = 9$ cm

$BC = 2x + 2 = 10 + 2 = 12$ cm

$AC = 3x = 15$ cm

In ΔDEF

DE = 18 cm, $EF = 3x + 9 = 15 + 9 = 24$ cm

$DF = 6x = 30$ cm **(1 Mark)**

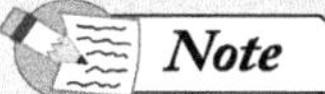

When two triangle are similar then their corres-ponding angles are equal and corresponding sides are proportional.

18.

Topper's Answer

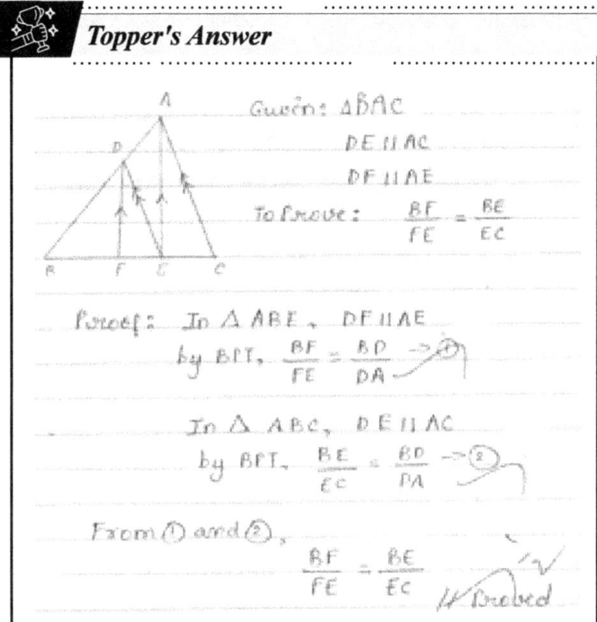
Given: ΔBAC
$DE \parallel AC$
$DF \parallel AE$
To Prove: $\frac{BF}{FE} = \frac{BE}{EC}$

Proof: In ΔABE, $DF \parallel AE$
by BPT, $\frac{BF}{FE} = \frac{BD}{DA}$ → (1)

In ΔABC, $DE \parallel AC$
by BPT, $\frac{BE}{EC} = \frac{BD}{DA}$ → (2)

From (1) and (2),
$\frac{BF}{FE} = \frac{BE}{EC}$
Proved

19. In ΔABC, $DE \,||\, AC$

$\therefore \quad \frac{BD}{AD} = \frac{BE}{EC}$ (By BPT) ....(i) **(1 Mark)**

In ΔABP, $CD \,||\, AP$

$\therefore \quad \frac{BD}{AD} = \frac{BC}{CP}$ (By BPT) ....(ii) **(1 Mark)**

from (i) and (ii)

$\frac{BE}{EC} = \frac{BC}{CP}$ **(1 Mark)**

Hence proved.

20. $\angle TPQ = \angle TQP$ [$\because$ TP = TQ] ....(i)

$\angle TPQ + \angle TQP + \angle PTQ = 180°$ [Angle sum property]

$2\angle TPQ + \angle PTQ = 180°$ ....(ii) [from (i)] **(1 Mark)**

$\angle OPQ + \angle TPQ = 90°$ [Radius $\perp$ to tangent]

$\angle TPQ = 90° - \angle OPQ$ **(1 Mark)**

Putting in (ii)

$2(90° - \angle OPQ) + \angle PTQ = 180°$

$180° - 2\angle OPQ + \angle PTQ = 180° \Rightarrow \angle PTQ = 2\angle OPQ$

(1 Mark)

Hence proved.

21. Given : $\angle D = \angle E$

$\frac{AD}{DB} = \frac{AE}{EC}$

To prove : ΔBAC is an isosceles triangle.

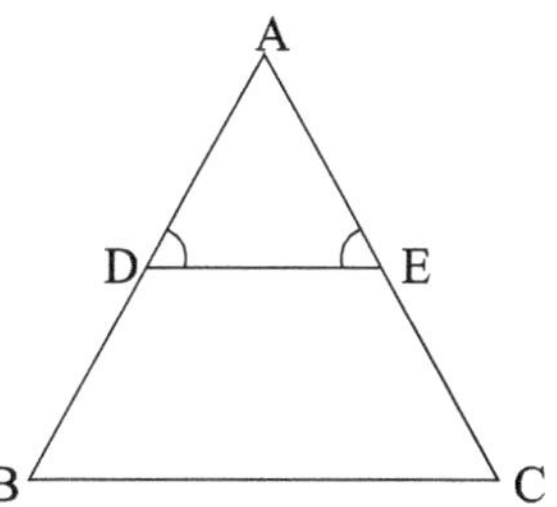

Proof: $\frac{AD}{DB} = \frac{AE}{EC}$ (Given)

$\therefore$ DE | | BC [By converse of B.P.T]

$\Rightarrow$ $\angle D = \angle B$ ....(i) [Corresponding angles]

$\angle E = \angle C$ ....(ii) [Corresponding angles]

(1 Mark)

But $\angle D = \angle E$ (Given)

From (i) and (ii)

$\therefore$ $\angle B = \angle C \Rightarrow AB = AC$ **(1 Mark)**

Hence, ΔBAC is an isosceles triangle.

Note

Side opposite to equal angles of triangle are equal.

22.

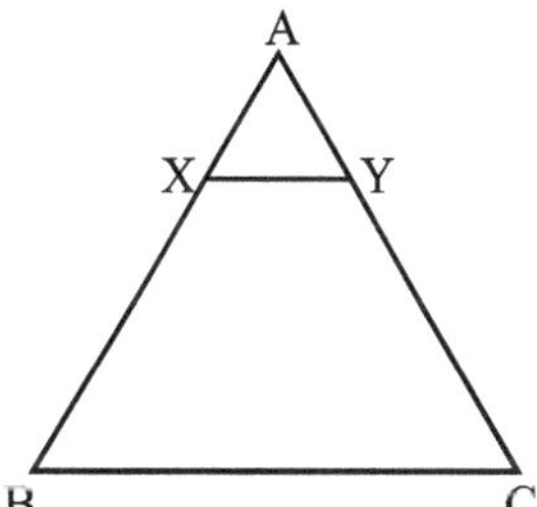

$\frac{AX}{XB} = \frac{3}{4}$, $AY = 5$, $YC = 9$ (Given)

$\frac{AX}{XB} = \frac{3}{4}$ and $\frac{AY}{YC} = \frac{5}{9}$ **(1 Mark)**

$\frac{AX}{XB} \neq \frac{AY}{YC}$ (By B.P.T.)

Hence XY is not parallel to BC. **(1 Mark)**

Note

A line divide two sides of triangle in same ratio then line will be parallel to third side.

23. $\Delta ABC \sim \Delta PQR$ (Given)

$$\frac{AB}{PQ}=\frac{BC}{QR}=\frac{AC}{PR}$$ (By similarity of triangles)

$$\Rightarrow \frac{z}{3}=\frac{8}{6}=\frac{4\sqrt{3}}{y}$$ **(1 Mark)**

$$\Rightarrow \frac{z}{3}=\frac{8}{6} \text{ and } \frac{8}{6}=\frac{4\sqrt{3}}{y}$$

$$\Rightarrow z=\frac{8\times 3}{6} \text{ and } y=\frac{4\sqrt{3}\times 6}{8}$$

$\therefore$ $z=4$ and $y=3\sqrt{3}$

$\therefore$ $y+z=4+3\sqrt{3}$ **(1 Mark)**

When two triangles are similar then their corresponding sides are proportional.

24.

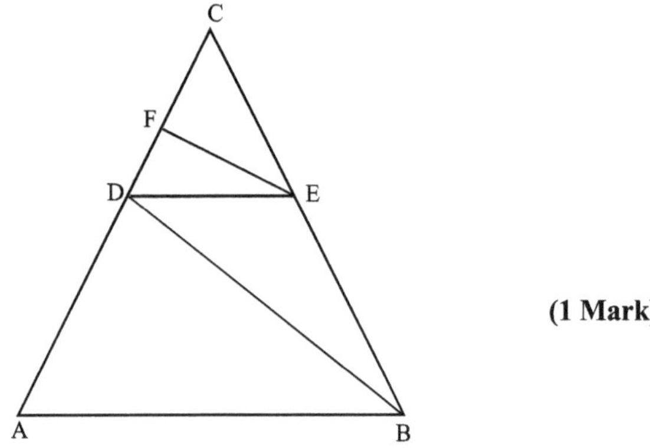

(1 Mark)

In ΔABC, $DE \parallel AB$

$$\Rightarrow \frac{CD}{AC}=\frac{CE}{BC} \quad \text{....... (1)}$$

[Cor. of Basic proportional theorem]

Again in ΔCDB, $EF \parallel BD$

$$\Rightarrow \frac{CF}{CD}=\frac{CE}{CB} \quad \text{....... (2)}$$ **(1 Mark)**

[Cor. of Basic proportoinal theorem]

From (1) and (2), we get

$$\frac{CD}{AC}=\frac{CF}{CD} \Rightarrow CD^2=CF\times AC$$ **(1 Mark)**

25. **(a) Statement:** If a line is drawn parallel to one side of a triangle to intersect the other two sides in distinct points, the other two sides are divided in the same ratio.

Proof: Suppose the given triangle is ABC in which a line parallel to side BC intersects other two sides AB & AC at D & E respectively.

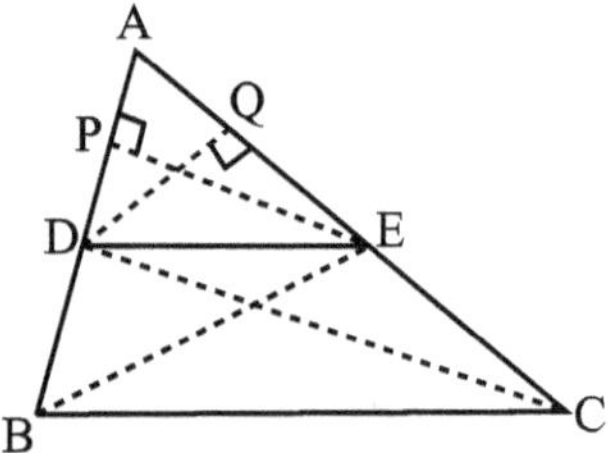

Claim: $\frac{AD}{DB}=\frac{AE}{EC}$

Construction: Join BE and CD and then draw $DQ \perp AC$ and $EN \perp AB$.

Now, area of $\Delta ADE = \frac{1}{2}\times \text{Base}\times \text{Height}$

$\Rightarrow ar(ADE)=\frac{1}{2}\times AD\times EP$

Similarly, $ar(BDE)=\frac{1}{2}\times DB\times EP$ **(1 Mark)**

$ar(ADE)=\frac{1}{2}\times AE\times DQ$

And $ar(DEC)=\frac{1}{2}\times EC\times DQ$

$$\text{Now, } \frac{ar(ADE)}{ar(BDE)}=\frac{\frac{1}{2}\times AD\times EP}{\frac{1}{2}\times DB\times EP}=\frac{AD}{DB} \quad \text{... (1)}$$

$$\frac{ar(ADE)}{ar(DEC)}=\frac{\frac{1}{2}\times AE\times DQ}{\frac{1}{2}\times EC\times DQ}=\frac{AE}{EC} \quad \text{... (2)}$$ **(1 Mark)**

Since, ΔBDE and ΔDEC are on the same base DE and between the same parallels BC & DE.

So, $ar(BDE)=ar(DEC)$ ... (3)

$$\text{Eq}^n\ (1)/(2) \Rightarrow \frac{ar(DEC)}{ar(BDE)}=\frac{\frac{AD}{DB}}{\frac{AE}{EC}}$$

$$\Rightarrow \frac{ar(DEC)}{ar(DEC)}=\frac{\frac{AB}{DB}}{\frac{AE}{EC}} \Rightarrow 1=\frac{\frac{AD}{DB}}{\frac{AE}{EC}}$$

$$\Rightarrow \boxed{\frac{AD}{DB}=\frac{AE}{EC}}$$ **(1 Mark)**

(b) Draw $DG \parallel BE$

In ΔABE, $\frac{AB}{BD}=\frac{AE}{GE}$ [BPT] **(½ Mark)**

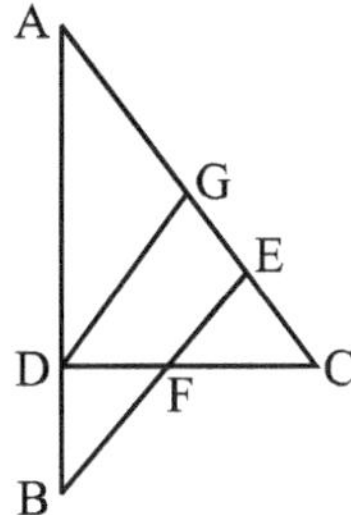

$CF = FD$ [F is the midpoint of DC] ...(i)(**½ Mark**)

In Δ CDG, $\frac{DF}{CF} = \frac{GE}{CE} = 1$ [Mid point theorem]

(½ Mark)

$GE = CE$ ...(ii)

$\angle CEF = \angle CFE$ [Given]

$CF = CE$ [Sides opposite to equal angles] ...(iii)

From (ii) & (iii) $CF = GE$ ...(iv)

From (i) & (iv) $GE = FD$

$\therefore \frac{AB}{BD} = \frac{AE}{GE} \Rightarrow \frac{AB}{BD} = \frac{AE}{FD}$ **(½ Mark)**

26. For the Theorem :

Given, To prove, Construction and figure

Proof

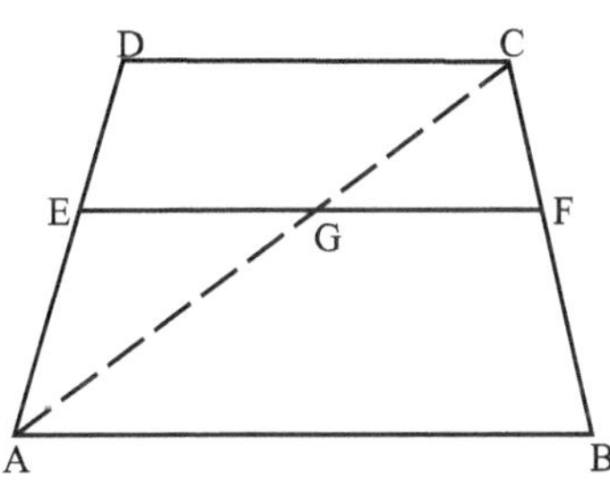

(1 Mark)

Let ABCD be a trapezium DC || AB and EF is a line parallel to AB and hence to DC.

To prove: $\frac{DE}{EA} = \frac{CF}{FB}$

Construction : Join AC, meeting EF in G.

Proof :

In ΔABC, we have

GF || AB

CG/GA = CF/FB [By BPT] ......(1) **(1 Mark)**

In ΔADC, we have

EG || DC (EF || AB & AB || DC)

DE/EA = CG/GA [By BPT] .....(2) **(1 Mark)**

From (1) & (2), we get,

$\frac{DE}{EA} = \frac{CF}{FB}$ **(1 Mark)**

27. Given: Let ABC be a triangle in which DE || BC and DE intersect AB and AC at D and E respectively.

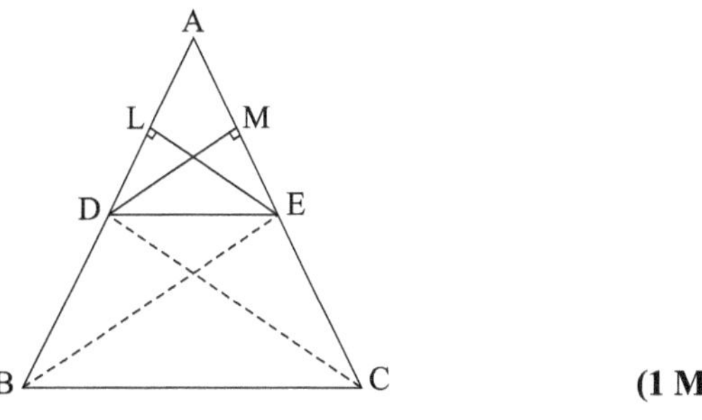

(1 Mark)

To prove: $\frac{AD}{DB} = \frac{AE}{EC}$

Construction: Join BE and CD

Draw $EL \perp AB$ and $DM \perp AC$

Proof: We have

$$\text{area } (\Delta\, ADE) = \frac{1}{2} \times AD \times EL$$

$$\text{and area } (\Delta DBE) = \frac{1}{2} \times DB \times EL \quad (\because \Delta = \frac{1}{2} \times b \times h)$$

$$\therefore \frac{\text{area}(\Delta ADE)}{\text{area}(\Delta DBE)} = \frac{\frac{1}{2} \times AD \times EL}{\frac{1}{2} \times DB \times EL}$$

$$= \frac{AD}{DB}$$ ...(1) **(1 Mark)**

Again, area (ΔADE) = area (ΔAED)

$$= \frac{1}{2} \times AE \times DM$$

$$\text{and area } (\Delta ECD) = \frac{1}{2} \times EC \times DM$$

$$\therefore \frac{\text{area}(\Delta\, ADE)}{\text{area}(\Delta ECD)} = \frac{\frac{1}{2} \times AE \times DM}{\frac{1}{2} \times EC \times DM} = \frac{AE}{EC} \quad ...(2)$$

(1 Mark)

Since, the area of triangles with same base and between same parallel lines are equal

$\therefore$ area (ΔDBE) = area (ΔECD) ...(3)

From equations (1), (2) and (3), we have

$$\frac{AD}{DB} = \frac{AE}{EC}$$ **(1 Mark)**

Hence proved.

28. 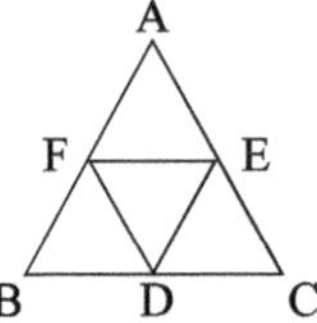

(½ Mark)

Given: In ΔABC, D, E and F are mid points of sides BC, AC and AB respectively.

To prove: ΔAEF, ΔDCE, ΔBFD and ΔFED are similar to ΔABC. **(½ Mark)**

Proof: In ΔABC, E and F are mid-point of AC and AB respectively.

∴ By mid-point theorem.

EF||BC and EF $\frac{1}{2}$ BC ...(i)

⇒ ∠AFE = ∠ABC (alternative angle)

∠A = ∠A (common)

∴ ΔAFE ~ ΔABC ...(ii) **(1 Mark)**

Similarly,

ΔFBD ~ ∠ABC ...(iii)

and ΔECD ~ ΔABC ...(iv)

Now, since EF||BC and EF = BD = CD [from (i)]

∴ BDEF and DCEF are parallelogram **(1 Mark)**

∴ ∠DBE = ∠DEF and ∠DCE = ∠EFD

∴ ∠DBF = ∠DEF and ∠DCE = ∠EFD

ΔDEF ~ ΔABC ... (v)

From (ii), (iii), (iv) and (v)

ΔDCE, ΔBFD, ΔAEF and ΔFED are similar to ΔABC.

(1 Mark)

A line joining mid-points of two sides of a triangle parallel and half the third side.

1. **(b)** Let the perimeter of ΔABC = x cm

Since the triangles are similar

$$\therefore \frac{\text{Perimeter of}\,\Delta ABC}{\text{Perimeter of}\,\Delta PQR} = \frac{AB}{PQ}$$

$$\frac{36}{x} = \frac{8}{6}$$

$$x = \frac{36 \times 6}{8} = 27\,\text{cm}$$ **(1 Mark)**

2. **(c)** 8cm **(1 Mark)**

3. **(b)** 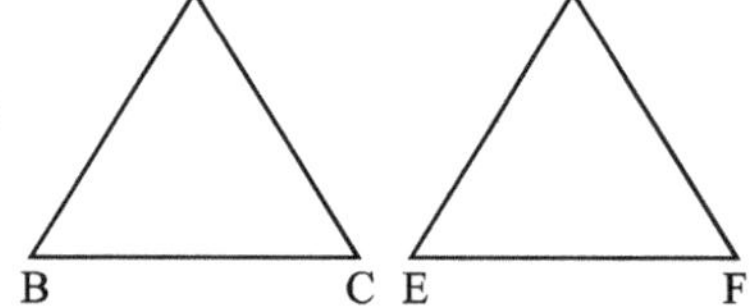

Given, ∠F = ∠C

∠B = ∠E

Then ΔABC ~ ΔDEF (by AA criterion)

Then, $\frac{AB}{DE} = \frac{BC}{EF} = \frac{AC}{DF} = \frac{1}{2}$

For congruent sides should be equal.

Therefore, triangles are similar but not congruent.

(1 Mark)

4. **(d)** 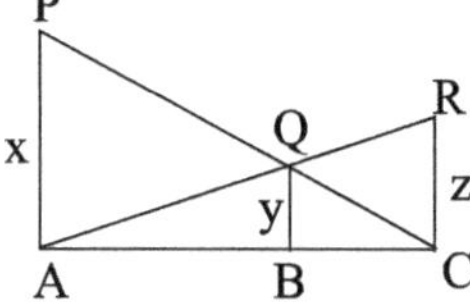

Here, AP ⊥ AC, QB ⊥ AC, RC ⊥ AC

Then AP || BQ, BQ || RC, AP || RC.

Given, x = 8 cm, z = 6 cm.

In ΔAQP & ΔRQC.

∠PQA = ∠RQC [vertically opp. angle]

∠QPA = ∠QCR [alternate interior angle]

ΔAQP ~ ΔRQC [by AA criterion]

So, $\frac{AP}{CR} = \frac{AQ}{RQ} \Rightarrow \frac{x}{z} = \frac{AQ}{RQ}$

$\frac{8}{6} = \frac{AQ}{RQ}$ ..... (i)

In ΔABQ & ΔACR.

$\angle A = \angle A$ [common]

$\angle AQB = \angle ARC$ [corresponding angle]

$\Delta ABQ \sim \Delta ACR$ [by AA criterion]

$$\frac{BQ}{CR} = \frac{AQ}{AR} \quad \text{..... (ii)}$$

from (i)

$$\frac{8}{6} = \frac{AQ}{RQ} \Rightarrow \frac{RQ}{AQ} = \frac{6}{8}$$

Add both side 1

$$\frac{8+6}{8} = \frac{AQ+RQ}{AQ}$$

$$\frac{14}{8} = \frac{AR}{AQ} \Rightarrow \frac{AQ}{AR} = \frac{8}{14}$$

Substitute the value in eq. (ii)

$$\frac{y}{z} = \frac{8}{14} \Rightarrow \frac{y}{6} = \frac{8}{14} \Rightarrow y = \frac{24}{7} \text{ cm.}$$ **(1 Mark)**

5. **(c)** $\Delta ACD \sim \Delta ABC$ (AA)

$\therefore \frac{AC}{AB} = \frac{AD}{AC}$ By corresponding parts of similar triangles

$$\frac{8}{AB} = \frac{3}{8}$$

This gives AB = 64/3 cm.

So BD = AB – AD = 64/3 – 3 = 55/3 cm. **(1 Mark)**

6. **(b)**

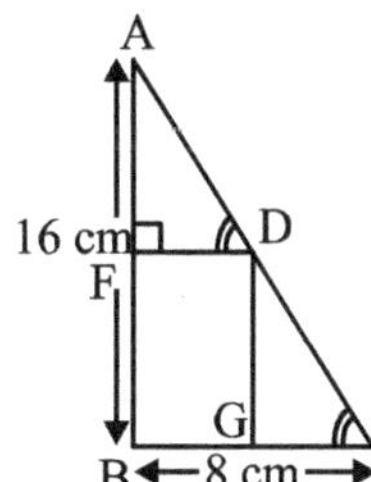

ΔABE is right triangle & FDGB is a square of side x cm

$\Delta AFD \sim \Delta DGE$ (AA)

$$\therefore \frac{AF}{DG} = \frac{FD}{GE} \text{ (CPST)}$$

$$\frac{16-x}{x} = \frac{x}{8-x}$$

$$(16 - x)(8 - x) = x^2$$

$$128 = 24x \text{ or } x = \frac{16}{3} \text{cm}$$ **(1 Mark)**

Sol. (7-11)

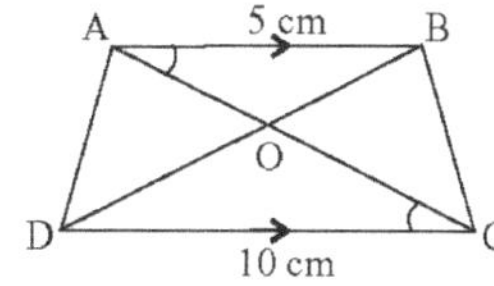

Common solution:

In ΔAOB and ΔCOD

$\angle AOB = \angle COD$ (Vertically opposite angle)

$\angle OAB = \angle OCD$ (Alternate interior angle)

$\Delta AOB \sim \Delta COD$ (by AA criterion)

So, $\frac{AB}{CD} = \frac{AO}{CO} = \frac{OB}{OD}, \frac{AB}{CD} = \frac{5}{10} = \frac{1}{2}$.

7. **(a)** Given ΔAOB and ΔCOD are similar by AA criterion. **(1 Mark)**

8. **(b)** As ΔAOB and ΔCOD are similar, then the ratio their corresponding sides will also equal.

So, $\frac{AO}{CO} = \frac{OB}{OD} = \frac{AB}{CD} = \frac{5}{10} = \frac{1}{2}$

By ratio of area of similar triangle theorem,

$$\frac{ar(\Delta AOB)}{ar(\Delta COD)} = \left(\frac{AB}{CD}\right)^2 = \left(\frac{1}{2}\right)^2 = \frac{1}{4}$$

$ar(\Delta AOB) : ar(\Delta COD) = 1 : 4$ **(1 Mark)**

9. **(d)** Given $\frac{OA+OB+AB}{OC+OD+CD} = \frac{1}{4}$, then the ratio of their corresponding sides also be 1 : 4.

So,

$\frac{AB}{CD} = \frac{1}{4}$ {If we add numerator and denominator. individually of the ratio of sides then, it will give the same ratio of the perimeter.}

CD = 4AB **(1 Mark)**

Ratio of corresponding sides of two similar triangles will also equal to the ratio of their perimeters.

10. **(b)** In ΔAOD and ΔBOC,

$$\frac{AO}{BC} = \frac{AD}{BO} = \frac{OD}{OC} \text{ (Given)}$$

So, the representation of triangles would be:

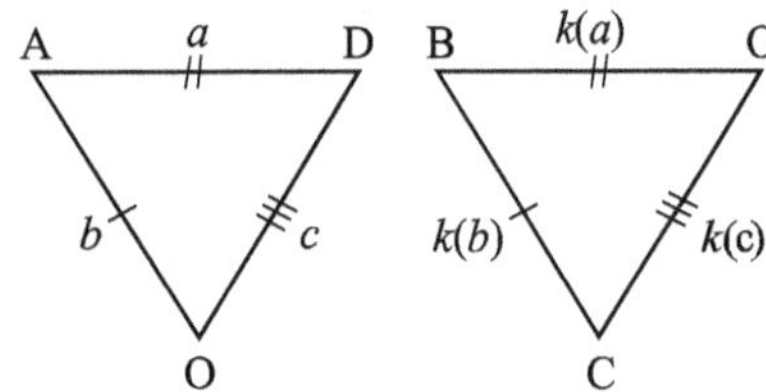

Therefore, $\Delta AOD \sim \Delta BCO$

(by SSS proportional criterion). **(1 Mark)**

11. **(b)** Given, ratio of areas of two similar triangles is 1 : 4.

$$\frac{ar(\Delta AOB)}{ar(\Delta COD)} = \left(\frac{AB}{CD}\right)^2$$

$$\frac{1}{4} = \left(\frac{AB}{CD}\right)^2$$

$$\frac{AB}{CD} = \frac{1}{2} = \frac{\text{alt. of } \Delta AOB}{\text{alt. of } \Delta COD}$$ **(1 Mark)**

The ratio of sides of two similar triangles will also equal to the ratio of their corresponding altitudes.

12. Two triangles are similar if their corresponding sides are in same ratio. **(1 Mark)**

13.

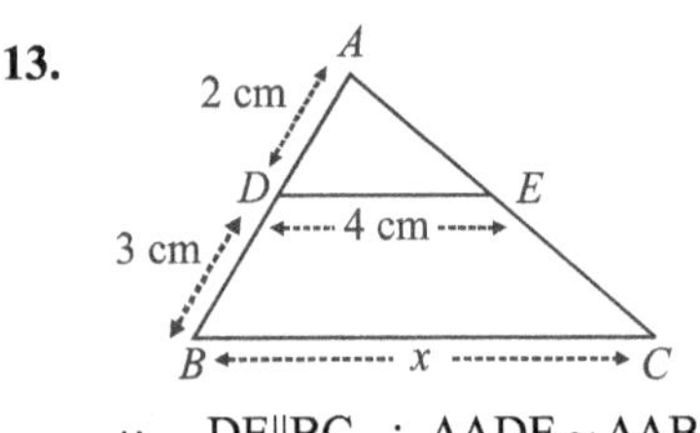

$\because$ DE||BC, $\therefore \Delta ADE \sim \Delta ABC$

$$\Rightarrow \frac{AD}{AB} = \frac{DE}{BC}$$

$$\Rightarrow \frac{2}{5} = \frac{4}{x} \Rightarrow x = 10 \text{ cm}$$ **(1 Mark)**

If a line DE is drawn parallel to one side of a ΔABC divide triangle in two part then smaller ΔADE similar to ΔABC and ratio of their corresponding sides are equal.

14. Given that ABCD is a parallelogram. **(½ Mark)**

Let AB = DC = a

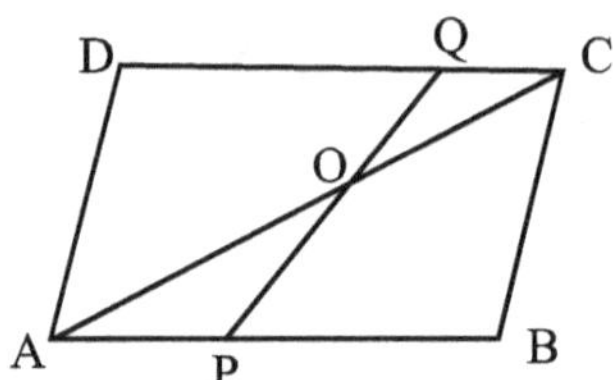

Point P divides AB in the ratio 2:3. Then we have

$$\Rightarrow AP = \frac{2}{5}a,\ BP = \frac{3}{5}a$$

Point Q divides DC in the ratio 4 : 1. Then we have

$$\Rightarrow DQ = \frac{4}{5}a, CQ = \frac{1}{5}a$$

$\Delta APO \sim \Delta CQO$ [AA similarity] **(½ Mark)**

$$\frac{AP}{CQ} = \frac{PO}{QO} = \frac{OA}{OC}$$

$$\text{Now } \frac{OA}{OC} = \frac{AP}{CQ} = \frac{OA}{OC} = \frac{\frac{2}{5}a}{\frac{1}{5}a} = \frac{2}{1} \Rightarrow OC = \frac{1}{2}OA$$

$\Rightarrow$ OC is half of OA **(½ Mark)**

15. Consider ΔABD and ΔECF

$\angle ADB = \angle EFC = 90°$ **(1 Mark)**

[$\because$ AD is perpendicular to CB and EF is perpedendicular to AC]

$\angle ABD = \angle ECF$ **(1 Mark)**

[$\because$ Angle opposite to equal sides are equal]

Thus, $\Delta ABD \sim \Delta ECF$ by AA criteria **(1 Mark)**

16. In ΔABC, $\angle 1 = \angle 2$

$\therefore$ AB = BD ......(i) **(½ Mark)**

Given,

AD / AE = AC / BD **(½ Mark)**

Using equation (i), we get

AD / AE = AC / AB .....(ii)

In ΔBAE and ΔCAD, by equation (ii),

AC / AB = AD / AE **(½ Mark)**

$\angle A = \angle A$ (common)

$\therefore \Delta BAE \sim \Delta CAD$ [By SAS similarity criterion]

(½ Mark)

17. Writes True(T) **(½ Mark)**

Writes that in ΔOSR and ΔOPQ:

$\angle ROS = \angle POQ = x°$ (vertically opposite angles)

$\angle ORS = \angle OSR = \angle OPQ = \angle OQP = \dfrac{180 - a°}{2}$ (angle sum property of isoceles triangles) **[1 Mark]**

Uses the above step to justify that ΔOSR – ΔOPQ by using the AAA similarity criterion **[½ Mark]**

18. Given: ΔABC, ΔDBC are right-angle triangles, right-angled at A and D, on the same side of BC. AC & BD intersect at P.

To prove: AP × PC = BP × DP.

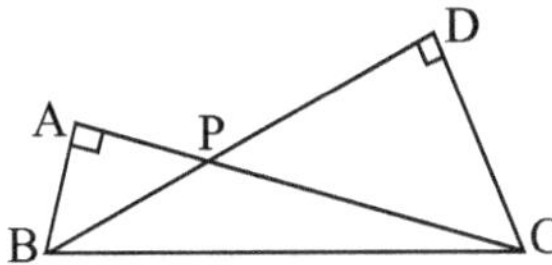

(1 Mark)

In ΔAPB and ΔPDC,

$\angle A = \angle D = 90°$

$\angle APB = \angle DPC$ (Vertically opposite)

ΔAPB ~ ΔDPC (By AA Similarity)

$\dfrac{AP}{DP} = \dfrac{BP}{PC}$ (by C.P.S.T.)

$\Rightarrow AP \times PC = BP \times PD.$ **(1 Mark)**

Hence proved.

19. ***Topper's Answer***

Given,

ΔABC ~ ΔPQR.

AD and PM are medians of ΔABC and ΔPQR respectively

Since, ΔABC ~ ΔPQR

$\dfrac{AB}{PQ} = \dfrac{BC}{QR} = \dfrac{AC}{PR}$. —①

D is the midpoint of BC (AD is median)

M is the midpoint of QR (PM is median)

∴ $BC = 2BD$
$QR = 2QM$ } ②

∴ $\dfrac{AB}{PQ} = \dfrac{BC}{QR}$ [from ①]

$\Rightarrow \dfrac{AB}{PQ} = \dfrac{2BD}{2QM}$ [from ②]

$\Rightarrow \dfrac{AB}{PQ} = \dfrac{BD}{QM}$ ⇒ ∴ ΔABD ~ ΔPQM

That is, $\dfrac{AB}{PQ} = \dfrac{BD}{QM} = \dfrac{AD}{PM}$ — ⓐ

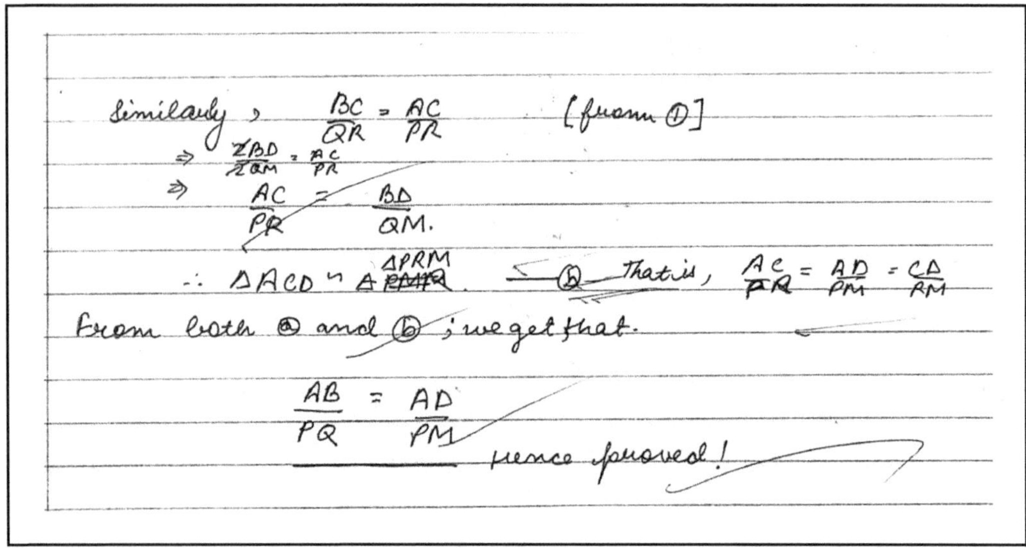

Similarly, $\frac{BC}{QR} = \frac{AC}{PR}$ [from ①]

$\Rightarrow \frac{2BD}{2QM} = \frac{AC}{PR}$

$\Rightarrow \frac{AC}{PR} = \frac{BD}{QM}$.

$\therefore \Delta ACD \sim \Delta PRM$ — ⓑ That is, $\frac{AC}{PR} = \frac{AD}{PM} = \frac{CD}{RM}$

From both ⓐ and ⓑ ; we get that.

$\frac{AB}{PQ} = \frac{AD}{PM}$

Hence proved!

20. Given that ABCD is rectangle and E is mid point of BC

i.e BE $= \frac{1}{2}$ BC $= \frac{1}{2}$ AD,

To prove: DF = 2FB and AF = 2FE.

Proof:

In ΔADF and ΔBEF

∠ADF = ∠EBF (Alternates angle) **(½ Mark)**

∠AFD = ∠BFE (V.O.A)

By AA – Similarity **(1 Mark)**

ΔADF ~ ΔEBF

By C.P.S.T.

$$\frac{DF}{BF} = \frac{AF}{EF} = \frac{AD}{BE}$$

$$\Rightarrow \frac{DF}{BF} = \frac{AF}{EF} = \frac{AD}{\frac{1}{2}AD} = 2$$

⇒ DF = 2BF **(1½ Marks)**

and AF = 2 EF. Hence proved.

21.

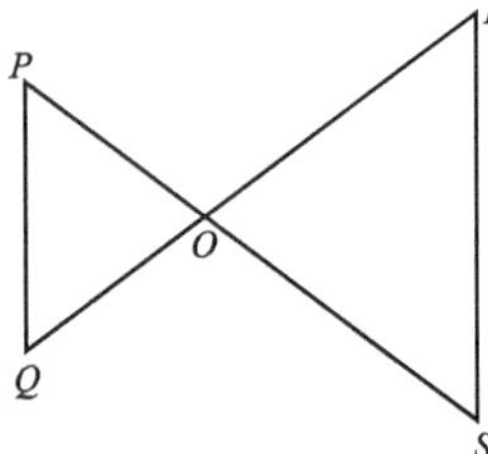

$PQ \parallel RS$ (Given)

So, $\angle P = \angle S$ (Alternate angles)

and $\angle Q = \angle R$ **(1 Mark)**

Also, $\angle POQ = \angle SOR$ (Vertically opposite angles)

Therefore, $\Delta\, POQ \sim \Delta\, SOR$ (*AAA* similarity criterion) **(2 Marks)**

22. We have, $AB = AP + PB = (3 + 6)$ cm = 9 cm

and, $AC = AQ + QC = (5 + 10)$ cm = 15 cm **(1 Mark)**

$$\therefore \quad \frac{AP}{AB} = \frac{3}{9} = \frac{1}{3} \text{ and } \frac{AQ}{AC} = \frac{5}{15} = \frac{1}{3}$$

$$\Rightarrow \quad \frac{AP}{AB} = \frac{AQ}{AC}$$

Thus, in triangles *APQ* and *ABC*, we have

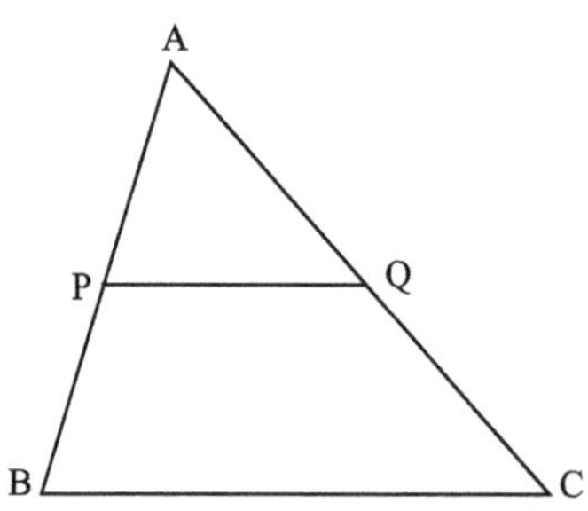

$\frac{AP}{AB} = \frac{AQ}{AC}$ and $\angle A = \angle A$ [Common]

$\Rightarrow \Delta\, APQ \sim \Delta\, ABC$ [SAS-criterion of similarity]

$\Rightarrow \frac{AP}{AB} = \frac{PQ}{BC} = \frac{AQ}{AC}$ **(1 Mark)**

$\Rightarrow \frac{PQ}{BC} = \frac{AQ}{AC}$

$\Rightarrow \frac{PQ}{BC} = \frac{5}{15} \Rightarrow \frac{PQ}{BC} = \frac{1}{3}$

$\Rightarrow BC = 3PQ$. **Proved.** **(1 Mark)**

23. Proof: In ΔACB & ΔADC

∠BCA = ∠ADC (Given) ∠A = ∠A

So, ΔACB~ΔADC (By A Acritenrian)

$\Delta ACB \sim \Delta ADC \Rightarrow \dfrac{AC}{AD} = \dfrac{AB}{AC} \Rightarrow \dfrac{8}{3} = \dfrac{AB}{8}$ **(2 Marks)**

$AB = \dfrac{64}{3} = 21.33$

$BD = AD - AB = 21.33 - 3 = 18.33$ cm **(2 Marks)**

24. Given: ΔABC where DE || BC

To Prove $\Rightarrow \dfrac{AD}{DB} = \dfrac{AE}{EC}$

Construction: Join BE & Co. Draw DM ⊥ AC & EN ⊥ AB

$ar.\Delta ADE = \dfrac{1}{2} \times \text{Base} \times \text{height} = \dfrac{1}{2} \times AD \times EN$

$ar.\Delta BDE = \dfrac{1}{2} \times DB \times EN$ **(1½ Marks)**

$$\frac{ar.\Delta ADE}{ar.\Delta BDE} = \frac{\frac{1}{2} \times AD \times EN}{\frac{1}{2} \times DB \times EN} = \frac{AD}{DB} \quad ...(i)$$

$ar.\Delta ABE = \dfrac{1}{2} \times AE \times DM \Rightarrow ar.\Delta DEC = \dfrac{1}{2} \times EC \times DM$

$$\frac{ar.\Delta ADE}{ar.\Delta DEC} = \frac{\frac{1}{2} \times AE \times DM}{\frac{1}{2} \times EC \times DM} = \frac{AE}{EC} \quad ...(ii)$$ **(1½ Marks)**

Now ΔBDE & ΔDEC are on the same base DE & between the same parallel line, BC & DE.

So, $ar.\Delta BDE = ar.\ \Delta DEC$ ...(iii)

in (i), (ii) and (iii)

$$\boxed{\frac{AD}{DB} = \frac{AE}{EC}}$$ **(1 Mark)**

So, other two sides are divided in the same.

25.

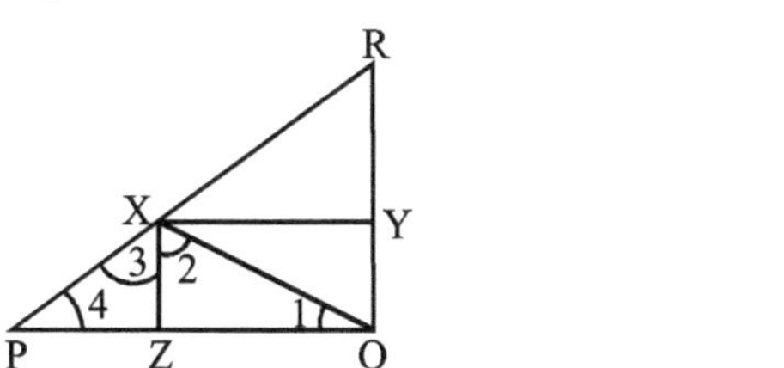

(1 Mark)

$RQ \perp PQ, XZ \perp PQ$

$\Rightarrow XZ \parallel YQ$

$\therefore XY \parallel ZQ$ ...(i)

$XYQZ$ is a rectangle. **(1 Mark)**

In $\Delta XZQ, \angle 1 + \angle 2 = 90°$ ...(ii)

In $\Delta PZX, \quad \angle 3 + \angle 4 = 90°$ ...(iii)

$XQ \perp PR \Rightarrow \angle 2 + \angle 3 = 90°$

From eqs. (i) and (iii)

$\angle 1 = \angle 3$

From eqs. (ii) and (iii)

$\angle 2 = \angle 4$ **(1 Mark)**

$\Delta PZX \sim \Delta XZQ$ (*AA* similarity)

$\dfrac{PZ}{XZ} = \dfrac{XZ}{ZQ}$

$\Rightarrow XZ^2 = PZ \times ZQ$ **(1 Mark)**

If a perpendicular is drawn from the vertex of the right angle of a triangle to the hypotenuse then triangles on both sides of the perpendicular are similar to the whole triangle and to each other

26.

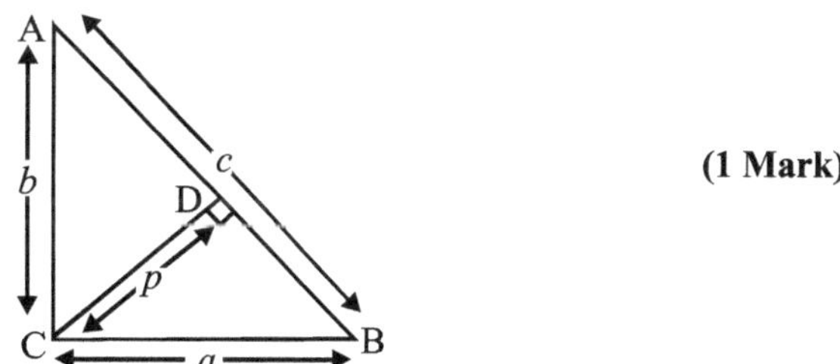

(1 Mark)

In ΔACB and ΔCDB

$\angle ACB = \angle CDB = 90°$

$\angle B = \angle B$ (common)

$\therefore \Delta ACB \sim \Delta CDB$ (by *AA* Similarity) **(1 Mark)**

$\Rightarrow \dfrac{b}{p} = \dfrac{c}{a}$

$\Rightarrow \dfrac{1}{p} = \dfrac{c}{ab}$ **(1 Mark)**

Squaring on both sides,

$$\frac{1}{p^2} = \frac{c^2}{a^2b^2}$$

$$\Rightarrow \quad \frac{1}{p^2} = \frac{a^2+b^2}{a^2b^2}$$

$[\because c^2 = a^2 + b^2]$

$$\therefore \quad \frac{1}{p^2} = \frac{1}{b^2} + \frac{1}{a^2}$$ Hence Proved.

(1 Mark)

If a perpendicular is drawn from the vertex of the right angle of a right triangle to the hypotenuse then triangles on both sides of the perpendicular are similar to the whole triangle and to each other.

27. To prove : $\frac{ar(\Delta ABC)}{ar(\Delta DBC)} = \frac{AO}{DO}$

Construction : Draw $AE \perp BC$ and $DF \perp BC$

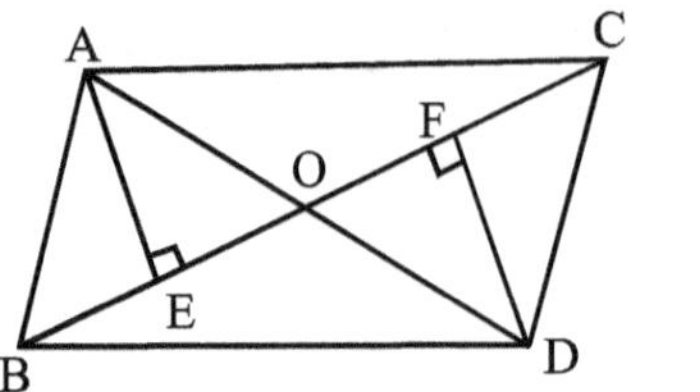

(1 Mark)

Proof :

In ΔAOE and ΔDOF,

$\angle AOE = \angle DOF$ (Vertically opposite angles)

$\angle AEO = \angle DFO = 90°$ (Construction)

$\Rightarrow \Delta AOE \sim \Delta DOF$ (By *AA* Similarity)

$\therefore \frac{AO}{DO} = \frac{AE}{DF}$ ...(i) **(1 Mark)**

Now $\frac{ar(\Delta ABC)}{ar(\Delta DBC)} = \frac{\frac{1}{2} \times BC \times AE}{\frac{1}{2} \times BC \times DF}$

$= \frac{AE}{DF}$

$= \frac{AO}{DO}$ **(2 Marks)**

Chapter 7 Coordinate Geometry

Topic-1: Distance Formula

1 Multiple Choice Questions

1. A point (x, y) is at a distance of 5 units from the origin. How many such points lie in the third quadrant? **[CBSE Sample Paper 2023-24, K]**

(a) 0 (b) 1
(c) 2 (d) infinitely many

2. The distance of the point (–6, 8) from x-axis is **[All India 2023 Set-II, Ap]**

(a) 6 units (b) – 6 units
(c) 8 units (d) 10 units

3. If end points of a diameter of a circle are (–5, 4) and (1, 0), then the radius of the circle is: **[All India 2023 Set-I, Ap]**

(a) $2\sqrt{13}$ units (b) $\sqrt{13}$ units
(c) $4\sqrt{2}$ units (d) $2\sqrt{2}$ units

4. The distance of the point (– 6, 8) from origin is: **[Delhi 2023, Ap]**

(a) 6 (b) – 6
(c) 8 (d) 10

5. The distance of the point (–1, 7) from x-axis is : **[Delhi 2023, K]**

(a) –1 (b) 7
(c) 6 (d) $\sqrt{50}$

6. If the vertices of a parallelogram PQRS taken in order are P(3,4), Q(–2,3) and R(–3,–2), then the coordinates of its fourth vertex S are **[CBSE Sample Paper 2022-23, U]**

(a) (–2,–1) (b) (–2,–3)
(c) (2,–1) (d) (1,2)

7. Points A(–1, y) and B(5, 7) lie on a circle with centre O(2, –3y). The values of y are **[All India 2022, Term-I, K]**

(a) 1, –7 (b) –1, 7
(c) 2, 7 (d) –2, –7

8. If A(4, –2), B(7, –2) and C(7, 9) are the vertices of a ΔABC, then ΔABC is **[All India 2022, Term-I, K]**

(a) equilateral triangle
(b) isosceles triangle
(c) right angled triangle
(d) isosceles right angled triangle

9. The distance of point A(–5, 6) from the origin is **[CBSE Sample Paper 2021-22, Term-I, U]**

(a) 11 units (b) 61 units
(c) $\sqrt{11}$ units (d) $\sqrt{61}$ units

10. The equation of the perpendicular bisector of line segment joining points A(4, 5) and B(–2, 3) is **[CBSE Sample Paper 2021-22 Term-I, U]**

(a) $2x - y + 7 = 0$ (b) $3x + 2y - 7 = 0$
(c) $3x - y - 7 = 0$ (d) $3x + y - 7 = 0$

11. ΔABC is a triangle such that AB : BC = 1 : 2. Point A lies on the y-axis and the coordinates of B and C are known. Which of the following formula can DEFINITELY be used to find the coordinates of A? **[CBSE CFPQ 2022, K]**

(i) Section formula
(ii) Distance formula

(a) only (i) (b) only (ii)
(c) both (i) and (ii) (d) neither (i) nor (ii)

12. A(5, 1), B(1, 4) and C(8, 5) are the coordinates of the vertices of a triangle. Which of the following types of triangle will ΔABC be? **[CBSE CFPQ 2022, K]**

(a) Equilateral triangle
(b) Scalene right-angled triangle
(c) Isosceles right-angled triangle
(d) Isosceles acute-angled triangle

13. The point P on *x*-axis equidistant from the points A(–1, 0) and B(5, 0) is **[All India 2020, K]**

(a) (2, 0) (b) (0, 2)
(c) (3, 0) (d) (2, 2)

14. The co-ordinates of the point which is reflection of point (–3, 5) in x-axis are **[All India 2020, Ap]**

(a) (3, 5) (b) (3, –5)

(c) (–3, –5) (d) (–3, 5)

15. The distance between the points $(a \cos\theta + b \sin\theta, 0)$ and $(0, a \sin\theta - b \cos\theta)$, is **[Delhi 2020, Ap]**

(a) $a^2 + b^2$ (b) $a^2 - b^2$

(c) $\sqrt{a^2+b^2}$ (d) $\sqrt{a^2-b^2}$

4 *Very Short Answer Questions (1 Mark)*

16. Point (x, y) is equidistant from points A(5, 1) and B(1, 5). Prove that x = y **[All India 2023 Set-II, Ap]**

17. Write the coordinates of a point P on x-axis which is equidistant from the points A(– 2, 0) and B(6, 0). **[All India 2019, Ap]**

18. Find the coordinates of a point A, where AB is diameter of a circle whose centre is (2, –3) and B is the point (1, 4). **[Delhi 2019, Ap]**

19. Find the distance of a point P (x, y) from the origin. **[All India 2018, Ap]**

5 *Short Answer Questions (2 or 3 Marks)*

20. Points A(3, 1), B(5, 1), C(a, b) and D(4, 3) are vertices of a parallelogram ABCD. Find the values of a and b. **[All India 2019, U]**

21. Find the point on y-axis which is equidistant from the points (5, –2) and (–3, 2). **[Delhi 2019, U]**

22. The line segment joining the points A(2, 1) and B(5, –8) is trisected at the points P and Q such that P is nearer to A. If P also lies on the line given by $2x - y + k = 0$, find the value of k. **[Delhi 2019, K]**

23. If the distances of P(x, y) from A(5, 1) and B(– 1, 5) are equal, then prove that $3x = 2y$. **[All India 2017, Term-II, K]**

24. The x-coordinate of a point P is twice its y-coordinate. If P is equidistant from Q(2, –5) and R(–3, 6), find the coordinates of P. **[Delhi 2016, Term-II, U]**

25. The points A(4, 7), B(p, 3) and C(7, 3) are the vertices of a right triangle, right-angled at B. Find the value of p. **[All India 2015, Term-II, Ap]**

26. If the point A(0, 2) is equidistant from the points B(3, p) and C(p, 5), find p. Also find the length of AB. **[Delhi 2014, Term-II, U]**

27. If the points A(–2, 1), B(a, b) and C(4, –1) are collinear and $a - b = 1$, find the values of a and b. **[Delhi 2014, Term-II, K]**

28. Prove that points (7, 10), (–2, 5) and (3, –4) are the vertices of an isosceles right triangle. **[All India 2013, Ap]**

Topic-2: Section Formula

1 *Multiple Choice Questions*

1. What is the ratio in which the line segment joining (2, –3) and (5, 6) is divided by x–axis? **[CBSE Sample Paper 2023-24, Ap]**

(a) 1 : 2 (b) 2 : 1

(c) 2 : 5 (d) 5 : 2

2. Three vertices of a parallelogram ABCD are A(1, 4), B(–2, 3) and C(5, 8). The ordinate of the fourth vertex D is **[All India 2022, Term-I, U]**

(a) 8 (b) 9

(c) 7 (d) 6

3. The ratio in which the line $3x + y - 9 = 0$ divides the line segment joining the points (1, 3) and (2, 7) is **[All India 2022, Term-I, K]**

(a) 3 : 2 (b) 2 : 3

(c) 3 : 4 (d) 4 : 3

4. The line segment joining the points P(–3, 2) and Q(5, 7) is divided by the y-axis in the ratio **[All India 2022, Term-I, K]**

(a) 3 : 1 (b) 3 : 4

(c) 3 : 2 (d) 3 : 5

5. The base BC of an equilateral ΔABC lies on the y-axis. The co-ordinates of C are (0, –3). If the origin is the mid-point of the base BC, what are the co-ordinates of A and B? **[All India 2022, Term-I, U]**

(a) A($\sqrt{3}$, 0); B(0, 3) (b) A($\pm 3\sqrt{3}$, 0); B(3, 0)

(c) A($\pm 3\sqrt{3}$, 0); B(0, 3) (d) A($-\sqrt{3}$, 0); B(3, 0)

6. In ΔABC right angled at B, if tan A = $\sqrt{3}$, then cos A cos C– sin A sin C = **[CBSE Sample Paper 2021-22, Term-I, Ap]**

(a) –1 (b) 0

(c) 1 (d) $\sqrt{3}/2$

7. The vertices of a parallelogram in order are A(1, 2), B(4, y), C(x, 6) and D(3, 5). Then (x, y) is

[CBSE Sample Paper 2021-22, Term-I, Ap]

(a) (6, 3) (b) 3, 6)

(c) (5, 6) (d) (1, 4)

8. Point P divides the line segment joining R(–1, 3) and S(9, 8) in ratio k : 1. If P lies on the line $x - y + 2 = 0$, then value of k is **[CBSE Sample Paper 2021-22, Term-I, K]**

(a) $\frac{2}{3}$ (b) $\frac{1}{2}$

(c) $\frac{1}{3}$ (d) $\frac{1}{4}$

Q. (9-13) are based on Case Study

A **hockey field** is the playing surface for the game of hockey. Historically, the game was played on natural turf (grass) but nowadays it is predominantly played on an artificial turf.

It is rectangular in shape - 100 yards by 60 yards. Goals consist of two upright posts placed equidistant from the centre of the backline, joined at the top by a horizontal crossbar. The inner edges of the posts must be 3.66 metres (4 yards) apart, and the lower edge of the crossbar must be 2.14 metres (7 feet) above the ground.

Each team plays with 11 players on the field during the game including the goalie.

Positions you might play include-

- **Forward :** As shown by players A, B, C and D.
- **Midfielders:** As shown by players E, F and G.
- **Fullbacks:** As shown by players H, I and J.

Goalie: As shown by players H, I and J.

Using the picture of a hockey field below, answer the questions that follow:

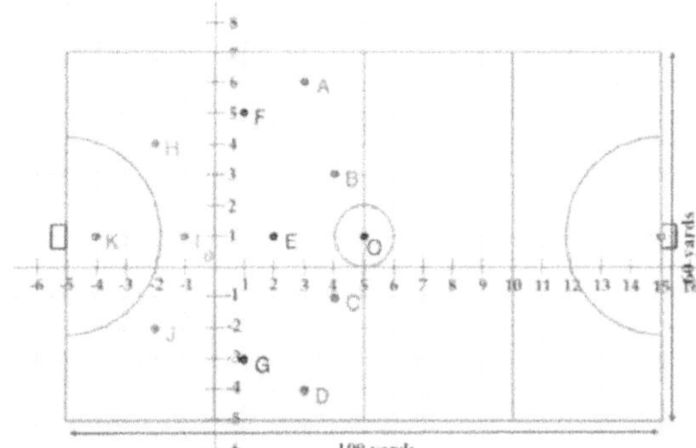

9. The coordinates of the centroid of ΔEHJ are

[CBSE Sample Paper 2021-22, Term-I, Ap]

(a) $\left(\frac{-2}{3},1\right)$ (b) $\left(1,\frac{-2}{3}\right)$

(c) $\left(\frac{2}{3},1\right)$ (d) $\left(\frac{-2}{3},1\right)$

10. If a player P needs to be at equal distances from A and G, such that A, P and G are in straight line, then position of P will be given by

[CBSE Sample Paper 2021-22, Term-I, Ap]

(a) $\left(\frac{-3}{2},2\right)$ (b) $\left(2,\frac{-3}{2}\right)$

(c) $\left(2,\frac{3}{2}\right)$ (d) (–2, –3)

11. The point on x axis equidistant from I and E is

[CBSE Sample Paper 2021-22, Term-I, K]

(a) $\left(\frac{1}{2},0\right)$ (b) $\left(0,\frac{-1}{2}\right)$

(c) $\left(\frac{-1}{2},0\right)$ (d) $\left(0,\frac{1}{2}\right)$

12. What are the coordinates of the position of a player Q such that his distance from K is twice his distance from E and K, Q and E are collinear?

[CBSE Sample Paper 2021-22, Term-I, K]

(a) (1, 0) (b) (0, 1)

(c) (–2, 1) (d) (–1, 0)

13. The point on y axis equidistant from B and C is

[CBSE Sample Paper 2021-22, Term-I, U]

(a) (–1, 0) (b) (0, –1)

(c) (1, 0) (d) (0, 1)

14. If the point P(6, 2) divides the line segment joining A(6, 5) and B(4, *y*) in the ratio 3 : 1, then the value of *y* is

[All India 2020, K]

(a) 4 (b) 3

(c) 2 (d) 1

15. If the point P(*k*, 0) divides the line segment joining the points A (2, –2) and B (–7, 4) in the ratio 1 : 2, then the value of *k* is **[Delhi 2020, K]**

(a) 1 (b) 2

(c) –2 (d) –1

16. If the points A(*x*, 2), B(–3, –4) and C(7, –5) are collinear, then the value of *x* is : **[Delhi 2014, Term-II, K]**

(a) – 63 (b) 63

(c) 60 (d) – 60

2 Assertion Reason/Two Statement Type Questions

17. **Assertion (A) :** If the points A(4, 3) and B(x, 5) lie on a circle with centre O(2, 3), then the value of x is 2

Reason (R) : Centre of a circle is the mid-point of each chord of the circle. **[All India 2023 Set-I, U]**

(a) Both Assertion (A) and Reason (R) are true and Reason (R) is the correct explanation of Assertion (A).
(b) Both Assertion (A) and Reason (R) are true and Reason (R) is not the correct explanation of Assertion (A).
(c) Assertion (A) is true but Reason (R) is false.
(d) Assertion (A) is false but Reason (R) is true.

18. **Assertion (A):** If the co-ordinates of the mid-points of the sides AB and AC of ΔABC are D(3,5) and E(-3,-3) respectively, then BC = 20 units

Reason (R): The line joining the mid points of two sides of a triangle is parallel to the third side and equal to half of it. **[CBSE Sample Paper 2022-23, Ap]**

(a) Both Assertion (A) and Reason (R) are true and Reason (R) is the correct explanation of Assertion (A).
(b) Both Assertion (A) and Reason (R) are true and Reason (R) is not the correct explanation of Assertion (A).
(c) Assertion (A) is true but Reason (R) is false.
(d) Assertion (A) is false but Reason (R) is true.

4 Very Short Answer Questions (1 Mark)

19. Find the ratio in which line y = x divides the line segment joining the points (6, –3) and (1, 6). **[All India 2023 Set-II, Ap]**

20. The line segment joining the points A(4, –5) and B(4, 5) is divided by the point P such that AP : AB = 2 : 5. Find the coordinates of P. **[All India 2023 Set-I, Ap]**

5 Short Answer Questions (2 or 3 Marks)

21. A line intersects y-axis and x-axis at point P and Q, respectively. If R(2, 5), is the mid-point of line segment PQ, then find the coordinates of P and Q. **[All India 2023 Set-II, Ap]**

22. Find the ratio in which the line segment joining the points A(6, 3) and B(–2, –5) is divided by x-axis. **[All India 2023 Set-II, Ap]**

23. On a playground, Parth, Qasim and Ragini are standing at the points P(2, 4), Q(8, 6) and R(8, 9) respectively. Sameer is standing exactly halfway between Parth and Qasim on the line joining Parth and Qasim.
What is the shortest distance, in units, between Sameer and Ragini? Show your steps. **[CBSE CFPQ 2022, K]**

24. If the mid-point of the line segment joining the points A(3, 4) and B(k, 6) is P(x, y) and $x + y - 10 = 0$, find the value of k. **[All India 2020, Ap]**

25. If the point C (–1, 2) divides internally the line segment joining A (2, 5) and B (x, y) in the ratio 3:4, find the coordinates of B. **[Delhi 2020, Ap]**

26. Find the ratio in which the y-axis divides the line segment joining the points (6, –4) and (–2, –7). Also find the point of intersection. **[All India 2020, K]**

27. Find the ratio in which the line x – 3y = 0 divides the line segment joining the points (– 2, – 5) and (6, 3). Find the coordinates of the point of intersection. **[All India 2019, U]**

28. Find the ratio in which the segment joining the points (1, –3) and (4, 5) is divide by x-axis. Also find the coordinates of this point on x-axis. **[Delhi 2019, Ap]**

29. Find the ratio in which P (4, m) divides the line segment joining the points A(2, 3) and B (6, –3). Hence find m. **[All India 2018, Ap]**

30. A line intersects the y-axis and x-axis at the points P and Q respectively. If (2, – 5) is the mid-point of PQ, then find the coordinates of P and Q. **[All India 2017, Term-II, U]**

31. In what ratio does the point $\left(\frac{24}{11}, y\right)$ divide the line segment joining the points P(2, – 2) and Q(3, 7) ? Also find the value of y. **[All India 2017, Term-II, K]**

32. Find the ratio in which y-axis divides the line segment joining the points A(5, –6) and B(–1, –4). Also find the coordinates of the point of division. **[Delhi 2016, Term-II, K]**

33. If the coordinates of points A and B are (– 2, – 2) and (2, – 4) respectively, find the coordinates of P such that AP $= \frac{3}{7}$AB, where P lies on the line segment AB. **[All India 2015, Term-II, K]**

34. Find the ratio in which the y-axis divides the line segment joining the points (–4, –6) and (10, 12). Also find the coordinates of the point of division. **[All India 2013, K]**

Long Answer Questions (4 or 5 Marks)

35. If the points A($k + 1$, $2k$), B($3k$, $2k + 3$) and C($5k - 1$, $5k$) are collinear, then find the value of k.

A (k+1, 2k)   B (3k, 2k + 3)   C C(5k–1, 5k)

[All India 2017, Term-II, K]

Let point B divide AC in ratio $\lambda : 1$.

36. Find the ratio in which the point P(x, 2) divides the line segment joining the points A(12, 5) and B(4, –3). Also find the value of x. **[Delhi 2014, Term-II, U]**

Case Based Questions (4 Marks)

37. Tharunya was thrilled to know that the football tournament is fixed with a monthly timeframe from 20th July to 20th August 2023 and for the first time in the FIFA Women's World Cup's history, two nations host in 10 venues. Her father felt that the game can be better understood if the position of players is represented as points on a coordinate plane.

[CBSE Sample Paper 2023-24, U]

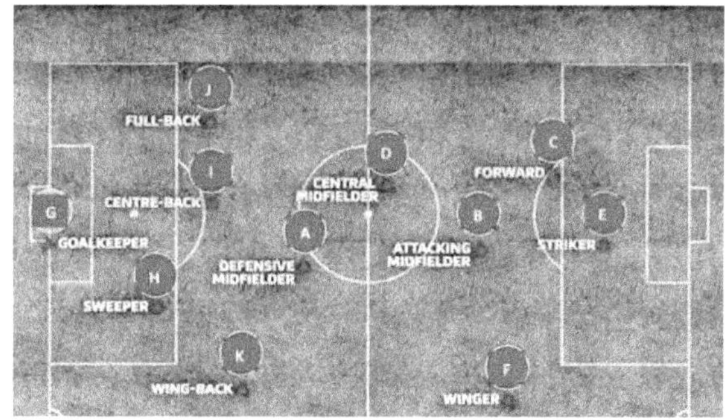

(i) At an instance, the midfielders and forward formed a parallelogram. Find the position of the central midfielder (D) if the position of other players who formed the parallelogram are : A(1, 2), B(4, 3) and C(6, 6)

(ii) Check if the Goal keeper G(–3, 5), Sweeper H(3, 1) and Wing–back K(0, 3) fall on a same straight line.

OR

Check if the Full–back J(5, –3) and Centre–back I (–4, 6) are equidistant from forward C(0, 1) and if C is the mid–point of IJ.

(iii) If Defensive midfielder A(1, 4), Attacking midfielder B(2, –3) and Striker E(a, b) lie on the same straight line and B is equidistant from A and E, find the position of E.

38. Jagdish has a field which is in the shape of a right angled triangle AQC. He wants to leave a space in the form of a square PQRS inside the field for growing wheat and the remaining for growing vegetables (as shown in the figure). In the field, there is a pole marked as O. **[Delhi 2023, U]**

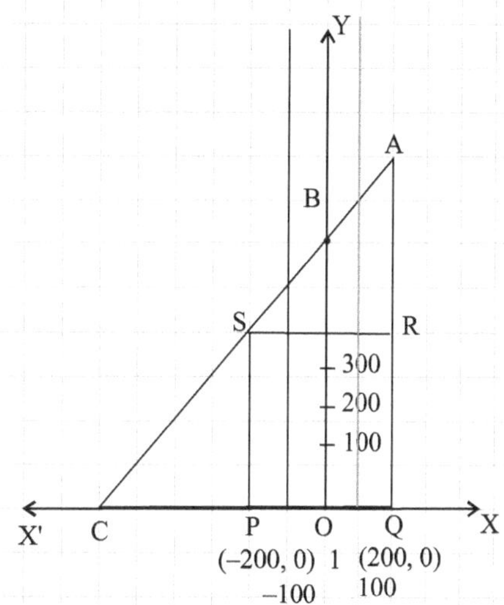

Based on the above information, answer the following questions:

(i) Taking O as origin, coordinates of P are (–200, 0) and Q are (200, 0). PQRS being a square, what are the coordinates of R and S?

(ii) (a) What is the area of square PQRS?

OR

(b) What is the length of diagonal PR in square PQRS?

(iii) If S divides CA in the ratio K:1, what is the value of K, where points A is (200, 800)?

39. A tiling or tessellation of a flat surface is the covering of a plane using one or more geometric shapes, called tiles, with no overlaps and no gaps. Historically, tessellations were used in ancient Rome and in Islamic art. You may find tessellation patterns on floors, walls, paintings etc. Shown below is a tiled floor in the archaeological Museum of Seville, made using squares, triangles and hexagons.

A craftsman thought of making a floor pattern after being inspired by the above design. To ensure accuracy in his work, he made the pattern on the Cartesian plane. He used regular octagons, squares and triangles for his floor tessellation pattern

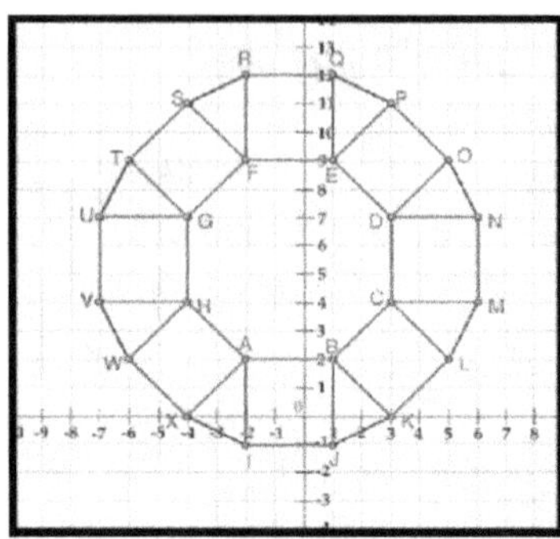

[CBSE Sample Paper 2022-23, U]

Use the above figure to answer the questions that follow:

(i) What is the length of the line segment joining points B and F?

(ii) The centre 'Z' of the figure will be the point of intersection of the diagonals of quadrilateral WXOP. Then what are the coordinates of Z?

(iii) What are the coordinates of the point on y axis equidistant from A and G?

OR

What is the area of Trapezium AFGH?

Hints & Solutions

Topic-1: Distance Formula

1. **(d)** infinitely many **(1 Mark)**

2. **(c)** The ordinates of a point represents the distance from x-axis. **(1 Mark)**

3. **(b)** Given points are (–5, 4) and (1, 0)

Diameter $= \sqrt{(-5-1)^2+(4-0)^2}$

$= \sqrt{36+16} = \sqrt{52} = 2\sqrt{13}$

Then radius $= \frac{\text{diameter}}{2} = \frac{2\sqrt{13}}{2} = \sqrt{13}$ units **(1 Mark)**

4. **(d)** (0, 0) (x_1, y_1) —— (–6, 8) (x_2, y_2)

Distance formula $= \sqrt{(x_1-x_2)^2+(y_1-y_2)^2}$

$D = \sqrt{36+64} = \sqrt{100} = 10$ **(1 Mark)**

5. **(b)** (–1, 7) —— (x, y0)

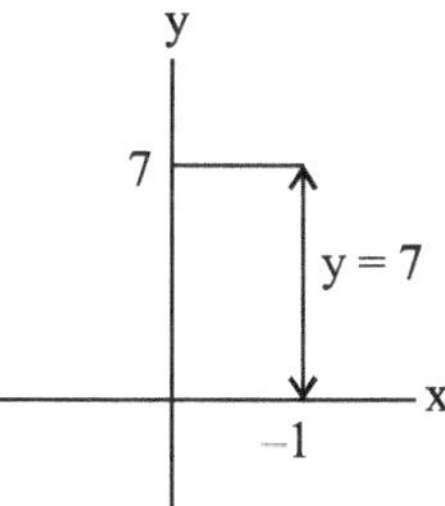

(1 Mark)

6. **(c)** (2,–1) **(1 Mark)**

7. **(b)** Centre O(2, –3*y*) and point A(–1, *y*) and B (5, 7).

OA and OB are radii of circle.

OA = OB

$\sqrt{(-1-2)^2+(y+3y)^2} = \sqrt{(5-2)^2+(7+3y)^2}$

Take square both sides.

$9 + 16y^2 = 9 + 49 + 9y^2 + 42y$

$7y^2 - 42y - 49 = 0$

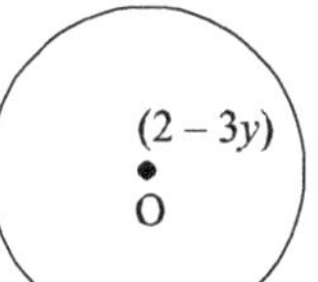

$7(y^2 - 6y - 7) = 0$

$y^2 - 6y - 7 = 0$

$y^2 - 7y + y - 7 = 0$

$y(y-7) + 1(y-7) = 0 \Rightarrow (y-7)(y+1) = 0$

$y = 7, -1$

Therefore, the values of y are 7 and –1. **(1 Mark)**

8. **(c)** Given vertices of triangle *ABC* is *A*(4, –2); *B*(7, –2) and *C*(7, 9)

$AB = \sqrt{(-2+2)^2+(7-4)^2} = 3$

$BC = \sqrt{(7-7)^2+(9+2)^2} = 11$

$AC = \sqrt{(7-4)^2+(9+2)^2} = \sqrt{130}$

A(4, –2)
B (7, –2) C(7, 9)

Apply pythagoras theorem,

$AC^2 = AB^2 + BC^2$

$\left(\sqrt{130}\right)^2 = (3)^2 + (11)^2$

$130 = 9 + 121$

$130 = 130$

So, these vertices forms the right angle triangle. **(1 Mark)**

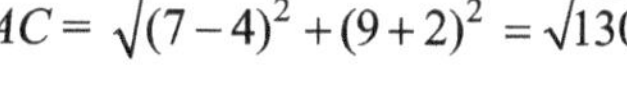

Note

We cannot say anything about triangle by coordinates. So, we need to find distances by using the coordinates.

9. **(d)** Distance of point A(–5, 6) from the origin (0, 0) is

$\sqrt{(0+5)^2+(0-6)^2} = \sqrt{25+36} = \sqrt{61}$ units **(1 Mark)**

10. **(d)** Any point (*x*, *y*) of perpendicular bisector will be equidistant from A & B.

$\therefore \sqrt{(x-4)^2+(y-5)^2} = \sqrt{(x+2)^2+(y-3)^2}$

Solving we get $-12x - 4y + 28 = 0$ or $3x + y - 7 = 0$

(1 Mark)

11. **(b)** **(1 Mark)**

12. **(c)** **(1 Mark)**

13. **(a)** $P(x, 0) = \left(\frac{5-1}{2}, 0\right) = (2, 0)$ **(1 Mark)**

[$\because$ A and B both lies on x-axis]

Three or more points lies in same line are called collinear.

14. **(c)** **(1 Mark)**

For reflection of a point with respect to x-axis change sign of y-coordinate and with respect to y-axis change sign of x-coordinate.

15. **(c)** Distance$= \sqrt{(a\cos\theta + b\sin\theta)^2 + (a\sin\theta - b\cos\theta)^2}$

$= \sqrt{a^2 + b^2}$ **(1 Mark)**

16. Length of AP = Length of BP

$\Rightarrow \sqrt{(5-x)^2 + (1-y)^2} = \sqrt{(1-x)^2 + (5-y)^2}$

$\Rightarrow \sqrt{x^2 + 25 - 10x + y^2 + 1 - 2y}$

$= \sqrt{x^2 + 1 - 2x + y^2 - 10y + 25}$

$\Rightarrow x^2 + 25 - 10x + y^2 + 1 - 2y = x^2 + 1 - 2x + y^2 - 10y + 25$

$\Rightarrow -10x - 2y = -2x - 10y$

$\Rightarrow 8x = 8y \Rightarrow y = x$ **(1 Mark)**

17. Let coordinates of P on x-axis is (x, 0)

$\because$ PA = PB

$\Rightarrow PA^2 = PB^2$

$(x + 2)^2 = (x - 6)^2$

$\Rightarrow x^2 + 4 + 4x = x^2 + 36 - 12x$

$\Rightarrow 4 + 4x = 36 - 12x \Rightarrow 16x = 32$

$\Rightarrow x = 2$

Co-ordinates of P are (2, 0) **(1 Mark)**

Note

If abscissa of point will be zero then point lies on x-axis. Hence points P, A and B are collinear. So, P is mid point of AB. $\therefore P = \left(\frac{-2+6}{2}, 0\right) = (2, 0)$

18. (x,y)A ——— C (2,–3) ——— B (1,4)

Let, the co-ordinate of point A is (x,y).

Since, C is the mid-point of line AB.

$\therefore 2 = \frac{x+1}{2} \Rightarrow x + 1 = 4 \Rightarrow x = 3$

and $-3 = \frac{y+4}{2} \Rightarrow y + 4 = -6 \Rightarrow y = -10.$ **(1 Mark)**

Therefore, the co-ordinates of the point A is (3,–10).

19. Origin has coordinates (0, 0)

$\therefore$ Distance of P (x, y) from origin (0, 0) is

$\sqrt{(x-0)^2 + (y-0)^2} = \sqrt{x^2 + y^2}$ **(1 Mark)**

20. ....

Topper's Answer

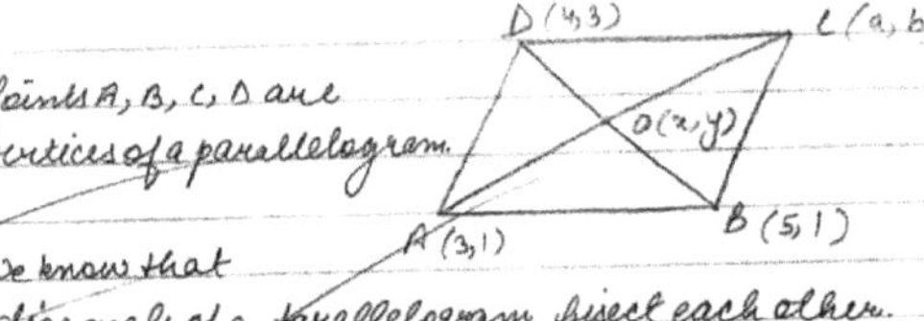

Points A, B, C, D are vertices of a parallelogram.

We know that diagonals of a parallelogram bisect each other.

$\therefore$ O is the midpoint of both AC and BD.

Using section formula for mid-point.

on BD,

$x = \frac{4+5}{2}$, $y = \frac{3+1}{2}$

$\Rightarrow x = \frac{9}{2}$, $y = 2$.

on AC

$x = \frac{3+a}{2}$, $y = \frac{b+1}{2}$

$\Rightarrow \frac{9}{2} = \frac{3+a}{2}$, $2 = \frac{b+1}{2}$ $\Rightarrow$ $a = 6$, $b = 3$

21. Let the point on y-axis is (0, y).

According to the question,

$$\sqrt{(0-5)^2+(y+2)^2}=\sqrt{(0+3)^2+(y-2)^2}$$ **(1 Mark)**

Square on both sides,

$25+(y+2)^2=9+(y-2)^2$

$\Rightarrow 25-9=(y-2)^2-(y+2)^2$

$\Rightarrow 16=y^2+4-4y-y^2-4-4y$

$\Rightarrow 16=-8y \quad \Rightarrow y=-2$

Hence, the point on y-axis which is equidistant from the points (5, –2) and (–3, 2) is (0, –2). **(1 Mark)**

22. Given P and Q be the points of trisection of AB i.e.,

AP = PQ = QB

Therefore, P divides AB internally in the ratio 1 : 2.

Therefore, the coordinates of P, by applying the section formula, are

$$\left(\frac{1(5)+2(2)}{1+2},\frac{1(-8)+2(1)}{1+2}\right)\text{, i.e., P}(3,-2)$$ **(1 Mark)**

Since, P also lies on the line $2x-y+k=0$.

Hence, (3, –2) satisfy $2x-y+k=0$

$\therefore\ 2(3)-(-2)+k=0\Rightarrow k=-8.$

Hence, the value of k is –8. **(1 Mark)**

23. Given that,

PA = PB

and to prove : $3x=2y$

Since, PA = PB

$$\Rightarrow \sqrt{(x-5)^2+(y-1)^2}=\sqrt{(x+1)^2+(y-5)^2}$$ **(½ Mark)**

$\Rightarrow (x-5)^2+(y-1)^2=(x+1)^2+(y-1)^2$

(Squaring both the sides) **(½ Mark)**

$\Rightarrow x^2-10x+25+y^2-2y+1$
$=x^2+2x+1+y^2-10y+25$

$\Rightarrow -10x-2y=2x-10y$

$\Rightarrow 8y=12x$

$\Rightarrow 3x=2y$ **(1 Mark)**

Hence Proved

Note

Use distance formula to find the distance AB between two points $A(x_1,y_1)$ and $B(x_2,y_2)$, $AB=\sqrt{(x_2-x_1)^2+(y_2-y_1)^2}$

24. Let y–coordinate of the point P be a.

So, x–coordinate will be $2a$

Point $P(2a, a)$ is equidistant from $Q(2, -5)$ and $R(-3, 6)$

Distance $=\sqrt{(x_2-x_1)^2+(y_2-y_1)^2}$

$PQ=\sqrt{(2a-2)^2+(a+5)^2}$

$=\sqrt{4a^2+4-8a+a^2+25+10a}$

$[\because (x-y)^2=x^2+y^2-2xy]$

$PQ=\sqrt{5a^2+2a+29}$ **(½ Mark)**

$PR=\sqrt{(2a+3)^2+(a-6)^2}$

$=\sqrt{4a^2+9+12a+a^2+36-12a}$

$[\because (x+y)^2=x^2+y^2+2xy]$

$=\sqrt{5a^2+45}$

$PQ=PR$ **(½ Mark)**

Squaring on both sides

$PQ^2=PR^2$

$\Rightarrow 5a^2+2a+29=5a^2+45$

$\Rightarrow 2a=16$

$\Rightarrow a = 8$

$\therefore$ Coordinates of P are (16, 8) **(1 Mark)**

25. **(1 Mark)**

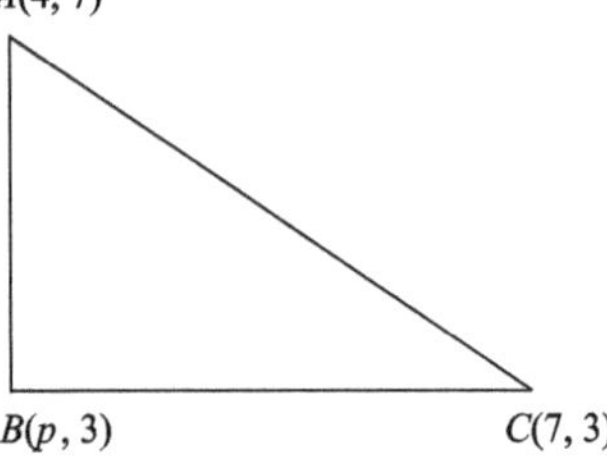

Distance = $\sqrt{(x_2 - x_1)^2 + (y_2 - y_1)^2}$

$AB = \sqrt{(p-4)^2 + (3-7)^2}$

$= \sqrt{(p)^2 + (4)^2 - 8p + 16}$

$= \sqrt{p^2 + 16 - 8p + 16}$

$= \sqrt{p^2 - 8p + 32}$ ...(1)

$BC = \sqrt{(7-p)^2 + (3-3)^2}$

$= \sqrt{(7-p)^2}$ ...(2)

$CA = \sqrt{(4-7)^2 + (7-3)^2} = \sqrt{9+16} = \sqrt{25}$ ...(3)

By Pythagoras theorem in ΔABC

$AC^2 = AB^2 + BC^2$

$\left(\sqrt{25}\right)^2 = \left(\sqrt{p^2 - 8p + 32}\right)^2 + \left(\sqrt{(7-p)^2}\right)^2$ **(1 Mark)**

$25 = p^2 - 8p + 32 + (7 - p)^2$

$\Rightarrow 25 = p^2 - 8p + 32 + p^2 + 49 - 14p$

$\Rightarrow 25 = 2p^2 - 22p + 81$

$\Rightarrow 2p^2 - 22p + 56 = 0$

$\Rightarrow p^2 - 11p + 28 = 0$

$\Rightarrow p^2 - 7p - 4p + 28 = 0$

$\Rightarrow (p - 7)(p - 4) = 0$

$\Rightarrow p = 7$ or $p = 4$

Since, co-ordinates of B are (7, 3)

$\therefore p \neq 7$

So, required value of p is 4 **(1 Mark)**

26. Given : Points A(0, 2), B(3, p) and C(p, 5)

A is equidistant from B and C

$\therefore$ AB = AC

Distance = $\sqrt{(x_2 - x_1)^2 + (y_2 - y_1)^2}$ **(½ Mark)**

$\sqrt{(3-0)^2 + (p-2)^2} = \sqrt{(p-0)^2 + (5-2)^2}$ **(½ Mark)**

Squaring on both sides

$9 + p^2 + 4 - 4p = p^2 + 9$

$13 - 4p = 9$

$4 = 4p$

$p = 1$

$\therefore$ B(3, 1), C(1, 5), A(0, 2) **(1 Mark)**

$AB = \sqrt{(3-0)^2 + (1-2)^2}$

$= \sqrt{9+1} = \sqrt{10}$ units. **(1 Mark)**

27. Given: Points A(–2, 1), B(a, b) and C(4, –1)

ABC are collinear

$\therefore$ Area of $\Delta ABC = 0$ **(½ Mark)**

$\frac{1}{2}[x_1(y_2 - y_3) + x_2(y_3 - y_1) + x_3(y_1 - y_2)] = 0$

$\frac{1}{2}[-2(b + 1) + a(-1 - 1) + 4(1 - b)] = 0$

$-2b - 2 - 2a + 4 - 4b = 0$

$-2a - 6b + 2 = 0$

$2a + 6b = 2$

$a + 3b = 1$ ...(1) **(1 Mark)**

Also $a - b = 1$ ...(2) (given)

Subtracting equation (1) from (2)

$4b = 0$

$b = 0$ **(1 Mark)**

Subtituting b = 0 in (1)

$a = 1$ **(½ Mark)**

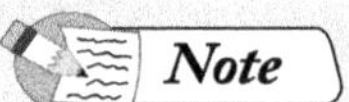

Note

If three points are collinear, then the points can not form any triangle.

28. Let $A(7, 10)$, $B(-2, 5)$, $C(3, -4)$

Distance = $\sqrt{(x_2 - x_1)^2 + (y_2 - y_1)^2}$

$AB = \sqrt{(-2-7)^2 + (5-10)^2}$ **(½ Mark)**

$= \sqrt{81+25} = \sqrt{106}$

$BC = \sqrt{(3+2)^2+(-4-5)^2}$ **(½ Mark)**

$= \sqrt{25+81} = \sqrt{106}$

$CA = \sqrt{(3-7)^2+(-4-10)^2}$

$= \sqrt{16+196} = \sqrt{212}$ **(½ Mark)**

$AB = BC$ **(½ Mark)**

$\therefore$ ABC is isoceles triangle

$BC^2 + AB^2 = 106 + 106 = 212$

$CA^2 = 212$

$\therefore \quad CA^2 = AB^2 + BC^2$ **(½ Mark)**

Reverse of pythagoras theorem: If sum of squares of two sides is equal to square of a side, then it is a right triangle.

ABC is also right triangle.

Hence, ABC is isoceles right triangle. **(½ Mark)**

Topic-2: Section Formula

1. **(a)** 1 : 2 **(1 Mark)**

2. **(b)** Let D(x, y)

Mid point $O = \left(\frac{1+5}{2}, \frac{4+8}{2}\right)$

$= \left(\frac{6}{2}, \frac{12}{2}\right) = (3, 6)$

A (1, 4), D (x, y), B (–2, 3), C (5, 8), O

Coordinate O will also the midpoint of BD.

$3 = \frac{x-2}{2}$ | $\frac{x+3}{2} = 6$

$6 = x - 2$ | $x + 3 = 12$

$x = 8$ | $x = 9$

Coordinate D(x, y) $\rightarrow$ D(8, 9), ordinate = 9. **(1 Mark)**

Note

Ordinate stands for 'y' coordinate of the ordered pair.

3. **(c)** (1, 3) (2, 7)

Let the ratio be k : 1

Apply section formula,

$x = \frac{2k+1}{k+1}, \quad y = \frac{7k+3}{k+1}$

These two coordinates also satisfied the line $3x + y - 9 = 0$

$3\left(\frac{2k+1}{k+1}\right)+\left(\frac{7k+3}{k+1}\right)-9=0$

$6k + 3 + 7k + 3 - 9k - 9 = 0$

$4k = 3$

$k = \frac{3}{4}$

Therefore, the required ratio is 3 : 4. **(1 Mark)**

4. **(d)** Given points of the line PQ is $P(-3, 2)$ & $Q(5, 7)$

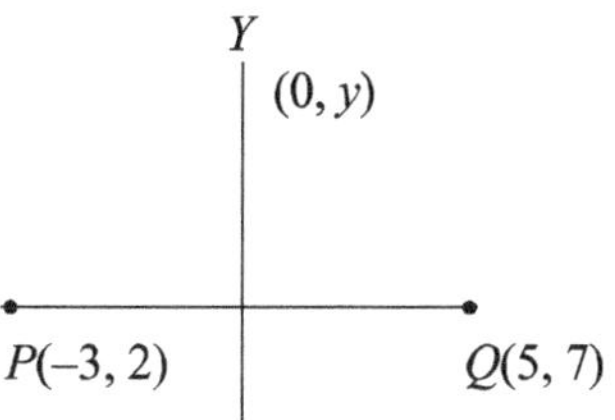

Let the ratio be k : 1

$x = \frac{k \times 5 + 1 \times (-3)}{k+1}$

$0 = \frac{5k-3}{k+1} \Rightarrow 5k - 3 = 0 = 5k = 3 \Rightarrow k = \frac{3}{5}$

Therefore, the ratio is 3 : 5 **(1 Mark)**

5. **(c)** Given origin is the midpoint of the line BC.

Let B(0, y) and A(x, 0).

Apply midpoint formula.

B (0, y), (0, 0), (x, 0) A x-axis, C (0, –3)

$0 = \frac{y-3}{2} \Rightarrow y = 3$

$\Rightarrow$ B $\rightarrow$ (0, 3)

ΔABC is an equilateral triangle.

AB = BC

$\sqrt{(x-0)^2+(0-3)^2} = \sqrt{(0-0)^2+(-3-3)^2}$

$\sqrt{x^2+9} = \sqrt{36}$

Take square both sides,

$x^2 + 9 = 36$

$x^2 = 27 \Rightarrow x \pm 3\sqrt{3}$

$A = (\pm 3\sqrt{3}, 0)$ **(1 Mark)**

6. **(b)** $\tan A = \sqrt{3} = \tan 60°$ so $\angle A = 60°$, Hence, $\angle C = 30°$.

So cos A cos C– sin A sin C or cos 60° cos 30° – sin 60° sin 30°

$$= \left(\frac{1}{2}\right)\times\left(\frac{\sqrt{3}}{2}\right)-\left(\frac{\sqrt{3}}{2}\right)\times\left(\frac{1}{2}\right)=0$$ **(1 Mark)**

7. **(a)** Since ABCD is a parallelogram, diagonals AC and BD bisect each other,

∴ Mid point of AC = mid point of BD.

$$\left(\frac{x+1}{2},\frac{6+2}{2}\right)=\left(\frac{3+4}{2},\frac{5+y}{2}\right)$$

Comparing the co-ordinates, we get,

$\frac{x+1}{2}=\frac{3+4}{2}$. So, x = 6

Similarly, $\frac{6+2}{2}=\frac{5+y}{2}$. So, y = 3

∴ (x, y) = 6, 3 **(1 Mark)**

8. **(a)** Since P divides the line segment joining R (–1, 3) and S (9, 8) in ratio k : 1 ∴ Coordinates of P are $\left(\frac{9k-1}{k+1},\frac{8k+3}{k+1}\right)$

Since P lies on the line x – y + 2 = 0, then Coordinates of point P will satisfy the given equation

So, $\frac{9k-1}{k+1}-\frac{8k+3}{k+1}+2=0$

9k – 1 – 8k – 3 + 2k + 2 = 0

which gives k = 2/3 **(1 Mark)**

9. **(a)** Centroid of ΔEHJ with E(2, 1), H(–2, 4) & J(–2, –2) is

Coordinates of centroid are $\left(\frac{x_1+x_2+x_3}{3},\frac{y_1+y_2+y_3}{3}\right)$

$$\left(\frac{2+(-2)+(-2)}{3},\frac{1+4+(-2)}{3}\right)=\left(\frac{-2}{3},1\right)$$ **(1 Mark)**

10. **(c)** If P needs to be at equal distance from A(3, 6) and G(1, –3), such that A, P and G are collinear, then P will be the mid-point of AG.

So coordinates of P will be $\left(\frac{3+1}{2},\frac{6+(-3)}{2}\right)=\left(2,\frac{3}{2}\right)$

(1 Mark)

11. **(a)** Let the point on x-axis equidistant from I(–1, 1) and E(2, 1) be (x, 0) then $\sqrt{(x+1)^2+(0-1)^2}$

$=\sqrt{(x-2)^2+(0-1)^2}$

$x^2 + 1 + 2x + 1 = x^2 + 4 - 4x + 1$

6x = 3 So $x = \frac{1}{2}$

∴ the required point is $\left(\frac{1}{2},0\right)$ **(1 Mark)**

12. **(b)** Let the coordinates of the position of a player Q such that his distance from K(–4,1) is twice his distance from E(2,1) be Q(x, y)

Then KQ : QE = 2 : 1

$$Q(x,y)=\left(\frac{2\times2+1\times(-4)}{3},\frac{2\times1+1\times1}{3}\right)=(0,1)$$ **(1 Mark)**

13. **(d)** Let the point on y-axis equidistant from B(4, 3) and C(4, –1) be (0, y)

then $\sqrt{(4-0)^2+(3-y)^2}=\sqrt{(4-0)^2+(y+1)^2}$

$16 + y^2 + 9 - 6y = 16 + y^2 + 1 + 2y$

–8y = – 8

So y = 1.

∴ the required point is (0, 1) **(1 Mark)**

14. **(d)** $P(6, 2)=\left(\frac{4\times3+1\times6}{3+1},\frac{3\times y+1\times5}{3+1}\right)$

$\because\ 6 \neq \frac{18}{4}$ (Question is wrong)

$2=\frac{3y+5}{4} \Rightarrow 3y+5=8$

$3y=3 \Rightarrow y=1$ **(1 Mark)**

15. **(d)** A(2, –2) —1— P(k,0) —2— B(–7,4)

$P(k, 0)=\left(\frac{-7+4}{1+2},\frac{4-4}{1+2}\right)$

= (–1, 0)

k = –1 **(1 Mark)**

16. **(a)** A (x, 2) —K— B (–3, –4) —I— C (7, –5)

let B divides AB in ratio of K : I

Applying section formula

$\frac{7k + x}{k+1} = -3$ ...(i)

$\frac{-5k + 2}{k+1} = -4$ ..(ii)

k = 6

substitute the obtained value of k in equation (1)

7(6) + x = – 3 (6 + 1)

42 + x = – 21

$\boxed{x = -63}$ **(1 Mark)**

17. **(c)** A : Lenght of OA = Length of OB

$\Rightarrow \sqrt{(4-2)^2 + (3-3)^2} = \sqrt{(x-2)^2 + (5-3)^2}$

$\Rightarrow 4 = x^2 + 4 - 4x + 4 \Rightarrow (x-2)^2 = 0 \Rightarrow x = 2$

R : Centre of circle is the mid point of each diameter of the circle. **(1 Mark)**

18. **(a)** Both Assertion (A) and Reason (R) are true and Reason (R) is the correct explanation of Assertion (A) **(1 Mark)**

19. Let the ratio is λ : 1

$x = \frac{\lambda+6}{\lambda+1}, y = \frac{6\lambda - 6}{\lambda+1}$

λ 1

(6, –3) (x, y) (1, 6)

for y = x

$\Rightarrow \frac{\lambda+6}{\lambda+1} = \frac{6\lambda-6}{\lambda+1} \Rightarrow 5\lambda = 9 \Rightarrow \lambda = \frac{9}{5}$

So the ratio is 9 : 5 **(1 Mark)**

20. Let coordinates of P is (a, b)

By section formula

$a = \frac{2\times4+3\times4}{5} = \frac{20}{5} = 4 \Rightarrow b = \frac{2\times5-3\times5}{5} = \frac{-5}{5} = -1$

coordinates of P is (4, –1) **(1 Mark)**

21.

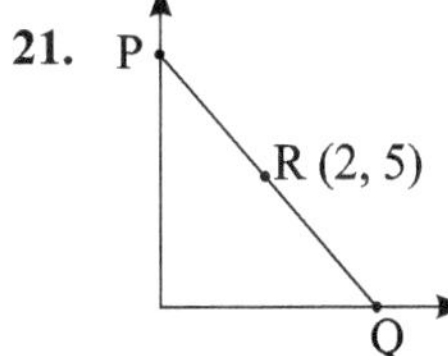

The coordinates of P will be (0, y) and the coordinates of Q will be (x, 0).

According to mid point formula

$\frac{x+0}{2} = 2$ and $\frac{y+0}{2} = 5$ **(1 Mark)**

$x = 4$ and $y = 10$

Hence, the coordinates of P are (0, 10) and Q are (4, 0). **(1 Mark)**

LCM (72, 120) = $2^3 \times 3^2 \times 5 = 360$ **(1 Mark)**

22.

d 1

A (6, 3) Q (x, 3) B (–2, –5)

At x-axis, $y = 0$

∴ Point be Q(x, 0)

Let the point Q divides the line segment AB in ratio d:1

Applying section formula

$\frac{-2d+6}{d+1} = x$ ...(i)

and

$\frac{-5d+3}{d+1} = 0$ ...(ii) **(1 Mark)**

From equation (ii)

–5d + 3 = 0

$d = \frac{3}{5}$ **(1 Mark)**

$d : 1 = \frac{3}{5} : 1 = 3 : 5$

Hence, the required ratio is 3:5 **(1 Mark)**

23. Uses the mid-point formula and finds the coordinates of Sameer's location as: **(1 Mark)**

$\left(\frac{2+8}{2}, \frac{4+6}{2}\right) = (5,5).$

Uses the distance formula and finds the shortest distance between Sameer and Ragini as $\sqrt{\{(8-5)^2 + (9-5)^2\}} = 5$ units. **(1 Mark)**

24. Since, mid-point of A(3, 4) and B(k, 6) is P(x, y).

$\therefore \quad P(x, y) = \left(\frac{3+k}{2}, \frac{4+6}{2}\right) = \left(\frac{3+k}{2}, 5\right)$

$\Rightarrow \quad x = \frac{3+k}{2}, y = 5$ **(1½ Marks)**

Putting values of x and y in

$x + y - 10 = 0$

$$\Rightarrow \quad \frac{3+k}{2} + 5 - 10 = 0$$

$$\Rightarrow \quad \frac{3+k}{2} = 5 \quad \Rightarrow \quad 3 + k = 10$$

$$\Rightarrow \quad k = 10 - 3 \quad \Rightarrow \quad k = 7$$ **(1½ Marks)**

25. Using section formula

3	4
A(2,5) ——— P(–1,2) ——— B(x,y)	

$$C(-1,2) = \left(\frac{3 \times x + 2 \times 4}{3+4}, \frac{3 \times y + 4 \times 5}{3+4}\right)$$

$$C(-1,2) = \left(\frac{3x+8}{7}, \frac{3y+20}{7}\right)$$ **(1 Mark)**

Comparing both sides

$$-1 = \frac{3x+8}{7}$$

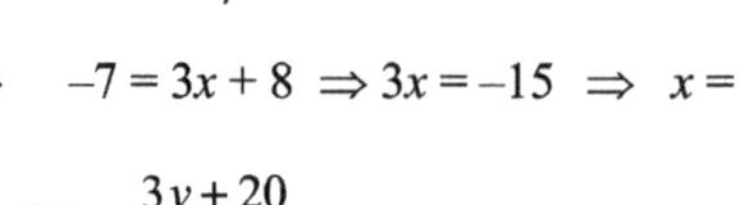

$$\Rightarrow \quad -7 = 3x + 8 \Rightarrow 3x = -15 \Rightarrow x = -5$$

And $2 = \frac{3y+20}{7}$

$$\Rightarrow \quad 14 = 3y + 20 \Rightarrow 3y = -6 \Rightarrow y = -2$$

$\therefore$ Coordinates of B are (–5,–2) **(1 Mark)**

Note

The co-ordinates of point P(x, y) which divides line segment m:n internally is

$$(x, y) = \left(\frac{mx_2 + nx_1}{m+n}, \frac{my_2 + ny_1}{m+n}\right)$$

26.

Topper's Answer

choice - ①

k : 1

A(6,–4) —— P(0,y) —— B(–2,–7)

Let the y axis meet the line segment joining points A(6,–4) and B(–2,–7) be P(0,y).

Let P divide AB in the ratio k:1

coordinates of P : $P\left(\frac{-2k+6}{k+1}, \frac{-7k-4}{k+1}\right)$

$\frac{-2k+6}{k+1} = 0$

$-2k + 6 = 0$

$2k = 6$

$k = \frac{3}{2}$ [sic]

Ans: Ratio in which y axis divides AB = 3 : 1

$y = \frac{-7(3)-4}{(3)+1}$

$y = \frac{-21-4}{4}$

$y = \frac{-25}{4}$

Ans: Point of intersection of y axis and line segment = $P\left(0, \frac{-25}{4}\right)$.

27. Let the ratio be k : 1

By section formula, we have

$x = \dfrac{mx_2 + nx_1}{m+n}$, $y = \dfrac{my_2 + ny_1}{m+n}$ **(1 Mark)**

Here, $x_1 = -2$, $x_2 = 6$, $y_1 = -5$, $y_2 = 3$

m = k, n = 1

$\Rightarrow x = \dfrac{k(6)+(-2)}{k+1} = \dfrac{6k-2}{k+1}$

$\Rightarrow y = \dfrac{k(3)+(-5)}{k+1} = \dfrac{3k-5}{k+1}$

$\left(\dfrac{6k-2}{k+1}, \dfrac{3k-5}{k+1}\right)$ points lie on the line x – 3y = 0

$\therefore \left(\dfrac{6k-2}{k+1}\right) - 3\left(\dfrac{3k-5}{k+1}\right) = 0$

$\Rightarrow \dfrac{6k-2}{k+1} - \dfrac{(9k-15)}{k+1} = 0 \Rightarrow 6k - 2 - 9k + 15 = 0$

$\Rightarrow -3k + 13 = 0 \Rightarrow k = \dfrac{13}{3}$

Hence, ratio = 13 : 3 **(1 Mark)**

$\therefore x = \dfrac{6k-2}{k+1} = \dfrac{\dfrac{6\times13}{3}-2}{\dfrac{13}{3}+1} = \dfrac{(26-2)\times3}{16} = \dfrac{72}{16} = \dfrac{9}{2}$

$= \dfrac{3\quad 5}{} = \dfrac{3\times\dfrac{13}{}-5}{\dfrac{13}{}} = \dfrac{(13-5)\times3}{13+3} = \dfrac{24}{16} = \dfrac{3}{2}$

$\therefore$ Intersection point is $\left(\dfrac{9}{2}, \dfrac{3}{2}\right)$ **(1 Mark)**

28. Let the ratio be k : 1.

Then by the section formula, the co-ordinates of the point which divides AB in the ratio k :1 are

$\left(\dfrac{4k+1}{k+1}, \dfrac{5k-3}{k+1}\right)$. **(1 Mark)**

This point lies on the x-axis, and we know that on the x-axis, y = 0

$\therefore \dfrac{5k-3}{k+1} = 0 \Rightarrow 5k - 3 = 0 \Rightarrow k = \dfrac{3}{5}$.

That is, the ratio is (3/5) : 1 that is 3 :5.

Putting $k = \dfrac{3}{5}$, we get the point of intersection as $\left(\dfrac{17}{8}, 0\right)$.

(1 Mark)

29. K : 1

A (2, 3) —— P (4, m) —— B (6, –3)

Let P (4, m) divide AB in the ratio of K : 1

By section formula, $4 = \dfrac{K(6)+1(2)}{K+1}$

$\Rightarrow$ 4K + 4 = 6K + 2

$\Rightarrow$ 2 = 2K

$\Rightarrow$ K = 1 **(1 Mark)**

So, P (4, m) is midpoint of AB as it divides AB in the ratio of 1 : 1.

$\therefore \quad m = \dfrac{1(-3)+1(3)}{1+1} = \dfrac{-3+3}{2} = \dfrac{0}{2} = 0$

Hence the value of m = 0 **(1 Mark)**

30. The line intersects the y-axis at P and x-axis at Q and also given that, M(2 – 5) is mid-point of PQ.

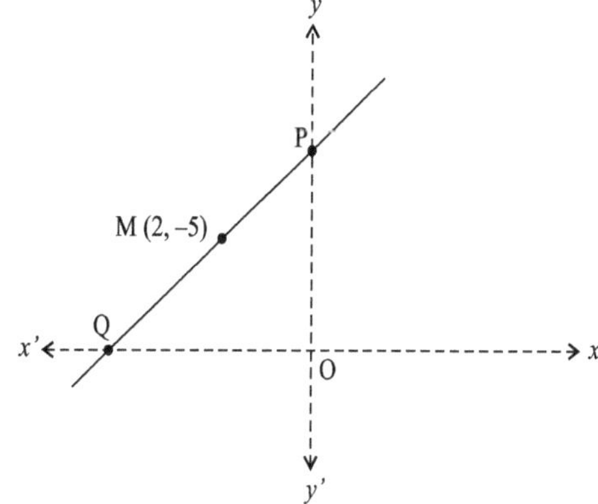

(1 Mark)

Using mid point formula, $M = \left(\frac{x_1+x_2}{2}, \frac{y_1+y_2}{2}\right)$

$$\left(\left(\frac{x+0}{2}\right), \left(\frac{0+y}{2}\right)\right) = (2, -5)$$

$$\Rightarrow \frac{x}{2} = 2, \frac{y}{2} = -5$$

$$\Rightarrow x = 4, y = -10$$

Thus the co-ordinates of P & Q are (0, –10) and (4, 0) respectively. **(1 Mark)**

31. Let point $R\left(\frac{24}{11}, y\right)$ divide the line segment joining the points P(2, –2) and Q(3, 7) in ratio k : 1, using

Then, by section formula.

$$x = \frac{kx_2 + x_1}{k+1}, y = \frac{ky_2 + y_1}{k+1}$$

$$\Rightarrow \frac{24}{11} = \frac{3k+2}{k+1}, y = \frac{7k-2}{k+1}$$ **(1 Mark)**

$$\Rightarrow 24(k+1) = 11(3k+2) \quad ...(i)$$

$$y(k+1) = 7k-2 \quad ...(ii)$$

From eqn. (i)

$$9k = 2 \Rightarrow k = \frac{2}{9}$$

Putting $k = \frac{2}{9}$ in eq. (ii), we have

$$y\left(\frac{2}{9}\right) + y = 7\left(\frac{2}{9}\right) - 2$$

$$\Rightarrow \frac{2y+9y}{9} = \frac{14-18}{9} \Rightarrow \frac{11y}{9} = \frac{-4}{9}$$

$$\Rightarrow y = \frac{-4}{11}$$

Thus, the given point $\left(\frac{24}{11}, y\right)$ divides the line segment in ratio 9 : 2 and value of y is $\frac{-4}{11}$ **(1 Mark)**

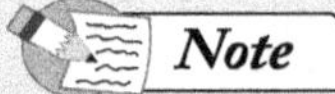

The other form of section formula is

$$(x, y) = \left(\frac{mx_2 + nx_1}{m+n}, \frac{my_2 + ny_1}{m+n}\right)$$

32. As the point lie on y axis, so it should be $(0, y)$

Let $P(0, y)$ divides $A(5, -6)$ and $B(-1, -4)$ into $k : 1$

$$P = \left(\frac{mx_2 + nx_1}{m+n}, \frac{my_2 + ny_1}{m+n}.\right)$$

$$\Rightarrow (0, y) = \left(\frac{-k+5}{k+1}, \frac{-4k+(-6)}{k+1}\right)$$

On equating x–coordinates

$$\Rightarrow \frac{-k+5}{k+1} = 0$$

$$\Rightarrow k = 5$$ **(1 Mark)**

Hence, P divides A and B in 5 : 1

Now equating y–coordinates

$$\frac{-4k-6}{k+1} = y$$

$$\Rightarrow \frac{-4(5)-6}{5+1} = y$$

$$\Rightarrow y = \frac{-26}{6} = \frac{-13}{3}$$

$\therefore$ Point P is $\left(0, -\frac{13}{3}\right)$ **(1 Mark)**

For finding ratio K:1 by equating x and y coordinate in section formula, if value of K is different then these three points are not collinear.

33.

A(–2, –2) ——3—— P ——4—— B(2, –4)

$$AP = \frac{3}{7}AB$$

$$\Rightarrow \frac{AP}{AB} = \frac{3}{7}$$ **(1 Mark)**

Taking reciprocal on both side

$$\frac{AB}{AP} = \frac{7}{3}$$

$$\Rightarrow \frac{AP+PB}{AP} = \frac{7}{3} \Rightarrow \frac{AP}{AP}+\frac{PB}{AP} = \frac{7}{3}$$

$$\Rightarrow 1 + \frac{PB}{AP} = \frac{7}{3} \Rightarrow \frac{PB}{AP} = \frac{7}{3}-1=\frac{4}{3}$$ **(1 Mark)**

Coordinates of $P = \left(\frac{mx_2+nx_1}{m+n}, \frac{my_2+ny_1}{m+n}\right)$

$$= \left(\frac{3(2)+4(-2)}{3+4}, \frac{3(-4)+4(-2)}{3+4}\right)$$

$$= \left(\frac{6-8}{7}, \frac{-12-8}{7}\right)$$

$$= \left(\frac{-2}{7}, \frac{-20}{7}\right)$$ **(1 Mark)**

34. $A(-4, -6)$ —— k —— $P(0, y)$ —— 1 —— $B(10, 12)$

Let P be the point on y-axis

$P(0, y)$

Let $P(0, y)$ divides $A(-4, -6)$, $B(10, 12)$ in $k : 1$

By section formula

$$P = \left(\frac{mx_2+nx_1}{m+n}, \frac{my_2+ny_1}{m+n}\right)$$ **(1 Mark)**

$$(0, y) = \left(\frac{10k-4}{k+1}, \frac{12k-6}{k+1}\right)$$

On equating x–coordinate

$$\frac{10k-4}{k+1} = 0$$

$$\Rightarrow 10k = 4$$

$$\Rightarrow k = \frac{4}{10} = \frac{2}{5}$$ **(1 Mark)**

Thus y axis divides AB in 2 : 5.

On equating y-coordinate

$$y = \frac{12k-6}{k+1}$$

$$\Rightarrow y = \frac{12\left(\frac{2}{5}\right)-6}{\frac{2}{5}+1} = \frac{\frac{24-30}{5}}{\frac{7}{5}} = -\frac{6}{7}$$

Thus, coordinates of the point of division are $\left(0, -\frac{6}{7}\right)$

(1 Mark)

Note

Distance between a point (x, y) from origin is given by $\sqrt{x^2+y^2}$

35. It is given that points A$(k+1, 2k)$, B $(3k, 2k+3)$ and C$((5k-1), 5k)$ are collinear **(1 Mark)**

$\therefore$ The area of triangle formed with these points = 0

$$\Rightarrow \frac{1}{2}\left[x_1(y_2-y_3)+x_2(y_3-y_1)+x_3(y_1-y_2)\right]=0$$ **(1 Mark)**

$$\Rightarrow \frac{1}{2}[(k+1)\{(2k+3)-5k\}+3k(5k-2k)+(5k-1)\{2k-(2k+3)\}] = 0$$

$$\Rightarrow (k+1)(-3k+3)+3k(3k)+(5k-1)(-3) = 0$$

$$\Rightarrow -3k^2+3k-3k+3+9k^2-15k+3 = 0$$

$$\Rightarrow 6k^2-15k+6 = 0$$ **(1 Mark)**

Dividing by 3 on both sides of equation we get

$$\Rightarrow 2k^2-5k+2 = 0$$

$$\Rightarrow 2k^2-4k-k+2 = 0$$

$$\Rightarrow 2k(k-2)-1(k-2) = 0$$

$$\Rightarrow (2k-1)(k-2) = 0$$

$\Rightarrow$ $(2k - 1) = 0$ or $(k - 2) = 0$

$\Rightarrow$ $k = \frac{1}{2}, 2$

Thus, the required values of k are $\frac{1}{2}$ and 2. **(1 Mark)**

36. Let point P (x, 2) divides the line segment joining the points A(12, 5) and B(4, –3) in the ratio k : 1

Coordinates of $P = \left(\frac{mx_2 + nx_1}{m+n}, \frac{my_2 + ny_1}{m+n}\right)$ **(1 Mark)**

$(x, 2) = \left(\frac{4k+12}{k+1}, \frac{-3k+5}{k+1}\right)$

On equating the corresponding coordinates

$x = \frac{4k+12}{k+1}, \ 2 = \frac{-3k+5}{k+1}$ **(½ Mark)**

$\frac{-3k+5}{k+1} = 2$

$\Rightarrow -3k + 5 = 2k + 2 \Rightarrow 5k = 3$

$k = \frac{3}{5}$ ...(1) **(½ Mark)**

$x = \frac{4k+12}{k+1}$

$x = \frac{4\left(\frac{3}{5}\right)+12}{\left(\frac{3}{5}\right)+1}$ (from (1))

$= \frac{12+60}{3+5} = \frac{72}{8} = 9$ **(1 Mark)**

Thus point P divides line segment A(12, 5) and B(4, –3) in the ratio 3:5. **(1 Mark)**

37. (i) Let D be (a, b) then

Mid point of AC = Midpoint of BD

$\left(\frac{1+6}{2}, \frac{2+6}{2}\right) = \left(\frac{4+a}{2}, \frac{3+b}{2}\right)$

$\Rightarrow \left(\frac{7}{2}, 4\right) = \left(\frac{4+a}{2}, \frac{3+b}{2}\right)$ **(½ Mark)**

So, we have

$4 + a = 7$ $\quad$ $3 + b = 8$

$a = 3$ $\quad$ $b = 5$

Central midfielder is at (3, 5) **(½ Mark)**

(ii) $GH = \sqrt{(-3-3)^2 + (5-1)^2} = \sqrt{36+16}$

$= \sqrt{52} = 2\sqrt{13}$ **(½ Mark)**

$GK = \sqrt{(0+3)^2 + (3-5)^2} = \sqrt{9+4} = \sqrt{13}$

(½ Mark)

$HK = \sqrt{(3-0)^2 + (1-3)^2} = \sqrt{9+4} = \sqrt{13}$

(½ Mark)

GK + HK = GH $\Rightarrow$ G, H & K lie on a same straight line **(½ Mark)**

OR

$CJ = \sqrt{(0-5)^2 + (1+3)^2} = \sqrt{25+16} = \sqrt{41}$

(½ Mark)

$CI = \sqrt{(0+4)^2 + (1-6)^2} = \sqrt{16+25} = \sqrt{41}$

(½ Mark)

Full–back J (5, –3) and centre–back I (–4, 6) are equidistant from forward C(0, 1) **(½ Mark)**

Mid–point of IJ = $\left(\frac{5-4}{2}, \frac{-3+6}{2}\right) = \left(\frac{1}{2}, \frac{3}{2}\right)$

(½ Mark)

C is NOT the mid–point of IJ

(iii) A, B and E lie on the same straight line and B is equidistant from A and E

$\Rightarrow$ B is the mid–point of AE **(½ Mark)**

$\left(\frac{1+a}{2}, \frac{4+b}{2}\right) = (2, -3)$ **(½ Mark)**

Then we get $\Rightarrow \frac{1+a}{2} = 2; \frac{4+b}{2} = -3$

38. (i) As PQRS being a square. So its all sides are equal.

PQ = PS = SR = RQ

By using distance formula,

$PQ = \sqrt{(200+200)^2 + (0-0)^2} = \sqrt{1600+0} = 400$

Here, S = (–200, y), P = (–200,0) **(1 Mark)**

$PS = \sqrt{(-200+200)^2 + (0-y)^2} = 400$

$\Rightarrow \sqrt{y^2} = 400 = 400$

S = (–200, 400)
R = (200, 400)

(ii) (a) Area of square PQRS = $(side)^2$

$= (400)^2 = 1600$ sq. units **(2 Marks)**

OR

(b) $PR^2 = PQ^2 + QR^2 = (400)^2 + (400)^2 = 3200$

$PR = 400\sqrt{2}$ unit **(2 Marks)**

(iii) C —K— S —1— A

C = (–600, 0); S = (–200, 400); A = (200, 800) **(1 Mark)**

39. (i) B(1,2), F(-2,9)

$BF^2 = (-2-1)^2 + (9-2)^2$

$= (-3)^2 + (7)^2$

$= 9 + 49 = 58$

So, $BF = \sqrt{58}$ units **(1 Mark)**

(ii)

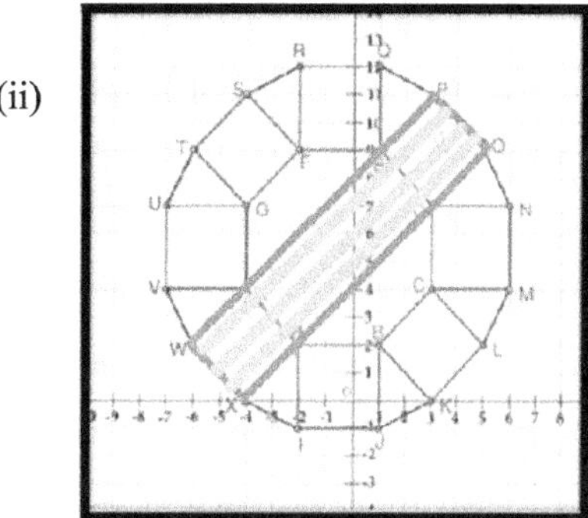

W(–6, 2), X(–4, 0), O(5, 9), P(3, 11) **(½ Mark)**

Clearly WXOP is a rectangle

Point of intersection of diagonals of a rectangle is the mid point of the diagonals. So the required point is mid point of WO or XP

$= \left(\frac{-6+5}{2}, \frac{2+9}{2}\right)$ **(½ Mark)**

$= \left(\frac{-1}{2}, \frac{11}{2}\right)$

(iii) A(–2, 2), G(–4, 7)

Let the point on y-axis be Z(0,y) **(½ Mark)**

$AZ^2 = GZ^2$ **(½ Mark)**

$(0+2)^2 + (y-2)^2 = (0+4)^2 + (y-7)^2$

$(2)^2 + y^2 + 4 - 4y = (4)^2 + y^2 + 49 - 14y$

$8 - 4y = 65 - 14y$

$10y = 57$

So, y= 5.7 **(1 Mark)**

i.e. the required point is (0, 5.7)

OR

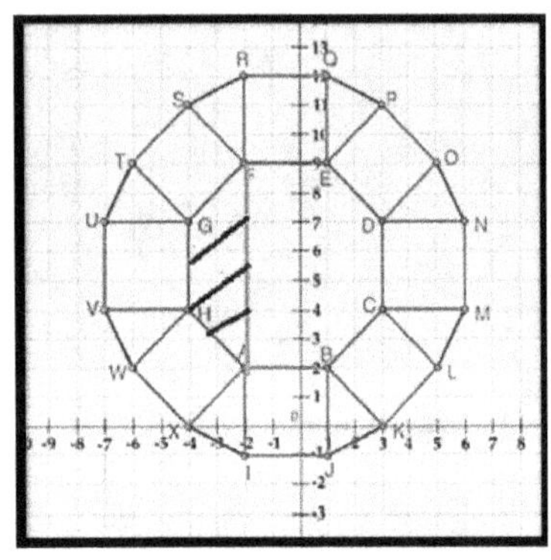

A(–2, 2), F(–2, 9), G(–4, 7), H(–4, 4)

Clearly GH = 7 – 4 =3units **(½ Mark)**

AF = 9 – 2 = 7 units **(½ Mark)**

So, height of the trapezium AFGH = 2 units

So, area of AFGH = $\frac{1}{2}$(AF + GH) × height

$= \frac{1}{2}(7 + 3) \times 2$ **(½ Mark)**

= 10 sq. units **(½ Mark)**

Chapter 8 Introduction to Trigonometry

Topic-1: Trigonometric Ratios

Multiple Choice Questions

1. Given that $\sin\theta = \frac{a}{b}$, then $\cos\theta$.

[CBSE Sample Paper 2023-24, K]

(a) $\frac{b}{\sqrt{b^2 - a^2}}$

(b) $\frac{b}{a}$

(c) $\frac{\sqrt{b^2 - a^2}}{b}$

(d) $\frac{a}{\sqrt{b^2 - a^2}}$

2. If $\tan\theta = \frac{5}{12}$, then the value of $\frac{\sin\theta + \cos\theta}{\sin\theta - \cos\theta}$ is :

[All India 2023, K]

(a) $-\frac{17}{7}$

(b) $\frac{17}{7}$

(c) $\frac{17}{13}$

(d) $-\frac{7}{13}$

3. Which of the following is true for all values of $\theta (0° \le \theta \le 90°)$? **[Delhi 2023, K]**

(a) $\cos^2\theta - \sin^2\theta = 1$

(b) $\text{cosec}^2\theta - \sec^2\theta = 1$

(c) $\sec^2\theta - \tan^2\theta = 1$

(d) $\cot^2\theta - \tan^2\theta = 1$

4. If 5 $\tan\beta$ =4, then $\frac{5\sin\beta - 2\cos\beta}{5\sin\beta + 2\cos\beta} =$

[CBSE Sample Paper 2022-23, K]

(a) 1/3

(b) 2/5

(c) 3/5

(d) 6

5. In ΔABC right angled at B, $\sin A \; \frac{\quad}{25}$, then the value of $\cos C$ is **[All India 2022, Term-I, K]**

(a) $\frac{7}{25}$

(b) $\frac{24}{25}$

(c) $\frac{7}{24}$

(d) $\frac{24}{7}$

6. If $4 \tan \beta = 3$, then $\frac{4\sin\beta - 3\cos\beta}{4\sin\beta + 3\cos\beta} =$

[CBSE Sample Paper 2021-22, Term-I K]

(a) 0

(b) 1/3

(c) 2/3

(d) $\frac{3}{4}$

7. In the given figure, D is the mid-point of BC, then the value of $\frac{\cot y^\circ}{\cot x^\circ}$ is

[CBSE Sample Paper 2021-22, Term-I, K]

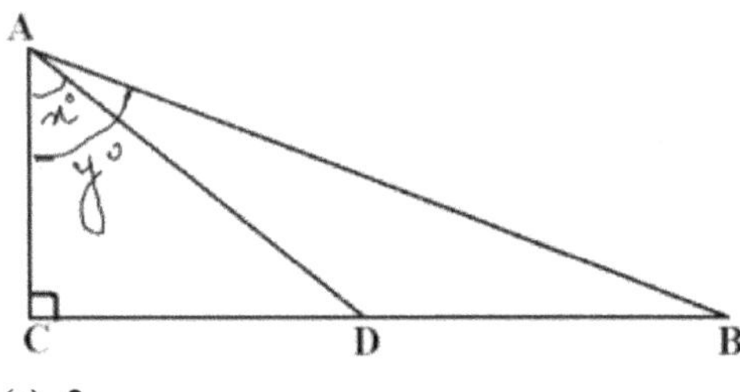

(a) 2

(b) $\frac{1}{2}$

(c) $\frac{1}{3}$

(d) $\frac{1}{4}$

4 *Very Short Answer Question (1 Mark)*

8. If $\sin A = \frac{3}{4}$, calculate sec A. **[All India 2019, K]**

5 *Short Answer Questions (2 or 3 Marks)*

9. The rod AC of a TV disc antenna is fixed at right angles to the wall AB and a rod CD is supporting the disc as shown in Fig. 4. If AC = 1.5 m long and CD = 3 m, find (i) $\tan \theta$, (ii) $\sec \theta + \text{cosec } \theta$ **[Delhi 2020, U]**

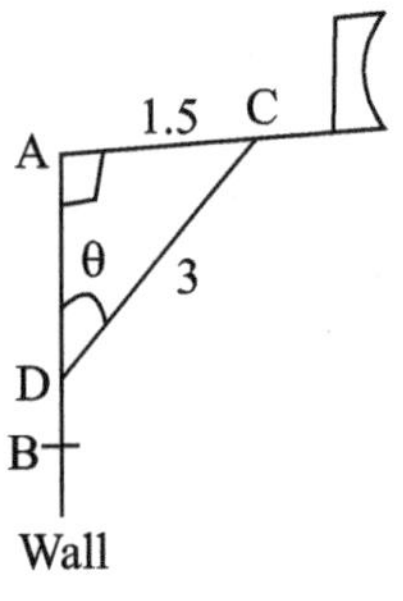

[Fig.]

10. If $4 \tan \theta = 3$, evaluate $\left(\frac{4\sin\theta - \cos\theta + 1}{4\sin\theta + \cos\theta - 1}\right)$

[All India 2018, K]

11. If in a triangle *ABC* right angled at *B*, *AB* = 6 units and *BC* = 8 units, then find the value of sin *A* . cos *C* + *cos A*. sin *C*. **[All India 2017 Term-I, A]**

12. P, 40, 41, Q 9 cm R

In the given ΔPQR, right-angled at *Q*, *QR* = 9 cm and *PR* – *PQ* = 1 cm. Determine the value of sin *R* + cos *R*.

[Delhi 2016 Term-I, A]

Topic-2: Trigonometric Ratios of Some Specific Angles

1 Multiple Choice Questions

1. $\left(\frac{1-\tan^2 30°}{1+\tan^2 30°}\right)$ is equal to : **[All India 2023, K]**

(a) sin 60

(b) cos 60°

(c) tan 60°

(d) cos 30°

2. If x tan 60°cos 60° = sin60°cot 60°, then x = **[CBSE Sample Paper 2022-23, K]**

(a) cos30°

(b) tan30°

(c) sin30°

(d) cot30°

3. If sinθ + cosθ = $\sqrt{2}$, then tanθ + cotθ = **[CBSE Sample Paper 2022-23, U]**

(a) 1

(b) 2

(c) 3

(d) 4

4. If $\cot\theta = \frac{1}{\sqrt{3}}$, then value of $\sec^2\theta + \text{cosec}^2\theta$ is **[All India 2022, Term-I, K]**

(a) 1

(b) $\frac{40}{9}$

(c) $\frac{38}{9}$

(d) $5\frac{1}{3}$

5. Given that $\sec\theta = \sqrt{2}$, the value of $\frac{1+\tan\theta}{\sin\theta}$ is **[All India 2022, Term-I, K]**

(a) $2\sqrt{2}$

(b) $\sqrt{2}$

(c) $3\sqrt{2}$

(d) 2

6. If the angles of ΔABC are in ratio 1 : 1 : 2, respectively (the largest angle being angle C), then the value of $\frac{\sec A}{\text{cosec}\, B} - \frac{\tan A}{\cot B}$ is **[CBSE Sample Paper 2021-22, Term-I, K]**

(a) 0

(b) 1/2

(c) 1

(d) $\sqrt{3}/2$

7. $\frac{2\tan 30°}{1-\tan^2 30°}$ = **[Delhi 2014, Term-I, K]**

(a) cos 60°

(b) sin 60°

(c) tan 60°

(d) sin 30°

4 Very Short Answer Questions (1 Mark)

8. Evaluate: $\frac{5}{\cot^2 30°} + \frac{1}{\sin^2 60°} - \cot^2 45° + 2\sin^2 90°$ **[Delhi 2023, K]**

9. If θ is an acute angle and sinθ = cosθ, find the value of $\tan^2\theta + \cot^2\theta - 2$. **[Delhi 2023, K]**

10. Evaluate :
$\sin^2 60° + 2\tan 45° - \cos^2 30°$ **[All India 2019, K]**

11. If $\sin(A+B) = 1$ and $\sin(A-B) = \frac{1}{2}$, $0 \le A+B = 90°$ and $A > B$, then find A and B. **[All India 2017, Term-I, U]**

12. If $\tan(3x + 30°) = 1$ then find the value of x. **[Delhi 2016, Term-I K]**

5 *Short Answer Questions (2 or 3 Marks)*

13. If $\tan(A + B) = \sqrt{3}$ and $\tan(A - B) = \frac{1}{\sqrt{3}}$, $0° < A + B < 90°$; $A > B$, find A and B.

[CBSE Sample Paper 2022-23, 2023-24, K]

14. Find the value of x if $2 \text{ cosec}^2 30 + x \sin^2 60 - \frac{3}{4}\tan^2 30 = 10$ **[CBSE Sample Paper 2023-24, K]**

15. If $\tan(A + B) = 1$ and $\tan(A - B) = \frac{1}{\sqrt{3}}$, $0° < A + B < 90°$, $A > B$, then find the values of A and B.

[All India 2019, K]

16. Evaluate :

$\tan^2 30° \sin 30° + \cos 60° \sin^2 90° \tan^2 60° - 2 \tan 45° \cos^2 0° \sin 90°$. **[Delhi 2016 Term-I, K]**

Topic-3: Trigonometric Identities

1 *Multiple Choice Questions*

1. $(\sec A + \tan A)(1 - \sin A) =$ **[CBSE Sample Paper 2023-24, U]**

   (a) sec A
   (b) sin A
   (c) cosec A
   (d) cos A

2. $\frac{\cos^2\theta}{\sin^2\theta} - \frac{1}{\sin^2\theta}$, in simplified form is :

   [All India 2023 Set-II, U]

   (a) $\tan^2\theta$
   (b) $\sec^2\theta$
   (c) 1
   (d) −1

3. If θ is an acute angle of a right angled triangle, then which of the following equation is **not** true?

   [All India 2023 Set-II, U]

   (a) $\sin\theta \cot\theta = \cos\theta$
   (b) $\cos\theta \tan\theta = \sin\theta$
   (c) $\text{cosec}^2\theta - \cot^2\theta = 1$
   (d) $\tan^2\theta - \sec^2\theta = 1$

4. If θ is an acute angle and $\tan\theta + \cot\theta = 2$, then the value of $\sin^3\theta + \cos^3\theta$ is **[All India 2022 Term-I, U]**

   (a) 1
   (b) $\frac{1}{2}$
   (c) $\frac{\sqrt{2}}{2}$
   (d) $\sqrt{2}$

5. If $a \cot\theta + b \text{ cosec}\theta = p$ and $b \cot\theta + a \text{ cosec}\theta = q$, then $p^2 - q^2 =$ **[All India 2022 Term-I, U]**

   (a) $a^2 - b^2$
   (b) $b^2 - a^2$
   (c) $a^2 + b^2$
   (d) $b - a$

6. If $\sec\theta + \tan\theta = p$, then $\tan\theta$ is

   [All India 2022 Term-I, A]

   (a) $\frac{p^2+1}{2p}$
   (b) $\frac{p^2-1}{2p}$
   (c) $\frac{p^2-1}{p^2+1}$
   (d) $\frac{p^2+1}{p^2-1}$

7. If $2\sin^2\beta - \cos^2\beta = 2$, then β is

[CBSE Sample Paper 2021-22, Term-I, U]

(a) 0°

(b) 90°

(c) 45°

(d) 30°

8. If $\tan\alpha + \cot\alpha = 2$, then $\tan^{20}\alpha + \cot^{20}\alpha =$

[CBSE Sample Paper 2021-22, Term-I, U]

(a) 0

(b) 2

(c) 20

(d) 2^{20}

9. If $1 + \sin^2\alpha = 3\sin\alpha\cos\alpha$, then values of $\cot\alpha$ are

[CBSE Sample Paper 2021-22, Term-I, A]

(a) –1, 1

(b) 0, 1

(c) 1, 2

(d) –1, –1

10. $(1 + \tan^2\theta).\cos^2\theta =$ **[Delhi 2014, Term-I, K]**

(a) $\dfrac{1}{\sin^2\theta - \cos^2\theta}$

(b) $\sec^2\theta$

(c) 1

(d) $\dfrac{1}{2}$

2 *Assertion Reason/Two Statement Type Questions*

11. **Statement A (Assertion):** For $0 < \theta \le 90°$, $\text{cosec}\,\theta - \cot\theta$ and $\text{cosec}\,\theta + \cot\theta$ are reciprocal of each other.
Statement R (Reasion): $\text{cosec}^2\theta - \cot^2\theta = 1$

[All India 2023 Set-II, A]

(a) Both Assertion (A) and Reason (R) are true; and Reason (R) is the correct explanation of Assertion (A).

(b) Both Assertion (A) and Reason (R) are true; but Reason (R) is not the correct explanation of Assertion (A).

(c) Assertion (A is true but Reason (R) is false.

(d) Assertion (A) is false but Reason (R) is true.

4 *Very Short Answer Questions (1 Mark)*

12. If $a\cos\theta + b\sin\theta = m$ and $a\sin\theta - b\cos\theta = n$, then prove that $a^2 + b^2 = m^2 + n^2$. **[All India 2023, A]**

13. Prove that:

$$\sqrt{\frac{\sec A - 1}{\sec A + 1}} + \sqrt{\frac{\sec A + 1}{\sec A - 1}} = 2\text{cosec}\,A$$

14. Prove that: **[All India 2023, U]**

$$\frac{\tan\theta}{1-\cot\theta} + \frac{\cot\theta}{1-\tan\theta} = 1 + \sec\theta\,\text{cosec}\,\theta$$

15. If $\sin A + \sin^2 A = 1$, then find the value of the expression $(\cos^2 A + \cos^4 A)$. **[All India 2020, K]**

16. The value of $\left(\sin^2\theta + \dfrac{1}{1+\tan^2\theta}\right) =$ ____________

[Delhi 2020, A]

17. The value of $(1+\tan^2\theta)(1-\sin\theta)(1+\sin\theta)$

= ____________. **[Delhi 2020, A]**

5 Short Answer Questions (2 or 3 Marks)

18. If $1 + \sin^2\theta = 3\sin\theta\cos\theta$, then prove that $\tan\theta = 1$ or $\frac{1}{2}$

[CBSE Sample Paper 2023-24, U]

19. Prove that $\frac{1+\sec A}{\sec A} = \frac{\sin^2 A}{1-\cos A}$.

[All India 2023 Set-II, U]

20. If $\frac{1}{\sin\theta-\cos\theta} = \frac{\operatorname{cosec}\theta}{\sqrt{2}}$, prove that $\left(\frac{1}{\sin\theta+\cos\theta}\right)^2 = \frac{\sec^2\theta}{2}$.

[CBSE CFPQ 2022, U]

21. Prove the following that-

$$\frac{\tan^3\theta}{1+\tan^2\theta} + \frac{\cot^3\theta}{1+\cot^2\theta} = \sec\theta\operatorname{cosec}\theta - 2\sin\theta\cos\theta$$

[CBSE CFPQ 2022, A]

22. Prove the following.

$$\frac{1}{\operatorname{cosec}\theta - \cot\theta} - \frac{\cot\theta}{\cos\theta} = \cot\theta$$

(CBSE CFPQ 2022, A)

23. Prove that: **(CBSE CFPQ 2022, A)**

$$\frac{\operatorname{cosec}^2 x - \sin^2 x\cot^2 x - \cot^2 x}{\sin^2 x} = 1$$

24. Prove that $1 + \frac{\cot^2\alpha}{1+\operatorname{cosec}\alpha} = \operatorname{cosec}\alpha$

[All India 2020, K]

25. Show that $\tan^4\theta + \tan^2\theta = \sec^4\theta - \sec^2\theta$

[All India 2020, K]

26. If $\sin\theta + \cos\theta = \sqrt{2}$, prove that $\tan\theta + \cot\theta = 2$.

[All India 2020, K]

27. If $\sin\theta + \cos\theta = \sqrt{3}$, then prove that $\tan\theta + \cot\theta = 1$.

[Delhi 2020, U]

28. Prove that:

$$\frac{2\cos^3\theta - \cos\theta}{\sin\theta - 2\sin^3\theta} - \cot\theta$$

[All India 2020, U]

29. Prove that

$(\sin\theta + \operatorname{cosec}\theta)^2 + (\cos\theta + \sec\theta)^2 = 7 + \tan^2\theta + \cot^2\theta$.

[Delhi 2019, A]

30. Prove that $(1 + \cot A - \operatorname{cosec} A)(1 + \tan A + \sec A) = 2$

[Delhi 2019, A]

31. Prove that

$$(\operatorname{cosec}\theta - \sin\theta)(\sec\theta - \cos\theta) = \sin\theta.\cos\theta = \frac{1}{\tan\theta + \cot\theta}$$

[All India 2017, Term-I, A]

32. Prove that : $(\cot\theta - \operatorname{cosec}\theta)^2 = \frac{1-\cos\theta}{1+\cos\theta}$

[Delhi 2016, Term-I, A]

33. Prove that $\frac{1+\cos^2\theta}{\sin^2\theta} = 2\operatorname{cosec}^2\theta - 1$

[All India 2015, Term-I, U]

34. Prove that: $\frac{\sin\theta}{\cot\theta + \operatorname{cosec}\theta} = 2 + \frac{\sin\theta}{\cot\theta - \operatorname{cosec}\theta}$

(All India 2015, Term-I, A)

35. Simplify : $\frac{\sin^3\theta + \cos^3\theta}{\sin\theta + \cos\theta} + \sin\theta\cos\theta$

[All India 2015 Term-I, A]

36. Prove that:

$$\tan^2 A - \tan^2 B = \frac{\cos^2 B - \cos^2 A}{\cos^2 B\cos^2 A} = \frac{\sin^2 A - \sin^2 B}{\cos^2 A\cos^2 B}$$

[All India 2015 Term-I, A]

37. Prove that:

$$\frac{\sin\theta - \cos\theta}{\sin\theta + \cos\theta} + \frac{\sin\theta + \cos\theta}{\sin\theta - \cos\theta} = \frac{2}{2\sin^2\theta - 1}$$

[Delhi 2014 Term-I, A]

38. If $x = p\sec\theta + q\tan\theta$

$y = p\tan\theta + q\sec\theta$

Prove that $x^2 - y^2 = p^2 - q^2$ **[Delhi 2014 Term-I, A]**

Long Answer Questions (4 or 5 Marks)

39. Prove that :

$$\frac{\tan\theta}{1-\cot\theta}+\frac{\cot\theta}{1-\tan\theta}=1+\sec\theta\ \text{cosec}\,\theta$$

[All India 2019, A]

40. Prove that :

$$\frac{\sin\theta}{\cot\theta+\text{cosec}\,\theta}=2+\frac{\sin\theta}{\cot\theta-\text{cosec}\,\theta}$$ **[All India 2019, A]**

41. Prove that $\frac{\sin A-\cos A+1}{\sin A+\cos A-1}=\frac{1}{\sec A-\tan A}$

[Delhi 2019, A]

42. Prove that : $\frac{\sin A-2\sin^3 A}{2\cos^3 A-\cos A}=\tan A$ **[All India 2018, A]**

43. If $m=\cos\theta-\sin\theta$ and $n=\cos\theta+\sin\theta$ than show that $\sqrt{\frac{m}{n}}+\sqrt{\frac{n}{m}}=\frac{2}{\sqrt{1-\tan^2\theta}}$ **[All India 2017 Term-I, A]**

44. Prove that

$$\frac{\sin A-\cos A+1}{\sin A+\cos A-1}=\frac{1}{\sec A-\tan A}.$$

[All India 2017 Term-I, A]

45. Prove that $b^2x^2-a^2y^2=a^2b^2$, if :

(i) $x=a\sec\theta, y=b\tan\theta$, or

(ii) $x=a\,\text{cosec}\,\theta, y=b\cot\theta$. **[Delhi 2016 Term-I, A]**

46. If $\sec\theta+\tan\theta=p$, show that $\sec\theta-\tan\theta=\frac{1}{p}$. Hence, find the values of $\cos\theta$ and $\sin\theta$. **[Delhi 2016 Term-I, A]**

47. Prove that

$$\frac{\tan\theta}{1-\cot\theta}+\frac{\cot\theta}{1-\tan\theta}=1+\tan\theta+\cot\theta=\sec\theta\,\text{cosec}\theta+1$$

[All India 2015 Term-I, A]

48. Prove : $\cot^2\theta\left(\frac{\sec\theta-1}{1+\sin\theta}\right)+\sec^2\theta\left(\frac{\sin\theta-1}{1+\sec\theta}\right)=0$

[All India 2015 Term-I, A]

49. If $\text{cosec}\theta+\cot\theta=P$, Prove that $\cos\theta=\frac{P^2-1}{P^2+1}$

[Delhi 2014 Term-I, A]

50. Prove that

$$\left(\frac{1+\sin\theta-\cos\theta}{1+\sin\theta+\cos\theta}\right)^2=\frac{1-\cos\theta}{1+\cos\theta}$$ **[Delhi 2014 Term-I, A]**

Hints & Solutions

Topic-1: Trigonometric Ratios

1. **(c)** $\frac{\sqrt{b^2-a^2}}{b}$ **(1 Mark)**

2. **(a)** Given, $\tan\theta = \frac{5}{12}$

$$\Rightarrow \frac{\sin\theta+\cos\theta}{\sin\theta-\cos\theta} = \frac{\cos\theta\left(\frac{\sin\theta}{\cos\theta}+1\right)}{\cos\theta\left(\frac{\sin\theta}{\cos\theta}-1\right)}$$

$$\Rightarrow \left(\frac{\tan\theta+1}{\tan\theta-1}\right) = \frac{\left(\frac{5}{12}+1\right)}{\left(\frac{5}{12}-1\right)} = -\frac{17}{7}$$ **(1 Mark)**

3. **(c)** As $1+\tan^2\theta = \sec^2\theta \Rightarrow \sec^2\theta - \tan^2\theta = 1$

$0° \le \theta \le 90$ **(1 Mark)**

4. **(a)** 1/3 **(1 Mark)**

5. **(a)** $\sin A = \frac{7}{25} = \frac{P}{H}$

Apply pythagoras theorem

$\cos C = \frac{B}{H} = \frac{BC}{AC}$

$= \frac{7}{25}$

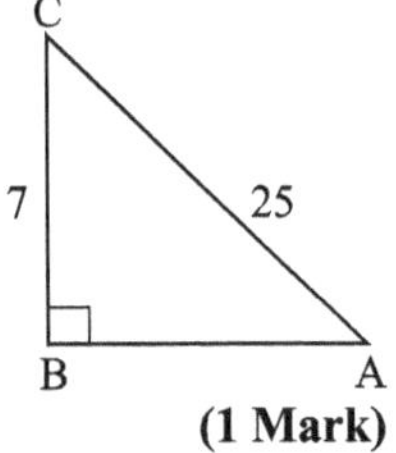

(1 Mark)

6. **(a)** Dividing both numerator and denominator by by $\cos\beta$,

$$\frac{4\sin\beta-3\cos\beta}{4\sin\beta+3\cos\beta} = \frac{4\tan\beta-3}{4\tan\beta+3} = \frac{3-3}{3+3} = 0$$ **(1 Mark)**

7. **(b)** From ΔACB

$$\frac{\cot y°}{\cot x°} = \frac{AC/BC}{AC/CD} = CD/BC = CD/2CD = \frac{1}{2}$$ **(1 Mark)**

8. $\sin A = \frac{P}{H} = \frac{3}{4}$

$\therefore$ P = 3k and H = 4k **(½ Mark)**

$P^2 + B^2 = H^2$

[Applying Pythagoras theorem]

$\Rightarrow 9k^2 + B^2 = 16k^2$

$\Rightarrow B^2 = 7k^2$

$\Rightarrow B = \sqrt{7}k$

$\therefore \sec A = \frac{H}{B} = \frac{4k}{\sqrt{7}k} = \frac{4}{\sqrt{7}}$ **(½ Mark)**

Note

Another way to find secA by using following formula. cosA $= \sqrt{1-\sin^2 A}$ and secA $= \frac{1}{\cos A}$

9. $AD = \sqrt{CD^2 - AC^2} = \sqrt{3^2-(1.5)^2} = \sqrt{9-2.25}$

$= \sqrt{6.75} = \frac{3\sqrt{3}}{2}$

(i) $\tan\theta = \frac{P}{B} = \frac{AC}{AD} = \frac{1.5}{3\sqrt{3}/2}$

$= \frac{3}{3\sqrt{3}} = \frac{1}{\sqrt{3}}$ **(1 Mark)**

(ii) $\sec\theta + \text{cosec}\theta = \frac{CD}{AD} + \frac{CD}{AC}$

$= \frac{3}{3\sqrt{3}/2} + \frac{3}{1.5} = \frac{2}{\sqrt{3}} + \frac{30}{15}$

$= \frac{2\times\sqrt{3}}{\sqrt{3}\times\sqrt{3}} + \frac{2}{1} = \frac{2\sqrt{3}}{3} + \frac{2}{1}$

$= \frac{2\sqrt{3}+6}{3} = \frac{2(\sqrt{3}+3)}{3}$ **(1 Mark)**

10.

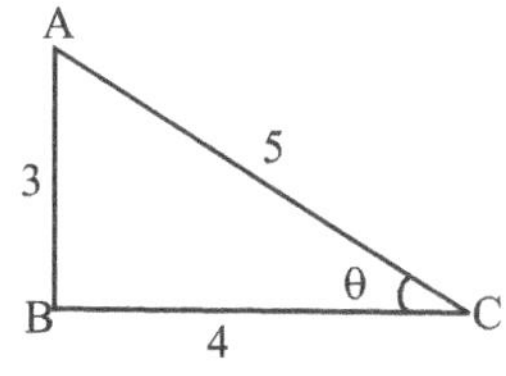

As $4\tan\theta = 3$

$$\Rightarrow \quad \tan\theta = \frac{3}{4} = \frac{\text{Perpendicular}}{\text{Base}} = \frac{AB}{BC}$$ **(1 Mark)**

By Pythagoras theorem, $AC = \sqrt{4^2 + 3^2} = \sqrt{25} = 5$

$$\therefore \sin\theta = \frac{\text{Perpendicular}}{\text{Hypotenuse}} = \frac{3}{5} \text{ and } \cos\theta = \frac{\text{Base}}{\text{Hypotenuse}} = \frac{4}{5}$$

$$\Rightarrow \quad \frac{4\sin\theta - \cos\theta + 1}{4\sin\theta + \cos\theta - 1} = \frac{4(3/5) - (4/5) + 1}{4(3/5) + \frac{4}{5} - 1}$$

$$= \frac{\frac{12-4+5}{5}}{\frac{12+4-5}{5}} = \frac{13/5}{\frac{11}{5}} = \frac{13}{11}$$ **(1 Mark)**

11.

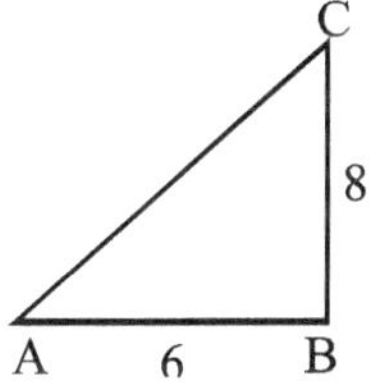

(By Pythagoras theorem)

$$AC^2 = (8)^2 + (6)^2 = 100$$

$$\Rightarrow \quad AC = 10$$ **(½ Mark)**

$$\therefore \quad \sin A = \frac{BC}{AC} = \frac{8}{10},$$

$$\cos A = \frac{AB}{AC} = \frac{6}{10}$$ **(½ Mark)**

and $\sin C = \dfrac{AB}{AC} = \dfrac{6}{10}$,

$$\cos C = \frac{BC}{AC} = \frac{8}{10}$$ **(½ Mark)**

$$\therefore \quad \sin A \cos C + \cos A \sin C$$

$$= \frac{8}{10} \times \frac{8}{10} + \frac{6}{10} \times \frac{6}{10}$$

$$\frac{64 + 36}{100} = 1$$ **(½ Mark)**

Note

Side opposite right angle of triangle is called hypotenuse and side opposite acute angle which we consider is called perpendicular and third side is called base.

12.

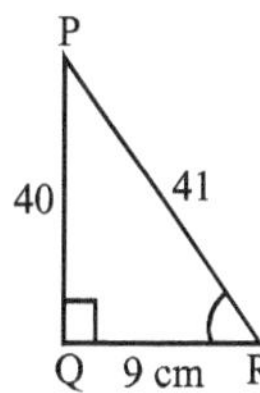

(By Pythagoras theorem)

$$PQ^2 + QR^2 = PR^2$$ **(½ Mark)**

$$\Rightarrow \quad PQ^2 + 9^2 = PR^2$$

$$PQ^2 + 81 = (PQ + 1)^2$$

$$PQ^2 + 81 = PQ^2 + 1 + 2PQ$$

$$\Rightarrow 2PQ = 80$$

$$\Rightarrow \quad PQ = 40$$ **(1 Mark)**

$$PR - PQ = 1$$ (Given)

$$\Rightarrow \quad PR = 1 + 40$$

$$\Rightarrow \quad PR = 41$$

$$\therefore \quad \sin R + \cos R = \frac{40}{41} + \frac{9}{41} = \frac{49}{41}$$ **(½ Mark)**

Topic-2: Trigonometric Ratios of Some Specific Angles

1. **(b)** $\left(\dfrac{1-\tan^2 30^\circ}{1+\tan^2 30^\circ}\right)$

$$\Rightarrow \left(\dfrac{1-\left(\dfrac{1}{\sqrt{3}}\right)^2}{1+\left(\dfrac{1}{\sqrt{3}}\right)^2}\right)=\dfrac{\left(1-\dfrac{1}{3}\right)}{\left(1+\dfrac{1}{3}\right)}=\dfrac{2}{4}$$

$\Rightarrow \dfrac{1}{2}=\sin 30^\circ \text{ or } \cos 60^\circ$ **(1 Mark)**

2. **(b)** $\tan 30^\circ$ **(1 Mark)**

3. **(b)** 2 **(1 Mark)**

4. **(d)** Given, $\cot\theta = \dfrac{1}{\sqrt{3}}$

$\cot\theta = \cot 60^\circ$

$\theta = 60^\circ$

$\sec^2\theta + \text{cosec}^2\theta = \sec^2 60 + \text{cosec}^2 60$

$= (2)^2 + \left(\dfrac{2}{\sqrt{3}}\right)^2 = 4+\dfrac{4}{3}=\dfrac{12+4}{3}=\dfrac{16}{3}=5\dfrac{1}{3}$ **(1 Mark)**

5. **(a)** $\sec\theta = \sqrt{2}$

$\sec\theta = \sec 45^\circ$

$\theta = 45^\circ$

Put $\theta = 45^\circ$ in the given expression,

$\dfrac{1+\tan\theta}{\sin\theta} = \dfrac{1+\tan 45^\circ}{\sin 45^\circ}=\dfrac{1+1}{\dfrac{1}{\sqrt{2}}}=2\sqrt{2}$ **(1 Mark)**

6. **(a)** $1x + 1x + 2x = 180^\circ$, $x = 45^\circ$.

$\angle A$, $\angle B$ and $\angle C$ are 45°, 45° and 90° resp.

$$\frac{\sec A}{\text{cosec } B}-\frac{\tan A}{\cot B}=\frac{\sec 45}{\text{cosec } 45}-\frac{\tan 45}{\cot 45}=\frac{\sqrt{2}}{\sqrt{2}}-\frac{1}{1}$$

$= 1 - 1 = 0$ **(1 Mark)**

7. **(c)** $\dfrac{2\tan 30^\circ}{1-\tan^2 30^\circ}=\dfrac{2\left(\dfrac{1}{\sqrt{3}}\right)}{1-\left(\dfrac{1}{\sqrt{3}}\right)^2}$

$=\dfrac{\dfrac{2}{\sqrt{3}}}{1-\dfrac{1}{3}}=\dfrac{2}{\sqrt{3}}\times\dfrac{3}{2}=\sqrt{3}=\tan 60^\circ.$ **(1 Mark)**

8. Put all values

$\dfrac{5}{(\sqrt{3})^2}+\dfrac{1}{(\sqrt{3}/2)^2}-(1)^2+2(1)^2 \Rightarrow \dfrac{5}{3}+\dfrac{4}{3}-1+2$ **(½ Mark)**

$\left[\begin{array}{l}\cot 30^\circ = \sqrt{3}, \sin 60^\circ = \dfrac{\sqrt{3}}{2}\\ \cot 45^\circ = 1, \sin 90^\circ = 1\end{array}\right]$

$\Rightarrow \dfrac{9}{3}+1=4$ **(½ Mark)**

9. $\tan^2\theta + \cot^2\theta - 2$ $\left[\text{put } \tan\theta = \dfrac{\sin\theta}{\cos\theta}\right]$.

$\Rightarrow \dfrac{\sin^2\theta}{\cos^2\theta}+\dfrac{\cos^2\theta}{\sin^2\theta}-2$ **(½ Mark)**

As $\sin\theta = \cos\theta$ put values $\Rightarrow \dfrac{\sin^2\theta}{\sin^2\theta}+\dfrac{\cos^2\theta}{\cos^2\theta}-2$

$\Rightarrow 1 + 1 - 2 = 0$ **(½ Mark)**

10. $\sin^2 60^\circ + 2\tan 45^\circ - \cos^2 30^\circ$

$=\left(\dfrac{\sqrt{3}}{2}\right)^2+2(1)-\left(\dfrac{\sqrt{3}}{2}\right)^2$ **(½ Mark)**

$=\dfrac{3}{4}+2-\dfrac{3}{4}=2$ **(½ Mark)**

11. $\sin(A+B) = 1 = \sin 90^\circ$

$\Rightarrow A + B = 90^\circ$ ...(i) **(½ Mark)**

$\sin(A - B) = \frac{1}{2} = \sin 30°$

$\Rightarrow A - B = 30°$ ...(ii)

By using elimination method

$A = 60°$ and $B = 30°$ **(½ Mark)**

12. $\tan(3x + 30°) = 1 = \tan 45°$ **(½ Mark)**

$\Rightarrow 3x + 30° = 45° \Rightarrow x = 5°$ **(½ Mark)**

13. $\tan(A + B) = \sqrt{3}$ $\therefore A + B = 60°$ ...(1) **(½ Mark)**

$\tan(A - B) = \frac{1}{\sqrt{3}}$ $\therefore A - B = 30°$ ...(2) **(½ Mark)**

Adding (1) & (2), we get $2A = 90° \Rightarrow A = 45°$ **(½ Mark)**

Also (1) – (2), we get $2B = 30° \Rightarrow B = 45°$ **(½ Mark)**

14. $2 \operatorname{cosec}^2 30 + x \sin^2 60 - \frac{3}{4}\tan^2 30 = 10$

$\Rightarrow 2(2)^2 + x\left(\frac{\sqrt{3}}{2}\right)^2 - \frac{3}{4}\left(\frac{1}{\sqrt{3}}\right)^2 = 10$ **(1 Mark)**

$\Rightarrow 2(4) + x\left(\frac{3}{4}\right) - \frac{3}{4}\left(\frac{1}{3}\right) = 10$ **(1 Mark)**

$\Rightarrow 8 + x\left(\frac{3}{4}\right) - \frac{1}{4} = 10$

$\Rightarrow 32 + x(3) - 1 = 40$

$\Rightarrow 3x = 9 \Rightarrow x = 3$ **(1 Mark)**

15.

Topper's Answer

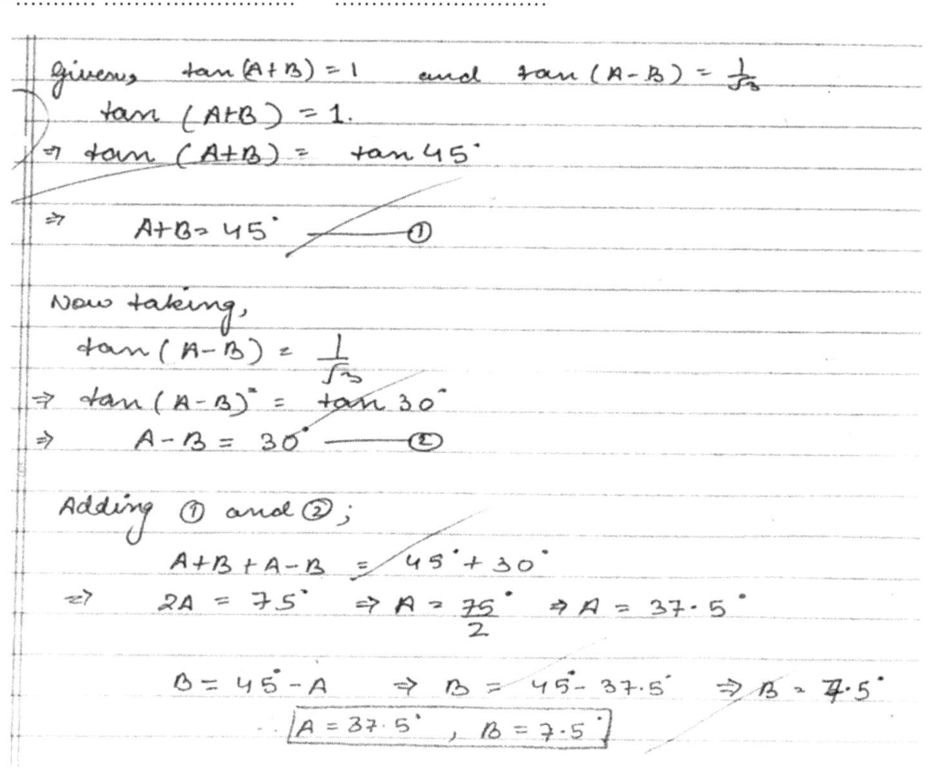

16. $\tan^2 30°\sin 30° + \cos 60°\sin^2 90° \tan^2 60° - 2\tan 45° \cos^2 0° \sin 90°$

$$= \frac{1}{3}\times\frac{1}{2}+\frac{1}{2}\times 1\times 3\times -2\times 1\times 1\times 1 = \frac{1}{6}+\frac{3}{2}-2 = -\frac{1}{3}$$

(2 Marks)

Topic-3: Trigonometric Identities

1. **(d)** cos A **(1 Mark)**

2. **(d)** $\frac{\cos^2\theta}{\sin^2\theta}-\frac{1}{\sin^2\theta} = -\left(\frac{1}{\sin^2\theta}-\frac{\cos^2\theta}{\sin^2\theta}\right)$

$$= -\left(\frac{1-\cos^2\theta}{\sin^2\theta}\right) = -\frac{\sin^2\theta}{\sin^2\theta} = -1$$ **(1 Mark)**

3. **(d)** Let $\theta = 45°$

Consider option (a)

$\sin(45°)\cdot\cot(45°) = \cos(45°)$

$\frac{1}{\sqrt{2}}\cdot 1 = \frac{1}{\sqrt{2}}$

$\frac{1}{\sqrt{2}} = \frac{1}{\sqrt{2}}$

Hence, LHS = RHS

Consider option (b)

$\cos(45°)\cdot\tan(45°) = \sin(45°)$

$\frac{1}{\sqrt{2}} = \frac{1}{\sqrt{2}}$

$\therefore$ LHS = RHS

Consider option (c)

$\text{cosec}^2(45°) - \cot^2(45°) = 1$

$2 - 1 = 1$

$1 = 1$

$\therefore$ LHS = RHS

Consider option (d)

$\tan^2(45°) - \sec^2(45°) = 1$

$1 - 2$

$-1 \neq 1$

$\therefore$ LHS $\neq$ RHS

Hence option (d) is incorrect **(1 Mark)**

4. **(c)** $\tan\theta + \cot\theta = 2$

$$\frac{\sin\theta}{\cos\theta}+\frac{\cos\theta}{\sin\theta} = 2$$

$$\frac{\sin^2\theta+\cos^2\theta}{\sin\theta\cos\theta} = 2$$

$$\frac{1}{2\sin\theta\cos\theta} = 1 \Rightarrow \sin 2\theta = 1$$

$$\sin 2\theta = \sin 90° \Rightarrow 2\theta = 90° \Rightarrow \theta = 45°$$

$$\sin^3\theta + \cos^3\theta = (\sin 45°)^3 + (\cos 45°)^3$$

$$= \left(\frac{1}{\sqrt{2}}\right)^3 + \left(\frac{1}{\sqrt{2}}\right)^3$$

$$= \frac{1}{2\sqrt{2}}+\frac{1}{2\sqrt{2}} = \frac{2}{2\sqrt{2}} = \frac{\sqrt{2}}{2}$$ **(1 Mark)**

5. **(b)** $a\cot\theta + b\,\text{cosec}\,\theta = p$ ..... (i)

$b\cot\theta + a\,\text{cosec}\,\theta = q$ ..... (ii)

$p^2 - q^2 = (p-q)(p+q)$ .....(iii)

Add (i) & (ii)

$p + q = (a+b)\cot\theta + (a+b)\text{cosec}\,\theta$

$p + q = (a+b)(\cot\theta - \text{cosec}\,\theta)$

Subtract (i) & (ii)

$p - q = (a-b)(\cot\theta - \text{cosec}\,\theta)$

Substitute the values in eq. (iii)

$(p^2 - q^2) = (p-q)(p+q)$

$= [(a-b)(\cot\theta - \text{cosec}\,\theta)][(a+b)(\cot\theta + \text{cosec}\,\theta)]$

$= (a^2 - b^2)(\cot^2\theta - \text{cosec}^2\theta)$

$p^2 - q^2 = -(a^2 - b^2) = b^2 - a^2$ **(1 Mark)**

6. **(b)** $\sec\theta + \tan\theta = p$ ...(i)

$$\frac{1}{\sec\theta+\tan\theta} = \frac{1}{p}$$

$$\frac{1}{\sec\theta+\tan\theta}\times\frac{\sec\theta-\tan\theta}{\sec\theta-\tan\theta} = \frac{1}{p}$$

$$\frac{\sec\theta-\tan\theta}{\sec^2\theta-\tan^2\theta} = \frac{1}{p}$$ $\therefore \{\sec^2\theta - \tan^2\theta = 1\}$

$\sec\theta - \tan\theta = \frac{1}{p}$ ...(ii)

Subtract (ii) from (i)

$\sec\theta + \tan\theta = p$

$\sec\theta - \tan\theta = \dfrac{1}{p}$

$\underline{-\qquad + \qquad -}$

$2\tan\theta = p - \dfrac{1}{p}$

$\tan\theta = \left(\dfrac{p^2-1}{2p}\right)$ **(1 Mark)**

7. **(b)** $2\sin^2\beta = \cos^2\beta = 2$

Then $2\sin^2\beta - (1-\sin^2\beta) = 2$

$3\sin^2\beta = 3$ or $\sin^2\beta = 1$

$\Rightarrow$ β is 90° **(1 Mark)**

8. **(b)** $\tan\alpha + \cot\alpha = 2$ gives $\alpha = 45°$. So $\tan\alpha = \cot\alpha = 1$

$\tan^{20}\alpha + \cot^{20}\alpha = 1^{20} + 1^{20} = 1 + 1 = 2$ **(1 Mark)**

9. **(c)** $1 + \sin^2\alpha = 3\sin\alpha\cos\alpha$

$\sin^2\alpha + \cos^2\alpha + \sin^2\alpha = 3\sin\alpha\cos\alpha$

$2\sin^2\alpha - 3\sin\alpha\cos\alpha + \cos^2\alpha = 0$

$2\sin^2\alpha - 2\sin\alpha\cos\alpha - \sin\alpha\cos\alpha + \cos^2\alpha = 0$

$(2\sin\alpha - \cos\alpha)(\sin\alpha - \cos\alpha) = 0$

$\therefore \cot\alpha = 2$ or $\cot\alpha = 1$ **(1 Mark)**

10. **(c)** $(1+\tan^2\theta).\cos^2\theta = \sec^2\theta\cos^2\theta = 1$ **(1 Mark)**

11. **(a)** Let $\theta = 45°$

Then,

$\text{cosec } 45° - \cot 45° = \sqrt{2}-1$

and

$\text{cosec } 45° + \cot 45° = \sqrt{2}+1$

$$\frac{1}{\sqrt{2}-1} = \frac{\sqrt{2}+1}{\sqrt{2}+1} \times \frac{1}{\sqrt{2}-1} = \frac{\sqrt{2}+1}{2-1} = \sqrt{2}+1$$

Hence, it is clear that $\sqrt{2}-1$ and $\sqrt{2}+1$ are reciprocal of each other.

$\therefore$ Assertion is true

$\text{cosec}^2\theta - \cot^2\theta = 1$

$(\text{cosec }\theta - \cot\theta)(\text{cosec }\theta + \cot\theta) = 1$

$(\text{cosec }\theta - \cot\theta) = \dfrac{}{(\text{cosec }\theta + \cot\theta)}$

Hence, reason is also true and reason correctly explain the assertion. **(1 Mark)**

12. $m^2 = a^2\cos^2\theta + b^2\sin^2\theta + 2ab\cos\theta\sin\theta$

$n^2 = a^2\sin^2\theta + b^2\cos^2\theta - 2ab\cos\theta\sin\theta$ **(½ Mark)**

$m^2 + n^2 = (a^2+b^2)\cos^2\theta + (a^2+b^2)\sin^2\theta$

$\Rightarrow m^2 + n^2 = (a^2+b^2)(\cos^2\theta + \sin^2\theta)$

$\Rightarrow m^2 + n^2 = a^2 + b^2 \quad [\therefore \cos^2\theta + \sin^2\theta = 1]$

(½ Mark)

13. $$\frac{\sqrt{\sec A - 1}}{\sqrt{\sec A + 1}} + \frac{\sqrt{\sec A + 1}}{\sqrt{\sec A - 1}} = \frac{\sec A - 1 + \sec A + 1}{\sqrt{\sec^2 A - 1}}$$

(½ Mark)

$$= \frac{2\sec A}{\sqrt{\tan^2 A}} = \frac{2\sec A}{\tan A} \qquad [\therefore \sec^2 A - 1 = \tan^2 A]$$

$$= 2\left(\frac{1}{\cos A}\right)\left(\frac{\cos A}{\sin A}\right) = 2\text{ cosec } A$$ **(½ Mark)**

14. $$\frac{\dfrac{\sin\theta}{\cos\theta}}{\dfrac{\sin\theta - \cos\theta}{\sin\theta}} + \frac{\dfrac{\cos\theta}{\sin\theta}}{\dfrac{\cos\theta - \sin\theta}{\cos\theta}}$$

$$\Rightarrow \frac{\sin^2\theta}{\cos\theta(\sin\theta - \cos\theta)} + \frac{\cos^2\theta}{\sin\theta(\cos\theta - \sin\theta)}$$

$$\Rightarrow \frac{\sin^3\theta - \cos^3\theta}{\sin\theta\cos\theta(\sin\theta - \cos\theta)}$$ **(½ Mark)**

$[\because a^3 - b^3 = (a-b)(a^2+b^2+ab)]$

$$= \frac{(\sin\theta - \cos\theta)(1 + \cos\theta\sin\theta)}{\sin\theta\cos\theta(\sin\theta - \cos\theta)} \qquad [\because \sin^2\theta + \cos^2\theta = 1]$$

$$\Rightarrow \frac{1 + \cos\theta\sin\theta}{\sin\theta\cos\theta} = 1 + \frac{1}{\sin\theta\cos\theta}$$

$= 1 + \sec\theta\text{ cosec }\theta$ **(½ Mark)**

15. $\sin A + \sin^2 A = 1$ ...(i)

$\sin A = 1 - \sin^2 A = \cos^2 A$ **(½ Mark)**

$\therefore \cos^2 A + \cos^4 A = \cos^2 A + (\cos^2 A)^2$

$= \sin A + \sin^2 A = 1$ [From (i)] **(½ Mark)**

16. $$\sin^2\theta + \frac{1}{1+\tan^2\theta} = \sin^2\theta + \frac{1}{\sec^2\theta}$$

$= \sin^2\theta + \cos^2\theta = 1$ **(1 Mark)**

17. $(1+\tan^2\theta)(1-\sin^2\theta) = \sec^2\theta \cdot \cos^2\theta$

$$= \frac{1}{\cos^2\theta}\cdot\cos^2\theta = 1$$ **(1 Mark)**

18. Given, $1 + \sin^2\theta = 3\sin\theta\cos\theta$

Dividing both sides by $\cos^2\theta$, we get **(½ Mark)**

$$\frac{1}{\cos^2\theta} + \tan^2\theta = 3\tan\theta$$

$\sec^2\theta + \tan^2\theta = 3\tan\theta$ **(½ Mark)**

$1 + \tan^2\theta + \tan^2\theta = 3\tan\theta$ **(½ Mark)**

$1 + 2\tan^2\theta = 3\tan\theta$ **(½ Mark)**

$2\tan^2\theta - 3\tan\theta + 1 = 0$

If $\tan\theta = x$, then the equation becomes $2x^2 - 3x + 1 = 0$

$\Rightarrow (x-1)(2x-1) = 0, x = 1$ or $\dfrac{1}{2}$

$x = \tan\theta \Rightarrow \tan\theta = 1$ or $\dfrac{1}{2}$ **(1 Mark)**

19. $\dfrac{1+\sec A}{\sec A}=\dfrac{\sin^2 A}{1-\cos A}$

LHS

$$\frac{1+\frac{1}{\cos A}}{\frac{1}{\cos A}}=\frac{\frac{\cos A+1}{\cos A}}{\frac{1}{\cos A}}=1+\cos A$$ **(1½ marks)**

RHS

$$\frac{\sin^2 A}{1-\cos A}=\frac{1-\cos^2 A}{1-\cos A}$$

$$=\frac{(1-\cos A)(1+\cos A)}{1-\cos A}$$

$$=1+\cos A$$ **(1½ marks)**

Hence, LHS = RHS

20. Squares both sides of the given equation as:

$$\frac{1}{\sin^2\theta+\cos^2\theta-2\sin\theta\cos\theta}=\frac{\text{cosec}^2\theta}{2}$$ **(½ Mark)**

Simplifies the above equation as:

$$\frac{2}{\text{cosec}^2\theta}=1-2\sin\theta\cos\theta$$ **(½ Mark)**

Simplifies the above equation as: **(½ Mark)**

$2\sin\theta\cos\theta = 1-2\sin^2\theta$

Squares the LHS of the equation to be proved as:

$$\frac{1}{\sin^2\theta+\cos^2\theta+2\sin\theta\cos\theta}$$ **(½ Mark)**

Uses step 3 and simplifies the above expression as: **(½ Mark)**

$$\frac{1}{2-2\sin^2\theta}$$

Simplifies the above expression as: **(½ Mark)**

$$\frac{1}{2\cos^2\theta}=\frac{\sec^2\theta}{2}$$

Concludes that LHS = RHS.

21. LHS: $\dfrac{\sin^3\theta/\cos^3\theta}{1+\sin^2\theta/\cos^2\theta}+\dfrac{\cos^3\theta/\sin^3\theta}{1+\cos^2\theta/\sin^2\theta}$ **(½ Mark)**

$$=\frac{\sin^3\theta/\cos^3\theta}{(\cos^2\theta+\sin^2\theta)/\cos^2\theta}+\frac{\cos^3\theta/\sin^3\theta}{(\sin^2\theta+\cos^2\theta)/\sin^2\theta}$$

$$=\frac{\sin^3\theta}{\cos\theta}+\frac{\cos^3\theta}{\sin\theta}$$ **(½ Mark)**

$$=\frac{\sin^4\theta+\cos^4\theta}{\cos\theta\sin\theta}$$ **(½ Mark)**

$$=\frac{(\sin^2\theta+\cos^2\theta)^2-2\sin^2\theta\cos^2\theta}{\cos\theta\sin\theta}$$ **(½ Mark)**

$$=\frac{1-2\sin^2\theta\cos^2\theta}{\cos\theta\sin\theta}$$ **(½ Mark)**

$$=\frac{1}{\cos\theta\sin\theta}-\frac{2\sin^2\theta\cos^2\theta}{\cos\theta\sin\theta}$$

$\sec\theta\,\text{cosec}\,\theta - 2\sin\theta\cos\theta$

= RHS **(½ Mark)**

22. (i) Simplifies the given LHS by rationalizing the first term as: **(1 Mark)**

$$\frac{\text{cosec}\,\theta+\cot\theta}{\text{cosec}^2\theta-\cot^2\theta}-\frac{\cot\theta}{\cos\theta}$$

Simplifies the above expression as: **(1 Mark)**

$\text{cosec}\,\theta + \cot\theta - \text{cosec}\,\theta = \cot\theta$

Concludes that LHS = RHS

23. Simplifies the given LHS as: **(1 Mark)**

$$\frac{1-\sin^2 x\cot^2 x}{\sin^2 x}$$

Simplifies the above expression as: **(½ Mark)**

$\text{cosec}^2 x - \cot^2 x$

Simplifies the above expression as 1 and concludes that LHS = RHS. **(½ Mark)**

24. L.H.S. $= 1+\dfrac{\cot^2\alpha}{1+\text{cosec}\,\alpha}=1+\dfrac{\text{cosec}^2\alpha-1}{\text{cosec}\,\alpha+1}$ **(1 Mark)**

$$=1+\frac{(\text{cosec}\,\alpha+1)(\text{cosec}\,\alpha-1)}{\text{cosec}\,\alpha+1}$$

$= 1 + \text{cosec}\,\alpha - 1 = \text{cosec}\,\alpha =$ R.H.S. **(1 Mark)**

Hence, proved.

25. L.H.S.$= \tan^4\theta + \tan^2\theta = (\tan^2\theta)^2 + \tan^2\theta$

$= (\sec^2\theta - 1)^2 + \sec^2\theta - 1$ **(1 Mark)**

$= \sec^4\theta - 2\sec^2\theta + 1 + \sec^2\theta - 1$

$= \sec^4\theta - \sec^2\theta =$ R.H.S. **(1 Mark)**

Hence, proved.

26. $\sin\theta + \cos\theta = \sqrt{2}$

Squaring both sides

$(\sin\theta + \cos\theta)^2 = (\sqrt{2})^2$

$\sin^2\theta + \cos^2\theta + 2\sin\theta\times\cos\theta = 2$ **(1 Mark)**

$1 + 2\sin\theta\cdot\cos\theta = 2$ $[\because \sin^2\theta+\cos^2\theta = 1]$

$2\sin\theta\cdot\cos\theta = 1 \Rightarrow \sin\theta\cdot\cos\theta = \dfrac{1}{2}$ ...(i)

L.H.S. $= \tan\theta + \cot\theta = \dfrac{\sin\theta}{\cos\theta}+\dfrac{\cos\theta}{\sin\theta}$

$$=\frac{\sin^2\theta+\cos^2\theta}{\sin\theta\cdot\cos\theta}=\frac{1}{\frac{1}{2}}\quad\text{[from (i)]}$$

= 2 = R.H.S. **(1 Mark)**

Hence, proved.

27. $\sin\theta + \cos\theta = \sqrt{3}$

Squaring both sides, we get

$\Rightarrow \quad \sin^2\theta + \cos^2\theta + 2\sin\theta\cos\theta = 3$

$\Rightarrow \quad 1 + 2\sin\theta\cos\theta = 3 \qquad [\because \sin^2\theta + \cos^2\theta = 1]$

$\Rightarrow \quad \sin\theta\cos\theta = 1$ **(1 Mark)** ...(i)

Now, $\tan\theta + \cot\theta$

$$= \frac{\sin\theta}{\cos\theta} + \frac{\cos\theta}{\sin\theta}$$

$$= \frac{\sin^2\theta + \cos^2\theta}{\sin\theta\cos\theta} = \frac{1}{1}$$ [By (i)]

$= 1 = \text{RHS}$ **(1 Mark)**

Hence Proved.

28.

Topper's Answer

$$\frac{2\cos^3\theta - \cos\theta}{\sin\theta - 2\sin^3\theta} = \cot\theta$$

LHS:

$$\frac{\cos\theta\,(2\cos^2\theta - 1)}{\sin\theta\,(1 - 2\sin^2\theta)}$$

$$\frac{\cos\theta\,[2(1-\sin^2\theta) - 1]}{\sin\theta\,(1 - 2\sin^2\theta)}$$

$$\frac{\cos\theta\,[2 - 2\sin^2\theta - 1]}{\sin\theta\,(1 - 2\sin^2\theta)} \Rightarrow \frac{\cos\theta}{\sin\theta} \times \frac{(1-2\sin^2\theta)}{(1-2\sin^2\theta)} \Rightarrow \cot\theta$$

LHS = RHS = $\cot\theta$ //

Proved.

29. $(\sin\theta + \text{cosec}\,\theta)^2 + (\cos\theta + \sec\theta)^2 = 7 + \tan^2\theta + \cot^2\theta$.

Taking left side,

LHS = $\sin^2\theta + \text{cosec}^2\theta + 2\sin\theta\,\text{cosec}\theta + \cos^2\theta + \sec^2\theta + 2\cos\theta\sec\theta$ **(1 Mark)**

$$= \sin^2\theta + \text{cosec}^2\theta + 2\sin\theta \times \frac{1}{\sin\theta} + \cos^2\theta + \sec^2\theta + 2\cos\theta \times \frac{1}{\cos\theta}$$

(1 Mark)

$= \sin^2\theta + \text{cosec}^2\theta + 2 + \cos^2\theta + \sec^2\theta + 2$

$= \sin^2\theta + \cos^2\theta + 4 + \text{cosec}^2\theta + \sec^2\theta$

$= 1 + 4 + \text{cosec}^2\theta + \sec^2 \quad [\because \sin^2\theta + \cos^2\theta = 1]$

$= 5 + 1 + \cot^2\theta + 1 + \tan^2\theta$

$[\because \tan^2\theta + 1 = \sec^2\theta \text{ and } \cot^2\theta + 1 = \text{cosec}^2\theta]$

$= 7 + \tan^2\theta + \cot^2\theta = \text{R.H.S.}$ **(1 Mark)**

30. $(1 + \cot A - \text{cosec}A)(1 + \tan A + \sec A) = 2$

Taking L.H.S, **(1 Mark)**

LHS = $(1 + \cot A - \text{cosec}A)(1 + \tan A + \sec A)$

$$= \left(1 + \frac{\cos A}{\sin A} - \frac{1}{\sin A}\right)\left(1 + \frac{\sin A}{\cos A} + \frac{1}{\cos A}\right)$$

$$= \left(\frac{\sin A + \cos A - 1}{\sin A}\right)\left(\frac{\cos A + \sin A + 1}{\cos A}\right)$$

$$= \frac{\sin^2 A + \cos^2 A + 2\sin A\cos A - 1}{\sin A\cos A}$$ **(1 Mark)**

$[\because (a-b)(a+b) = a^2 - b^2]$

$$= \frac{1 + 2\sin A\cos A - 1}{\sin A\cos A} \quad [\because \sin^2 A + \cos^2 A = 1]$$

$$= \frac{2\sin A\cos A}{\sin A\cos A} = 2 = \text{R.H.S.}$$ **(1 Mark)**

If more than two trigonometry functions are given in a problem, then convert all functions in the form of sin θ cos θ.

31. (cosec θ – sin θ) (secθ – cos θ)

$$= \left(\frac{1}{\sin\theta} - \sin\theta\right)\left(\frac{1}{\cos\theta} - \cos\theta\right)$$

$$= \left(\frac{1-\sin^2\theta}{\sin\theta}\right)\left(\frac{1-\cos^2\theta}{\cos\theta}\right)$$ **(1 Mark)**

$$= \frac{\cos^2\theta}{\sin\theta} \times \frac{\sin^2\theta}{\cos\theta} \quad \left[\because 1-\sin^2\theta = \cos^2\theta, \; 1-\cos^2\theta = \sin^2\theta\right]$$

= sin θ. cos θ. ...(i)

Now $\frac{1}{\tan\theta + \cot\theta} = \frac{1}{\frac{\sin\theta}{\cos\theta} + \frac{\cos\theta}{\sin\theta}}$

$$= \frac{1}{\frac{\sin^2\theta + \cos^2\theta}{\sin\theta.\cos\theta}} = \frac{\sin\theta.\cos\theta}{\sin^2\theta + \cos^2\theta}$$

= sin θ. cos θ. ...(ii) **(1 Mark)**

From (i) and (ii)

(cosec θ – sin θ) (sec θ – cos θ)

= sin θ. cosθ $\frac{1}{\tan\theta + \cot\theta}$ Hence proved. **(1 Mark)**

32. To prove $(\cot\theta - \text{cosec}\theta)^2 = \frac{1-\cos\theta}{1+\cos\theta}$

LHS = $(\cot\theta - \text{cosec}\theta)^2$ $\left[\cot\theta = \frac{\cos\theta}{\sin\theta}\right]$

$$= \left(\frac{\cos\theta}{\sin\theta} - \frac{1}{\sin\theta}\right)^2 \quad \left[\text{cosec}\,\theta = \frac{1}{\sin\theta}\right]$$

(1 Mark)

$$= \left(\frac{\cos\theta - 1}{\sin\theta}\right)^2$$

$$= \frac{(1-\cos\theta)^2}{\sin^2\theta}$$ **(1 Mark)**

$$= \frac{(1-\cos\theta)^2}{(1-\cos^2\theta)} \quad (\sin^2\theta + \cos^2\theta = 1)$$

$$= \frac{1-\cos\theta}{1+\cos\theta}$$ **(1 Mark)**

= RHS

33. L.H.S. $= \frac{1+\cos^2\theta}{\sin^2\theta} = \frac{1}{\sin^2\theta} + \frac{\cos^2\theta}{\sin^2\theta}$ **(1 Mark)**

$= \text{cosec}^2\theta + \cot^2\theta$

$= \text{cosec}^2\theta + (\text{cosec}^2\theta - 1)$

$= 2\text{cosec}\,\theta - 1$ = R.H.S. **(1 Mark)**

34. To prove $\frac{\sin\theta}{\cot\theta + \text{cosec}\theta} = 2 + \frac{\sin\theta}{\cot\theta - \text{cosec}\theta}$

i.e. $\frac{\sin\theta}{\cot\theta + \text{cosec}\theta} - \frac{\sin\theta}{\cot\theta - \text{cosec}\theta} = 2$ **(½ Mark)**

$$\text{LHS} = \sin\theta\left(\frac{1}{\cot\theta + \text{cosec}\theta} - \frac{1}{\cot\theta - \text{cosec}\theta}\right)$$

$$= \sin\theta\left(\frac{\cot\theta - \text{cosec}\theta - \cot\theta - \text{cosec}\theta}{(\cot\theta + \text{cosec}\theta)(\cot\theta - \text{cosec}\theta)}\right)$$ **(1 Mark)**

$$= \frac{\sin\theta\,(-2\text{cosec}\theta)}{\cot^2\theta - \text{cosec}^2\theta} \quad \left[\because \text{cosec}^2\theta - \cot^2\theta = 1\right]$$

$$= \frac{-2\sin\theta \times \frac{1}{\sin\theta}}{-1}$$ **(1 ½ Marks)**

= 2

35. $\frac{\sin^3\theta + \cos^3\theta}{\sin\theta + \cos\theta} + \sin\theta\cos\theta$ **(1 Mark)**

$$= \frac{(\sin\theta + \cos\theta)(\sin^2\theta + \cos^2\theta - \sin\theta\cos\theta)}{(\sin\theta + \cos\theta)} + \sin\theta\cos\theta$$

$= \sin^2\theta + \cos^2\theta - \sin\theta\cos\theta + \sin\theta\cos\theta$

$= \sin^2\theta + \cos^2\theta = 1$ **(1 Mark)**

36. LHS

$$= \tan^2 A - \tan^2 B = \frac{\sin^2 A}{\cos^2 A} - \frac{\sin^2 B}{\cos^2 B}$$

$$= \frac{\sin^2 A\cos^2 B - \cos^2 A\sin^2 B}{\cos^2 A\cos^2 B}$$ **(1 Mark)**

$$= \frac{(1-\cos^2 A)\cos^2 B - \cos^2 A(1-\cos^2 B)}{\cos^2 A\cos^2 B}$$

$$= \frac{\cos^2 B - \cos^2 A\cos^2 B - \cos^2 A + \cos^2 A\cos^2 B}{\cos^2 A\cos^2 B}$$

$$= \frac{\cos^2 B - \cos^2 A}{\cos^2 A\cos^2 B}$$ **(1 Mark)**

Also $\frac{\cos^2 B - \cos^2 A}{\cos^2 A\cos^2 B} = \frac{(1-\sin^2 B) - (1-\sin^2 A)}{\cos^2 A\cos^2 B}$

$$= \frac{\sin^2 A - \sin^2 B}{\cos^2 A\cos^2 B} = \text{RHS}.$$ **(1 Mark)**

37. We have,

$$\text{L.H.S.} = \frac{\sin\theta - \cos\theta}{\sin\theta + \cos\theta} + \frac{\sin\theta + \cos\theta}{\sin\theta - \cos\theta}$$

$$= \frac{(\sin\theta - \cos\theta)^2 + (\sin\theta + \cos\theta)^2}{(\sin^2\theta) - (\cos^2\theta)}$$ **(1 Mark)**

$$= \frac{(\sin^2\theta + \cos^2\theta - 2\sin\theta\cos\theta) + (\sin^2\theta + \cos^2\theta + 2\sin\theta\cos\theta)}{\sin^2\theta - (1 - \sin^2\theta)}$$

$$= \frac{2}{\sin^2\theta - 1 + \sin^2\theta}$$

$$= \frac{2}{2\sin^2\theta - 1}$$ **(1 Mark)**

= R.H.S.

38. L.H.S $= x^2 - y^2$

$= (p \sec\theta + q \tan\theta)^2 - (p \tan\theta + q \sec\theta)^2$

$= p^2 \sec^2\theta + q^2 \tan^2\theta + 2pq \tan\theta \sec\theta$ **(1 Mark)**

$-(p^2 \tan^2\theta + q^2 \sec^2\theta + 2pq \tan\theta \sec\theta)$

$= p^2 (\sec^2\theta - \tan^2\theta) - q^2 (\sec^2\theta - \tan^2\theta)$

$= (p^2 - q^2)(1 + \tan^2\theta - \tan^2\theta)$

$= (p^2 - q^2)(1) = p^2 - q^2 =$ R.H.S **(1 Mark)**

39. $$\text{L.H.S.} = \frac{\tan\theta}{1 - \cot\theta} + \frac{\cot\theta}{1 - \tan\theta} = \frac{\frac{\sin\theta}{\cos\theta}}{1 - \frac{\cos\theta}{\sin\theta}} + \frac{\frac{\cos\theta}{\sin\theta}}{1 - \frac{\sin\theta}{\cos\theta}}$$

$$= \frac{\frac{\sin\theta}{\cos\theta}}{\frac{\sin\theta - \cos\theta}{\sin\theta}} + \frac{\frac{\cos\theta}{\sin\theta}}{\frac{\cos\theta - \sin\theta}{\cos\theta}}$$ **(1 Mark)**

$$= \frac{\sin^2\theta}{\cos\theta(\sin\theta - \cos\theta)} + \frac{\cos^2\theta}{\sin\theta(\cos\theta - \sin\theta)}$$

$$= \frac{\sin^2\theta}{\cos\theta(\sin\theta - \cos\theta)} - \frac{\cos^2\theta}{\sin\theta(\sin\theta - \cos\theta)}$$ **(1 Mark)**

$$= \frac{1}{\sin\theta - \cos\theta}\left[\frac{\sin^2\theta}{\cos\theta} - \frac{\cos^2\theta}{\sin\theta}\right]$$

$$= \frac{1}{\sin\theta - \cos\theta}\left[\frac{\sin^3\theta - \cos^3\theta}{\cos\theta.\sin\theta}\right]$$ **(1 Mark)**

$$= \frac{[\sin\theta - \cos\theta][\sin^2\theta + \cos^2\theta + \sin\theta.\cos\theta]}{(\sin\theta - \cos\theta).(\cos\theta \times \sin\theta)}$$

$[\because a^3 - b^3 = (a - b)(a^2 + b^2 + ab)]$

$$\Rightarrow \frac{\sin^2\theta + \cos^2\theta + \sin\theta.\cos\theta}{(\cos\theta \times \sin\theta)}$$ $[\because \sin^2\theta + \cos^2\theta = 1]$

$$\Rightarrow \frac{1 + \sin\theta.\cos\theta}{\cos\theta \times \sin\theta} = \frac{1}{\cos\theta.\sin\theta} + \frac{\sin\theta.\cos\theta}{\sin\theta.\cos\theta}$$

$= 1 + \sec\theta.\ \text{cosec}\ \theta =$ R.H.S. **(1 Mark)**

$$\left(\because \frac{1}{\cos\theta} = \sec\theta, \frac{1}{\sin\theta} = \text{cosec}\theta\right)$$

Hence proved.

40. $$\text{L.H.S.} = \frac{\sin\theta}{\cos\theta + \text{cosec}\theta} = \frac{\sin\theta}{\frac{\cos\theta}{\sin\theta} + \frac{1}{\sin\theta}}$$

$$\Rightarrow \frac{\sin\theta}{\frac{\cos\theta + 1}{\sin\theta}} = \frac{\sin^2\theta}{\cos\theta + 1}$$ **(1 Mark)**

$$\Rightarrow \frac{\sin^2\theta}{1 + \cos\theta} \times \frac{(1 - \cos\theta)}{(1 - \cos\theta)} = \frac{\sin^2\theta(1 - \cos\theta)}{1 - \cos^2\theta}$$

$$= \frac{\sin^2\theta(1 - \cos\theta)}{1 - \cos^2\theta} = \frac{\sin^2\theta(1 - \cos\theta)}{\sin^2\theta}$$ **(1 Mark)**

$= 1 - \cos\theta$ ...(1)

$$\text{R.H.S.} = 2 + \frac{\sin\theta}{\cot\theta - \text{cosec}\theta} = 2 + \frac{\sin\theta}{\frac{\cos\theta}{\sin\theta} - \frac{1}{\sin\theta}}$$

$$= 2 + \frac{\sin^2\theta}{\cos\theta - 1}$$ **(1 Mark)**

$$\Rightarrow 2 - \frac{\sin^2\theta}{(1 - \cos\theta)} = 2 - \frac{\sin^2\theta \times (1 + \cos\theta)}{(1 - \cos\theta) \times (1 + \cos\theta)}$$

$$\Rightarrow 2 - \frac{\sin^2\theta(1 + \cos\theta)}{1 - \cos^2\theta} = 2 - \frac{\sin^2\theta(1 + \cos\theta)}{\sin^2\theta}$$

$= 2 - (1 + \cos\theta)$

$= 1 - \cos\theta$ ...(2)

From equations (1) and (2), we get

L.H.S. = R.H.S. **(1 Mark)**

Hence proved.

41. $$\frac{\sin A - \cos A + 1}{\sin A + \cos A - 1} = \frac{1}{\sec A - \tan A}.$$

Taking L.H.S,

$$\text{L.H.S} = \frac{\sin A - \cos A + 1}{\sin A + \cos A - 1}$$

Taking cosA common in numerator and denominator,

$$= \frac{\tan A - 1 + \sec A}{\tan A + 1 - \sec A}$$ **(1 Mark)**

Multiplying (tanA – secA) in numerator and denominator,

$$= \frac{\{(\tan A + \sec A) - 1\}(\tan A - \sec A)}{\{(\tan A - \sec A) + 1\}(\tan A - \sec A))}$$ **(1 Mark)**

$$=\frac{(\tan^2 A-\sec^2 A)-(\tan A-\sec A)}{(\tan A-\sec A+1)(\tan A-\sec A)}$$ **(1 Mark)**

$$=\frac{-1-\tan A+\sec A}{(\tan A-\sec A+1)(\tan A-\sec A)}$$

$$=\frac{-1}{\tan A-\sec A}=\frac{1}{\sec A-\tan A}=\text{R.H.S.}$$ **(1 Mark)**

42. Prove that $\frac{\sin A-2\sin^3 A}{2\cos^3 A-\cos A}=\tan A$

$$\text{L.H.S}=\frac{\sin A-2\sin^3 A}{2\cos^3 A-\cos A}$$

$$=\frac{\sin A(1-2\sin^2 A)}{\cos A(2\cos^2 A-1)}$$ **(1 Mark)**

$$=\frac{\sin A(1-2(1-\cos^2 A))}{\cos A(2\cos^2 A-1)}$$ [using $\sin^2\theta+\cos^2\theta=1$]

$$=\frac{\sin A(1-2+2\cos^2 A)}{\cos A(2\cos^2 A-1)}$$ **(1 Mark)**

$$=\frac{\sin A(2\cos^2 A-1)}{\cos A(2\cos^2 A-1)}$$ **(1 Mark)**

$$=\frac{\sin A}{\cos A}=\tan A=\text{RHS}$$ **(1 Mark)**

Hence proved.

43. Given: $m=\cos\theta-\sin\theta$ and $n=\cos\theta+\sin\theta$.

$$\text{L.H.S}=\sqrt{\frac{m}{n}}+\sqrt{\frac{n}{m}}=\sqrt{\frac{\cos\theta-\sin\theta}{\cos\theta+\sin\theta}}+\sqrt{\frac{\cos\theta+\sin\theta}{\cos\theta-\sin\theta}}$$

(1 Mark)

$$=\sqrt{\frac{(\cos\theta-\sin\theta)^2}{\cos^2\theta-\sin^2\theta}}+\sqrt{\frac{(\cos\theta+\sin\theta)^2}{\cos^2\theta-\sin^2\theta}}$$ [Rationalize the denominator]

$$=\frac{\cos\theta-\sin\theta}{\sqrt{\cos^2\theta-\sin^2\theta}}+\frac{\cos\theta+\sin\theta}{\sqrt{\cos^2\theta-\sin^2\theta}}$$ **(1 Mark)**

$$=\frac{\cos\theta-\sin\theta+\cos\theta+\sin\theta}{\sqrt{\cos^2\theta-\sin^2\theta}}$$ **(1 Mark)**

$$=\frac{2\cos\theta}{\sqrt{\cos^2\theta\left(1-\frac{\sin^2\theta}{\cos^2\theta}\right)}}=\frac{2\cos\theta}{\cos\theta\sqrt{1-\tan^2\theta}}$$

$$=\frac{2}{\sqrt{1-\tan^2\theta}}=\text{R.H.S}$$ **(1 Mark)**

44. $\text{L.H.S}=\frac{\sin A-\cos A+1}{\sin A+\cos A-1}$

Divide each term of numerator and denominator by cos A

$$=\frac{\frac{\sin A}{\cos A}-\frac{\cos A}{\cos A}+\frac{1}{\cos A}}{\frac{\sin A}{\cos A}+\frac{\cos A}{\cos A}-\frac{1}{\cos A}}$$ **(1 Mark)**

$$=\frac{\tan A+\sec A-1}{\tan A-\sec A+1}$$ **(1 Mark)**

$$=\frac{\tan A+\sec A-1}{\tan A-\sec A+\sec^2 A-\tan^2 A}$$ **(1 Mark)**

$$=\frac{\tan A+\sec A-1}{-(\sec A-\tan A)+(\sec A-\tan A)(\sec A+\tan A)}$$

$$=\frac{\tan A+\sec A-1}{(\sec A-\tan A)(\tan A+\sec A-1)}=\frac{1}{\sec A-\tan A}$$

(1 Mark)

Another method to prove by rationalising numerator . i.e

$$\frac{\sin A-\cos A+1}{\sin A+\cos A-1}\times\frac{(\sin A-\cos A)-1}{(\sin A-\cos A)-1}.$$

45. (i) Now, $\frac{x^2}{a^2}=\sec^2\theta,\ \frac{y^2}{b^2}=\tan^2\theta$

$$\Rightarrow\ \frac{x^2}{a^2}-\frac{y^2}{b^2}=\sec^2\theta-\tan^2\theta=1.$$

$\therefore\ b^2x^2-a^2y^2=a^2b^2$ **(2 Marks)**

(ii) Now, $\frac{x^2}{a^2}=\text{cosec}^2\theta,\ \frac{y^2}{b^2}=\cot^2\theta$

$$\Rightarrow\ \frac{x^2}{a^2}-\frac{y^2}{b^2}=\text{cosec}^2\theta-\cot^2\theta=1.$$

$\therefore\ b^2x^2-a^2y^2=a^2b^2$ **(2 Marks)**

46. By elimination method

$\sec\theta+\tan\theta=p$ ...(i)

$\sec\theta-\tan\theta=\frac{1}{p}$ ...(ii)

$+\quad+\quad+$

$2\sec\theta=p+\frac{1}{p}$ **(1 Mark)**

$\Rightarrow \quad 2\sec\theta = \frac{p^2+1}{p}$

$\Rightarrow \quad \sec\theta = \frac{p^2+1}{2p}$

$\sec\theta = \frac{1}{\cos\theta}$

$\cos\theta = \frac{2p}{p^2+1}$ **(1 Mark)**

By Elimination Method

$\sec\theta + \tan\theta = p$ ...(i)

$\sec\theta - \tan\theta = \frac{1}{p}$ ...(ii)

$- \quad + \quad -$

$2\tan\theta = p - \frac{1}{p}$ **(1 Mark)**

$\tan\theta = \frac{p^2-1}{2p}$

Now, $\tan\theta = \frac{\sin\theta}{\cos\theta}$

$\Rightarrow \quad \sin\theta = \tan\theta \,.\, \cos\theta$

$= \frac{p^2-1}{2p} \times \frac{2p}{p^2+1}$

$= \frac{p^2-1}{p^2+1}$ **(1 Mark)**

Another method to find sin θ by formula $Sin^2\theta = 1 - cos^2\theta$.

47. LHS $= \frac{\tan\theta}{1-\cot\theta} + \frac{\cot\theta}{1-\tan\theta}$

$= \frac{\sin\theta}{\cos\theta.\left(\frac{\sin\theta-\cos\theta}{\sin\theta}\right)} + \frac{\cos\theta}{\sin\theta.\left(\frac{\cos\theta-\sin\theta}{\cos\theta}\right)}$

(1 Mark)

$= \frac{\sin^2\theta}{\cos\theta(\sin\theta-\cos\theta)} + \frac{\cos^2\theta}{\sin\theta(\cos\theta-\sin\theta)}$

$= \frac{\sin^2\theta}{\cos\theta(\sin\theta-\cos\theta)} - \frac{\cos^2\theta}{\sin\theta(\sin\theta-\cos\theta)}$ **(1 Mark)**

$= \frac{\sin^2\theta\times\sin\theta-\cos^2\theta\times\cos\theta}{\sin\theta\cos\theta(\sin\theta-\cos\theta)}$

$= \frac{\sin^3\theta-\cos^3\theta}{\sin\theta\cos\theta(\sin\theta-\cos\theta)}$ **(1 Mark)**

$= \frac{(\sin\theta-\cos\theta)(\sin^2\theta+\cos^2\theta+\sin\theta\cos\theta)}{\sin\theta\cos\theta(\sin\theta-\cos\theta)}$

$= \sec\theta\,\text{cosec}\,\theta + 1$

RHS : $1 + \tan\theta + \cot\theta$

$= \frac{\sin\theta\cos\theta+1}{\sin\theta\cos\theta} = 1 + \sec\theta\,\text{cosec}\,\theta$ = LHS

LHS = RHS Hence Proved. **(1 Mark)**

48. Consider $\cot^2\theta\left(\frac{\sec\theta-1}{1+\sin\theta}\right) + \sec^2\theta\left(\frac{\sin\theta-1}{1+\sec\theta}\right)$

$= \frac{\cot^2\theta(\sec\theta-1)(\sec\theta+1) + \sec^2\theta(\sin\theta-1)(\sin\theta+1)}{(1+\sin\theta)(1+\sec\theta)}$ **(1 Mark)**

$= \frac{\cot^2\theta(\sec^2\theta-1)+\sec^2\theta(\sin^2\theta-1)}{(1+\sin\theta)(1+\sec\theta)}$

$= \frac{\cot^2\theta\tan^2\theta-\sec^2\theta\cos^2\theta}{(1+\sin\theta)(1+\sec\theta)}$ **(1 Mark)**

$= \frac{\frac{1}{\tan^2\theta}\times\tan^2\theta-\frac{1}{\cos^2\theta}\times\cos^2\theta}{(1+\sin\theta)(1+\sec\theta)}$ **(1 Mark)**

$= \frac{1-1}{(1+\sin\theta)(1+\sec\theta)}$

$= \frac{0}{(1+\sin\theta)(1+\sec\theta)}$

$= 0$ **(1 Mark)**

LHS = RHS

Hence proved.

49. We have

$\text{cosec}\theta + \cot\theta = P$

$\frac{1}{\sin\theta} + \frac{\cos\theta}{\sin\theta} = P$ **(1 Mark)**

$\frac{1+\cos\theta}{\sin\theta} = P$

Squaring both sides, we have

$\frac{(1+\cos\theta)^2}{\sin^2\theta} = P^2$ **(1 Mark)**

[Appliging C & D]

$\frac{P^2-1}{P^2+1} = \frac{\frac{(1+\cos\theta)^2}{\sin^2\theta}-1}{\frac{(1+\cos\theta)^2}{\sin^2\theta}+1}$ **(1 Mark)**

$$\frac{P^2-1}{P^2+1}=\frac{1+\cos^2\theta+2\cos\theta-\sin^2\theta}{1+\cos^2\theta+2\cos\theta+\sin^2\theta}$$

$$\frac{P^2-1}{P^2+1}=\frac{\cos^2\theta+2\cos\theta+\left(1-\sin^2\theta\right)}{1+\left(\cos^2\theta+\sin^2\theta\right)+2\cos\theta}$$

$$\frac{P^2-1}{P^2+1}=\frac{\cos^2\theta+2\cos\theta+\cos^2\theta}{1+1+2\cos\theta}$$ **(1 Mark)**

$$\frac{P^2-1}{P^2+1}=\frac{2\cos^2\theta+2\cos\theta}{2+2\cos\theta}$$

$$\frac{P^2-1}{P^2+1}=\frac{2\cos\theta(\cos\theta+1)}{2(1+\cos\theta)}$$

$$\frac{P^2-1}{P^2+1}=\cos\theta$$ **(1 Mark)**

Hence Proved

If $\frac{a}{b}=\frac{c}{d}$ then by componendo and dividendo (C & D) method $\frac{a+b}{a-b}=\frac{c+d}{c-d}$

50. $$\frac{1+\sin\theta-\cos\theta}{1+\sin\theta+\cos\theta}=\frac{1+\sin\theta-\cos\theta}{1+\sin\theta+\cos\theta}\times\frac{1+\sin\theta+\cos\theta}{1+\sin\theta+\cos\theta}$$

Multiplying numerator and denominator by $(1+\sin\theta+\cos\theta)$

$$=\frac{(1+\sin\theta)^2-\cos^2\theta}{(1+\sin\theta+\cos\theta)^2}$$ **(1 Mark)**

$$=\frac{1+\sin^2\theta+2\sin\theta-\cos^2\theta}{1+\sin^2\theta+\cos^2\theta+2\sin\theta+2\cos\theta+2\sin\theta\cos\theta}$$

$$=\frac{(1-\cos^2\theta)+\sin^2\theta+2\sin\theta}{1+1+2\sin\theta+2\cos\theta+2\sin\theta\cos\theta}$$ **(1 Mark)**

$$=\frac{2\sin^2\theta+2\sin\theta}{2(1+2\sin\theta)+2\cos\theta(1+\sin\theta)}$$

$$=\frac{2\sin\theta(\sin\theta+1)}{2(1+\sin\theta)(1+\cos\theta)}=\frac{\sin\theta}{1+\cos\theta}$$ **(1 Mark)**

$$\text{L.H.S}=\left(\frac{1+\sin\theta-\cos\theta}{1+\sin\theta+\cos\theta}\right)^2=\left(\frac{\sin\theta}{1+\cos\theta}\right)^2$$

$$=\frac{\sin^2\theta}{(1+\cos\theta)^2}=\frac{1-\cos^2\theta}{(1+\cos\theta)^2}$$

$$=\frac{(1-\cos\theta)\times(1+\cos\theta)}{(1+\cos\theta)^2}=\frac{1-\cos\theta}{1+\cos\theta}=\text{R.H.S.}$$ **(1 Mark)**

9 Chapter Some Applications of Trigonometry

Topic-1: Heights and Distances

Multiple Choice Questions

1. If a pole 6 m high casts a shadow $2\sqrt{3}$m long on the ground, then the Sun's elevation is **[CBSE Sample Paper 2023-24, Ap]**

(a) 60° (b) 45°
(c) 30° (d) 90°

2. If a pole 6 m high casts a shadow $2\sqrt{3}$ m long on the ground, then sun's elevation is: **[Delhi 2023, Ap]**

(a) 60° (b) 45°
(c) 30° (d) 90°

3. A ladder makes an angle of 60° with the ground when placed against a wall. If the foot of the ladder is 2m away from the wall, then the length of the ladder (in meters) is : **[Delhi 2014 Term-II, Ap]**

(a) $\frac{4}{\sqrt{3}}$ (b) $4\sqrt{3}$
(c) $2\sqrt{2}$ (d) 4

4. The angle of depression of a car, standing on the ground, from the top of a 75 m high tower, is 30°. The distance of the car from the base of the tower (in m.) is : **[All India 2013, Ap]**

(a) $25\sqrt{3}$ (b) $50\sqrt{3}$
(c) $75\sqrt{3}$ (d) 150

4 Very Short Answer Questions (1 Mark)

5. The angles of depressions from the observing positions O_1 and O_2 respectively of the object A are _________, _________. **[All India 2020, Ap]**

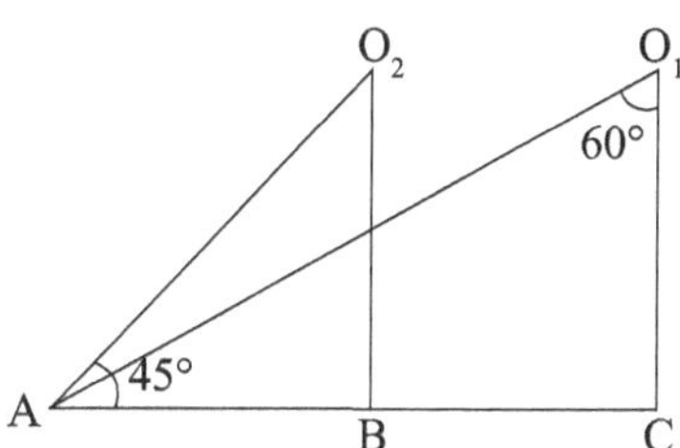

6. The ratio of the length of a vertical rod and the length of its shadow is 1: $\sqrt{3}$. Find the angle of elevation of the sum at that moment? **[Delhi 2020, Ap]**

7. If a tower 30 m high, casts a shadow $10\sqrt{3}$ m long on the ground, then what is the angle of elevation of the sun ? **[All India 2017 Term-II, Ap]**

8. AB is a 6 m high pole and CD is a ladder inclined at an angle of 60° to the horizontal and reaches up to a point D of pole. If AD = 2.54 m, find the length of the ladder. (use $\sqrt{3}$ = 1.73) **[Delhi 2016 Term-II, Ap]**

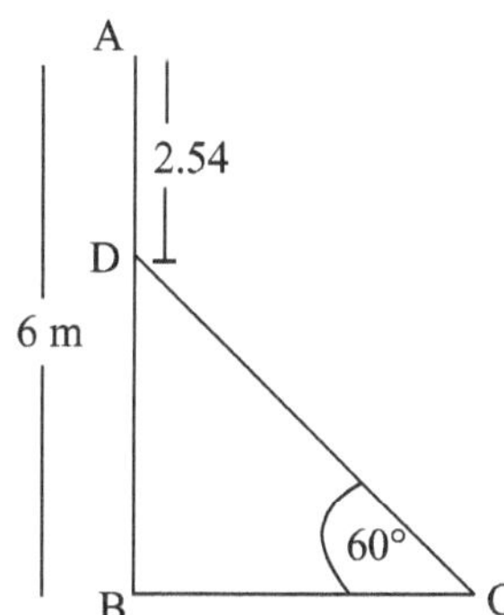

9. A tower AB is 20 m high and BC, its shadow on the ground, is $20\sqrt{3}$ m long. Find the Sun's altitude. **[All India 2015 Term-II, Ap]**

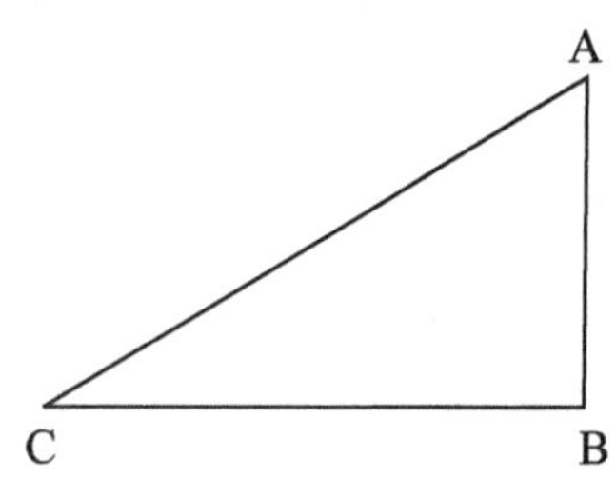

5 *Short Answer Questions (2 or 3 Marks)*

10. Find the length of the shadow on the ground of a pole of height 18 m when angle of elevation θ of the sun is such that $\tan\theta = \frac{6}{7}$. **[All India 2023 Set-II, Ap]**

11. Two men on either side of a cliff 75 m high observe the angles of elevation of the top of the cliff to be 30° and 60°. Find the distance between the two men.

[All India 2022 Term-II, Ap]

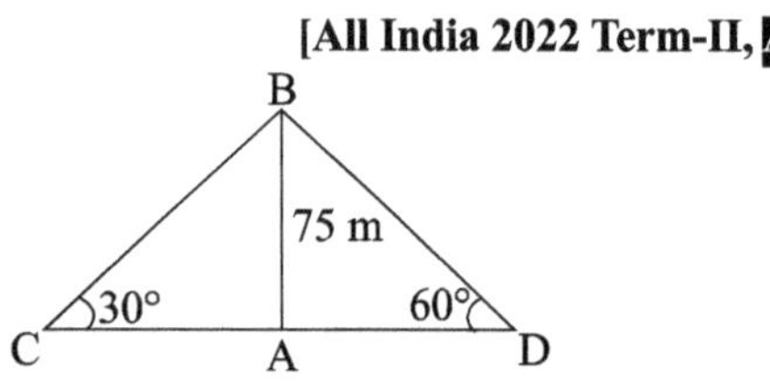

12. The position of an eagle and two identical geese are shown in the figure below. All the birds are at the same height from the ground. Assume that the Eagle can fly at the same speed in all directions and that the geese are unaware of the Eagle's intention and will not move from their positions. **[CBSE CFPQ 2022, Ap]**

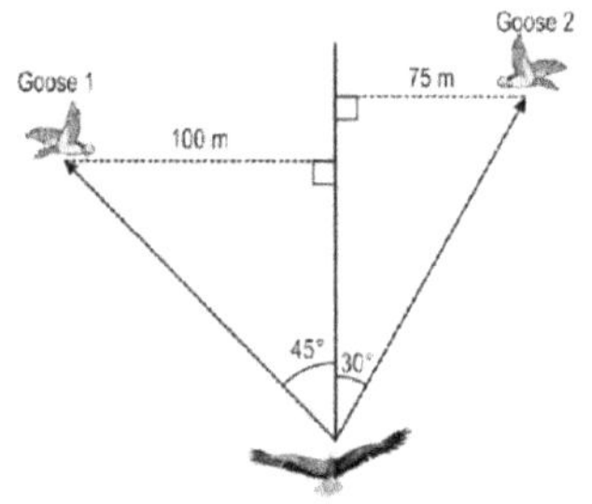

(**Note:** The figure is not to scale.)

If the eagle wants to attack the goose that is nearer to it, which one should it attack? Show your steps.

(**Note:** Use $\sqrt{2} = 1.41$, $\sqrt{3} = 1.73$)

13. Two boats are sailing in the sea 80 m apart from each other towards a cliff AB. The angles of depression of the boats from the top of the cliff are 30° and 45° respectively, as shown in Figure. Find the height of the cliff.

[All India 2022, Ap]

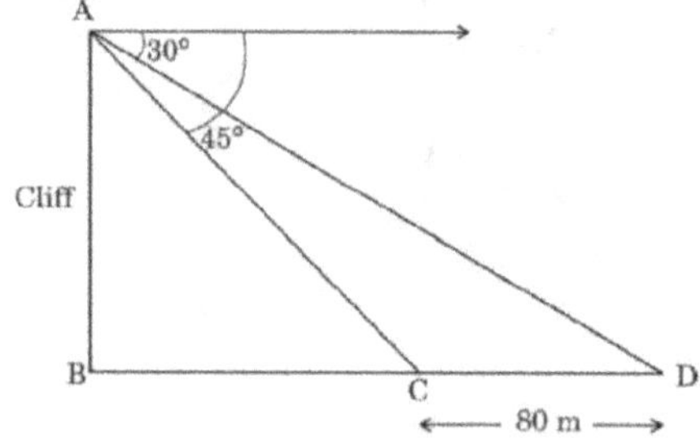

14. On a straight line passing through the foot of a tower, two points C and D are at distances of 4 m and 16 m from the foot respectively. If the angles of elevation from C and D of the top of the tower are complementary, then find the height of the tower. **[All India 2017 Term-II, Ap]**

15. The angles of depression of the top and bottom of a 50 m high building from the top of a tower are 45° and 60° respectively. Find the height of the tower and the horizontal distance between the tower and the building. (use $\sqrt{3} = 1.73$

[Delhi 2016 Term-II, Ap]

16. The angle of elevation of an aeroplane from a point A on the ground is 60°. After a flight of 15 seconds, the angle of elevation changes to 30°. If the aeroplane is flying at a constant height of $1500\sqrt{3}$ m, find the speed of the plane in km/hr. **[All India 2015 Term-II, Ap]**

17. Two ships are there in the sea on either side of a light house in such a way that the ships and the light house are in the same straight line. The angles of depression of two ships are observed from the top of the light house are 60° and 45°. If the height of the light house is 200 m, find the distance between the two ships. [Use $\sqrt{3} = 1.73$]

[Delhi 2014 Term-II, Ap]

18. The horizontal distance between two poles is 15 cm. The angle of depression of the top of first pole as seen from the top of second pole is 30°. If the height of the second pole is 24 m, find the height of the first pole. $\left[\text{Use } \sqrt{3} = 1.732\right]$ **[All India 2013, Ap]**

6 *Long Answer Questions (4 or 5 Marks)*

19. The angle of elevation of the top of a vertical tower from a point P on the ground is 60°. From another point Q, 10 m vertically above the first point P, its angle of elevation is 30°. Find : **[All India 2023, Ap]**

(a) The height of the tower.

(b) The distance of the point P from the foot of the tower.

(c) The distance of the point P from the top of the tower.

20. A straight highway leads to the foot of a tower. A man standing on the top of the 75 m high tower observes two cars at angles of depression of 30° and 60°, which are approching the foot of the tower. If one car is exactly behind the other on the seme side of the tower, find the distance between the two cars. (use $\sqrt{3} = 1.73$) **[Delhi 2023, Ap]**

21. From the top of 7 m high building, the angle of elevation of the top of a cable tower is 60° and the angle of depression of its foot is 30¦. Determine the height of the tower. **[Delhi 2023, Ap]**

22. From a point on the ground, the angles of elevation of the bottom and the top of a tower fixed at the top of a 20 m high building are 45° and 60° respectively. Find the height of the tower. **[All India 2020, Ap]**

23. A vertical tower stands on a horizontal plane and is surmounted by a vertical flag-staff of height 6 m. At a point on the plane, the angle of elevation of the bottom and top of the flag-staff are 30° and 45° respectively. Find the height of the tower. (Take $\sqrt{3} = 1.73$)

[Delhi 2020, Ap]

24. Amit, standing on a horizontal plane, finds a bird flying at a distance of 200 m from him at an elevation of 30°. Deepak standing on the roof of a 50 m high building, finds the angle of elevation of the same bird to be 45°. Amit and Deepak are on opposite sides of the bird. Find the distance of the bird from Deepak. **[All India 2019, Ap]**

25. The shadow of a tower standing on a level ground is found to be 40 m longer when the Sun's altitude is 30° than when it was 60°. Find the height of the tower. (Given $\sqrt{3} - 1.732$)

[All India 2019, Ap]

26. A man in a boat rowing away from a light house 100 m high takes 2 minutes to change the angle of elevation of the top of the light house from 60° to 30°. Find the speed of the boat in metres per minute. [Use $\sqrt{3} = 1.732$]

[Delhi 2019, Ap]

27. Two poles of equal heights are standing opposite each other on either side of the road, which is 80 m wide. From a point between them on the road, the angles of elevation of the top of the poles are 60° and 30° respectively. Find the height of the poles and the distances of the point from the poles. **[Delhi 2019, Ap]**

28. As observed from the top of a 100 m high light house from the sea-level, the angles of depression of two ships are 30° and 45°. If one ship is exactly behind the other on the same side of the light house, find the distance between the two ships. **[All India 2018, Ap]**

29. An aeroplane is flying at a height of 300 m above the ground. Flying at this height, the angles of depression from the aeroplane of two points on both banks of a river in opposite directions are 45° and 60° respectively. Find the width of the river. [Use $\sqrt{3} = 1.732$]

[All India 2017 Term-II, Ap]

30. A bird is sitting on the top of a 80 m high tree. From a point on the ground, the angle of elevation of the bird is 45°. The bird flies away horizontally in such a way that it remained at a constant height from the ground. After 2 seconds, the angle of elevation of the bird from the same point is 30°. Find the speed of flying of the bird. (Take $\sqrt{3} = 1.732$)

[Delhi 2016 Term-II, Ap]

31. At a point A, 20 metres above the level of water in a lake, the angle of elevation of a cloud is 30°. The angle of depression of the reflection of the cloud in the lake, at A is 60°. Find the distance of the cloud from A.

[All India 2015 Term-II, Ap]

32. A farmer has a triangular field *ABC* as shown in the figure given below. He decided to divide his field among his two children's –Piyush of age 12 years and Reena of age 16 years. He divided his field in two triangular parts *ABD* and *ADC*. He gave triangular part *ABD* to Piyush and triangular part *ADC* to Reena. Find the area of each triangular part of the field. (Take $\sqrt{3} = 1.7$)

[All India 2015 Term-I, Ap]

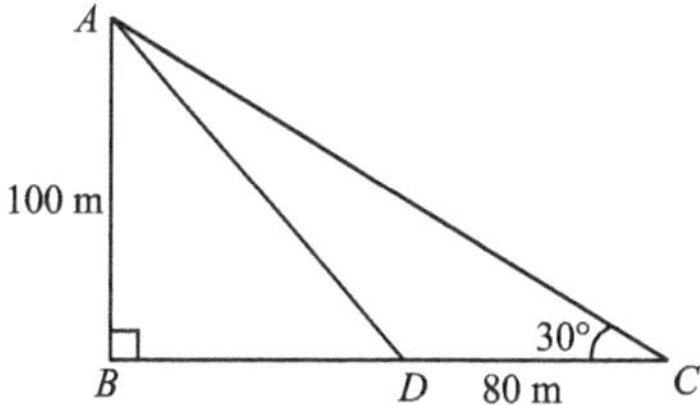

33. The angles of elevation and depression of the top and the bottom of a tower from the top of a building, 60 m high, are 30° and 60° respectively. Find the difference between the heights of the building and the tower and the distance between them. **[Delhi 2014 Term-II, Ap]**

34. The angle of elevation of the top of a building from the foot of the tower is 30° and the angle of elevation of the top of the tower from the foot of the building is 60°. If the tower is 60 m high, find the height of the building. **[All India 2013, Ap]**

Case Based Questions (4 Marks)

35. One evening, Kaushik was in a park. Children were playing cricket. Birds were singing on a nearby tree of height 80m. He observed a bird on the tree at an angle of elevation of 45°.

When a sixer was hit, a ball flew through the tree frightening the bird to fly away. In 2 seconds, he observed the bird flying at the same height at an angle of elevation of 30° and the ball flying towards him at the same height at an angle of elevation of 60°. **[CBSE Sample Paper 2023-24, Ap]**

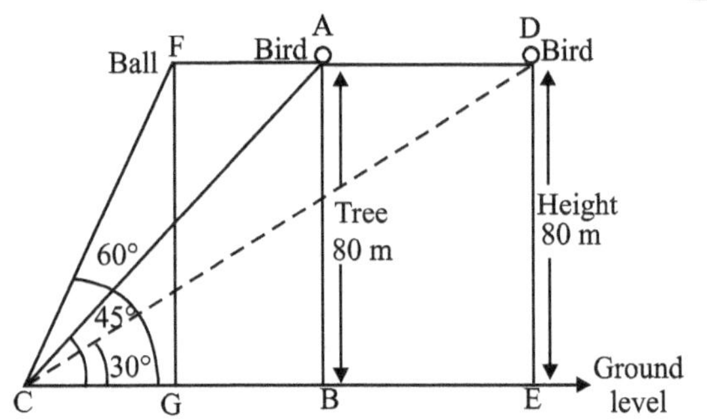

(i) At what distance from the foot of the tree was he observing the bird sitting on the tree?

(ii) How far did the bird fly in the mentioned time?

OR

After hitting the tree, how far did the ball travel in the sky when Kaushik saw the ball?

(iii) What is the speed of the bird in m/min if it had flown $20(\sqrt{3}+1)$m?

36. Radio towers are used for transmitting a range of communication services including radio and television, The tower will either act as an antenna itself or support one or more antennas on its structure. On a similar concept, a radio station tower was built in two Section A and B. Tower is supported by wires from a point O.

Distance between the base of the tower and point O is 36 cm. From point O, the angle of elevation of the top of the Section B is 30° and the angle of elevation of the top of Section A is 45°. **[All India 2023 Set-II, Ap]**

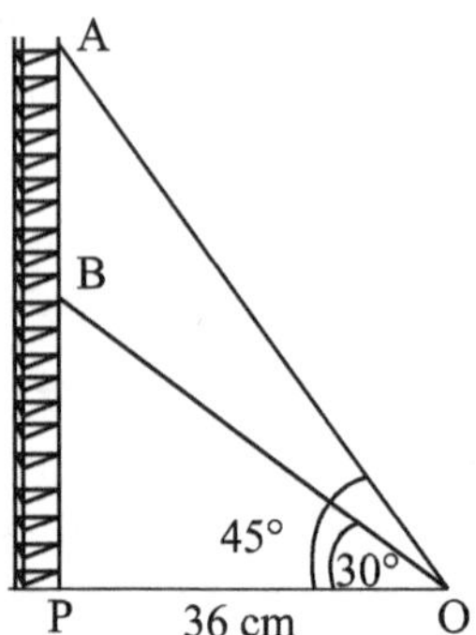

Based on the above information, answer the following questions:

(i) Find the length of the wire from the point O to the top of Section B.

(ii) Find the distance AB.

OR

Find the area of ΔOPB.

(iii) Find the height of the Section A from the base of the tower.

37. We all have seen the airplanes flying in the sky but might have not thought of how they actually reach the correct destination. Air Traffic Control (ATC) is a service provided by ground-based air traffic controllers who direct aircraft on the ground and through a given section of controlled airspace, and can provide advisory services to aircraft in non-controlled airspace. Actually, all this air traffic is managed and regulated by using various concepts based on coordinate geometry and trigonometry.

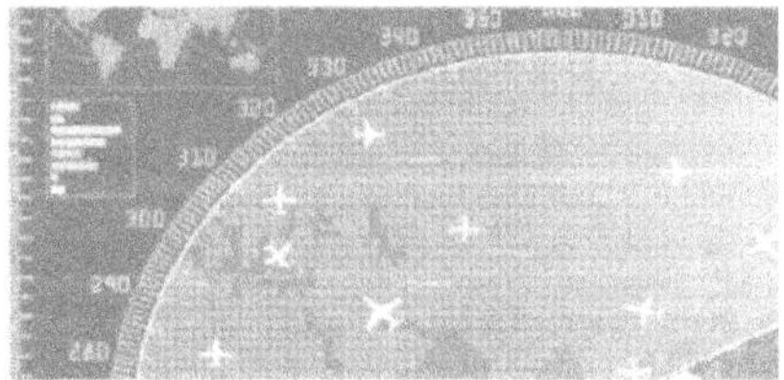

At a given instance, ATC finds that the angle of elevation of an airplane from a point on the ground is 60°. After a flight of 30 seconds, it is observed that the angle of elevation changes to 30°. The height of the plane remains constantly as $3000\sqrt{3}$ m. Use the above information to answer the questions that follow-

(i) Draw a neat labelled figure to show the above situation diagrammatically.

[CBSE Sample Paper 2022-23, Ap]

(ii) What is the distance travelled by the plane in 30 seconds? **[CBSE Sample Paper 2022-23, Ap]**

OR

Keeping the height constant, during the above flight, it was observed that after $15(\sqrt{3}-1)$ seconds, the angle of elevation changed to 45°. How much is the distance travelled in that duration.

(iii) What is the speed of the plane in km/hr.

[CBSE Sample Paper 2022-23, Ap]

38. Kite Festival

Kite festival is celebrated in many countries at different times of the year. In India, every year 14th January is celebrated as International Kite Day. On this day many people visit India and participate in the festival by flying various kinds of kites.

The picture given below, shows three kites flying together.

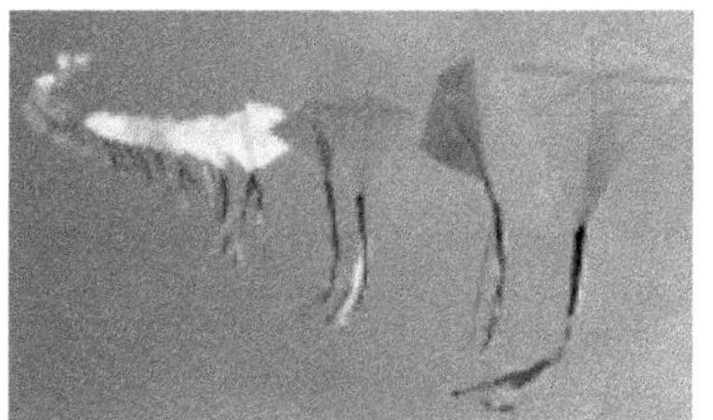

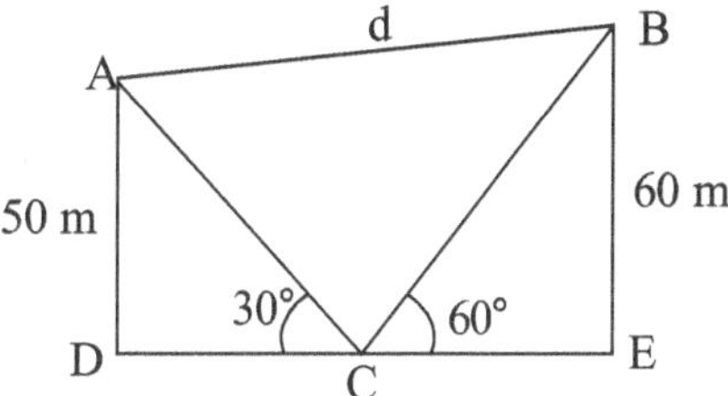

In Fig., the angles of elevation of two kites (Points A and B) from the hands of a man (Point C) are found to be 30° and 60° respectively. Taking AD = 50 m and BE = 60 m, find

[All India 2022, Term-II, Ap]

(1) the lengths of strings used (take them straight) for kites A and B as shown in the figure.

(2) the distance 'd' between these two kites.

Hints & Solutions

Topic-1: Heights and Distances

1. (d) 60° **(1 Mark)**

2. (a) $\frac{AB}{BC} = \frac{\text{Perp.}}{\text{Base}} = \tan\theta$

$\Rightarrow \frac{6}{2\sqrt{3}} = \tan\theta$

$\Rightarrow \sqrt{3} = \tan\theta \Rightarrow \theta = 60°$

A, 6, B, C, $2\sqrt{3}$

(1 Mark)

3. (d)

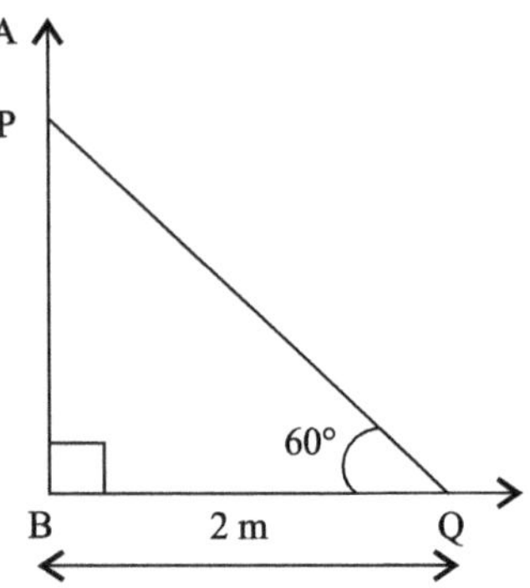

In fig. PQ is the length of ladder which is placed against the wall AB and makes an angle 60° with the ground.

BQ = 2 m

In right triangle PBQ:

$\cos 60° = \frac{BQ}{PQ} = \frac{2}{PQ}$ $[\because \cos\theta = \frac{\text{Base}}{\text{Hypotenuse}}]$

$\Rightarrow \frac{1}{2} = \frac{2}{PQ}$

$\Rightarrow PQ = 4$ m

$\therefore$ Length of the ladder is 4 m. **(1 Mark)**

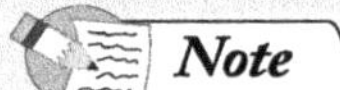

Note

It is also can be solved by using tanθ as

$tan 60° = \frac{BP}{BQ} \Rightarrow BP = \sqrt{3}\ BQ = 2\sqrt{3}$

By Pythagoras theorem in ΔPBQ.

$PQ^2 = BP^2 + BQ^2 = (2\sqrt{3})^2 + (2)^2 = 12 + 4 = 16$

$\therefore PQ = 4$

4. (c) To find: *BC*

In right Δ*ABC*

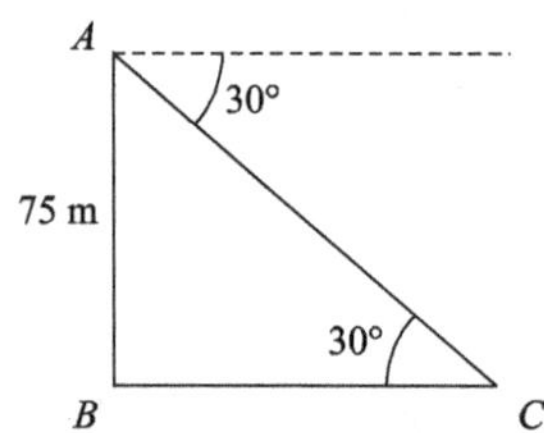

$\tan\theta = \frac{P}{B}$

$\tan 30° = \frac{AB}{BC}$

$\frac{1}{\sqrt{3}} = \frac{75m}{BC}$

$BC = 75\sqrt{3}m$ **(1 Mark)**

Note

The angle of depression of a point on the object being viewed is the angle formed by the line of sight with the horizontal when the point is below the horizontal level.

5. [30°, 45°]

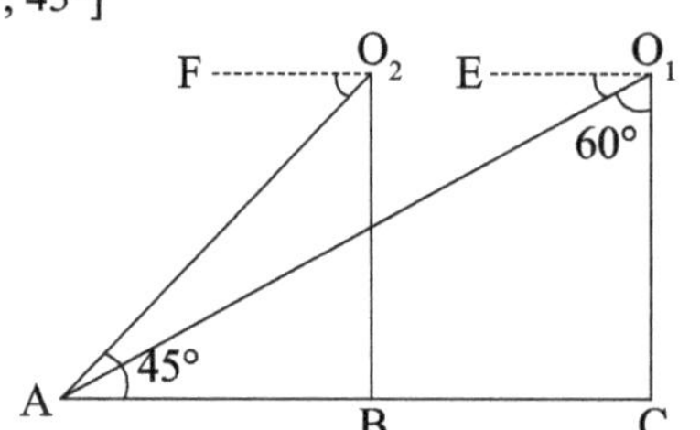

(½ Mark)

Depression angle at $O_1 = 90° - 60° = 30°$

Depression angle at $O_2 = 45° = \angle BAO_2$ **(½ Mark)**

6. $\tan\theta = \frac{\text{length of vertical rod}}{\text{length of shadow}}$

$= \frac{1}{\sqrt{3}} = \tan 30°$

$\Rightarrow \theta = 30°$ **(1 Mark)**

7. Let PQ be the height of tower and QR be its shadow

PQ = 30 m

QR = $10\sqrt{3}$ m

Now, In ΔPQR

$$\tan\theta = \frac{PQ}{QR}$$

$$\tan\theta = \frac{30}{10\sqrt{3}}$$ **(½ Mark)**

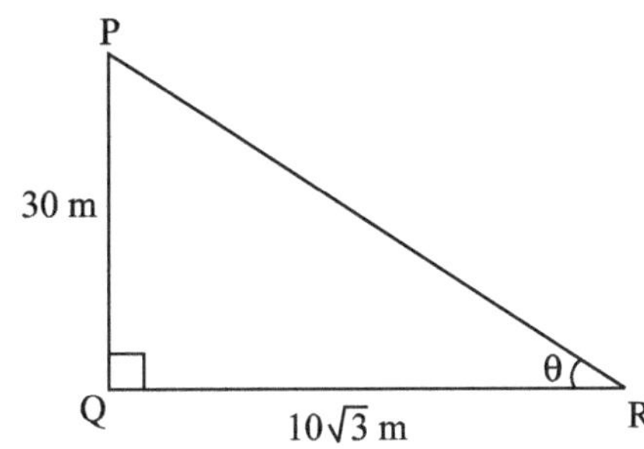

$$\tan\theta = \frac{30\times\sqrt{3}}{10\sqrt{3}\times\sqrt{3}} = \sqrt{3}$$

$\Rightarrow \tan\theta = \sqrt{3}$

$\tan\theta = \tan 60^\circ$

$\Rightarrow \theta = 60^\circ$ **(½ Mark)**

Thus, angle of elevation of sun is 60°

8. Given: $AD = 2.54$ m

$AB = AD + DB = 6$ m

$2.54 + DB = 6$

$DB = 3.46$ m **(½ Mark)**

In right triangle BCD

$$\sin 60^\circ = \frac{BD}{CD} \qquad \left[\because \sin\theta = \frac{p}{H}\right]$$

$$\frac{\sqrt{3}}{2} = \frac{3.46}{CD}$$

$$CD = \frac{2\times 3.46}{\sqrt{3}} = \frac{2\times 3.46}{1.73} = 4 \text{ m}$$

$\therefore$ Length of the ladder = 4 m **(½ Mark)**

9. Given: $AB = 20$ m, $BC = 20\sqrt{3}$

In right ΔABC

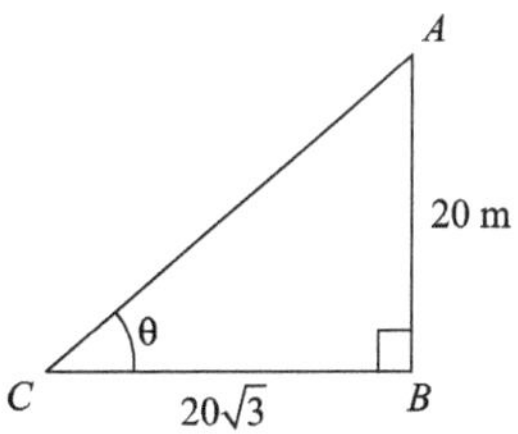

$$\tan\theta = \frac{AB}{BC}$$

$$\tan\theta = \frac{20}{20\sqrt{3}} = \frac{1}{\sqrt{3}}$$ **(½ Mark)**

$\Rightarrow \tan\theta = \tan 30^\circ$

$\Rightarrow \theta = 30^\circ$

Thus, the sun's altitude is 30° **(½ Mark)**

10. (a)

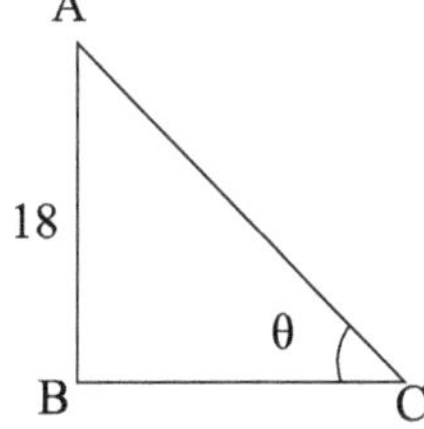

Let AB represent the pole of height 18 m.

$$\tan\theta = \frac{6}{7}$$ **(1 Mark)**

Let BC represent the length of shadow.

In the triangle ABC, AB represent the perpendicular BC represent the base and AC is the hypotenuse of triangle.

For any right triangle, $\tan\theta$ is the ratio of perpendicular to base.

Hence for the given triangle, perpendicular is 6 m and base is 7 m.

But according to diagram, perpendicular is 18 m.

$$\therefore \tan\theta = \frac{6}{7} = \frac{6\times 3}{7\times 3} = \frac{18}{21}$$ **(1 Mark)**

11. Let AD = 'x'm & AC = 'y'm.

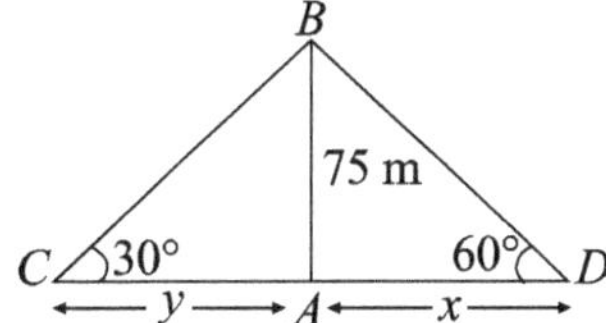

In ΔBAD

$$\tan 60^\circ = \frac{AB}{AD}$$

$$\sqrt{3} = \frac{75}{x}$$

$$x = \frac{75}{\sqrt{3}} \text{ m.}$$ **(1 Mark)**

In ΔBAC

$$\tan 30^\circ = \frac{AB}{AC}$$

$$\frac{1}{\sqrt{3}} = \frac{75}{y}$$

$$y = 75\sqrt{3} \text{ m.}$$

Required distance $AC = x + y$

$$= \frac{75}{\sqrt{3}} \times \frac{\sqrt{3}}{\sqrt{3}} + 75\sqrt{3} = 100\sqrt{3} \text{ m}$$ **(1 Mark)**

12. Applies trigonometric ratio to determine the distance of the first goose from Eagle as $100\sqrt{2}$ m or 141m.

(1 Mark)

Applies trigonometric ratio to determine the distance of the second goose from Eagle as 150 m.
Argues that since goose 1 is closer, the Eagle would attack it.

(1 Mark)

13.

Topper's Answer

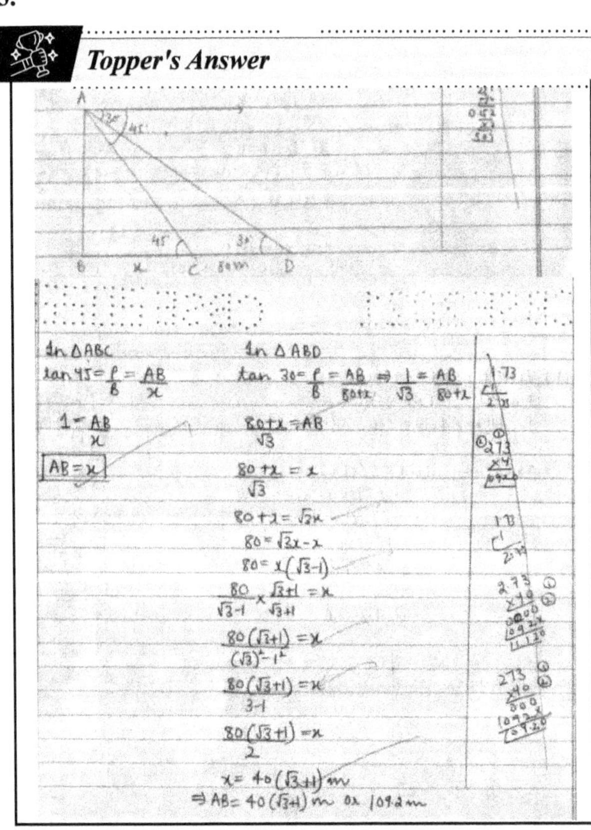

14. Let AB is the height of tower 'h' m. Suppose the angle of elevation of top of tower from point C on ground be θ.

The angle of elevation of the top of the tower from point D is (90° – θ)

Here, BC = 4 m & BD = 16 m

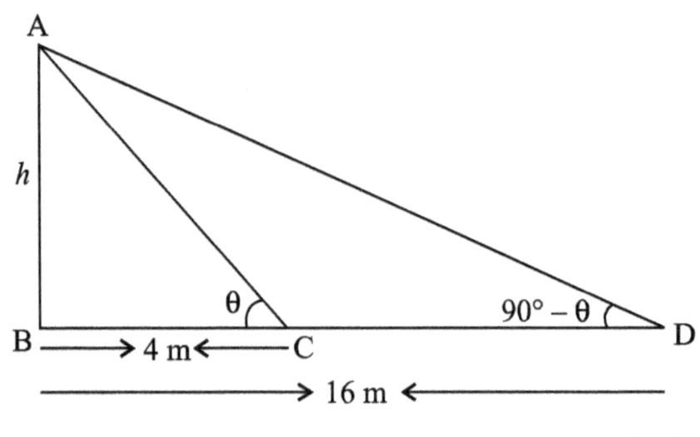

(½ Mark)

In ΔABC, $\tan\theta = \frac{\text{Perpendicular}}{\text{Base}}$

$$\tan\theta = \frac{AB}{BC} = \frac{h}{4} \quad \text{...(i)}$$ **(½ Mark)**

In Δ ABD,

$$\tan(90 - \theta) = \frac{AB}{BC} = \frac{h}{16}$$

$$\Rightarrow \cot\theta = \frac{h}{16} \quad \text{...(ii)}$$ **(1 Mark)**

Multiplying (i) and (ii), we get

$$(\tan\theta)(\cot\theta) = \frac{h}{4} \times \frac{h}{16}$$

$$\Rightarrow 1 = \frac{h^2}{64} \Rightarrow h^2 = 64 \Rightarrow h = \sqrt{64} = 8 \text{ m}$$

Thus, the height of tower is 8 m. **(1 Mark)**

15. Let height of the tower AB be h m and the horizontal distance between tower and the building be $BC = x$ m.

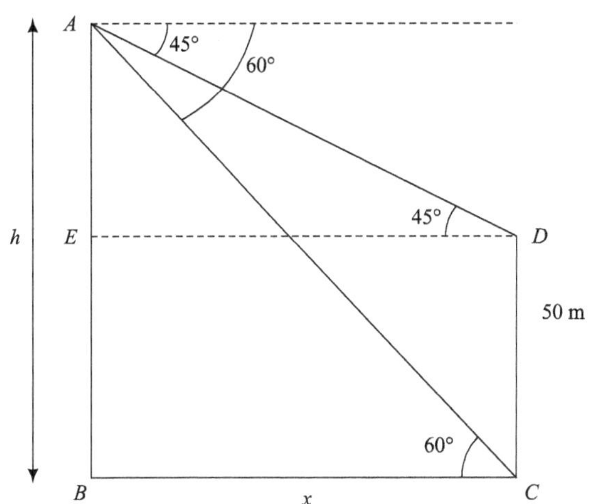

So $AE = (h - 50)m$ **(½ Mark)**

In ΔAED,

$$\tan 45° = \frac{AE}{ED} \qquad \left[\because \tan\theta = \frac{P}{B}\right]$$

$$1 = \frac{h-50}{x}$$

$$x = h - 50 \qquad ...(1)$$ **(½ Mark)**

In ΔABC

$$\Rightarrow \tan 60° = \frac{AB}{BC}$$

$$\Rightarrow \sqrt{3} = \frac{h}{x}$$

$$h = \sqrt{3}\, x \qquad ...(2)$$ **(½ Mark)**

From (1) and (2)

$$x = \sqrt{3}\, x - 50$$

$$\Rightarrow \sqrt{3}\, x - x = 50$$

$$\Rightarrow x(\sqrt{3}-1) = 50$$

$$\Rightarrow x = \frac{50}{\sqrt{3}-1} \times \frac{\sqrt{3}+1}{\sqrt{3}+1}$$

$$= \frac{50(\sqrt{3}+1)}{(\sqrt{3})^2-(1)^2} \qquad [\because (a-b)(a+b) = a^2 - b^2]$$

$$= \frac{50(\sqrt{3}+1)}{2}$$

$= 25 \times 2.73 = 68.25$ m **(1 Mark)**

Substituting value of x in (1)

$68.25 = h - 50$

$h = 68.25 + 50$

$h = 118.25$ m

$\therefore$ Height of tower is 118.25 m and Horizontal distance between the tower and the building is 68.25 m.

(½ Mark)

Trignometry ratios are applicable for right triangle, when one side and one acute angle are given and we have to find other sides.

16. Height of aeroplane $= DB = CE = 1500\sqrt{3}$ m

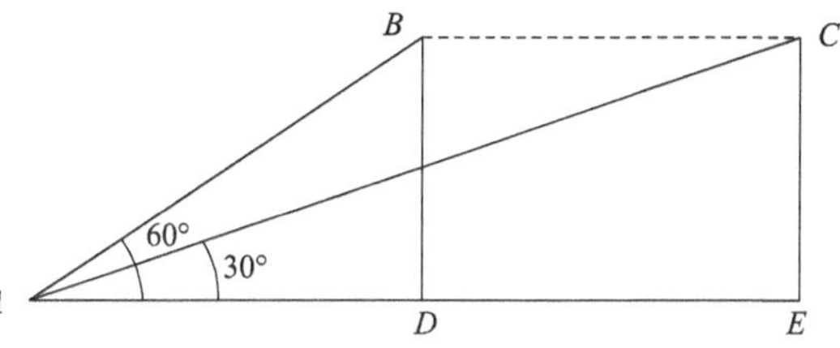

(½ Mark)

$\angle BAE = 60°$, $\angle CAE = 30°$

In right ΔAOB,

$$\Rightarrow \tan 60° = \frac{BD}{AD}$$

$$\Rightarrow \sqrt{3} = \frac{1500\sqrt{3}}{AD} \Rightarrow AD = 1500 \text{ m}$$ **(½ Mark)**

In right ΔACE

$$\tan 30° = \frac{CE}{AE}$$

$$\Rightarrow \frac{1}{\sqrt{3}} = \frac{1500\sqrt{3}}{AE}$$

$AE = 4500$ m **(1 Mark)**

$\therefore$ Distance covered by plane in 15 seconds $= BC$

$= DE = AE - AD$

$= 4500 - 1500 = 3000$ m

$\because$ Speed $= \dfrac{\text{Distance}}{\text{Time}}$

$\therefore$ Speed of aeroplane $= \dfrac{3000\text{m}}{15\text{sec}}$

$= 200$ m/s

$= 200 \times \dfrac{1}{1000} \times 60 \times 60$ km/hr

$= 720$ km/hr. **(1 Mark)**

17. Let d be the distance between two ships and x m be the distance of one of the ships from the light house.

Distance of other ship from light house = $(d - x)$ mt.

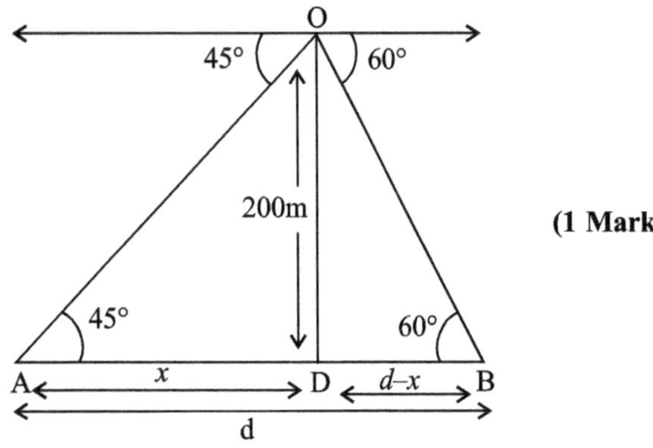

(1 Mark)

In rt ΔADO

$\tan 45° = \dfrac{OD}{AD} = \dfrac{200}{x}$ $\left[\tan\theta = \dfrac{P}{B}\right]$

$1 = \dfrac{200}{x}$

$x = 200$ ...(1)

In right ΔBDO

$\tan 60° = \dfrac{OD}{BD} \Rightarrow \sqrt{3} = \dfrac{200}{d - x}$

$\Rightarrow d - x = \dfrac{200}{\sqrt{3}}$

$\Rightarrow d - 200 = \dfrac{200}{\sqrt{3}}$ [From (1)]

$\Rightarrow d = \dfrac{200}{\sqrt{3}} + 200$ **(1 Mark)**

$\Rightarrow d = \dfrac{200}{\sqrt{3}} + 200 \Rightarrow d = 200\left[\dfrac{\sqrt{3}+1}{\sqrt{3}}\right]$

$\Rightarrow d = 200\left[\dfrac{\sqrt{3}+1}{\sqrt{3}} \times \dfrac{\sqrt{3}}{\sqrt{3}}\right]$

$= 200\left[\dfrac{3+\sqrt{3}}{3}\right] = 200 \times 1.58 = 316$ (approx)

Thus, distance between two ships is approximately 316 m.

(1 Mark)

18. Let height of first pole, CE be h metres

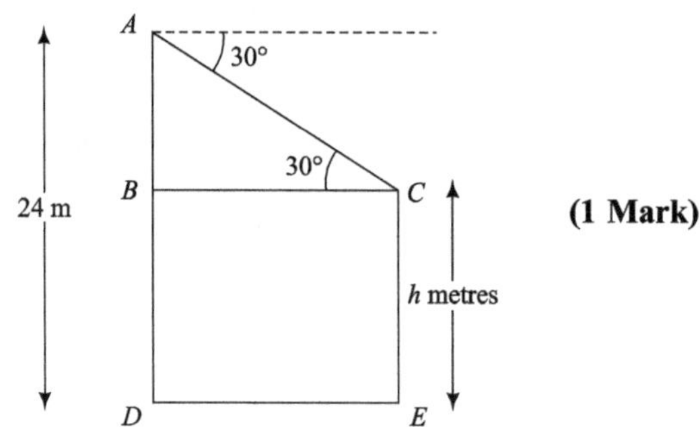

(1 Mark)

Height of second pole,

$AD = 24\ m$

$AB = AD - BD$

$AB = AD - CE$ $(\because BD = CE)$

$AB = 24 - h$

Horizontal distance between two poles, $DE = 15$ m

In right ΔABC

$\tan\theta = \dfrac{P}{B}$

$\Rightarrow \tan 30° = \dfrac{AB}{BC}$

$\Rightarrow \dfrac{1}{\sqrt{3}} = \dfrac{24-h}{15}$ $(\because BC = DE = 15)$ **(1 Mark)**

$\Rightarrow 15 = \sqrt{3}(24 - h)$

$\Rightarrow 15 = 24\sqrt{3} - h\sqrt{3}$

$\Rightarrow h\sqrt{3} = 24\sqrt{3} - 15$

$\Rightarrow h = \dfrac{24\sqrt{3}-15}{\sqrt{3}} \times \dfrac{\sqrt{3}}{\sqrt{3}}$

$\Rightarrow h = \dfrac{72 - 15\sqrt{3}}{3} = 24 - 5\sqrt{3}$

$\Rightarrow h = (24 - 5\sqrt{3})$ m

$\Rightarrow h = 15.34$ m **(1 Mark)**

19. In ΔAQO

$\tan 45° = \dfrac{h}{OQ}$

In $\Delta APB \Rightarrow \tan 60° = \dfrac{h+10}{PB}$

where PB = OQ

$\Rightarrow \dfrac{h}{\tan 45°} = \dfrac{h+10}{\tan 60°}$

$\Rightarrow h = \dfrac{h+10}{\sqrt{3}}$

$\Rightarrow \sqrt{3}h - h = 10 \Rightarrow h = \dfrac{10}{\sqrt{3}-1}$ **(1 Mark)**

(a) height of tower = h + 10 = $\dfrac{10}{\sqrt{3}-1} + 10 = \dfrac{10\sqrt{3}}{\sqrt{3}-1}$ **(1 Mark)**

(b) distance of PB = h = $\dfrac{10}{\sqrt{3}-1}$ **(1 Mark)**

(c) distance of P

$A = \sqrt{(h+10)^2 + h^2} = \sqrt{h^2 + 100 + 20h + h^2}$

$\Rightarrow \sqrt{\dfrac{300}{(\sqrt{3}-1)^2} + \dfrac{100}{(\sqrt{3}-1)^2}} = \dfrac{20}{(\sqrt{3}-1)}$ **(1 Mark)**

20. CD = ?

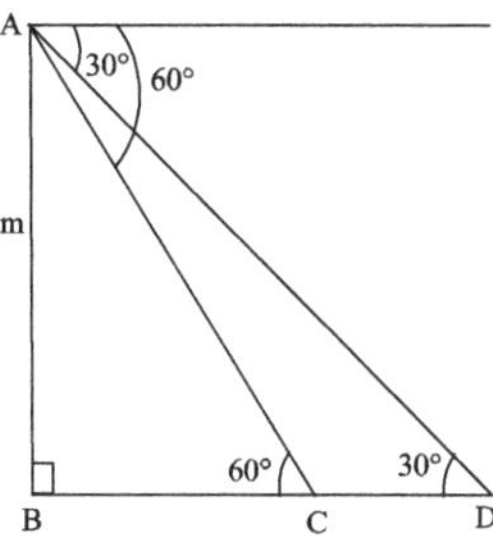

Let AB be the 75m high tower,

In ΔABC, $\angle B = 90°$

$\dfrac{AB}{BC} = \tan 60°$

$\Rightarrow \quad BC = \dfrac{AB}{\tan 60^0} = \dfrac{75m}{\sqrt{3}}$

$25\sqrt{3}m$ ...(i)

Now In ΔABD, $\dfrac{AB}{BD} = \tan 30^0$ **(2 Marks)**

$BD = \dfrac{AB}{\tan 30^0} = 75 \times \sqrt{3} = 75 \times \sqrt{3}$ ...(ii)

CD = BD – BC (using (i) & (ii), we get)

$\Rightarrow 75\sqrt{3} - 25\sqrt{3} = 50\sqrt{3}$ **(2 Marks)**

Note

sin θ = P/H, cos θ = B/H, tan θ = P/B, where P = perpendicular, B = base, H = Hypotenuse]

21. BD ll CE

So BD = CE = 7m.

Now, In ΔBCD

$\Rightarrow \dfrac{BC}{BD} = \dfrac{BC}{7} = \cot 30^0$

$\Rightarrow BC = 7 \times \sqrt{3} = 7\sqrt{3}$ **(2 Marks)**

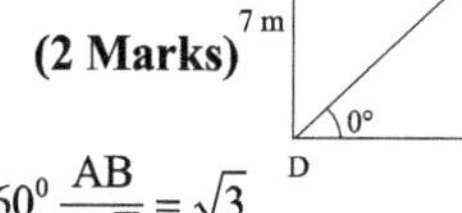

Now in ΔABC, $\dfrac{AB}{BC} = \tan 60^0 \; \dfrac{AB}{7\sqrt{3}} = \sqrt{3}$

$AB = 7\sqrt{3} \times \sqrt{3} = 21$ m

Total height of tower = AB + BD = 21 + 7 = 28 m

(2 Marks)

22. AB be the building of height 20 m

Let height of tower AC is *h* m.

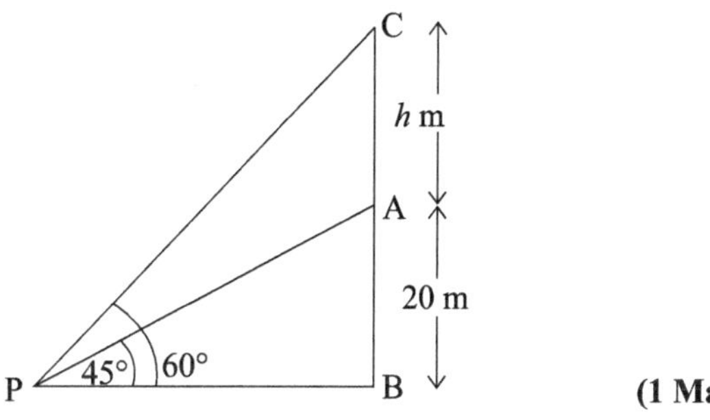

(1 Mark)

In right ΔAPB.

$\tan 45° = \dfrac{AB}{PB}$ $\left[\tan\theta = \dfrac{P}{B}\right]$

$1 = \dfrac{20}{PB}$ PB $\Rightarrow$ = 20 m **(1½ Marks)**

In right ΔPCB

$\tan 60° = \dfrac{BC}{PB}, \quad \sqrt{3} = \dfrac{20+h}{20}$

$20\sqrt{3} = 20 + h$

$h = 20\sqrt{3} - 20 = 20(\sqrt{3} - 1)$ m **(1½ Marks)**

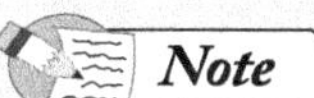

Note

The angle of elevation of a point viewed, is the angle formed by the line of sight with horizontal when it is above horizontal level.

23. AB = height of flag-staff = 6m

Let BC = height of tower = h m

In right ΔBCD

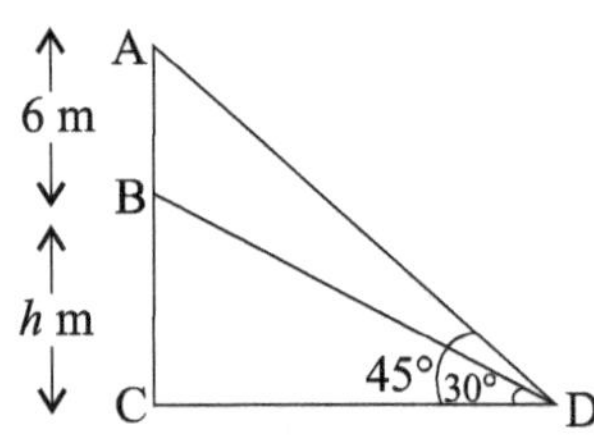

(1 Mark)

$$\tan 30° = \frac{P}{B} = \frac{BC}{CD}$$

$$\Rightarrow \frac{h}{CD} = \frac{1}{\sqrt{3}} \Rightarrow CD = h\sqrt{3} \quad ....(i)$$

In right ΔACD, $\tan 45° = \frac{P}{B} = \frac{AC}{CD}$ **(1 Mark)**

$$\Rightarrow \frac{h+6}{CD} = 1 \Rightarrow h = CD - 6$$

$$\Rightarrow h = h\sqrt{3} - 6 \quad \text{[From (i)]}$$

$$\Rightarrow h(\sqrt{3}-1) = 6$$

$$\Rightarrow h = \frac{6}{\sqrt{3}-1} \times \frac{\sqrt{3}+1}{\sqrt{3}+1} \Rightarrow h = \frac{6(\sqrt{3}+1)}{2}$$ **(1 Mark)**

$$\Rightarrow h = 3(\sqrt{3}+1)$$

$h = 3 \times 2.73 \Rightarrow h = 8.19$m **(1 Mark)**

$\therefore$ Height of the tower is 8.19m

24. Let Amit be at C point and the bird is at point A such that $\angle ACB = 30°$. Let AB be the height of bird from point B on ground and Deepak is at D point, DE is the building of height 50 m.

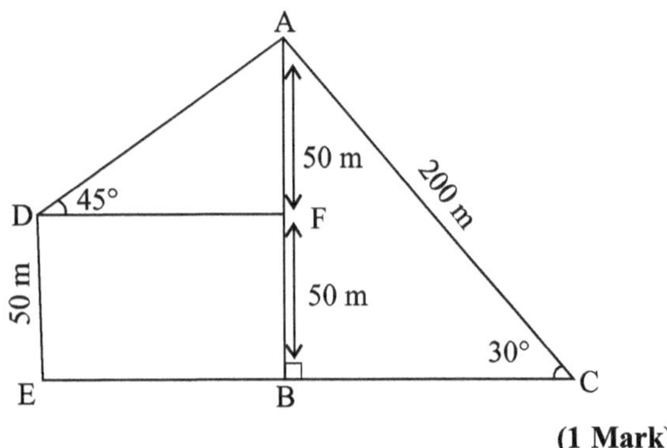

(1 Mark)

In right triangle ABC, we have

$$\sin 30° = \frac{P}{H} = \frac{AB}{AC}$$

$$\frac{1}{2} = \frac{AB}{200}$$

AB = 100 m **(1 Mark)**

In right ΔAFD, we have

$$\sin 45° = \frac{P}{H} = \frac{AF}{AD}$$

$\therefore$ AB = AF + BF **(1 Mark)**

100 = AF + 50

AF = 50

$$\therefore \sin 45° = \frac{AF}{AD} \Rightarrow \frac{1}{\sqrt{2}} = \frac{50}{AD}$$

$AD = 50\sqrt{2}$m **(1 Mark)**

Hence, the distance of bird from Deepak is $50\sqrt{2}$m

25.

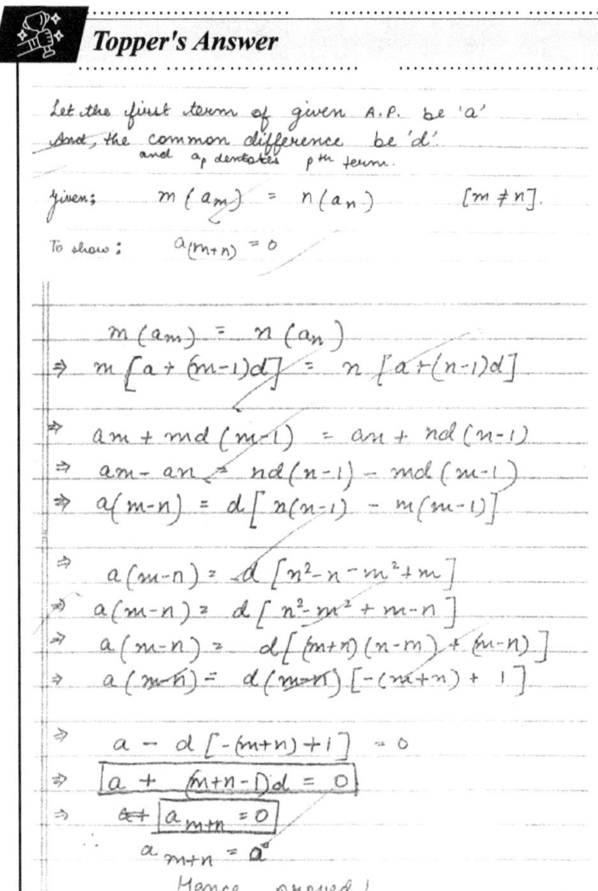
Topper's Answer

Let the first term of given A.P. be 'a'
And, the common difference be 'd'.
and a_p denotes p^{th} term.

Given; $m(a_m) = n(a_n)$ $[m \neq n]$.

To show: $a_{(m+n)} = 0$

$m(a_m) = n(a_n)$
$\Rightarrow m[a+(m-1)d] = n[a+(n-1)d]$
$\Rightarrow am + md(m-1) = an + nd(n-1)$
$\Rightarrow am - an = nd(n-1) - md(m-1)$
$\Rightarrow a(m-n) = d[n(n-1) - m(m-1)]$

$\Rightarrow a(m-n) = d[n^2 - n - m^2 + m]$
$\Rightarrow a(m-n) = d[n^2 - m^2 + m - n]$
$\Rightarrow a(m-n) = d[(m+n)(n-m) + (m-n)]$
$\Rightarrow a(m-n) = d(m-n)[-(m+n)+1]$

$\Rightarrow a - d[-(m+n)+1] = 0$
$\Rightarrow a + (m+n-1)d = 0$
$\Rightarrow a_{m+n} = 0$
$\therefore a_{m+n} = 0$
Hence, proved!

26.

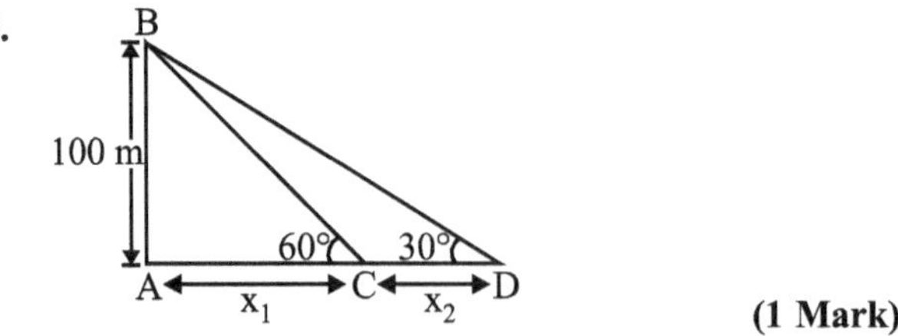

(1 Mark)

Given, height of the light house is 100 m.

According to the question the man takes 2 minutes to rowing the boat from C to D.

Let AC = x_1 metre and CD = x_2 metre

In ΔABC, **(1 Mark)**

$$\tan 60° = \frac{100}{x_1} \Rightarrow \sqrt{3} = \frac{100}{x_1} \Rightarrow x_1 = \frac{100}{\sqrt{3}} \quad ...(1)$$

In ABD,

$$\tan 30° = \frac{100}{(x_1 + x_2)} \Rightarrow \frac{1}{\sqrt{3}} = \frac{100}{(x_1 + x_2)}$$

$$\Rightarrow x_1 + x_2 = 100\sqrt{3}$$

Using equation (1) in above equation,

$$\frac{100}{\sqrt{3}} + x_2 = 100\sqrt{3} \Rightarrow x_2 = 100\sqrt{3} - \frac{100}{\sqrt{3}}$$ **(1 Mark)**

$$\text{or, } x_2 = \frac{200}{\sqrt{3}}$$

$$\text{Since, speed} = \frac{\text{distance}}{\text{time}} = \frac{x_2}{2} = \frac{200}{2\sqrt{3}}$$

$$\therefore \text{speed} = \frac{100}{\sqrt{3}} = \frac{100}{1.732} = 57.738$$

Therefore, the speed of the boat is 57.738 metres per minute. **(1 Mark)**

27.

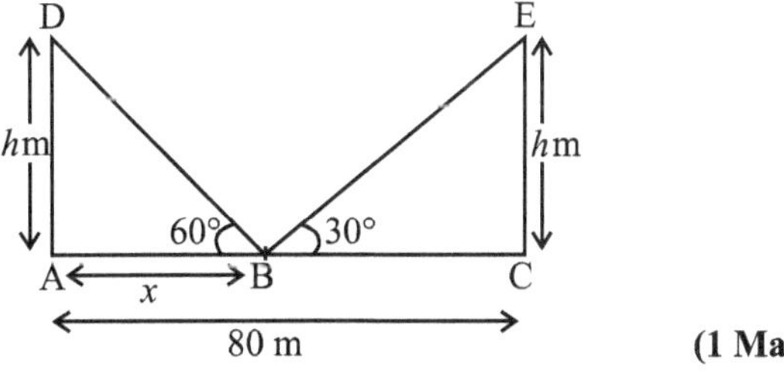

(1 Mark)

Let the height of the poles is hm and the distance of the point B from A is x m.

In right ΔADB,

$$\tan 60° = \frac{h}{x} \Rightarrow x\sqrt{3} = h \quad ...(1)$$ **(1 Mark)**

In ΔBEC,

$$\tan 30° = \frac{h}{80 - x} \Rightarrow \frac{1}{\sqrt{3}} = \frac{h}{80 - x}$$

$$\Rightarrow 80 - x = \sqrt{3}h$$

$$\Rightarrow h = \frac{80 - x}{\sqrt{3}} \quad .....(2)$$ **(1 Mark)**

From equations (1) and (2),

$$x\sqrt{3} = \frac{80 - x}{\sqrt{3}} \Rightarrow 3x = 80 - x \Rightarrow 4x = 80 \Rightarrow x = 20 \text{ m.}$$

Since, $h = x\sqrt{3} \Rightarrow h = 20\sqrt{3}$ m

Therefore, the height of the poles is $20\sqrt{3}$ metre, the distance of the point B from the pole AD is 20 metre and the distance of the point B from the pole CE = 80 – 20 = 60 metre. **(1 Mark)**

Angle of elevation is larger at nearest point of vertical object.

28.

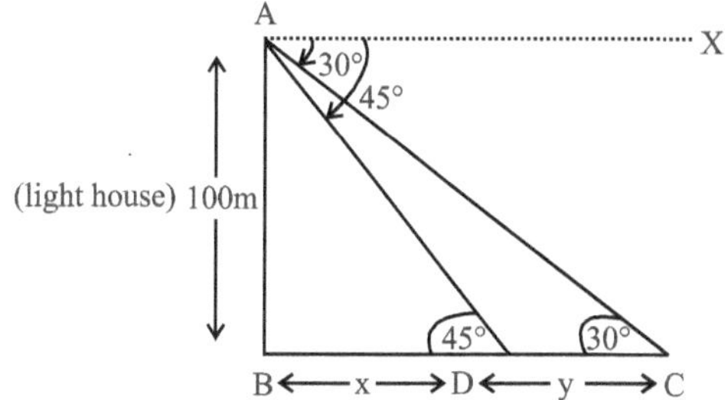

The height of the light house AB = 100 m **(1 Mark)**

Here $\angle ADB = 45°$ and $\angle ACB = 30°$ (Given)

In right ΔABD,

$$\tan 45° = \frac{AB}{BD}$$

$$1 = \frac{100}{x}$$

$$x = 100$$ **(1 Mark)**

In right ΔABC,

$$\tan 30° = \frac{AB}{BC} = \frac{100}{x + y}$$ **(1 Mark)**

$$\Rightarrow \frac{1}{\sqrt{3}} = \frac{100}{100 + y}$$

$$\Rightarrow 1.732 \times 100 = 100 + y$$

$$\Rightarrow y = 173.2 - 100 = 73.2 \text{ m}$$ **(1 Mark)**

Hence, the distance between two ships CD = 73.2 m

29. Let 'D' be the point of location of aeroplane lying 300 m height above the ground from where it makes angles of depression as 45° & 60° of the two banks A & B of the river.

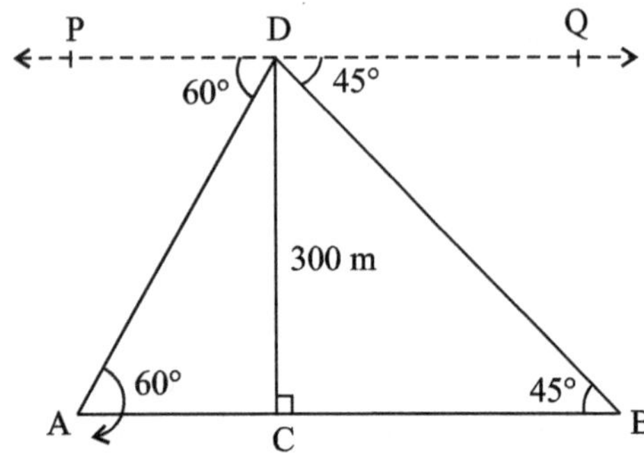

(1 Mark)

Here,

$$\angle CAD = \angle PDA = 60^\circ$$

$$\angle CBD = \angle QDB = 45^\circ$$

Now in right ΔACD

$$\tan 60^\circ = \frac{CD}{AC}$$

$$\sqrt{3} = \frac{300}{AC}$$

$$\Rightarrow \quad AC = \frac{300}{\sqrt{3}}$$

$$\Rightarrow \quad AC = \frac{300\sqrt{3}}{\sqrt{3}} = 100\sqrt{3}$$

$$\Rightarrow \quad AC = 100 \times 1732 = 173.2 \text{ m}$$ **(1½ Mark)**

Also, in ΔBCD

$$\tan 45^\circ = \frac{CD}{BC}$$

$$\Rightarrow \quad 1 = \frac{300}{BC}$$

$$\Rightarrow \quad BC = 300 \text{ m}$$

∴ width of the river

$$AB = AC + BC = 173.2 + 300 = 473.2 \text{ m}$$

Thus, the width of the river is 473.2 m **(1½ Mark)**

An angle of elevation is the angle made by the line of sight to the top of the object and horizontal line, while angle of depression is made when the observer needs to look down to see the object.

30. Given: The angles of elevations of the bird in two positions P and Q from point A are 45° and 30° respectively.

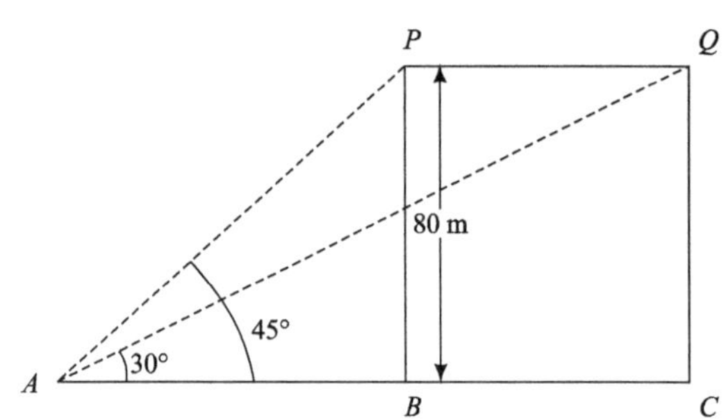

$\therefore \angle PAB = 45^\circ$ and $\angle QAB = 30^\circ$ **(1 Mark)**

Also $PB = 80$ m

In right ΔABP

$$\tan 45^\circ = \frac{BP}{AB} \qquad \left[\because \tan\theta = \frac{P}{B}\right]$$

$$\Rightarrow \quad 1 = \frac{80}{AB}$$ **(1 Mark)**

$$\Rightarrow \quad AB = 80 \text{ m}$$

⇒ In right ΔACQ

$$\Rightarrow \quad \tan 30^\circ = \frac{CQ}{AC}$$

$$\Rightarrow \quad \frac{1}{\sqrt{3}} = \frac{80}{AC}$$

$$\Rightarrow \quad AC = 80\sqrt{3}\text{m}$$

$$\therefore \ PQ = BC = AC - AB$$

$$= 80\sqrt{3} - 80$$

$$= 80(\sqrt{3}-1)\text{m}$$ **(1 Mark)**

So, the bird covers $80(\sqrt{3}-1)$m in 2 sec.

$$\text{Speed of bird} = \frac{\text{Distance covered}}{\text{Time taken}}$$

$$= \frac{80(\sqrt{3}-1)}{2} \text{ m/sec}$$

$$= \frac{40(\sqrt{3}-1)}{1000} \times 60 \times 60$$

$= 144(1.732 - 1)$ km/hr

$= 105.408$ km/h **(1 Mark)**

Angle of elevation is the angle from the horizontal upward and angle of depression is horizontal downward to an object.

31. Let vertical height of cloud from level of A be h, then the reflection is seen from A at a depth of h + 20 from ground level in the lake.

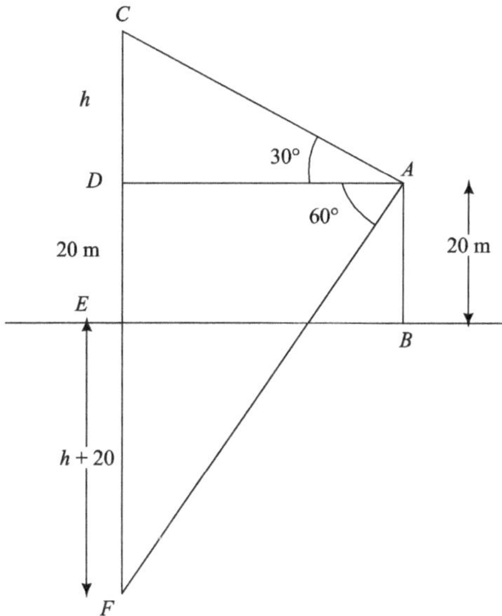

(1 Mark)

In right ΔACD

$$\tan 30° = \frac{CD}{AD} = \frac{h}{AD}$$

$$\frac{1}{\sqrt{3}} = \frac{h}{AD} \Rightarrow AD = \sqrt{3}h \quad ...(1)$$

In right ΔADF **(1 Mark)**

$$\tan 60° = \frac{FD}{AD}$$

$$\Rightarrow \sqrt{3} = \frac{h+40}{AD}$$

$$\Rightarrow \sqrt{3} = \frac{h+40}{\sqrt{3}h} \quad \text{(from (1))}$$

(1 Mark)

$h + 40 = 3h \Rightarrow 40 = 2h \Rightarrow h = 20$

In right ΔAOC

$$\Rightarrow \sin 30° = \frac{CD}{AC} \quad [\because CD = h = 20]$$

$$\Rightarrow \frac{1}{2} = \frac{20}{AC}$$

$\Rightarrow AC = 40$

$\therefore$ Distance of cloud from $A = AC = 40$ m **(1 Mark)**

32.

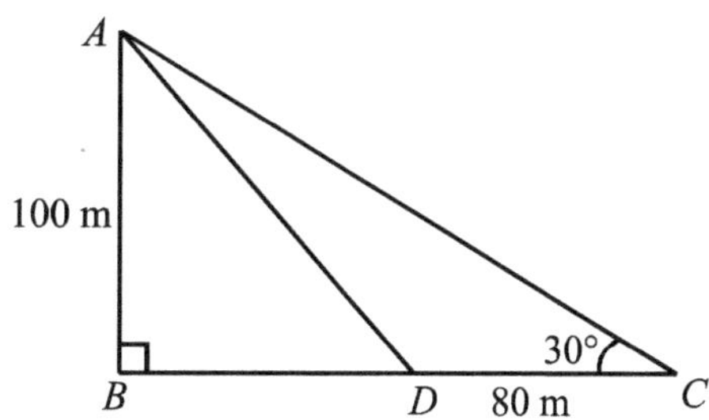

Given : In ΔABC

$AB = 100$ m and $\theta = 30°$. **(1 Mark)**

Consider ΔABC

$$\frac{AB}{BC} = \tan 30°$$

$$\Rightarrow \frac{100}{BC} = \frac{1}{\sqrt{3}}$$

$$\Rightarrow BC = 100\sqrt{3}\, m = 100\sqrt{3} \times 1.7$$

$= 170$ m **(1 Mark)**

$\Rightarrow BD = BC - CD$

$= 100\sqrt{3} - 80$

$= 170 - 80$

$= 90$ m

We know, area of a triangle

$$= \frac{1}{2} \times \text{base} \times \text{height}$$

$\therefore$ area of ΔABC $= \frac{1}{2} \times BC \times AB$

$= \frac{1}{2} \times 170 \times 100$

$= 8500 \text{ m}^2$ **(1 Mark)**

area of ΔABD $= \frac{1}{2} \times BD \times AB$

$= \frac{1}{2} \times 90 \times 100$

$= 4500 \text{ m}^2$

area of ΔACD = area of ΔABC – area of ΔABD

$= (8500 - 4500) \text{ m}^2$

$= 4000 \text{ m}^2$. **(1 Mark)**

The area of portion given to Piyush is 4500 m^2 and the area of portion given to Reena is 4000 m^2.

Hence, the distribution of field among his son and daughter is unfair, he gave bigger piece of field to his son as compare to his daughter which reflects gender inequality.

(1 Mark)

33.

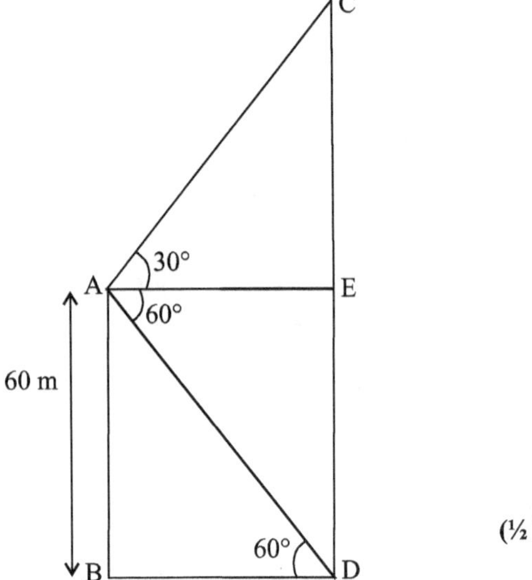

(½ Mark)

Let AB be the building and CD be the tower.

In right ΔABD

$\tan 60° = \frac{AB}{BD}$

$\sqrt{3} = \frac{60}{BD}$

$BD = \frac{60}{\sqrt{3}} \times \frac{\sqrt{3}}{\sqrt{3}} = \frac{60\sqrt{3}}{3}$

$BD = 20\sqrt{3}$ ...(1) **(1 Mark)**

In right ΔACE

$\tan 30° = \frac{CE}{AE}$

$\frac{1}{\sqrt{3}} = \frac{CE}{BD}$ $(\because AE = BD)$

$\frac{1}{\sqrt{3}} = \frac{CE}{20\sqrt{3}}$ [From (1)]

CE = 20 **(½ Mark)**

Height of tower = CE + ED = CE + AB

= 20 + 60

= 80 m **(½ Mark)**

Difference between heights of tower and the building

= 80 – 60

= 20 m **(½ Mark)**

Distance between the tower and the building = BD

$BD = 20\sqrt{3}$m **(1 Mark)**

34. Let *AB* be building and *CD* be tower

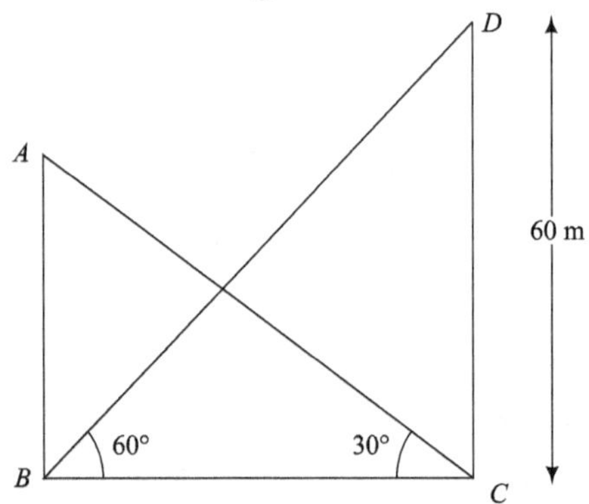

(1 Mark)

Height of tower = *CD* = 60 m

In right Δ*BDC*

$\Rightarrow \tan\theta = \frac{P}{B}$

$\Rightarrow \tan 60° = \frac{DC}{BC}$

$\sqrt{3} = \frac{60}{BC}$

$\Rightarrow BC = \frac{60}{\sqrt{3}} \times \frac{\sqrt{3}}{\sqrt{3}} = \frac{60\sqrt{3}}{3}$

$BC = 20\sqrt{3}$m **(1½ Marks)**

In Δ*ABC*

$\tan 30° = \frac{AB}{BC}$

$\frac{1}{\sqrt{3}} = \frac{AB}{20\sqrt{3}}$

AB = 20 m

∴ Height of building is 20 m. **(1½ Marks)**

35. (i) In ΔACB **(1 Mark)**

$\tan 45° = \frac{80}{CB} \Rightarrow CB = 80m$

So, the distance from the foot of the tree was 80m.

(ii) $\tan 30° = \frac{80}{CE}$ {In Δ DCE} **(½ Mark)**

$\Rightarrow \frac{1}{\sqrt{3}} = \frac{80}{CE}$ **(½ Mark)**

$\Rightarrow CE = 80\sqrt{3}$ **(½ Mark)**

Distance the bird flew

$= AD = BE = CE - CB = 80\sqrt{3} - 80 = 80(\sqrt{3} - 1)$ m **(½ Mark)**

OR

Given: $\tan 60° = \frac{80}{CG}$ **(½ Mark)**

$\Rightarrow \sqrt{3} = \frac{80}{CG}$ **(½ Mark)**

$\Rightarrow CG = \frac{80}{\sqrt{3}}$ **(½ Mark)**

Distance the ball travelled after hitting the tree
= FA = GB = CB – CG

$GB = 80 - \frac{80}{\sqrt{3}} = 80\left(1 - \frac{1}{\sqrt{3}}\right) m$ **(½ Mark)**

(iii) Speed of the bird

$= \frac{\text{Distance}}{\text{Time taken}} = \frac{20\left(\sqrt{3}+1\right)}{2} m/sec$ **(½ Mark)**

$= \frac{20\left(\sqrt{3}+1\right)}{2} \times 60$ m/min = 600 ($\sqrt{3}$ + 1) m/min **(½ Mark)**

The required speed of the bird is $600(\sqrt{3}+1)$ m/min

36. (i) The length of wire from point O to the top of section B is given by OB

Consider ΔBOP

$\cos 30° = \frac{\text{Base}}{\text{Hypotenuse}}$

$\frac{\sqrt{3}}{2} = \frac{36}{OB}$

$OB = \frac{72}{\sqrt{3}} cm$

$OB = \frac{72\sqrt{3}}{3} cm$

$\boxed{OB = 24\sqrt{3}}$ **(1 Mark)**

(ii) In ΔBOP

$\tan 30 = \frac{\text{perpendicular}}{\text{base}}$

$\frac{1}{\sqrt{3}} = \frac{BP}{36}$

$\Rightarrow BP = \frac{36}{\sqrt{3}} = \frac{36}{\sqrt{3}} \times \frac{\sqrt{3}}{\sqrt{3}} = 12\sqrt{3}$ cm

In ΔAOP

$\tan 45° = \frac{AP}{PO}$

$1 = \frac{AP}{PO} \Rightarrow AP = PO$ **(1 Mark)**

As, AP = AB + BP and PO = 36 cm

Hence,

BP + AB = 36

AB = 36 – BP

$= 36 - \frac{36}{\sqrt{3}}$

$AB = 36\left(\frac{\sqrt{3}-1}{\sqrt{3}}\right)$ cm

$= 36\left(\frac{\sqrt{3}-1}{\sqrt{3}} \times \frac{\sqrt{3}}{\sqrt{3}}\right)$ cm

$= 36\left(\frac{3-\sqrt{3}}{3}\right)$ cm

$= 12\sqrt{3}(\sqrt{3}-1)$ cm **(1 Mark)**

OR

Area of ΔOPB = ½(Base)×(Height) **(1 Mark)**

= ½(36 cm)×(BP)

= ½(36 cm)×($12\sqrt{3}$) cm

= $216\sqrt{3}$ cm² **(1 Mark)**

(iii) Height of section A from Base = AB + BP = 36 cm **(1 Mark)**

37. (i)

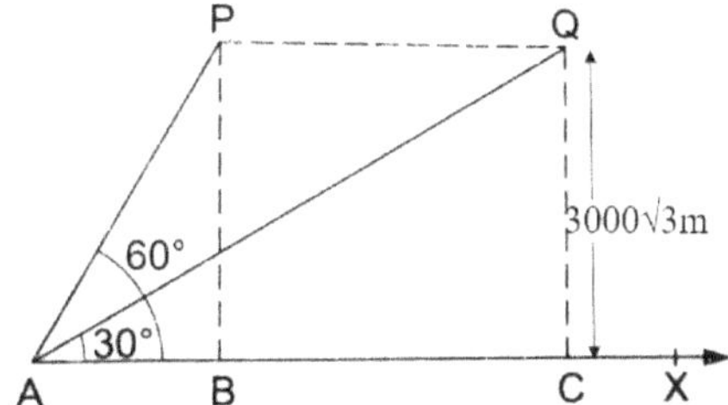

P and Q are the two positions of the plane flying at a height of $3000\sqrt{3}$ m. A is the point of observation. **(1 Mark)**

(ii) In Δ PAB, tan 60° = PB/AB

Or $\sqrt{3} = 3000\sqrt{3}$ /AB

So AB = 3000 m **(1 Mark)**

tan 30° = QC/AC

$1/\sqrt{3} = 3000\sqrt{3}$ / AC

AC = 9000 m **(½ Mark)**

distance covered = 9000 – 3000

= 6000 m. **(½ Mark)**

OR

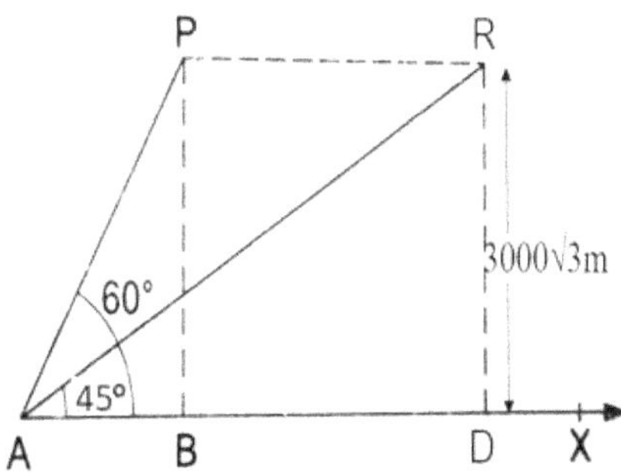

In ΔPAB, tan 60° = PB/AB

Or $\sqrt{3} = 3000\sqrt{3}$ / AB **(½ Mark)**

So AB =3000 m

tan 45° = RD/AD (½ Mark)

$1 = 3000\sqrt{3}$ / AD (½ Mark)

AD = $3000\sqrt{3}$ m

distance covered = $3000\sqrt{3} - 3000$ (½ Mark)

= $3000(\sqrt{3} - 1)$ m.

(iii) speed = 6000/30 (½ Mark)

= 200 m/s

= 200 × 3600/1000 (½ Mark)

= 720 km/hr

Alternatively: speed = $\frac{3000(\sqrt{3}-1)}{15(\sqrt{3}-1)}$ (½ Mark)

= 200 m/s

= 200 × 3600/1000 (½ Mark)

= 720 km/hr

38. (1) Given, figure of two flying kites is represented as:

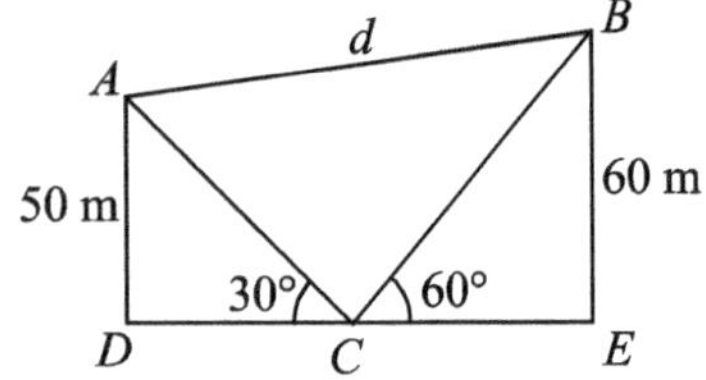

In ΔADC

$\sin 30° = \frac{P}{H} = \frac{AD}{AC}$

$\frac{1}{2} = \frac{50}{AC}$

$AC = 100$ cm

(1 Mark)

In ΔBEC

$\sin 60° = \frac{P}{H} = \frac{BE}{BC}$

$\frac{\sqrt{3}}{2} = \frac{60}{BC}$

$BC = \frac{120}{\sqrt{3}} \times \frac{\sqrt{3}}{\sqrt{3}}$

Hence $BC = 40\sqrt{3}$m.

(1 Mark)

(2) In the above figure $\angle ACB = 180 - (60 + 30) = 90°$

(1 Mark)

In ΔACB

$AB^2 = AC^2 + BC^2$

$d^2 = (100)^2 + (40\sqrt{3})^2$

$d^2 = 10000 + 1600 \times 3$

$d^2 = 10000 + 4800$

$d^2 = 14800$

$d = 20\sqrt{37}$m. **(1 Mark)**

10 Chapter Circles

Topic-1: Revisiting Tangent to a Circle

Multiple Choice Questions

1. If O is centre of a circle and chord PQ makes an angle 50° with the tangent PR at the point of contact P, then the angle subtended by the chord at the centre is **[CBSE Sample Paper 2023-24, Ap]**

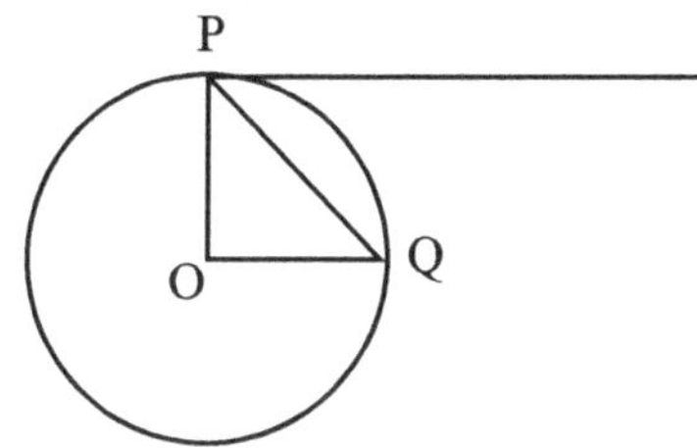

(a) 130°
(b) 100°
(c) 50°
(d) 30°

2. In the given figure, AB is a tangent to the circle centered at O. If OA = 6 cm and ∠OAB = 30°, then the redius of the circle is: **l India 2023, Ap]**

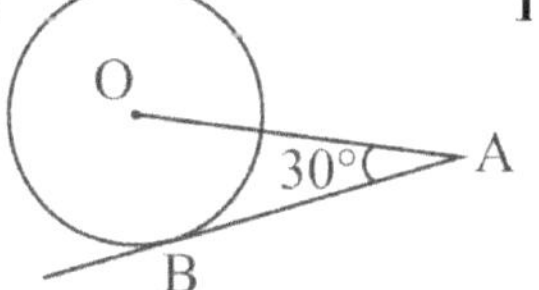

(a) 3 cm
(b) $3\sqrt{3}$ cm
(c) 2 cm
(d) $\sqrt{3}$ cm

3. The length of tangent drawn to a circle of radius 9 cm from a point 41 cm from the centre is: **[Delhi 2023, A]**

(a) 40 cm (b) 9 cm
(c) 41 cm (d) 50 cm

4. In the given figure, O is the centre of the circle and PQ is the chord. If the tangent PR at P makes an angle of 50° with PQ, then the measure of ∠POQ is: **[Delhi 2023, U]**

(a) 50°
(b) 40°
(c) 100°
(d) 130°

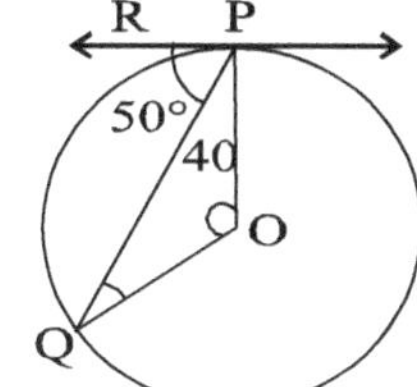

4 Very Short Answer Questions (1 Mark)

5. In the given figure, PQ is a chord of the circle centered at O. PT is a tangent to the circle at P. If ∠QPT = 55°, then find ∠PRQ. **[All India 2023, A]**

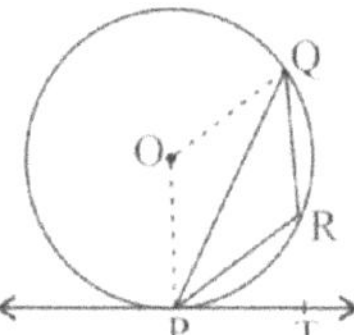

6. In given Fig. the length PB = ____________ cm. **[All India 2020, Ap]**

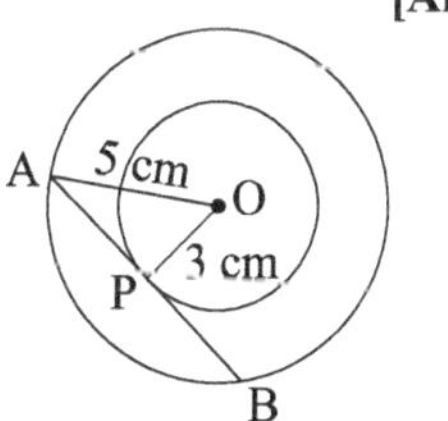

7. In Figure PQ is a chord of a circle with centre O and PT is a tangent. If ∠ QPT = 60°, find ∠ PRQ. **[All India 2015, Term-II, K]**

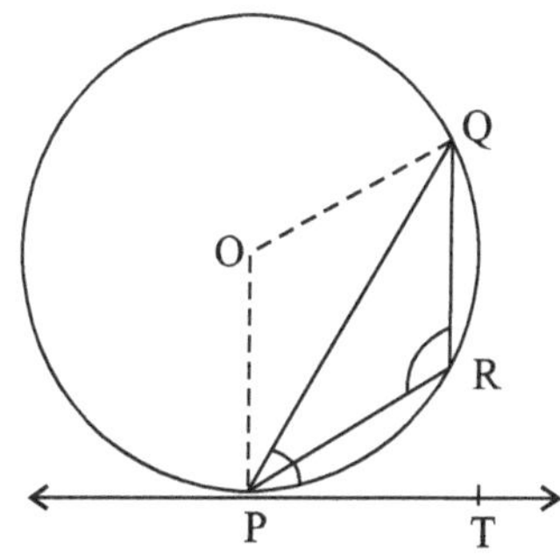

Short Answer Questions (2 or 3 Marks)

8. In the given figure, PA is a tangent to the circle drawn from the external point P and PBC is the secant to the circle with BC as diameter.
If $\angle AOC = 130°$, then find the measure $\angle APB$, where O is the centre of the circle. **[All India 2023 Set-II, K]**

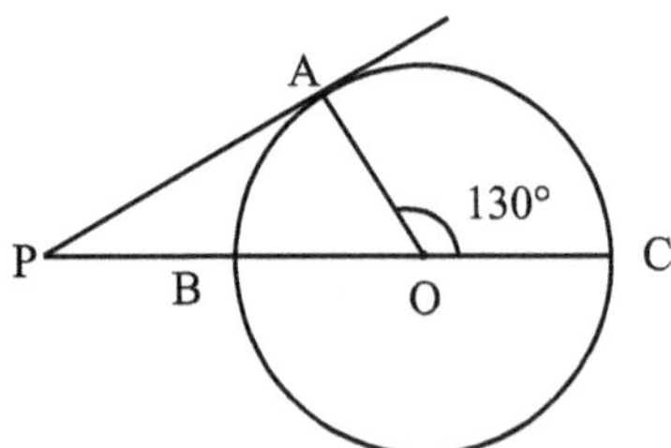

9. In Fig., AB is diameter of a circle centered at O. BC is tangent to the circle at B. If OP bisects the chord AD and $\angle AOP = 60°$, then find m$\angle$C. **[All India 2022, K]**

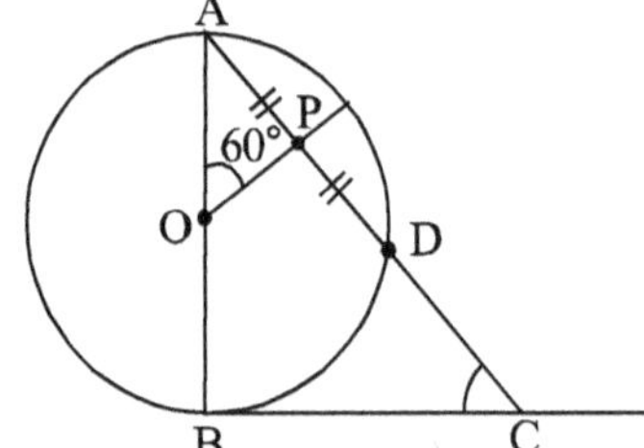

10. In Fig., XAY is a tangent to the circle centered at O. If $\angle ABO = 40°$, then find m$\angle$BAY and m$\angle$AOB.

[All India 2022, K]

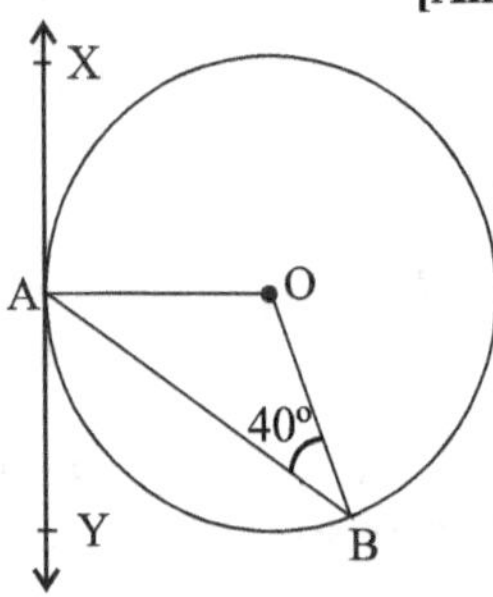

Long Answer Question (4 or 5 Mark)

11. Two circles with centres O and O′ of radii 6 cm and 8 cm, respectively intersect at two points P and Q such that OP and O′P are tangents to the two circles. Find the length of the common chord PQ. **[All India 2023, Set-I, Ap]**

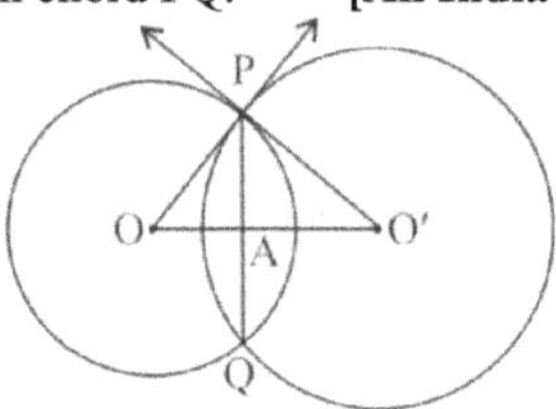

Topic-2: Number of Tangents from a Point on a Circle

Multiple Choice Questions

1. A quadrilateral PQRS is drawn to circumscribe a circle. If PQ = 12 cm, QR = 15 cm and RS = 14 cm, then find the length of SP is **[CBSE Sample Paper 2023-24, Ap]**

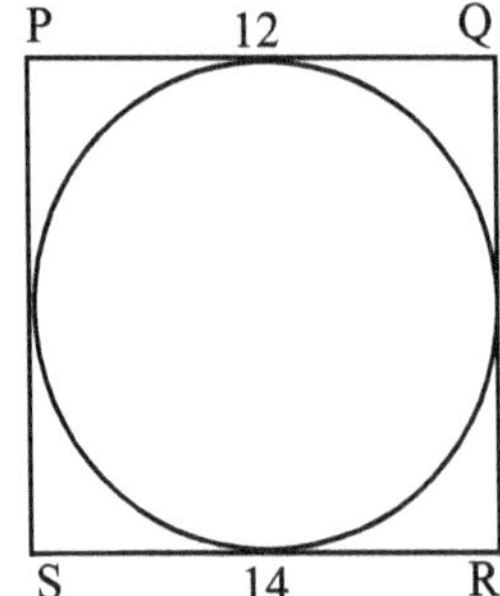

(a) 15 cm (b) 14 cm
(c) 12 cm (d) 11 cm

2. In the given figure, PA and PB are tangents from external point P to a circle with centre C and Q is any point on the circle. Then the measure of $\angle AQB$ is

[All India 2023 Set-II, A]

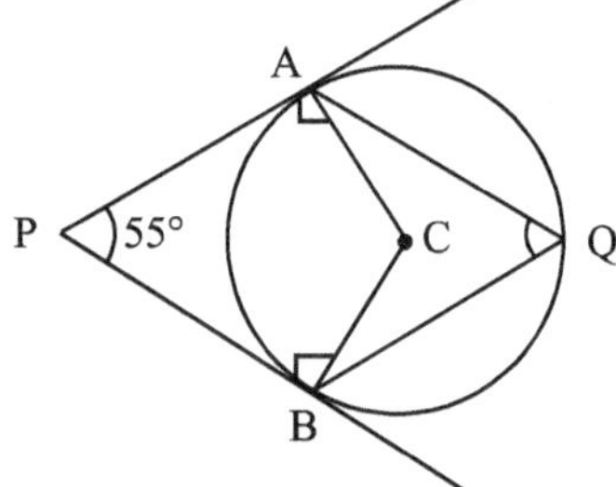

(a) $62\frac{1}{2}°$ (b) 125°
(c) 55° (d) 90°

3. In the given figure, AB = BC = 10 cm. If AC = 7 cm, then the length of BP is **[All India 2023 Set-II, Ap]**

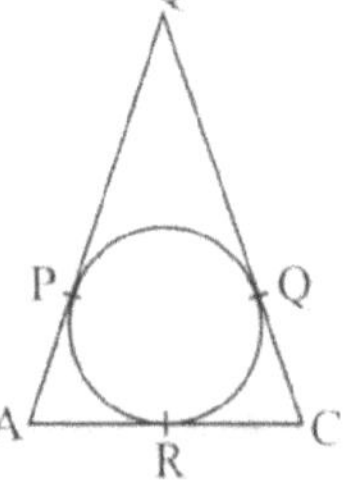

(a) 3·5 cm (b) 7 cm (c) 6·5 cm (d) 5 cm

4. In the given figure, AC and AB are tangents to a circle centered at O. If ∠COD = 120°, then ∠BAO is equal to: **[All India 2023 Set-I, Ap]**

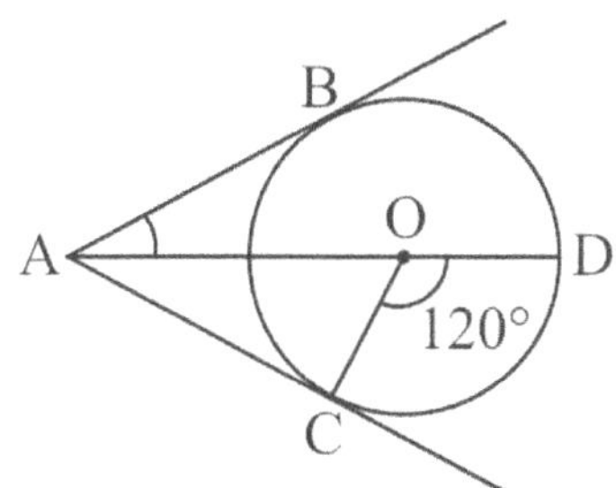

(a) 30° (b) 60°
(c) 45° (d) 90°

5. If two tangents inclined at an angle of 60° are drawn to a circle of radius 3cm, then the length of each tangent is equal to **[CBSE Sample Paper 2022-23, Ap]**

(a) $\frac{3\sqrt{3}}{2}$ cm (b) 3cm
(c) 6cm (d) $3\sqrt{3}$ cm

6. The area of the circle that can be inscribed in a square of 6cm is **[CBSE Sample Paper 2022-23, K]**

(a) $36\,\pi$ cm^2 (b) $18\,\pi$ cm^2
(c) $12\,\pi$ cm^2 (d) $9\,\pi$ cm^2

7. A circle has a centre O and radii OQ and OR. Two tangents, PQ and PR, are drawn from an external point, P.

In addition to the above information, which of these must also be known to conclude that the quadrilateral PQOR is a square? **[CBSE CFPQ 2022, K]**

(i) OQ and OR are at an angle of 90°.

(ii) The tangents meet at an angle of 90°.

(a) Only (i) (b) Only (ii)
(c) Either (i) or (ii) (d) Both (i) and (ii)

8. The circumference of a circle is 100 cm. The side of a square inscribed in the circle is

[CBSE Sample Paper 2021-22, Term-I, K]

(a) $50\sqrt{2}$ cm (b) $\frac{100}{\pi}$ cm (c) $50\frac{\sqrt{2}}{\pi}$ cm (d) $100\frac{\sqrt{2}}{\pi}$ cm

9. In Fig. QR is a common tangent to the given circles, touching externally at the point T. The tangent at T meets QR at P. If PT = 3.8 cm, then the length of QR (in cm) is :

[Delhi 2014, Term-II, U]

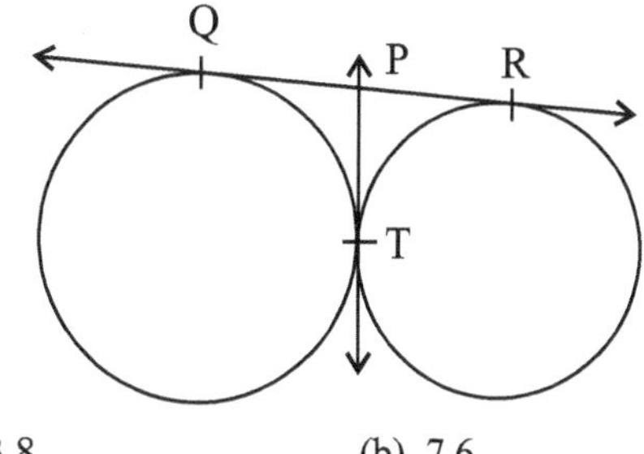

(a) 3.8 (b) 7.6
(c) 5.7 (d) 1.9

10. In Fig. PQ and PR are two tangents to a circle with centre O. If ∠QPR = 46°, that ∠QOR equals:

[Delhi 2014, Term-II, Ap]

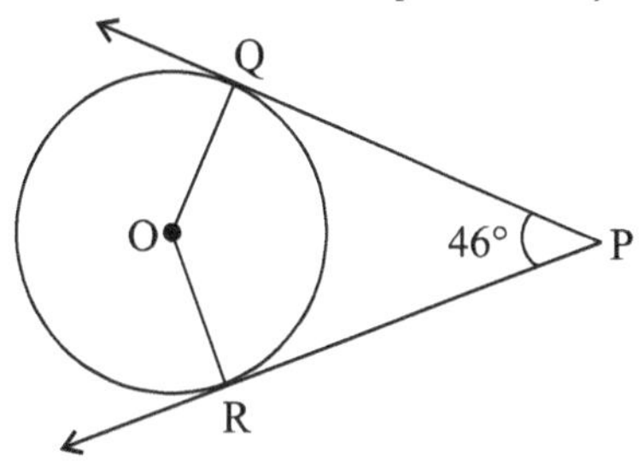

(a) 67° (b) 134°
(c) 44° (d) 46°

11. In Fig. PA and PB are two tangents drawn from an external point P to a circle with centre C and radius 4 cm. If PA ⊥ PB, then the length of each tangent is :

[All India 2013, Ap]

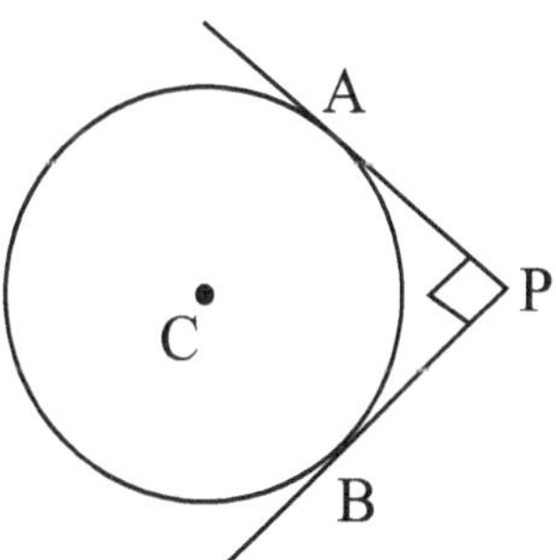

(a) 3 cm (b) 4 cm
(c) 5 cm (d) 6 cm

12. In Fig. a circle with centre O is inscribed in a quadrilateral ABCD such that, it touches the sides BC, AB, AD and CD at points P, Q, R and S respectively. If AB = 29 cm, AD = 23 cm, ∠ B = 90° and DS = 5 cm, then the radius of the circle (in cm.) is :

[All India 2013, A]

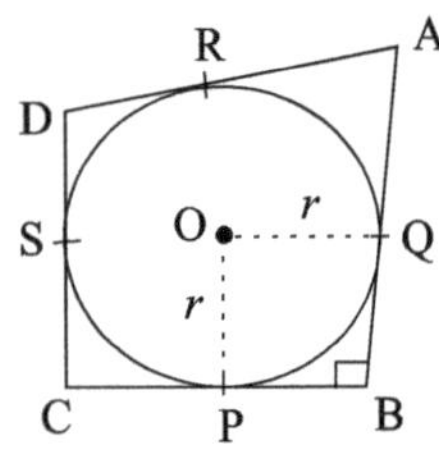

(a) 11 (b) 18

(c) 6 (d) 15

4 Very Short Answer Questions (1 Mark)

13. A point is 25 cm from the centre of a circle of radius 15 cm.

Find the length of the tangent from the point to the circle. Show your steps.

(CBSE CFPQ 2022, K)

14. In Fig. ΔABC is circumscribing a circle, the length of BC is ___________ cm. **[Delhi 2020, K]**

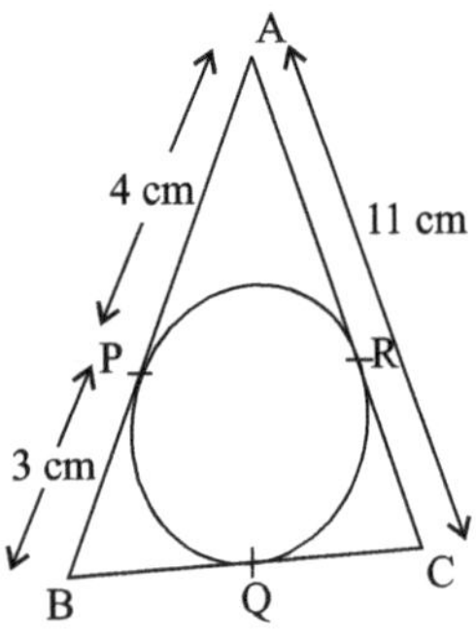

15. If the angle between two tangents drawn from an external point P to a circle of radius a and centre O, is 60°, then find the length of OP. **[All India 2017, Term-II, K]**

16. From an external point P, tangents PA and PB are drawn to a circle with centre O. If $\angle$PAB = 50°, then find $\angle$AOB.

[Delhi 2016, Term-II, U]

Short Answer Questions (2 or 3 Marks)

17. From an external point P, two tangents, PA and PB are drawn to a circle with centre O. At a point E on the circle, a tangent is drawn to intersect PA and PB at C and D, respectively. If PA = 10 cm, find the perimeter of ΔPCD.

[CBSE Sample Paper 2023-24, A]

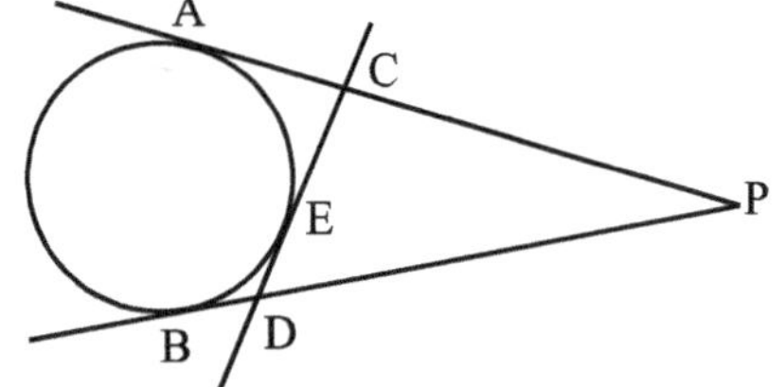

18. PA and PB are tangents drawn to a circle of centre O from an external point P. Chord AB makes an angle of 30° with the radius at the point of contact.

If length of the chord is 6 cm, find the length of the tangent PA and the length of the radius OA.

[CBSE Sample Paper 2023-24, U]

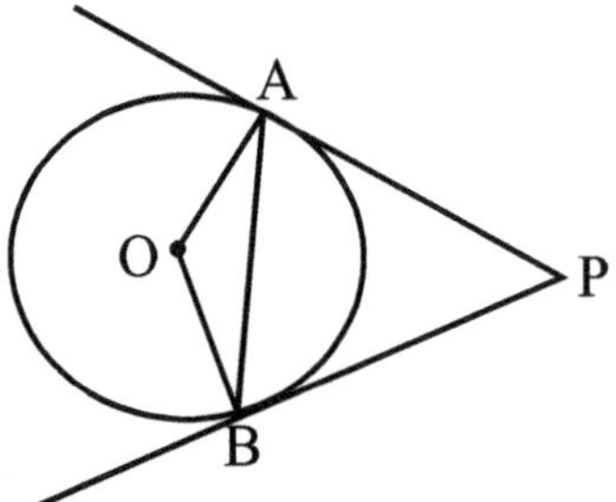

19. Two tangents TP and TQ are drawn to a circle with centre O from an external point T. Prove that $\angle$PTQ = 2 $\angle$OPQ.

[CBSE Sample Paper 2023-24, U]

20. Two concentric circles are of radii 5 cm and 3 cm. Find the length of the chord of the larger circle which touches the smaller circle. **[Delhi 2023, A]**

21. Prove that the angle between the two tangents drawn from an external point to a circle is supplementary to the angle subtended by the line segment joining the points of contact at the centre. **[Delhi 2023, A]**

22. In the given figure, O is the centre of circle. Find $\angle$AQB, given that PA and PB are tangents to the circle and $\angle$APB= 75°. **[CBSE Sample Paper 2022-23, A]**

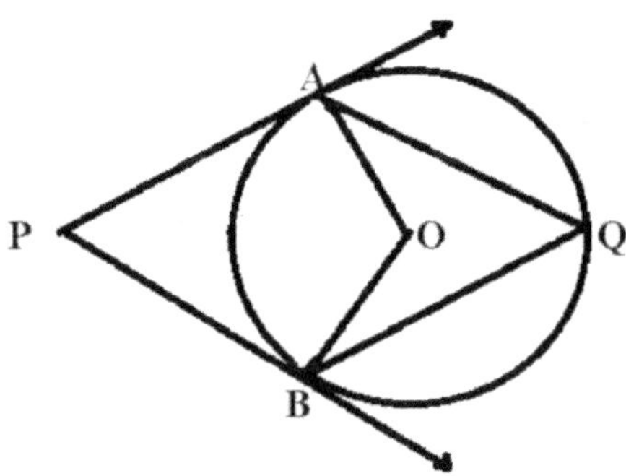

23. Prove that a parallelogram circumscribing a circle is a rhombus **[CBSE Sample Paper 2022-23, K]**

24. In the figure XY and X'Y' are two parallel tangents to a circle with centre O and another tangent AB with point of contact C interesting XY at A and X'Y' at B, what is the measure of ∠AOB. **[CBSE Sample Paper 2022-23, Ap]**

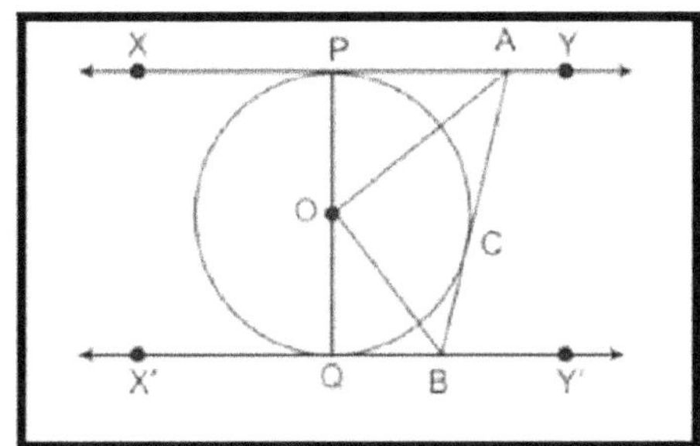

25. If a circle touches the side BC of a triangle ABC at P and extended sides AB and AC at Q and R, respectively, prove that $AQ = \frac{1}{2}(BC + CA + AB)$ **[All India 2020, A]**

26. In Figure, a quadrilateral ABCD is drawn to circumscribe a circle. Prove that AB + CD = BC + AD.

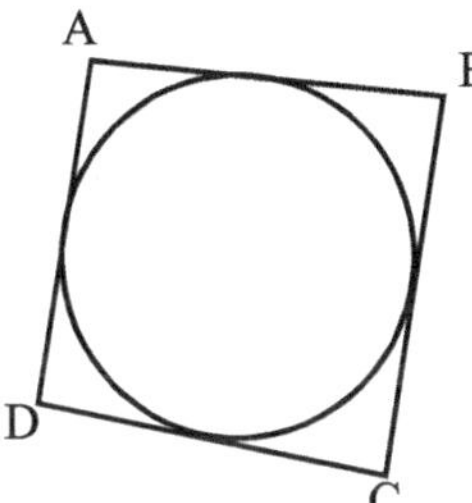

[All India 2020, U]

27. Prove that opposite sides of a quadrilateral circumscribing a circle subtend supplementary angles at the centre of the circle. **[All India 2019, U]**

28. In Figure, PQ and RS are two parallel tangents to a circle with centre O and another tangent AB with point of contact C intersecting PQ at A and RS at B. Prove that ∠AOB = 90°. **[All India 2019, U]**

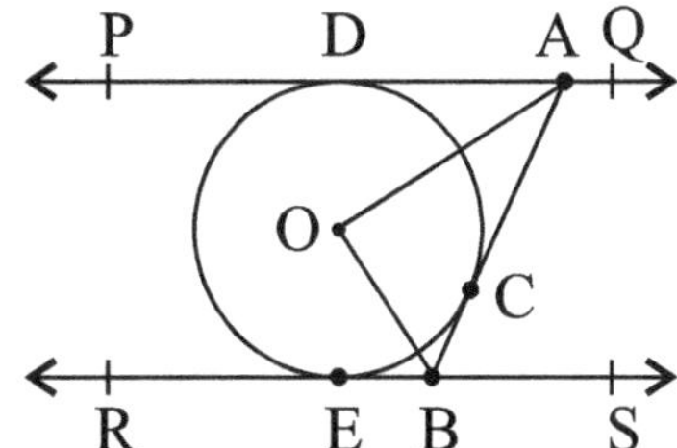

29. In Fig. PQ is a chord of length 8 cm of a circle of radius 5 cm and centre O. The tangents at P and Q intersect at point T. Find the length of TP. **[Delhi 2019, Ap]**

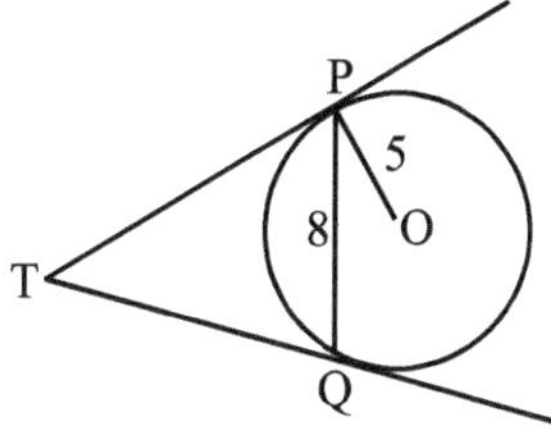

30. Prove that the lengths of tangents drawn from an external point to a circle are equal. **[All India 2018, A]**

31. Prove that the tangents drawn at the end points of a chord of a circle make equal angles with the chord.

[All India 2017, Term-II, K]

32. A circle touches all the four sides of a quadrilateral ABCD. Prove that

AB + CD = BC + DA **[All India 2017, Term-II, A]**

33. In Fig. a circle is inscribed in a ΔABC, such that it touches the sides AB, BC and CA at points D, E and F respectively. If the lengths of sides AB, BC and CA are 12 cm, 8 cm and 10 cm respectively, find the lengths of AD, BE and CF. **[Delhi 2016, Term-II, Ap]**

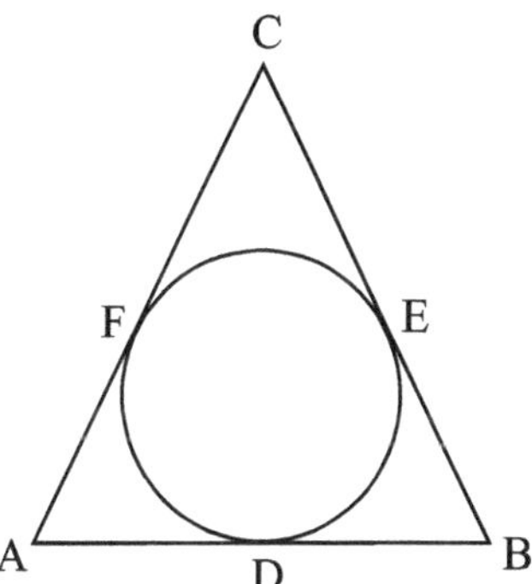

34. In Fig. 3, AP and BP are tangents to a circle with centre O, such that AP = 5 cm and ∠APB = 60°. Find the length of chord AB. **[Delhi 2016, Term-II, Ap]**

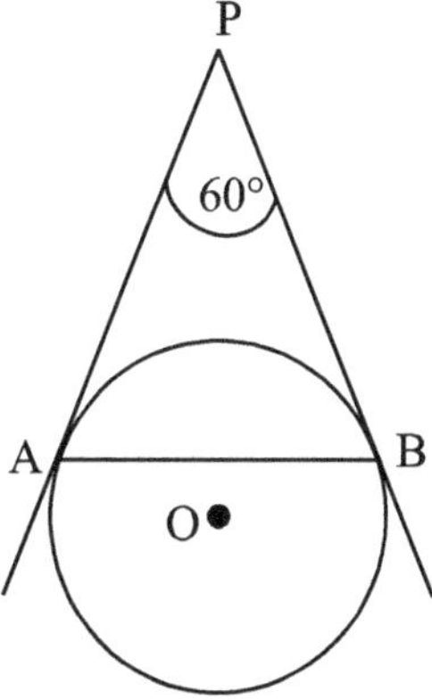

35. In Figure, two tangents RQ and RP are drawn from an external point R to the circle with centre O. If PRQ = 120°, then prove that OR = PR + RQ.

[All India 2015, Term-II, A]

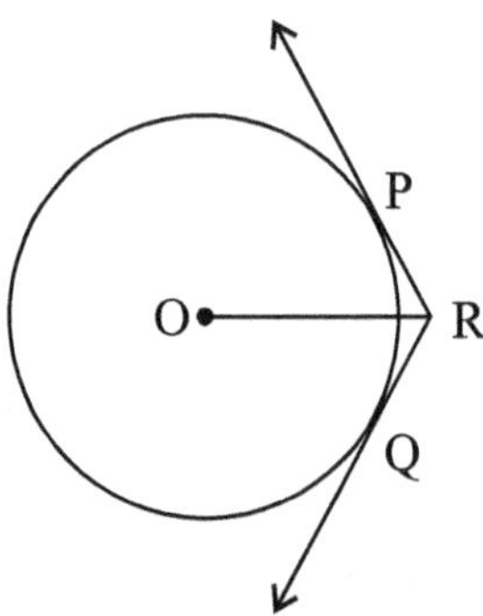

36. In Figure, a triangle ABC is drawn to circumscribe a circle of radius 3 cm, such that the segments BD and DC are respectively of lengths 6 cm and 9 cm. If the area of ΔABC is 54 cm², then find the lengths of sides AB and AC.

[All India 2015, Term-II, K]

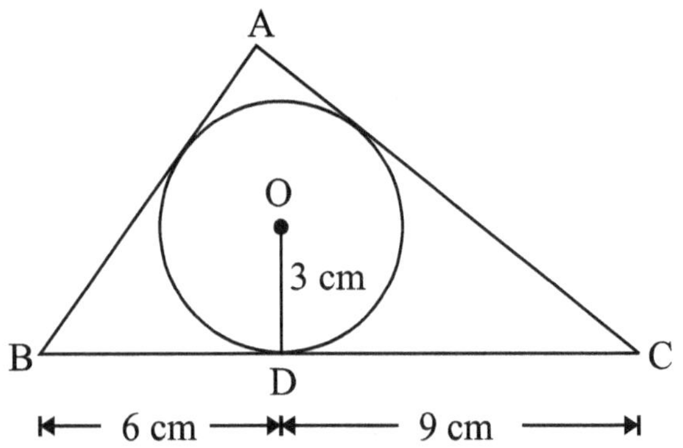

37. Prove that the line segment joining the points of contact of two parallel tangents of a circle, passes through its centre. **[Delhi 2014, Term-II, A]**

38. If from an external point P of a circle with centre O, two tangents PQ and PR are drawn such that ∠QPR = 120°, prove that 2PQ = PO. **[Delhi 2014, Term-II, Ap]**

39. In Fig. a circle is inscribed in an equilateral triangle ABC of side 12 cm. Find the radius of inscribed circle and the area of the shaded region. **[Delhi 2014, Term-II, A]**

(Use $\pi = 3.14$ and $\sqrt{3} = 1.73$]

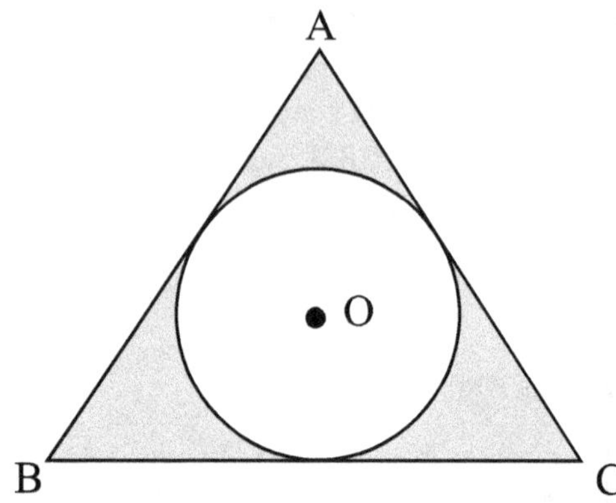

40. In Fig. a circle inscribed in triangle ABC touches its sides AB, BC and AC at points D, E and F respectively. If AB = 12 cm, BC = 8 cm and AC = 10 cm, then find the lengths of AD, BE and CF. **[All India 2013, K]**

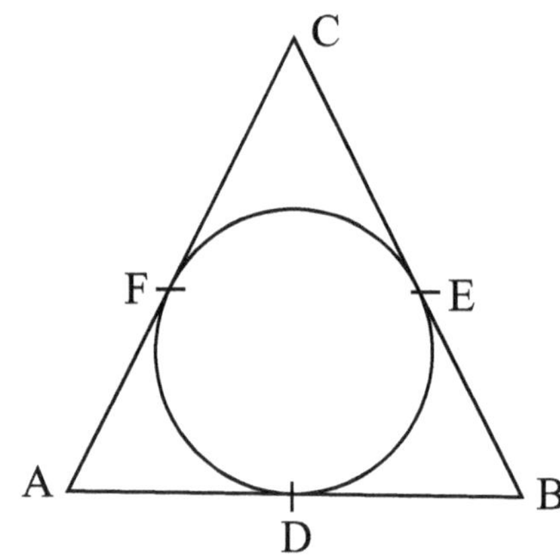

41. Prove that the parallelogram circumscribing a circle is a rhombus. **[All India 2013, U]**

42. In Figure, PQ and PR are tangents to the circle centred at O. If ∠OPR = 45°, then prove that ORPQ is a square.

[All India 2022, U]

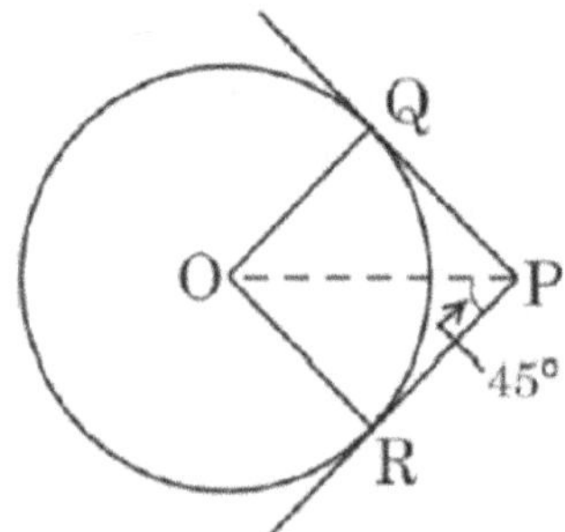

Long Answer Questions (4 or 5 Marks)

43. Two tangents TP and TQ are drawn to a circle with centre O from an external point T. Prove that ∠PTQ = 2 ∠OPQ. **[All India 2023 Set-II, A]**

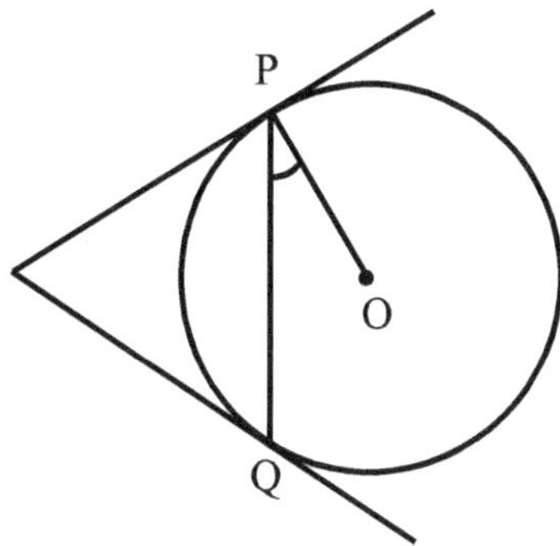

44. A circle touches the side BC of a ΔABC at a point P and touches AB and AC when produced at Q and R respectively. Show that AQ = $\frac{1}{2}$ (Perimeter of ΔABC).

[All India 2023 Set-II, A]

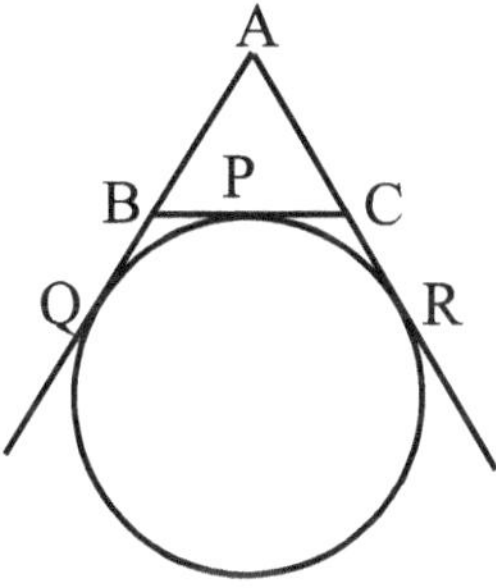

45. A triangle ABC is drawn to circumscribe a circle of radius 4 cm such that the segments BD and DC are of lengths 10 cm and 8 cm respectively. Find the lengths of the sides of AB and AC, if it is given that area ΔABC = 90 cm^2.

[All India 2023, A]

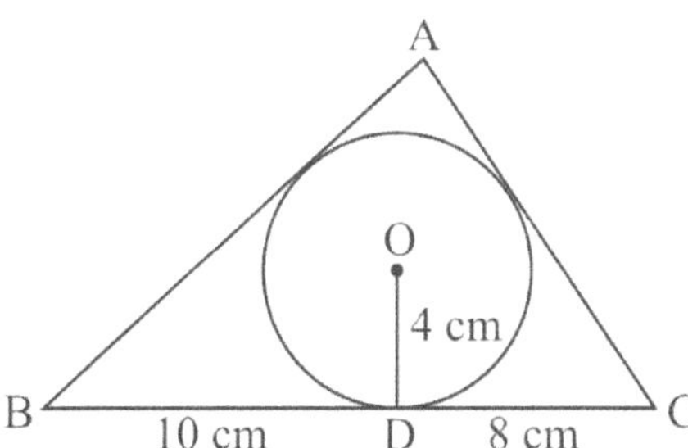

46. In Fig., PQ is a chord of length 8 cm of a circle of radius 5 cm. The tangents at P and Q meet at a point T. Find the length of TP. **[All India 2022, Term-II, A]**

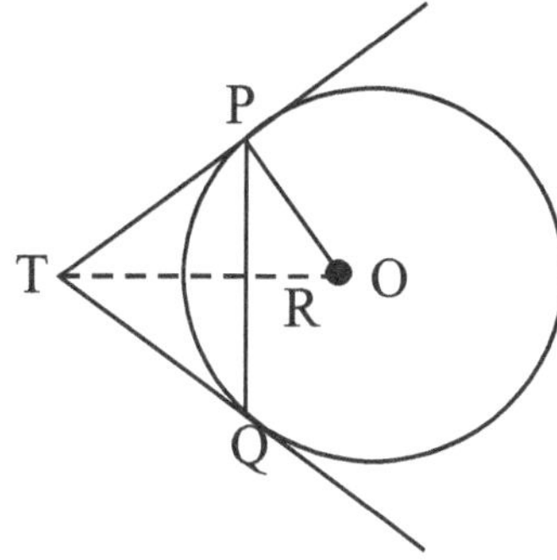

47. Prove that the lengths of two tangents drawn from an external point to a circle are equal.

[All India 2017, Term-II, Ap]

48. In the given figure, XY and X′Y′ are two parallel tangents to a circle with centre O and another tangent AB with point of contact C, is intersecting XY at A and X′Y′ at B. Prove that ∠AOB = 90°. **[All India 2017, Term-II, A]**

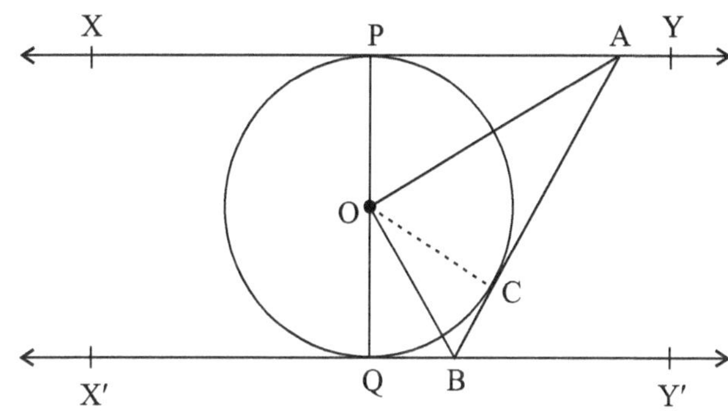

49. Prove that the lengths of tangents drawn from an external point to a circle are equal. **[Delhi 2016, Term-II, Ap]**

50. In Fig. O is the centre of a circle of radius 5 cm. T is a point such that OT = 13 cm and OT intersects circle at E. If AB is a tangent to the circle at E, find the length of AB, where TP and TQ are two tangents to the circle.

[Delhi 2016, Term-II, Ap]

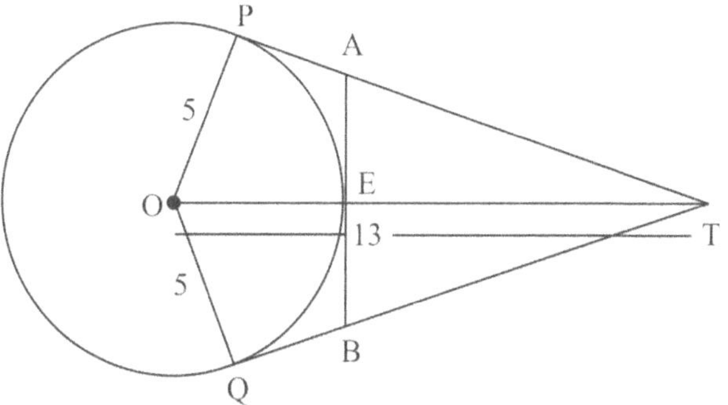

51. An elastic belt is placed around the rim of a pulley of radius 5 cm. From one point C on the belt, the elastic belt is pulled directly away from the centre O of the pulley until it is at P, 10 cm from the point O. Find the length of the belt that is still in contact with the pulley. Also find the shaded area. (use $\pi = 3.14$ and $\sqrt{3} = 1.73$)

[Delhi 2016, Term-II, Ap]

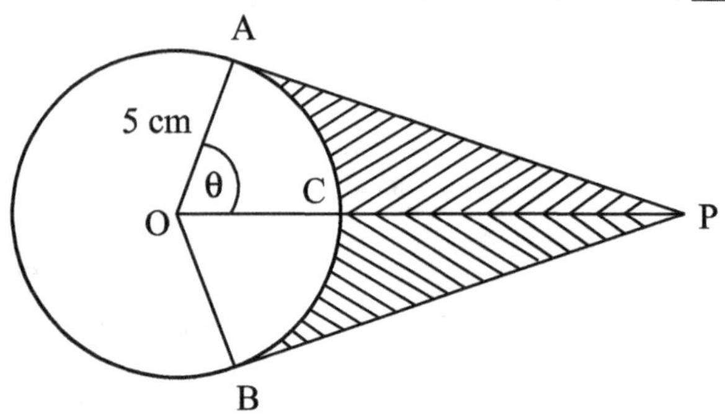

52. Prove that the lengths of the tangents drawn from an external point to a circle are equal.

[All India 2015, Term-II, A]

53. Prove that the tangent drawn at the mid-point of an arc of a circle is parallel to the chord joining the end points of the arc. **[All India 2015, Term-II, A]**

54. Prove that the length of the tangents drawn from an external point to a circle are equal.

[Delhi 2014, Term-II, U]

55. Prove that a parallelogram circumscribing a circle is a rhombus. **[Delhi 2014, Term-II, U]**

56. Prove that the tangent at any point of a circle is perpendicular to the radius through the point of contact.

[All India 2013, A]

57. In Fig. l and m are two parallel tangents to a circle with centre O, touching the circle at A and B respectively. Another tangent at C intersects the line l at D and m at E. Prove that $\angle DOE = 90°$. **[All India 2013, U]**

Hints & Solutions

Topic-1: Tangent to a Circle

1. **(b)** 100° **(1 Mark)**

2. **(a)** For ΔOAB

$\sin 30° = \frac{r}{6}$

$\Rightarrow \quad r = 6 \sin 30°$

$= 6 \times \frac{1}{2} = 3$ cm **(1 Mark)**

3. **(a)** $(41)^2 = (9)^2 + (AC)^2$; $1681 = 81 + (AC)^2$

$AC = \sqrt{1600}$; AC = 40 cm **(1 Mark)**

4. **(c)** RP ⊥ OP (Tangent to the circle).

$\angle OPQ = 90° - \angle RPQ = 90° - 50 = 40°$

$\angle OPQ = \angle OPQ = 40°$ $\angle QOP = 180° - 40° - 40°$

$= 180° - 80° = 100°$ [sum of triangle angle] **(1 Mark)**

5. $\angle QPT + \angle OPQ = 90°$

$\Rightarrow \quad \angle OPQ = 90° - 55° = 35°$

In ΔOPQ

$\Rightarrow \quad 35° + 35° + \angle POQ = 180°$

$\Rightarrow \quad \angle POQ = 180° - 70° = 110°$

The major arc of $\angle POQ = 360° - 110° = 250°$

And, $\angle QRP = \frac{1}{2}(\angle POQ) = \frac{250°}{2} = 125°$ **(1 Mark)**

6. **[4 cm]**

$PB = AP = \sqrt{5^2 - 3^2}$ $(\because OP \perp AB)$

$= \sqrt{25 - 9} = 4$ cm **(1 Mark)**

7. *PT* is tangent

$\therefore \angle OPT = 90°$ [Radii is perpendicular to the tangent]

$\angle QPT = 60°$

$\angle OPQ = \angle OPT - \angle QPT$

$= 90° - 60° = 30°$

$OP = OQ$ (Radii of circle)

$\angle OPQ = \angle OQP = 30°$ (Angle opposite to equal sides are equal) **(½ Mark)**

In Δ*OPQ*

$\angle OPQ + \angle OQP + \angle POQ = 180°$ (Angle sum property)

$30° + 30° + \angle POQ = 180°$

$\angle POQ = 180° - 60° = 120°$

$\angle PRQ = \frac{1}{2}$ (Reflex angle *POQ*) ...(1)

Reflex angle *POQ* = 360 – 120 = 240

$\angle PRQ = \frac{1}{2} \times 240 = 120°$ **(½ Mark)**

Note

All angles inscribed in a circle and substended by same chord are equal.

8. In the given figure.

$\angle AOC + \angle AOP = 180°$ (linear pair)

$\therefore \angle AOP = 180° - 180° \angle AOC$

$= 180° - 130°$

$= 50°$ **(1 Mark)**

Also $\angle PAO = 90°$ (The tangent at any point of circle is perpendicular to radius through point of contact)

In ΔAPO

$\angle PAO + \angle AOP + \angle APO = 180°$

(angle sum property)

$90° + 50° + \angle APO = 180°$

$\angle APO = 180 - 140 = 40°$ **(1 Mark)**

9. Since, *OP* bisects the chord *AD*.

So *OP* will be perpendicular to *AD*.

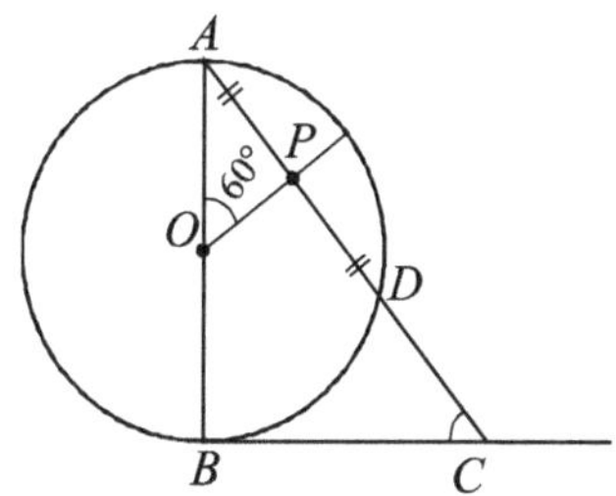

In ΔAOP **(1 Mark)**

Thus $\angle OAP = 180° - 60° - 90° = 30°$

Now In ΔABC

$\angle A = 30°$

$\angle B = 90°$

($\therefore$ BC is tangent to AB)

Thus $\angle ACB = 180 - 90 - 30 = 60°$ **(1 Mark)**

10. From the given figure

$OA = OB$ (Radii of a circle)

so $\angle A = \angle B = 40°$ (each)

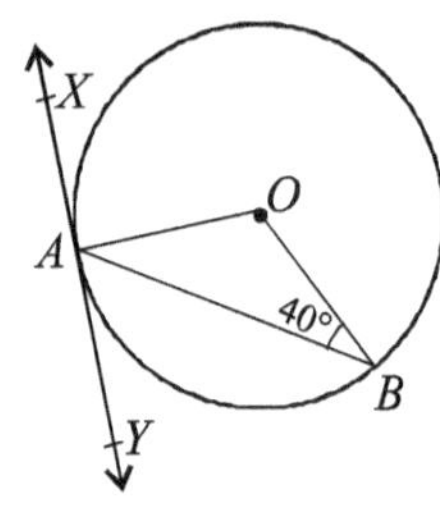

Hence $\angle A + \angle B + \angle AOB = 180°$ **(1 Mark)**

$M\angle AOB = 180° - 40° - 40°$

$= 100°$

Here, $\angle OAY = 90°$ ($\because$ XAY is tangent of OA)

and $M\angle BAY = \angle OAY - \angle OAB$

$= 90° - 40° = 50°$ **(1 Mark)**

11. By $\Delta POO'$

$(OO')^2 = 64 + 36 = 100$ **(1 Mark)**

$\Rightarrow \quad OO' = 10$

By ΔPOA, and $\Delta PO'A$

$36 = x^2 + (PA)^2$

$\Rightarrow \quad (PA)^2 = 36 - x^2$

$64 = (10 - x)^2 + (PA)^2$

$\Rightarrow \quad (PA)^2 = 64 - (10 - x)^2$

$\Rightarrow \quad 36 = x^2 = 64 - (10 - x)^2 \Rightarrow x = \frac{18}{5}$ **(1 Mark)**

Then $(PA) = \sqrt{36 - \left(\frac{18}{5}\right)^2} = \sqrt{\frac{900 - 324}{25}} = \frac{24}{25}$ **(1 Mark)**

Then $PQ = 2(PA) = 2 \times \frac{24}{25} = \frac{48}{5}$ **(1 Mark)**

Topic-2: Number of Tangents from a Point on a Circle

1. **(d)** 11 cm **(1 Mark)**

2. **(a)** In the gien figure

$\angle PAO = \angle PBO = 90°$

The tangent at any point of circle is perpendicular to the radius through point of contact.

Consider the quadrilateral PAOB.

$55° + 90° + 90° + \angle AOB = 360°$ (sum of all angles of quadrilateral)

$\angle AOB = 360° - 235°$

$\angle AOB = 125°$

Now,

$\angle AQB = ½\angle AOB$ (Angle subtended by an arc at the center is double the angle subtended by it at any point on remaing part of circle.)

$\angle AQB = ½(125)° = 62.5°$ **(1 mark)**

3. **(c)** AP = AR and CR = CQ

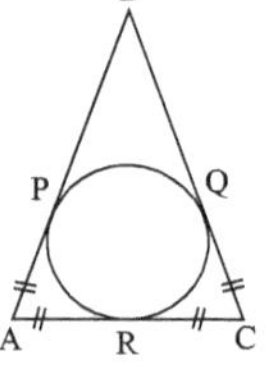

$\Rightarrow \quad AR + CR = 7$

or $\quad AP + CQ = 7$

$\Rightarrow \quad (AB - BP) + (BC - BQ) = 7$

$\Rightarrow \quad (10 - BP) + (10 - BQ) = 7$

$\Rightarrow \quad 20 - 7 = 2x \qquad [BP = BQ = x]$

(1 Mark)

4. **(a)** Given ΔOAC

$\angle DOA = 120° + \angle AOC = 180°$

$\Rightarrow \quad \angle AOC = 60° \Rightarrow 60° + 90° + \angle OAC = 180°$

$\Rightarrow \quad \angle OAC = 180° - 150° = 30°$ **(1 Mark)**

5. **(d)** $3\sqrt{3}$ cm **(1 Mark)**

6. **(d)** $9\pi \text{ cm}^2$ **(1 Mark)**

7. **(c)** **(1 Mark)**

8. **(c)** $2\pi r = 100$. So diameter $= 2r = \frac{100}{\pi}$ = diagonal of the square.

side $\sqrt{2}$ = diagonal of square $= \frac{100}{\pi}$

$\because$ side $= \frac{100}{\sqrt{2}\pi} = \frac{50\sqrt{2}}{\pi}$ **(1 Mark)**

9. **(b)** Length of tangents drawn from an external point to a circle is equal.

$\therefore$ QP = PT = 3.8 cm (1)

PR = PT = 3.8 cm (2)

From equation (1) and (2)

QP = PR = 3.8 cm

Now, QR = PQ + PR

= 3.8 cm + 3.8 cm

= 7.6 cm **(1 Mark)**

10. **(b)** Given : $\angle$QPR = 46°

PQ and PR are tangents.

$\therefore$ Radius drawn to these tangents are perpendicular to the tangents

OQ $\perp$ PQ, OR $\perp$ RP

$\Rightarrow$ $\angle$OQP = $\angle$ORP = 90°

In quadrilateral PQOR

$\angle$OQP + $\angle$QPR + $\angle$PRO + $\angle$ROQ = 360°

90° + 46° + 90° + $\angle$ROQ = 360°

$\angle$ROQ = 360° – 226° = 134° **(1 Mark)**

11. **(b)** As we know that radius of *a* circle is perpendicular to the tangent

$CA \perp AP$, $CB \perp BP$

$AC = BC = 4$ cm (Radii of circle)

$AP = PB$ (Tangents drawn from an external point to the circle are equal in length)

$\angle APB = \angle CAP = \angle CBP = 90°$

$\angle ACB + \angle APB + \angle CAP + \angle CBP = 360°$ (Sum of angles of quadrilateral)

$\angle ACB + 90° + 90° + 90° = 360°$

$\angle ACB = 90°$

As all angles of quadrilateral are of 90°. It may be square or rectangle.

In rectangle opposite sides are equal.

But here $AC = BC$ and $AP = PB$

$\therefore$ *ACBP* is a square.

$AC = BP = CB = AP = 4$ cm

Length of tangents are 4 cm each **(1 Mark)**

12. **(a)** Given: $DS = 5$ cm, $AB = 29$ cm, $AD = 23$ cm, $\angle B = 90°$

DS and *DR* are tangents.

Since tangents to the circle from same external point are equal in length.

$DS = DR = 5$ cm

$AR = AD - DR$

$AR = 23 - 5 = 18$ cm

AR and *AQ* are tangents

$\therefore$ $AR = AQ = 18$ cm [Tangents from external point are equal in length]

$AB = 29$ cm

$BQ = AB - AQ$

$BQ = 29 - 18 = 11$ cm

$\angle B = 90°$ [Given]

$\angle OQB = 90°$ [Radii is perpendicular to tangent]

$\angle OPB = 90°$, hence $\angle POQ = 90°$

$PB = BQ$ [Tangents from external point are equal in length]

As all angles are of 90° and adjacent sides are equal, *OQBP* is a square

$BQ = 11$ cm

$OQ = QB = BP = OP = 11$ cm

$\therefore$ Radius of the circle is 11 cm. **(1 Mark)**

13. Finds the length of the tangent as

$\sqrt{(25^2 - 15^2)} = 20$ cm. **(1 Mark)**

14. BP = BQ = 3 cm, AP = AR = 4 cm.

BC = BQ + QC = 3 + (11 – 4) = 10 cm **(1 Mark)**

15. Let PQ and PR be the two tangents drawn to the circle with radius 'a' and centre 'O' such that $\angle QPR = 60°$

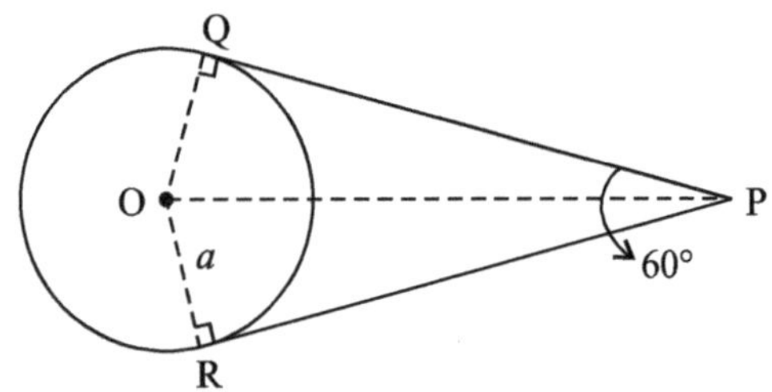

In ΔOPQ and ΔOPR

$OQ = OR = a$ (radius)

$\angle OQP = \angle ORP = 90°$

(tangent perpendicular to radius at point of contact)

$PQ = PR$ (tangents drawn from an external point are equal)

So, $\Delta OPR \cong \Delta OPR$ (SAS Axiom) [By CPCT]

$\therefore \quad \angle OPQ = \angle OPR = 30°$

$\Rightarrow$ In ΔOPR

$$\sin 30° = \frac{OQ}{OP}$$

$$\Rightarrow \quad \frac{1}{2} = \frac{a}{OP}$$

$\Rightarrow \quad OP = 2a$

Thus, the length of OP is '$2a$' **(1 Mark)**

16. Given: PA and PB are tangents

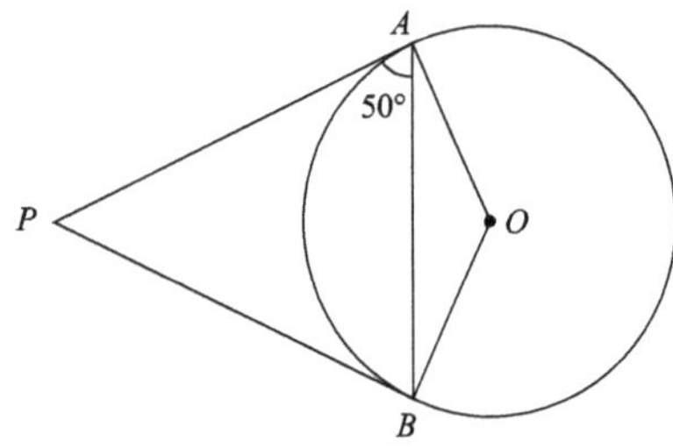

$\therefore$ $\angle PAO = 90°$ [Radius is perpendicular to the tangent at the point of contact]

$\angle PAB = 50°$ (given)

$\therefore$ $\angle OAB = \angle PAO - \angle PAB$

$= 90° - 50° = 40°$

In ΔOAB

$OB = OA$ (Radii of circle)

$\angle OAB = \angle OBA = 40°$ [Angles opposite to equal sides are equal]

$\angle OAB + \angle AOB + \angle OBA = 180°$ (Angle sum property)

$\angle AOB = 180° - 40 - 40$

$\angle AOB = 100°$ **(1 Mark)**

The tangent line never cross the circle it just touches the circle.

17. Given that PA = 10 cm PA = PB; CA = CE; DE = DB

(½ Mark)

[Tangents to a circle]

Perimeter of $\Delta PCD = PC + CD + PD$

$= PC + CE + DE + PD$

$= PC + CA + DB + PD$ { CE = CA & DE = B}

$= PA + PB$ { PA = PC + CA & PB = DB + PD}

(1 Mark)

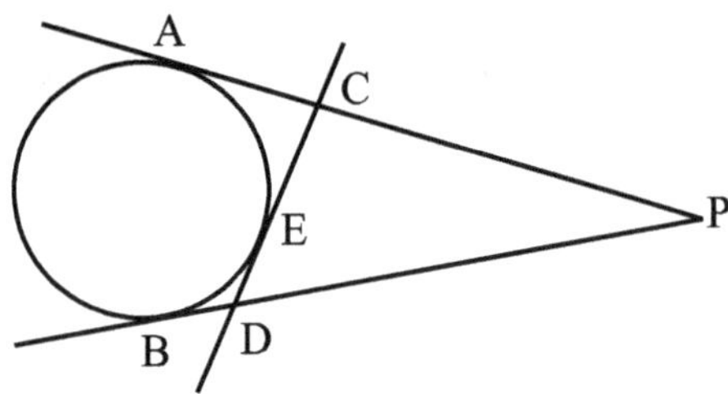

$\Rightarrow$ Perimeter of $\Delta PCD = PA + PA = 2PA = 2(10) = 20$cm

(½ Mark)

18. Given that $\angle OAB = 30°$, AB = 6

$\angle OAP = 90°$ [Angle between the tangent and the radius at the point of contact]

$\angle PAB = 90° - 30° = 60°$ **(½ Mark)**

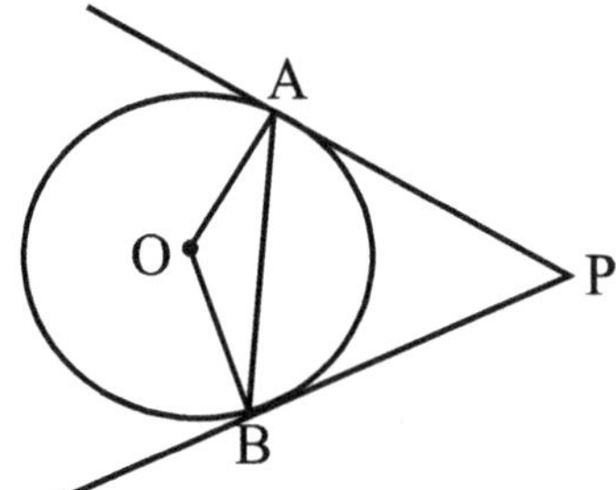

AP = BP [Tangents to a circle from an external point]

$\angle PAB = \angle PBA$

[Angles opposite to equal sides of a triangle] **(½ Mark)**

In ΔABP, $\angle PAB + \angle PBA + \angle APB = 180°$

[Angle Sum Property]

$60° + 60° + \angle APB = 180°$

$\angle APB = 60°$ **(½ Mark)**

$\therefore$ ΔABP is an equilateral triangle, where PA = BP = AB.

PA = 6 cm **(½ Mark)**

In right ΔOAP, $\angle OPA = 30° \left\{\because \angle OPA = \frac{\angle APB}{2} = \frac{60}{2} = 30°\right\}$

$\tan 30° = \frac{OA}{PA}$

i.e. $\frac{1}{\sqrt{3}} = \frac{OA}{6}$ **(½ Mark)**

i.e. $OA = \frac{6}{\sqrt{3}} = 2\sqrt{3}cm$ **(½ Mark)**

19. Let $\angle TPQ = \theta$

$\angle TPO = 90°$ [Angle between the tangent and the radius at the point of contact] **(½ Mark)**

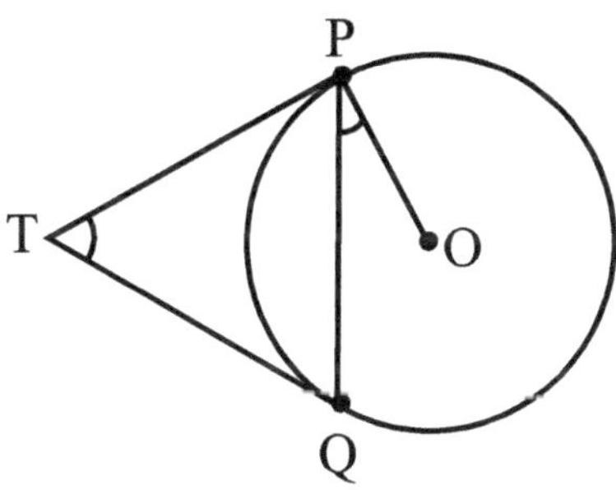

$\angle OPQ = 90° - \theta$ ... (1)

Also, $\angle$ TP = TQ

[Tangents to a circle from an external point] **(½ Mark)**

$\angle TPQ = \angle TQP = \theta$

[Angles opposite to equal sides of a triangle] **(½ Mark)**

In ΔPQT, $\angle PQT + \angle QPT + \angle PTQ = 180°$

[Angle Sum Property] **(½ Mark)**

$\theta + \theta + \angle PTQ = 180°$

$\angle PTQ = 180° - 2\theta$ **(½ Mark)**

$\angle PTQ = 2(90° - \theta)$ **(½ Mark)**

$\angle PTQ = 2\angle OPQ$ [using (1)]

20. OM be the radius of inner circle = 3 cm

outer circle = 5 cm

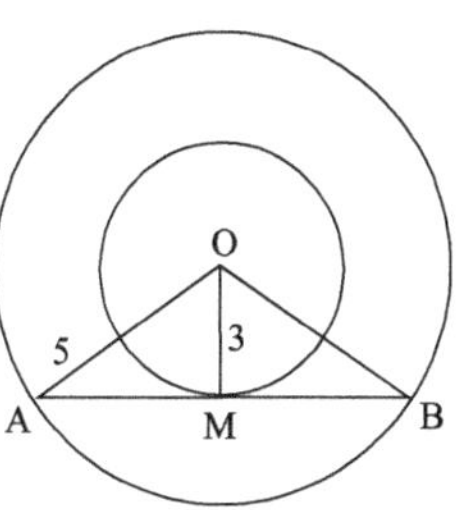

$AM^2 = OA^2 - OM^2$

$\Rightarrow AM^2 = (5)^2 - (3)^2$

$= 25 - 9 = 16$

$\Rightarrow AM = 4$

(1 Mark)

Chord AB = 2AM = 2 × 4 = 8 cm **(1 Mark)**

21. As tangents are peapendicular to radii it of circle.

$\Rightarrow \angle CAO = \angle CBO = 90$

Now ACBO is qualrileteral.

Sum of angles = 360^0

$90° + \angle AOB + 90° + \angle ACB = 360°$

$\Rightarrow \angle AOB + \angle ACB = 180^0$ **(1 Mark)**

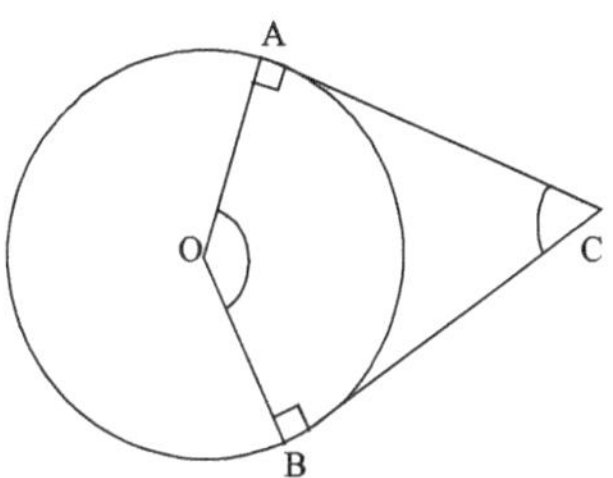

(1 Mark)

So, angle b/w two tangents drawn from an external point to a circle is supplementary to the angle subtended by the line segment joining the points of contact at the centre.

22. $\angle PAO - \angle PBO = 90°$ (angle b/w radius and tangent)

(1 Mark)

$\angle AOB = 105°$ (By angle sum property of a triangle)

(1 Mark)

$\angle AQB = ½ \times 105° = 52.5°$ (Angle at the remaining part of the circle is half the angle subtended by the arc at the centre)

23. Let ABCD be the rhombus circumscribing the circle with centre O, such that AB, BC, CD and DA touch the circle at points P, Q, R and S respectively.

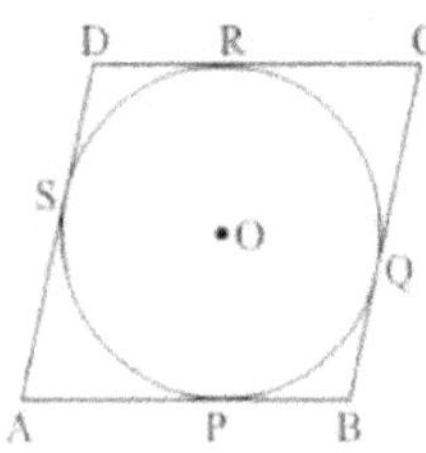

We know that the tangents drawn to a circle from an exterior point are equal in length.

$\therefore$ AP = AS ....(1)

BP = BQ ....(2)

CR = CQ ....(3)

DR = DS ....(4)

(1 Mark)

Adding (1), (2), (3) and (4) we get

AP + BP + CR + DR = AS + BQ + CQ + DS

(AP + BP) + (CR + DR) = (AS + DS) + (BQ + CQ)

$\therefore$ AB + CD = AD + BC ....(5)

(1 Mark)

Since AB = DC and AD = BC (opposite sides of parallelogram ABCD) putting in (5) we get, 2AB = 2AD or AB = AD. **(½ Mark)**

$\therefore$ AB=BC=DC=AD

Since a parallelogram with equal adjacent sides is a rhombus, so ABCD is a rhombus **(½ Mark)**

24.

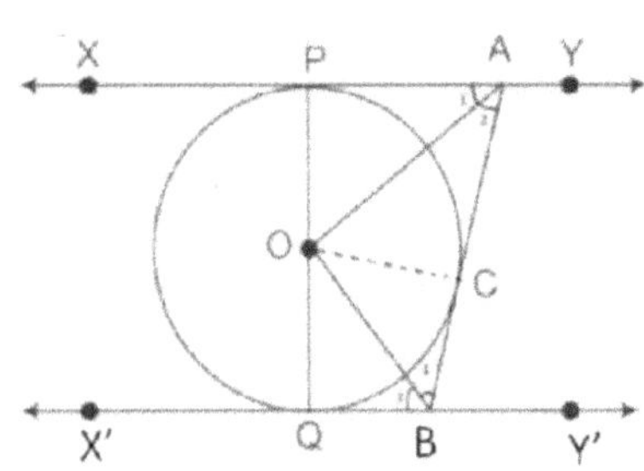

Join OC In ΔOPA and ΔOCA

OP = OC (radii of same circle)

PA = CA (length of two tangents from an external point)

(½ Mark)

AO = AO (Common)

Therefore, ΔOPA ≅ ΔOCA (By SSS congruency criterion)

(½ Mark)

Hence, $\angle 1 = \angle 2$ (CPCT)

Similarly $\angle 3 = \angle 4$ **(½ Mark)**

$\angle PAB + \angle QBA = 180°$ (co interior angles are supplementary as XY ∥ X'Y') (½ mark)

$2\angle 2 + 2\angle 4 = 180°$

$\angle 2 + \angle 4 = 90°$ ....(1)

$\angle 2 + \angle 4 + \angle AOB = 180°$ (Angle sum property)

Using (1), we get, $\angle AOB = 90°$ **(½ Mark)**

25. Given: A circle touches the side BC of a ΔABC at P and extended sides AB and AC at Q and R.

To prove: $AQ = \frac{1}{2}(BC + CA + AB)$

Proof: Lengths of tangents drawn to a circle from an external point are equal.

$\therefore$ AQ = AR ...(i) [Tangents from A]

BP = BQ ...(ii) [Tangents from B]

CP = CR ...(iii) [Tangents from C]

$$\text{R.H.S.} = \frac{1}{2}(BC + CA + AB)$$

$$= \frac{1}{2}(BP + PC + CA + AB)$$ **(1 Mark)**

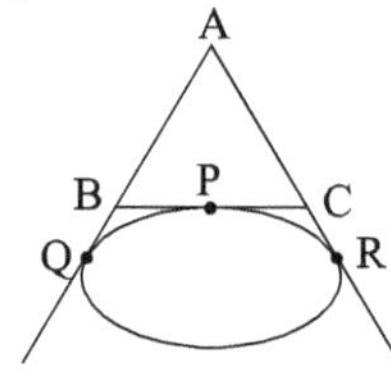

$$= \frac{1}{2}(AB + BQ + AC + CR)$$ [from (ii) & (iii)]

$$= \frac{1}{2}[AQ + AR] = \frac{1}{2}[AQ + AQ]$$ [from (i)]

$$= \frac{1}{2}[2AQ] = AQ = \text{L.H.S.}$$ **(1 Mark)**

Hence, proved.

An excircle of the triangle is a circle lying outside the triangle, tangent to one of its sides and tangent to the extensions of the other two. The length of tangents to the extensions side is equal to the semi perimeter of triangle.

26.

Topper's Answer

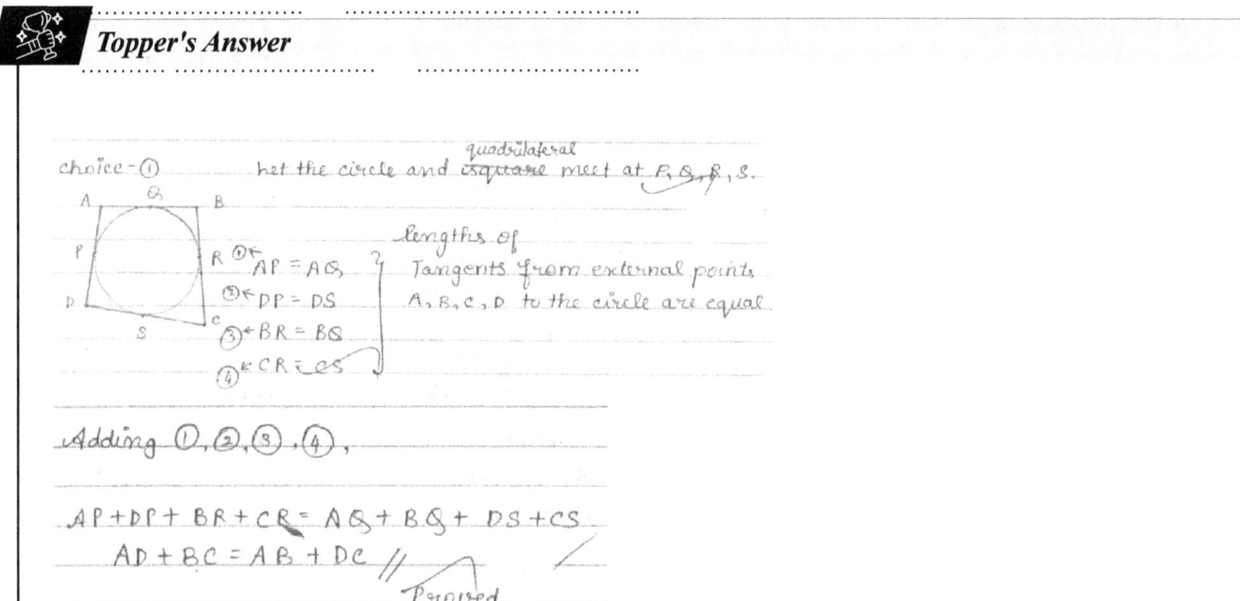

choice-① Let the circle and quadrilateral meet at P, Q, R, S.

① AP = AQ
② DP = DS
③ BR = BQ
④ CR = CS

} lengths of Tangents from external points A, B, C, D to the circle are equal

Adding ①, ②, ③, ④,

AP + DP + BR + CR = AQ + BQ + DS + CS

AD + BC = AB + DC // Proved.

27.

Topper's Answer

To prove: opposite sides of a quadrilateral circumscribing a circle subtend equal angles at the centre.

Construction: Constructed a quadrilateral ABCD, circumscribing a circle (centre O). Circle touches AB, BC, CD, DA at P, Q, R, S respectively.

To prove: $\angle AOB + \angle COD = 180^\circ$
Or $\angle AOD + \angle BOC = 180^\circ$

We know, that tangents from same exterior point subtend equal angle at the centre of circle with radius.

$\therefore \angle AOP = \angle AOS = \angle 1$ (say)

Similarly, $\angle BOP = \angle BOQ = \angle 2$

$\angle COQ = \angle COR = \angle 3$

$\angle DOR = \angle DOS = \angle 4$.

$\therefore \angle AOP + \angle BOP + \angle BOQ + \angle COQ + \angle COR + \angle DOR + \angle DOS + \angle AOS = 360^\circ$ [Complete angle around a point]

$\Rightarrow 2\angle 1 + 2\angle 2 + 2\angle 3 + 2\angle 4 = 360^\circ$

$\Rightarrow \angle 1 + \angle 2 + \angle 3 + \angle 4 = 180^\circ$

$\Rightarrow (\angle 1 + \angle 2) + (\angle 3 + \angle 4) = 180^\circ$.

$\Rightarrow \angle AOB + \angle COD = 180^\circ$

Or $(\angle 1 + \angle 4) + (\angle 2 + \angle 3) = 180^\circ$

$\Rightarrow \angle AOD + \angle BOC = 180^\circ$

Hence, proved!

28. Given: PQ || RS

To prove: $\angle AOB = 90°$

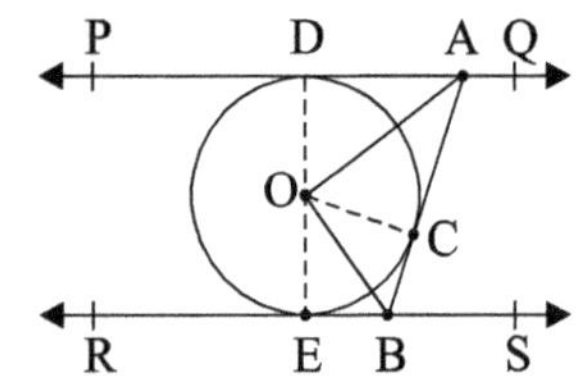

Construction: Join from O to C, D and E

In ΔODA and ΔOCA

OD = OC (radii of circle)

OA = OA (common)

AD = AC (tangent drawn from the external point)

By SSS congruency

$\Delta ODA \cong \Delta OCA$ **(1 Mark)**

$\angle DOA = \angle AOC$ ...(i) (By C.P.C.T)

Similarly,

$\Delta EOB \cong \Delta COB$ **(1 Mark)**

$\angle EOB = \angle BOC$ ...(ii) (By C.P.C.T)

EOD is a diameter of the circle, therefore it is a straight line.

Hence, $\angle DOA + \angle AOC + \angle EOB + \angle BOC = 180°$

$\Rightarrow 2(\angle AOC) + 2(\angle BOC) = 180°$ [from (i) and (ii)]

$\Rightarrow \angle AOC + \angle BOC = 90°$

$\Rightarrow \angle AOB = 90°$ **(1 Mark)**

Hence proved.

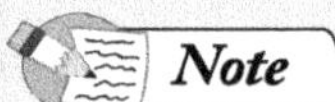

A line joining centre to external point bisect the angle between tangents from that point. Another method to prove use this property.

29.

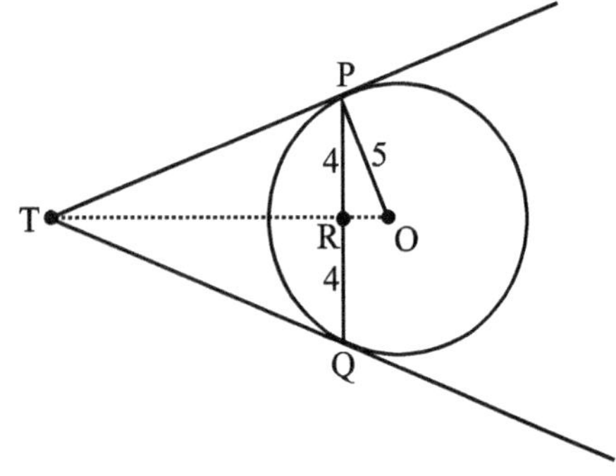

Join OT. Let it intersect PQ at the point R. Then ΔTPQ is isosceles and TO is the angle bisector of $\angle PTQ$. So, $OT \perp PQ$ and therefore, OT bisects PQ which gives PR = RQ = 4 cm.

Also, $OR = \sqrt{(OP)^2 - (PR)^2} = \sqrt{5^2 - 4^2} = 3$ cm

(1 Mark)

Now $\angle TPR + \angle RPO = 90° = \angle TPR + \angle PTR$

So, $\angle RPO = \angle PTR$ **(1 Mark)**

Therefore, right triangle TRP is similar to the right triangle PRO by AA similarity.

This gives

$\frac{TP}{PO} = \frac{RP}{RO}$, i.e., $\frac{TP}{5} = \frac{4}{3}$ or $TP = \frac{20}{3}$ cm. **(1 Mark)**

30.

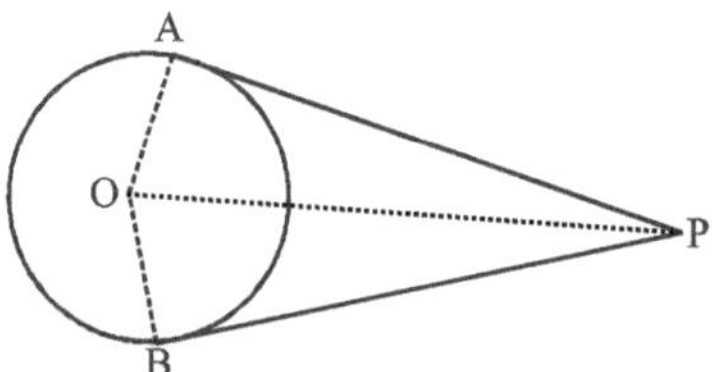

Given : A circle C(O, r) with p as its external point. tangents PA and PB are drawn to the circle

To prove : PA = PB

Construction :- Join OA, OB and OP

Proof : In Δ PAO and Δ PBO, we have

OA = OB (radii of same circle)

OP = OP (common)

$\angle OAP = \angle OBP = 90°$ (Radius is perpendicular to tangent)

$\therefore$ By RHS Congruency rule

$\Delta PAO \cong \Delta PBO$ **(1 Mark)**

$\Rightarrow$ PA = PB

Hence, tangents drawn from external point to a circle are equal in length. **(1 Mark)**

31. Let AB is the chord of circle with centre 'O' and Let AC & BC to the same circle. Join OC to cut AB at D. **(1 Mark)**

Now, we have to prove that

$\angle CAD = \angle CBD,$

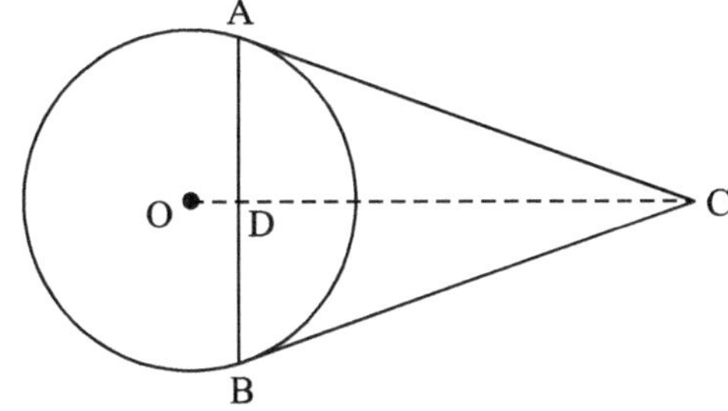

As line segment joining the centre to the external point from where tangents are drawn, bisects the angle between two tangents.

So, $\angle ACD = \angle BCD$ ...(i)

In ΔACD & $\angle BCD$

CA = CB [tangents from external point are equal]

$\angle ACD = \angle BCD$ [from (i)]

CD = CD (Common line)

$\therefore$ $\Delta ACD \cong \Delta BCD$ (By SAS Axiom)

$\Rightarrow$ $\angle CAD = \angle CBD$ (By CPCT)

(1 Mark)

In any circle, the angle between a chord and a tangent through one and point of the chord is equal to the angle in the alternate segment.

32. Let ABCD be a quadrilateral and a circle touches the side AB, BC, CD & DA of quadrilateral at P, Q, R, S respectively.

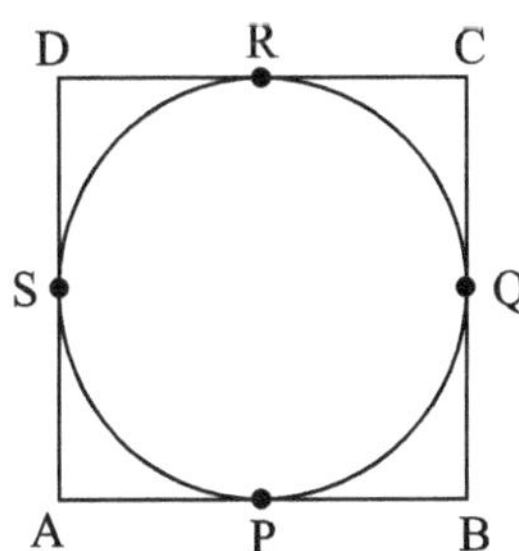

Since, we know the length of tangents drawn from an external point to a circle are equal.

DR = DS ...(i)

CR = CQ ...(ii)

BP = BQ ...(iii)

AP = AS ...(iv) **(1 Mark)**

Adding (i), (ii), (iii) and (iv)

DR + CR + BP + AP = DS + CQ + BQ + AS

(DR + CR) + (BP + AP) = (DS + AS) + (CQ + BQ)

$\Rightarrow$ CD + AB = AD + BC

Or, AB + CD = BC + DA **(1 Mark)**

Hence, proved.

33. Let $AD = x$ cm

$\therefore$ $AD = AF = x$ cm [Tangents drawn from external points are equal]

$\because$ $AD + BD = AB = 12$ **(1 Mark)**

$\Rightarrow$ $BD = 12 - x$

$\therefore$ $BD = BE = 12 - x$ ...(1)

Now, $AF + CF = AC = 10$

$\Rightarrow$ $CF = 10 - x$

$\therefore$ $CE = CF = 10 - x$ ...(2)

$BE + CE = BC = 8$

$\Rightarrow$ $12 - x + 10 - x = 8$ [From 1 and 2]

$\Rightarrow$ $22 - 8 = 2x$

$\Rightarrow$ $x = 7$ **(1 Mark)**

$\therefore$ $AD = x = 7$ cm

$BE = 12 - x = 5$ cm

$CF = 10 - x = 3$ cm

$\therefore$ Lengths of AD, BE and CF are 7cm, 5 cm and 3 cm respectively. **(1 Mark)**

34. PA and PB are tangents from an external point P

$\therefore$ $PA = PB$ [Tangents from an external points are equal in length]

In ΔPAB

$PA = PB$ **(1 Mark)**

$\therefore$ ΔPAB is isoceles

$\angle PAB = \angle PBA = x$ (say) [Angles opposite to equal sides will also be equal]

$\angle APB = 60°$ (given)

$\angle PAB + \angle PBA + \angle APB = 180°$ (Angle sum property)

$x + x + 60° = 180°$

$2x = 120$

$\Rightarrow x = 60°$ **(1 Mark)**

$\therefore \angle PAB = \angle PBA = \angle APB = 60°$

All angles are 60°, therefore ΔPAB is equilateral

$\because AP = 5$ cm

In equilateral triangle all sides are equal

$\therefore AB = AP = 5$ cm

Length of chord AB is 5 cm. **(1 Mark)**

In circle, radius is perpendicular to the tangent drawn from external point to the circle at point of contact.

35. PR and PQ are tangents to the circle

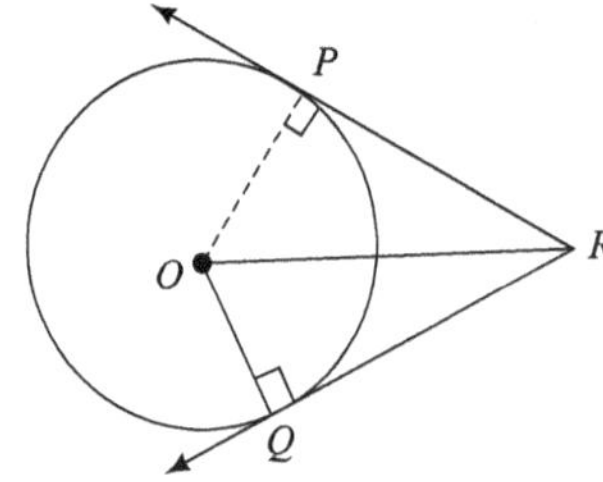

$\angle OPR = \angle OQR = 90°$ [Radii is perpendicular to the tangent of a circle] ...(1)

In ΔOPR and ΔOQR

$\angle OPR = \angle OQR = 90°$

$\Rightarrow OP = OQ$ [Radii of same circle]

$OR = OR$ (common side)

$\Rightarrow \Delta OPR \cong \Delta OQR$ (By *RHS* congruency) **(1 Mark)**

$\therefore RP = RQ$ (By *CPCT*) ...(2)

$\angle ORP = \angle ORQ$ (By *CPCT*) ...(3)

$\angle PRQ = \angle ORP + \angle ORQ \Rightarrow \angle PRQ = 120°$

$\Rightarrow \angle ORP + \angle ORP = 120°$ (from (3))

$\Rightarrow 2\angle ORP = 120° \Rightarrow \angle ORP = 60°$

In ΔOPR

$\Rightarrow \cos\theta = \frac{PR}{OR}$

$\Rightarrow \cos(\angle ORP) = \frac{PR}{OR} \Rightarrow \cos 60° = \frac{PR}{OR}$

$\Rightarrow \frac{PR}{OR} = \frac{1}{2} \Rightarrow OR = 2PR$

$\Rightarrow OR = 2PR \Rightarrow OR = PR + PR$

$\Rightarrow OR = PR + RQ$ (from (2))

Hence proved. **(1 Mark)**

36. Let circle touches AB at E, CA at F and BC at D.

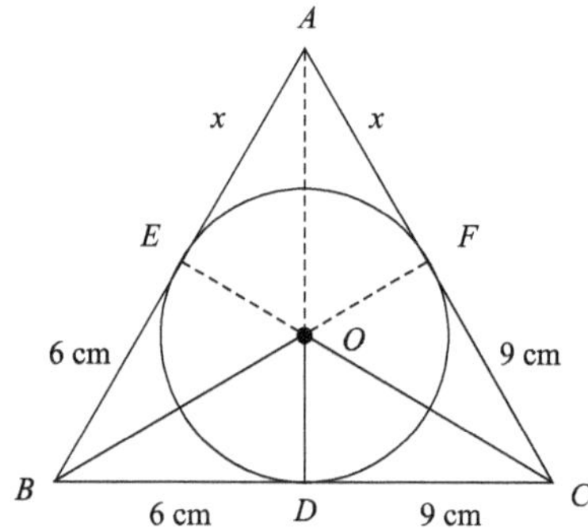

Const: Join OA, OF, OE, OB, OC

Let AF be x cm

$AF = AE = x$ [Radii is perpendicular to tangents]

Similarly $CD = CF = 9$ cm

$BD = BE = 6$ cm **(1 Mark)**

$\therefore BA = 6 + x$

$\Rightarrow AC = x + 9$

$BC = BD + DC = 6 + 9 = 15$ cm

Area of $\Delta OBC = \frac{1}{2} \times$ Base $\times$ Height

$= \frac{1}{2} \times BC \times OD = \frac{1}{2} \times 15 \times 3 = \frac{45}{2}$

Area of $\Delta OCA = \frac{1}{2} \times AC \times OE$

$= \frac{1}{2} \times (x + 9) \times 3 = \frac{3}{2}(x + 9)$

Area of $\Delta OAB = \frac{1}{2} \times AB \times OF$

$= \frac{1}{2} \times (x + 6) \times 3 = \frac{3}{2}(x + 6)$ **(1 Mark)**

Area of ΔABC = Area of ΔOBC + Area of ΔOCA + Area of ΔOAB

$54 = \frac{45}{2} + \frac{3}{2}(x+9) + \frac{3}{2}(x+6)$

$54 = 45 + 3x$

$3x = 54 - 45 = 9$

$\Rightarrow x = 3$

$\therefore AB = x + 6 = 6 + 3 = 9$ cm

$AC = 9 + x = 9 + 3 = 12$ cm **(1 Mark)**

37.

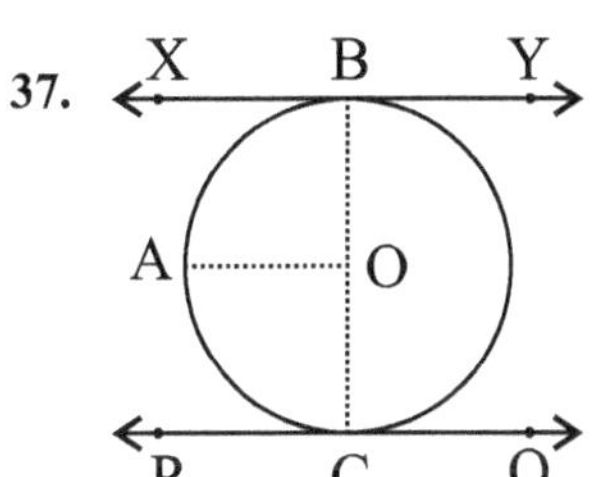

Let XBY and PCQ be two parallel tangents to a circle with centre O.

Construction : Join OB and OC

XB || AO

$\angle XBO + \angle AOB = 180°$ (Sum of adjacent angle is 180°)

As tangent to a circle is always perpendicular to the radius through point of contact.

$\angle XBO = 90°$

$90° + \angle AOB = 180°$

$\therefore \angle AOB = 90°$ ...(1) **(1 Mark)**

Similarly $\angle AOC = 90°$ ...(2)

Adding (1) and (2)

$\angle AOB + \angle AOC = 90° + 90° = 180°$

Hence, BOC is a straight line passing through O. Thus, the line segment joining the points of contacts of two parallel tangents of a circle passing through its centre. **(1 Mark)**

38.

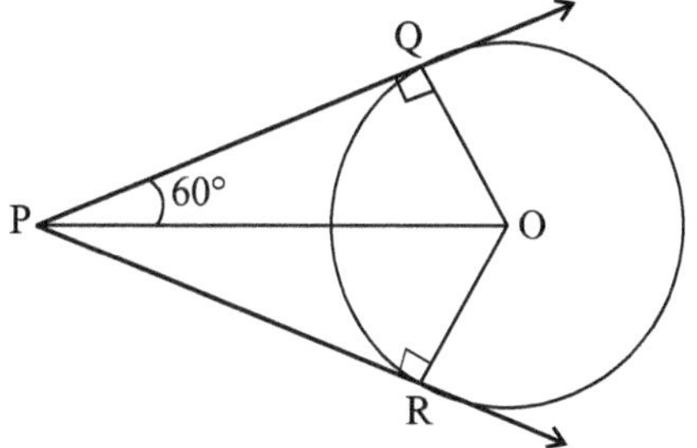

Let P be the external point to the circle and PQ and PR be two tangents.

PQ = PR (Tangents to the circle)

OP = OP (Common)

OQ = OR (Radius of circle are equal)

$\therefore \Delta OPQ \cong \Delta OPR$ (By SSS congruency) **(½ Mark)**

$\therefore \angle QPO = \angle OPR$

$\because \angle QPR = 120°$

$\therefore \angle OPQ = \frac{1}{2}\angle QPR = \frac{1}{2} \times 120°$

$\angle OPQ = 60°$ **(½ Mark)**

In right triangle QPO

$\cos 60° = \frac{PQ}{PO}$ $[\cos\theta = \frac{\text{Base}}{\text{Hypotenuouse}}]$

$\frac{1}{2} = \frac{PQ}{PO}$

PO = 2 PQ **(1 Mark)**

Hence Proved.

39. Given: ABC is equilateral triangle of side 12 cm

To find: Radius of inscribed circle and area of shaded region.

Construction: Join OA, OB and OC.

Draw OP ⊥ BC

OQ ⊥ AC

OR ⊥ AB

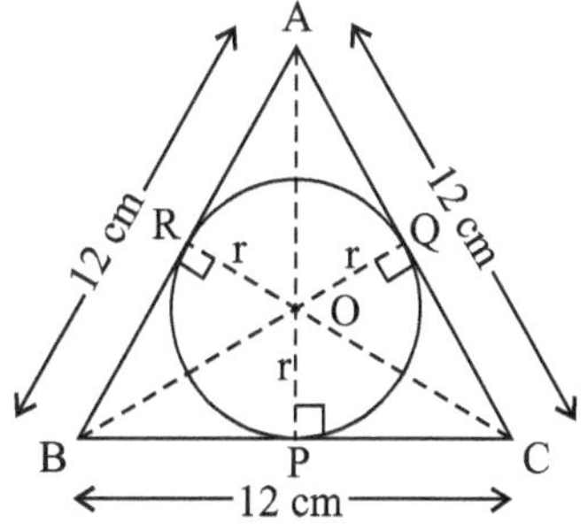

Let r cm be radius of circle.

Area of ΔABC = Area of ΔAOB + Area of ΔBOC + Area of ΔAOC **(½ Mark)**

$$\frac{\sqrt{3}}{4}\times(\text{side})^2=\frac{1}{2}\times AB\times OR+\frac{1}{2}\times BC\times OP+\frac{1}{2}\times AC\times OQ$$

$$\frac{\sqrt{3}}{4}\times(12)^2=\frac{1}{2}\times 12\times r+\frac{1}{2}\times 12\times r+\frac{1}{2}\times 12\times r$$

$$\frac{\sqrt{3}}{4}\times 144=3\times\frac{1}{2}\times 12\times r \Rightarrow \frac{\sqrt{3}}{4}\times 144=18r$$

$$r=\frac{\sqrt{3}\times 144}{4\times 18}=3.46 \text{ cm}$$

$\therefore$ Radius of inscribed circle is 3.46 cm **(1 Mark)**

Area of shaded region = Area of ΔABC – Area of the inscribed circle **(½ Mark)**

$$=\frac{\sqrt{3}}{4}\times(12)^2-\pi r^2 \quad =\frac{\sqrt{3}}{4}\times 144-\pi(3.46)^2$$

$= [62.28 - 37.68]\ cm^2$

$= 24.6\ cm^2$

$\therefore$ Area of shaded region = $24.6\ cm^2$ **(1 Mark)**

40. Since tangents drawn from external point are equal in length

$AD = AF$

$CF = CE$

$BD = BE$

Let $BD = BE = x$ **(½ Mark)**

Given that: $AB = 12$ cm, $BC = 8$ cm and $AC = 10$ cm

$CE = BC - BE = 8 - x = CF$ ...(i)

$AD = AB - BD = 12 - x = AF$ ...(ii) **(½ Mark)**

$AC = AF + FC = 10$

$8 - x + 12 - x = 10$ [from (i) & (ii)]

$2x = 20 - 10 = 10$

$x = 5$

$AD = 12 - x = 7$ cm

$BE = x = 5$ cm

$CF = 8 - x = 3$ cm **(1 Mark)**

41. Given: $ABCD$ is parallelogram circumscribing a circle with centre O.

To prove: $ABCD$ is a rhombus **(½ Mark)**

Proof: Tangents drawn from external point are equal in length

$\therefore$ $AP = AS$, $BP = BQ$, $CR = CQ$ and $DR = DS$

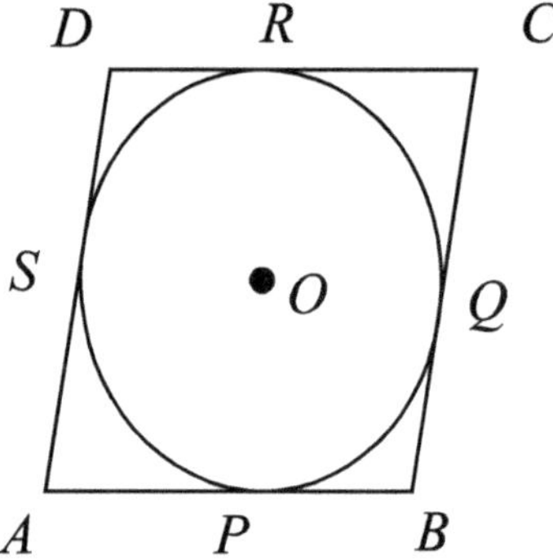

On adding above equations

$AP + BP + CR + DR = AS + BQ + CQ + DS$

$(AP + BP) + (CR + DR) = (AS + DS) + (BQ + CQ)$

$AB + CD = AD + BC$ ...(1) **(1 Mark)**

Since $ABCD$ is parallelogram

$AD = BC$ ...(2)

[Opposite sides of parallelogram are equal]

$AB = DC$ ...(3)

from (1)

$AB + AB = BC + BC$

$2AB = 2CB$

$AB = CB$ ...(4)

From (2), (3) and (4)

$AB = BC = CD = DA$. Rhombus has equal sides

$\therefore$ $ABCD$ is rhombus. **(½ Mark)**

42.

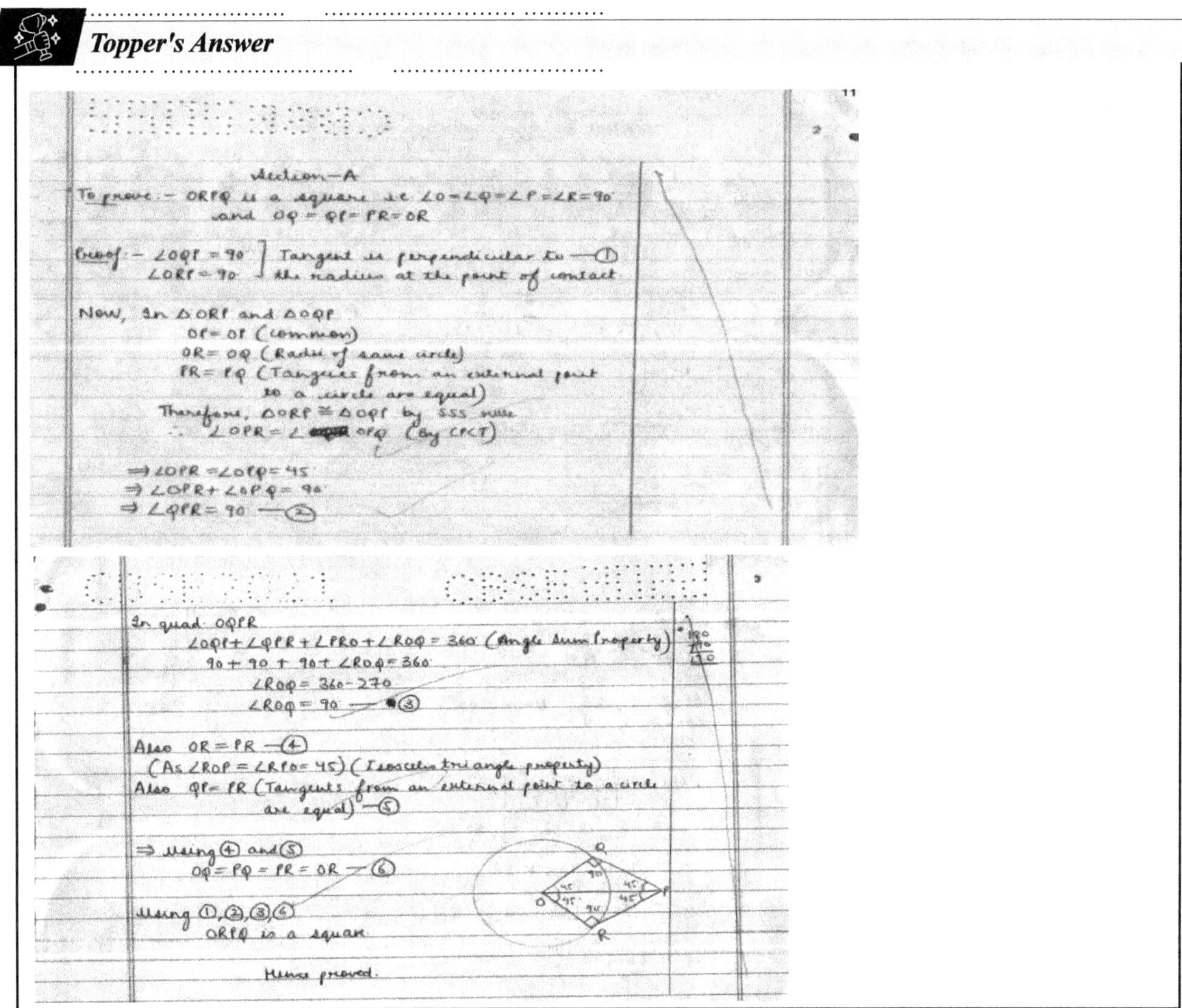

Topper's Answer

Section-A

To prove:- ORPQ is a square i.e ∠O = ∠Q = ∠P = ∠R = 90° and OQ = QP = PR = OR

Proof:- ∠OQP = 90°] Tangent is perpendicular to — (1)
∠ORP = 90°] the radius at the point of contact

Now, In ΔORP and ΔOQP
OP = OP (common)
OR = OQ (Radii of same circle)
PR = PQ (Tangents from an external point to a circle are equal)
Therefore, ΔORP ≅ ΔOQP by SSS rule
∴ ∠OPR = ∠OPQ (By CPCT)

⇒ ∠OPR = ∠OPQ = 45°
⇒ ∠OPR + ∠OPQ = 90°
⇒ ∠QPR = 90° — (2)

In quad. OQPR
∠OQP + ∠QPR + ∠PRO + ∠ROQ = 360° (Angle Sum Property)
90 + 90 + 90 + ∠ROQ = 360°
∠ROQ = 360 − 270
∠ROQ = 90° — (3)

Also OR = PR — (4)
(As ∠ROP = ∠RPO = 45°) (Isosceles triangle property)
Also QP = PR (Tangents from an external point to a circle are equal) — (5)

⇒ using (4) and (5)
OQ = PQ = PR = OR — (6)

Using (1), (2), (3), (6)
ORPQ is a square

Hence proved.

43. Let $\angle PTQ = \theta$

Also,

TP = TQ (∴ Tangent drawn from an external point to a circle are equal.) **(1 Mark)**

∴ ΔTPQ is isosceles triangle.

$$\therefore \ \angle TPQ = \angle TQP = \frac{1}{2}(180° - \theta) = 90° - \frac{\theta}{2}$$

(1 Mark)

$\angle OPT = 90°$ [Tangent at any point of circle is perpendicular to the radius through the point of contact]

$$\angle OPQ = \angle OPT - \angle TPQ$$

$$= 90° - \left(90° - \frac{Q}{2}\right)$$

$$= \frac{\theta}{2}$$ **(1 Mark)**

$$= \frac{1}{2}\angle PTQ$$

$\therefore \ \angle PTQ = 2\angle OPQ$ **(1 Mark)**

Hence proved.

44. In the figure

AG = AR
CP = CR
BQ = BP
[tangent drawn from external point are equal]

From the figure, it is clear that

AR = AC + CR

and

AQ = AB + BQ **(1 Mark)**

$\therefore$ AQ = AR

Hence,

AB + BQ = AC + CR **(2 Marks)**

Substituting BP for BQ and CP for CR

AB + BP = AC + CP (i)

Perimeter of ΔABC = AB + BC + CA

= AB + BP + PC + CA

= 2(AB + BP) [from eq. (i)]

= 2(AB + BQ) [$\because$ BP = BQ]

= 2AQ

Hence, AQ = $\frac{1}{2}$ Perimeter of ΔABC **(1 Mark)**

45. **(a)** BD = BE = 10; DC = CF = 8

And, AE = AF = x

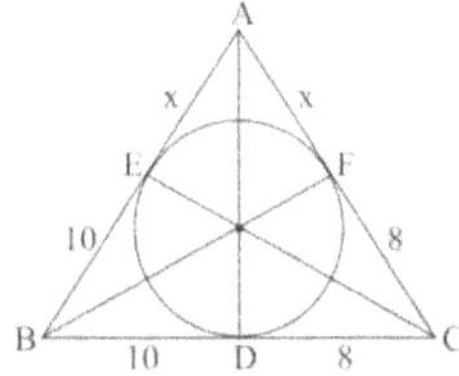

(1 Mark)

In ΔABC

$$\text{Area of } \Delta ABC = \frac{1}{2}\left[\begin{array}{r}\text{Area of } \Delta AOE + \text{Area of } \Delta OBD \\ + \text{Area of } \Delta ODC\end{array}\right]$$

$$\text{Area} = \frac{1}{2}\left[\frac{1}{2}(4x)+\frac{1}{2}(10\times4)+\frac{1}{2}(8\times4)\right]=90$$

(2 Marks)

$\Rightarrow$ 4x + 40 + 32 = 90 $\Rightarrow$ 4x = 18 $\Rightarrow$ x = $\frac{18}{4}$ = 4.5

(1 Mark)

Then, AB = 10 + 4.5 = 14.5

And AC = 8 + 4.5 = 12.5

46. Given, $PQ = 8$ cm, $OP = 5$ cm.

Since, A line joining external point to centre of circle bisect the angle between tangents drawn from that point. Here, TP & TQ are tangents with equal lengths. If join PQ then ΔTPQ is an isosceles triangle and $OT \perp PQ$.

So, $PR = RQ$.

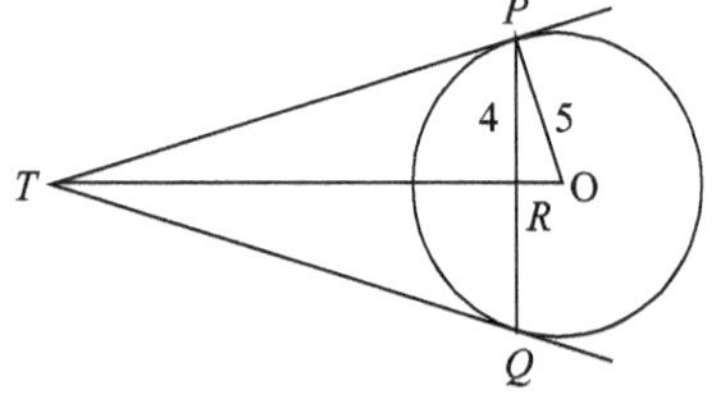

(1 Mark)

$$PR = \frac{PQ}{2} = \frac{8}{2} = 4 \text{ cm.}$$

In ΔPRO

$PO^2 = PR^2 + RO^2$

$5^2 = 4^2 + RO^2$

$25 = 16 + RO^2$

$RO^2 = 9.$ **(1 Mark)**

$RO = 3$ cm.

Let $TP = x$ cm, $TR = y$ cm.

In ΔPRT

$TP^2 = TR^2 + PR^2$

$x^2 = y^2 + 16$ ... (i)

In ΔTPO

$TO^2 = TP^2 + OP^2$

$(y + 3)^2 = x^2 + 25$

$y^2 + 9 + by = y^2 + 16 + 25$ {from (i)}

$6y = 32$

$y = \frac{16}{3}$ **(1 Mark)**

From (i)

$x^2 = y^2 + 16$

$$x^2 = \frac{256}{9} + 16 = \frac{256+144}{9}$$

$$x^2 = \frac{400}{9}$$

$$x = \frac{20}{3}\text{cm.}$$

Therefore, the length of TP is $\frac{20}{3}$ cm. **(1 Mark)**

47. Given : A circle with centre O; PA and PB are two tangents to the circle drawn from an external point P.

To prove : PA = PB

Construction : Join OA, OB, and OP. **(1 Mark)**

Since tangent at any point of a circle is perpendicular to the radius through the point of contact.

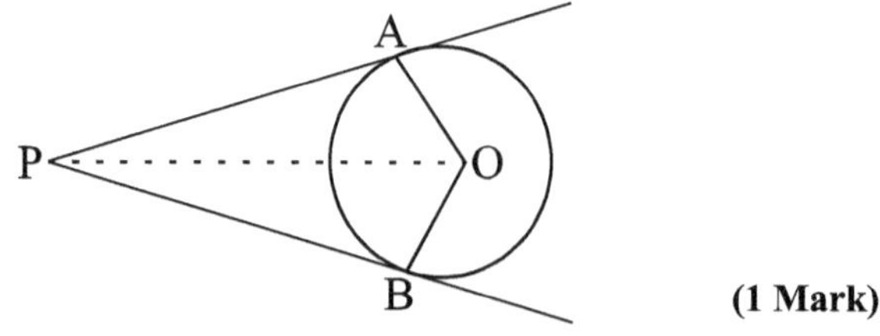

(1 Mark)

$\Rightarrow OA \perp PA$ and $OB \perp PB$

In ΔOPA and ΔOPB

$\angle OAP = \angle OBP = (90°)$

OA = OB (Radii of the same circle)

OP = OP (Common side)

Therefor $\Delta OPA \cong \Delta OPB$ (RHS congruency criterion)

(1 Mark)

PA = PB (By CPCT)

Hence, it is proved that the lengths of the two tangents drawn from an external point to a circle are equal.

(1 Mark)

48. Given that XY and X'Y' are two parallel tangents to the circle with centre 'O'.

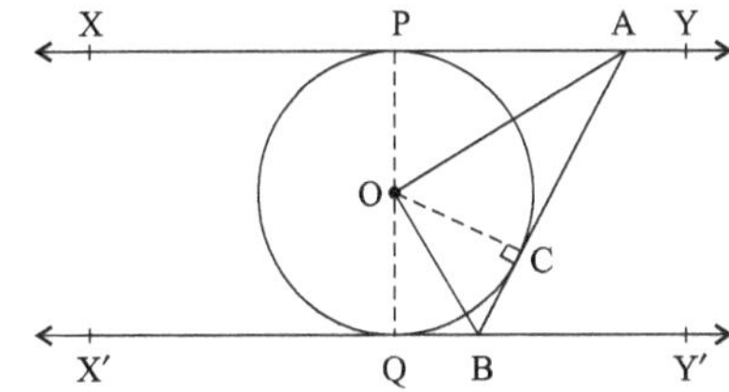

AB is another tangent at point C, which intersects XY at A and X'Y' at B.

In ΔOAP and ΔOAC

OP = OC (Radius of same circle)

OA = OA (common side)

AP = AC

(lengths of tangents drawn from an external point to circles)

$\Rightarrow \Delta OAP \cong \Delta OAS$ (SSS congruence) **(2 Marks)**

$\therefore \angle AOP = \angle COA$ ...(i) By CPCT]

Similary, $\Delta OQB \cong \Delta OCB$

$\therefore \angle BOQ = \angle COB$ ...(ii)

Since, POQ is a diameter of the circle, it is a straight line

$\Rightarrow \angle AOP + \angle COA + \angle BOQ + \angle COB = 180°$

$\Rightarrow 2\angle COA + 2\angle COB = 180°$ {Using (i) and (ii)

$\Rightarrow \angle COA + \angle COB = 90°$

$\Rightarrow \angle AOB = 90°$ **(2 Marks)**

Hence, proved.

49. Given: *P* be an external point and *PA* and *PB* are tangents to the circle.

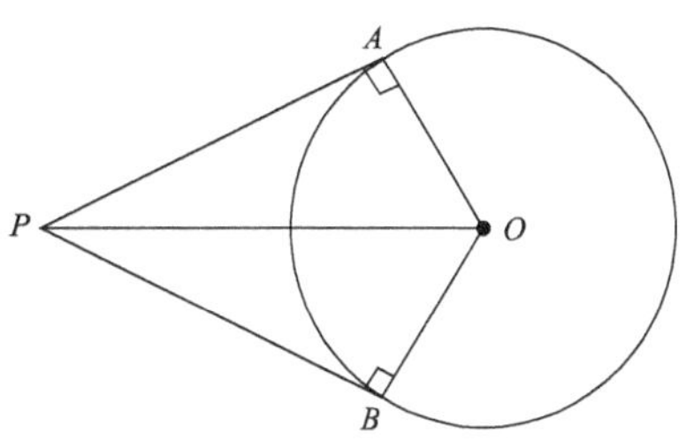

To prove: PA = PB

Construction: Join OA and OB. **(1 Mark)**

Proof: In ΔOAP and ΔOBP

$\angle A = \angle B = 90°$ [Radius of the circle is perpendicular to the tangents of the circle drawn from external point.]

$OP = OP$ (common)

$OA = OB$ = radii of the circle

$\Delta OAP \cong \Delta OBP$ (By *RHS* criterion of congruence)

$\therefore PA = PB$ (By *CPCT*) **(2 Marks)**

Hence proved. **(1 Mark)**

50. In Δ OPT, $\angle OPT = 90°$

By pythagoras theorem

$OP^2 + PT^2 = OT^2$ **(1 Mark)**

$\Rightarrow (5)^2 + (PT)^2 = (13)^2$

$PT^2 = 169 - 25 = 144$

PT = 12 cm ...(1)

OT = OE + ET

13 = 5 + ET (OE is radius)

ET = 8 cm ...(2) **(1 Mark)**

In ΔOPT and ΔEAT

$\angle OPT = \angle AET = 90°$

$\angle ATE = \angle PTO$ [common]

By AA – similarity

$\Delta OPT \sim \Delta AET$ **(1 Mark)**

$\frac{OP}{AE} = \frac{PT}{ET}$

$\frac{5}{AE} = \frac{12}{8}$ [From 1 and 2]

$AE = \frac{5 \times 8}{12} = \frac{10}{3}$ cm

Similarly, $BE = \frac{10}{3}$ cm

So, $AB = 2 \times \frac{10}{3} = \frac{20}{3}$ cm. **(1 Mark)**

51. Given: $OA = 5$ cm

$OP = 10$ cm

As tangent at any point of a circle is perpendicular to the radius through the point of contact.

$\therefore \angle OAP = 90°$

ΔOAP is right triangle

By pythagoras theorem

$H^2 = P^2 + B^2$ **(1 Mark)**

$OP^2 = OA^2 + AP^2$

$10^2 = 5^2 + AP^2$

$AP^2 = 100 - 25$

$AP^2 = 75$

$AP = 5\sqrt{3}$cm

$\cos\theta = \frac{OA}{OP} = \frac{5}{10}$ $\left[\because \cos\theta = \frac{B}{H}\right]$

$\cos\theta = \frac{1}{2}$

$\cos\theta = \cos 60°$

$\theta = 60°$

In ΔOAP and ΔOBP

$OP = OP$ (common)

$\angle OAP = \angle OBP = 90°$ [Radii is perpendicular to tangent of circle]

$OA = OB$ [Radii of circle]

$\therefore \Delta OAP \cong \Delta OBP$ [By RHS congruency]

$\angle AOP = \angle BOP$ [By CPCT]

$\therefore \angle AOP = \angle BOP = 60°$

$\angle AOB = \angle AOP + \angle BOP$

$= 60° + 60° = 120°$ **(1 Mark)**

Length of the belt still in contact with the pulley = circumference of the circle – length of the arc ACB

$= 2 \times 3.14 \times 5 - \frac{120°}{360°} \times 2 \times 3.14 \times 5$

$= 2 \times 3.14 \times 5\left[1-\frac{1}{3}\right]$

$= 2\times 3.14 \times 5 \times \frac{2}{3}$

$= 20.93$ cm

Area of $\Delta OAP = \frac{1}{2} \times$ Base $\times$ height

$= \frac{1}{2} \times AP \times OA$

$= \frac{1}{2}\times 5\sqrt{3}\times 5$

$= \frac{25\sqrt{3}}{2}\text{cm}^2$

Similarly

Area of $\Delta OBP = \frac{25\sqrt{3}}{2}\text{cm}^2$ **(1 Mark)**

$\therefore$ Area of ΔOBP + Area of Δ OAP

$= \frac{25\sqrt{3}}{2}+\frac{25\sqrt{3}}{2}$

$= 25\sqrt{3}$

$= 25 \times 1.73$

$= 43.25$ cm²

Area of sector OACB $= \frac{8}{360}\pi r^2$

$= \frac{120}{360}\times 3.14\times(5)^2$

$= 26.17$ cm²

$\therefore$ Area of the shaded region = (Area of ΔOAP + Area of ΔOBP) – Area of sector $OACB$

$= 43.25$ cm² – 26.17 cm²

$= 17.08$ cm² (approx.) **(1 Mark)**

52. To prove: $PA = PB$

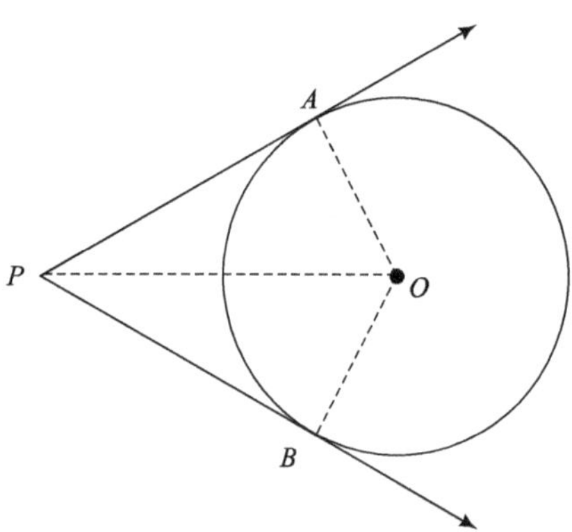

Construction: Join OA, OB and OP **(1 Mark)**

Proof:

It is known that a tangent at any point of a circle is perpendicular to the radius through the point of contact.

$\therefore$ $OA \perp PA$ and $OB \perp PB$

In ΔOPA and ΔOPB

$\angle OAP = \angle OBP = 90°$ **(1 Mark)**

$OA = OB$ (Radii of the same circle)

$OP = OP$ (Common side)

$\therefore$ $\Delta OPA \cong \Delta OPB$ (By RHS congruency)

$PA = PB$ (By $CPCT$) **(2 Marks)**

53. Given: A circle with centre O, P is the midpoint of arc APB. PT is a tangent to the circle at P.

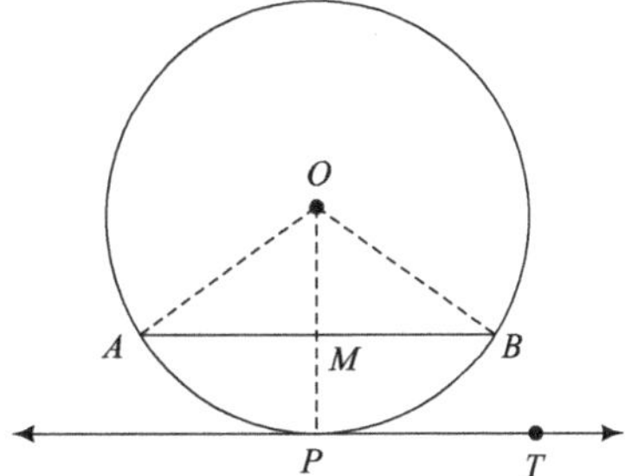

To prove: $AB \parallel PT$

Construction: Join OA, OB and OP **(1 Mark)**

Proof: $OP \perp PT$ [$\because$ Radius is perpendicular to tangent through point of contact]

$\angle OPT = 90°$

Since P is the midpoint of arc APB

arc AP = arc BP **(1 Mark)**

$\angle AOP = \angle BOP$ [If two arcs are equal, then they subtend equal angles at the centre of the circle]

$\angle AOM = \angle BOM$

In ΔAOM and ΔBOM

$OA = OB$ [Radii of circle]

$OM = OM$ [common]

$\angle AOM = \angle BOM$

$\Delta AOM \cong \Delta BOM$ [By SAS congruency] **(1 Mark)**

$\angle AMO = \angle BMO$ [By $CPCT$]

$\Rightarrow \angle AMO + \angle BMO = 180°$

$\Rightarrow \angle AMO + \angle AMO = 180°$

$\Rightarrow 2\angle AMO = 180°$

$\Rightarrow \angle AMO = \angle BMO = 90°$

$\Rightarrow \angle BMO = \angle OPT = 90°$

But, they are corresponding angles

$\therefore$ $AB \parallel PT$ **(1 Mark)**

54.

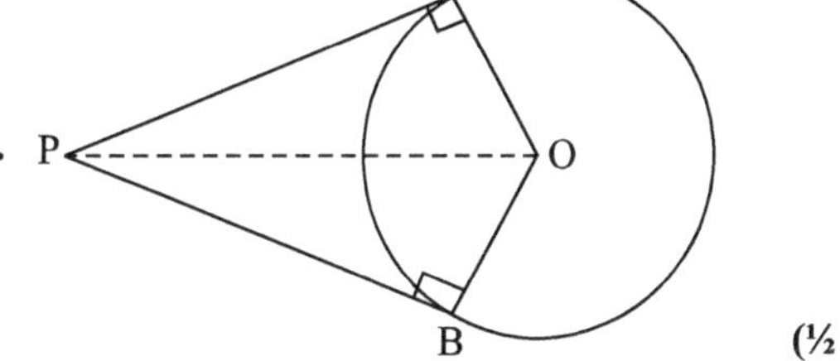

(½ Mark)

Given : PA and PB are tangents to the circle from external point P.

To prove : PA = PB

Construction : Join OP

Proof : In ΔAOP and ΔBOP

OA = OB [radii of same circle]

OP = OP [common]

∠OAP = ∠OBP = 90° [∵Tangents at any point on circle is perpendicular to the radius through the point of contact] **(½ Mark)**

∴ ΔAOP ≅ ΔOBP [By R.H.S congruence criterion] **(2 Marks)**

∴ AP = BP [Corresponding parts of congruent triangles] **(1 Mark)**

Hence proved.

55. **Given:** ABCD is a parallelogram circumscribing circle with centre O.

To prove: ABCD is rhombus

Proof:

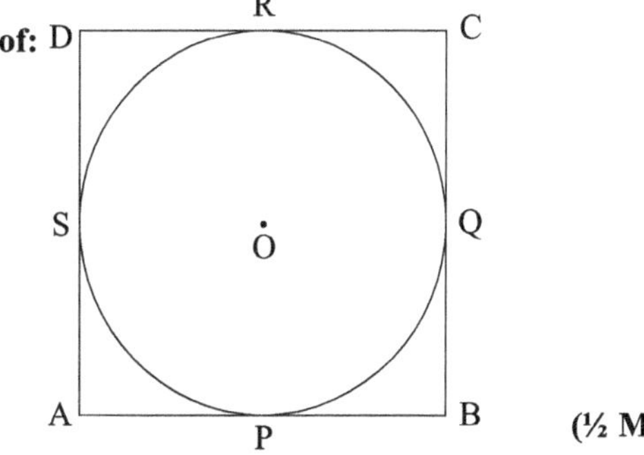

(½ Mark)

As tangents drawn to the circle from an extension points are equal in length.

$\therefore$ AP = PS ...(1)

BP = BQ ...(2)

CR = CQ ...(3) **(1 Mark)**

DR = DS ...(4)

Adding (1), (2), (3) and (4)

AP + BP + CR + DR = AS + BQ + CQ + DS

(AP + BP) + (CR + DR) = (AS + DS) + (BQ + CQ)

AB + CD = AD + BC **(1 Mark)**

Since, ABCD is a parallelogram

AB = CD (Opposite sides of parallelogram are equal)

BC = AD **(½ Mark)**

$\therefore$ AB + AB = BC + BC

2AB = 2BC

AB = BC

$\therefore$ AB = BC = AD = DC

Therefore, ABCD is a rhombus. **(1 Mark)**

56. Given that : A circle with centre *O*. *AX* is a tangent at point *A* of a circle.

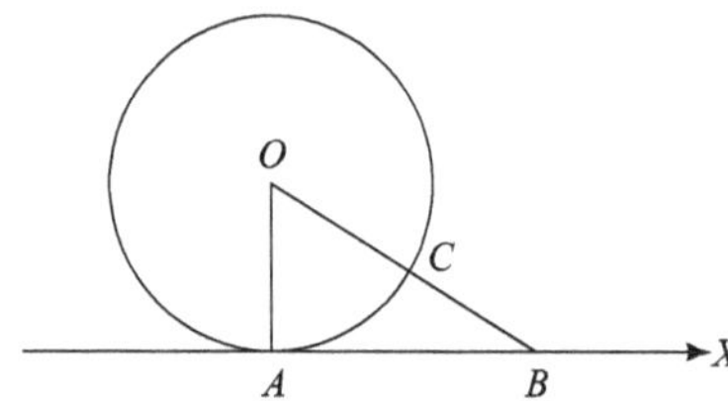

To prove : $OA \perp AB$

Construction : Take any point *B* on *AX* and Join *OB* which

intersect circle at C. **(1 Mark)**

Proof: $OA = OC$ [Radii of circle]

$OB = OC + CB$

$\therefore$ $OB > OC$ [*OC* is radius and *B* is any point on tangent]

$OB > OA$ [$\because OA = OC$] **(1 Mark)**

B is arbitary point on the tangent.

Thus, *OA* is shorter than any other line segment joining *O* to any point on tangent. And shortest distance of any point from a given line is perpendicular distance from that line.

Hence, tangent at any point of circle is perpendicular to the radius. **(2 Marks)**

57. Const: Join *OC*

Proof: In ΔOAD and ΔODC

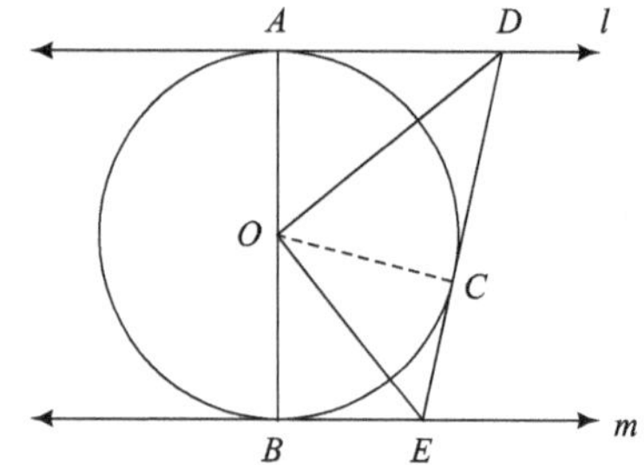

$OA = OC$ (Radii of the same circle)

$AD = DC$ (Length of tangents drawn from an external point to a circle are equal)

$OD = OD$ (common side)

$\Delta ODA \cong \Delta ODC$ (By SSS congruency) **(1 Mark)**

$\angle DOA = \angle COD$ (By CPCT) ...(1)

Similarly $\Delta OEB \cong \Delta OEC$

$\therefore$ $\angle EOB = \angle COE$ ...(2) **(1 Mark)**

$\therefore$ *AB* is diameter of circle

$\angle DOA + \angle COD + \angle COE + \angle EOB = 180°$ (straight line)

$\angle COD + \angle COD + \angle COE + \angle COE = 180°$

[From (1) and (2)]

$2(\angle COD + \angle COE) = 180°$

$\angle COD + \angle COE = 90°$

$\angle DOE = 90°$ **(2 Marks)**

Hence proved.

A line joining from centre of circle to outside point, bisect the angle between tangents from that out side point.

Chapter 11 Areas Related to Circles

Topic-1: Areas of Sector and Segment of a Circle

1 Multiple Choice Questions

1. If the perimeter and the area of a circle are numerically equal, then the radius of the circle is **[CBSE Sample Paper 2023-24, K]**
(a) 2 units (b) π unit
(c) 4 units (d) 7 units

2. It is proposed to build a new circular park equal in area to the sum of areas of two circular parks of diameters 16 m and 12 m in a locality. The radius of the new park is **[CBSE Sample Paper 2023-24, K]**
(a) 10m (b) 15m
(c) 20m (d) 24m

3. What is the area of a semi-circle of diameter 'd'? **[Delhi 2023, K]**
(a) $\frac{1}{16}\pi d^2$ (b) $\frac{1}{4}\pi d^2$ (c) $\frac{1}{8}\pi d^2$ (d) $\frac{1}{2}\pi d^2$

4. The number of revolutions made by a circular wheel of radius 0.25m in rolling a distance of 11km is **[CBSE Sample Paper 2022-23, K]**
(a) 2800 (b) 4000 (c) 5500 (d) 7000

5. The area of a quadrant of a circle where the circumference of circle is 176 m, is **[All India 2022, Term-I, A]**
(a) 2464 m^2 (b) 1232 m^2 (c) 616 m^2 (d) 308 m^2

6. The number of revolutions made by a circular wheel of radius 0.7m in rolling a distance of 176m is **[CBSE Sample Paper 2021-22, Ap]**
(a) 22 (b) 24 (c) 75 (d) 40

7. Given below is the picture of the Olympic rings made by taking five congruent circles of radius 1cm each, intersecting in such a way that the chord formed by joining the point of intersection of two circles is also of length 1 cm. Total area of all the dotted regions assuming the thickness of the rings to be negligible is **[CBSE Sample Paper 2021-22, Term-I, A]**

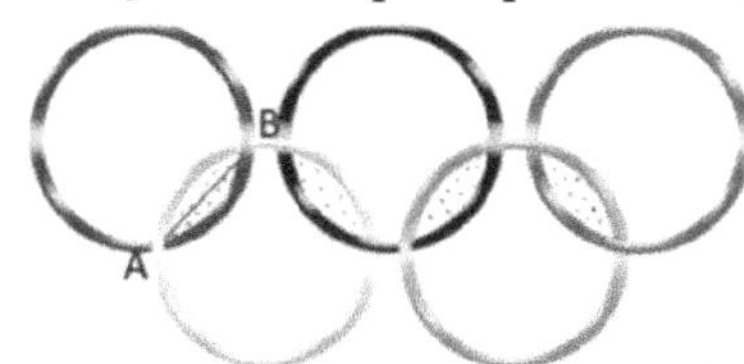

(a) $4\left(\frac{\pi}{12}-\frac{\sqrt{3}}{4}\right)$ cm² (b) $\left(\frac{\pi}{6}-\frac{\sqrt{3}}{4}\right)$ cm²
(c) $4\left(\frac{\pi}{6}-\frac{\sqrt{3}}{4}\right)$ cm² (d) $8\left(\frac{\pi}{6}-\frac{\sqrt{3}}{4}\right)$ cm²

8. If the difference between the circumference and radius of a circle is 37 cm, then using $\pi = \frac{22}{7}$, the circumference (in cm) of the circle is : **[All India 2013, A]**
(a) 154 (b) 44
(c) 14 (d) 7

4 Very Short Answer Question (1 Mark)

9. In fig. is a sector of circle of radius 10.5 cm. Find the perimeter of the sector. $\left(\text{Take } \pi = \frac{22}{7}\right)$ **[All India 2020, A]**

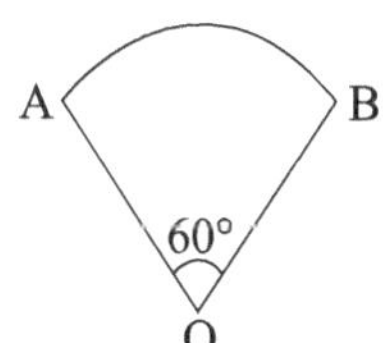

5 Short Answer Questions (2 or 3 Marks)

10. In a circle of radius 21 cm, an arc subtends an angle of 60° at the centre. Find the area of the sector formed by the arc. Also, find the length of the arc. **[All India 2023, Set-II, K]**

11. The length of the minute hand of a clock is 6cm. Find the area swept by it when it moves from 7:05 p.m. to 7:40 p.m. **[CBSE Sample Paper 2022-23, K]**

12. In the given figure, arcs have been drawn of radius 7cm each with vertices A, B, C and D of quadrilateral ABCD as centres. Find the area of the shaded region.

[CBSE Sample Paper 2022-23, Ap]

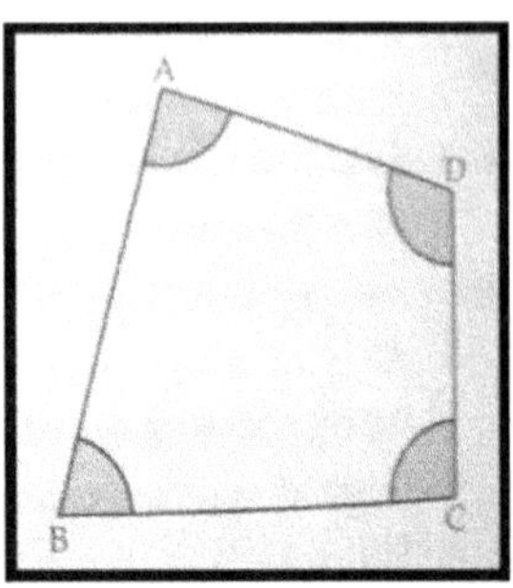

13. The area of a circular play ground is 22176 cm^2. Find the cost of fencing this ground at the rate of ₹50 per metre.

[All India 2020, Ap]

14. A piece of wire 22 cm long is bent into the form of an arc of a circle subtending an angle of 60° at its centre. Find the radius of the circle. $\left[\text{Use } \pi = \frac{22}{7}\right]$ **[Delhi 2020, K]**

15. In Figure, a square OABC is inscribed in a quadrant OPBQ. If OA = 15 cm, find the area of the shaded region. (Use $\pi = 3{\cdot}14$) **[All India 2019, K]**

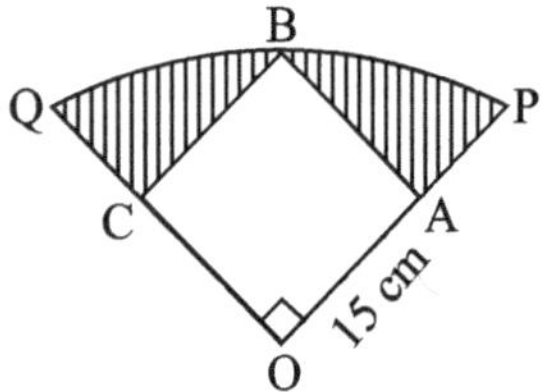

16. Find the area of the shaded region in Fig., if ABCD is a rectangle with sides 8 cm and 6 cm and O is the centre of circle. (Take $\pi = 3.14$) **[Delhi 2019, Ap]**

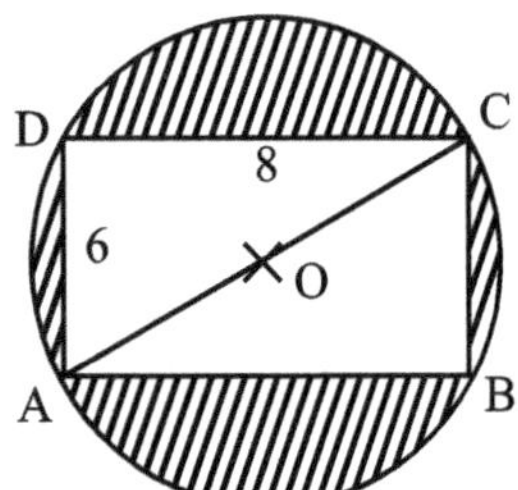

17. In the given figure, two concentric circles with centre O have radii 21 cm and 42 cm. If $\angle AOB = 60°$, find the area of the shaded region. $\left[\text{Use } \pi = \frac{22}{7}\right]$

[All India 2017, Term-II, K]

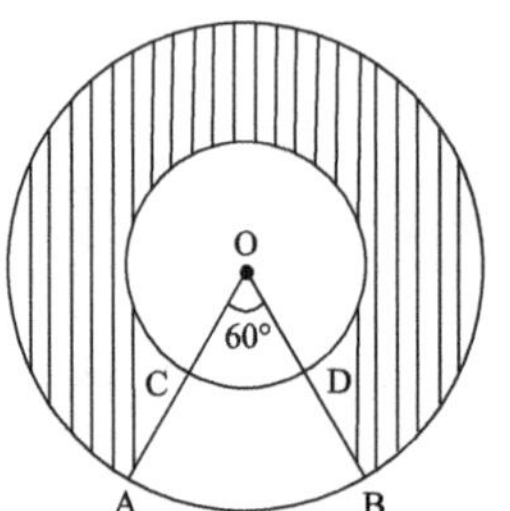

18. In Fig., are shown two arcs PAQ and PBQ. Arc PAQ is a part of circle with centre O and radius OP while arc PBQ is a semi-circle drawn on PQ as diameter with centre M. If OP = PQ = 10 cm. Show that area of shaded region is $25\left(\sqrt{3} - \frac{\pi}{6}\right) cm^2$. **[Delhi 2016, Term-II, U]**

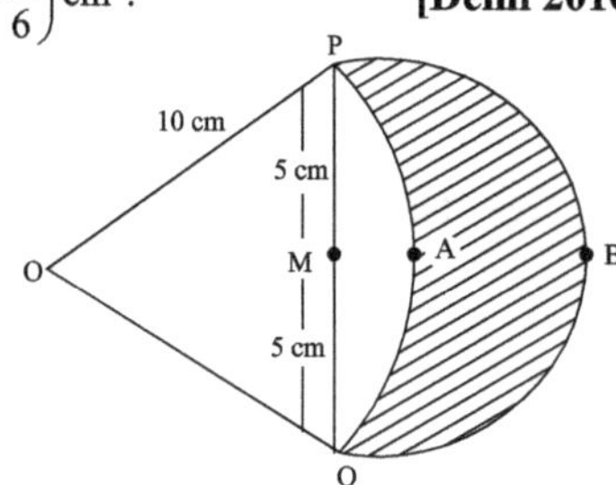

19. Find the area of the minor segment of a circle of radius 14 cm, when its central angle is 60°. Also find the area of the corresponding major segment. $\left[\text{Use } \pi = \frac{22}{7}\right]$.

[All India 2015, Term-II, K]

20. In a circle of radius 21 cm, an arc subtends an angle of 60° at the centre. Find : (i) the length of the arc (ii) area of the sector formed by the arc. $\left[\text{Use } \pi = \frac{22}{7}\right]$

[All India 2013, K]

Long Answer Questions (4 or 5 Marks)

21. A horse is tied to a peg at one corner of a square shaped grass field of side 15 m by means of a 5 m long rope. Find the area of that part of the field in which the horse can graze. Also, find the increase in grazing area if length of rope is increased to 10 m. (Use $\pi = 3.14$)

[All India 2023, Set I, K]

22. Find the area of the shaded region in fig., if PQ = 24 cm, PR = 7 cm and O is the centre of the circle.

[All India 2020, Ap]

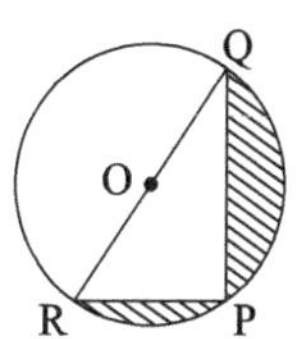

Topic-2: *Problem based on Area and Perimeter of Plane Figures*

Multiple Choice Questions

1. The minute hand of a clock is 84 cm long. The distance covered by the tip of minute hand from 10:10 am to 10:25 am is **[All India 2022, Term-I, Ap]**

(a) 44 cm (b) 88 cm (c) 132 cm (d) 176 cm

2. The area of a square that can be inscribed in a circle of area $\frac{1408}{7}$ cm^2 is **[All India 2022, Term-I, Ap]**

(a) 321 cm^2 (b) 642 cm^2 (c) 128 cm^2 (d) 256 cm^2

3. If the perimeter of a circle is half to that of a square, then the ratio of the area of the circle to the area of the square is **[All India 2022, Term-I, U]**

(a) 22 : 7 (b) 11 : 7 (c) 7 : 11 (d) 7 : 22

4. In the figure given below, ABCD is a square of side 14 cm with E, F G and H as the mid points of sides AB, BC, CD and DA respectively. The area of the shaded portion is

[CBSE Sample Paper 2021-22, Term-I, U]

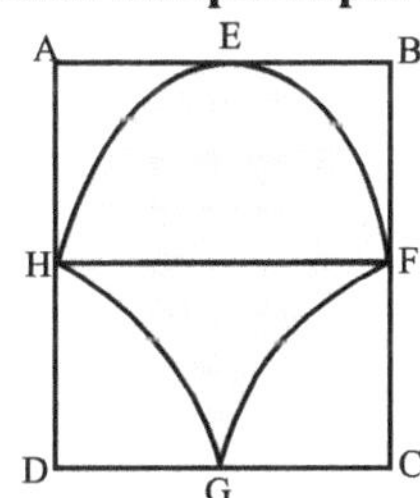

(a) 44cm^2 (b) 49 cm^2

(c) 98 cm^2 (d) $\frac{49\pi}{2}$ cm^2

Short Answer Questions (2 or 3 Marks)

5. With vertices A, B and C of ΔABC as centres, arcs are drawn with radii 14 cm and the three portions of the triangle so obtained are removed. Find the total area removed from the triangle.

[CBSE Sample Paper 2023-24, A]

6. Find the area of the unshaded region shown in the given figure. **[CBSE Sample Paper 2023-24, A]**

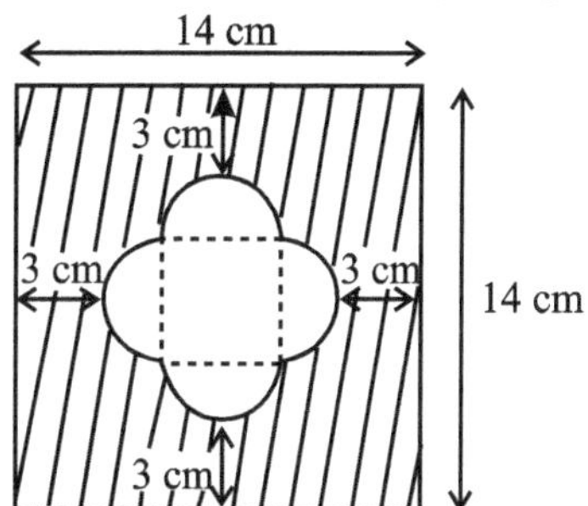

7. Sneha had a rectangular tablecloth with one side measuring 30 cm which she wanted to keep on her circular table of radius 25 cm. After keeping it on the table, she realised that the corners of the tablecloth just touched the edge of the circular table as shown in the figure. **[CBSE CFPQ 2022, Ap]**

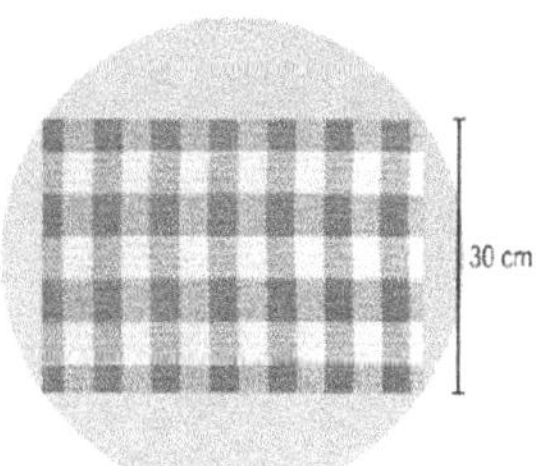

(**Note:** The figure is not to scale.)
Find the area of the table not covered by the tablecloth. Show your steps with valid reasons.
(**Note:** Use π = 3.14)

8. In Figure, a square OPQR is inscribed in a quadrant OAQB of a circle. If the radius of the circle is $6\sqrt{2}$ cm, find the area of shaded region.

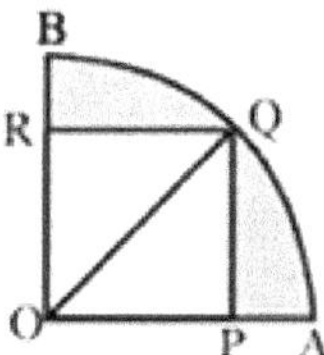

[All India 2020, U]

9. In Figure, ABCD is a square with side $2\sqrt{2}$ cm and inscribed in a circle. Find the area of the shaded region. (Use $\pi = 3\cdot14$) **[All India 2019, K]**

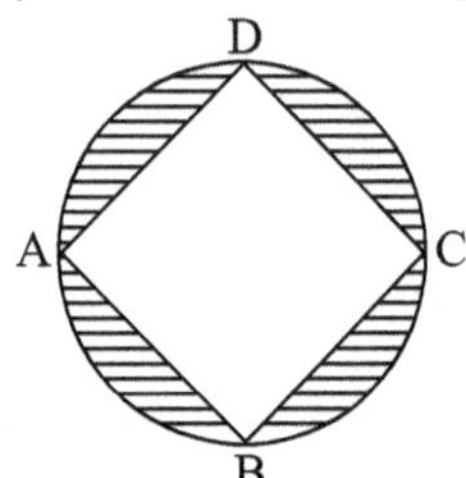

10. Find the area of the shaded region in Fig., where arcs drawn with centres A, B, C and D intersect in pairs at mid-points P, Q, R and S of the sides AB, BC, CD and DA respectively of a square ABCD of side 12 cm. [Use $\pi = 3.14$] **[All India 2018, A]**

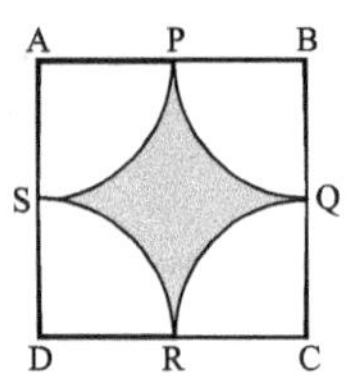

11. Three semicircles each of diameter 3 cm, a circle of diameter 4.5 cm and a semicircle of radius 4.5 cm are drawn in the given figure. Find the area of the shaded region. **[All India 2017, Term-II, Ap]**

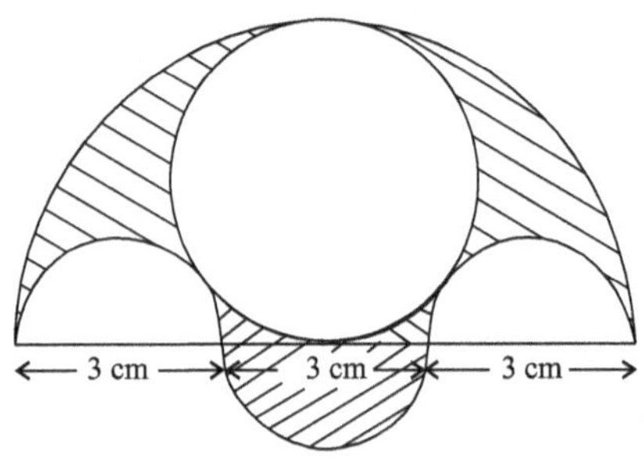

12. In Fig., ABCD is a square of side 14 cm. Semi-circles are drawn with each side of square as diameter. Find the area of the shaded region. $\left(\text{use } \pi = \frac{22}{7}\right)$

[Delhi 2016, Term-II, A]

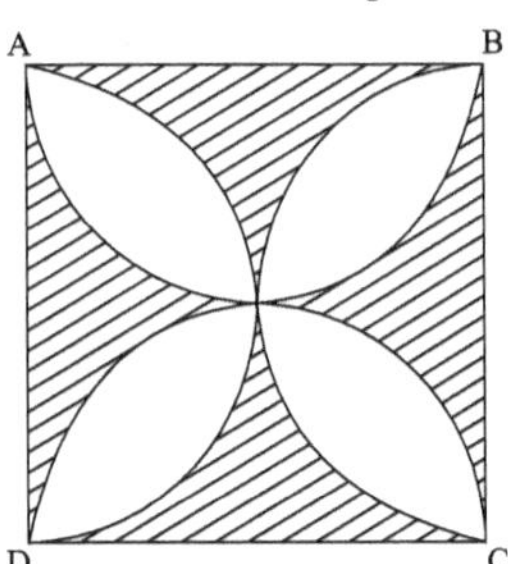

13. In Fig., a square OABC is inscribed in a quadrant OPBQ of a circle. If OA = 20 cm, find the area of the shaded region. (Use $\pi = 3.14$) **[Delhi 2014, Term-II, A]**

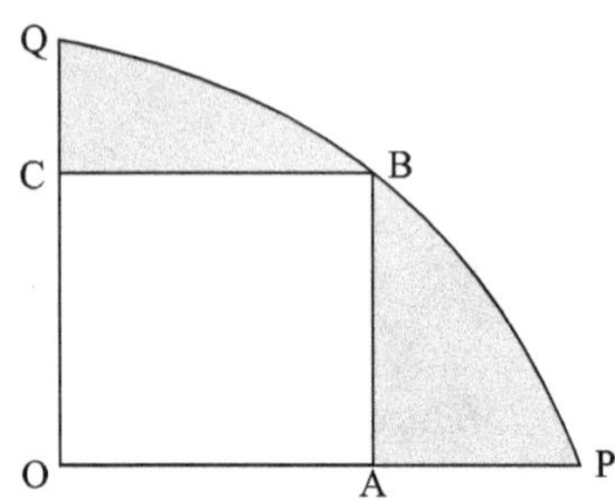

14. In Fig., PSR, RTQ and PAQ are three semicircles of diameters 10 cm, 3 cm and 7 cm respectively. Find the perimeter of the shaded region. [Use $\pi = 3.14$]

[Delhi 2014, Term-II, A]

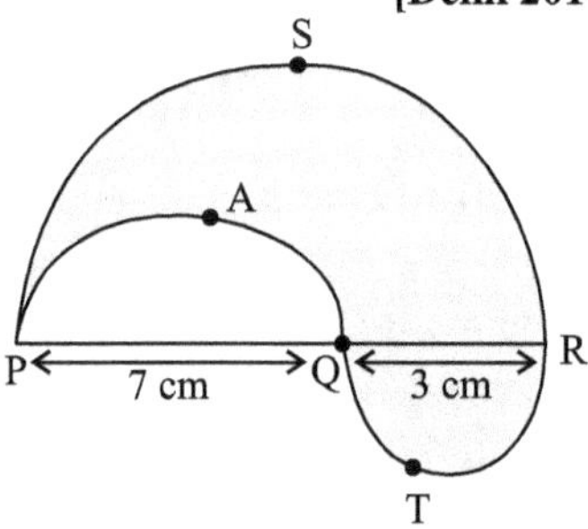

15. Two circular pieces of equal radii and maximum area, touching each other are cut out from a rectangular card board of dimensions 14 cm × 7 cm. Find the area of the remaining card board. $\left[\text{Use } \pi = \frac{22}{7}\right]$ **[All India 2013, A]**

16. In Fig., AB and CD are two diameters of a circle with centre O, which are perpendicular to each other. OB is the diameter of the smaller circle. If OA = 7 cm, find the area of the shaded region. $\left[\text{Use } \pi = \frac{22}{7}\right]$ **[All India 2013, Ap]**

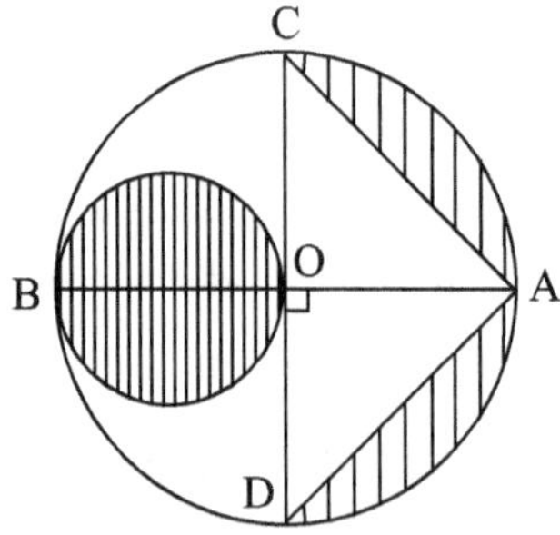

Long Answer Questions (4 or 5 Marks)

17. In the given figure, ABCD is a rectangle of dimensions 21 cm × 14 cm. A semicircle is drawn with BC as diameter. Find the area and the perimeter of the shaded region in the figure. **[All India 2017, Term-II, A]**

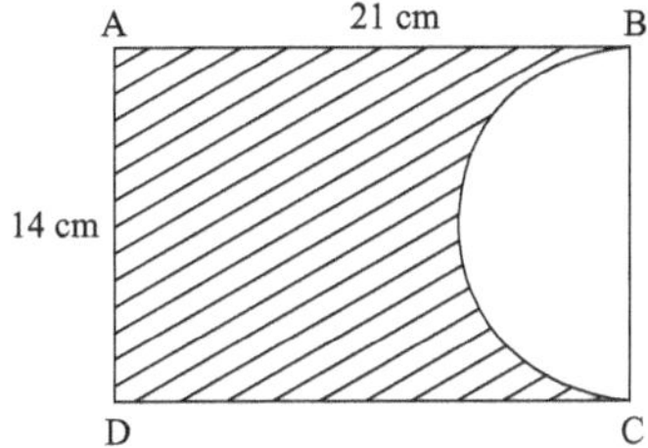

18. In Figure, PQRS is a square lawn with side PQ = 42 metres. Two circular flower beds are there on the sides PS and QR with centre at O, the intersection of its diagonals. Find the total area of the two flower beds (shaded parts).

[All India 2015, Term-II, Ap]

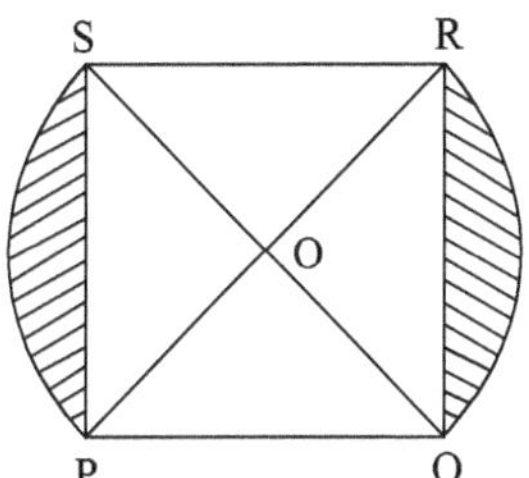

Hints & Solutions

Topic-1: Areas of Sector and Segment of a Circle

1. (a) 2 units **(1 Mark)**

2. (a) 10m **(1 Mark)**

3. (b) Area of semi-circle is πr^2

Here, d = 2r

$$r = \frac{d}{2};\ A = \pi\left[\frac{d}{2}\right]^2 = \pi \times \frac{1}{4}d^2 = \frac{1}{4}\pi d^2$$ **(1 Mark)**

4. (d) 7000 **(1 Mark)**

5. (c) Given, circumference of circle = 176

$2\pi r = 176$

$2 \times \frac{22}{7} \times r = 176$

$r = 28$ m

Area of quadrant $= \frac{\theta}{360} \times \pi r^2$

$= \frac{90}{360} \times \frac{22}{7} \times 28 \times 28$

$= 616\ m^2$. **(1 Mark)**

6. (d) Number of revolutions $= \frac{\text{total distance}}{\text{circumference}}$

$= \frac{\text{total distance}}{2\pi r} = \frac{176}{2 \times \frac{22}{7} \times 0.7} = 40$ **(1 Mark)**

7. (d)

Let O be the centre of the circle OA = OB = AB = 1 cm.

So ΔOAB is an equilateral triangle and $\therefore \angle AOB = 60°$

Required area = 8x Area of one segment with r = 1cm, $\theta = 60°$

Area of sector OAB – Area of an equilateral ΔOAB,

$$= 8x\left(\frac{60}{360} \times \pi \times 1^2 - \frac{\sqrt{3}}{4} \times 1^2\right)$$

$$= 8\left(\frac{\pi}{6} - \frac{\sqrt{3}}{4}\right)cm^2$$ **(1 Mark)**

8. (b) Circumference of a circle = $2\pi r$

$2\pi r - r = 37$

$r(2\pi - 1) = 37$

$$r\left(2 \times \frac{22}{7} - 1\right) = 37 \Rightarrow r\left(\frac{44-7}{7}\right) = 37$$

$$r\left(\frac{37}{7}\right) = 37$$

r = 7 cm

Circumference = $2\pi r$

$= 2 \times \frac{22}{7} \times 7$

= 44 cm **(1 Mark)**

9. Length of arc AB $= \frac{60°}{360°} \times 2\pi \times 10.5$

$= \frac{1}{6} \times 2 \times \frac{22}{7} \times \frac{105}{10} = 11$ cm

Perimeter of the sector = Length of arc AB + 2r

$= 11 + 2 \times 10.5 = 11 + 21 = 32$ cm **(1 Mark)**

10. Area of sector $= \frac{\theta}{360} \times \pi r^2$

$= \frac{60}{360} \times \frac{22}{7} \times 21 \times 21$

$= 231\ cm^2$ **(1½ Marks)**

Length of arc of sector $= \frac{\theta}{360} \times 2\pi r$

$= \frac{60}{360} \times 2 \times \frac{22}{7} \times 21$

= 22 cm **(1½ Marks)**

11. We know that, in 60 minutes, the tip of minute hand moves 360°

In 1 minute, it will move = 360°/60 = 6° **(½ Mark)**

$\therefore$ From 7 : 05 pm to 7: 40 pm i.e. 35 min, it will move through = 35 × 6° = 210° **(½ Mark)**

$\therefore$ Area of swept by the minute hand in 35 min = Area of sector with sectorial angle θ of 210° and radius of 6 cm

$= \frac{210}{360} \times \pi \times 6^2$ **(½ Mark)**

$= \frac{7}{12} \times \frac{22}{7} \times 6 \times 6 = 66\ cm^2$ **(½ Mark)**

12. Let the measure of $\angle A$, $\angle B$, $\angle C$ and $\angle D$ be θ_1, θ_2, θ_3 and θ_4 respectively

Required area = Area of sector with centre A + Area of sector with centre B + Area of sector with centre C + Area of sector with centre D **(½ Mark)**

$$=\frac{\theta_1}{360}\times\pi\times7^2+\frac{\theta_2}{360}\times\pi\times7^2+\frac{\theta_3}{360}\times\pi\times7^2+\frac{\theta_4}{360}\times\pi\times7^2$$

(½ Mark)

$$=\frac{(\theta_1+\theta_2+\theta_3+\theta_4)}{360}\times\pi\times7^2$$ **(½ Mark)**

(By angle sum property of a triangle)

$= 154\text{ cm}^2$ **(½ Mark)**

13. Area of circular play ground = πr^2

$22176=\frac{22}{7}\times r^2$ **(1 Mark)**

$r^2=\frac{22176\times7}{22}=7056 \Rightarrow r=\sqrt{7056}=84\text{ cm}$

Length of fencing (circumference of circle)

$=2\pi r=2\times\frac{22}{7}\times84=528\text{ cm}$

Cost of fencing = 528 × 0.5 = ₹ 264 **(1 Mark)**

14. Length of arc $=\frac{\theta}{360^\circ}\cdot2\pi r$

$22=\frac{60}{360}\times2\times\frac{22}{7}\times r$ **(1 Mark)**

$\frac{22\times6\times7}{2\times22}=r$ **(1 Mark)**

$r = 21\text{cm}$

15. Given: OABC is a square with OA = 15 cm

Let radius (OB) of circle = r cm

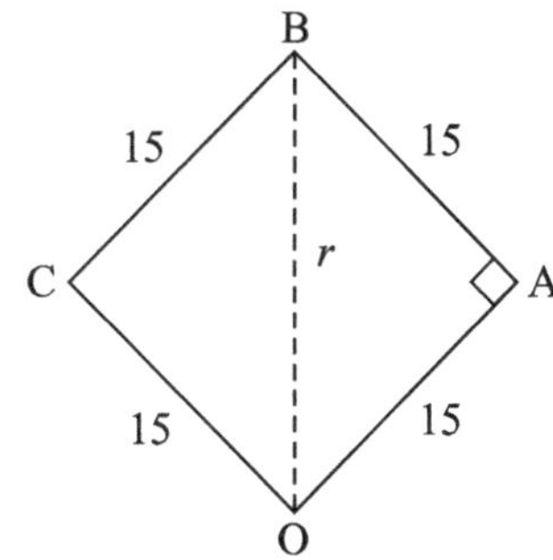

In right ΔAOB

$r^2 = 15^2 + 15^2 = 2 \times 15^2$

$r = 15\sqrt{2}$

Area of square = side × side = 15 × 15 = 225 cm^2

(1 Mark)

Area of quadrant OPBQ $=\frac{1}{4}\times\pi r^2$

$=\frac{1}{4}\times3.14\times15\sqrt{2}\times15\sqrt{2}$

$=\frac{225\times2\times3.14}{4}$

$= 225 \times 1.57$

$= 353.25\text{ cm}^2$ **(1 Mark)**

Area of shaded region

= Area of quadrant OPBQ – Area of square OABC

$= 353.25 - 225 = 128.25\text{ cm}^2$ **(1 Mark)**

16.

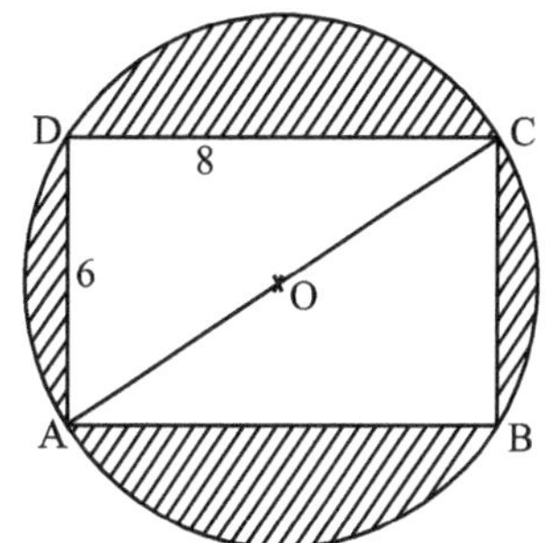

Area of the rectangle ABCD = 6 × 8 = 48

Using Pythagoras theorem in ΔABC,

$(AC)^2 = (AB)^2 + (BC)^2$

$= 8^2 + 6^2$ $[\because AB = CD \text{ and } AD = BC]$

$= 64 + 36 = 100$

$\Rightarrow AC = 10\text{ cm}$

Since, AC is the diameter of the circle.

Hence, radius of the circle is 5 cm.

$\therefore$ Area of the circle $= \pi r^2 = \pi(5)^2 = 25\pi$. **(1 Mark)**

Hence, the area of the shaded region is,

$= 25\pi - 48 = 25 \times 3.14 - 48$

$= 78.50 - 48 = 30.50\text{ cm}^2$. **(1 Mark)**

17. Radius of inner circle,

r = 21 cm

and Radius of outer circle, R = 42 cm.

Also, $\angle AOB = 60^\circ$ **(1 Mark)**

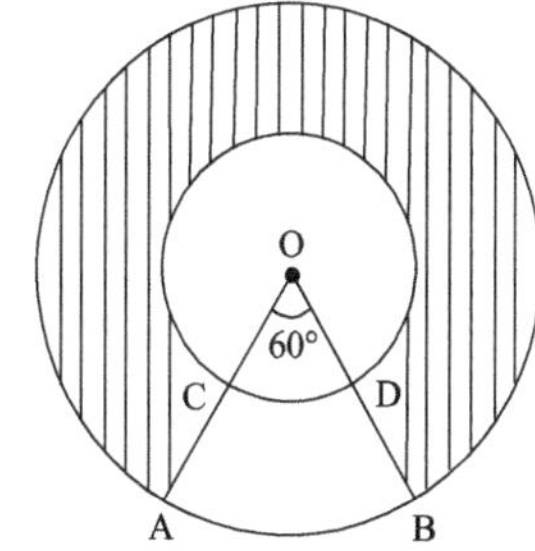

Now, area of the shaded region

= (Area of ring) – (Area of ABCD)

$$= \pi R^2 - \pi r^2 - \left[\frac{60}{360} \times \pi \times R^2 - \frac{60}{360} \times \pi \times r^2\right]$$

$$\left[\because \text{Area of section} = \frac{\theta}{360} \times \pi r^2\right]$$

$$= \pi(R^2 - r^2) - \frac{60}{360} \times \pi(R^2 - r^2)$$

$$= \pi(R^2 - r^2)\left[1 - \frac{60}{360}\right]$$

$$= \frac{22}{7}(42^2 - 21^2)\left(\frac{5}{6}\right)$$

$$= \frac{22}{7}(42+21)(42-21) \times \frac{5}{6}$$

$$= \frac{22}{7} \times 63 \times 21 \times \frac{5}{6}$$

$= 3465 \text{ cm}^2$

Thus, the required area of shaded region = 3465 cm^2.

(1 Mark)

Area of ring = $\pi R^2 - \pi r^2$

18. As OP = PQ = OQ = 10 cm

ΔOPQ is equilateral triangle

∠POQ = 60°

[∵ All angles in equilateral triangle are 60°]

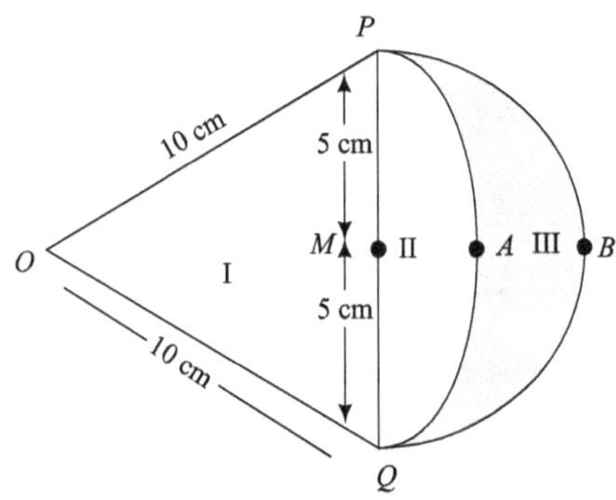

(1 Mark)

Area of II = Area of sector – Area of ΔPOQ

$$= \frac{\theta}{360} \times \pi r^2 - \frac{\sqrt{3}}{4}(a)^2$$

$$= \frac{60°}{360°} \times \pi(10^2) - \frac{\sqrt{3}}{4} \times (10)^2$$

$$= 100\left(\frac{\pi}{6} - \frac{\sqrt{3}}{4}\right)$$ **(1 Mark)**

Area of the semicircle on diameter PQ = Area of part II + Area of part III

Area of semicircle = $\frac{1}{2}\pi r^2$

$$= \frac{1}{2} \times \pi(5)^2 \qquad (\because r = 5)$$

$$= \frac{25}{2}\pi$$

$$\frac{25}{2}\pi = 100\left(\frac{\pi}{6} - \frac{\sqrt{3}}{4}\right) + \text{Area of part III}$$

$$\text{Area of part III} = \frac{25}{2}\pi - 100\left(\frac{\pi}{6} - \frac{\sqrt{3}}{4}\right)$$

$$= \frac{25}{2}\pi - \frac{100\pi}{6} + \frac{100\sqrt{3}}{4}$$

$$= 25\left(\sqrt{3} - \frac{\pi}{6}\right)$$

Hence proved. **(1 Mark)**

19. Radius of circle, r = 14 cm

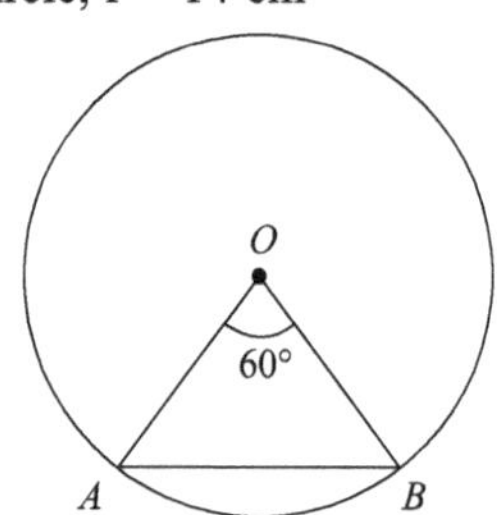

Chord AB subtends an angle 60° at the centre of circle

∠AOB = 60°

$$\text{Area of sector AOB} = \frac{\theta}{360°} \times \pi r^2 \Rightarrow = \frac{60°}{360°} \times \frac{22}{7} \times (14)^2$$

$$= \frac{1}{6} \times \frac{22}{7} \times 14 \times 14 = 102.67 \text{ cm}^2$$ **(1 Mark)**

$$\text{Area of circle} = \pi r^2 = \frac{22}{7} \times (14)^2 = 616 \text{ cm}^2$$

In ΔAOB

OA = OB (Radii of circle)

∴ ∠OAB = ∠OBA (Angles opposite to equal sides are equal)

∠OAB + ∠OBA + ∠AOB = 180° (Angle sum property)

∠OAB + ∠OAB + 60° = 180°

2∠OAB = 120° ⇒ ∠OAB = 60°

∴ ∠OAB = ∠OBA = ∠AOB = 60° **(1 Mark)**

Thus, ΔOAB is equilateral triangle

Area of equilateral triangle = $\frac{\sqrt{3}}{4} \times (\text{side})^2$

Area of ΔAOB = $\frac{\sqrt{3}}{4} \times (14)^2 = 84.87 \text{ cm}^2$

Area of minor segment = Area of the sector AOB – Area of ΔAOB

$= 102.67 - 84.87 = 17.85 \text{ cm}^2$

Area of major segment = Area of the circle – Area of the minor segment

$= 616 - 17.8 = 598.2 \text{ cm}^2$ **(1 Mark)**

20. r = 21 cm

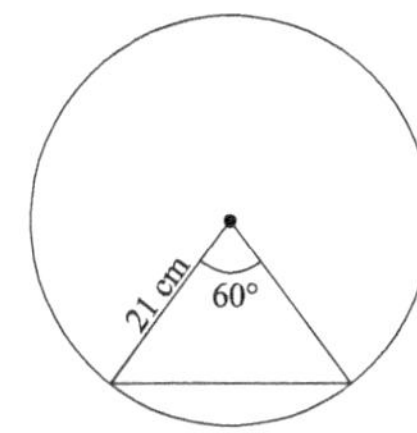

(i) Length of arc = $\frac{\theta}{360} \times 2\pi r$

$= \frac{60}{360} \times 2 \times \frac{22}{7} \times 21$

= 22 cm **(1½ Marks)**

(ii) Area of sector = $\frac{\theta}{360} \times \pi r^2$

$= \frac{60}{360} \times \frac{22}{7} \times 21 \times 21$

$= 231 \text{ cm}^2$ **(1½ Marks)**

Length of major arc = $\left(\frac{360-\theta}{360}\right)^{\circ} \times 2\pi r$.

21. Side of square = 15 m

Length of rope = 5 m

Area of quadrant of circle = $\frac{\pi r^2}{4} = \frac{\pi(5)^2}{4}$ **(2 Marks)**

$= 19.625 \text{ m}^2$

If length is increased to 10 m, then r = 10 m

Area of quadrant = $= 78.5 \text{ m}^2$

∴ Increase in area = $78.5 - 19.625 = 58.875 \text{ m}^2$

$\frac{\pi \times (10)^2}{4}$ **(2 Marks)**

Area of Sector = $\frac{\theta}{360^\circ} \times \pi r^2$; For Q adrant θ = 90°

22. In ΔRPQ, ∠P = 90°

∴ $RQ^2 = PR^2 + PQ^2 = (7)^2 + (24)^2 = 49 + 576$

$RQ^2 = 625 \Rightarrow RQ = \sqrt{625} = 25$

(Negative values is not possible)

Radius of circle (r) = $\frac{RQ}{2} = \frac{25}{2}$ **(2 Marks)**

∴ Area of the shaded region = Area of semicircle – Area ΔRPQ

$= \frac{1}{2}\pi r^2 - \frac{1}{2} \times \text{base} \times \text{height}$

$= \frac{1}{2} \times \frac{22}{7} \times \frac{25}{2} \times \frac{25}{2} - \frac{1}{2} \times 24 \times 7$

$= 245.54 - 84 = 161.54 \text{ cm}^2$ **(2 Marks)**

Angle in semicircle is right angle.

Topic-2: *Problem based on Area and Perimeter of Plane Figures*

1. **(a)** Angle of 1 division = $\frac{360}{12} = 30^\circ$

Angle between 10 : 10 am to 10 : 25 am = 30 × 3 = 90°

Distance covered by minute tip = $\frac{\theta}{360} \times 2\pi r$

$= \frac{30}{360} \times 2 \times \frac{22}{7} \times 84$

= 44 cm **(1 Mark)**

There are 3 divisions in the given time interval.

2. **(c)** Area of circle = $\frac{1408}{7}$ cm²

$\pi r^2 = \frac{1408}{7}$

$\frac{22}{7} \times r^2 = \frac{1408}{7} \Rightarrow r = 8\text{cm}$

In ΔAOB

Apply pythagoras theorem,

$AB^2 = OA^2 + OB^2$

$AB^2 = 8^2 + 8^2 = 64 + 64 = 128$

$AB = 8\sqrt{2}$ cm

Area of square = $(\text{side})^2 = \left(8\sqrt{2}\right)^2$

$= 128 \text{ cm}^2$ **(1 Mark)**

3. **(d)** Perimeter of circle = $\frac{1}{2}$(Perimeter of square)

$$2\pi r = \frac{1}{2} \times a \times 4$$

$$\frac{a}{r} = \frac{22}{7} \Rightarrow \frac{r}{a} = \frac{7}{22} \quad ......(i)$$

$$\frac{\textit{area of circle}}{\textit{area of square}} = \frac{\pi r^2}{a^2}$$

$$= \frac{22}{7} \times \frac{7}{22} \times \frac{7}{22} = \frac{7}{22} \quad \text{[from (i)]}$$

Required ratio is 7 : 22 **(1 Mark)**

4. **(c)** Shaded area = Area of semicircle + (Area of half square – Area of two quadrants)

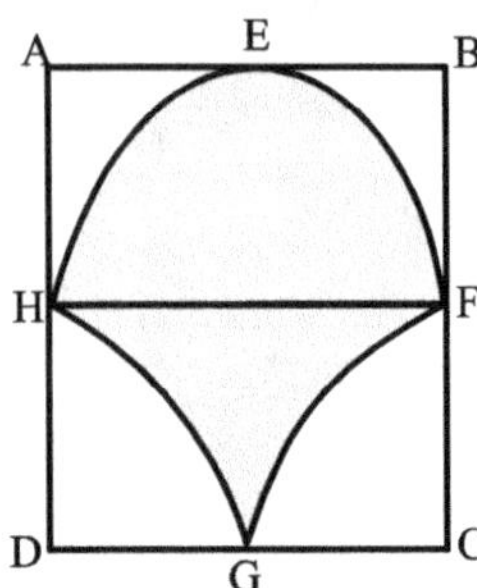

= Area of semicircle + (Area of half square – Area of semicircle).

= Area of half square $\frac{1}{2} \times 14 \times 14 = 98 \text{cm}^2$ **(1 Mark)**

5. Given that r = 14 cm

Total area removed $= \frac{\angle A}{360}\pi r^2 + \frac{\angle B}{360}\pi r^2 + \frac{\angle C}{360}\pi r^2$

$\frac{\angle A + \angle B + \angle C}{360}\pi r^2$ **(1 Mark)**

$= \frac{180}{360}\pi r^2 \quad \{\because \angle A + \angle B + \angle C = 180°\}$

$= \frac{180}{360} \times \frac{22}{7} \times (14)^2 = 308 \text{ cm}^2$ **(1 Mark)**

6. The side of the inner square = Diameter of the semi–circle = a

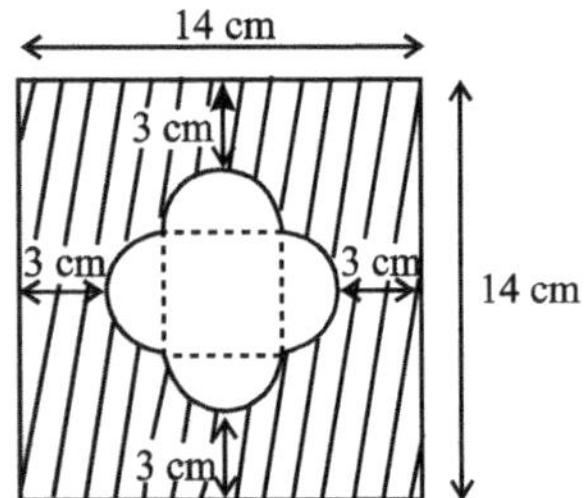

Area of the unshaded region

= Area of the inner square of side 'a' + 4 (Area of a semi–circle of diameter 'a') **(½ Mark)**

The horizontal/vertical extent of the white region

= 14 – 3 – 3 = 8 cm **(½ Mark)**

Radius of the semi–circle + side of a square + Radius of the semi–circle = 8 cm

2 (radius of the semi–circle) + side of a square = 8 cm

$\Rightarrow 2 \times \frac{9}{2} + a = 8 \text{ cm}$

2a = 8 cm ⇒ a = 4 cm **(½ Mark)**

Area of the unshaded region

= Area of a square of side 4 cm + 4 (Area of a semi–circle of diameter 4 cm)

$= (4)^2 + 4 \times \frac{1}{2}\pi(2)^2 = (16 + 8\pi)\text{cm}^2$ **(½ Mark)**

7. Writes that since ABCD is a rectangle, the diagonal of the tablecloth will be equal to the diameter of the circular table, which is 50 cm. **(½ Mark)**

Uses Pythagoras theorem to find the measure of the other side of the tablecloth as $\sqrt{(50^2 - 30^2)} = 40$ cm. **(1 Mark)**

Finds the area of the table as $3.14 \times (25)^2 = 1962.5 \text{ cm}^2$.

(½ Mark)

Finds the area of the tablecloth as $30 \times 40 = 1200 \text{ cm}^2$.

(½ Mark)

Finds the area not covered by the tablecloth as area of the table – area of the table = $1962.5 - 1200 = 762.5 \text{ cm}^2$.

(½ Mark)

8.

Topper's Answer

Area of Quadrant – Area of Square.

$\frac{22}{7} \times 6 \times 6 \times 2 - 6 \times 6.$

$6 \times 6 \left[\frac{11}{7} - 1\right]$

$6 \times 6 \times \frac{4}{7} \Rightarrow 20.57 \text{ cm}^2$ (approx)

.57 cm² (approx)

9. Given: ABCD is a square with side $2\sqrt{2}$ cm

Let radius of circle be r cm

$\therefore$ BD = 2r

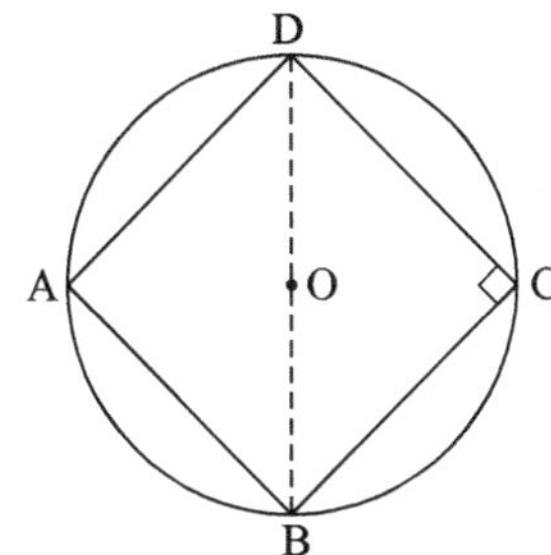

In ΔBDC,

$BD^2 = DC^2 + BC^2$

$\Rightarrow 4r^2 = (2\sqrt{2})^2 + (2\sqrt{2})^2$

$\Rightarrow 4r^2 = 8 + 8$

$\Rightarrow 4r^2 = 16$

$\Rightarrow r^2 = 4$

$\Rightarrow r = 2$ cm **(1 Mark)**

Area of square BCDA = Side × Side = DC × BC

$= 2\sqrt{2} \times 2\sqrt{2} = 8 \text{ cm}^2$

Area of circle = $\pi r^2 = 3.14 \times 2 \times 2 = 12.56 \text{ cm}^2$

(1 Mark)

Area of shaded region = Area of circle – Area of square

$= 12.56 - 8 = 4.56 \text{ cm}^2$ **(1 Mark)**

Angle in semicircle is right angle and each angle of square is right angle. So, diagonal of square and a diameter of circle is same.

10. 

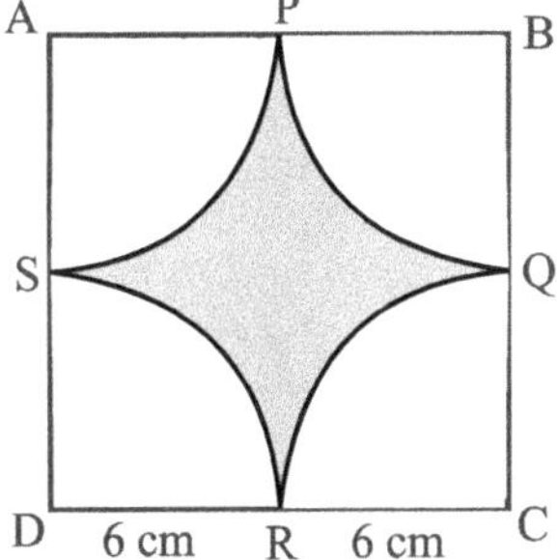

The area of shaded region.

= Area of square ABCD – Area of 4 quadrants **(1 Mark)**

$= 12 \times 12 - 4\left(\dfrac{\pi r^2 \theta}{360°}\right)$

$= 144 - \dfrac{4 \times 3.14 \times 6 \times 6 \times 90}{360}$

$= 144 - 3.14 \times 36 = 144 - 113.04$

$= 30.96 \text{ cm}^2$ **(1 Mark)**

11.

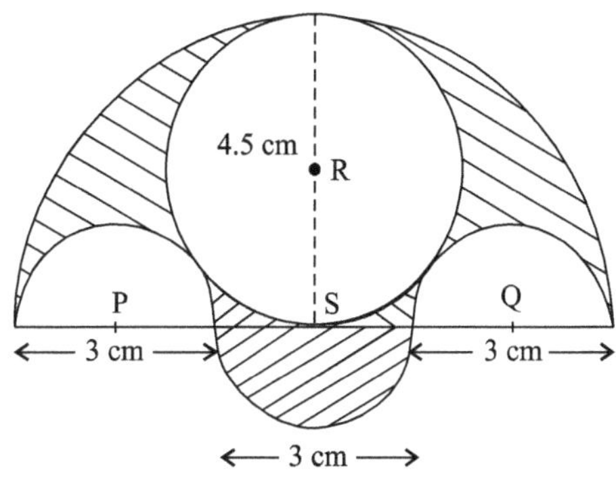

Here, area of shaded region = (Area of largest semicircle – Area of circle with centre R) – (Sum of areas of two semicircles with centres as P & Q respectively) + (Area of semicircle with centre S)

$= \dfrac{1}{2}\pi r_1^2 - \pi R^2 - 2\pi r_2^2 + \dfrac{1}{2}\pi r_3^2$ **(1 Mark)**

$= \left(\dfrac{\pi \times 4.5 \times 4.5}{2}\right) - \left(\pi \times \dfrac{4.5}{2} \times \dfrac{4.5}{2}\right) - \left(\dfrac{2\pi \times 3 \times 3}{2 \times 2 \times 2}\right) + \left(\dfrac{\pi \times 3 \times 3}{2 \times 2 \times 2}\right)$

$= \pi \times \dfrac{(4.5)^2}{2}\left[1 - \dfrac{1}{2}\right] - \dfrac{\pi \times 3 \times 3}{2 \times 2 \times 2}$

$= \pi \times \dfrac{20.25}{4} - \pi \times \dfrac{9}{8}$

$= \pi(5.06 - 1.12)$

$= \dfrac{22}{7} \times 3.94 = 12.38 \text{ cm}^2$ **(1 Mark)**

Thus, the required area of shaded region = 12.38 cm^2.

12. Let four shaded regions be I, II, III and IV and centres of the semicircle be P, Q, R and S.

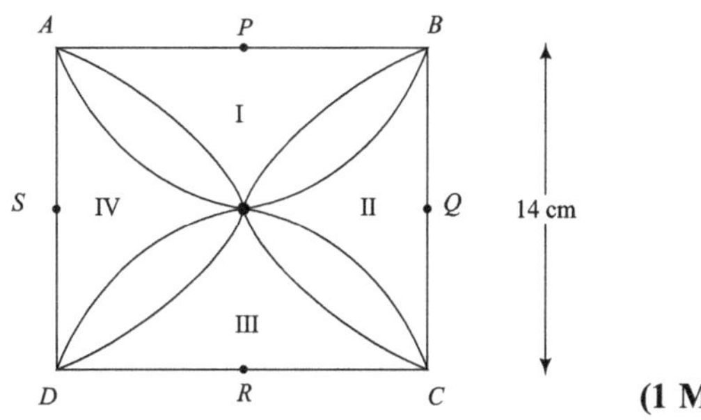

(1 Mark)

Given: Side of square = 14 cm

Area of region I + Area of region III = Area of square – Areas of the semicircles with centres S and Q

$= (\text{Side})^2 - 2 \times \frac{1}{2} \pi r^2$ **(½ Mark)**

$= (14)^2 - \frac{2}{2} \pi (7)^2$ $\left[\because r = \frac{d}{2} = \frac{14}{2} = 7\right]$

$= 196 - 49 \times \frac{22}{7} = 196 - 154 = 42 \text{ cm}^2$ **(½ Mark)**

Similarly

Area of region III + Area of region IV = 42 cm^2

∴ Area of shaded region = Area of region I + Area of region II + Area of region III + Area of region IV

= 42 + 42

= 84 cm^2 **(1 Mark)**

13. 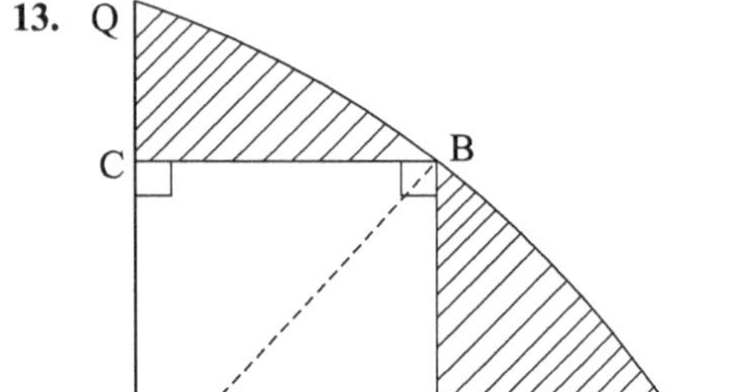

Let us join OB.

In right triangle OAB

$OA^2 + AB^2 = OB^2$ (By Pythagoras theorem)

$OB^2 = (20)^2 + (20)^2$

$OB^2 = 2(20)^2$

$OB = 20\sqrt{2}$ **(1 Mark)**

∴Radius of circle = OB = $20\sqrt{2}$ cm

Area of quadrilateral OPBQ = $\frac{1}{4}$ × Area of circle

$= \frac{1}{4} \times \pi r^2$

$= \frac{1}{4} \times \pi(20\sqrt{2})^2$

$= \frac{1}{4} \times 800\pi$

$= 200 \times 3.14$

= 628 cm^2 **(½ Mark)**

Area of square OABC = (side)^2 = (20)^2 = 400 cm^2

(½ Mark)

Area of shaded region = Area of quadrant OPBQ – Area of square OABC

= (628 – 400) cm

= 228 cm^2 **(1 Mark)**

14. Radius of semicircle PSR = $\frac{1}{2} \times 10$ cm = 5 cm

Radius of semicircle RTQ = $\frac{1}{2} \times 3 = 1.5$ cm

Radius of semicircle PAQ = $\frac{1}{2} \times 7 = 3.5$ cm **(1 Mark)**

Perimeter of shaded region = Circumference of semicircle PSR + Circumference of RTQ + Circumference of semicircle PAQ. **(1 Mark)**

$= \frac{1}{2} \times 2\pi (5) + \frac{1}{2} \times 2\pi (1.5) + \frac{1}{2} \times 2\pi (3.5)$

[∵ Circumference of semicircle = $\frac{1}{2}(2\pi r)$]

$= \pi (5 + 1.5 + 3.5)$ cm

$= 3.14 \times 10$ cm

= 31.4 cm **(1 Mark)**

15. Dimension of rectangular card board = 7 cm × 14 cm

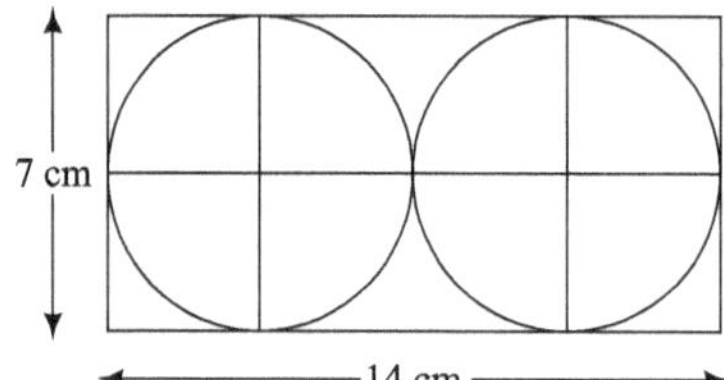

Since two circular pieces of equal radii and maximum area touching each other are cut from the rectangular card board. **(1 Mark)**

∴ Diameter of each circular piece = $\frac{14}{2} = 7$ cm

Radius of each circular piece = $\frac{7}{2}$cm $\left[\because r = \frac{d}{2}\right]$

Sum of areas of two circular piece

$= \pi r^2 + \pi r^2$

$= 2\pi r^2$

$= 2\times\frac{22}{7}\times\frac{7}{2}\times\frac{7}{2}$

$= 77\ cm^2$ **(1 Mark)**

Area of remaining card board = Area of the card board – Area of two circular pieces

$= (14 \times 7) - 77$

$= 98 - 77$

$= 21\ cm^2$ **(1 Mark)**

16. Radius of larger circle, (OA), R = 7 cm

Diameter of smaller circle, (OB) = 7 cm

Radius of smaller circle = $\frac{7}{2}$ cm

Height of ΔACD (OA) = 7 cm

Base of ΔACD (CD) = 14 cm **(½ Mark)**

Area of $\Delta ACD = \frac{1}{2} \times$ Base × Height

$= \frac{1}{2} \times CD \times OA = \frac{1}{2} \times 7 \times 14 = 49\ cm^2$ **(½ Mark)**

Area of larger semicircle with radius (OA) $= \frac{1}{2}\pi r^2$

$= \frac{1}{2}\times\frac{22}{7}\times(7)^2 = 77\ cm^2$ **(½ Mark)**

Area of smaller circle = πr^2

$= \frac{22}{7}\times\frac{7}{2}\times\frac{7}{2} = \frac{77}{2} cm^2$ **(½ Mark)**

Area of shaded region = Area of smaller circle + Area of larger semicircle – Area pf ΔACD

$= \frac{77}{2} + 77 - 49 = \frac{77}{2} + 28 = 66.5\ cm^2$ **(1 Mark)**

17. Given that dimensions of rectangle are 21 cm × 14 cm

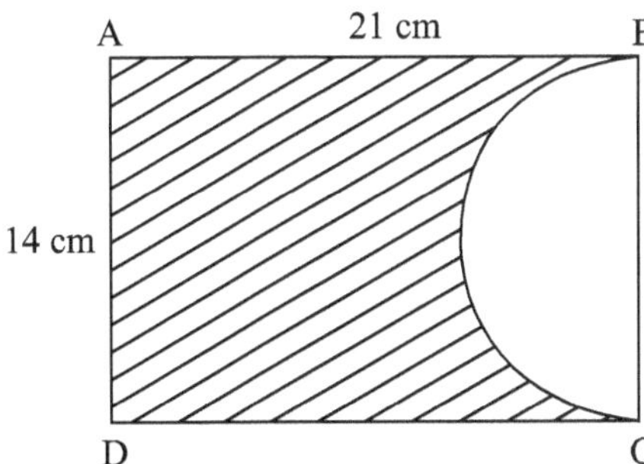

Diameter of semi circle = CB = 14 cm

$\therefore$ radius of semi circle, $r = \frac{14}{2} = 7$ cm **(1 Mark)**

$\Rightarrow$ area of shaded region = (Area of rectangle ABCD) – (Area of semi circle with radius 7 cm)

$= l \times b - \frac{1}{2}\pi r^2$

$= (21\times14) - \left(\frac{1}{2}\times\frac{22}{7}\times7\times7\right)$

$= 294 - 77 = 217\ cm^2$ **(1 Mark)**

Thus, required area of shaded region = 217 cm^2

Now, perimeter of shaded region = AB + AD + DC + BC

Now, perimeter of arc BC $= \pi r = \frac{22}{7}\times 7 = 22\,cm$

(1 Mark)

Thus, perimeter of shaded region = 21 + 14 + 21 + 22 = 78 cm

(1 Mark)

18. Area of square = $(side)^2$ **(1 Mark)**

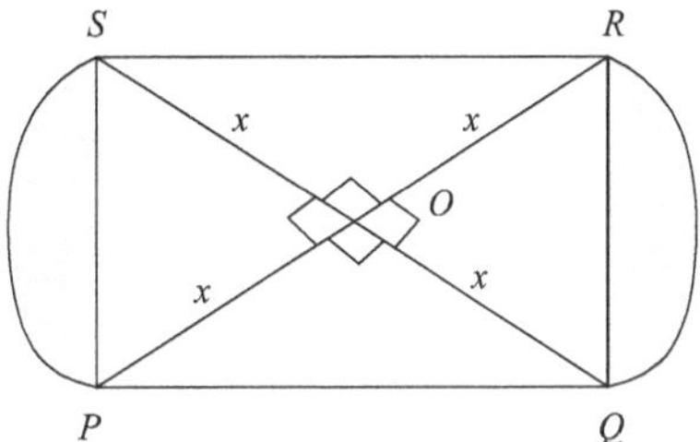

Area of the square lawn PQRS = 42 m × 42 m

We know that diagonal of square perpendicularly bisect each other

Let PR = QS = 2x

$\therefore$ OP = OR = OS = OQ = x **(1 Mark)**

[$\because$ Diagonal bisect each other]

In right ΔOPS

$OS^2 + OP^2 = PS^2$ [By Pythagoras theorem]

$\Rightarrow x^2 + x^2 = PS^2$

$\Rightarrow 2x^2 = (42)^2$

$\Rightarrow x^2 = \frac{42\times42}{2} = 21 \times 42$ ...(1) **(1 Mark)**

Area of sector POS $= \frac{\theta}{360} \times \pi r^2 = \frac{90°}{360°} \times \pi x^2$

$= \frac{1}{4}\times\frac{22}{7} \times 21 \times 42$ ...(2) (from (1))

Area of $\Delta POS = \frac{1}{4} \times$ Area of square lawn PQRS

$= \frac{1}{4} \times (42 \times 42)^2 \text{ m}^2$ ...(3) **(1 Mark)**

Area of flower bed PSP = Area of sector POS – Area of ΔPOS

$= \frac{1}{4} \times \frac{22}{7} \times 21 \times 42 - \frac{1}{4} \times 42 \times 42$ (from (2) and (3))

$= \frac{1}{4} \times 21 \times 42 \times \left(\frac{22}{7} - 2\right)$

$= \frac{1}{4} \times 21 \times 42 \times \left(\frac{8}{7}\right) \text{m}^2$

Area of 2 flower beds $= 2 \times \frac{1}{4} \times 21 \times 42 \times \frac{8}{7}$

$= 504 \text{ m}^2$

Hence, the total area of the two flower beds 504 m^2

(1 Mark)

12 Chapter Surface Areas and Volumes

Topic-1: Surface Area of a Combination of Solids

1 Multiple Choice Question

1. The sum of the length, breadth and height of a cuboid is $6\sqrt{3}$ cm and the length of its diagonal is $2\sqrt{3}$ cm. The total surface area of the cuboid is

[CBSE Sample Paper 2022-23, K]

(a) 48 cm^2 (b) 72 cm^2 (c) 96 cm^2 (d) 108 cm^2

2 Assertion Reason/Two Statement Type Question

2. **Statement A (Assertion):** Total surface area of the top is the sum of the curved surface area of the hemisphere and the curved surface area of the cone.

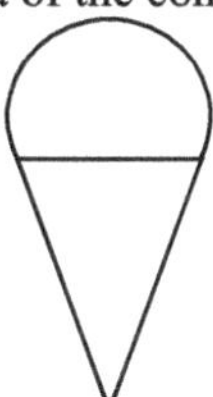

Statement R (Reason): Top is obtained by joining the plane surfaces of the hemisphere and cone together.

[CBSE Sample Paper 2023-24, K]

(a) Both assertion (A) and reason (R) are true and reason (R) is the correct explanation of assertion (A)
(b) Both assertion (A) and reason (R) are true and reason (R) is not the correct explanation of assertion (A)
(c) Assertion (A) is true but reason (R) is false.
(d) Assertion (A) is false but reason (R) is true.

5 Short Answer Questions (2 or 3 Marks)

3. Shifali made a lampshade using cane web as shown below.

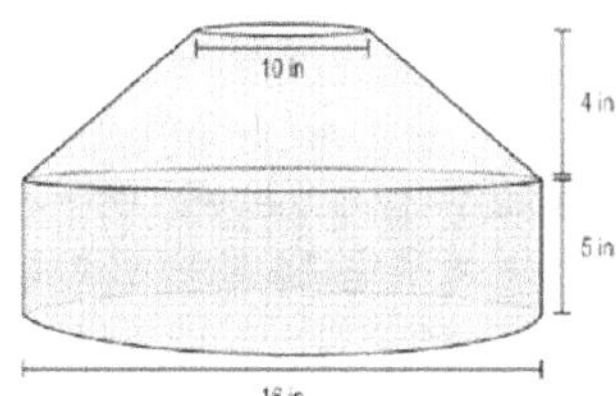

[CBSE CFPQ 2022, U]

4. Shown below is a solid made of a cone, a cylinder and a hemisphere.

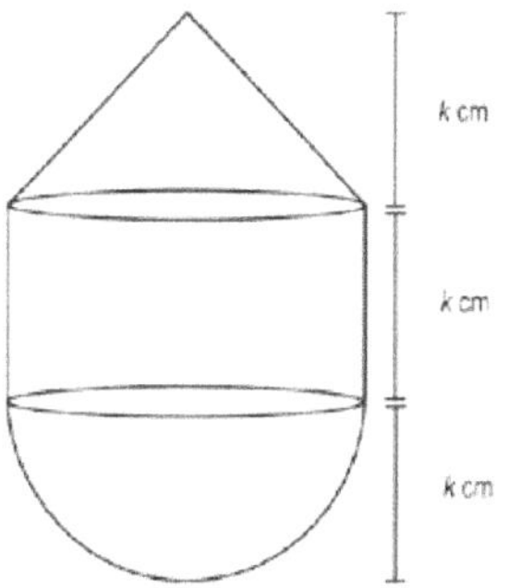

(Note: The figure is not to scale.)
Prove that the total volume of the solid is twice the volume of the cylinder.

[CBSE CFPQ 2022, U]

5. Three cubes of side 6 cm each, are joined as shown in Figure. Find the total surface area of the resulting cuboid.

[All India 2022, A]

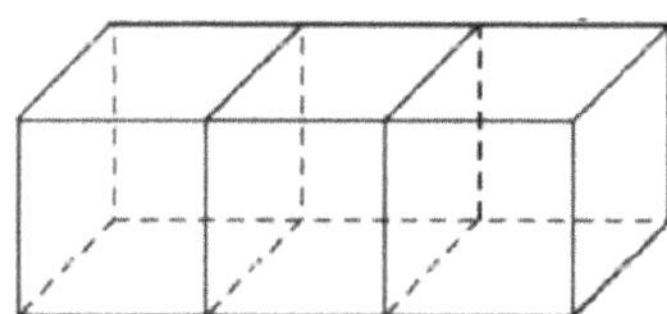

6. A wooden article was made by scooping out a hemisphere from each end of a solid cylinder, as shown in Fig.. If the height of the cylinder is 10 cm and its base is of radius 3.5 cm. Find the total surface area of the article.

[All India 2018, U]

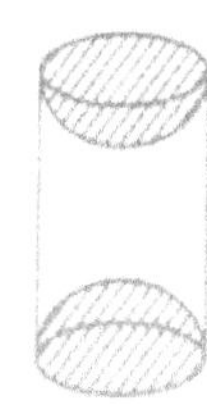

7. In Fig., is a decorative block, made up of two solids – a cube and a hemisphere. The base of the block is a cube of side 6 cm and the hemisphere fixed on the top has a diameter of 3.5 cm. Find the total surface area of the block. $\left(\text{use } \pi = \frac{22}{7}\right)$

[Delhi 2016, Term-II, Ap]

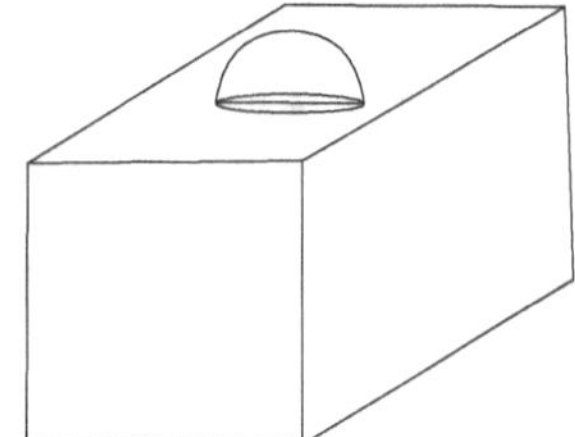

8. Due to sudden floods, some welfare associations jointly requested the government to get 100 tents fixed immediately and offered to contribute 50% of the cost. If the lower part of each tent is of the form of a cylinder of diameter 4.2 m and height 4 m with the conical upper part of same diameter but of height 2.8 m, and the canvas to be used costs ₹100 per sq. m, find the amount, the associations will have to pay. What values are shown by these associations ? $\left[\text{Use } \pi = \frac{22}{7}\right]$. **[All India 2015, Term-II, AP]**

9. A cubical block of side 10 cm is surmounted by a hemisphere. What is the largest diameter that the hemisphere can have ? Find the cost of painting the total surface area of the solid so formed, at the rate of ₹5 per 100 sq. cm. [Use $\pi = 3.14$] **[All India 2015, Term-II, U]**

10. A vessel is in the form of a hemispherical bowl surmounted by a hollow cylinder of same diameter. The diameter of the hemispherical bowl is 14 cm and the total height of the vessel is 13 cm. Find the total surface area of the vessel. $\left[\text{Use } \pi = \frac{22}{7}\right]$ **[All India 2013, AP]**

6 Long Answer Questions (4 or 5 Marks)

11. From a solid cylinder of height 20 cm and diameter 12 cm, a conical cavity of height 8 cm and radius 6 cm is hallowed out. Find the total surface area of the remaining solid. **[Delhi 2023, A]**

12. Due to heavy floods in a state, thousands were rendered homeless. 50 schools collectively decided to provide place and the canvas for 1500 tents and share the whole expenditure equally. The lower part of each tent is cylindrical with base radius 2.8 m and height 3.5 m and the upper part is conical with the same base radius, but of height 2.1 m. If the canvas used to make the tents costs ₹120 per m^2, find the amount shared by each school to set up the tents. **[CBSE Sample Paper 2022-23, K]**

13. From a solid cylinder of height 2.8 cm and diameter 4.2 cm, a conical cavity of the same height and same diameter is hollowed out. Find the total surface area of the remaining solid. $\left[\text{Take } \pi = \frac{22}{7}\right]$ **[Delhi 2014, Term-II, K]**

7 Case Based Questions (4 Marks)

14. Governing council of a local public development authority of Dehradun dicided to build an adventurous playground on the top of a hill, which will have adequate space for parking.

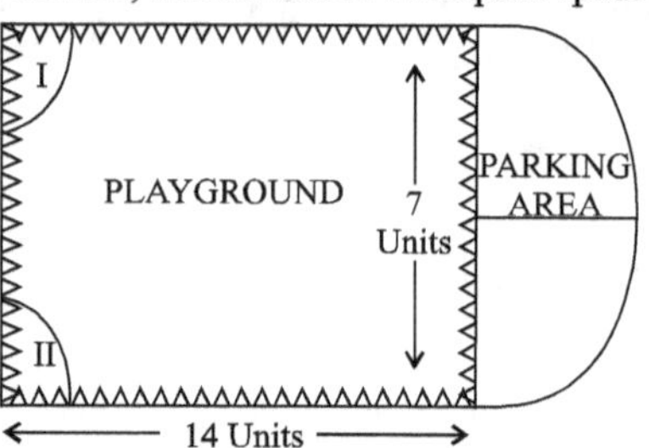

After survey, it was decided to build rectangular playground, with a semi-circular area allotted for parking at one end of the playground. The length and breadth of the rectangular playground are 14 units and 7 units, respectively. There are two quadrants of radius 2 units on one side for special seats. **[Delhi 2023, U]**

Based on the above information, answer the following questions:

(i) What is the total perimeter of the parking area?

(ii) (a) What is the total area of the parking and the two quadrants?

OR

(b) What is the ratio of area of playground to the area of parking area?

(iii) Find the cost of fencing the playground and parking area at the rate of ₹ 2 per unit.

15. Case Study

A 'circus' is a company of performers who put on shows of acrobats, clowns etc. to entertain people started around 250 years back, in open fields, now generally performed in tents. **[All India 2022, Term-II, K]**

One such 'Circus tent' is shown below.

The tent is in the shape of a cylinder surmounted by a conical top. If the height and diameter of cylindrical part are 9 m and 30 m respectively and height of conical part is 8 m with same diameter as that of the cylindrical part, then find

(1) the area of the canvas used in making the tent;

(2) the cost of the canvas bought for the tent at the rate ₹ 200 per sq. m, if 30 sq m canvas was wasted during stitching.

Topic-2: *Volume of a Combination of Solids*

Multiple Choice Questions

1. The volume of a right circular cone whose area of the base is 156 cm^2 and the vertical height is 8 cm, is **[All India 2023, Set-II, K]**

(a) 2496 cm^3 (b) 1248 cm^3

(c) 1664 cm^3 (d) 416 cm^3

2. Water in a river which is 3 m deep and 40 m wide is flowing at the rate of 2 km/h. How much water will fall into the sea in 2 minutes? **[All India 2023, Set-I, K]**

(a) 800 m^3 (b) 4000 m^3

(c) 8000 m^3 (d) 2000 m^3

Very Short Answer Question (1 Mark)

3. Two cones have their heights in the ratio 1:3 and radii in the ratio 3:1. What is the ratio of their volumes? **[Delhi 2020, Ap]**

Short Answer Questions (2 or 3 Marks)

4. The volume of a right circular cylinder with its height equal to the radius is $25\frac{1}{7}$ cm^3. Find the height of the cylinder. (Use $\pi = \frac{22}{7}$) **[All India 2020, Ap]**

5. A solid is in the form of a cylinder with hemispherical ends. The total height of the solid is 20 cm and the diameter of the cylinder is 7 cm. Find the total volume of the solid. (Use $\pi = \frac{22}{7}$) **[All India 2019, A]**

6. A well of diameter 4 m is dug 21 m deep. The earth taken out of it has been spread evenly all around it in the shape of a circular ring of width 3 m to form an embankment. Find the height of the embankment. **[Delhi 2016, Term-II, A]**

7. The sum of the radius of base and height of a solid right circular cylinder is 37 cm. If the total surface area of the solid cylinder is 1628 sq. cm, find the volume of the cylinder. $\left(\text{use } \pi = \frac{22}{7}\right)$ **[Delhi 2016, Term-II, U]**

8. A hemispherical bowl of internal diameter 36 cm contains liquid. This liquid is filled into 72 cylindrical bottles of diameter 6 cm. Find the height of the each bottle, if 10% liquid is wasted in this transfer. **[All India 2015, Term-II, U]**

9. A wooden toy was made by scooping out a hemisphere of the same radius from each end of a solid cylinder. If the height of the cylinder is 10 cm, and its base is of radius 3.5 cm, find the volume of wood in the toy. $\left[\text{Use } \pi = \frac{22}{7}\right]$ **[All India 2013, U]**

Long Answer Questions (4 or 5 Marks)

10. Water is flowing at the rate of 15 km/h through a pipe of diameter 14 cm into a cuboidal pond which is 50 m long and 44 m wide. In what time will the level of water in pond rise by 21 cm?
What should be the speed of water if the rise in water level is to be attained in 1 hour? **[CBSE Sample Paper 2023-24, U]**

11. A tent is in the shape of a cylinder surmounted by a conical top. If the height and radius of the cylindrical part are 3 m and 14 m respectively, and the total height of the tent is 13.5 m, find the area of the canvas required for making the tent, keeping a provision of 26 m^2 of canvas for stitching and wastage. Also, find the cost of the canvas to be purchased at the rate of ₹ 500 per m^2. **[CBSE Sample Paper 2023-24, K]**

12. A solid is in the shape of a right-circular cone surmounted on a hemisphere, the radius of each of them being 7 cm and the height of the cone is equal to its diameter. Find the volume of the solid. **[All India 2023, Set-II, A]**

13. There are two identical solid cubical boxes of side 7cm. From the top face of the first cube a hemisphere of diameter equal to the side of the cube is scooped out. This hemisphere is inverted and placed on the top of the second cube fs surface to form a dome. Find
(i) the ratio of the total surface area of the two new solids formed.
(ii) volume of each new solid formed. **[CBSE Sample Paper 2022-23, A]**

14. A solid toy in the form of a hemisphere surmounted by a right circular cone of same radius. The height of the cone is 10 cm and the radius of its base is 7 cm. Determine the volume of the toy. Also find the area of the coloured sheet required to cover the toy. (Use $\pi = \frac{22}{7}$ and $\sqrt{149} = 12.2$) **[All India 2020, U]**

15. A solid iron pole consists of a cylinder of height 220 cm and base diameter 24 cm, which is surmounted by another cylinder of height 60 cm and radius 8 cm. Find the mass of the pole, given that 1 cm^3 of iron has approximately 8 gm mass. (Use $\pi = 3{\cdot}14$) **[All India 2019, Ap]**

16. From each end of a solid metal cylinder, metal was scooped out in hemispherical form of same diameter. The height of the cylinder is 10 cm and its base is of radius 4.2 cm. The rest of the cylinder is melted and converted into a cylindrical wire of 1.4 cm thickness. Find the length of the wire. $\left[\text{Use } \pi = \frac{22}{7}\right]$. **[All India 2015, Term-II, Ap]**

17. Sushant has a vessel, of the form of an inverted cone, open at the top, of height 11 cm and radius of top as 2.5 cm and is full of water. Metallic spherical balls each of diameter 0.5 cm are put in the vessel due to which $\frac{2}{5}$ of the water in the vessel flows out. Find how many balls were put in the vessel. Sushant made the arrangement so that the water that flows out irrigates the flower beds. What value has been shown by Sushant ? **[Delhi 2014, Term-II, A]**

18. Water is flowing through a cylindrical pipe, of internal diameter 2 cm, into a cylindrical tank of base radius 40 cm, at the rate of 0.4 m/s. Determine the rise in level of water in the tank in half an hour. **[All India 2013, Ap]**

Case Based Questions (4 Marks)

19. A golf ball is spherical with about 300 – 500 dimples that help increase its velocity while in play. Golf balls are traditionally white but available in colours also. In the given figure, a golf ball has diameter 4.2 cm and the surface has 315 dimples (hemi-spherical) of radius 2 mm.

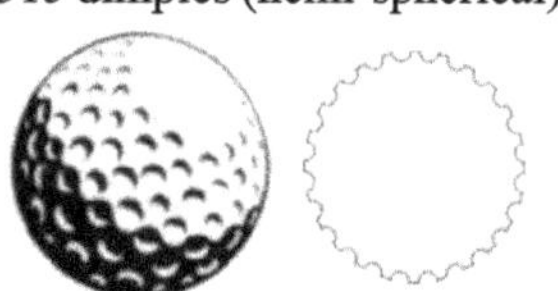

Based on the above, answer the following questions:

(i) Find the surface area of one such dimple. **[All India 2023, Set-I, K]**

(ii) Find the volume of the material dug out to make one dimple. **[All India 2023, Set-I, K]**

(iii) (a) Find the total surface area exposed to the surroundings. **[All India 2023, Set-I, K]**

OR

(iii) (b) Find the volume of the golf ball. **[All India 2023, Set-I, K]**

20. John planned a birthday party for his younger sister with his friends. They decided to make some birthday caps by themselves and to buy a cake from a bakery shop. For these two items, they decided the following dimensions :
Cake : Cylindrical shape with diameter 24 cm and height 14 cm.
Cap : Conical shape with base circumference 44 cm and height 24 cm.

Based on the above information, answer the following questions :

(a) How many square cm paper would be used to make 4 such caps ?

(b) The bakery shop sells cakes by weight (0·5 kg, 1 kg, 1·5 kg, etc.). To have the required dimensions, how much cake should they order, if 650 cm^3 equals 100 g of cake ? **[All India 2022, A]**

Hints & Solutions

Topic-1: Surface Area of a Combination of Solids

1. **(c)** $96\ cm^2$ **(1 Mark)**
2. **(a)** Both assertion (A) and reason (R) are true and reason (R) is the correct explanation of assertion (A) **(1 Mark)**
3. Finds the CSA of the top portion of the lampshade as $\pi(8 + 5)5$ sq in. **(1 Mark)**

   Finds the CSA of the bottom portion of the lampshade as $(2 \times \pi \times 8 \times 5)$ sq in. **(1 Mark)**

   Finds the total area of the cane web used to make the lampshade as 145π sq in and the minimum number of sheets of cane web required to make this lamp as $\frac{145 \times 22}{44 \times 7} = 11$ sheets. **(1 Mark)**

   Find the minimum number of sheets of cane web required to make this lamp if each sheet has an area of 44 square inches.

   (Note: Take $\pi = \frac{22}{7}$.)
4. Finds the volume of the cone as $\frac{\pi}{3} k^3\ cm^3$. **(½ Mark)**

   Finds the volume of the cylinder as $\pi k^3\ cm^3$. **(½ Mark)**

   Finds the volume of the hemisphere as $\frac{2}{3} \pi k^3\ cm^3$. **(½ Mark)**

   Finds the total volume of the solid as $\frac{\pi}{3} k^3 + \pi k^3 + \frac{2}{3} \pi k^3 = 2\pi k^3\ cm^3$. **(1 Mark)**

   Uses steps 2 and 4 and concludes that the total volume of the solid is twice the volume of the cylinder. **(½ Mark)**
5.

Topper's Answer

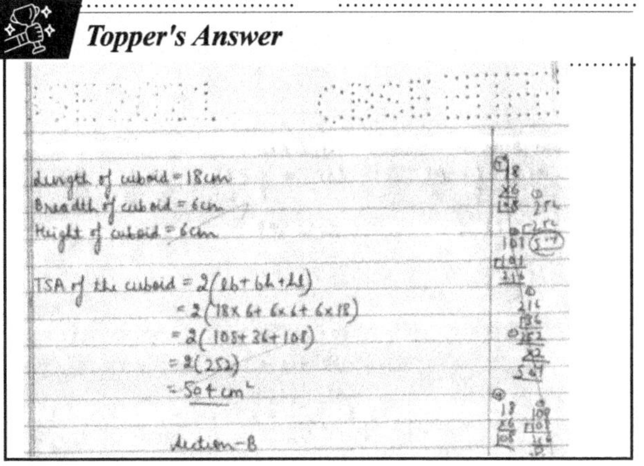

Length of cuboid = 18cm
Breadth of cuboid = 6cm
Height of cuboid = 6cm

TSA of the cuboid = 2(lb+bh+hl)
= 2(18×6+6×6+6×18)
= 2(108+36+108)
= 2(252)
= 504 cm²

Section-B

6.

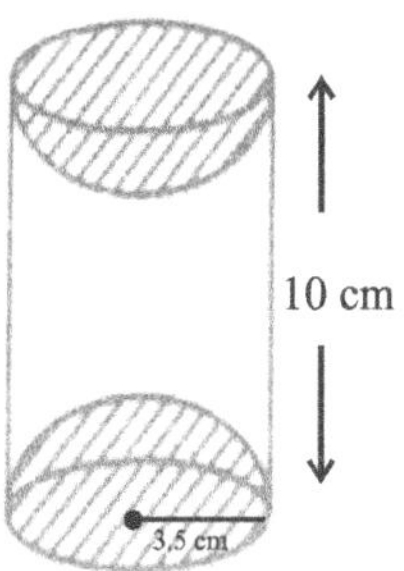

Total surface area of the article.

$= \text{CSA of cylinder} + 2\ (\text{CSA of Hemisphere})$ **(1 Mark)**

$= 2\pi rh + 2\ (2\pi r^2)$

$= 2\pi r\ (h + 2r)$

$= 2 \times \frac{22}{7} \times 3.5 \times (10 + 2 \times 3.5)$

$= 22 \times (17)$

$= 374\ cm^2$. **(1 Mark)**

CSA of hemisphere and cylinder are always added either case of hemisphere scooping out or surmounted.

7. Surface area of the block = Total surface area of the cube – Base area of the hemisphere + Curved surface area of the hemisphere

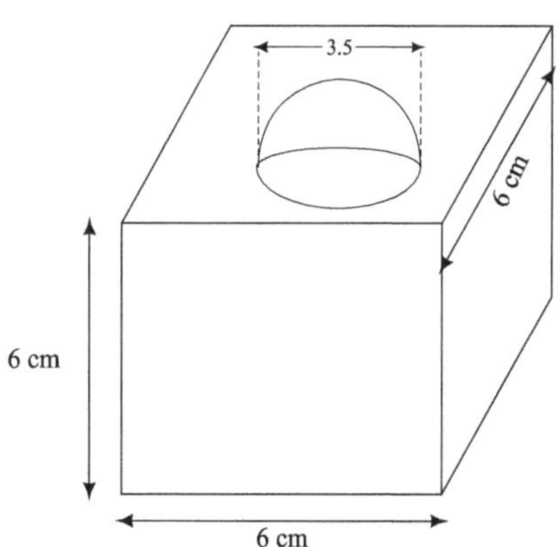

$= 6 \times (\text{Edge})^2 - \pi r^2 + 2\pi r^2$ **(1 Mark)**

$= 6(6)^2 + \pi r^2$

$= 216 + \frac{22}{7} \times \frac{3.5}{2} \times \frac{3.5}{2}$ $\left[\because r = \frac{d}{2} = \frac{3.5}{2}\right]$

$= 216 + 9.625$

$= 225.625\ cm^2$ **(1 Mark)**

8. Given: Height of cylindrical part = 4m

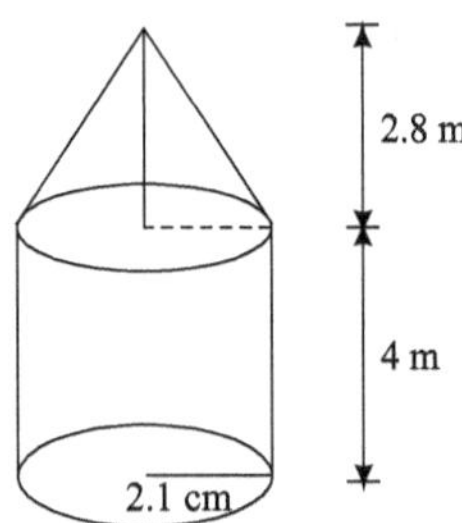

Height of conical part = 2.8 m

Diameter of cylindrical part = Diameter of conical part = 4.2 cm **(½ Mark)**

∴ Radius of cylindrical part = Radius of conical part

$= \frac{4.2}{2} m$ $\left[\because r = \frac{d}{2}\right]$

$= 2.1$ m **(½ Mark)**

Surface area of tent = Curved surface area of cylindrical part + Curved surface area of conical part

Curved surface are of cylinder = $2\pi rh$

$= 2 \times \frac{22}{7} \times 2.1 \times 4$

$= 52.80\ m^2$ **(1 Mark)**

slant height $l = \sqrt{h^2 + r^2} = \sqrt{(2.8)^2 + (2.1)^2}$

$= \sqrt{7.84 + 4.41} = \sqrt{12.25} = 3.5$

∴ *CSA* of cone = $\pi rl = \frac{22}{7} \times 2.1 \times 3.5 = 23.10\ m^2$

∴ Surface area of tent = $(52.8 + 23.1)\ m^2 = 75.9\ m^2$

Surface area of 100 tents = $100 \times 75.9 = 7590\ m^2$

Total cost of 100 tents = ₹ 100 × 7590 = ₹ 759000

Association offered 50% of the cost

Amount paid by association = 50% of 759000

$= \frac{50}{100} \times 759000$ = ₹ 379500 **(1 Mark)**

Areas of complex figures can be broken down and analysed as simpler known shapes by finding out the areas of these known shapes we can find out the required area of the unknown figure.

9. Hemisphere will touch the side of cubical block, so largest diameter of it will be equal to side of cubical block

∴ Largest diameter of the hemisphere = 10 cm

Surface area = Surface area of cube + surface area of hemisphere – Area of circular part of hemisphere

Surface area of cube = $6a^2$

$= 6(10)^2 = 600\ cm^2$

Surface area of hemisphere = $2\pi r^2$

$= 2 \times \frac{22}{7} \times (5)^2 = 157.14$ $\left(\because r = \frac{d}{2} = \frac{10}{2} = 5\right)$ **(1 Mark)**

Area of circular part = πr^2

$= \frac{22}{7} \times (5)^2$

$= \frac{550}{7} = 78.57$

∴ Surface area = 600 + 157.14 – 78.57

$= 678.57\ cm^2$ **(1 Mark)**

∴ Cost of painting the block at the rate of Rs 5/ cm^2

Cost of total solid = 678.57 × 5

= ₹ 3392.85 **(1 Mark)**

10. Diameter of hemispherical bowl = 14 cm

Radius of hemispherical bowl, $r = \frac{14}{2}\left(r = \frac{d}{2}\right)$

$r = 7$ cm

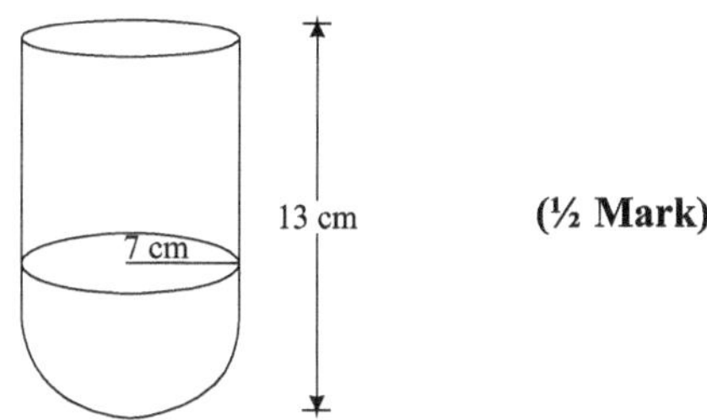

(½ Mark)

Radius of cylinder = Radius of hemispherical bowl

= 7 cm

Total height of vessel = 13 cm

∴ Height of cylinder, $h = 13 - 7 = 6$ cm **(½ Mark)**

Total surface area of the vessel = 2(*CSA* of cylinder + *CSA* of hemisphere) [∵ Vessel is hollow]

$= 2(2\pi rh + 2\pi r^2)$ **(1 Mark)**

$= 4\pi r(h + r)$

$= 4 \times \frac{22}{7} \times 7 \times (6 + 7)$

$= 88\ (13) = 1144$ cm^2 **(1 Mark)**

11. For solid cylinder, H = 20 cm, D = 120 cm, R = 6 cm

For cone, H = 8 cm, R = 6 cm **(1 Mark)**

$\ell = \sqrt{H^2 + R^2} = \sqrt{(8)^2 + (6)^2} = 10$ cm **(1 Mark)**

Total surface area of remaining soild = CSA of cone + CSA of cyclinder + area of circle

$\Rightarrow \pi rl + 2\pi rh + \pi r^2 = \pi r(l + 2h + r)$ **(2 Marks)**

12. Radius of the base of cylinder (r) = 2.8 m = Radius of the base of the cone (r)

Height of the cylinder (h) =3.5 m

Height of the cone (H) = 2.1 m.

Slant height of conical part (l) = $\sqrt{r^2} + H^2$

$= \sqrt{(2.8^2 + (2.1)^2}$

$= \sqrt{7.84} + 4.41$ **(1 Mark)**

$= \sqrt{12.25} = 3.5$ m **(1 Mark)**

Area of canvas used to make tent = CSA of cylinder + CSA of cone = $2 \times \pi \times 2.8 \times 3.5 + \pi \times 2.8 \times 3.5$

(1 Mark)

$= 61.6 + 30.8 = 92.4$m^2

Cost of 1500 tents at ₹120 per sq.m **(1 Mark)**

$= 1500 \times 120 \times 92.4$

$= 16{,}632{,}000$

Share of each school to set up the tents = 16632000/50

= ₹332,640 **(1 Mark)**

13.

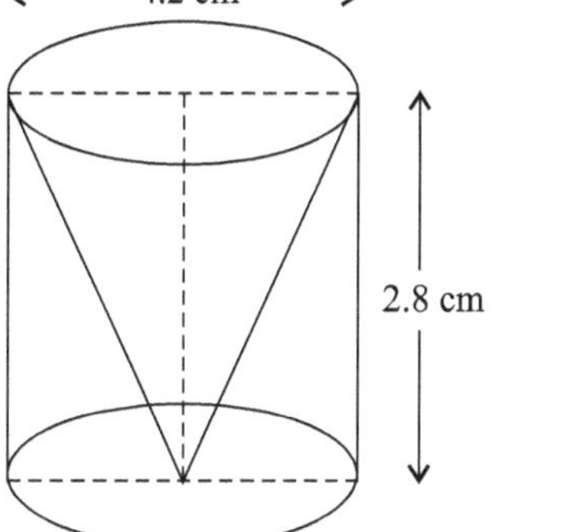

(1 Mark)

Given: Height (h_1) of the conical part = Height (h) of the cylinder part = 2.8 cm

Diameter of cylinder part = Diameter of conical part = 4.2 cm

Radius of cylindrical part = Radius of conical part

$= \frac{4.2}{2} = 2.1$ cm

Slant height of the conical part, $l = \sqrt{r^2 + h^2}$

$l = \sqrt{(2.1)^2 + (2.8)^2} = \sqrt{4.41 + 7.81} = \sqrt{12.25}$

= 3.5 cm **(1 Mark)**

Total surface area of remaining solid = curved surface area of the cylindrical part + Curved surface area of the conical part + Area of the cylindrical base **(1 Mark)**

$= 2\pi rh + \pi rl + \pi r^2$

$= 2 \times \frac{22}{7} \times 2.1 \times 2.8 + \frac{22}{7} \times 2.1 \times 3.5 + \frac{22}{7} \times 2.1 \times 2.1$

= [36.96 + 23.1 + 13.86] cm^2

= 73.92 cm^2

Thus, total surface area of the remaining solid is 73.92 cm^3 **(1 Mark)**

If a solid in molded by two or more than two solids then we need to divide it in separate solids to calculate its surface area.

14. **(i)** Perimeter of parking Area $= \frac{1}{4} \times 2\pi r + \frac{7}{2} + \frac{7}{2}$

$= \frac{22}{7} \times \frac{1}{2} \times \frac{7}{2} + 7 = \frac{5.5}{2} + 7 = 12.5$ **(1 Mark)**

(ii) **(a)** Total Area of parking + two quadrants

$\Rightarrow \frac{1}{4} \times \pi r^2 + \frac{1}{4} \times 2 \times \pi r^2$ **(1 Mark)**

$= \frac{1}{4} \times \frac{22}{7} \times \frac{7}{2} \times \frac{7}{2} + \frac{1}{4} \times 2 \times \frac{22}{7} \times 2 \times 2$

$\Rightarrow \frac{77}{8} + \frac{44}{7} = 16$ **(1 Mark)**

OR

(b) $\frac{\text{Area of playground}}{\text{Area of parking Area}} = \frac{14 \times 7 - 2 \times \frac{1}{4} \times \frac{22}{7} \times 2 \times 2}{\frac{1}{4} \times \frac{22}{7} \times \frac{7}{2} \times \frac{7}{2}}$

$\frac{\frac{98}{1} - \frac{44}{7}}{\frac{77}{8}} = \frac{686 - 44}{7} \times \frac{8}{77}$

$= \frac{642 \times 8}{7 \times 77} = \frac{5136}{539}$ **(2 Marks)**

(iii) Playground Area $\Rightarrow \frac{642}{7}$; Parking Area $\Rightarrow \frac{77}{8}$

Total cost of fencing $= 2\left(\frac{642}{7} + \frac{77}{8}\right) \Rightarrow 2\left(\frac{5136 + 539}{56}\right)$

$= \frac{5675}{28}$ Rs. $= 202.6$ Rs.

$= 203$ Rs. **(1 Mark)**

15. **(1)** Given diameter of cylinder = 30 m

hence, $r = \frac{30}{2} = 15$cm.

In ΔABC

$AC^2 = AB^2 + BC^2$

$AC^2 = (8)^2 + (15)^2$

$= 64 + 225$

or $AC = 17$ m. (say, 'l')

Area of canvas used = C.S.A of cone + C.S.A of cylinder.

$= \pi rl + 2\pi rh$ **(1 Mark)**

$= \pi r (l + 2h)$

$= \frac{22}{7} \times 15\,(17 + 2 \times 9)$

$= \frac{22}{7} \times 15 \times 35 = 110 \times 15 = 1650\text{m}^2$ **(1 Mark)**

(2) Cost of the canvas bought of $1\text{m}^2 \rightarrow$ ₹ 200

Total area of canvas bought = $(1650 + 30)$ m^2

$= 1680$ m^2 **(1 Mark)**

Cost of total canvas = 1680×200

= ₹ 3,36,000 **(1 Mark)**

Wasted area of canvas will be included in the area of canvas used in the tent to find the total cost of canvas bought.

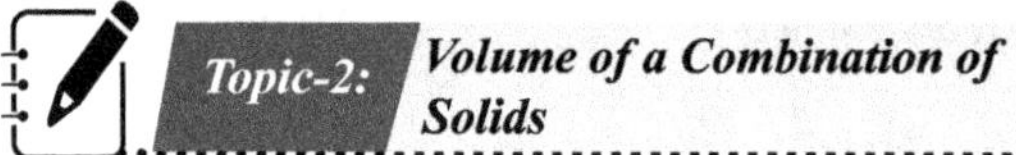

Topic-2: Volume of a Combination of Solids

1. **(d)** Volume of cone is calculated by the formula $\frac{\pi r^2 h}{3}$ where r and h are the radius of base and height of cone respectively.

As the base is in circular shape, hence area of base is πr^2.

$\therefore \pi r^2 = 156$ cm^2 (given)

height (h) = 8 cm

$\therefore$ volume $= \frac{156 \times 8}{3} = 416\text{cm}^3$ **(1 Mark)**

2. **(c)** Area of river $= 40 \times 3 = 120$ m^2

Rate of flowing $= \frac{2000}{60} = \frac{200}{6} = \frac{100}{3}$

Rate of flowing in 2 min $\frac{100}{3} \times 2 = \frac{200}{3}$

Water fall into the sea $= \frac{200}{3} \times 120$ **(1 Mark)**

3. Let height of both cones are h and $3h$

and radii of both cones are $3r$ and $1r$

Ratio of their volume $= \frac{\pi(3r)^2 h}{\pi(1r)^2 3h} = \frac{9\pi r^2 h}{3\pi r^2 h} = 3 : 1$

(1 Mark)

4. Since height of cylinder = radius (i.e., $h = r$)

Volume = $\pi r^2 h$ **(1 Mark)**

$$25\frac{1}{7} = \frac{22}{7} \times h^2 \times h$$

$$\frac{176}{7} = \frac{22}{7} \times h^3 \Rightarrow h^3 = \frac{176}{7} \times \frac{7}{22} = 8$$

$h = 2$ cm **(1 Mark)**

5. ABCD is a cylinder and BFC and AED are two hemisphere which has radius (r) = $-$ cm

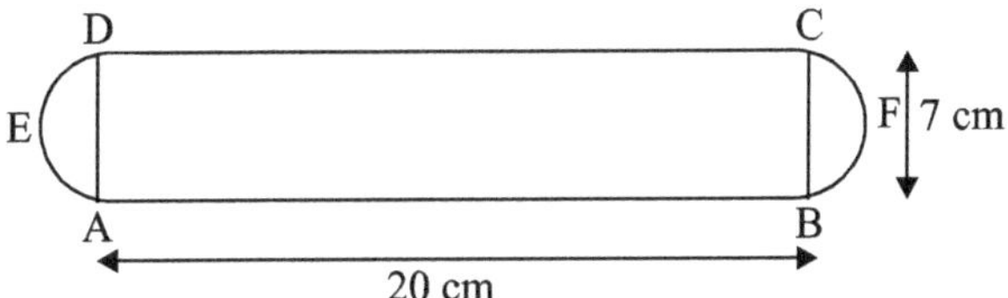

Height of cylinder (h):

$$AB = 20 - 2\times\frac{7}{2} = 13 \text{ cm}$$

Volume of cylinder = $\pi r^2 h$

$$= \frac{22}{7}\times\frac{7}{2}\times\frac{7}{2}\times 13 = \frac{11\times13\times7}{2} = \frac{1001}{2}$$

$= 500.5$ cm^3 **(1 Mark)**

Volume of two hemisphere = $2\times\frac{2}{3}\pi r^3$

$$= 2\times\frac{2}{3}\times\frac{22}{7}\times\frac{7}{2}\times\frac{7}{2}\times\frac{7}{2}$$

$$= \frac{49\times11}{3} = \frac{539}{3} = 179.67 \text{ cm}^3$$ **(1 Mark)**

Total volume of solid

= Volume of two hemisphere + Volume of cylinder

$= 179.67 + 500.5 = 680.17$ cm^3 **(1 Mark)**

6. Let r and h be the radius and depth of the well.

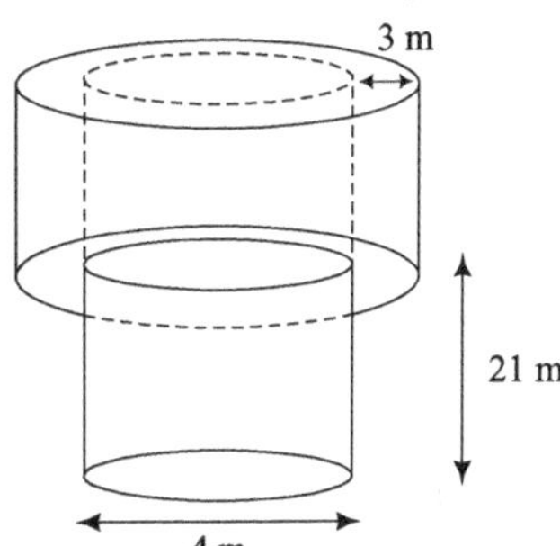

(½ Mark)

$$\therefore r = \frac{d}{2} = \frac{4}{2} = 2\text{m}$$

$h = 21$ m

Let R and H be the outer radius and height of the embankment respectively.

$\therefore R = r + 3 = 2 + 3 = 5$m **(½ Mark)**

Volume of the earth used to form the embankment

= Volume of earth dug out of the well.

$\pi(R^2 - r^2)H = \pi r^2 h$

$$H = \frac{r^2 h}{R^2 - r^2}$$ **(1 Mark)**

$$= \frac{2^2\times21}{5^2-2^2} = \frac{4\times21}{25-4} = \frac{4\times21}{21} = 4$$

$H = 4$ m **(1 Mark)**

$\therefore$ Height of the embankment is 4m

7. Let the radius of base and height of the solid right circular cylinder be r and h cm, respectively.

$r + h = 37$ ...(1)

Total surface are = 1628 sq. cm

$T.SA = 2\pi r (h + r)$

$1628 = 2\pi r (37)$ [From (1)]

$$r = \frac{1628}{37\times2\times\pi} = \frac{1628}{37\times2\times\left(\frac{22}{7}\right)} = \frac{1628\times7}{37\times2\times22}$$

$= 7$ cm **(1 Mark)**

Substituting value of r in (1)

$h + 7 = 37$

$h = 30$ cm

Volume of cylinder = $\pi r^2 h$

$= \pi (7)^2(30)$

$$= \frac{22}{7}\times 7\times 7\times 30$$

$= 4{,}620$ cm^3

$\therefore$ Volume of cylinder is 4,620 cm^3. **(1 Mark)**

8. Diameter of hemispherical bowl = 36 cm

Radius of hemispherical bowl = $\frac{36}{2}$ $\left(\because r = \frac{d}{2}\right)$

= 18 cm

Volume of hemispherical bowl = $\frac{2}{3}\pi r^3$

= $\frac{2}{3} \times \pi \times (18)^3 = 3888\ \pi\ \text{cm}^3$ **(1 Mark)**

Volume of the liquid transferred

= 3888 π – 10% of 3888π

= $3888\pi - \frac{10}{100} \times 3888\pi$

= $3499.2\pi\ \text{cm}^3$

Diameter of cylindrical bottles = 6 cm

Radius of cylindrical bottles, $R = \frac{6}{2} = 3$ cm

Let height of cylindrical bottle be h

Volume of each cylindrical bottle = $\pi r^2 h$

= $\pi(3)^2 h$

= $9\pi h$ **(1 Mark)**

Total volume of 72 such cylindrical bottles = $72 \times 9\pi h$

= $648\ \pi\ h\ \text{cm}^3$

Also, total volume of 72 such cylindrical bottles = Volume of the liquid transferred

$648\ \pi\ h = 3499.2\ \pi$

$h = \frac{3499.2}{648} = 5.4$ cm

Height of each cylindrical bottle = 5.4 cm **(1 Mark)**

9. Height of cylinder, h = 10 cm

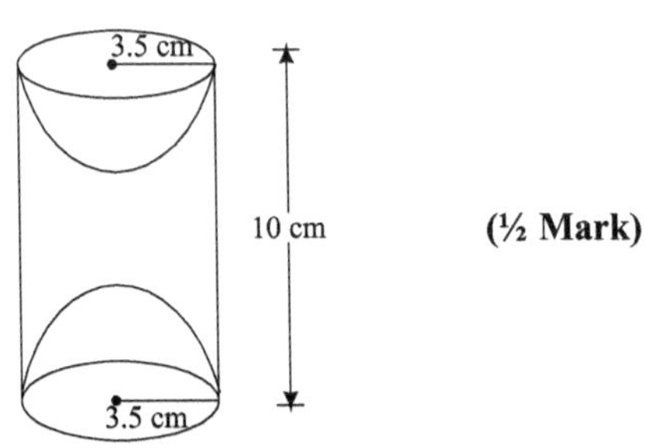

(½ Mark)

Radius of the cylinder = Radius of each hemisphere = 3.5 cm

Volume of cylinder = $\pi r^2 h$

= $\frac{22}{7}(3.5)^2\ (10)$ **(½ Mark)**

Volume of each hemisphere = $\frac{2}{3}\pi r^3$

= $\frac{2}{3} \times \frac{22}{7} \times (3.5)$ **(½ Mark)**

Volume of wood in the toy = Volume of the cylinder – 2 × Volume of each hemisphere

= $\frac{22}{7} \times (3.5)^2 \times 10 - 2 \times \frac{2}{3} \times \frac{22}{7} \times (3.5)^3$

= $\frac{22}{7}(3.5)^2\left(10 + \frac{4}{3}(3.5)\right)$

= 38.5 (10 – 4.67)

= 38.5 × 5.33

= $205.205\ \text{cm}^3$ **(1½ Marks)**

Note

Volume for a conical cavity in a cylinder = $\frac{2}{3}pr^2h$

10. **Given:** Length of the pond l = 50m, width of the pond b = 44m

Water level is to rise by, h = 21 cm = $\frac{21}{100}$ m

Volume of water in the pond = lbh = $50 \times 44 \times \frac{21}{100}\ \text{m}^3$

= $462\ \text{m}^3$ **(½ Mark)**

Diameter of the pipe = 14 cm

Radius of the pipe, r = 7cm = $\frac{7}{100}$ m

Area of cross–section of pipe = πr^2

= $\frac{22}{7} \times \frac{7}{100} \times \frac{7}{100} = \frac{154}{10000}\ \text{m}^2$ **(½ Mark)**

Rate at which the water is flowing through the pipe

= 15 km/h = 15000 m/h **(½ Mark)**

Volume of water flowing in 1 hour = Area of cross–section of pipe x height of water coming out of pipe **(½ Mark)**

$= \left(\frac{154}{10000} \times 15000\right) m^3$ **(1 Mark)**

Time required to fill the pond

$= \frac{\text{Volume of the pond}}{\text{Volume of water flowing in 1 hour}} = \frac{462}{\left(\frac{154 \times 15000}{10000}\right)}$

(1 Mark)

$= \frac{462 \times 10000}{154 \times 15000} = 2 \text{ hours}$

Speed of water if the rise in water level is to be attained in 1 hour = 2 × 15 = 30 km/h **(1 Mark)**

11. **Given:** Radius of the cylindrical tent (r) = 14 m

Total height of the tent = 13.5 m

Height of the cylinder = 3 m

Height of the conical part = 10.5 m **(½ Mark)**

Slant height of the cone (l) = $\sqrt{h^2 + r^2}$

$= \sqrt{(10.5)^2 + (14)^2}$

$= \sqrt{110.25 + 196}$

$= \sqrt{306.25} = 17.5 m$ **(1 Mark)**

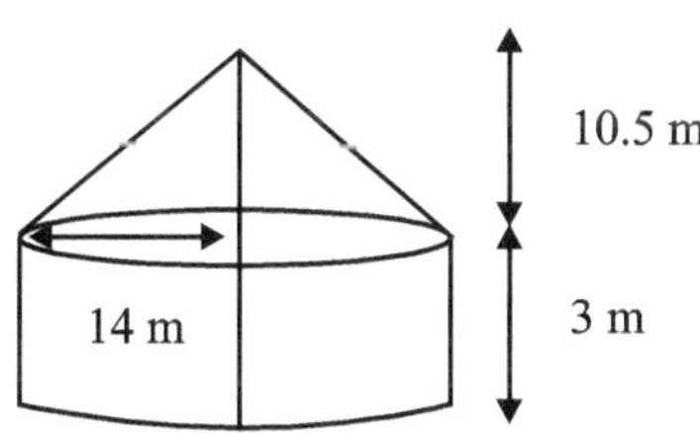

Curved surface area of cylindrical portion

$= 2\pi rh$

$= 2 \times \frac{22}{7} \times 14 \times 3$ **(1 Mark)**

$= 264 \text{ m}^2$

Curved surface area of conical portion

$= \pi rl$

$= \frac{22}{7} \times 14 \times 17.5$ **(1 Mark)**

$= 770 \text{ m}^2$ **(½ Mark)**

Total curved surface area = 264 m^2 + 770 m^2 = 1034 m^2

Provision for stitching and wastage = 26 m^2

Area of canvas to be purchased = 1034 + 26 = 1060 m^2

(½ Mark)

Cost of canvas = Rate × Surface area **(½ Mark)**

= 500 × 1060 = ₹ 5,30,000/-

12.

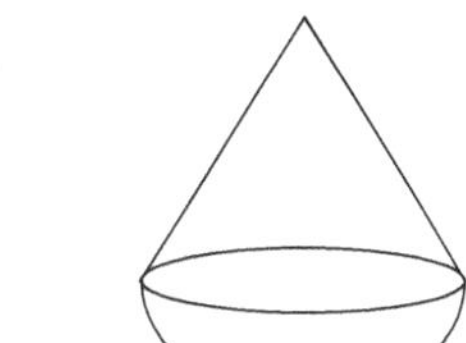

Radius = 7 cm

Diameter = 14 cm = Height of cone [given]

Volume of solid

= volume of hemisphere + volume of cone

(2 Marks)

Volume of cone = $\frac{\pi r^2 h}{3}$

Volume of hemishpere = $\frac{2}{3}\pi r^3$

Volume of solid $= \frac{2}{3}\pi r^3 + \frac{\pi r^2 h}{3}$ **(2 Marks)**

$= \frac{\pi r^2}{3}(2r + h)$

$= \frac{\pi r^2}{3}(14 + 14)$

$= \frac{28}{3} \times \frac{22}{7} \times 7 \times 7$

$= 1437.3 \text{ cm}^3$ **(1 Mark)**

Hence the volume of solid is 1437.3 cm^3

13. First Solid Second Solid

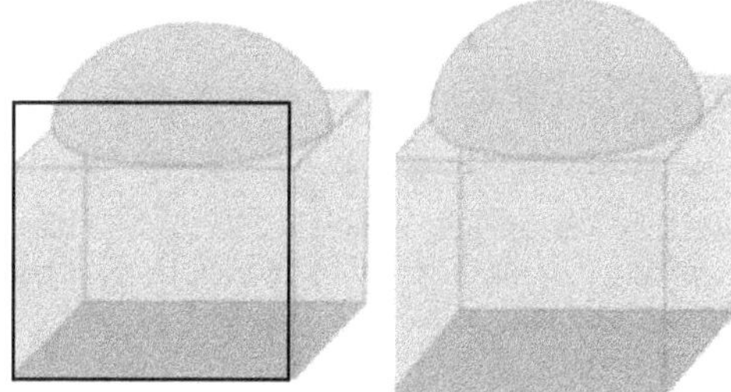

(i) SA for first new solid (S.): **(1 Mark)**

$6 \times 7 \times 7 + 2\pi \times 3.5^2 - \pi \times 3.5^2$

$= 294 + 77 - 38.5 = 332.5 \text{ cm}^2$

SA for second new solid (S.): **(1 Mark)**

$6 \times 7 \times 7 + 2\,\pi \times 3.5^2 - \pi \times 3.5^2$

$= 294 + 77 - 38.5 = 332.5 \text{ cm}^2$ **(1 Mark)**

So $S_1 : S_2 = 1:1$

(ii) Volume for first new solid $(V_1) = 7 \times 7 \times 7 - \frac{2}{3}\pi \times 3.5^3$

$= 343 - \frac{539}{6} = \frac{1519}{6} \text{cm}^2$ **(1 Mark)**

Volume for second new solid $(V_2) = 7 \times 7 \times 7 + \frac{2}{3}\pi \times 3.5^3$

$= 343 + \frac{539}{6} = \frac{2597}{6} \text{cm}^2$ **(1 Mark)**

14.

Topper's Answer

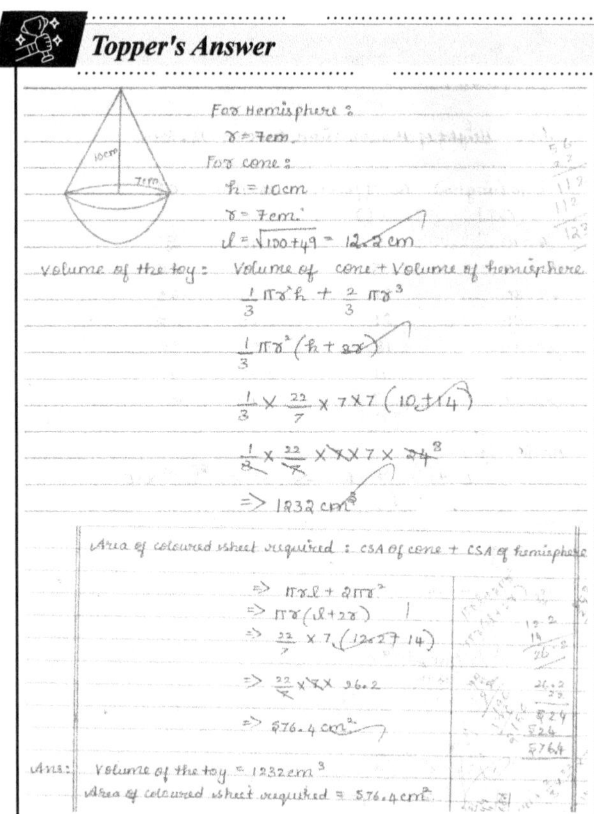
For Hemisphere :
r = 7cm
For cone :
h = 10cm
r = 7cm
l = √(100+49) = 12.2 cm
Volume of the toy : Volume of cone + Volume of hemisphere
1/3 πr²h + 2/3 πr³
1/3 πr² (h + 2r)
1/3 × 22/7 × 7 × 7 (10 + 14)
1/3 × 22/7 × 7 × 7 × 24
=> 1232 cm³
Area of coloured sheet required : CSA of cone + CSA of hemisphere
=> πrl + 2πr²
=> πr(l + 2r)
=> 22/7 × 7 (12.2 + 14)
=> 22/7 × 7 × 26.2
=> 576.4 cm²
Ans: Volume of the toy = 1232 cm³
Area of coloured sheet required = 576.4 cm²

15. Let AB be the iron pole of height 220 cm with base radius 12 cm and there is the other cylinder CD of height 60 cm whose base radius is 8 cm.

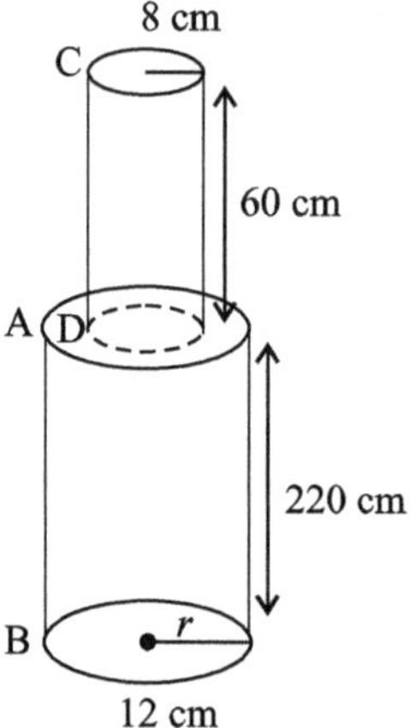

Let r_1 be the radius of the pole AB, r_2 be the radius of the pole CD, h, be the height of the pole AB and h_2 be the height of the pole CD.

Volume of AB pole $= \pi r_1^2 h_1 = 3.14 \times 12 \times 12 \times 220$
$= 99475.2 \text{ cm}^3$ **(1 Mark)**

Volume of CD pole $= \pi r_2^2 h_2 = 3.14 \times 8 \times 8 \times 60$
$= 12057.6 \text{ cm}^3$ **(1 Mark)**

Total volume of the poles $= 99475.2 + 12057.6$
$= 111532.8 \text{ cm}^3$ **(1 Mark)**

It is given that, mass of 1 cm^3 of iron = 8 gm
Then mass of 111532.8 cm^3 of iron = 111532.8 × 8 gm
= 892262.4 gm

Hence, required mass of the pole = 892262.4 gm **(1 Mark)**

Note

For finding the total surface area of that figure by, Total surface area = Total surface area of AB cylinder + Total surface area of CD cylinder – 2 × area of base of CD cylinder.

16. Height of the cylinder, $h = 10$ cm

Radius of cylinder, $r = 4.2$ cm

Volume of cylinder $= \pi r^2 h$

$= \pi(4.2)^2\, 10$

$= 176.4\, \pi \text{ cm}^3$ **(1 Mark)**

Volume of hemisphere (scoped part) $= \frac{4}{3}\pi r^3$

$= \frac{4}{3} \times \pi \times (4.2)^3$

$= 98.8\, \pi \text{ cm}^3$

Volume of the scooped metal cylinder

= Volume of cylinder – Volume of hemisphere

$= 176.4\pi - 98.8\pi$

$= 77.6\pi \text{ cm}^3$ **(1 Mark)**

Let height (length) of wire be H

Diameter of wire, $d = 1.4$ cm

Radius of wire, $R = \frac{d}{2} = \frac{1.4}{2} = 0.7$

Volume of cylindrical wire = $\pi R^2 H$

$= \pi (0.7)^2 H$ **(1 Mark)**

Volume of scooped metal cylinder = Volume of the wire

$\Rightarrow 77.6\pi = (0.7)^2 \pi H$

$\Rightarrow H = \frac{77.6}{(0.7)^2} = \frac{77.6}{0.49}$

$\Rightarrow H = 158.36$ cm ≈ 158.4 cm

$\therefore$ Length of the wire would be approximately 158.4 cm

(1 Mark)

When a solid is converted into another solid of a different shape (by melting or casting), the volume remains constant.

17.

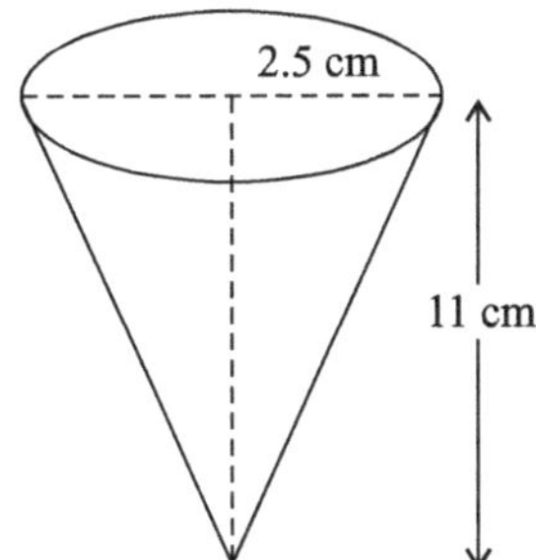

(1 Mark)

Height of the conical vessel (h) = 11 cm

Radius of the conical vessel (r_1) = 2.5 cm

Radius of the metallic sphere balls (r_2) = $\frac{0.5}{2} = 0.25$ cm

Let n be the number of spherical balls.

Volume of water spilled = Volume of the spherical balls dropped

$\frac{2}{5}$ × volume of cone = n × volume of one spherical ball.

(1 Mark)

$$\frac{2}{5} \times \left(\frac{1}{3}\pi r^2 h\right) = n \times \left(\frac{4}{3}\pi r_2^3\right)$$

$$\frac{2}{5} \times \frac{1}{3} \times \pi \times (2.5)^2 \times 11 = n \times \frac{4}{3} \pi \times (0.25)^3$$

$(2.5)^2 \times 11 = n \times 10 \times (0.25)^3$

n = 400

Hence, the number of spherical balls that were dropped in the vessel is 440. **(1 Mark)**

Sushant made the arrangement so that the water that flows out irrigates the flower beds. This shows the judicious usage of water. **(1 Mark)**

18. Diameter of circular end pipe = 2 cm

$\therefore$ Radius of circular end pipe, $r_1 = \frac{2}{2}$ cm $= \frac{1}{100} = 0.01$ m

Area of cross-section = $\pi r_1^{\,2}$

$= \pi(0.01)^2$

$= 0.0001\pi\ m^2$

Speed of water = 0.4 m/s

= 0.4 × 60 m/min = 24 metre/min

Volume of water flowing in 1 min = (Area of cross section of pipe) × (Speed of water)

$= 24 \times 0.0001\ \pi\ m^3$

$= 0.0024\ \pi\ m^3$

Volume of water flowing in 30 min

$= 30 \times 0.0024$

$= 0.072\ \pi\ m^3$ **(2 Marks)**

Radius of base of cylindrical tank,

$r_2 = 40$ cm

$= \frac{40}{100}$m $= 0.4$ m

Let the cylindrical tank be filled up to h metre in 30 minutes.

Volume of water filled in tank in 30 minutes = Volume of water flowed Out in 30 min. from the pipe

$\pi r_2^2 h = 0.072\ \pi$

$(0.4)^2 h = 0.072$

$h = \frac{0.072}{0.16} = 0.45$ m $= 0.45 \times 100$ cm

= 45 cm

$\therefore h = 45$ cm

Rise in level of water in the tank in half an hour in 45 cm. **(2 Marks)**

In other case, when water is flowing through a canal, which is b metre wide and h metre height then area of cross section = b × h.

19. (i) Surface area of half circle = $2\pi r^2$

$\Rightarrow\ 2\pi\left(\frac{2}{10}\right)^2 = \frac{8\pi}{100}$ cm^2 **(1 Mark)**

(ii) Volume of half sphere = $\frac{2}{3}\pi r^3$

One half sphere volume = $\frac{2}{3}\pi\left(\frac{2}{10}\right)^3 = \frac{16\pi}{3000}$ cm^3

(1 Mark)

(iii) (a) Total surface area exposed to surrounding = surface area of ball – surface area of 315 dimples

$= 4\pi r^2 - 315 \times \frac{8\pi}{100}$

$= 70.56\pi - 252\pi = 45.36\pi$ cm^2 **(2 Marks)**

OR

(b) Volume of ball $= \frac{4}{3}\pi r^3$ – (volume of dimples)

$= \frac{4}{3}\pi r^3 - 315 \times \frac{16\pi}{3000}$

$= \frac{4}{3}\pi(2.1)^3 - 315 \times \frac{16\pi}{3000}$

$= 38.78 - 5.28 = 33.5$ **(2 Marks)**

20.

Topper's Answer

(a) CSA of one cap = Square cm paper required for one cap

$2\pi r = 44$ $\quad l^2 = h^2 + r^2$

$2 \times \frac{22}{7} \times r = 44$ $\quad l^2 = 24^2 + 7^2$

$l^2 = 576 + 49$

$r = \frac{44 \times 7}{22 \times 2} = 7$ cm $\quad l^2 = 625$

$l = 25$ cm

CSA of one cap $= \pi r l$

$= \frac{22}{7} \times 7 \times 25$

$= 550$ cm^2

CSA of four caps i.e. square cm paper required for four caps $= 4 \times 550$

$= 2200$ cm^2

(b) Volume of cake $= \pi r^2 h$ $\quad$ | $d = 24$ cm, $r = \frac{d}{2} = 12$ cm

$= \frac{22}{7} \times 12 \times 12 \times 14$

$= 6336$ cm^3

650 cm^3 = 100 g or 0.1 kg

6336 cm$^3 = \frac{0.1 \text{ kg} \times 6336}{650} = \frac{6336}{6500} = \frac{95.9}{100} = 0.95$ kg

So they should order a 1 kg cake

Chapter 13 Statistics

Topic-1: Mean of Grouped Data

Multiple Choice Questions

1. If every term of the statistical data consisting of n terms is decreased by 2, then the mean of the data: **[All India 2023, Set-I, K]**
   (a) decreases by 2 (b) remains unchanged
   (c) decreases by 2n (d) decreases by 1

2. The numbers 3, 5, 7 and 9 have their respective frequencies $x-2$, $x+2$, $x-3$ and $x+3$. If the arithmetic mean is 6.5 then the value of x is **[Delhi 2014, Term-I, A]**
   (a) 3 (b) 4
   (c) 5 (d) 6

Very Short Answer Questions (1 Mark)

3. Find the mean of the following distribution **[All India 2023, Set-II, K]**

Classes	0–15	15–30	30–45	45–60	60–75	75–90
Frequency	17	20	18	21	15	9

4. Find the class-marks of the classes 10-25 and 35-55. **[All India 2020, K]**

5. Consider the following distribution: **[All India 2015, Term-I, K]**

Marks Obtained	0 or more	10 or more	20 or more	30 or more	40 or more	50 or more
Number of students	63	58	55	51	48	42

   (i) Calculate the frequency of the class 30 – 40.
   (ii) Calculate the class mark of the class 10 – 25

Short Answer Questions (2 or 3 Marks)

6. The length of 40 leaves of a plant are measured correct to nearest millimetre, and the data obtained is represented in the following table. **[CBSE Sample Paper 2023-24, A]**

Length [in mm]	Number of leaves
118 – 126	3
127 – 135	5
136 – 144	9
145 – 153	12
154 – 162	5
163 – 171	4
172 – 180	2

   Find the mean length of the leaves.

7. The mean of the following frequency distribution is 25. Find the value of f. **[All India 2022, Term-II, AP]**

Classes:	0-10	10-20	20-30	30-40	40-50
Frequency:	5	18	15	f	6

8. Find the mean of the following data using assumed mean method: **[All India 2022, Term-II, AP]**

Classes:	0-5	5-10	10-15	15-20	20-25
Frequency:	8	7	10	13	12

9. The frequency distribution of daily rainfall in a town during a certain period is shown below. **(CBSE CFPQ 2022, A)**

Rainfall (in) mm	Number of days
0-20	7
20-40	x
40-60	10
60-80	4

   Unfortunately, due to manual errors, the information on the 20–40 mm range got deleted from the data.
   If the mean daily rainfall for the period was 35 mm, find the number of days when the rainfall ranged between 20-40 mm. Show your work.

10. Find the mean of the following distribution: **[Delhi 2020, Ap]**

Class:	3-5	5-7	7-9	9-11	11-13
Frequency:	5	10	10	7	8

11. A class teacher has the following absentee record of 40 students of a class for the whole term. Find the mean number of days a student was absent.

Number of days:	0-6	6-12	12-18	18-24	24-30	30-36	36-42
Number of students:	10	11	7	4	4	3	1

[All India 2019, K]

12. The marks obtained by 110 students in an examination are given below : **[All India 2019, AP]**

Marks:	30 – 35	35 – 40	40 – 45	45 – 50	50 – 55	55 – 60	60 – 65
Number of Students:	14	16	28	23	18	8	3

Find the mean marks of the students.

13. The mean of the following data is 42. Find the missing frequency x and y, if the sum of the frequency is 100

Class intervals	0 – 10	10 – 20	20 – 30	30 – 40	40 – 50	50 – 60	60 – 70	70 – 80
f	7	10	x	13	y	10	14	9

[Delhi 2016, Term-I, Ap]

14. Find the mean of the following distribution: **[All India 2015, Term-I, Ap]**

xi	4	6	9	10	15
fi	5	10	10	7	8

15. If the mean of the following distribution is 6, find the value of p. **[All India 2015, Term-I, K]**

xi	2	4	6	10	p + 5
fi	3	2	3	1	2

16. Following table shows the weight of 12 students:

Weight (in kgs)	67	70	72	73	75
Number of students	4	3	2	2	1

Find the mean weight of the students.

[Delhi 2014, Term-I, Ap]

Long Answer Questions (4 or 5 Marks)

17. The mean of the following frequency distribution is 18. The frequency f in the class interval 19 – 21 is missing. Determine f. **[All India 2020, Ap]**

Class interval	11–13	13–15	15–17	17–19	19–21	21–23	23–25
Frequency	3	6	9	13	f	5	4

18. The mean of the following distribution is 18. Find the frequency of the class 19 - 21. **[All India 2018, Ap]**

Class	11-13	13-15	15-17	17-19	19-21	21-23	23-25
Frequency	3	6	9	13	f	5	4

Topic-2: Mode of Grouped Data

Multiple Choice Question

1. The upper limit of the modal class from the given distribution is **[CBSE Sample Paper 2023-24, Ap]**

Height [in cm]	Below 140	Below 145	Below 150	Below 155	Below 160	Below 165
Number of girls	4	11	29	40	46	51

(a) 165 (b) 160
(c) 155 (d) 150

Very Short Answer Question (1 Mark)

2. Find the value of λ, if the mode of the following data is 20:
15, 20, 25, 18, 13, 15, 25, 15, 18, 17, 20, 25, 20, λ, 18. **[Delhi 2016, Term-I, Ap]**

5

Short Answer Questions (2 or 3 Marks)

3. If mode of the following frequency distribution is 55, then find the value of x. **[All India 2022, Term-II, Ap]**

Class:	0-15	15-30	30-45	45-60	60-75	75-90
Frequency:	10	7	x	15	10	12

4. Compute the mode for the following frequency distribution: **[All India 2020, Ap]**

Size of items (in cm)	0 – 4	4 – 8	8 – 12	12 – 16	16 – 20	20 – 24	24 – 28
Frequency	5	7	9	17	12	10	6

5. Find the mode of the following data: **[Delhi 2020, Ap]**

Class:	0-20	20-40	40-60	60-80	80-100	100-120	120-140
Frequency:	6	8	10	12	6	5	3

6. Find the mode of the following frequency distribution : **[All India 2019, Ap]**

Class Interval:	25 – 30	30 – 35	35 – 40	40 – 45	45 – 50	50 – 55
Frequency:	25	34	50	42	38	14

7. Find the mode of the following frequency distribution. **[Delhi 2019, Ap]**

Class	**Frequency**
0–10	8
10–20	10
20–30	10
30–40	16
40–50	12
50–60	6
60–70	7

8. The data regarding marks obtained by 48 students of a class in a class test is given below. Calculate the modal marks of students.

Marks Obtained	**0 – 5**	**5 – 10**	**10 – 15**	**15 – 20**	**20 – 25**	**25 – 30**	**30 – 35**	**35 – 40**	**40 – 45**	**45 – 50**
Number of students	1	0	2	0	0	10	25	7	2	1

[Delhi 2016, Term-I, Ap]

9. On the sports day of a school, 300 students participated. Their ages are given in the following distribution:

Age (in years)	5–7	7–9	9–11	11–13	13–15	15–17	17–19
Number of students	67	33	41	95	36	13	15

Find the mean and mode of the data. **[Delhi 2016, Term-I, Ap]**

10. Find the mode of the following distribution :

Daily wages	31–36	37–42	43–48	49–54	55–60	61–66
No. of workers	6	12	20	15	9	4

[All India 2015, Term-I, Ap]

Long Answer Questions (4 or 5 Marks)

11. The median of the following data is 50. Find the values of 'p' and 'q', if the sum of all frequencies is 90. Also find the mode of the data.

Marks obtained	**Number of students**
20 – 30	p
30 – 40	15
40 – 50	25
50 – 60	20
60 – 70	q
70 – 80	8
80 – 90	10

[CBSE Sample Paper 2023-24, Ap]

12. 250 apples of a box were weighed and the distribution of masses of the apples is given in the following table: **[All India 2023, Set-II, Ap]**

Mass (in grams)	80-100	100-120	120-140	140-160	160-180
Number of apples	20	60	70	x	60

(i) Find the value of x and the mean mass of the apples.

(ii) Find the modal mass of the apples.

13. Find the mode of the given frequency distribution:

Class	Frequency
15-25	6
25-35	11
35-45	22
45-55	23
55-65	14
65-75	5

[All India 2022, K]

14. The following expenditure gives the state-wise teacher-student ratio in higher secondary schools of India. Find the mean and mode of this data and interpret it. **[All India 2015, Term-I, Ap]**

Number of Students Per Teacher	Number of States/ U.T.
15 – 20	3
20 – 25	8
25 – 30	9
30 – 35	10
35 – 40	3
40 – 45	0
45 – 50	0
50 – 55	2

15. The following table shows the ages of the patients admitted in a hospital during a year:

Age (in years)	5 – 15	15 – 25	25 – 35	35 – 45	45 – 55	55 – 65
Number of patients	6	11	21	23	14	5

Find the mean and the mode of the data given above. Compare and interpret the two measures of central tendency. **[All India 2015, Term-I, Ap]**

16. The runs made by players in some cricket matches are tabulated below : **[Delhi 2014, Term-I, Ap]**

Runs made	0–20	20–40	40–60	60–80	80–100	100–120
No. of players	6	8	f1	12	6	5

If mode of the above frequency distribution is 65, find the value of f_1.

What is your impression about the players whose performance is given in the table ? To discourage young students watching TV for hours together, will you encourage them to play games ? Why?

Topic-3: Median of Grouped Data

Multiple Choice Questions

1. If the mean and the median of a data are 12 and 15 respectively, then its mode is: **[All India 2023, Set-II, K]**

(a) 13·5 (b) 21 (c) 6 (d) 14

2. For the following distribution:

Class	0-5	5-10	10-15	15-20	20-25
Frequency	10	15	12	20	9

The sum of lower limits of median class and modal class is: **[Delhi 2023, A]**

(a) 15 (b) 25 (c) 30 (d) 35

3. If the difference of Mode and Median of a data is 24, then the difference of median and mean is **[CBSE Sample Paper 2022-23, U]**

(a) 8 (b) 12 (c) 24 (d) 36

4. For the following distribution,

Class	0-5	5-10	10-15	15-20
Frequency	10	15	12	20

the sum of the lower limits of the median and modal class is **[CBSE Sample Paper 2022-23, U]**

(a) 15 (b) 25 (c) 30 (d) 35

5. In statistics, and outlier is a data point that differs significantly from other observations of a data set.

If and outlier is included in the following data set, which measure(s) of central tendency would change?

12, 15, 22, 44, 44, 48, 50, 51 **[CBSE CFPQ, K]**

(a) only mean

(b) only mean and median

(c) all - mean, median, mode

(d) (cannot be said without knowing the outlier.)

Very Short Answer Question (1 Mark)

6. The mean and median of 100 observations are 50 and 52 respectively. The value of the largest observation is 100. It was later found that it is 110 not 100. Find the true mean and median. **[All India 2017, Term-I, K]**

Short Answer Questions (2 or 3 Marks)

7. Heights of 50 students of class X of a school are recorded and following data is obtained:

[All India 2022 ,Term-II, Ap]

Height (in cm):	130-135	135-140	140-145	145-150	150-155	155-160
Number of students:	4	11	12	7	10	6

8. The table blow shows the salaries of 280 persons :

Salary (In thousand ₹)	No. of Persons
5 – 10	49
10 – 15	133
15 – 20	63
20 – 25	15
25 – 30	6
30 – 35	7
35 – 40	4
40 – 45	2
45 – 50	1

Calculate the median salary of the data.

[All India 2018, Ap]

9. Find the unknown values in the following table :

[All India 2017, Term-I, Ap]

Class Interval	Frequency	Comulative Frequency
0 – 10	5	5
10 – 20	7	x_1
20 – 30	x_2	18
30 – 40	5	x_3
40 – 50	x_4	30

10. Monthly expenditures of milk in 100 families of a housing society are given in the following frequency distribution:

[All India 2017, Term-I, Ap]

Monthly expenditure (in ₹)	0–175	175–350	350–525	525–700	700–875	875–1050	1050–1225
Number of families	10	14	15	21	28	7	5

Find the mode and median for this distribution.

11. Find the median of the following frequency distribution

Marks	0-10	10-20	20- 30	30- 40	40- 50	Total
Number of students	8	20	36	24	12	100

[Delhi 2014, Term-I, Ap]

12. If the median for the following frequency distribution is 28.5, find the value of x and y :**[Delhi 2014, Term-I, Ap]**

Class	Frequencies
0 – 10	5
10 – 20	x
20 – 30	20
30 – 40	15
40 – 50	y
50 – 60	5
Total	**60**

Long Answer Questions (4 or 5 Marks)

13. The monthly expenditure on milk in 200 families of a Housing Society is given below:

Monthly Expenditure (in ₹)	1000-1500	2000-2500	2500-3000	3000-3500	3500-4000	4000-4500	4500-5000
Number of falimilies	24	40	33	x	30	22	167

Find the value of x and also, find the median and mean expenditure on milk. **[Delhi 2023, A]**

14. The median of the following data is 525. Find the values of x and y, if the total frequency is 100

[CBSE Sample Paper 2022-23, K]

Class interval	0-100	100-200	200-300	300-400	400-500	500-600	600-700	700-800	800-900	900-1000
Frequency	2	5	x	12	17	20	y	9	7	4

15. The median of the following data is 525. Find the values of x and y, if total frequency is 100: **[Delhi 2020, K]**

Class	Frequency
0–100	2
100–200	5
200–300	x
300–400	12
400–500	17
500–600	20
600–700	y
700–800	9
800–900	7
900–1000	4

16. If the median of the following frequency distribution is 32.5. Find the values of f_1 and f_2. **[Delhi 2019, A]**

Class	Frequency
0–10	f_1
10–20	5
20–30	9
30–40	12
40–50	f_2
50–60	3
60–70	2
Total	40

17. If median of the number of patients attending a hospital is 36, then find the missing frequencies f_1 and f_2 in the following frequency distribution, when it is given that total number of days is 100: **[All India 2017, Term-I, U]**

Number of patients	0–10	10–20	20–30	30–40	40–50	50–60	60–70
Number of days	5	12	f1	f2	15	11	14

18. Find the median of the following data :

Height (in cm)	Less than 120	Less than 140	Less than 160	Less than 180	Less than 200
Number of students	12	26	34	40	50

[Delhi 2016, Term-I, K]

Hints & Solutions

Topic-1: Mean of Grouped Data

1. (a) Let $\frac{a+b+c...+n \text{ terms}}{n} = Z$

And, $\frac{(a-2)+(b-2)+...+n \text{ terms}}{n}$

$\Rightarrow \frac{(a+b+...+n \text{ terms})-(2+2...n \text{ terms})}{n}$

$\Rightarrow \frac{(a+b+...n \text{ terms})}{n} - \frac{2n}{n} = Z - 2$ **(1 Mark)**

2. (c) Arithmetic mean

$= \frac{3(x-2)+5(x+2)+7(x-3)+9(x+3)}{x-2+x+2+x-3+x+3} = 6.5$

$\Rightarrow \frac{24x+10}{4x} = 6.5$

$\Rightarrow 24x+10 = 26x$

$\Rightarrow x = 5$ **(1 Mark)**

3.

Classes	Frequency	x_i	$f_i x_i$
0–15	17	7.5	127.5
15–30	20	22.5	450
30–45	18	37.5	675
45–60	21	52.5	1102.5
60–75	15	67.5	1012.5
75–90	9	82.5	742.5
	$\Sigma f = 100$	$\Sigma x_i = 270$	$\Sigma f_i x_i = 4110$

Now, Mean $= \frac{\sum f_i x_i}{\sum f_i} = \frac{4110}{100} = 41.1$ **(1 Mark)**

4. Class Marks $= \frac{U+L}{2}$

Class Marks of (10 – 25) $= \frac{10+25}{2} = 17.5$

Class Marks of (35 – 55) $= \frac{35+55}{2} = 45$ **(1 Mark)**

5. (i) So, frequency of the class 30 – 40 is 51 – 48 = 3. **(½ Mark)**

(ii) Class Mark of the class :

$10-25 = \frac{10+25}{2}$

$= \frac{35}{2} = 17.5$ **(½ Mark)**

6.

Length [in mm]	Number of leaves (f)	CI	Mid x	d	fd
118 – 126	3	117.5 –126.5	122	–27	–81
127 – 135	5	126.5 – 135.5	131	–18	–90
136 – 144	9	135.5 – 144.5	140	–9	–81
145 – 153	12	144.5 – 153.5	a = 149	0	0
154 – 162	5	153.5 – 162.5	158	9	45
163 – 171	4	162.5 – 171.5	167	18	72
172 – 180	2	171.5 – 181.5	176	27	54

(1 Mark, ½ Mark, ½, Mark)

Mean $= a + \frac{\Sigma fd}{\Sigma f} = 149 + \frac{-81}{40}$

$= 149 - 2.025 = 146.975$

Average length of the leaves = 146.975 **(1 Mark)**

7. Given, Mean = 25

Class interval	f_i	x_i	$f_i x_i$
0 – 10	5	5	25
10 – 20	18	15	270
20 – 30	15	25	375
30 – 40	f	35	35f
40 – 50	6	45	270
	$44+f$		$940+35f$

(1 Mark)

$\bar{x} = \frac{\sum f_i x_i}{\sum f_i} = \frac{940+35f}{44+f}$ **(1 Mark)**

$25 = \frac{5(188+7f)}{44+f}$

$5 = \frac{188+7f}{44+f}$

220 + 5f = 188 + 7f

32 = 2f

$\boxed{f = 16}$ **(1 Mark)**

Therefore, the value of f = 16

8.

Class interval	frequency	x_i	$d_i = x_i - A$	$f_i d_i$
0 – 5	8	2.5	–10	–80
5 – 10	7	7.5	–5	–35
10 – 15	10 A←	12.5	0	0
15 – 20	13	17.5	5	65
20 – 25	12	22.5	10	120
	50			70

(1 Mark)

$\bar{x} = A + \frac{\sum f_i d_i}{\sum f_i}$ **(1 Mark)**

$= 12.5 + \frac{70}{50} = 12.5 + 1.4$

$\bar{x} = 13.9$ **(1 Mark)**

Note

Suppose the assume mean to middle class mark among all the class mark.

9. Completes the frequency distribution table as:

Rainfall (in mm)	Number of days/ Frequency (f_i)	Class-mark (x_i)	($f_i x_i$)
0-20 mm	7	10	70
20-40 mm	x	30	30x
40-60 mm	10	50	500
60-80 mm	4	70	280
Total	21 + x		850 + 30x

Writes the equation for mean as: **(2 Marks)**

$$\frac{850 + 30x}{21 + x} = 35$$

Solves the equation in step 2 to find the value of x as 23. **(1 Mark)**

10.

Class Interval	Class Mark (x_i)	Frequency (f_i)	$x_i f_i$
3-5	4	5	20
5-7	6	10	60
7-9	8	10	80
9-11	10	7	70
11-13	12	8	96
Total		40	326

(2 Marks)

$$\text{Mean} = \frac{\Sigma x_i f_i}{\Sigma f_i} = \frac{326}{40} = 8.15$$ **(1 Mark)**

11.

Topper's Answer

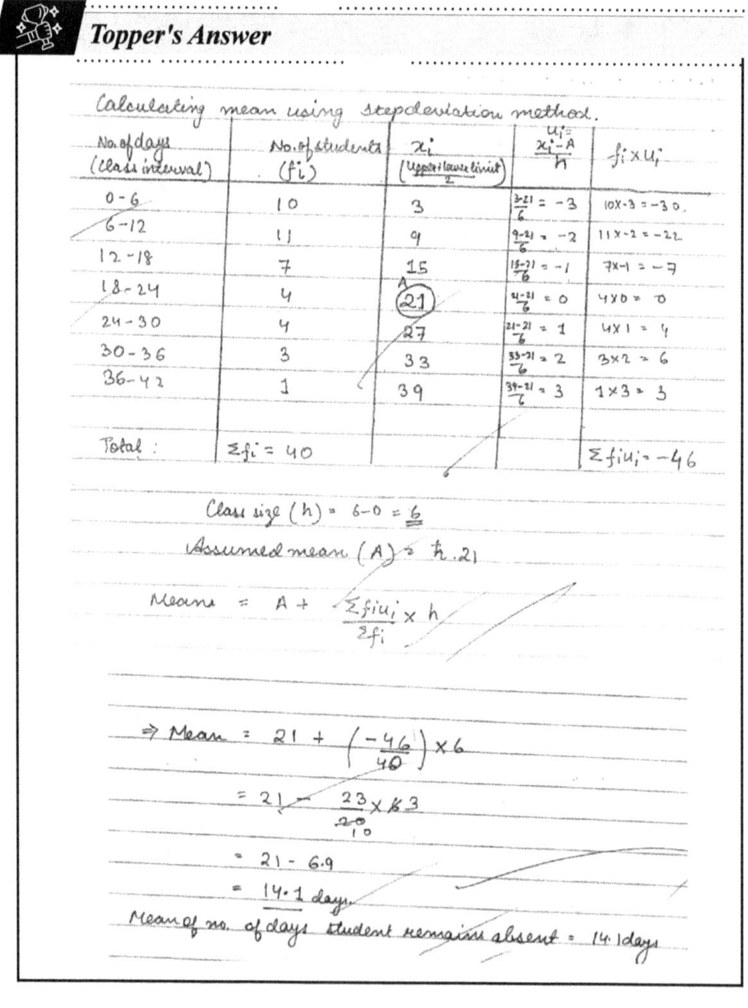

Calculating mean using stepdeviation method.

No. of days (Class interval)	No. of students (f_i)	x_i (Upper+lower limit)/2	$u_i = \frac{x_i - A}{h}$	$f_i \times u_i$
0-6	10	3	$\frac{3-21}{6} = -3$	$10 \times -3 = -30$
6-12	11	9	$\frac{9-21}{6} = -2$	$11 \times -2 = -22$
12-18	7	15	$\frac{15-21}{6} = -1$	$7 \times -1 = -7$
18-24	4	21	$\frac{21-21}{6} = 0$	$4 \times 0 = 0$
24-30	4	27	$\frac{27-21}{6} = 1$	$4 \times 1 = 4$
30-36	3	33	$\frac{33-21}{6} = 2$	$3 \times 2 = 6$
36-42	1	39	$\frac{39-21}{6} = 3$	$1 \times 3 = 3$
Total:	$\Sigma f_i = 40$			$\Sigma f_i u_i = -46$

Class size (h) = 6 − 0 = 6

Assumed mean (A) = 21

Mean = $A + \frac{\Sigma f_i u_i}{\Sigma f_i} \times h$

⇒ Mean = $21 + \left(\frac{-46}{40}\right) \times 6$

$= 21 - \frac{23}{10} \times 3$

$= 21 - 6.9$

$= 14.1$ days

Mean of no. of days student remains absent = 14.1 days

12.

Class Interval (Marks)	No. of Students (f_i)	Mid-value (x_i)	f_ix_i
30 - 35	14	32.5	455
35 - 40	16	37.5	600
40 - 45	28	42.5	1190
45 - 50	23	47.5	1092.5
50 - 55	18	52.5	945
55 - 60	8	57.5	460
60 - 65	3	62.5	187.5
	$\Sigma f_i = 110$		$\Sigma f_ix_i = 4930$

(2 Marks)

$$\text{Mean} = \frac{\sum f_i x_i}{\sum f_i}$$

$$= \frac{4930}{110}$$

$= 44.81$ **(1 Mark)**

13.

C.I.	f_i	Mid-value x_i	$u_i = \frac{x_i - A}{h}$	$f_i u_i$
0 – 10	7	5	– 4	– 28
10 – 20	10	15	– 3	– 30
20 – 30	x	25	– 2	– 2x
30 – 40	13	35	– 1	– 13
40 – 50	y	45 (A)	0	0
50 – 60	10	55	1	10
60 – 70	14	65	2	28
70 – 80	9	75	3	27
	100			$-6-2x$

(1 Mark)

$$\text{Mean} = A + \frac{\Sigma f_i \mu_i}{\Sigma fi} \times h$$

$$42 = 45 + \frac{-6-2x}{100} \times 10$$

$$-3 = \frac{-6-2x}{10}$$

$-30 = -6 - 2x$

$2x = 30 - 6 = 24$

$x = 12.$ **(1 Mark)**

Now, $\Sigma f_i = 100$ given

$\Rightarrow 63 + x + y = 100$

$\Rightarrow 63 + 12 + y = 100$

$\Rightarrow y = 100 - 75 = 25.$ **(1 Mark)**

14. Calculation of Arithmetic Mean

x_i	f_i	f_ix_i
4	5	20
6	10	60
9	10	90
10	7	70
15	8	120
	$N = \Sigma f_i = 40$	$\Sigma f_ix_i = 360$

(2 Marks)

$\therefore$ Mean $\overline{X} = \frac{\sum f_i x_i}{\sum f_i} = \frac{360}{40} = 9$ **(1 Mark)**

15. Calculation of Mean

x_i	f_i	f_ix_i
2	3	6
4	2	8
6	3	18
10	1	10
p + 5	2	2 p + 10
	$N = \Sigma f_i = 11$	$\Sigma f_ix_i = 2p + 52$

(1 Mark)

where, $N = \Sigma f_i = 11$, $\Sigma f_ix_i = 2p + 52$ **(1 Mark)**

$\therefore$ Mean $= \frac{\sum f_i x_i}{N}$

$\Rightarrow 6 = \frac{2p+52}{11} \Rightarrow 66 = 2p + 52$

$\Rightarrow 2p = 14 \Rightarrow p = 7$ **(1 Mark)**

16. Calculation of Arithmetic Mean

Weight (in kg) x_i	Frequency f_i	f_ix_i
67	4	268
70	3	210
72	2	144
73	2	146
75	1	75
	$N = \Sigma f_i = 12$	$\Sigma f_ix_i = 843$

(1 Mark)

$\therefore$ Mean $= \overline{X} = \frac{\sum f_i x_i}{N} = \frac{843}{12} = 70.25$ kg **(1 Mark)**

When each observation is multiply by some constant then mean is also multiply by that constant.

17.

Class-interval	11–13	13–15	15–17	17–19	19–21	21–23	23–25	Total
Class-Mark (x_i)	12	14	16	18	20	22	24	
Frequency (f_i)	3	6	9	13	f	5	4	40 + f
$x_i f_i$	36	84	144	234	20f	110	96	704 + 20f

(2 Marks)

$$\text{Mean} = \frac{\Sigma x_i f_i}{\Sigma f_i}$$ **(1 Mark)**

$$18 = \frac{704 + 20f}{40 + f}$$ **(1 Mark)**

18(40 + f) = 704 + 20f

720 + 18f = 704 + 20f

720 – 704 = 20f – 18f

16 = 2f

$$f = \frac{16}{2} = 8$$ **(1 Mark)**

18.

Class	Frequency	x_i	$f_i x_i$
11 - 13	3	12	36
13 - 15	6	14	84
15 - 17	9	16	144
17 - 19	13	18	234
19 - 21	f	20	20f
21 - 23	5	22	110
23 - 25	4	24	96
	40 + f = Σ f		$\Sigma f_i x_i$ = 704 + 20 f

(2 Marks)

Mean = 18 [Given]

$\Rightarrow \frac{\Sigma f_i x_i}{\Sigma f} = 18$

$\Rightarrow \frac{704 + 20f}{40 + f} = 18$ **(1 Mark)**

$\Rightarrow$ 704 + 20 f = 720 + 18 f

$\Rightarrow$ 2f = 16

$\Rightarrow f = \frac{16}{2} = 8$

∴ The value of f = 8 **(1 Mark)**

Topic-2: *Mode of Grouped Data*

1. **(d)** 150 **(1 Mark)**

2. Writing the data as discrete frequency distribution, we get

x_i	13	15	17	18	20	λ	25
f_i	1	3	1	3	3	1	3

For 20 to be mode of the frequency distribution, λ = 20. **(1 Mark)**

3. Given, mode = 55

Then, the modal class in the given class interval is 45–60.

Here, $l = 45, f_1 = 45, f_0 = x, f_2 = 10, h = 15$

$$\text{Mode} = l + \frac{f_1 - f_0}{2f_1 - f_0 - f_2} \times h$$ **(1 Mark)**

$$55 = 45 + \frac{15 - x}{(2 \times 15 - x - 10)} \times 15$$

$$10 = \frac{15(15 - x)}{(30 - x - 10)}$$

$$\frac{2}{3} = \frac{(15 - x)}{(20 - x)}$$

40 – 2x = 45 – 3x

$\boxed{x = 5}$

Therefore, the value of x is 5. **(1 Mark)**

4. Maximum frequency = 17

∴ Model class = 12 – 16

∴ $L = 12, F_0 = 9, F_1 = 17, F_2 = 12$ and h = 4

$$\text{Mode} = L + \frac{F_1 - F_0}{2F_1 - F_0 - F_2} \times h$$ **(1 Mark)**

$$= 12 + \frac{17 - 9}{2 \times 17 - 12 - 9} \times 4$$

$$= 12 + \frac{32}{34 - 21} = 12 + \frac{32}{13}$$

= 12 + 2.46 = 14.46 **(1 Mark)**

5. Maximum frequency = 12

∴ Modal class is 60 – 80.

∴ $L = 60, h = 20, f_0 = 10, f_1 = 12$ and $f_2 = 6$.

$$\text{Mode} = L + \frac{f_1 - f_0}{2f_1 - f_0 - f_2} \times h$$ **(1 Mark)**

$$= 60 + \frac{12 - 10}{24 - 10 - 6} \times 20 = 60 + \frac{2}{8} \times 20$$

= 60 + 5 = 65 **(1 Mark)**

6.

Class Interval	Frequency
25 – 30	25
30 – 35	34(f_0)
35 – 40	50(f_1)
40 – 45	42(f_2)
45 – 50	38
50 – 55	14

Here, the maximum frequency is 50. **(1 Mark)**

So, 35 – 40 will be the modal class.

$l = 35, f_0 = 34, f_1 = 50, f_2 = 42$ and h = 5

$$\text{Mode} = l + \left(\frac{f_1 - f_0}{2f_1 - f_0 - f_2}\right) \times h$$ **(1 Mark)**

$$= 35 + \left(\frac{50-34}{2 \times 50 - 34 - 42}\right) \times 5 \quad = 35 + \left(\frac{16}{100-76}\right) \times 5$$

$$= 35 + \frac{16}{24} \times 5 \quad = 35 + \frac{80}{24} \quad = 35 + 3.33$$

$= 38.33$ **(1 Mark)**

7.

Class	0–10	10–20	20–30	30–40	40–50	50–60	60–70
Frequency	8	10	10	16	12	6	7

Here, the maximum class frequency is 16, and the class corresponding to this frequency is 30 – 40.

So, the modal class is 30 – 40.

Now, modal class = 30 - 40, lower limit (l) of modal class = 30, class size (h) = 40 – 30 = 10.

frequency (f_1) of the modal class = 16. **(1 Mark)**

frequency (f_0) of the class preceding the modal class = 10

frequency (f_2) of the class succeding the modal class = 12

Since, $\text{Mode} = l + \left(\frac{f_1 - f_0}{2f_1 - f_0 - f_2}\right) \times h$ **(1 Mark)**

$$= 30 + \left(\frac{16-10}{2 \times 16 - 10 - 12}\right) \times 10$$

$= 30 + \left(\frac{6}{10}\right) \times 10 = 36.$ **(1 Mark)**

Therefore, the mode of the given frequency distribution is 36.

8. Modal class is 30 – 35, $l = 30$, $f_1 = 25$, $f_0 = 10$, $f_2 = 7$, $h = 5$

$\text{Mode} = l + \left(\frac{f_1 - f_0}{2f_1 - f_0 - f_2}\right) \times h$ **(1 Mark)**

$\Rightarrow \text{Mode} = 30 + \frac{25-10}{50-10-7} \times 5 = 32.27$ approx.

(1 Mark)

9. Here, maximum frequency = 95,

so Modal class= 11 –13

$l = 11$, $f_1 = 95$, $f_0 = 41$, $f_2 = 36$, $h = 2$

$\text{Mode} = l + \left(\frac{f_1 - f_0}{2f_1 - f_0 - f_2}\right) \times h$ **(½ Mark)**

$$= 11 + \left(\frac{95-41}{190-41-36}\right) \times 2$$

$$= 11 + \frac{54}{113} \times 2$$

$\therefore$ Mode = 11 + 0.95 = 11.95 **(½ Mark)**

Now, let us calculate Mean :

C.I.	f_i	Mid-value x_i	$u_i = \frac{x_i - A}{h}$	$f_i u_i$
0 – 10	7	5	– 4	– 28
10 – 20	10	15	– 3	– 30
20 – 30	x	25	– 2	– 2x
30 – 40	13	35	– 1	– 13
40 – 50	y	45 (A)	0	0
50 – 60	10	55	1	10
60 – 70	14	65	2	28
70 – 80	9	75	3	27
	100			– 6 – 2x

$\text{Mean} = \frac{3198}{300} = 10.66$ **(2 Marks)**

10. The class interval has to be made continuous and overlapping 37 – 36 = 1, 43 – 42 = 1 and so on. So, we subtract 0.5 in the lower limit and add 0.5 to the upper limit of each class interval and make the class continuous as 31 – 0.5 = 30.5, 36 + 0.5 = 36.5 and so on. So, classes are 30.5 to 36.5, 36.5 to 42.5, 42.5 to 48.5, etc. We draw the table with continuous class and find the modal class.

Daily wages	No. of workers
30.5–36.5	6
36.5–42.5	12
42.5–48.5	20
48.5–54.5	15
54.5–60.5	9
60.5–66.5	4

(1 Mark)

Modal class is 42.5 – 48.5 and mode lies in this class which is given by formula,

$\text{Mode} = \ell + \left(\frac{f_1 - f_0}{2f_1 - f_0 - f_2}\right) \times h$ **(1 Mark)**

Here, $\ell = 42.5$, $f_1 = 20$, $f_0 = 12$, $f_2 = 15$, $h = 6$

$$\therefore \text{Mode} = 42.5 + \frac{20-12}{2(20)-12-15} \times 6$$

$\therefore$ Mode = 46.2 **(1 Mark)**

When we have to find mean, median and mode from discontinuous class interval then convert class interval into continuous and overlapping by adding 0.5 in upper limit and subtracting 0.5 in lower limit.

11. Given 'n' = 90, median = 50

Marks obtained	Number of students	Cumulative frequency
20 – 30	p	p
30 – 40	15	p + 15
40 – 50	25	p + 40
50 – 60	20	p + 60
60 – 70	q	p + q + 60
70 – 80	8	p + q + 68
80 – 90	10	p + q + 78
	90	

(1 Mark)

$p + q + 78 = 90$

$p + q = 12$ ... (1)

$$\text{Median} = (l) + \frac{\frac{n}{2} . f}{f} . h$$

$$50 = 50 + \frac{45-(p+40)}{20} . 10$$ **(1 Mark)**

$$\frac{45-(p+40)}{20} . 10 = 0$$

$45 - (p + 40) = 0$

$P = 5$

From eq (1) $\Rightarrow 5 + q = 12$ **(1 Mark)**

$q = 7$

$$\text{Mode} = l + \frac{f_1 - f_0}{2f_1 - f_0 - f_2} . h = 40 + \frac{25-25}{2(25)-15-20} . 10$$

$$= 40 + \frac{100}{15} = 40 + 6.67 = 46.67$$ **(1 Mark)**

12. (i) The total number of apples are 250

$20 + 60 + 70 + x + 60 = 250$

$x = 250 - 210$

$x = 40$ **(1½ Marks)**

Mass in grams	Number of apples (f_i)	Mid value (x_i)	$f_i \cdot x_i$
80–100	20	90	1800
100–120	60	110	6600
120–140	70	130	9100
140–160	40	150	6000
160–180	60	170	10200
	$\sum f_i = 250$		$\sum f_i x_i = 33700$

$$\bar{x} = \frac{\sum x_i f_i}{\sum fi} = \frac{33700}{250} = 134.8 \text{gm}$$ **(1½ Marks)**

(ii) Modal mass is calculated as

$$\text{Mode} = \ell + \left(\frac{f_i - f_0}{2f_i - f_0 - f_2}\right) \times h$$

Where ℓ = lower limit of modal class

f_i = frequency of modal class

f_0 = frequency of class precedding two modal

f_2 = frequency of class succeeding the modal

h = class size

From the table it is clear that highest frequency is to 60. the modal class is 120 – 140

$\ell = 120, f_i = 70, f_0 = 60, f_2 = 40, h = 20$ **(1 Mark)**

Modal mass of mode

$$= 120 + \left(\frac{70-60}{(2\times 70)-60-40}\right) \times 20$$

$$= 120 + \frac{200}{140-100}$$

$$= 120 + \frac{200}{40} = 125$$ **(1 Mark)**

Modal mass of apples = 125 gm

13.

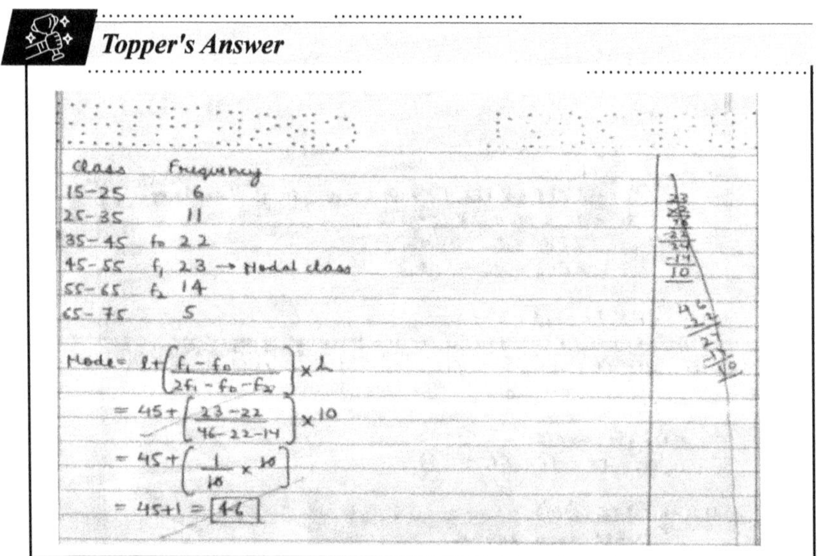

Topper's Answer

Class	Frequency
15-25	6
25-35	11
35-45	f_0 22
45-55	f_1 23 → Modal class
55-65	f_2 14
65-75	5

Mode = $l + \left(\frac{f_1 - f_0}{2f_1 - f_0 - f_2}\right) \times h$

$= 45 + \left(\frac{23-22}{46-22-14}\right) \times 10$

$= 45 + \left(\frac{1}{10} \times 10\right)$

$= 45 + 1 = \boxed{46}$

14.

Class	fi	xi	$u_i = \frac{x_i - 37.5}{5}$	fi ui
15–20	3	17.5	– 4	–12
20–25	8	22.5	– 3	–24
25–30	9	27.5	– 2	–18
30–35	10	32.5	– 1	–10
35–40	3	37.5	0	0
40–45	0	42.5	1	0
45–50	0	47.5	2	0
50–55	2	52.5	3	6
		Σfi = 35	**Σfiui = –58**	

(2 Marks)

a = 37.5, h = 5

$$\bar{x} = a + \frac{\Sigma f_i u_i}{\Sigma f_i} \times h = 37.5 + \frac{(-58)}{35} \times 5 = 29.2$$

Now, $\ell = 30$, h = 5, $f_1 = 10$, $f_0 = 9$, $f_2 = 3$

$$\text{Mode} = \ell + \left(\frac{f_1 - f_0}{2f_1 - f_0 - f_2}\right) \times h$$

$$= 30 + \frac{(10-9)}{2 \times 10 - 9 - 3} \times 5 = 30 + \left(\frac{1}{20-12}\right) \times 5$$

= 30.62 **(1 Mark)**

Mode = 30.62 and Mean = 29.2

Most states/U.T. have a student-teacher ratio of 30.62, on an average this ratio is 29.2. **(1 Mark)**

15.

Age (in years)	Number of patients (f_i)	Mid-values (x_i)	$f_i x_i$
5–15	6	10	60
15–25	11	20	220
25–35	21	30	630
35–45	23	40	920
45–55	14	50	700
55–65	5	60	300
Total	80		2830

$$\text{Mean} = \frac{\Sigma f_i x_i}{\Sigma f_i} = \frac{2830}{80} = 35.37 \text{ years.}$$ **(2 Marks)**

Here, maximum class frequency is 23, and the class corresponding to this frequency is 35 – 45. So, the modal class is 35 – 45.

Now, $\ell = 35$, h = 10, $f_1 = 23$, $f_0 = 21$, $f_2 = 14$

∴ Mode

$$= \ell + \left(\frac{f_1 - f_0}{2f_1 - f_0 - f_2}\right) \times h = 35 + \left(\frac{20}{46-35}\right)$$

= 36.8 year. **(1 Mark)**

Mode = 36.8 years, Mean = 35.37 years. Maximum number of patients admitted in the hospital are of the age 36.8 years (approx.), while on an average the age of a patient admitted to the hospital is 35.37 years. **(1 Mark)**

16. Since mode is 65, the modal class should be 60 – 80. We have,

$\ell = 60$, h = 20, f_m modal = 12, $f_o = f_1$ (Preceeding) and $f_2 = 6$. **(1 Mark)**

$$\text{mode} = l + \frac{f_m - f_o}{2f_m - f_o - f_2} \times h$$ **(1 Mark)**

$$65 = 60 + \left(\frac{12 - f_1}{2 \times 12 - f_1 - 6}\right) \times 20$$

$$5 = \left(\frac{12 - f_1}{24 - f_1 - 6}\right) \times 20$$

$$5 = \frac{(12 - f_1) \times 20}{18 - f_1}$$

$5(18 - f_1) = (12 - f_1) \times 20$

$18 - f_1 = 4(12 - f_1)$

$18 - f_1 = 48 - 4f_1$

$18 - 48 = -4f_1 + f_1$

$-30 = -3f_1$

$f_1 = 10$ **(1 Mark)**

Hence the value of f_1 is 10.

Since mode is 65 i.e., on an average a player is making 65 runs, we can say that players are good.

Playing outdoor games is certainly better than watching T.V.

For good health, playing games is very useful. **(1 Mark)**

Topic-3: Median of Grouped Data

1. **(b)** Mode = 3(median) – 2(mean)

$\Rightarrow$ Mode = 3(15) – 2(12)

= 45 – 24 = 21 **(1 Mark)**

2. **(b)** lower limit of modal class = 15

lower limit of medain class = 10

Total = 25 **(1 Mark)**

3. **(b)** 12 **(1 Mark)**

4. **(b)** 25 **(1 Mark)**

5. **(a)** **(1 Mark)**

6. $\text{Mean} = \dfrac{\Sigma f(x)}{\Sigma f}$

$\Rightarrow 50 = \dfrac{\Sigma f(x)}{100}$

$\Rightarrow \Sigma f(x) = 5000$ ...(i) **(½ Mark)**

Correct, $\Sigma f(x) = 5000 - 100 + 110$

$= 5010$

$\therefore$ Correct Mean $\dfrac{5010}{100}$

$= 50.1$

Median will remain same i.e., median = 52 **(½ Mark)**

Note

Since middle value (values) of observations is called median therefore when we change any observation except middle value (values) then median will not change.

7.

Class interval	f_i	(C.f)	
130 – 135	4	4	
135 – 140	11	15	→ (C. f)
140 – 145	12	27	→ Median class
145 – 150	7	34	$\frac{N}{2} = \frac{50}{2} = 25$
150 – 155	10	44	
155 – 160	6	50	$l = 140$

(1 Mark)

Apply Median formula,

$$\text{Median} = l + \frac{\left(\frac{N}{2} - \text{C.f}\right)}{f} \times h$$

$$= 140 + \frac{(25-15)}{12} \times 5$$

$$= 140 + \frac{10}{12} \times 5$$

$$= 140 + \frac{25}{6} = 140 + 4.16$$

Median = 144.16 **(1 Mark)**

8.

Salary (in thousands)	No. of Persons	Cumulative Frequency
5-10	49	49
10-15	133	182
15-20	63	245
20-25	15	260
25-30	6	266
30-35	7	273
35-40	4	277
40-45	2	279
45-50	1	280
Total	**280**	

(1 Mark)

Median class has $\dfrac{280}{2}$ or 140th observation

$\therefore$ Medium class is 10 – 15

L = 10, h = 15 – 10 = 5, f = 133, N = 280,

Cf = 49

$\therefore$ Median salary $= L + \frac{h}{f}(N/2 - Cf)$ **(1 Mark)**

$$= 10 + \frac{5}{133}(140 - 49)$$

$$= 10 + \frac{5 \times 91}{133} = 10 + \frac{455}{133}$$

= 10 + 3.4 = 13.4 (approx.) **(1 Mark)**

9. $x_1 = 7 + 5 = 12$ **(1 Mark)**

$x_2 = 18 - x_1 = -5 = 6$

$x_3 = 18 + 5 = 23$ **(1 Mark)**

and $x_4 = x_3 + 5 = 28$ **(1 Mark)**

10.

Class Interval	f	c.f.
0 – 175	10	10
175 – 350	14	24
350 – 525	15	39
525 – 700	21	60
700 – 875	28	88
875 – 1050	7	95
1050 – 1225	5	100

(1 Mark)

$$\frac{N}{2}=\frac{\Sigma f}{2}=\frac{100}{2}=50$$

Median class = 525 – 700

$\therefore$ l = 525, C.F = 39, f = 21, h = 175

$$\text{Median}=1+\frac{\left(\frac{N}{2}-C.F\right)}{f}\times h$$

$$\text{Median}=525+\frac{175}{21}\times[50-39]$$

$= 525 + 91.6$

$= 616.6$ **(1 Mark)**

Here $f_1 = 20$, $f_0 = 21$, $f_2 = 7$

$$\text{Mode } L+\left(\frac{f_1-f_0}{2f_1-f_0-f_2}\right)$$

$$700+\left(\frac{28-21}{2\times 28-21-7}\right)\times 175$$

$$700+\frac{7}{28}\times 175$$

$= 700 + 43.75$

$= 743.75$ **(1 Mark)**

11. Let us write the cumulative frequency distribution table from the given data as below:

Class	Frequency	Cumulative Frequency
0 – 10	8	8
10 – 20	20	28
20 – 30	36	64
30 – 40	24	88
40 – 50	12	100
Total	**100**	

(1 Mark)

$$50=\frac{n}{2}$$

We have n = 100 (the total number of the entries). Then $\frac{n}{2} = 50$ is greater than 28 but less than 64 in the column of cumulative frequency in the above table. Therefore, 20 - 30 is the median class of the data. We have l = 20, n = 100, f = 36 cf = 28 and h = 10.

$$\text{Median} = l+\left\{\frac{\frac{n}{2}-cf}{f}\right\}\times h$$ **(1 Mark)**

$$=20+\left\{\frac{50-28}{36}\right\}\times 10$$

$$=20+\frac{55}{9}$$

$= 20 + 6.11 = 26.11$ **(1 Mark)**

Median divides observations into two equal parts

12.

Class	f	c.f.
0 – 10	5	5
10 – 20	x	x + 5
20 – 30	20	x + 25
30 – 40	15	x + 40
40 – 50	y	x + y + 40
50 – 60	5	x + y + 45
	Σ f = 60	

(1 Mark)

$\therefore$ 45 + x + y = 60

x + y = 15 ....(i)

Now, given that median is 28.5 which is lies in interval 20–30. So, median class is 20–30.

$\therefore$ l = 20, N = 60, c.f = 5 + x, f = 20 and h = 10

$$\text{Median} = l+\frac{\left(\frac{N}{2}-c.f.\right)}{f}\times h$$ **(1 Mark)**

$$28.5 = 20+\frac{[30-(5+x)]}{20}\times 10$$

$8.5 = \frac{30-5-x}{2}$

$17 = 25 - x$

$x = 25 - 17 = 8$

Putting value of x in eqn. (i), we get

$8 + y = 15 \Rightarrow y = 7.$

Hence, x = 8, y = 7. **(1 Mark)**

13.

Exp (₹)	Family	Cf	m_i	$m_i x_i$
1000 – 1500	24	24	1250	30, 000
1500 – 2000	40	64	1750	70, 000
2000 – 2500	33	97	2250	74, 250
2500 – 3000	x = 28	25	2750	77, 000
3000 – 3500	30	155	3250	97500
3500 – 4000	22	177	3750	82500
4000 – 4500	16	193	4250	68000
4500 – 5000	7	200	N 4750	33250
	200			**Total 532,500**

(2 Marks)

$200 = 172 + x$

$\boxed{x = 28}$; $\frac{N}{2} = \frac{200}{2} = 100$

l = lower limit = 2500; h = 500; cf = 97; f = 28

$$\text{Median} = l + \frac{\frac{N}{2} - Cf}{f} \times h = 2500 + \frac{100-97}{28} \times 500$$

(1 Mark)

$$\text{Median} = 2500 + \frac{1500}{28} = 2553.57$$

$$\text{Mean} = \frac{\sum f_i x_i}{\sum f_i} = \frac{532500}{200} = ₹\ 2662.5$$ **(1 Mark)**

14. Median = 525, so Median Class = 500 – 600 **(½ Mark)**

Class interval	Frequency	Cumulative Frequency
0-100	2	2
100-200	5	7
200-300	x	7 + x
300-400	12	19 + x
400-500	17	36 + x
500-600	20	56 + x
600-700	y	56 + x + y
700-800	9	65 + x + y
800-900	7	72 + x + y
900-1000	4	76 + x + y

(1½ Marks)

$76 + x + y = 100 \Rightarrow x + y = 24$ ....(i)

(1 Mark)

$$\text{Median} = l + \frac{\frac{n}{2} - cf}{f} \times h$$ **(½ Mark)**

Since, l = 500, h = 100, f = 20, cf = 36 + x and n = 100

Therefore, putting the value in the Median formula, we get;

$$525 = 200 + \frac{50-(36+x)}{20} \times 100$$ **(½ Mark)**

so x = 9

y = 24 – x (from eq.i)

y = 24 – 9 = 15

Therefore, the value of x = 9 **(½ Mark)**

and y = 15. **(½ Mark)**

15.

Class	Frequency (f_i)	c.f.
0–100	2	2
100–200	5	7
200–300	x	7 + x
300–400	12	19 + x
400–500	17	36 + x
500–600	20	56 + x
600–700	y	56 + x + y
700–800	9	85 + x + y
800–900	7	72 + x + y
900–1000	4	76 + x + y = N

(1 Mark)

Here, Total frequency (N) = 100

$\Rightarrow\ 76 + x + y = 100$

$x + y = 24$

Median = 525 lies in class 500–600

$\therefore$ Median class = 500 – 600

L = 500, h = 100

f = 20 **(1 Mark)**

Previous c.f. = 36 + x

$$\text{Median} = L + \left[\frac{\frac{N}{2} - \text{c.f.}}{f}\right] \times h$$

$$\Rightarrow \quad 525 = 500 + \left[\frac{50 - 36 - x}{20}\right] \times 100$$

$\Rightarrow \quad 25 = (14 - x)5$

$\Rightarrow \quad 14 - x = 5$

$\Rightarrow \quad x = 9$ **(1 Mark)**

Now, from (i)

$9 + y = 24$

$y = 15$ **(1 Mark)**

16.

Class	0–10	10–20	20–30	30–40	40–50	50–60	60–70
Frequency	f_1	5	9	12	f_2	3	2
Cumulative frequency	f_1	$f_1 + 5$	$f_1 + 14$	$f_1 + 26$	$f_1 + f_2 + 26$	$f_1 + f_2 + 29$	$f_1 + f_2 + 31$

(1 Mark)

It is given that total frequency n = 40

So, $f_1 + f_2 + 31 = 40 \Rightarrow f_1 + f_2 = 9$ ....(1) **(1 Mark)**

The median is 32.5, which lies in the class 30–40

$\therefore \ \ell = 30, f = 12, cf = f_1 + 14, h = 40 - 30 = 10$

$$\text{Now, median} = \ell + \left(\frac{\frac{n}{2} - cf}{f}\right)h$$

$$\Rightarrow 32.5 = 30 + \left(\frac{\frac{40}{2} - (f_1 + 14)}{12}\right) \times 10$$

$$\Rightarrow \ 2.5 = \frac{20 - f_1 - 14}{12} \times 10 \ \Rightarrow \ 2.5 \times 6 = 5(6 - f_1)$$

$\Rightarrow 15 = 30 - 5f_1 \Rightarrow 5f_1 = 15 \Rightarrow f_1 = 3$ **(1 Mark)**

Now, from equation (1),

$f_1 + f_2 = 9$ or, $3 + f_2 = 9 \Rightarrow f_2 = 6$ **(1 Mark)**

Therefore, the values of f_1 and f_2 are 3 and 6 respectively.

17.

C.I	fi	c.f
0-10	8	5
10-20	12	17
20-30	f_1	$17 + f_1$
30-40	f_2	$17 + f_1 + f_2$
40-50	15	$32 + f_1 + f_2$
50-60	11	$43 + f_1 + f_2$
60-70	14	$57 + f_1 + f_2$

(1 Mark)

$$\sum fi = 57 + f_1 + f_2$$

Given that median is 36

$\therefore$ Median class is 30 – 40

$\therefore$ L = 30, C.F = $17 + f_1$, f = f_2, h = 10 **(1 Mark)**

$$\text{Median} = L + \frac{\frac{N}{2} - C.F.}{f} \times h$$

$$36 = 30 + \frac{50 - 17 - f_1}{f_2} \times 10 \quad 6 = \frac{33 - f_1}{f_2} \times 10$$

$6f_2 = 330 - 10 f_1$ ...(i)

$57 + f_1 + f_2 = 100$ [given]

$f_2 = 43 - f_1$ **(1 Mark)**

Putting in (i)

$258 - 6 f_1 = 330 - 10 f_1$

$4f_1 = 72$

$f_1 = 18$

$f_2 = 43 - 18 = 25$ **(1 Mark)**

18.

Height	**Frequency**	**c.f.**
100 – 120	12	12
120 –140	14	26
140 – 160	8	34
160 – 180	6	40
180 – 200	10	50
Total	**50**	

(1 Mark)

Here, $N = 50 \Rightarrow \frac{N}{2} = \frac{50}{2} = 25$ **(1 Mark)**

So, Median Class = 120 – 140

Here, l = 120, h = 20, c.f. = 12, f = 14 **(1 Mark)**

$$\text{Median} = l + \left(\frac{\frac{N}{2} - c.f.}{f}\right) \times h$$

$$= 120 + \left(\frac{25-12}{14}\right) \times 20$$

$$= 120 + \frac{260}{14} = 120 + 18.57$$

Median = 138.57 **(1 Mark)**

Chapter 14 Probability

Topic-1: A Theoretical Approach

1 Multiple Choice Questions

1. 2 cards of hearts and 4 cards of spades are missing from a pack of 52 cards. A card is drawn at random from the remaining pack. What is the probability of getting a black card? **[CBSE Sample Paper 2023-24, Ap]**

(a) $\frac{22}{52}$ (b) $\frac{22}{46}$

(c) $\frac{24}{52}$ (d) $\frac{24}{46}$

2. A bag contains 5 pink, 8 blue and 7 yellow balls. One ball is drawn at random from the bag. What is the probability of getting neither a blue nor a pink ball? **[All India 2023 Set-II, K]**

(a) $\frac{1}{4}$ (b) $\frac{2}{5}$

(c) $\frac{7}{20}$ (d) $\frac{13}{20}$

3. A card is drawn at random from a well shuffled deck of 52 playing cards. The probability of getting a face card is **[All India 2023 Set-II, K]**

(a) $\frac{1}{2}$ (b) $\frac{3}{13}$

(c) $\frac{4}{13}$ (d) $\frac{1}{13}$

4. Which of the following numbers cannot be the probability of happening of an event: **[All India 2023, A]**

(a) 0 (b) $\frac{7}{0\cdot01}$

(c) 0.07 (d) $\frac{0\cdot07}{3}$

5. Two dice are rolled together. What is the probability of getting a sum greater than 10? **[All India 2023, K]**

(a) $\frac{1}{9}$ (b) $\frac{1}{6}$

(c) $\frac{1}{12}$ (d) $\frac{5}{18}$

6. A card is drawn at random from a well-shuffled pack of 52 cards. The probability that the card drawn is not an ace is: **[Delhi 2023, A]**

(a) $\frac{1}{13}$ (b) $\frac{9}{13}$

(c) $\frac{4}{13}$ (d) $\frac{12}{13}$

7. A bag contains 5 red balls and n green balls. If the probability of drawing a green ball is three times that of a red ball, then the value of *n* is: **[Delhi 2023, A]**

(a) 18 (b) 15

(c) 10 (d) 20

8. Two dice are rolled simultaneously. What is the probability that 6 will come up at least once? **[CBSE Sample Paper 2022-23, Ap]**

(a) 1/6 (b) 7/36

(c) 11/36 (d) 13/36

9. For an event E, $P(E)+P(\bar{E})=x$, then the value of x^3-3 is **[All India 2022, Term-I, A]**

(a) –2 (b) 2

(c) 1 (d) –1

10. The probability that the drawn card from a pack of 52 cards is neither an ace nor a spade is **[All India 2022, Term-I, A]**

(a) $\frac{9}{13}$ (b) $\frac{35}{52}$

(c) $\frac{10}{13}$ (d) $\frac{19}{26}$

11. Which of the following cannot be the probability of an event ? **[All India 2022, Term-I, K]**

(a) 0.01 (b) 3%

(c) $\frac{16}{17}$ (d) $\frac{17}{16}$

12. The diameter of a car wheel is 42 cm. The number of complete revolutions it will make in moving 132 km is **[All India 2022, Term-I, K]**

(a) 10^4 (b) 10^5

(c) 10^6 (d) 10^3

13. A dice is rolled twice. The probability that 5 will not come up either time is **[All India 2022, Term-I, A]**

(a) $\frac{11}{36}$ (b) $\frac{1}{3}$

(c) $\frac{13}{36}$ (d) $\frac{25}{36}$

14. Two fair coins are tossed. What is the probability of getting at the most one head?

[CBSE Sample Paper 2021-22, Term-I, Ap]

(a) $\frac{3}{4}$ (b) $\frac{1}{4}$

(c) $\frac{1}{2}$ (d) $\frac{3}{8}$

15. A letter of English alphabets is chosen at random. What is the probability that it is a letter of the word **'MATHEMATICS'**?

[CBSE Sample Paper 2021-22, Term-I, U]

(a) $\frac{4}{13}$ (b) $\frac{9}{26}$

(c) $\frac{}{13}$ (d) $\frac{11}{26}$

16. A card is drawn from a well shuffled deck of cards. What is the probability that the card drawn is neither a king nor a queen? **[CBSE Sample Paper 2021-22, Term-I, U]**

(a) $\frac{11}{13}$ (b) $\frac{12}{13}$

(c) $\frac{11}{26}$ (d) $\frac{11}{52}$

17. Two fair dice are rolled simultaneously. The probability that 5 will come up at least once is

[CBSE Sample Paper 2021-22, Term-I, A]

(a) $\frac{5}{36}$ (b) $\frac{11}{36}$

(c) $\frac{12}{36}$ (d) $\frac{23}{36}$

18. If two different dice are rolled together, the probability of getting an even number on both dice, is :

[Delhi 2014, Term-II, Ap]

(a) $\frac{1}{36}$ (b) $\frac{1}{2}$

(c) $\frac{1}{6}$ (d) $\frac{1}{4}$

19. A number is selected a random from the numbers 1 to 30. The probability that it is a prime number is :

[Delhi 2014, Term-II, A]

(a) $\frac{2}{3}$ (b) $\frac{1}{6}$

(c) $\frac{1}{3}$ (d) $\frac{11}{30}$

20. The probability of getting an even number, when a die is thrown once, is : **[All India 2013, Ap]**

(a) $\frac{1}{2}$ (b) $\frac{1}{3}$

(c) $\frac{1}{6}$ (d) $\frac{5}{6}$

21. A box contains 90 discs, numbered from 1 to 90. If one disc is drawn at random from the box, the probability that it bears a prime-number less than 23, is :

[All India 2013, Ap]

(a) $\frac{7}{90}$ (b) $\frac{10}{90}$

(c) $\frac{4}{45}$ (d) $\frac{9}{89}$

2 *Assertion Reason/Two Statement Type Question*

22. **Assertion (A) :** The probability that a leap year has 53 Sundays is $\frac{2}{7}$.

Reason (R) : The probability that a non-leap year has 53 Sundays is $\frac{5}{7}$. **[Delhi 2023, A]**

(a) Both Assertion (A) and Reason (R) are true and Reason (R) is the correct explanation of Assertion (A).

(b) Both Assertion (A) and Reason (R) are true and Reason (R) is not the correct explanation of Assertion (A).

(c) Assertion (A) is true but Reason (R) is false.

(d) Assertion (A) is false but Reason (R) is true.

4 *Very Short Answer Questions (1 Mark)*

23. If a fair coin is tossed twice, find the probability of getting 'atmost one head'. **[Delhi 2023, K]**

24. If a number x is chosen at random from the numbers $-3, -2, -1, 0, 1, 2, 3$, then find the probability of $x^2 < 4$.

[All India 2020, K]

25. What is the probability that a randomly taken leap year has 52 Sundays? **[All India 2020, A]**

26. A die is thrown once. What is the probability of getting a prime number. **[All India 2020, An]**

27. A letter of English alphabet is chosen at random. What is the probability that the chosen letter is a consonant. **[Delhi 2020, An]**

28. A die is thrown once. What is the probability of getting a number less than 3? **[Delhi 2020, An]**

29. If the probability of winning a game is 0.07, what is the probability of losing it? **[Delhi 2020, A]**

30. The probability of selecting a rotten apple randomly from a heap of 900 apples is 0.18. What is the number of rotten apples in the heap ? **[All India 2017, Term-II, K]**

31. Cards marked with number 3, 4, 5, ..., 50 are placed in a box and mixed thoroughly. A card is drawn at random from the box. Find the probability that the selected card bears a perfect square number. **[Delhi 2016, Term-II, U]**

5 *Short Answer Questions (2 or 3 Marks)*

32. Two coins are tossed simultaneously. What is the probability of getting **[CBSE Sample Paper 2022-23, A]**
(i) At least one head?
(ii) At most one tail?
(iii) head and a tail?

33. Jenin has four 50-rupee notes, seven 100-rupee notes and two 2000-rupee notes in her purse. She doesn't have any other denomination of currency with her. She goes for shopping and buys a skirt for Rs 799. She takes out a note from her purse at random. **(CBSE CFPQ 2022, A)**
(i) Find the probability that the note will be sufficient to pay for the dress.
(ii) Find the probability that she will be able to give exactly Rs 799 to the shopkeeper.
Show your work.

34. Farah and Sheena are playing a game with number tokens. Each of them has four number tokens, 2, 3, 4 and 5. A token is randomly picked by each of them from their stack simultaneously. If the sum of the numbers picked by each of them is a prime number, Farah wins the game and if it is a composite number, then Sheena wins the game.
Find the probability of each of them winning the game and state who has a higher probability of winning the game. Show your work.
(ii) Writes that the probability that jenin will be able to give exactly Rs 799 to the shopkeeper is 0.
(CBSE CFPQ 2022, A)

35. A child has a die whose six faces show the letters as shown below : **[All India 2020, A]**

A	B	C	D	E	A

The die is thrown once. What is the probability of getting (i) A, (ii) D ?

36. If a number x is chosen at random from the numbers $-3, -2, -1, 0, 1, 2, 3$. What is probability that $x^2 \leq 4$? **[Delhi 2020, K]**

37. A die is thrown once. Find the probability of getting (i) a composite number, (ii) a prime number. **[All India 2019, K]**

38. The probability of selecting a blue marble at random from a jar that contains only blue, black and green marbles is $\frac{1}{5}$. The probability of selecting a black marble at random from the same jar is $\frac{1}{4}$. If the jar contains 11 green marbles, find the total number of marbles in the jar. **[All India 2019, K]**

39. A game consists of tossing a coin 3 times and noting the outcome each time. If getting the same result in all the tosses is a success, find the probability of losing the game. **[Delhi 2019, U]**

40. A die is thrown once. Find the probability of getting a number which (i) is a prime number (ii) lies between 2 and 6. **[Delhi 2019, U]**

41. Two different dice are tossed together. Find the probability:
(i) of getting a doublet
(ii) of getting a sum 10, of the numbers on the two dice. **[All India 2018, K]**

42. An integer is chosen at random between 1 and 100. Find the probability that it is : **[All India 2018, K]**
(i) divisible by 8. (ii) not divisible by 8.

43. A bag contains 15 white and some black balls. If the probability of drawing a black ball from the bag is thrice that of drawing a white ball, find the number of black balls in the bag. **[All India 2017, Term-II, A]**

44. In a single throw of a pair of different dice, what is the probability of getting (i) a prime number on each die? (ii) a total of 9 or 11 ? **[Delhi 2016, Term-II, Ap]**

45. The probability of selecting a red ball at random from a jar that contains only red, blue and orange balls is $\frac{1}{4}$. The probability of selecting a blue ball at random from the same jar is $\frac{1}{3}$. If the jar contains 10 orange balls, find the total number of balls in the jar. **[All India 2015, Term-II, A]**

46. Rahim tosses two different coins simultaneously. Find the probability of getting at least one tail. **[Delhi 2014, Term-II, A]**

47. A card is drawn at random from a well shuffled pack of 52 playing cards. Find the probability that the drawn card is neither a king nor a queen. **[All India 2013, A]**

6 *Long Answer Questions (4 or 5 marks)*

48. Two different dice are thrown together. Find the probability that the numbers obtained have **[All India 2017, Term-II, K]**

(i) even sum, and

(ii) even product.

49. A game of chance consists of spinning an arrow on a circular board, divided into 8 equal parts, which comes to rest pointing at one of the numbers 1, 2, 3, ..., 8, which are equally likely outcomes. What is the probability that the arrow will point at (i) an odd number (ii) a number greater than 3 (iii) a number less than 9. **[Delhi 2016, Term-II, A]**

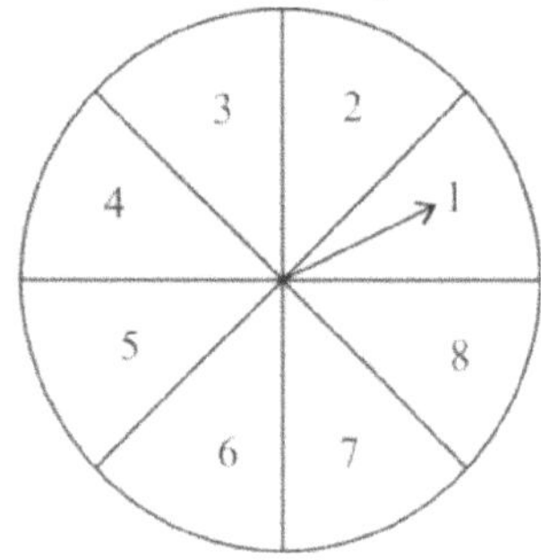

50. A card is drawn at random from a well-shuffled deck of playing cards. Find the probability that the card drawn is **[All India 2015, Term-II, A]**

(i) a card of spade or an ace.

(ii) a black king.

(iii) neither a jack nor a king.

(iv) either a king or a queen.

51. A bag contains cards numbered from 1 to 49. A card is drawn from the bag at random, after mixing the cards thoroughly. Find the probability that the number on the drawn card is : **[Delhi 2014, Term-II, K]**

(i) an odd number (ii) a multiple of 5

(iii) a perfect square (iv) an even prime number

52. A group consists of 12 persons, of which 3 are extremely patient, other 6 are extremely honest and rest are extremely kind. A person from the group is selected at random. Assuming that each person is equally likely to be selected, find the probability of selecting a person who is (i) extremely patient (ii) extremely kind or honest. Which of the above values you prefer more. **[All India 2013, A]**

Case Based Questions (4 marks)

53. "Eight Ball" is a game played on a pool table with 15 balls numbered 1 to 15 and a "cue ball" that is solid and white. Of the 15 numbered balls, eight are solid (non-white) coloured and numbered 1 to 8 and seven are striped balls numbered 9 to 15. **[All India 2023 Set-II, A]**

The 15 numbered pool balls (no cue ball) are placed in a large bowl and mixed, then one ball is drawn out at random. Based on the above information, answer the following questions:

(i) What is the probability that the drawn ball bears number 8 ?

(ii) What is the probability that the drawn ball bears an even number?

OR

What is the probability that the drawn ball bears a number, which is a multiple of 3?

(iii) What is the probability that the drawn ball is a solid coloured and bears an even number?

54. A middle school decided to run the following spinner game as a fund-raiser on Christmas Carnival. **[All India 2023 Set-I, A]**

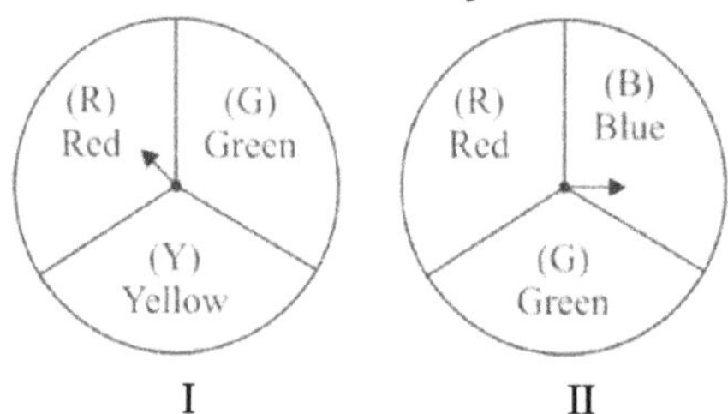

Making Purple : Spin each spinner once. Blue and red make purple. So, if one spinner shows Red (R) and another Blue (B), then you 'win'. One such outcome is written as 'RB'.

Based on the above, answer the following questions:

(i) List all possible outcomes of the game.

(ii) Find the probability of 'Making Purple'.

(iii) (a) For each win, a participant gets ₹10, but if he/she loses, he/she has to pay ₹5 to the school. If 99 participants played, calculate how much fund could the school have collected.

OR

(iii) (b) If the same amount of ₹ 5 has been decided for winning or losing the game, then how much fund had been collected by school? (Number of participants = 99)

Topic-2: Probability Related to Area and Volume

Multiple Choice Question

1. There is a square board of side '2a' units circumscribing a red circle. Jayadev is asked to keep a dot on the above said board. The probability that he keeps the dot on the shaded region is **[CBSE Sample Paper 2023-24, K]**

(a) $\frac{\pi}{4}$ (b) $\frac{4-\pi}{4}$

(c) $\frac{\pi-4}{4}$ (d) $\frac{4}{\pi}$

Hints & Solutions

Topic-1: A Theoretical Approach

1. (b) $\frac{22}{46}$ **(1 Mark)**

2. (c) Probability of getting neither a blue nor a pink ball is the same as probability of getting yellow ball

$$P(\text{Yellow}) = \frac{7}{5+8+7} = \frac{7}{20}$$ **(1 Mark)**

3. (b) There are total 12 face cards (4 Jacks, 4 queens, 4 kings)

$$P(\text{face card}) = \frac{12}{52} = \frac{3}{13}$$ **(1 Mark)**

4. (b) Probability always should be ≤ 1

$\frac{7}{0.01} = 700 > 1$ So, $\frac{7}{0.01}$ is not possible. **(1 Mark)**

Note

If E be any event then $0 \leq P(E) \leq 1$

5. (c) Getting a sum greater than 10 = (5, 6), (6, 5), (6, 6)

$\Rightarrow$ Total cases = 6 × 6 = 36

$$\text{Probability} = \frac{\text{Number of event}}{\text{Total cases}} = \frac{3}{36} = \frac{1}{12}$$ **(1 Mark)**

6. (d) Total ace in well-shuffled pack of cards = 4

Probability that the card drawn is not an acce

$$\Rightarrow \frac{52-4}{52} = \frac{48}{52} = \frac{12}{13}$$ **(1 Mark)**

7. (b) Prob. of green ball = 3 Prob. of red ball.

$$\frac{n}{5+n} = 3 \times \frac{5}{5+n} = n = 15$$ **(1 Mark)**

8. (c) 11/36 **(1 Mark)**

9. (a) Given, $P(E) + P(\bar{E}) = x$

Sum of probabilities is 1.

so, $P(E) + P(\bar{E}) = 1$

$x^3 - 3 = (1)^3 - 3 = 1 - 3 = -2.$ **(1 Mark)**

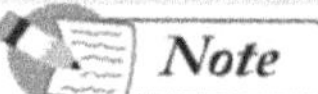

Note

Sum of all probabilities is 1.
Then, $x = 1$.

10. (a) There are total 4 ace and 13 spade in a well shuffled card.

Number of cards other than ace and spade

$= 52 - (4 + 12) = 52 - 16 = 36$

$$\text{Probability } \overline{(\text{ace and spade})} = \frac{36}{52} = \frac{9}{13}$$ **(1 Mark)**

11. (b) Probability of an event cannot be in the percentage and cannot be greater than one. **(1 Mark)**

12. (b) Diameter of car wheel = 42 cm

$$\text{radius} = \frac{42}{2} = 21 \text{ cm.}$$

Let the number of revolutions is n

$n \times 2\pi r = 10^5 \times 132$ cm

$$n \times 2 \times \frac{22}{7} \times 21 = 10^5 \times 132 \Rightarrow n = 10^5$$ **(1 Mark)**

13. (d) Total sample space = $6^2 = 36$

$$S = \begin{cases} (1,1)\ (1,2)\ (1,3)\ (1,4)\ (1,5)\ (1,6) \\ (2,1)\ (2,2)\ (2,3)\ (2,4)\ (2,5)\ (2,6) \\ (3,1)\ (3,2)\ (3,3)\ (3,4)\ (3,5)\ (3,6) \\ (4,1)\ (4,2)\ (4,3)\ (4,4)\ (4,5)\ (4,6) \\ (5,1)\ (5,2)\ (5,3)\ (5,4)\ (5,5)\ (5,6) \\ (6,1)\ (6,2)\ (6,3)\ (6,4)\ (6,5)\ (6,6) \end{cases}$$

$$P(5 \text{ not come either time}) = \frac{25}{36}$$ **(1 Mark)**

14. (a) Possible outcomes are (HH), (HT), (TH), (TT)

Favourable outcomes (at the most one head) are (HT), (TH), (TH), (TT)

So probability of getting at the most one head = $\frac{3}{4}$

(1 Mark)

15. **(a)** Number of possible outcomes are 26

Favourable outcomes are M, A, T, H, E, I, C, S

Probability $= \frac{8}{26} = \frac{4}{13}$ **(1 Mark)**

16. **(a)** Probability that the card drawn is neither a king nor a queen,

$$= \frac{52-8}{52} = \frac{44}{52} = \frac{11}{13}$$

(There are four cards of king and four cards of queen in a deck) **(1 Mark)**

17. **(b)** Outcomes when 5 will come up at least once are-

(1, 5), (2, 5), (3, 5), (4, 5), (5, 5), (6, 5), (5, 1), (5, 2), (5, 3), (5, 4) and (5, 6)

Probability that 5 will come up at least once $= \frac{11}{36}$

(1 Mark)

18. **(d)** Possible outcomes on rolling the two dice are given below.

[(1, 1), (1, 2), (1, 3), (1, 4), (1, 5), (1, 6), (2, 1), (2, 2), (2, 3), (2, 4), (2, 5), (2, 6), (3, 1), (3, 2), (3, 3), (3, 4), (3, 5), (3, 6), (4, 1), (4, 2), (4, 3), (4, 4), (4, 5), (4, 6), (5, 1), (5, 2), (5, 3), (5, 4), (5, 5), (5, 6), (6, 1), (6, 2), (6, 3), (6, 4), (6, 5), (6, 6)]

Total number of outcomes = 36

Favourable outcomes:

[(2, 2), (2, 4), (2, 6), (4, 2), (4, 4), (4, 6), (6, 2), (6, 4), (6, 6)]

Total number of favourable outcomes = 9

∴ Probability of getting an even number on both dice = P(E)

$$P(E) = \frac{\text{Total Number of favourable outcomes}}{\text{Total number of outcomes}}$$

$$= \frac{9}{36} = \frac{1}{4}$$ **(1 Mark)**

19. **(c)** Total number of possible outcomes = 30

Prime numbers between 1 to 30 are:

2, 3, 5, 7, 11, 13, 17, 19, 23 and 29

Total number of favourable outcomes = 10

∴ Probability of selecting a prime number from 1 to 30,

$$P(E) = \frac{\text{Total number of favourable outcomes}}{\text{Total number of outcomes}}$$

$$= \frac{10}{30} = \frac{1}{3}$$ **(1 Mark)**

20. **(a)** Numbers in a die: 1, 2, 3, 4, 5, 6

Total number of possible outcomes = 6

Even number: 2, 4, 6

Number of favourable outcomes = 3

Probability of an event

$$= \frac{\text{Number of favourable outcomes}}{\text{Total number of possible outcomes}}$$

$P(E) = \frac{3}{6} = \frac{1}{2}$ **(1 Mark)**

21. **(c)** Total number of outcomes = 90

Prime number less than 23 = {2, 3, 5, 7, 11, 13, 17, 19}

∴ Number of favourable outcomes = 8

$$P(E) = \frac{\text{Number of favourable outcomes}}{\text{Total number of outcomes}}$$

$P(E) = \frac{8}{90} = \frac{4}{45}$ **(1 Mark)**

22. **(c)** As in leap year 366 days.

in one week = 7 days

$\frac{366}{7}$ = 52 weeks + 2 days, may be Sunday.

So probability $= \frac{2}{7}$

But for reason (R), a non leap year has 365 days = 52 weaks + 1 days

$P = \frac{1}{7}$ Not $\frac{5}{7}$ **(1 Mark)**

23. S = {HH, HT, TH, TT} atmost one head = {HT, TH, TT}]

Prob. of getting atmost one head $\Rightarrow \frac{3}{4}$ **(1 Mark)**

24. Total numbers = 7

$\because \quad x^2 < 4 \Rightarrow -2 < x < 2$

i.e. $x = -1, 0, 1$

$\therefore$ Number of favourable outcomes = 3

$P(x^2 < 4) = \frac{3}{7}$ **(1 Mark)**

25. Total number of days in leap year = 366

So, a leap year with have 52 weeks and other two days can be, (Sun, Mon), (Mon, Tue), (Tue, Wed), (Wed, Thu), (Thu, Fri), (Fri, Sat), (Sat, Sun).

Total outcomes = 7

Number of out comes (Not Sunday) = 5

P(Exactly 52 Sundays) = $\frac{5}{7}$ **(1 Mark)**

26. A die is thrown once

$\therefore$ Number of total outcomes = 6

Prime number = 2, 3, 5

$\therefore$ P(Prime number) = $\frac{3}{6} = \frac{1}{2}$ **(1 Mark)**

27. Total number of English alphabet = 26

Number of consonant = 21

$P = \frac{\text{Number of consonant}}{\text{Number of alphabet}} = \frac{21}{26}$ **(1 Mark)**

28. Total outcomes = 6

Number less than 3 = 1, 2.

Number of favourable outcomes = 2

$P = \frac{2}{6} = \frac{1}{3}$ **(1 Mark)**

29. Probability of winning a game = 0.07

Probability of losing the game = 1 – 0.07 = 0.93

(1 Mark)

30. Probability of an event (E) = $\frac{\text{No. of favourable outcomes}}{\text{Total No. of outcomes}}$

Let K be the number of rotten apples in the heap

$\therefore \quad P(E) = \frac{K}{900}$

Since, P(E) = 0.18

$\therefore \quad 0.18 = \frac{K}{900}$

$\Rightarrow K = 162$

Thus, total rotten apples = 162 **(1 Mark)**

31. Cards: 3, 4, 5 ... 50

$\therefore$ Total number of outcomes = 48

Perfect squares are 4, 9, 16, 25, 36 and 49

$\therefore$ Total number of favourable outcomes = 6

$\text{Probability} = \frac{\text{Number of favourable outcomes}}{\text{Total number of outcomes}}$

$= \frac{6}{48} = \frac{1}{8}$ **(1 Mark)**

32. (i) P (At least one head) = 3/4 **(1 Mark)**

(ii) P(At most one tail) = 3/4 **(1 Mark)**

(iii) P(A head and a tail) = 2/4 = 1/2 **(1 Mark)**

33. (i) Identifies total number of outcomes as 4 + 7 + 2 = 13 and favourable number of outcomes as 2. **(½ Mark)**

Finds the Probability that the note will be sufficient to pay for the dress as $\frac{2}{13}$. **(½ Mark)**

(ii) Here, favourable number of outcome is 0 (as she cant be able to pay ₹ 799 exactly). **(1 Mark)**

$\therefore$ The required probability = 0

34. Writes that the total number of outcomes is 16.

(½ Mark)

Writes that the number of favourable outcomes for Farah to win the game is 6. **(½ Mark)**

Finds the probability that Farah wins the game as $\frac{6}{16} = \frac{3}{8}$.
(½ Mark)

Finds the probability that Sheena wins the game as $1 - \frac{3}{8} = \frac{5}{8}$. **(1 Mark)**

Uses steps 3 and 4 to conclude that Sheena has a higher probability of winning the game. **(½ Mark)**

35. Total outcomes (No. of faces) = 6

(i) Number of A = 2

$\therefore \quad P(A) = \dfrac{\text{No. of favourable outcomes}}{\text{Total outcomes}}$

$= \dfrac{2}{6} = \dfrac{1}{3}$ **(1 Mark)**

(ii) Number of D = 1

$\therefore \quad P(D) = \dfrac{\text{No. of favourable outcomes}}{\text{Total outcomes}} = \dfrac{1}{6}$ **(1 Mark)**

The outcome that we are looking in an experiment is a favourable outcome.

36. Total outcomes = 7

$x^2 \leq 4 \Rightarrow x \leq 2 \text{ or } x \geq -2$

$\therefore \quad x = -2, -1, 0, 1, 2$ **(1 Mark)**

Number of favourable outcomes = 5

$P(x^2 \leq 4) = \dfrac{\text{No. of favourable outcomes}}{\text{Total outcomes}}$

$= \dfrac{5}{7}$ **(1 Mark)**

37. ***Topper's Answer***

Event : Dice is thrown.

Outcomes : 1, 2, 3, 4, 5, 6 (6 outcomes)

Favourable events :-

i) Composite number = 4, 6

Probability of getting a composite no. = $\dfrac{\text{no. of favourable outcomes}}{\text{Total outcomes}}$

$= \dfrac{2}{6} = \dfrac{1}{3}$

ii) prime no. : 2, 3, 5.

Probability = $\dfrac{\text{no. of outcomes favourable to the event}}{\text{Total possible outcomes}}$

or $\left(\dfrac{\text{no. of prime nos.}}{\text{Total outcomes}}\right)$

$= \dfrac{3}{6} = \dfrac{1}{2}$

38. P(blue) + P(black) + P(green) = 1

$\dfrac{1}{5} + \dfrac{1}{4} + P(\text{green}) = 1$

$P(\text{green}) = 1 - \left(\dfrac{1}{5} + \dfrac{1}{4}\right)$

$= 1 - \dfrac{9}{20} = \dfrac{11}{20}$ **(1 Mark)**

$\because \; P(\text{green}) = \dfrac{\text{No. of green marbles}}{\text{Total no. of marbles}}$

$\dfrac{11}{20} = \dfrac{11}{\text{Total no. of marbles}}$

Total no. of marbles = 20 **(1 Mark)**

Probability of all elementary outcomes greater than and equal to zero and less than and equal to one. Also, sum of all elementary outcomes equal to one.

39. Possible outcomes are {HTH, HHT, THT, TTH, THH, HTT, HHH, TTT}
Since, success represent getting the same result in all 3 tosses. **(1 Mark)**
$\therefore$ Set of favourable outcomes for losing the game is {HTH, HHT, THT, TTH, THH, HTT} that is 6 outcomes

Hence, the probability of losing the game $= \frac{6}{8} = \frac{3}{4}$ **(1 Mark)**

40. Possible outcomes for throwing a die once is

{1, 2, 3, 4, 5, 6}.

(i) Prime number on the dice is {2, 3, 5}.i.e. 3 outcomes.

$\therefore$ The probability of getting a prime number

$= \frac{3}{6} = \frac{1}{2}$ **(1 Mark)**

(ii) Number between 2 and 6 are {3, 4, 5} i.e. 3 outcomes.

$\therefore$ The probability of getting a number lies between 2 and 6 $= \frac{3}{6} = \frac{1}{2}$. **(1 Mark)**

Total number of possible outcomes for throwing a die n times are equal to $6 \times 6 \times$ .... n times $= 6^n$

41. When two different dice are tossed, the total number of outcomes is 36.

(i) Getting a doublet means getting (1, 1), (2, 2), (3, 3), (4, 4), (5, 5), (6, 6)

So, number of favourable outcomes = 6

Hence, probability of getting a doublet

$= \frac{6}{36} = \frac{1}{6}$ **(1 Mark)**

(ii) Outcomes in which the sum of numbers obtained is 10 are

(4, 6), (5, 5), (6, 4)

$\therefore$ Probability of getting a sum of 10

$= \frac{3}{36} = \frac{1}{12}$ **(1 Mark)**

42. An integer is chosen at random between 1 and 100. So, total number of outcomes are 98 as 1 and 100 are excluded.

(i) Numbers divisible by 8 are 8, 16, 24, 32, 40, 48, 56, 64, 72, 80, 88, and 96

Number of favourable outcomes = 12

Hence, probability of getting a

number divisible by 8 $= \frac{12}{98} = \frac{6}{49}$ **(1 Mark)**

(ii) Probability of getting a number not divisible by 8

$= 1 - \frac{6}{49} = \frac{49-6}{49}$

$= \frac{43}{49}$ **(1 Mark)**

43. Suppose number of black ball be x

It is given that, white balls = 15

$\therefore$ Total number of outcomes $= 15 + x$ **(1 Mark)**

According to question,

P (black balls) = 3 × P (white balls)

$$\left[\because \text{Probability} = \frac{\text{Number of favourable outcomes}}{\text{Total number of outcomes}}\right]$$

$$\Rightarrow \frac{x}{x+15} = 3\times\left(\frac{15}{15+x}\right)$$

$\Rightarrow x = 45$

Hence, number of black balls in the bag is 45. **(1 Mark)**

44. Total number of outcomes on throwing a pair of dice = $6 \times 6 = 36$

(i) Let E be the event of getting a prime number on each die.

$\therefore$ Favourable outcomes = {(2, 2)(2, 3)(2, 5)(3, 2)(3, 3) (3, 5)(5, 2)(5, 3), (5, 5)}

Number of favourable outcomes = 9

$$\text{Probability} = \frac{\text{Number of favourable outcomes}}{\text{Total number of outcomes}}$$

$P(E) = \frac{9}{36} = \frac{1}{4}$ **(1 Mark)**

(ii) Let F be the event of getting a total of 9 or 11

$\therefore$ Favourable outcomes = {(3, 6), (4, 5), (5, 4), (6, 3), (5, 6), (6, 5)}

Number of favourable outcomes = 6

$P(F) = \frac{6}{36} = \frac{1}{6}$

$P(F) = \frac{1}{6}$ **(1 Mark)**

45. Let total number of balls be x

Given: $P(\text{getting red balls}) = \frac{1}{4}$

$P(\text{getting blue balls}) = \frac{1}{3}$ **(1 Mark)**

$\text{Probability} = \frac{\text{Number of favorable outcomes}}{\text{Total number of outcomes}}$

$\therefore P(\text{getting orange balls}) = \frac{10}{x}$

[$\because$ number of orange balls = 10]

As we know that sum of probability of all possible event is 1.

P(getting red balls) + P(getting blue balls) + P(getting orange balls) = 1

$\Rightarrow \frac{1}{4}+\frac{1}{3}+\frac{10}{x} = 1$

$\Rightarrow \frac{10}{x} = 1-\frac{1}{4}-\frac{1}{3}$

$\Rightarrow \frac{10}{x} = \frac{12-3-4}{12}$

$\Rightarrow \frac{10}{x} = \frac{5}{12} \Rightarrow x = 24$

$\therefore$ Total number of balls = 24 **(1 Mark)**

46. Sample space for tossing two coins is [HH, HT, TH, TT]

Total number of outcomes = 4

Sample space of getting at least one tail on tossing:

[HT, TH, TT]

$\therefore$ Number of favourable outcomes = 3 **(½ Mark)**

Probability of getting at least one tail

$= \frac{\text{Number of favourable outcomes}}{\text{Total number of outcomes}}$

$= \frac{3}{4}$ **(1½ Marks)**

Note

If E be any event then P(E) + $P(\overline{E}) = 1$

So, to find probability of getting no tail = $P(\overline{E}) = 1 - P(E)$

$= 1-\frac{3}{4} = \frac{1}{4}$

47. Total number of outcomes = 52

Total Queens = 4

Total Kings = 4

$P(E) = \frac{\text{Number of favourable outcomes}}{\text{Total number of outcomes}}$

Probability of getting either a king or a queen $= \frac{4+4}{52} = \frac{8}{52}$

(1 Mark)

$\therefore$ Probability of getting neither a king nor a queen

$= 1-\frac{8}{52}$

$= \frac{44}{52} = \frac{11}{13}$ **(1 Mark)**

Note

A pack of playing cards consists of four suits called Hearts, Spades, Diamonds and Clubs. Each suite consists of 13 cards.

48. On throwing the two different dice the various outcomes obtained are as follows:-

(1, 1) (1, 2) (1, 3) (1, 4) (1, 5) (1, 6)

(2, 1) (2, 2) (2, 3) (2, 4) (2, 5) (2, 6)

(3, 1) (3, 2) (3, 3) (3, 4) (3, 5) (3, 6)

(4, 1) (4, 2) (4, 3) (4, 4) (4, 5) (4, 6)

(5, 1) (5, 2) (5, 3) (5, 4) (5, 5) (5, 6)

(6, 1) (6, 2) (6, 3) (6, 4) (6, 5) (6, 6)

Thus total outcomes are 36 **(1 Mark)**

(i) Even sum outcomes are

(1, 1), (1, 3), (1, 5),

(2, 2), (2, 4), (2, 6),

(3, 1), (3, 3), (3, 5),

(4, 2), (4, 4), (4, 6),

(5, 1), (5, 3), (5, 5),

(6, 2), (6, 4), (6, 6),

Number of favourable outcomes = 18

$\therefore P(E) = \frac{\text{Number of favourable outcomes}}{\text{Total number of outcomes}}$

$\Rightarrow$ P (even sum) = $\frac{18}{36} = \frac{1}{2}$ **(1 Mark)**

(ii) Even product outcomes are as follows:

(1, 2), (1, 4), (1, 6), (2, 1), (2, 2), (2, 3), (2, 4), (2, 5), (2, 6), (3, 2), (3, 4), (3, 6), (4, 1), (4, 2), (4, 3), (4, 4), (4, 5), (4, 6), (5, 2), (5, 4), (5, 6), (6, 1), (6, 2), (6, 3), (6, 4), (6, 5), (6, 6)

Number of favourable outcomes = 27 **(1 Mark)**

$\therefore P(E) = \frac{\text{Number of favourable outcomes}}{\text{Total number of outcomes}}$

P(even product) = $\frac{27}{36} = \frac{3}{4}$ **(1 Mark)**

Hence, the probability of getting even sum is $\frac{1}{2}$ and getting even product is $\frac{3}{4}$

49. Numbers are from 1 to 8

Total numbers of event = 8

(i) Odd numbers are 1, 3, 5 and 7

Number of favourable outcomes = 4

Let E be the event that arrow will point an odd number

Probability = $\frac{\text{Number of favourable outcomes}}{\text{Total number of outcomes}}$

$P(E) = \frac{4}{8} = \frac{1}{2}$ **(1 Mark)**

(ii) Numbers greater than 3 are 4, 5, 6, 7, 8

Number of favourable outcomes = 5

Let F be the event that arrow will point number greater than 3

$P(F) = \frac{5}{8}$ **(1½ Marks)**

(iii) Numbers less than 9 are 1, 2, 3, 4, 5 ,6, 7, 8

Number of favourable outcomes = 8

Let G be event that arrow points at a number less than 9

$P(G) = \frac{8}{8} = 1$ **(1½ Marks)**

The numerator (number of favourable outcomes) is always less than or equal to the denominator (the number of total possible outcomes) $\therefore 0 \le P(E) \le 1$.

50. Probability of an event = $\frac{\text{Number of favorable outcomes}}{\text{Total number of outcomes}}$

(i) Let E_1 be the event of getting spade or an ace

Total spade cards = 13

Ace each of hearts, Diamonds and Clubs = 3

Number of favourable outcomes = 13 + 3 = 16

$P(E_1) = \frac{16}{52} = \frac{4}{13}$ **(1 Mark)**

(ii) Let E_2 be the event of getting *a* black king

Number of favourable outcomes = 2 [king of spades clubs]

$P(E_2) = \frac{2}{52} = \frac{1}{26}$ **(1 Mark)**

(iii) Let E_3 be the event of getting neither *a* jack nor *a* king

Total jacks = 4, Total kings = 4

Probability (getting a jack or *a* king) = $\frac{8}{52}$

Probability (getting neither *a* jack nor *a* king) = $1 - \frac{8}{52}$

$= \frac{44}{52} = \frac{11}{13}$ **(1 Mark)**

(iv) Let E be the event of getting a king or *a* queen

Total Queens = 4, Total Kings = 4

Probability (getting a king or a queen) = $\frac{8}{52} = \frac{2}{13}$

(1 Mark)

51. Total number of cards = 49

$\therefore$ Total number of outcomes = 49

(i) Odd numbers between 1 to 49 are

1, 3, 5, 7, 9, 11, 13, 15, 17, 19, 21, 23, 25, 27, 29, 31, 33, 35, 37, 39, 41, 43, 45, 47, 49

Total number of favourable outcomes = 25

$\therefore$ Required probability

$= \frac{\text{Total number of favourable outcomes}}{\text{Total number of outcomes}}$

$= \frac{25}{49}$ **(1 Mark)**

(ii) Multiples of 5 between 1 to 49 are

5, 10, 15, 20, 25, 30, 35, 40, 45

Total number of favourable outcomes = 9

$\therefore$ Required probability = $\frac{9}{49}$ **(1 Mark)**

(iii) Perfect square numbers are

1, 4, 9, 16, 25, 36, and 45

Total number of favourable outcomes = 7

$\therefore$ Required probability = $\frac{7}{49} = \frac{1}{7}$ **(1 Mark)**

(iv) Even prime number is 2

total number of favorable outcomes = 1

$\therefore$ Required Probability = $\frac{1}{49}$ **(1 Mark)**

Probability P of any event A is P(A) ≥ 0.

52. The group consists of 12 persons

$\therefore$ Total number of possible outcomes = 12

(i) Let E_1 be the event of selecting person who are extremely patient

$\therefore$ Number of favourable outcome = 3

$$P(E_1) = \frac{\text{Number of favourable outcome}}{\text{Total number of possible outcome}}$$

$$= \frac{3}{12} = \frac{1}{4}$$

$P(E_1) = \frac{1}{4}$ **(1½ Marks)**

(ii) Let E_2 be the event of selecting persons who are extremely kind or honest.

Number of persons who are extremely honest = 6

Number of kind persons = 12 – (6 + 3)

= 3

$\therefore$ Number of favourable outcomes = 6 + 3 = 9

$$P(E_2) = \frac{9}{12} = \frac{3}{4}$$

$\therefore P(E_2) = \frac{3}{4}$ **(1½ Marks)**

Each of the three values, patience, honesty and kindnes is important in one's life. **(1 Mark)**

The chances of occurence of head and tail when tossing a coin is always same then that outcomes are called equally likely.

53. (i) Number of ball that bear number 8 = 1

$$\text{Probability} = \frac{\text{Numbers of favourable outcome}}{\text{Total Number of outcomes}}$$

P(ball bearing number 8) = $\frac{1}{15}$ **(1 Mark)**

(ii) Even numbers up to 15 are 2, 4, 6, 8, 10, 12, 14. **(1 Mark)**

Hence, the favourable outcomes are 7 and

total outcomes are 15

P(even number ball) = $\frac{7}{15}$ **(1 Mark)**

(OR)

Multiple of 3 up to 15 are 3, 6, 9, 12, 15 **(1 Mark)**

Hence favourable outcomes are 5 and total outcome! are 15

P (multiple of 3) = $\frac{5}{15} = \frac{1}{3}$ **(1 Mark)**

(iii) Solid balls are numbered 1 to 8

Total even number upto 8 are = 4

Total balls = 15

P(even number solid balls) = $\frac{4}{15}$ **(1 Mark)**

54. (i) The total possible outcomes of a player spinning the game is 9. **(1 Mark)**

(ii) The probability of making purple is $\frac{1}{9}$.

For making purple we need R in spinner 1 and B in spinner 2. So favourable outcome is 1

And the total outcomes is 9 **(1 Mark)**

(iii) (a) $P(W) = \frac{1}{9}$, $P(L) = 1 - \frac{1}{9} = \frac{8}{9}$

Total fund collected = $\left(99 \times \frac{1}{9}\right)(-10) + \frac{1}{9}5$

$= -110 + 11 \times 40 = 330$ **(2 Marks)**

OR

(b) Fund collected by school.

$= 99 \times \frac{1}{9} \times (-5) + 99 \times \frac{8}{9} \times 5$

$= 11(-5) + (11 \times 40) = 385$ **(2 Marks)**

Topic-2: Probability Related to Area and Volume

1. **(b)** $\frac{4-\pi}{4}$ **(1 Mark)**

www.ingramcontent.com/pod-product-compliance
Lightning Source LLC
LaVergne TN
LVHW080058170826

845677LV00024B/1785
* 9 7 8 9 3 5 5 6 4 6 3 2 3 *